Environmental Economics and Policy

The Addison-Wesley Series in Economics

Abel/Bernanke
Macroeconomics

Berndt
The Practice of Econometrics

Bierman/Fernandez
Game Theory with Economic
Applications

Binger/Hoffman
Microeconomics with Calculus

Boyer
Principles of Transportation
Economics

Branson
Macroeconomic Theory and
Policy

Bruce
Public Finance and the
American Economy

Burgess
The Economics of Regulation
and Antitrust

Byrns/Stone
Economics

Carlton/Perloff
Modern Industrial Organization

Caves/Frankel/Jones
World Trade and Payments:
An Introduction

Chapman
Environmental Economics:
Theory, Application, and Policy

Cooter/Ulen
Law and Economics

Downs
An Economic Theory of
Democracy

Eaton/Mishkin
Online Readings to Accompany
The Economics of Money,
Banking, and Financial Markets

Ehrenberg/Smith
Modern Labor Economics

Ekelund/Tollison
Economics: Private Markets
and Public Choice

Fusfeld
The Age of the Economist

Gerber
International Economics

Ghiara
Learning Economics:
A Practical Workbook

Gordon
Macroeconomics

Gregory
Essentials of Economics

Gregory/Stuart
Russian and Soviet Economic
Performance and Structure

Gros/Steinherr
Winds of Change: Economic
Transition in Central and
Eastern Europe

Hartwick/Olewiler
The Economics of Natural
Resource Use

Hubbard
Money, the Financial System,
and the Economy

Hughes/Cain
American Economic History

Husted/Melvin
International Economics

Jehle/Reny
Advanced Microeconomic Theory

Klein
Mathematical Methods for
Economics

Krugman/Obstfeld
International Economics:
Theory and Policy

Laidler
The Demand for Money: Theo-
ries, Evidence, and Problems

Lesser/Dodds/Zerbe
Environmental Economics and
Policy

Lipsey/Courant/Ragan
Economics

McCarty
Dollars and Sense: An Introduction to Economics

Melvin
International Money and Finance

Miller
Economics Today

Miller/Benjamin/North
The Economics of Public Issues

Mills/Hamilton
Urban Economics

Mishkin
The Economics of Money,
Banking, and Financial Markets

Parkin
Economics

Parkin/Bade
Economics in Action Software

Perloff
Microeconomics

Phelps
Health Economics

Riddell/Shackelford/Stamos
Economics: A Tool for Critically
Understanding Society

Ritter/Silber/Udell
Principles of Money, Banking,
and Financial Markets

Rohlf
Introduction to Economic
Reasoning

Ruffin/Gregory
Principles of Economics

Sargent
Rational Expectations and
Inflation

Scherer
Industry Structure, Strategy,
and Public Policy

Schotter
Microeconomics

Sherman/Kolk
Business Cycles and Forecasting

Smith
Case Studies in Economic
Development

Studenmund
Using Econometrics

Su
Economic Fluctuations and
Forecasting

Tietenberg
Environmental and Natural
Resource Economics

Tietenberg
Environmental Economics and
Policy

Todaro
Economic Development

Waldman/Jensen
Industrial Organization:
Theory and Practice

Environmental Economics and Policy

THIRD EDITION

TOM TIETENBERG
Colby College

Boston San Francisco New York
London Toronto Sydney Tokyo Singapore Madrid
Mexico City Munich Paris Cape Town Hong Kong Montreal

Publisher: Frank Ruggirello
Executive Editor: Denise Clinton
Acquisitions Editor: Victoria Warneck
Development Editor: Roxanne Hoch
Supplements Editor: Meredith Gertz
Media Producer: Melissa Honig
Marketing Manager: Adrienne D'Ambrosio
Managing Editor: James Rigney
Production Supervisor: Katherine Watson
Project Coordination and Composition: Electronic Publishing Services Inc., N.Y.C.
Production Assistant: Andrea Basso
Manufacturing Buyer: Hugh Crawford
Design/Art Direction: Regina Hagen
Text Design: Electronic Publishing Services Inc., N.Y.C.
Cover Designer: Joyce Cosentino
Cover Photo ©2001 PhotoDisk, Inc.

Library of Congress Cataloging-in-Publication Data

Tietenberg, Thomas H.
  Environmental economics and policy / Tom Tietenberg. — 3rd ed.
      p.   cm.
  Includes index.
  ISBN 0-321-07813-6
    1. Environmental economics.   I. Title.
HD75.6.T54 2000
333.7—dc21   00-046220

ISBN 0-321-07813-6
1 2 3 4 5 6 7 8 9 10—MA—04 03 02 01 00

Brief Contents

Detailed Contents vii

Preface xix

1 Visions of the Future   1

2 Valuing the Environment: Concepts   15

3 Valuing the Environment: Methods   32

4 Property Rights, Externalities, and Environmental Problems   59

5 Sustainable Development: Defining the Concept   84

6 The Population Problem   98

7 Natural Resource Economics: An Overview   122

8 Energy   136

9 Water   157

10 Agriculture   176

11 Biodiversity I: Forest Habitat   198

12 Biodiveristy II: Commercially Valuable Species   220

13 Environmental Economics: An Overview   243

14 Stationary-Source Local Air Pollution   263

15 Acid Rain and Atmosphere Modification   287

16 Transportation   311

17 Water Pollution   336

18 Solid Waste and Recycling   363

19 Toxic Substances and Hazardous Wastes   382

20 Development, Poverty, and the Environment   410

21 The Quest for Sustainable Development   434

22 Visions of the Future Revisited   463

Glossary   *473*

Index   *483*

Detailed Contents

PREFACE   xix

1 Visions of the Future 1

INTRODUCTION 1
The Self-Extinction Premise 1
Environmental and Natural Resource Economics 3
Thinking About the Future 3

THE BASIC PESSIMIST MODEL 3
Conclusions of the Pessimist Model 3
EXAMPLE 1.1 THE DANGERS OF PROGNOSTICATION 4
The Nature of the Model 6

THE BASIC OPTIMIST MODEL 7
Conclusions of the Optimist Model 8
The Nature of the Model 8

THE ROAD AHEAD 10
The Issues 10
An Overview of the Book 11
Summary 12
Further Reading 13
Additional References 13
Web Sites of Interest 13
Discussion Questions 14

2 Valuing the Environment: Concepts 15

INTRODUCTION 15

THE HUMAN ENVIRONMENT RELATIONSHIP 16
The Environment as an Asset 16
The Economic Approach 18

NORMATIVE CRITERIA FOR DECISION MAKING 18

EVALUATING PREDEFINED OPTIONS 18
EXAMPLE 2.1 NATURE KNOWS BEST 20

FINDING THE OPTIMAL OUTCOME 25
Static Efficiency 26
Dynamic Efficiency 27

APPLYING THE CONCEPTS 27
Pollution Control 27
EXAMPLE 2.2 DOES REDUCING POLLUTION MAKE ECONOMIC SENSE? 28

EXAMPLE 2.3 CHOOSING BETWEEN PRESERVATION AND DEVELOPMENT IN AUSTRALIA 29
Preservation Versus Development 29
Summary 30
Further Reading 30
Additional References 30
Web Sites of Interest 31
Discussion Questions 31

3 Valuing the Environment: Methods 32

INTRODUCTION 32
VALUING BENEFITS 33
Types of Values 34
Classifying Valuation Methods 35
EXAMPLE 3.1 VALUING THE NORTHERN SPOTTED OWL 37
EXAMPLE 3.2 VALUING DAMAGE FROM GROUNDWATER CONTAMINATION USING AVERTING EXPENDITURES 40
EXAMPLE 3.3 VALUING DIESEL ODOR REDUCTION BY CONTINGENT RANKING 41
EXAMPLE 3.4 THE VALUE OF WILDLIFE VIEWING 42
Issues in Benefit Estimation 44
Approaches to Cost Estimation 45
The Treatment of Risk 46
Choosing the Discount Rate 48
A Critical Appraisal 48
EXAMPLE 3.5 THE IMPORTANCE OF THE DISCOUNT RATE 49
COST-EFFECTIVENESS ANALYSIS 51
IMPACT ANALYSIS 52
EXAMPLE 3.6 NO_2 CONTROL IN CHICAGO: AN EXAMPLE OF COST-EFFECTIVE ANALYSIS 53
Summary 54
Further Reading 55
Additional References 56
Web Sites of Interest 57
Discussion Questions 57

4 Property Rights, Externalities, and Environmental Problems 59

INTRODUCTION 59
PROPERTY RIGHTS 60
Property Rights and Efficient Market Allocations 60
Efficient Property Right Structres 60
EXAMPLE 4.1 POLLUTION IN CENTRALLY PLANNED ECONOMICS 61
Producer's Surplus, Scarcity Rent, and Long-Run Competitive Equilibrium 64
EXTERNALITIES AS A SOURCE OF MARKET FAILURE 64
The Concept Introduced 64
Types of Externalities 66

IMPROPERLY DESIGNED PROPERTY RIGHTS SYSTEM 66
  Other Property Rights Regimes 66
    EXAMPLE 4.2 SHRIMP FARMING EXTERNALITIES IN THAILAND 67
  Public Goods 69
    EXAMPLE 4.3 PUBLIC GOODS PRIVATELY PROVIDED: THE NATURE CONSERVANCY 72
IMPERFECT MARKET STRUCTURES 72
DIVERGENCE OF SOCIAL AND PRIVATE DISCOUNT RATES 74
GOVERNMENT FAILURE 74
THE PURSUIT OF EFFICIENCY 75
  Private Resolution through Negotiation 75
    EXAMPLE 4.4 RELIGION AS THE SOURCE OF ENVIRONMENTAL PROBLEMS 76
  The Courts: Property Rules and Liability Rules 77
  Legislative and Executive Regulation 79
AN EFFICIENT ROLE FOR GOVERNMENT 79
Summary 80
Further Reading 81
Additional References 82
Web Sites of Interest 82
Discussion Questions 82

5 Sustainable Development: Defining the Concept 84
INTRODUCTION 84
A TWO-PERIOD MODEL 85
DEFINING INTERTEMPORAL FAIRNESS 89
ARE EFFICIENT ALLOCATIONS FAIR? 90
APPLYING THE SUSTAINABILITY CRITERION 91
IMPLICATIONS FOR ENVIRONMENTAL POLICIES 92
    EXAMPLE 5.1 NAURU: WEAK SUSTAINABILITY IN THE EXTREME 93
Summary 94
Further Reading 95
Additional References 95
Web Sites of Interest 96
Discussion Questions 96

6 The Population Problem 98
INTRODUCTION 98
HISTORICAL PERSPECTIVE 99
  World Population Growth 99
  Population Growth in the United States 100
  Effects of Population Growth on Economic Development 101
  Effects of Economic Development on Population Growth 108
  The Economic Approach to Population Control 109
    EXAMPLE 6.1 THE VALUE OF AND AVERTED BIRTH 111
    EXAMPLE 6.2 FERTILITY DECLINE IN KOREA: A CASE STUDY 115

EXAMPLE 6.3 INCOME-GENERATING ACTIVITIES OF FERTILITY CONTROL: BANGLADESH 117
Summary 118
Further Reading 119
Additional References 119
Web Sites of Interest 120
Discussion Questions 121

7 Natural Resource Economics: An Overview 122

INTRODUCTION 122

A RESOURCE TAXONOMY 123
   EXAMPLE 7.1 THE PITFALLS OF MISUSING RESERVE DATA 125

EFFICIENT INTERTEMPORAL ALLOCATIONS 127
   The Two-Period Model Revisited 128
   The N-Period Model 127
   Transition to a Renewable Substitute 130
   Exploration and Technological Progress 131

MARKET ALLOCATIONS 131
   EXAMPLE 7.2 TECHNOLOGICAL PROGRESS IN THE IRON ORE INDUSTRY 132
   Appropriate Property-Right Structure 132
   Environmental Costs 133
Summary 134
Further Reading 134
Additional References 135
Discussion Questions 135

8 Energy 136

INTRODUCTION 136

NATURAL GAS: PRICE CONTROLS 138
   EXAMPLE 8.1 PRICE CONTROLS AND SUBSTITUTION BIAS 140

OIL: THE CARTEL PROBLEM 142
   Price Elasticity of Demand 142
   EXAMPLE 8.2 ARE "SOFT ENERGY" PATHS DOOMED? 143
   Income Elasticity of Demand 144
   Non-OPEC Suppliers 144
   Compatibility of Member Interests 144

TRANSITION FUELS: ENVIRONMENTAL PROBLEMS 146

CONSERVATION AND LOAD MANAGEMENT 150

THE LONG RUN 152
Summary 154
Further Reading 154
Additional References 155
Web Sites of Interest 156
Discussion Questions 156

9 Water 157

INTRODUCTION 157

THE POTENTIAL FOR WATER SCARCITY 158

THE EFFICIENT ALLOCATION OF SCARCE WATER 160
Surface Water 160
Groundwater 160

THE CURRENT ALLOCATION SYSTEM 161
Riparian and Prior-Appropriation Doctrine 161
Sources of Inefficiency 162

POTENTIAL REMEDIES 166
EXAMPLE 9.1 USING ECONOMIC PRINCIPLES TO CONSERVE WATER IN CALIFORNIA 167
EXAMPLE 9.2 PROTECTING INSTREAM USES THROUGH ACQUIRING WATER RIGHTS 168
EXAMPLE 9.3 WATER PRICING IN ZURICH, SWITZERLAND 170
EXAMPLE 9.4 POLITICS AND THE PRICING OF SCARCE WATER 171

Summary 172
Further Reading 173
Additional References 173
Web Sites of Interest 174
Discussion Questions 175

10 Agriculture 176

INTRODUCTION 176

GLOBAL SCARCITY 177
Examining Global Scarcity 178
Outlook for the Future 180
The Role of Agriculture Policies 185
A Summing Up 186

DISTRIBUTION OF FOOD RESOURCES 186
Defining the Problem 186
Domestic Production in LCDs 187
The Underevaluation Bias 188
EXAMPLE 10.1 THE PRICE RESPONSIVENESS OF SUPPLY: THAILAND 189
Feeding the Poor 190
EXAMPLE 10.2 PERVERSE GOVERNMENT INTERVENTION: THE CASE OF COLOMBIA 191
EXAMPLE 10.3 THE DISTRIBUTION DILEMMA: INDIA'S GREEN REVOLUTION 193

FEAST AND FAMINE CYCLES 193
Summary 195
Further Reading 195
Additional References 196
Web Sites of Interest 197
Discussion Questions 197

11 Biodiversity I: Forest Habitat 198

INTRODUCTION 198

DEFINING PROFIT-MAXIMIZING MANAGEMENT 199
Special Attributes of the Forest 199
The Biological Dimension 200
The Economics of Forest Harvesting 201

LAND CONVERSION 202

SOURCES OF INEFFICIENCY 205
Perverse Incentives for the Landowner 205
Perverse Incentives for Nations 207

POVERTY AND DEBT 208

SUSTAINABLE FORESTRY 208

PUBLIC POLICY 209
EXAMPLE 11.1 PRODUCING SUSTAINABLE FORESTRY THROUGH CERTIFICATION 212
EXAMPLE 11.2 SUCCESS STORIES IN CONSERVING TROPICAL FORESTS 214
EXAMPLE 11.3 THE INTERNATIONAL TROPICAL TIMBER AGREEMENT 215
EXAMPLE 11.4 TRUST FUNDS FOR CONSERVATION 216
Summary 216
Further Reading 217
Additional References 218
Web Sites of Interest 218
Discussion Questions 219

12 Biodiversity II: Commercially Valuable Species 220

INTRODUCTION 220

EFFICIENT HARVESTS 221
The Biological Dimension 221
Static-Efficient Sustained Yield 223

APPROPRIABILITY AND MARKET SOLUTIONS 224
EXAMPLE 12.1 PROPERTY RIGHTS AND FISHERIES: OYSTERS 226

PUBLIC POLICY TOWARD FISHERIES 227
EXAMPLE 12.2 FREE-ACCESS HARVESTING OF THE MINKE WHALE 228
Aquaculture 228
EXAMPLE 12.3 HARBOR GANGS OF MAINE 229
Raising the Real Cost of Fishing 230
Taxes 233
Individual Transferable Quotas (ITQs) 233
EXAMPLE 12.4 EFFICIENT VS. MARKET EXPLOITATION OF LOBSTERS 234
The 200-Mile Limit 237
EXAMPLE 12.5 LOCAL APPROACHES TO WILDLIFE PROTECTION: ZIMBABWE 238

PREVENTING POACHING 238
Summary 239

Further Reading 240
Additional References 240
Discussion Questions 241
Web Sites of Interest 242

13 Environmental Economics: An Overview 243

INTRODUCTION 243

A POLLUTANT TAXONOMY 244

DEFINING THE EFFICIENT ALLOCATION OF POLLUTION 245
Fund Pollutants 245

MARKET ALLOCATION OF POLLUTION 247

EFFICIENT POLICY RESPONSES 249
   EXAMPLE 13.1 ENVIRONMENTAL TAXATION IN CHINA 249

COST-EFFECTIVE POLICIES FOR EMISSION REDUCTION 250
Defining a Cost-Effective Allocation 250
Cost-Effective Pollution Control Policies 252
Emission Standards 252
Emission Charges 253
Transferable Emission Permits 255

OTHER POLICY DIMENSIONS 256

Summary 258
   EXAMPLE 13.2 ENERGY-DEMAND UNCERTAINTY AND THE COST OF BEING WRONG: PERMITS VS. CHARGES 259
Further Reading 260
Additional References 260
Web Sites of Interest 260
Discussion Questions 262

14 Stationary-Source Local Air Pollution 263

INTRODUCTION 263

CONVENTIONAL POLLUTANTS 264
The Command-and-Control Policy Framework 264
The Efficiency of the Command-and-Control Approach 267
   EXAMPLE 14.1 THE PARTICULATE AND SMOG AMBLENT STANDARDS CONTROVERSY 269
Cost-Effectiveness of the Command-and-Control Approach 270
Air Quality 273

INNOVATIVE APPROACHES 273
The Emissions Trading Program 273
   EXAMPLE 14.2 THE BUBBLE AND OFFSET POLICIES IN ACTION 275
Smog Trading 276
The Effectiveness of Emissions Trading 276
Emission Charges 279

Hazardous Pollutants 280
Emissions Fees 282
    EXAMPLE 14.3 EFFICIENT REGULATION OF HAZARDOUS POLLUTANTS: THE BENZENE CASE 283
Summary 284
Further Reading 285
Additional References 285
Web Sites of Interest 286
Discussion Questions 286

15 Acid Rain and Atmosphere Modification 287

INTRODUCTION 287

REGIONAL POLLUTANTS 288
Acid Rain 288
    EXAMPLE 15.1 ADIRONDACK ACIDIFICATION 290
    EXAMPLE 15.2 THE SULFUR ALLOWANCE PROGRAM 294
    EXAMPLE 15.3 WHY AND HOW DO ENVIRONMENTALISTS BUY POLLUTION? 295

GLOBAL POLLUTANTS 297
Ozone Depletion 297
Global Warming 299
    EXAMPLE 15.4 TRADEABLE PERMITS FOR OZONE-DEPLETING CHEMICALS 300
    EXAMPLE 15.5 ETHICS, RISK AVERSION, AND THE GREENHOUSE EFFECT 302
Summary 306
Further Reading 308
Additional References 308
Web Sites of Interest 310

16 Transportation 311

INTRODUCTION 311

THE ECONOMICS OF MOBILE-SOURCE POLLUTION 313
Implicit Subsidies 313
Externalities 314
The Consequences 315

POLICY TOWARD MOBILE SOURCES 316
Some History 316
Structure of the U.S. Approach 316
    EXAMPLE 16.1 PROJECT XL—THE QUEST FOR EFFECTIVE, FLEXIBLE REGULATION 319
European Approaches 319

AN ECONOMIC AND POLITICAL ASSESSMENT 320
    EXAMPLE 16.2 CAR SHARING: BETTER USE OF AUTOMOTIVE CAPITAL? 321
Technology Forcing and Sanctions 322
Differentiated Regulation 322
Uniformity of Control 323
The Deterioration of New-Car Emission Rates 323
    EXAMPLE 16.3 SETTING THE NATIONAL AUTOMOBILE EMISSION STANDARDS 324
Lead Phaseout Program 326

Alternative Fuels 327
Air Quality 327
 EXAMPLE 16.4 GETTING THE LEAD OUT: THE LEAD PHASEOUT PROGRAM 328
POSSIBLE REFORMS 329
 EXAMPLE 16.5 INNOVATIVE MOBILE-POLLUTION CONTROL STRATEGIES: SINGAPORE AND HONG KONG 330
Summary 331
 EXAMPLE 16.6 COUNTERPRODUCTIVE POLICY DESIGN 332
Further Reading 334
Additional References 334
Web Sites of Interest 334
Discussion Questions 335

17 Water Pollution 336

INTRODUCTION 336

THE NATURE OF WATER POLLUTION PROBLEMS 337
Types of Waste-Receiving Water 337
Sources of Contamination 337
 EXAMPLE 17.1 INCIDENTS OF GROUNDWATER POLLUTION 338
Types of Pollutants 339

WATER POLLUTION CONTROL POLICY 342
Traditional Water Pollution Control Policy 342
Early Legislation 342
Subsequent Legislation 343
The TDML Program 345
The Safe-Drinking Water Act 345
Ocean Pollution 345
Private Enforcement 346

EFFICIENCY AND COST-EFFECTIVENESS 347
Ambient Standards and the Zero Discharge Goal 347
National Effluent Standards 348
 EXAMPLE 17.2 MARKETABLE EMISSION PERMITS ON THE FOX RIVER 351
Municipal Waste Treatment Subsidies 352
Pretreatment Standards 353
Nonpoint Pollution 353
 EXAMPLE 17.3 COST-EFFECTIVE PRETREATMENT STANDARDS 354
Oil Spills 355
 EXAMPLE 17.4 ANATOMY OF AN OIL SPILL SUIT: THE AMOCO CADIZ 356
Citizen Suits 356
An Overall Assessment 357
Summary 359
Further Reading 360
Additional References 360
Web Sites of Interest 362
Discussion Questions 362

18 Solid Waste and Recycling 363

INTRODUCTION 363

EFFICIENT RECYCLING 364
Extraction and Disposal Costs 364
EXAMPLE 18.1 POPULATION DENSITY AND RECYCLING: THE JAPANESE EXPERIENCE 365
Recycling: A Closer Look 365
EXAMPLE 18.2 LEAD RECYCLING 366

WASTE DISPOSAL AND POLLUTION DAMAGE 366
Disposal Costs and Efficiency 367
The Disposal Decision 367
Disposal Costs and the Scrap Market 369
Public Policies 369
EXAMPLE 18.3 PRICING TRASH IN MARIETTA, GEORGIA 370
Pollution Damage 371
EXAMPLE 18.4 IMPLEMENTING THE íTAKE-BACKí PRINCIPLE 372

PRODUCT DURABILITY 373
Functional Obsolescence 375
Fashion Obsolescence 375
Durability Obsolescence 376
Summary 378
EXAMPLE 18.5 THE BET 379
Further Reading 379
Additional References 380
Web Sites of Interest 381
Discussion Questions 381

19 Toxic Substances and Hazardous Wastes 382

INTRODUCTION 382

NATURE OF TOXIC SUBSTANCE POLLUTION 383
Health Effects 384
Policy Issues 385

MARKET ALLOCATIONS OF TOXIC SUBSTANCES 387
Occupational Hazards 387
EXAMPLE 19.1 SUSCEPTIBLE POPULATIONS IN THE HAZARDOUS WORKPLACE 389
Product Safety 389
Third Parties 390

CURRENT POLICY 391
Common Law 391
EXAMPLE 19.2 JUDICIAL REMEDIES IN TOXIC SUBSTANCE CONTROL: THE KEPONE CASE 392
Criminal Law 393
Statutory Law 394
International Agreements 397

AN ASSESSMENT OF THE LEGAL REMEDIES 397
The Common Law 397
The Statutory Law 401
EXAMPLE **19.3** WEIGHING THE RISKS: SACCHARIN 403
Assurance Bonds: An Innovative Proposal 405
EXAMPLE **19.4** PERFORMANCE BONDS FOR BROMINATED FLAME RETARDANTS 406
Summary 406
Further Reading 407
Additional References 408
Web Sites of Interest 409
Discussion Questions 409

20 Development, Poverty, and the Environment 410

INTRODUCTION 410
THE GROWTH PROCESS 412
The Nature of the Process 412
Potential Sources of Reduced Growth 412
Environmental Policy 415
Energy 416
EXAMPLE **20.1** JOBS VS. THE ENVIRONMENT: WHAT IS THE EVIDENCE? 417
OUTLOOK FOR THE NEAR FUTURE 419
Population Impacts 419
The Information Economy 419
THE GROWTH-DEVELOPMENT RELATIONSHIP 420
Conventional Measures 420
Alternative Measures 423
GROWTH AND POVERTY: THE INDUSTRIALIZED NATIONS 425
The Effects on Income Inequality 425
EXAMPLE **20.2** DOES MONEY BUY HAPPINESS? 426
POVERTY IN THE LESS INDUSTRIALIZED NATIONS 426
The Appropriateness of the Traditional Model 427
Barriers to Development 428
Summary 431
Further Reading 432
Additional References 432
Web Sites of Interest 433
Discussion Questions 433

21 The Quest for Sustainable Development 434

INTRODUCTION 434
SUSTAINABILITY AND DEVELOPMENT 425
Market Allocations 437
Efficiency and Sustainability 438

EXAMPLE 21.1 RESOURCE DEPLETION AND ECONOMIC SUSTAINABILITY: MALAYSIA 440

TRADE AND THE ENVIRONMENT 442

A MENU OF OPPORTUNITIES 443

Agriculture 444

Energy 444

Waste Reduction 445

EXAMPLE 21.2 SUSTAINABLE DEVELOPMENT: THREE SUCCESS STORIES 446

MANAGING THE TRANSITION 447

EXAMPLE 21.3 CONTROLLING LAND USE DEVELOPMENT WITH TDRs 448

Prospects for International Cooperation 449

Opportunities for Cooperation 449

Restructuring Incentives 450

FORCED TRANSITION 456

Defining the Target 456

EXAMPLE 21.4 REPUTATIONAL STRATEGIES FOR POLLUTION CONTROL IN INDONESIA 457

Institutional Structure 457

Administration 459

Summary 459

Further Reading 460

Additional References 461

Web Sites of Interest 462

Discussion Questions 462

22 Visions of the Future Revisited 463

ADDRESSING THE ISSUES 463

Conceptualizing the Problem 464

Institutional Responses 466

Sustainable Development 468

A Concluding Comment 471

GLOSSARY 473

INDEX 483

Preface to
the Third Edition

About two decades ago, while on a plane heading for a conference, I struck up a conversation with the passenger next to me. During the course of that conversation he asked me what I did for a living. After mulling over my response that I was an environmental economist, he asked, "Isn't that a contradiction in terms?"

He had a point. The economy has been a major source of environmental degradation. Developers pave over wetlands. Timber companies denude the forests. Fishermen deplete the oceans. Industries pollute the waters. And on and on.

Recently, however, those same powerful forces that have historically been associated with environmental degradation have been enlisted in the struggle to protect the environment. Buying and selling quotas have helped restore New Zealand fisheries. Pharmaceutical companies are investing in biodiversity preservation. Peak-load and congestion pricing have encouraged the better use of existing power plants and roads rather than the building of new ones. By-the-bag charging for solid waste has stimulated recycling and reduced the volume of waste. "Green fees" are raising revenues for environmental improvement while discouraging environmentally destructive behavior. The list goes on.

The success of these approaches in providing a politically feasible and effective means of changing environmentally destructive behavior has attracted much wider interest in the field of environmental economics. Environmental groups, states, local governments, national governments, and even international organizations are beginning to incorporate the principles and techniques of environmental economies in their efforts to preserve and protect the environment.

But environmental economics is not a naturally hospitable field. Most of the economic principles that underlie these approaches flow from some intimidating mathematical models, making them inaccessible to all but those who are willing to invest the time and effort to learn the underlying mathematics. This lack of accessible textbooks has created a void. *Environmental Economics and Policy* is designed specifically to fill that void. It was written to communicate the powerful insights of the field to those taking economics courses designed for nonmajors or, more generally, to an audience with little or no training in economics.

With its strong emphasis on public policy, this book shows how economics can be used both to understand the behavioral sources of environmental problems and to provide the foundation for innovative solutions. Chapters 1 through 5 of the book describe the basic economic approach to the environment, laying out the underlying values, as well as the procedures used to translate those values into policy-relevant principles. Chapters 6 through 19 deal with natural resource economics (analyzing the flow of materials and energy from the environment into the economy) and environmental economics (analyzing the flow of waste products into the environment). Chapters 20 through 22 focus on sustainable development, reflecting the demonstrated, current global interest in finding new, environmentally compatible means of lifting the world's poor out of poverty. Throughout, the manner in which the principles can be applied is illustrated by a host of specific international examples. Considerable attention has been paid to environmental problems and policies in Eastern and Western Europe, Japan, and the developing nations, as well as in the United States.

This third edition of *Environmental Economics and Policy* is an economics book, but it goes beyond economics. Insights from the natural and physical sciences, literature, and political science, as well as other disciplines, are scattered liberally throughout the text. In some cases, these references raise unresolved issues that economic analysis can help resolve, whereas in others they affect the structure of the economic analysis or provide a contrasting point of view.

Students looking for additional sources of information on this subject don't have to look very far. A number of journals are now devoted either exclusively or mostly to the topics covered in this book. One, *Ecological Economics,* is a journal dedicated to bringing economists and ecologists closer together in a common search for appropriate solutions for environmental challenges. Interested readers can also find advanced work in the field in *Land Economics, Journal of Environmental Economics and Management, Environmental and Resource Economics, Resource and Energy Economics,* and *Natural Resources Journal,* among others.

New resources for student research projects have been made available in response to the growing popularity of the field. Original research on topics related to international environmental and natural resource issues was formerly very difficult for students to conduct because of the paucity of data. A number of good sources now exist; among these are *World Resources* (Washington, DC: Oxford University Press, published annually), which has an extensive data appendix, and *OECD Environmental Data* (Paris: Organization for Economic Co-operation and Development, published periodically).

Further sources on the field and the profession of environmental economics can be found on my web site. The address is: http://www.colby.edu/personal/thtieten/sustain.html.

NEW TO THIS EDITION

The third edition has increased the international focus of the book. Greater attention has been paid to environmental problems and policies in Eastern and Western Europe, Japan, and the developing nations than was the case in the previous edition.

The introductory material on sustainable development now appears as a separate chapter. Economic valuation of the environment is now addressed in two chapters, rather than one. While the first deals with the concepts that lie behind economic valuation, the second focuses on measurement concepts. Both chapters contain several practical illustrations. The two chapters on forestry and fisheries have been rewritten to focus on the two threats to biodiversity coming from destruction of habitat (with forests as the main example) and over exploitation of species (with fisheries as the main example). A large number of related web site addresses have been added to chapters. A new glossary defines and explains over 200 terms.

New boxed examples highlight special topics, including: (1) Does Reducing Pollution Make Economic Sense?; (2) Valuing Damage from Groundwater Contamination Using Averting Expenditures; (3) Valuing Diesel Odor Reduction by Contingent Ranking; (4) Shrimp Farming Externalities in Thailand; (5) Nauru: Weak Sustainability in the Extreme; (6) Water Pricing in Zurich, Switzerland; (7) Producing Sustainable Forestry Through Certification; (8) Environmental Taxation in China; (9) The Particulates and Smog Ambient Standards Controversy; (10) Project XL—The Quest for Effective, Flexible Regulation; (11) Car Sharing: Better use of Automotive Capital?; (12) Pricing Trash in Marietta, Georgia; (13) Jobs versus the

Environment; What Is the Evidence?; (14) Resource Depletion and Economic Sustainability: Malaysia; and (15) Controlling Land Use Development with TDRs.

New topics covered include:

Averting expenditures

Contingent ranking

Economic pressures for converting habitat to alternative uses

Sustainable forestry

Forestry certification

Preventing poaching

Voluntary programs for controlling pollution

Kyoto protocol and emissions trading of greenhouse gases

The "hot air" problem

The Total Maximum Daily Load program to control water pollution

Controlling land use with transferable development rights

Some completely new data and artwork have been added.

This edition retains a strong policy orientation. Though a great deal of theory and empirical evidence is discussed, their inclusion is motivated by the desire to increase understanding of intriguing policy problems, and these aspects are discussed in the context of those problems. This explicit integration of research and policy within each chapter avoids the problem frequently encountered in applied economics textbooks—that is, in such texts the theory developed in earlier chapters is often only loosely connected to the rest of the book. The many insights gleaned from other disciplines have an important role to play in overcoming the typical textbook's tendency to accept the material uncritically at a superficial level; instead, this text highlights those characteristics that make the economics approach unique.

ACKNOWLEDGMENTS

Perhaps the most rewarding part of writing this book has been that it has put me in touch with so many thoughtful people I had not previously met. I very much appreciate the faculty and students who pointed out areas of particular strength or areas where coverage could be expanded in this edition. The support this book has received from faculty and students has been gratifying and energizing. One can begin to understand the magnitude of my debt to my colleagues by glancing at the several hundred names in the lists of references contained in the name index. Because their research contributions make this an exciting field, full of insights worthy of being shared, my task was easier and a lot more fun than it might otherwise have been.

Valuable assistance was received during various stages of the writing from the following people:

Michael Balch	University of Iowa
Maurice Ballabon	Baruch College
A. Paul Baroutsis	Slippery Rock University of Pennsylvania
Fikret Berkes	Brock University
Trond Björndahl	Norwegian School of Economics and Business Administration

Sidney M. Blumner	California State Polytechnic University—Pomona
Vic Brajer	California State University, Fullerton
Richard Bryant	University of Missouri—Rolla
David Burgess	University of Western Ontario
Richard V. Butler	Trinity University
Trudy Ann Cameron	UCLA
Duane Chapman	Cornell University
Charles J. Chicchetti	University of Wisconsin—Madison
Gregory B. Christiansen	California State University—Hayward
Hal Cochrane	Colorado State University
Jon Conrad	Cornell University
William Corcoran	University of Nebraska at Omaha
Maureen L. Cropper	University of Maryland
John H. Cumberland	University of Maryland
Herman E. Daly	University of Maryland
Diane P. Dupont	University of Guelph
Randall K. Filer	Hunter College
Ann Fisher	Pennsylvania State University
Anthony C. Fisher	University of California—Berkeley
Marvin Frankel	University of Illinois—Urbana-Champaign
A. Myrick Freeman III	Bowdoin College
James Gale	Michigan Technological University
Haynes Goddard	University of Cinncinati
Nicholas Gotsch	Institute of Agricultural Economics (Zurich)
Doug Greer	San Jose State University
Ronald Griffin	Texas A&M University
W. Eric Gustafson	University of California—Davis
A. R. Gutowsky	California State University—Sacramento
Jon D. Harford	Cleveland State University
Gloria E. Helfand	University of Michigan
Ann Helwege	Tufts University
John J. Hovis	University of Maryland
Paul Huszar	Colorado State University
Craig Infanger	University of Kentucky
James R. Kahn	State University of New York—Binghamton
John O. S. Kennedy	LaTrobe University
Thomas Kinnaman	Bucknell University
Andrew Kliet	Louisiana State University
Richard F. Kosobud	University of Illinois at Chicago
Dwight Lee	University of Georgia
Joseph N. Lekakis	University of Crete
Ingemar Leksell	University of Goteberg
Randolph M. Lyon	Executive Office of the President (U.S.)
Giadomenico Majone	Harvard University
David Martin	Davidson College
Charles Mason	University of Wyoming

Frederic C. Menz	Clarkson University
Nicholas Mercuro	University of New Orleans
David E. Merrifield	Western Washington University
Michael J. Mueller	Clarkson University
Thomas C. Noser	University of Alabama
Lloyd Orr	Indiana University
Peter J. Parks	Rutgers University
Alexander Pfaff	Columbia Unviersity
Raymond Prince	University of Colorado—Boulder
H. David Robison	La Salle University
J. Barkley Rosser, Jr.	James Madison University
Jonathan Rubin	Unversity of Tennessee—Knoxville
Milton Russell	University of Tennessee
Frederick O. Sargent	University of Vermont
Salah El Serafy	World Bank
W. Douglas Shaw	University of Nevada—Reno
Aharon Shapiro	St. John's University
James S. Shortle	Pennsylvania State University
Leah J. Smith	Swarthmore College
V. Kerry Smith	Duke University
Rob Stavins	Harvard University
Joe B. Stevens	Oregon State University
Gert Svendsen	The Aarhus School of Business
Kenneth N. Townsend	Hampden-Sydney College
Wallace E. Tyner	Purdue University
Nora Underwood	University of California—Davis
Myles Wallace	Clemson University
Frank Ward	New Mexico State University
Patrick Welle	Bemidji State University
Anthony Yezer	George Washington University

In preparing this edition, I am especially indebted to the following reviewers for their detailed, helpful suggestions:

Gregory S. Amacher	Virginia Polytechnic Institute and State University
Michael Balch	University of Iowa
Mary A. Burke	Florida State University
David E. Gallo	California State University—Chico
Joseph A. Herriges	Iowa State University
Donn Johnson	Quinnipiac College
Richard F. Kosobud	University of Illinois—Chicago
Douglas M. Larson	University of California—Davis
Ross McKitrick	University of Guelph
Kankana Mukherjee	Clarkson University
Dan S. Olexio	U.S. Military Academy at West Point

Their support and willingness to share ideas on how the manuscript could be improved are much appreciated.

I have been fortunate to have been aided by many extremely capable student research assistants over the years. Andrea Murphy and Andrew Townsend helped me to produce this edition. Working with such fine young men and women has made it all the more obvious to me why teaching is the world's most satisfying profession.

Finally, I should like to express publicly my deep appreciation to my wife Gretchen, my daughter Heidi, and my son Eric for their love and support.

Tom Tietenberg
Sand Cove
Prospect Harbor, Maine

Visions of the Future

From the arch of the bridge to which his guide has carried him, Dante now sees the Diviners . . . coming slowly along the bottom of the fourth Chasm. By help of their incantations and evil agents, they had endeavored to pry into the future which belongs to the almighty alone, and now their faces are painfully twisted the contrary way; and being unable to look before them, they are forced to walk backwards.

DANTE ALIGHIERI, *DIVINE COMEDY: THE INFERNO*, TRANSLATED BY CARLYLE (1867)

◆ INTRODUCTION

The Self-Extinction Premise

About the time the American colonies became independent, Edward Gibbon completed his monumental work, *The History of the Decline and Fall of the Roman Empire*. In a particularly poignant passage that opens the last chapter of his opus, he re-creates a scene in which the learned Poggius, a friend, and two servants ascend the Capitoline Hill after the fall of Rome. They are awed by the contrast between what Rome once was and what Rome had become:

> In the time of the poet it was crowned with the golden roofs of a temple; the temple is overthrown, the gold has been pillaged, the wheel of fortune has accomplished her revolution, and the sacred ground is again disfigured with thorns and brambles. . . . The forum of the Roman people, where they assembled to enact their laws and elect their magistrates is now enclosed for the cultivation of potherbs, or thrown open for the reception of swine and buffaloes. The public and private edifices, that were founded for eternity lie prostrate, naked, and broken, like the limbs of a mighty giant; and the ruin is the more visible, from the stupendous relics that have survived the injuries of time and fortune. [Vol. 6, pp. 650–51]

What could cause the demise of such a grand and powerful society? Gibbon weaves a complex thesis to answer this question, suggesting ultimately that the seeds for Rome's destruction were sown by the Empire itself.[1] Though Rome finally succumbed to such external forces as fires and invasions, its vulnerability was based upon internal weakness.

The premise that societies germinate the seeds of their own destruction has long fascinated scholars. In one historically significant study in the early nineteenth century, Thomas Malthus foresaw a time when the urge to reproduce would create a situation in which population growth would outstrip the growth of food supply, resulting in starvation and death.

The 1970s and 1980s ushered in a revival of interest in Malthus's premise, mainly because of the growing number of writers who believe that modern society has embarked on a path that leads to self-destruction. Modern ecologists, for example, have suggested that the environment possesses a unique carrying capacity for the population; once that capacity is exceeded, widespread ecological disruption occurs with disastrous consequences for humanity. The focus is no longer on individual societies, but rather on the survival of the planet.

Sources of concern are not difficult to find. Since mid-century the world has lost nearly one fifth of the topsoil from its cropland, a fifth of its tropical rain forests, and tens of thousands of plant and animal species. Human activity has increased carbon dioxide levels to the point where the global climate is being affected. The protective ozone shield is being depleted. Dead forests and lakes are common in parts of Europe.[2]

Writers have begun to suggest that we have reached a turning point. Bill McKibben put it this way:

> We can no longer imagine that we are part of something larger than ourselves. . . . now we make the world, affect every operation. . . . This is, I suppose, the victory we have been pointing to at least since the eviction from Eden—the domination some have always dreamed of. But it is the story of King Midas writ large—the power looks nothing like we thought it would. It is a brutish, cloddish power, not a creative one.[3]

Humans have negotiated the transition from "adapting to" nature to "managing" nature.[4] The scale of activity has become so large that we affect the life processes of the planet. Where will it all lead?

---

[1]Rome does not provide the only historical example of a powerful society that followed a path of self-extinction. It has been suggested, for example, that the classic Maya civilization succumbed when its concentrated population proved too large to be supported by the soils around it. See Jeremy A. Sabloff, "The Collapse of Classic Maya Civilization," in *Patient Earth,* John Harte and Robert H. Socolow, eds. (New York: Holt, Rinehart and Winston, 1971): 16–27; Lester R. Brown, "World Population Growth, Soil Erosion, and Food Security," *Science* 214 (27 November, 1981): 995–1002.

[2]For an up-to-date examination of the earth's vital signs see the first chapter of the current edition of *State of the World* (New York: W. W. Norton), an annual published by the staff of the Worldwatch Institute in Washington, DC.

[3]Bill McKibben, *The End of Nature* (New York: Random House, 1989): 83–84.

[4]Symptomatic of this transition was the title of the September 1989 issue of *Scientific American.* This special issue on the environment was titled "Managing Planet Earth."

Environmental and Natural Resource Economics

For several decades economists have been concerned with topics such as exhaustible resources and pollution, but during the last two decades, the frequency of related books and articles has accelerated rapidly.[5] Consequently, we've come to better understand the relationship between humanity and the environment and how that relationship affects, and is affected by, economic and political institutions.

This knowledge has allowed political leaders to forge new solutions to old problems. Economic principles underlie fundamentally new approaches to controlling pollution, making better use of scarce water supplies, stemming deforestation, and limiting climate change—to name but a few of the areas that have been transformed. In this book you will be introduced to these economic principles and the entire spectrum of economic approaches to producing better environmental outcomes derived from them.

Thinking About the Future

The two visions presented in this chapter (the basic pessimist model and the basic optimist model) demonstrate areas of concern that will be given closer scrutiny later in this text. They also highlight the key relationships that motivate the conclusions drawn by authors of those visions so that we can assess the adequacy of these relationships as guides to reality.

As Example 1.1 points out, speculating about the future is a risky business. The pessimist and optimist visions we examine were chosen from the literally hundreds that exist because they define, in some sense, the endpoints of a spectrum. We shall, of course, explore not only these endpoints, but the vast intervening territory as we proceed through the book.

◆ THE BASIC PESSIMIST MODEL

One end of the spectrum is defined by an ambitious study published in 1972 under the title *The Limits to Growth* and subsequently updated and revised in 1992 under the title *Beyond the Limits.* Based on a technique known as *systems dynamics,* developed by Professor Jay Forrester at MIT, a large-scale computer model was constructed to simulate likely future outcomes of the world economy. The most prominent feature of systems dynamics is the use of feedback loops to explain behavior. The *feedback loop* is a closed path that connects an action to its effect on the surrounding conditions, which in turn can influence further action. As the examples presented subsequently in this chapter demonstrate, depending on how the relationships are described, a wide variety of complex behavior can be explained by this technique.

Conclusions of the Pessimist Model

Three main conclusions were reached by this study. The first suggests that within a time span of less than a hundred years with no major change in the physical, economic, or social relationships that have traditionally governed world development, society will run out of

---

[5]One article that is generally credited with sparking a renewed interest in natural resource problems is John Krutilla, "Conservation Reconsidered," *The American Economic Review* 57 (September 1968): 777–786.

Example 1.1

The Dangers of Prognostication

Our view of the future can be limited by our understanding of the past and present, as well as of the technological possibilities that lie around the corner. Often that understanding is not what it should be, and the forecasts based on it can seem rather absurd in retrospect.

In 1486, for example, a committee headed by Fray Hernando de Talavera was established by King Ferdinand and Queen Isabella to advise them on the merits of funding Christopher Columbus's plan to sail to the West Indies. Following four years of work, the committee reported its conclusion that a voyage of the type contemplated was impossible because (1) the Western Ocean was infinite and probably not navigable; (2) even if the Antipodes (the expected landfall) were reached, the return journey would be impossible; and (3) there probably were no Antipodes to be reached, because most of the world was presumably covered by water—St. Augustine said so.

In 1835 Thomas Tredgold, a British railroad designer, declared, "Any general system of conveying passengers—at a velocity exceeding 10 miles an hour, or thereabouts—is extremely improbable."

The chief geologist of the U.S. Geological Survey reported in 1920 that only 7 billion barrels of petroleum remained to be recovered with existing techniques. He predicted that, at the contemporary annual rate of consumption of a half billion barrels, American oil resources would be exhausted in 14 years—by 1934. However, when that fateful year arrived, 12, not 7, billion barrels had been produced and there was an additional 12 billion barrels of proved reserves.

Economists are certainly not immune from the dangers of prognostication. In *The Coal Question: An Inquiry Concerning the Progress of the Nation and the Probable Exhaustion of Our Coal Mines,* published in 1865, Stanley Jevons concluded that the rapid increase in coal consumption coupled with the finite nature of the supply of coal would cause progress to stop in the near future. In his discussion of Jevons's work, John Maynard Keynes notes in passing that Jevons had a similar fear of an increasing scarcity of paper. Jevons apparently acted on those fears for, some 50 years after his death, his children had not used up the stock of paper he had accumulated.

Sources: Glen Hueckel, "A Historical Approach to Future Economic Growth," *Science* 191 (14 March 1975): 925–31; Harry U. Spiegel, ed., *The Development of Economic Thought* (New York: Wiley, 1952): 490–525; Edward Cornish et al., *The Study of the Future* (Washington, DC: World Future Society, 1977): 106–08.

the nonrenewable resources on which the industrial base depends. When the resources have been depleted, a precipitous collapse of the economic system will result, manifested in massive unemployment, decreased food production, and a decline in population as the death rate soars. There is no smooth transition, no gradual slowing down of activity; rather, the economic system consumes successively larger amounts of the depletable resources until suddenly they are gone. The characteristic behavior of the system is overshoot and collapse (see Figure 1.1).

FIGURE 1.1   The Limits-to-Growth Standard Run

Senario 1

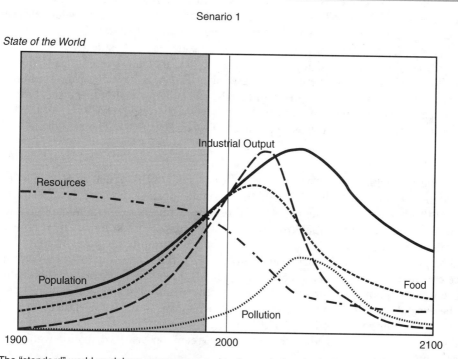

State of the World

Industrial Output

Resources

Population

Food

Pollution

1900   2000   2100

The "standard" world model run assumes no major change in the physical, economic, or social relationships that have governed the development of the world system. All variables plotted here follow historical values from 1900 to 1970. Food, industrial output, and population grow exponentially until the rapidly diminishing resource base forces a slowdown in industrial growth. Because of natural delays in the system, both population and pollution continue to increase for some time after the peak of industrialization. Population growth is finally halted by a rise in the death rate due to decreased food and medical services.

Source: Reprinted from *Beyond the Limits* copyright © 1992 by Meadows, Meadows and Randers. With permission from Chelsea Green Publishing Co., White River Junction, Vermont.

The second conclusion of the study is that piecemeal approaches to solving the individual problems will not be successful. To demonstrate this point, the authors arbitrarily double their estimates of the resource base and allow the model to trace out an alternative vision based on this new, higher level of resources. In this alternative vision the collapse still occurs, but this time it is caused by excessive pollution generated by the increased pace of industrialization permitted by the greater availability of resources. The authors then suggest that if the depletable resource and pollution problems were somehow jointly solved, population would grow unabated and the availability of food would become the binding constraint. In this model the removal of one limit merely causes the system to bump subsequently into another one, usually with more dire consequences.

As its third and final conclusion, the study suggests that overshoot and collapse can be avoided only by an immediate limit on population and pollution as well as a cessation of economic growth. The portrait painted shows only two possible outcomes: the termination of growth by self-restraint and conscious policy—an approach that avoids the collapse—or the termination of growth by a collision with the natural limits, resulting in societal collapse. Thus, according to this study, one way or the other, growth will cease. The only issue is whether the conditions under which it will cease will be congenial or hostile.

The 1992 update concluded that in the intervening 20 years many of the limits identified in the earlier study have been reached and exceeded. Fisheries have been overexploited; forests are being cut down at an unprecedented rate; soil is being depleted, and the air over some cities cannot be breathed without causing damage to the respiratory system. Still, the authors conclude, it is possible to avoid the collapse if we make the right choices now.

The Nature of the Model

Why were these conclusions reached? Clearly, they depend on the structure of the model. By identifying the characteristics that yield these conclusions, we can then, in subsequent chapters of this book, examine the realism of those characteristics. The dominant characteristic of the model is exponential growth coupled with fixed limits. Exponential growth in any variable (e.g., 3 percent per year) implies that the absolute increases in that variable will be greater and greater each year.[6] Furthermore, the higher the rate of growth in resource consumption, the faster a fixed stock of it will be exhausted. Suppose, for example, current reserves of a resource are 100 times current use and the supply of reserves cannot be expanded. If consumption were not growing, this stock would last 100 years. However, if consumption were to grow at 2 percent per year, the reserves would be exhausted in 55 years, and if growth increased to 10 percent per year, exhaustion would occur after only 24 years.

Several resources are held in fixed supply by the model. These include the amount of available land and the stock of depletable resources. In addition, the supply of food is fixed relative to the supply of land. The combination of exponential growth in demand and fixed sources of supply necessarily implies that, at some point, resource supplies must be exhausted. The extent to which those resources are essential thus creates the conditions for collapse.

This basic structure of the model is in some ways reinforced and in some ways tempered by the presence of a large number of positive and negative feedback loops. *Positive feedback loops* are those in which secondary effects tend to reinforce the basic trend. An example of a positive feedback loop is the process of capital accumulation. New investment generates greater output, which, when sold, generates profits. These profits, in turn, can be used to fund additional new investments. This example suggests a manner in which the growth process is self-reinforcing.

Positive feedback loops may also be involved in global warming. Scientists believe that the relationship between emissions of methane and global warming, for example, may be described as a positive feedback loop. Because methane is a greenhouse gas, increases in

---

[6]Suppose, for example, that in some initial year there are 100 units of a specific variable. If that variable is growing at 10 percent per year, then it will grow by 10 units during the first year and 11 units the second year.

methane emissions contribute to global warming. As the planetary temperature rises, however, it could cause the release of extremely large quantities of methane currently trapped in the permafrost; the larger quantities of methane would trigger further temperature increases, which could release more methane, and so on.

Human responses can intensify environmental problems. When shortages of a commodity are imminent, consumers typically begin to hoard the commodity. Hoarding intensifies the shortage. Similarly, people faced with shortages of food commonly eat the seed that is the key to more plentiful food in the future. Situations giving rise to this kind of downward spiral are particularly troublesome.

A *negative feedback loop* is self-limiting rather than self-reinforcing, as illustrated by the role of death rates in limiting population growth in the model. As growth occurs, it causes larger increases in industrial output, which in turn cause more pollution. The increase in pollution triggers a rise in death rates, retarding population growth. From this example it can be seen that negative feedback loops can provide a tempering influence on the growth process, though not necessarily a desirable one.

Perhaps the best-known example of negative feedback on a planetary scale is provided in a theory advanced by James Lovelock, an English scientist. Called the *Gaia hypothesis* after the Greek concept for Mother Earth, this view of the world suggests that the earth is a living organism with a complex feedback system that seeks an optimal physical and chemical environment. Deviations from this optimal environment trigger natural, nonhuman response mechanisms that restore the balance. According to the Gaia hypothesis, the planetary environment is (at least in part) a self-regulating process.

The model of the world envisioned by proponents of the Gaia hypothesis is incompatible with that envisioned by the *Beyond the Limits* team. Because of the dominance of positive feedback loops, coupled with fixed limits on essential resources, the structure of the *Beyond the Limits* model preordains its conclusion that human activity is on a collision course with nature. Although the values assumed for various parameters (e.g., the size of the stock of depletable resources) affect the timing of the various effects, they do not substantially affect the nature of the outcome.

The dynamics implied by the notion of a feedback loop is helpful in a more general sense than the specific relationships embodied in this model. As we proceed with our investigation, the degree to which our economic and political institutions serve to intensify or to limit emerging environmental problems will be a key concern.

◆ THE BASIC OPTIMIST MODEL

Is the portrait of the world economy presented by *Beyond the Limits* accurate? Many think not. One of the most vocal critics was the late Julian Simon, a well-known population economist. His alternative vision, published under the title *The Ultimate Resource*, rejects the overshoot-and-collapse scenario in favor of a more optimistic vision.[7]

---

[7]Julian L. Simon, *The Ultimate Resource* (Princeton, NJ: Princeton University Press, 1981).

Conclusions of the Optimistic Model

The Simon vision of the future concludes:

> The standard of living has arisen along with the size of the world's population since the beginning of recorded time. And with increases in income and population have come less severe shortages, lower costs, and an increased availability of resources, including a cleaner environment and greater access to natural recreation areas. And there is no convincing reason why these trends toward a better life, and toward lower prices for raw materials (including food and energy), should not continue indefinitely. [p. 345]

The Nature of the Model

What concepts of how the world works underlie this optimistic vision? Simon's argument is founded on two main tenets. First, his reading of the evidence suggests that, historically, human resourcefulness has always overcome both scarcities of resources and environmental problems associated with economic activity. Second, he finds no compelling reason that this trend cannot continue indefinitely into the future.

To bolster his argument, Simon offers several observations that are documented in this book:

- The amount of land being committed to agriculture is still increasing. Even where it is decreasing (e.g., in the United States), agricultural production has increased. Food production is therefore not likely to be a limiting factor.

- Contrary to popular belief, natural resources have not become more scarce over time. Apparent shortages are due more to (correctable!) problems with human behavior than to any physical lack of availability.

- Pollution levels have declined as populations and incomes have increased. Pollution is not the inevitable consequence of economic activity; rather, it results from societal choices about how resources should be invested.

What are the driving forces behind these outcomes? Simon suggests that our economic and, to a lesser extent, political systems respond to scarcity in ways that eliminate or diminish its impact. In the language of industrial dynamics, negative feedbacks to impending scarcity create a self-limiting process.

Consider, for example, just one such feedback. Impending scarcity triggers higher prices. Higher prices stimulate suppliers to find more of the resource. They also stimulate users to use less, to search for alternative (perhaps renewable) inputs. Both of these reactions tend to diminish the scarcity. Indeed, Simon's analysis suggests that these reactions have been so powerful that usable supplies of many resources are more abundant now than they were several decades ago!

Simon's optimism also extends to pollution. Pollution levels decline with higher income because both the demand for better environmental quality and the ability to pay for it increase with income. It therefore follows that one of the consequences of rising incomes is a decline in pollution. (Some of these pollution-income relationships were quantified by the World Bank in 1992; the study results are presented as Figure 1.2.)

FIGURE 1.2 Environmental Indicators for Various Country Income-Levels

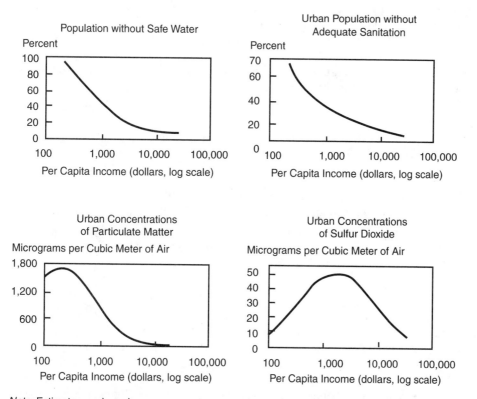

Note: Estimates are based on cross-country regression analysis of data from the 1980s.

Sources: From World Development Report 1992 by World Bank, copyright 1992 by The International Bank for Reconstruction and Development / The World Bank. Used by permissions of Oxford University Press.

Simon expects a continuation of these trends, because the one resource on which all future activity ultimately depends—the ultimate resource—is not limited. In his words:

> The natural world allows, and the developed world promotes through the marketplace, responses to human needs and shortages in such a manner that one backward step leads to 1.001 steps forward, or thereabouts. That's enough to keep us headed in a life-sustaining direction. The main fuel to speed our progress is our stock of knowledge, and the brake is our lack of imagination. The ultimate resource is people—skilled, spirited, and hopeful people who will exert their wills and imaginations for their own benefit, and so, inevitably, for the benefit of us all.

Simon believes that the fatal flaw in the *Beyond the Limits* vision is its "myopia." He believes that the authors of that study fail to understand the power of human imagination as it is unleashed by the feedback mechanisms in our economic and political systems as they respond to scarcity and environmental degradation. The immutable limits that are responsible for overshoot and collapse in the *Beyond the Limits* study turn out, in the Simon vision, to be purely transitory.

◆ THE ROAD AHEAD

We have introduced our study by reference to two rather different world visions—one optimistic and one pessimistic. In part, the differences between them depend on how human behavior is perceived. If intensifying pressure on the environment results in a behavioral response that intensifies the pressures, pessimism is justified. If, on the other hand, the human responses either currently are reducing those pressures or could be reformed so as to reduce those pressures, then optimism may be justified.

This is an important issue. Everywhere we look, we encounter environmental problems:

- Scientists believe that the mean temperature of the planet is increasing over time and is likely to exceed the highest levels ever experienced by humans so far.
- The diversity of species is being reduced at an unprecedented rate.
- Rates of population growth continue at levels that are likely to exceed rates of growth in the production of food for many countries of the world.
- Modern agriculture in some areas has become dependent on irrigation, which is drawing down groundwater supplies, and the use of pesticides, which are contaminating the quality of remaining water.

And the list goes on.

The field of environmental and natural resource economics has become an important source of ideas for coping with these problems. Not only does the field provide a firm basis for understanding the human sources of environmental problems, this understanding provides a firm foundation for crafting specific solutions to these problems. In subsequent chapters, for example, you shall be exposed to how economic analysis can be (and has been) used to forge solutions to global warming (Chapter 14), biodiversity loss (Chapter 10), population growth (Chapter 6), and water scarcity (Chapter 8). Many of the solutions are quite novel.

The search for solutions must recognize that market forces are extremely powerful. Attempts to solve environmental problems that ignore these forces run a high risk of failure. It is both possible and desirable to harness these forces and channel them into directions that protect the environment. Environmental and natural resource economics provides a specific set of directions for how that can be accomplished.

The Issues

Obviously, the two opposing visions of the future present us with rather different conceptions of what the future holds, as well as different views of what policy choices should be made. They also suggest that to act as if one vision is correct, when it is not, could prove to be a costly error. Thus, it is important to determine whether one of these two views or, alternatively, some third view, is correct.

In order to assess any model or view, it is necessary to address the basic issues:

1. Is the problem correctly conceptualized as exponential growth with fixed, immutable resource limits? Does the earth have a finite carrying capacity?

2. If these limits do exist, have they been measured correctly, or, as Simon argues, has the *Beyond the Limits* team been rather myopic in the way it treats resources? How can the carrying-capacity concept be operationalized? Do current levels of economic activity exceed the earth's carrying capacity?

3. How does the economic system respond to scarcities? Does the process involve mainly negative feedback loops? Would it intensify or ameliorate any initial scarcities? Is the overshoot-and-collapse syndrome an accurate portrayal of the future?

4. What is the role of the political system in controlling these problems? In what circumstances is government intervention necessary? Is this intervention uniformly benign, or can it make the situation worse? What roles are appropriate for our executive, legislative, and judicial branches?

5. Many environmental problems involve a considerable degree of uncertainty about the severity of the problem and the effectiveness of possible solutions. Can our economic and political institutions respond to this uncertainty in reasonable ways?

6. Can the economic and political systems work together to eradicate poverty while respecting our obligation to future generations? Or does our obligation to future generations inevitably conflict with the desire to raise the living standards of those currently in absolute poverty? Can short-term and long-term goals be harmonized? Is sustainable development feasible? How could it be achieved? What does it imply about the future of economic activity in the industrialized nations? in the less industrialized nations?

We will use economic analysis to suggest answers to these questions in the rest of the book.

An Overview of the Book

In the following chapters you will study the rich and rewarding field of environmental and natural resource economics. The menu of topics is broad and varied. Economics provides a powerful analytical framework for examining the relationships between the environment on the one hand and the economic and political systems on the other. The study of economics can assist in identifying circumstances that give rise to environmental problems, in discovering causes of these problems, and in searching for solutions. Each chapter is an introduction to a unique topic in environmental and natural resource economics, and our overarching focus on growth in a finite environment weaves these topics into a single theme.

We begin by comparing perspectives being brought to bear on these problems by economists and noneconomists. The manner in which scholars in various disciplines view problems and potential solutions depends on how they organize the available facts, how they interpret those facts, and what kinds of values they apply in translating these interpretations into policy. Before taking a detailed look at environmental problems, we shall compare the ideology of conventional economics to other prevailing ideologies in both the natural and social sciences. This comparison both explains why reasonable people may, upon examining the same set of facts, reach different conclusions and conveys some sense of the strengths and weaknesses of economic analysis as it is applied to environmental problems. Specific evaluation criteria are defined and examples are developed to show how economic criteria can be applied to specific environmental problems.

After examining the major perspectives shaping environmental policy, we shall turn to the physical limits identified by *Beyond the Limits,* the manner in which the economic and political institutions have dealt with the resulting problems, and the potential for improvement in the future. We begin our examination with an inquiry into the nature, causes, and consequences of population growth, a major factor in determining how rapidly the limits could be reached.

The next section of the book deals with several topics traditionally falling within natural resource economics. Energy is discussed as an example of a depletable, nonrecyclable resource. Minerals illustrate how depletable, recyclable resources are allocated over time, including the appropriate role for recycling. The degree to which the current situation approximates this ideal is assessed, with particular attention paid to aspects such as tax policy, disposal costs, and product durability.

The chapters on renewable or replenishable resources (e.g., water, food, forestry, fisheries) show that the effectiveness with which current institutions manage renewable resources depends on whether the resources are living or inanimate and whether they are treated as private or as common property.

We then move on to an area of public policy—pollution control—that is coming to rely much more heavily on the use of economic incentives to produce the desired response. The overview chapter emphasizes not only the nature of the problems but also differences among policy approaches taken to resolve them. The unique aspects of local air pollution, regional and global air pollution, automobile air pollution, water pollution, and the control of toxic substances are dealt with individually in five subsequent chapters.

Following this examination of the individual environmental and natural resource problems and the policies that can be, and have been, used to ameliorate these problems, the book turns to the growth process itself. Certain questions must be asked: What are the causes and consequences of economic growth? What roles do natural resources and environmental control play in the growth process? What is the likely future for economic growth? Is an immediate transition to a zero-economic-growth path (as suggested by *Beyond the Limits*) necessary? Or, if unnecessary, is it desirable?

The book closes by assembling the bits and pieces of evidence accumulated in each of the preceding chapters and fusing them into an overall response to the questions posed in this chapter. The last chapter also suggests some of the major unresolved issues in environmental policy that are likely to be among those commanding center stage over the next several years or decades.

SUMMARY

Is our society so myopic that it has chosen a path that can only lead to the destruction of society as we now know it? We have examined briefly two studies that provide two different answers to that question. *Beyond the Limits* responds in the affirmative, whereas Simon responds negatively. The pessimistic view is based upon the inevitability of exceeding the carrying capacity of the planet as the population and the level of economic activity grow. The optimistic view sees initial scarcity triggering sufficiently powerful reductions in population growth and increases in technological progress such that the future brings abundance, not deepening scarcity.

Our examination of these rather different visions has revealed a number of questions that must be answered if we are to assess what the future holds. Seeking answers to these questions requires that we accumulate a much better understanding about how choices are made in economic and political systems and how those choices affect, and are affected by, the natural environment. We shall begin that process in Chapter 2, where the economic approach is developed in broad terms and is contrasted with other conventional approaches.

FURTHER READING

Cairncross, F. *Green, Inc.: A Guide to Business and the Environment* (Washington, D.C.: Island Press, 1995). A noted economic journalist explores how business can become part of the solution.

Lovins, A., L. H. Lovins, P. Hawken. "A Road Map for Natural Capitalism." *Harvard Business Review* (1999): 145–158. A vision suggesting that business strategies built on a more productive use of natural resources can solve many environmental problems at a profit.

Oates, W. E., ed., *The RFF Reader in Environmental and Resource Management* (Washington, D.C.: Resources for the Future, Inc., 1999). A collection of short, highly readable commentaries on subjects ranging from biodiversity and climate change to environmental justice.

Stavins, R., ed. *Economics of the Environment: Selected Readings,* 4th ed. (New York: W. W. Norton & Company, Inc., 2000). An excellent set of complementary readings that captures both the power of the discipline and the controversy it provokes.

World Commission on Environment and Development. *Our Common Future* (Oxford: Oxford University Press, 1987). An enormously influential book that has set the tone for international discussions of sustainable development.

ADDITIONAL REFERENCES

Ascher, William. *Why Governments Waste Natural Resources: Policy Failures in Developing Countries* (Baltimore, MD: Johns Hopkins University Press, 1999).

Brander, James A. and M. Scott Taylor. "The Simple Economics of Easter Island: A Ricardo-Malthus Model of Renewable Resource Use," *American Economic Review* Vol. 88, No. 1 (March, 1998): 119–138.

Portney, P. R. "The Growing Role of Economics in Environmental Decisionmaking," *Environment* Vol. 40, No. 2 (1998): 14.

WEB SITES OF INTEREST

1. *www.igc.apc.org/desip/malthus/index.html*
   This is the homepage of the International Society of Malthus. Contains background, predictions, links to related sites, maps showing changes in human population throughout history, and the complete text of Malthus's "Essay on the Principle of Population."

2. *www.sun.rhbnc.ac.uk/~uhss021/ESP/BeyondTheLimits.html*
   This web site provides an overview of Beyond the Limits. Mac users can download a World3 computer program simulation that also allows the user to change variables and see the resultant consequences.

3. *www.bmgt.umd.edu/~jsimon/*
   This is the homepage of Julian Simon. It contains links and unpublished books and articles including The Ultimate Resource II.

DISCUSSION QUESTIONS

1. A central concept in the *Beyond the Limits* view of the future is the finiteness of resources. In *The Ultimate Resource,* Julian Simon makes the point that calling the resource base "finite" is misleading. To illustrate this point he uses a yardstick, with its one-inch markings, as an analogy. The distance between two markings is finite—one inch—but an infinite number of points is contained within that finite space. Therefore, in one sense, what lies between the markings is finite, but in another, equally meaningful sense, it is infinite. Is the concept of a finite resource base useful or not? Why?

2. This chapter contains two rather different views of the future. Because the validity of these views cannot completely be tested until the time period covered by the forecast has passed (so that predictions can be matched against actual events), how can we ever hope to establish whether one is a better view than the other? What criteria might be proposed for evaluating predictions?

3. Positive and negative feedback loops lie at the core of systematic thinking about the future. As you examine the key forces shaping the future, what examples of positive and negative feedback loops can you uncover?

2

Valuing the Environment: Concepts

When you have eliminated the impossible, whatever remains, however improbable, must be the truth.

SHERLOCK HOLMES, FROM SIR ARTHUR CONAN DOYLE'S *THE SIGN OF FOUR* (1890)

◆ INTRODUCTION

Before examining specific environmental problems and the policy responses to them, it is important that we develop and clarify the economics approach, so that we will have some sense of the forest before examining each of the trees. By having a feel for the conceptual framework, it becomes easier not only to deal with individual cases, but, perhaps more importantly, to see how they fit into a comprehensive approach.

In this chapter we develop the general conceptual framework used in economics to approach environmental problems. We begin by examining the relationship between human actions, as manifested through the economic system, and the environmental consequences of those actions. We can then establish criteria for judging the desirability of the outcomes of this relationship. These criteria provide a basis for identifying the nature and severity of environmental problems, and a foundation for designing effective policies to deal with them.

Throughout this chapter the economic point of view is contrasted with alternative points of view. These contrasts bring the economic approach into sharper focus and stimulate deeper and more critical thinking about all possible approaches.

◆ THE HUMAN ENVIRONMENT RELATIONSHIP

The Environment as an Asset

In economics the environment is viewed as a composite asset that provides a variety of services. It is a very special asset, to be sure, since it provides the life support systems that sustain our very existence, but it is an asset nonetheless. As with other assets, we wish to prevent undue depreciation of the value of this asset so that it may continue to provide aesthetic and life-sustaining services.

The environment provides the economy with raw materials, which are transformed into consumer products by the production process, and energy, which fuels this transformation. Ultimately these raw materials and energy return to the environment as waste products (see Figure 2.1).

The environment also provides services directly to consumers. The air we breathe, the nourishment we receive from food and drink, and the protection we derive from shelter and

FIGURE 2.1   The Economic System and the Environment

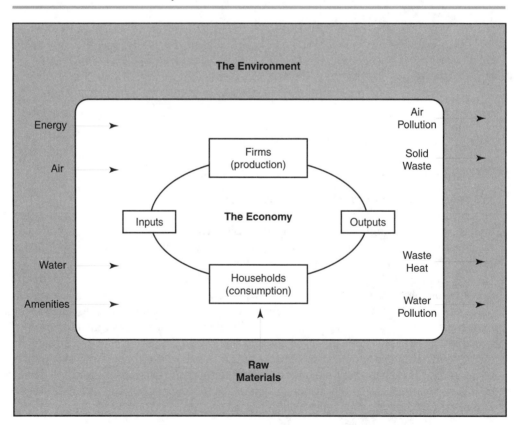

clothing are all benefits we receive either directly or indirectly from the environment. In addition, anyone who has experienced the exhilaration of white-water canoeing, the total serenity of a wilderness trek, or the breathtaking beauty of a sunset will readily recognize that the environment provides us with a variety of amenities for which no substitute exists.

If the environment is defined broadly enough, the relationship between the environment and the economic system can be considered a *closed system*. For our purposes, a closed system is one in which no inputs (energy, matter, and so on) are received from outside the system and no outputs are transferred outside the system. An *open system,* by contrast, is one in which the system imports or exports matter or energy.

If we restrict our conception of the relationship in Figure 2.1 to our planet and the atmosphere around it, then clearly we do not have a closed system. We derive most of our energy from the sun, either directly or indirectly. We have also sent spaceships well beyond the boundaries of our atmosphere. Nonetheless, historically speaking, for *material* inputs and outputs (not including energy), this system can be treated as a closed system because the amount of exports (such as abandoned space vehicles) and imports (moon rocks, for example) are negligible. Whether the system remains closed depends on the degree to which space exploration opens up the rest of our solar system as a source of raw materials.

The treatment of our planet and its immediate environs as a closed system has an important implication which is summed up in the *first law of thermodynamics*—energy and matter cannot be created or destroyed.[1] The law implies that the mass of materials flowing into the economic system from the environment has to either accumulate in the economic system or return to the environment as waste. When accumulation stops, the mass of materials flowing into the economic system is equal in magnitude to the mass of waste flowing into the environment.

Excessive wastes can, of course, depreciate the asset; when they exceed the absorptive capacity of nature, wastes reduce the services that the asset provides.[2] Examples are easy to find: air pollution can cause respiratory problems; polluted drinking water can cause cancer; smog obliterates scenic vistas.

The relationship of people to the environment is also conditioned by another physical law, the *second law of thermodynamics*. Known popularly as the *entropy law*, this law states that entropy increases. *Entropy* is the amount of energy not available for work. Applied to energy processes, this law implies that no conversion from one form of energy to another is completely efficient and that the consumption of energy is an irreversible process. Some energy is always lost during conversion, and the rest, once used, is no longer available for further work. The second law also implies that in the absence of new energy inputs, any closed system must eventually use up its energy. Since energy is necessary for life, life ceases when energy ceases.

We should remember that our planet is not even approximately a closed system with respect to energy; we gain energy from the sun. The entropy law does suggest, however,

---

[1] We know, however, from Einstein's famous equation ($E = mc^2$) that matter can be transformed into energy. This transformation is the source of energy in nuclear power.

[2] A detailed economic model, known as the materials balance model, has been constructed to integrate physical mass flows and the economic system. A description of this model can be found in Allen V. Kneese, Robert U. Ayers, and Ralph d'Arge. *Economics and the Environment: A Materials Balance Approach* (Washington, DC: Resources for the Future, Inc., 1970).

that this flow of solar energy establishes an upper limit on the flow of energy that can be sustained. Once the stocks of stored energy (such as fossil fuels and nuclear energy) are gone, the amount of energy available for useful work will be determined solely by this flow and by the amount that can be stored (dams, trees, and so on). Thus, over the very long run, the growth process will be limited by the availability of solar energy and our ability to put it to work.

The Economic Approach

Two different types of economic analysis can be applied to increase our understanding of the relationship between the economic system and the environment: Positive economics attempts to describe *what is, what was,* or *what will be. Normative* economics, by contrast, deals with what *ought to be.* Disagreements within positive economics can usually be resolved by an appeal to the facts. Normative disagreements, however, involve value judgments.

Both branches are useful. Suppose, for example, we want to investigate the relationship between trade and the environment. Positive economics could be used to describe the kinds of impacts trade would have on the economy and the environment. It could not, however, provide any guidance on the question of whether trade was desirable. That judgment would have to come from normative economics.

Normative analysis can arise in several different contexts It might be used, for example, to evaluate the desirability of either a proposed new pollution control regulation or a proposal to preserve an area currently scheduled for development. In these cases the analysis helps to provide guidance on the desirability of a program before that program is put into place. In other contexts it might be used to evaluate how an already-implemented program has worked out. Both of these types of situations share the characteristic that the alternatives being evaluated are well defined in advance. Here the relevant question is: Should we do it or shouldn't we?

A rather different context for normative economics can arise when the possibilities are more open-ended. For example, we might ask how much should we control emissions of greenhouse gases (which contribute to global warming) and how should we achieve that degree of control? Or we might ask how much forest of various types should be preserved? Answering these questions requires us to consider the entire range of possible outcomes and to select the best or optimal one. Although that is a much more difficult question to answer than one which asks us only to compare two predefined alternatives, the basic normative analysis framework is the same in both cases.

◆ NORMATIVE CRITERIA FOR DECISION MAKING

Evaluating Predefined Options

If you were asked to evaluate the desirability of some proposed action, you would probably begin by attempting to identify both the gains from that action and the losses. If the gains exceed the losses, then it seems natural to support the action.

That simple framework provides the starting point for the economic approach. Economists suggest that actions have both benefits and costs. If the benefits exceed the costs, then the action is desirable. On the other hand, if the costs exceed the benefits, then the action is not desirable.

FIGURE 2.2   The Individual Demand Curve

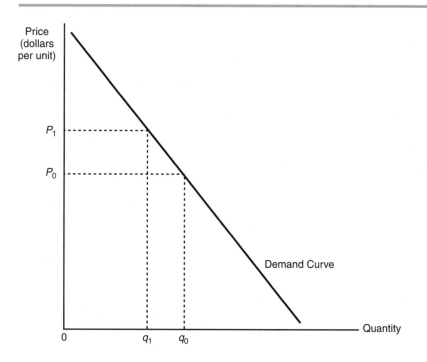

We can formalize this in the following way. Let B be the benefits from a proposed action and C be the costs. Our decision rule would then be:

If B > C, then support the action.

Otherwise, oppose the action.[3]

As long as B and C are positive an equivalent formulation would be:

If B/C > 1, support the action.

Otherwise, oppose the action.

So far so good, but how do we measure benefits and costs? In economics the system of measurement is anthropocentric, which simply means human-centered. All benefits and costs are valued in terms of their effects (broadly defined) on humanity. As shall be pointed out later, that does *not* imply (as it might first appear) that ecosystem effects are ignored unless they *directly* affect humans. The fact that large numbers of humans contribute voluntarily to organizations that are dedicated to environmental protection provides ample evidence that humans place a value on environmental preservation which goes well beyond any direct use they might make of it. Nonetheless the notion that humans are doing the valuing is a controversial point (Example 2.1).

Benefits can be derived from the demand curve for the good or service provided by the action. Demand curves measure the amount of a particular good people would be willing to purchase at various prices. In a typical situation, a person will purchase less of a commodity (or environmental service) the higher is its cost. In Figure 2.2, when the price is p_0, q_0 will be purchased, but if the price rises to p_1, purchases will fall to q_1.

---

[3]Actually if B = C, it wouldn't make any difference if the action occurs or not; the benefits and costs are a wash.

Example 2.1

Nature Knows Best

The view that the environment should be managed by humans is rather controversial, particularly among ecologists. In *The Closing Circle*, Barry Commoner poses what he calls the third law of ecology: nature knows best. Commoner elaborates on this view:

> ...living things accumulate a complex organization of compatible parts; those possible arrangements that are not compatible with the whole are screened out over the long course of evolution. Thus, the structure of a present living thing or the organization of a current natural ecosystem is likely to be "best" in the sense that it has been so heavily screened for disadvantageous components that any new one is very likely to be worse than the present one. [p. 43]

Don't interfere with the ecosystem is the underlying message.

The conflict between the economic approach and that proposed by Commoner is perhaps best illustrated by the controversy over the Tellico Dam and the snail darter. The Tellico Dam was an ambitious water project on the Little Tennessee River authorized by Congress in 1967. During the summer of 1973, a Tennessee ichthyologist, Dr. David A. Etnier, Jr., discovered a previously unknown species of perch called the snail darter. During 1975, with the dam 75 percent complete, the Secretary of the Interior declared the snail darter an endangered species, which, under the Endangered Species Act of 1973, was sufficient to stop construction of the dam. The Supreme Court in 1978 upheld the act. The final turn of events, however, in this twisted saga came in 1979 when Congress passed, as a rider on an energy and water appropriations bill, an exemption from the Endangered Species Act for the snail darter.

The economic approach stacks up the worth of the project against the worth of the snail darter, both as a species and as a member of the larger ecological system. The principle of minimum interference suggests that regardless of the importance of the snail darter and regardless of the cost, it should be preserved. The extinction of a species is never justified regardless of the circumstances.

Ironically, this clash of principles need not have taken place. An economic analysis showed the dam to be a poor investment, and the snail darter was subsequently successfully transplanted to the neaby Hiwasee River. Nonetheless, this issue serves to illustrate that the seemingly abstract conflict between alternative sets of values can have very practical implications.

Sources: "Endangered Species Curbs," *Congressional Quarterly Almanac*, 34 (1978): 707; "Public Works Energy Development Funds," *Congressional Quarterly Almanac*, 35 (1979): 223, "Endangered Species Act," *Congressional Quarterly Almanac*, 35 (1979): 661; Barry Commoner, *The Closing Circle* (New York: Alfred A. Knopf, 1972).

The meaning of these demand curves can be illustrated with this hypothetical experiment: suppose you were asked: At a price of X dollars, how much commodity Y would you buy? Your answer could be recorded as a point on a diagram such as Figure 2.2. By repeating

FIGURE 2.3 The Relationship of Demand to Willingness to Pay

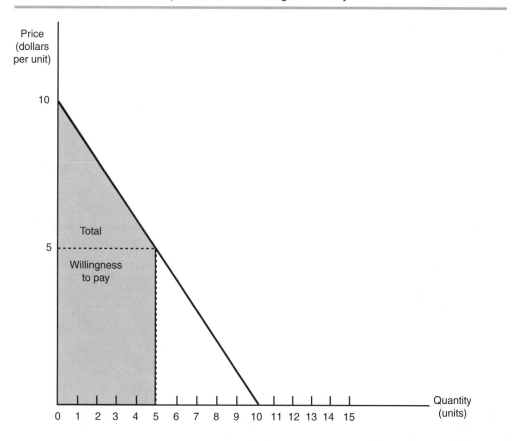

the question many times for different prices, we could trace out a locus of points. Connecting these points would yield an individual *demand curve*. Adding up all of the individual amounts demanded by all individuals at some stipulated price yields one point on the market demand curve. Connecting the points for various prices reveals the market demand curve.

For each quantity purchased, the corresponding point on the market demand curve represents the amount of money some person is willing to pay for the last unit of the good. The *total willingness to pay* for some quantity of this good—say, 3 units—is the sum of the willingness to pay for each of the three units. Thus the total willingness to pay for 3 units would be measured by the sum of the willingness to pay for the first, second, and third units, respectively. It is now a simple extension to determine that the total willingness to pay is the area under the continuous market demand curve to the left of the allocation in question. For example, in Figure 2.3 the total willingness to pay for 5 units of the commodity is the shaded area.[4] Total willingness to pay is the concept we shall use to define *total benefits*. Thus total

---

[4]From simple geometry it can be noticed that for linear demand curves this area is the sum of the areas of the triangle on top plus the rectangle on the bottom. The area of a right triangle is ½ × base × height. Therefore, in our example this area is ½ × \$5 × 5 + \$5 × 5 = \$37.50.

FIGURE 2.4 The Relationship of Marginal Cost and Total Cost

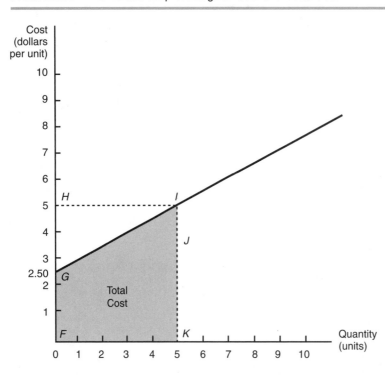

benefits are equal to the area under the market demand curve from the origin to the allocation of interest.

Measuring total costs on the same set of axes involves logic similar to measuring total benefits. It is important to stress that environmental services have costs even though they are produced without any human input. All costs should be measured as opportunity costs.

For environmental services their *opportunity cost* is the net benefit forgone because the resources providing the service can no longer be used in their next most beneficial use. Resources are not free if they can be put to alternative uses. For example, suppose a particular stretch of river can be used either for white-water canoeing or to generate electric power. Since the dam that generates the power would flood the rapids, the two uses are incompatible. The opportunity cost of producing power is the forgone net benefit that would have resulted from the white-water canoeing.

In graphing costs, we shall use the marginal opportunity cost curve to correspond to the marginal willingness-to-pay function used above to graph benefits. The *marginal opportunity cost curve* defines the additional cost of producing the last unit. In purely competitive markets, the marginal opportunity cost curve is identical to the supply curve.

Total cost is simply the sum of the marginal costs.[5] The total cost of producing 3 units is equal to the cost of producing the first unit plus the cost of producing the second

---

[5]Strictly speaking, the sum of the marginal costs is equal to total variable cost. In the short run, this is smaller than total cost by the amount of the fixed cost. For our purposes this distinction is not important.

FIGURE 2.5   The Derivation of Net Benefits

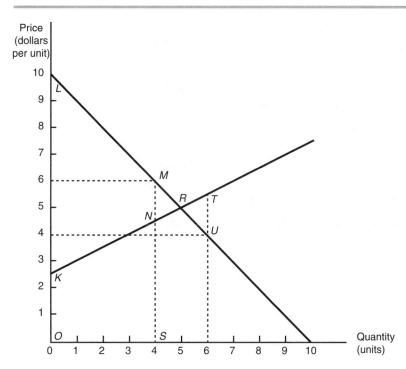

unit plus the cost of producing the third unit. As with total willingness to pay, the geo-metric representation of the sum of the individual elements of a continuous marginal cost curve is the area under the marginal cost curve, as illustrated in Figure 2.4 by the shaded area *FGIJK*.[6]

Since net benefit is defined as the excess of benefits over costs, it follows that net benefit is equal to that portion of the area under the demand curve which lies above the supply curve. Consider Figure 2.5, which combines the information in Figures 2.3 and 2.4.

Let's now use this apparatus to illustrate the use of the decision rules introduced ear-lier. Let's suppose for example that we are considering preserving a four-mile stretch of river and that the benefits and costs of that action are reflected in Figure 2.5. Should that stretch be preserved?

The analysis we have covered so far is very useful for thinking about actions where time is not an important factor. Yet many of the decisions made now have consequences which per-sist well into the future. Time is a factor. Exhaustible energy resources, once used, are gone. Biological renewable resources (such as fisheries or forests) can be overharvested, leaving smaller and possibly weaker populations for future generations. Persistent pollutants can ac-cumulate over time. How can we make choices when the benefits and costs may occur at dif-ferent points in time?

---

[6]Notice again that this area is the sum of a right triangle and a rectangle. In Figure 2.4 the total variable cost of pro-ducing 5 units is $18.75. Why?

Incorporating time into the analysis requires an extension of the concepts we have already developed. This extension provides a way for thinking not only about the magnitude of benefits and costs, but also about timing. In order to incorporate timing, the decision rule must provide a way to compare the net benefit received in one period with the net benefit received in another. The concept that allows this comparison is called *present value*. Therefore, before introducing this expanded decision rule, we must define present value.

Present value explicitly incorporates the time value of money. A dollar today invested at 10 percent interest yields $1.10 a year from now (the return of the $1 principal plus $0.10 interest). The present value of $1.10 received one year from now is, therefore, $1 because, given $1 now, you can turn it into $1.10 a year from now by investing it at 10 percent interest. We can find the present value of any amount of money (X) received one year from now by computing $X/(1 + r)$, where r is the appropriate interest rate (10% in our above example).

What could your dollar earn in two years at r percent interest? Because of compound interest, the amount would be $\$1(1 + r)(1 + r) = \$1(1 + r)^2$. It follows then that the present value of X received two years from now is $X/(1 + r)^2$.

By now the pattern should be clear. The present value of a *one-time* net benefit received n years from now is

$$PV\left[B_n\right] = \frac{B_n}{\left(1 + r\right)^n}.$$

The present value of a stream of net benefits $\{B_0, \ldots, B_n\}$ received over a period of n years is computed as

$$PV\left[B_0,\ldots,B_n\right] = \sum_{i=0}^{n} \frac{B_i}{\left(1 + r\right)^i},$$

where r is the appropriate interest rate and B_0 is the amount of net benefits received immediately. The process of calculating the present value is called *discounting*, and the rate r is referred to as the discount rate.[7]

The number resulting from a present-value calculation has a straightforward interpretation. Suppose you were investigating an allocation that would yield the following pattern of net benefits on the last day of each of the next five years: $3000, $5000, $6000, $10,000, $12,000. If you use an interest rate of 6% ($r = 0.06$) and the above formula, you will discover that this stream has a present value of $29,210.

What does that number mean? If you put $29,210 in a savings account earning 6 percent interest and wrote yourself checks, respectively, for $3000, $5000, $6000, $10,000, and $12,000 on the last day of each of the next five years, your last check would just restore the account to a zero balance. Thus, you should be indifferent about receiving $29,210 now or in the specific five–year stream of benefits totaling $36,000; given one, you can get the other. Hence, the method is called present value because it translates everything back to its current worth.

---

[7]The discount rate should equal the social opportunity cost of capital. We examine in Chapter 4 the questions of whether private firms can be expected to use the socially correct discount rate. In Chapter 3, we discuss how the discount rate is chosen by the government.

It is now possible to show how this analysis can be used to evaluate actions. First calculate the present value of net benefits from the action. If the present value is greater than zero, the action should be supported. Otherwise it should not.

◆ FINDING THE OPTIMAL OUTCOME

In the preceding section we have examined how benefit-cost analysis can be used to evaluate the desirability of specific actions. In this section we want to examine how this approach can be used to identify "optimal" or best approaches.

In subsequent chapters which address individual environmental problems, the normative analysis will proceed in three steps. First we will identify an optimal outcome. Second we will attempt to discern the extent to which our institutions produce optimal outcomes and, where divergences occur between actual and optimal outcomes, to attempt to uncover the behavioral sources of the problems. Finally we can use both our knowledge of the nature of the problems and their underlying behavioral causes as a basis for designing appropriate policy solutions. Though how these three steps are applied to each of the environmental problems will reflect the uniqueness of each situation, the overarching framework used to shape that analysis will be the same.

To provide some concreteness of this approach, consider two examples, one drawn from natural resource economics and another from environmental economics. These are meant to be illustrative and to convey a flavor of the argument; the details are left to upcoming chapters.

Consider the rising number of depleted ocean fisheries. Depleted fisheries, which involve fish populations that have fallen so low as to threaten their viability as commercial fisheries, not only jeopardize oceanic biodiversity, but also pose a threat to both the individuals who make their living from the sea and the communities that have depended on fishing to support their local economies.

How would an economist attempt to understand and to resolve this problem? The first step would involve defining the optimal stock or the optimal rate of harvest of the fishery. The second step would compare this level with the actual stock and harvest levels. Once this economic framework is applied, not only does it become clear that stocks are much lower than optimal for many fisheries, but the reason for excessive exploitation becomes clear as well. Understanding the nature of the problem has led quite naturally to some solutions. Once implemented, these policies have allowed some fisheries to begin the process of renewal. The details of this analysis and the policy implications which flow from it are covered in Chapter 13.

Another problem involves solid waste. As local communities run out of room for landfills in the face of an increasing generation of waste, what can be done?

Economists start by thinking about how one would define the optimal amount of waste. The definition necessarily incorporates waste reduction and recycling as aspects of the optimal outcome. The analysis not only reveals that current waste levels are excessive, but also suggests some specific behavioral sources of the problem. Based upon this understanding, specific economic solutions have been identified and implemented. Communities that have adopted these measures have generally experienced lower levels of waste and higher levels of recycling.

In the rest of the book, similar analysis is applied to population, energy, minerals, agriculture, air and water pollution, and a host of other topics. In each case the economic analysis helps to point the way toward solutions. To initiate that process we must begin by defining what is meant by optimal.

Static Efficiency

The chief normative economic criterion for choosing among various allocations occurring at the same point in time is called *static efficiency,* or merely *efficiency.* An allocation of resources is said to satisfy the static efficiency criterion if the net benefit from the use of those resources is maximized by that allocation.

Let's show how this concept can be applied by returning to Figure 2.5. Previously we asked whether an action which preserved four miles of river was worth doing? The answer was yes because the net benefits from that action were positive.

Static efficiency, however, requires us to ask a rather different question; namely, what is the efficient number of miles to be preserved? We know from the definition that the efficient amount of preservation would maximize net benefits. Do four units maximize net benefits?

We can answer that question by establishing whether it is possible to increase the net benefit by preserving more or less of the river. If the net benefit can be increased by preserving more miles, clearly preserving four miles could not have maximized the net benefit and, therefore, could not have been efficient.

Consider what would happen if society were to choose to preserve five miles instead of four. What happens to the net benefit? It increases by area MNR. Since we can find another allocation with greater net benefit, four miles of preservation could not have been efficient. Are five? Yes. Let's see why.

We know that five miles of preservation convey more net benefits than four. If this allocation is efficient, then it must also be true that the net benefit is smaller for levels of preservation higher than five. Notice that the additional cost of preserving the sixth unit (the area under the marginal cost curve) is larger than the additional benefit received from preserving it (the corresponding area under the demand curve). Therefore, the triangle RTU represents the reduction in net benefit that occurs if six miles are preserved rather than five.

Since the net benefit is reduced, both by preserving less than five and by preserving more than five, we conclude that five units is the preservation level that maximizes net benefit. Therefore, from our definition, preserving five miles constitutes an efficient allocation.[8]

One implication of this example, which shall be very useful in succeeding chapters, is what we shall call the first equimarginal principle:

> First Equimarginal Principle (the "Efficiency Equimarginal Principle"): Net benefits are maximized when the marginal benefits from an allocation equal the marginal costs.

This criterion helps to minimize wasted resources, but is it fair? The ethical basis for this criterion is derived from a concept called *Pareto optimality,* named after the Italian-born Swiss economist Vilfredo Pareto, who first proposed it around the turn of the twentieth century.

> Allocations are said to be Pareto optimal if no other feasible allocation could benefit some people without any deleterious effects on at least one other person.

---

[8]The monetary worth of the net benefit is the sum of two right triangles, and it equals ($\frac{1}{2}$)(5)(5) + ($\frac{1}{2}$)(2.50)(5) or $18.75. Can you see why?

Allocations that do not satisfy this definition are suboptimal. Suboptimal allocations can always be rearranged so that some people are better off and no one is hurt by the rearrangement. Therefore, the gainers could use a portion of their gains to compensate the losers sufficiently to ensure they were at least as well off as they were prior to the reallocation. Efficient allocations are Pareto optimal. Since net benefits are maximized by an efficient allocation, it is not possible to increase the net benefit by rearranging the allocation. Without an increase in the net benefit, there is no way the gainers could sufficiently compensate the losers; the gains to the gainers would necessarily be smaller than the losses to the losers.

Inefficient allocations are judged inferior because they do not maximize the net benefit. By failing to maximize net benefit, they are forgoing an opportunity to make some people better off without harming others.

Dynamic Efficiency

The static efficiency criterion is very useful for comparing resource allocations when time is not an important factor. How can we make choices when the benefits and costs may occur at different points in time?

The traditional criterion used to find an optimal allocation when time is involved is called *dynamic efficiency,* a generalization of the static efficiency concept already developed. In this generalization, the present-value criterion provides a way for comparing the net benefits received in one period with the net benefits received in another.

An allocation of resources across n time periods satisfies the dynamic efficiency criterion if it maximizes the present value of net benefits that could be received from all the possible ways of allocating those resources over the n periods.

◆ APPLYING THE CONCEPTS

Having now spent some time developing the concepts we need, let's take a moment to examine some actual studies in which they have been used.

Pollution Control

Benefit-cost analysis has been used to assess the desirability of efforts to control pollution. Pollution control certainly confers many benefits, but it also has costs. Do the benefits justify the costs? That was a question the U.S. Congress wanted answered, so in Section 812 of the Clean Air Act Amendments of 1990, it required the U.S. Environmental Protection Agency (EPA) to evaluate the benefits and costs of the U.S. air pollution control policy over the 1970–1990 period (Example 2.2).

In responding to this congressional mandate, the EPA set out to quantify and to monetize both the benefits and the costs of achieving the emissions reductions required by U.S. policy. Benefits quantified by this study included reduced death rates and lower incidences of chronic bronchitis, lead poisoning, strokes, respiratory diseases, and heart disease as well as the benefits of better visibility, reduced damage to structures, and improved agricultural productivity. They were unable to quantify many suspected ecosystem effects.

Two categories of costs were also quantified. The first category included the higher costs of goods and services as the costs of installing, operating, and maintaining pollution control

Example 2.2

Does Reducing Pollution Make Economic Sense?

In its 1997 report to Congress, the EPA presented the results of its attempt to discover whether the Clean Air Act had produced positive net benefits over the period 1970 to 1990. The results suggested that the present value of benefits (using a discount rate of 5%) was $22.2 trillion, while the costs were $0.523 trillion. Performing the necessary subtraction reveals that the net benefits were therefore equal to $21.7 trillion. According to this study, U.S. air pollution control policy during this period made very good economic sense.

TABLE 2.1   Monetized Benefits and Costs of the U.S. Clean Air Act, 1970–1990
              (Billions of 1990 Dollars)

	1975	*1980*	*1985*	*1990*	*Present Value*
Benefits[a]	355	930	1,155	1,248	22,200
Costs[b]	14	21	25	26	523
Net Benefits	341	909	1,130	1,220	21,700

[a]These are the mean (average) benefits. Due to the uncertainties involved, EPA also calculated low and high estimates.

[b]These are the annualized costs. (Many investments in pollution control involve the purchase of durable equipment which lasts many years). Rather than put all of the expense in the year of purchase, EPA distributed the costs over the useful lives of this equipment.

Source: Created by the author from information presented in U.S. Environmental Protection Agency, *The Benefits and Costs of the Clean Air Act, 1970 to 1990* (Washington, DC: Environmental Protection Agency, 1997): Table 18 on p. 56.

equipment were passed on to the consumers in the form of higher prices. The second category included the costs associated with designing and implementing the regulations as well as monitoring and enforcing compliance with them.

Though we shall return to this study later in the book for a deeper look at how these estimates were derived, a couple of comments are relevant now. First, despite the fact that this study did not attempt to value the pollution damage to ecosystems which was avoided by this policy, the net benefits are strongly positive. While presumably the case for controlling pollution would have been even stronger had they been included, the case is strong enough even when they are not included. An inability to monetize everything does not necessarily jeopardize the ability to reach sound policy conclusions.

Although these results justify the conclusion that pollution control made economic sense, they do not justify the stronger conclusion that the policy was efficient. Notice that to justify that conclusion the study would have to have shown that the present value of net benefits was maxi-

Example 2.3

Choosing Between Preservation And Development In Australia

The KCZ, a 50-square-kilometer area lying entirely within the Kakadu National Park (KNP), was initially set aside as part of a government grazing lease. The current issue was whether it should be mined (it was believed to contain significant deposits of gold, platinum, and palladium) or added to the KNP, one of Australia's major parks. In recognition of its unique ecosystem and extensive wildlife as well as its aboriginal archeological sites, much of the park has been placed on the United Nation's World Heritage List. Mining would produce income and employment, but it could also cause the ecosystems in both the KCZ and KNP to experience irreversible damage. What value was to be placed on those risks? Would those risks outweigh the employment and income effects from mining?

To provide answers to these crucial questions, economists conducted a benefit cost analysis using a technique known as contingent valuation. (We shall go into some detail about how this technique works in the next chapter, but for now it can suffice to note that this is a technique for eliciting "willingness to pay" information.) The value of preserving the site was estimated to be A$435 million, while the present value of mining the site was estimated to be A$102.

According to this analysis preservation was the preferred option and it was the option chosen by the government.

Source: Richard T. Carson, Leanne Wilks, and David Imber, "Valuing the Preservation of Australia's Kakadu Conservation Zone," *Oxford Economic Papers* Vol. 46 Supplement (1994): 727–749.

mized, not merely positive. In fact this study did not attempt to calculate the maximum net benefits outcome and if it had, it would have discovered that the policy during this period was not completely efficient. With an optimal policy mix, the net benefits would have been even higher.

Preservation Versus Development

One of the most basic conflicts faced by environmental policy occurs when a currently underdeveloped but ecologically significant piece of land becomes a candidate for development. If developed, the land may provide jobs for workers, wealth for owners, and goods for consumers, but it may also degrade the ecosystem, possibly in irreversible ways. Wildlife habitat may be eliminated, wetlands may be paved over, and recreational opportunities may be gone forever. On the other hand, if the land is preserved, the ecosystem benefits will be retained, but the opportunity for increased income and employment will have been lost. These conflicts become intensified if unemployment rates in the area are high and the local ecology is rather unique.

One such conflict arose in Australia from a proposal to mine a piece of land which was in an area known as the Kakadu Conservation Zone (KCZ). Should it be mined? Or should it be preserved? One way to examine that question is to use the techniques above to examine the net benefits of the two alternatives (Example 2.3).

SUMMARY

The relationship between humanity and the environment requires many choices. Some basis for making rational choices is absolutely necessary. If not made by design, decisions will be made by default.

The economics approach views the environment as a composite asset, supplying a variety of services to humanity. The intensity and composition of those services depend on the actions of humans as constrained by physical laws, such as the first and second laws of thermodynamics.

Economics has two rather different means of enhancing understanding of environmental and natural resource economics. Positive economics is useful in describing the actions of people and the impact of those actions on the environmental asset. Normative economics can provide guidance on how optimal service flows can be defined and achieved.

Normative economics invokes benefit-cost analysis for judging the desirability of the level and composition of provided services. A static efficient allocation is one that maximizes the net benefit over all possible uses of those resources. The dynamic efficiency criterion, which is appropriate when time is an important consideration, is satisfied when the outcome maximizes the present value of net benefits from all possible uses of the resources. Future chapters examine the degree to which our social institutions yield allocations that conform to these criteria.

FURTHER READING

Freeman, A. Myrick III. *The Measurement of Environmental and Resource Values* (Washington, DC: Resources for the Future, Inc., 1993). A comprehensive and analytically rigorous survey of the concepts and methods for environmental valuation.

Hanley, Nick, and Clive L. Spash. *Cost-Benefit Analysis and the Environment* (Brookfield, VT: Edward Elgar Publishing Company, 1994). An up-to-date account of the theory and practice of benefit-cost analysis applied to environmental problems. Contains a number of specific case studies.

Kelman, Steven. "Cost-Benefit Analysis—An Ethical Critique," *Regulation* (January/February 1981), 33–40. Kelman suggests that attempts to expand the use of benefit-cost analysis in the areas of environmental, health, and safety regulation raise troubling ethical questions.

ADDITIONAL REFERENCES

Burness, Stuart, Ronald Cummings, Glenn Morris, and Inga Paik. "Thermodynamic and Economic Concepts as Related to Resource–Use Policies," *Land Economics* 56 (February 1980): 1–9.

Krutilla, John. "Conservation Reconsidered," *The American Economic Review* 57 (September 1968): 777–786.

WEB SITES OF INTEREST

1. *http://www.rff.org/*
   The homepage for Resources for the Future, Inc., a leading environmental economics research organization. The section on Methods, Tools and Techniques is particularly relevant for this chapter.

2. *http://www.epa.gov/docs/oppe/eaed/eedhmpg.htm*
   EPA has prepared Economic Analyses (EAs) since 1981 on most major regulations. EAs analyze alternative approaches to achieving regulatory objectives and the economic benefits and costs of these alternatives. The Economy and the Environment Program has built an inventory of most EPA EAs and some related reports and other materials as well as file copies of most of them on paper, and also provides a limited number as downloadable reports.

DISCUSSION QUESTION

1. It has been suggested that we should use the "net energy" criterion to make choices among various types of energy. Net energy is defined as the total energy content in the energy source minus the energy required to extract, process, and deliver it to consumers. According to this criterion, we should use those sources with the highest net energy content first. Would the dynamic efficiency criterion and the net energy criterion be expected to yield the same choice? Why or why not?

Valuing
the Environment:
Methods

For it so falls out, That what we have, we prize not to the worth, Whiles we enjoy it, but being lack'd and lost, Why, then we rack the value, then we find The virtue that possession would not show us, Whiles it was ours.

WILLIAM SHAKESPEARE, MUCH ADO ABOUT NOTHING.

◆ INTRODUCTION

Soon after the Exxon Valdex oil tanker ran aground on the Bligh Reef in Prince William Sound off the coast of Alaska on March 24, 1989, the Exxon corporation accepted the liability for the damage caused by the leaking oil. This liability consisted of two parts: (1) the cost of clearing up the spilled oil and restoring the site insofar as possible, and (2) compensation for the damage caused to the local ecology.

In the last chapter we examined the concepts used by economists to calculate this damage. Yet implementing these concepts is far from a trivial exercise. While the costs of cleanup were fairly transparent (specific bills for labor, materials, and equipment appeared at Exxon corporate headquarters with great regularity), estimating the damage was more complex. How can we move from the general concepts to the actual estimates of compensation required by the courts?

A series of special techniques has been developed to value the benefits from environmental improvement or, conversely, to value the damage done by environmental degradation. Special techniques were necessary because most of the normal valuation techniques which have been used over the years cannot be applied to environmental resources. While demand curves for normal commodities such as bread or automobiles can be estimated from readily available market data, no such data exist for environmental resources that do not pass through markets. It is not possible to check your local grocery store for the current price of clean air.

In this chapter we shall examine these valuation methods. We begin with an examination of how benefit/cost can be implemented in an environmental context. In this section we identify and discuss the various valuation techniques that are used to value environmental resources in both *ex ante* and *ex post* settings. This is followed by a discussion of the strategies that exist for using economics to protect the environment when valuation information cannot reliably be obtained. One of these strategies, cost-effectiveness analysis, has become extremely important in guiding pollution control policy. Its popularity is not only due to the very practical consideration that it can be a valuable component of the policy process even when reliable valuation estimates cannot be obtained, but also because it responds to the concerns of those who reject the anthropomorphic basis for economic valuation. It has become the technique of choice for those who recognize the importance of economics for protecting the environment, but are skeptical of any efforts to monetize the value of environmental resources.

◆ VALUING BENEFITS

While the valuation techniques we shall cover can be applied to both valuing the damage caused by pollution and valuing the services provided by the environment, each context offers its own unique problems. We begin our investigation of valuation techniques by exposing some of the difficulties associated with one of those contexts, pollution control.

In the United States, damage estimates not only are used in the design of policies, they have also become important in the courts. Under the Comprehensive Environmental Response, Compensation, and Liability Act, local, state, or federal governments can seek monetary compensation from responsible parties for natural resources that are injured or destroyed by spills and releases of hazardous wastes. Some basis for deciding the magnitude of the award is necessary.[1]

The damage caused by pollution can take many different forms. The first, and probably most obvious, is the effect on human health. Polluted air and water can cause disease when ingested. Other forms of damage include loss of enjoyment from outdoor activities and damage to vegetation, animals, and materials.

Assessing the magnitude of this damage requires (1) identifying the affected categories; (2) estimating the physical relationship between the pollutant emissions (including natural sources) and the damage caused to the affected categories; (3) estimating responses by the affected parties toward averting or mitigating some portion of the damage; and (4) placing a monetary value on the physical damages. Each step is often difficult to accomplish.

Because the experiments used to track down causal relationships are uncontrolled, identifying the affected categories is a complicated matter. Obviously we cannot run large numbers of people through controlled experiments. If people were subjected to different levels of some pollutant, such as carbon monoxide, so that we could study the short-term and long-term effects, some might become ill and even die. Ethical concern precludes human experimentation of this type.

---

[1]The rules for determining these damages are defined in Department of Interior regulations. See 40 Code of Federal Regulations 300:72–74.

This leaves us essentially two choices. We can try to infer the impact on humans from controlled laboratory experiments on animals, or we can do statistical analysis of differences in mortality or disease rates for various human populations living in polluted environments to see the extent to which they are correlated with pollution concentrations. Neither approach is completely acceptable.

Animal experiments are expensive, and the extrapolation from effects on animals to effects on humans is tenuous at best. Many of the significant effects do not appear for a long time. To determine these effects in a reasonable period of time, test animals must be subjected to large doses for a relatively short period of time. The researcher then extrapolates from the results of these high-dosage, short-duration experiments to estimate the effects of lower doses over a longer period of time on a human population. Because these extrapolations move well beyond the range of experimental experience, many scientists disagree on how the extrapolations should be accomplished.

Statistical studies, on the other hand, deal with human populations subjected to low doses for long periods, but, unfortunately, they have another set of problems—correlation does not imply causation. To illustrate, the fact that death rates are higher in cities with higher pollution levels does not prove that the higher pollution caused the higher death rates. Perhaps those same cities averaged older populations, which would tend to lead to higher death rates. Or perhaps they had more smokers. The existing studies have been sophisticated enough to account for many of these other possible influences but, because of the relative paucity of data, they have not been able to cover them all.

The problems discussed so far arise when identifying whether a particular effect results from pollution. The next step is to estimate how strong the relationship is between the effect and the pollution concentrations. In other words, it is necessary not only to discover *whether* pollution causes an increased incidence of respiratory disease, but also to estimate *how much* reduction in respiratory illness could be expected from a given reduction in pollution.

The nonexperimental nature of the data makes this a difficult task. It is not uncommon for researchers analyzing the same data to come to remarkably different conclusions. Diagnostic problems are compounded when the effects are synergistic—that is, when the effect depends in a nonadditive way on what other elements are in the surrounding air or water at the time of the analysis.

Once physical damages have been identified, the next step is to place a monetary value on them. It is not difficult to see how complex an undertaking this is. Consider, for example, the difficulties in assigning a value to extending a human life by several years or to the pain, suffering, and grief borne by a cancer victim and the victim's family.

How can these difficulties be overcome? What valuation techniques are available not only to value pollution damage, but also to value the large number of services that the environment provides?

Types of Values

Depending upon the circumstance, we may need to place a value on either a *stock* or a *flow*. For example, the standing forest is a stock of trees, while the harvest of timber from that forest represents one of the service flows. The two are connected in that the value of a stock should be equal to the present value of the stream of services flowing from the stock. If the present value of the stream of services is maximized, then we say the resource is being used efficiently. This is equivalent to maximizing the value of that resource.

Economists have decomposed the total economic value conferred by resources into three main components: (1) use value, (2) option value, and (3) nonuse value. Use value reflects the direct use of the environmental resource. Examples would include fish harvested from the sea, timber harvested from the forest, water extracted from a stream for irrigation, even the scenic beauty conferred by a natural vista. Pollution can cause a loss of use value such as when air pollution increases the vulnerability to illness, an oil spill adversely affects a fishery, or when smog enshrouds a scenic vista.

A second category of value, the option value, reflects the value people place on a future ability to use the environment. Option value reflects the willingness to preserve an option to use the environment in the future even if one is not currently using it. Whereas use value reflects the value derived from current use, option value reflects the desire to preserve a potential for possible future use.

The third and final category of value, nonuse value, reflects the common observation that people are more than willing to pay for improving or preserving resources that they will never use. If the federal government decided to sell the Grand Canyon to a chicken farmer to serve as a place to store manure, feathers, and chicken entrails, it is not hard to imagine that citizens across the country (indeed around the world) would rise up in protest. The loss in value of this unique resource would evidently be enormous even to those who have never visited the place and never will. Because this value does not derive either from direct use or potential use, it represents a very different category of value.

These categories of value can be combined to produce the total willingness to pay (TWP): TWP = Use Value + Option Value + Nonuse value.

Since nonuse values are derived from motivations other than personal use, they are obviously less tangible than use values. Furthermore, as Example 3.1 makes clear, estimated nonuse values can be quite large. It is therefore not surprising that they are controversial. Indeed when the Department of Interior drew up its regulations on the appropriate procedures for performing natural resource damage assessment, it prohibited the inclusion of nonuse values unless use values for the incident under consideration were zero. A subsequent 1989 decision by the District of Columbia Court of Appeals (880 F. 2nd 432) overruled this decision and allowed passive-use values to be included as long as they could be measured.

Classifying Valuation Methods

Several methods are available to estimate these values. In this section a brief overview will be provided to convey some sense of the range of possibilities and how they are related. Subsequent sections will provide more specific information about how they are actually used.

The possibilities are presented in Table 3.1. Direct observation methods are those which are based on actual observable choices and from which actual resource values can be directly inferred. For example, in calculating how much local fishermen lost from the oil spill, the direct observation method might calculate how much the catch declined and the resulting value of the lost consumer surplus (as reflected by the area under the demand curve which can be traced out using observable prices). In this case prices are directly observable, and their use allows the direct calculation of the loss in value.

TABLE 3.1 Economic Methods for Measuring Environmental and Resource Values

Methods	Observed Behavior	Hypothetical
Direct	Market Price Simulated Markets	Contingent Valuation
Indirect	Travel Cost Hedonic Property Values Hedonic Wage Values Avoidance Expenditures	Contingent Ranking

Source: Adapted from Table 2-1 in A. Myrick Freeman, III, *The Measurement of Environmental and Resource Values: Theory and Methods* (Washington, D.C.: Resources of the Future Inc., 1993). Reproduced with permission of Resources for the Future.

Compare this with the direct hypothetical case which might be used when the value is not directly observable. In Example 3.1, for example, the nonuse value of the Northern Spotted Owl was not directly observable. Hence the authors attempted to derive this value by using a survey which attempted to elicit the respondents' willingness to pay for the preservation of the species.

This approach, called contingent valuation, provides a means of deriving values which cannot be obtained in more traditional ways. The simplest version of this approach merely asks respondents what value they would place on an environmental change (such as the loss of a wetlands or increased exposure to pollution) or on preserving the resource in its current state. More complicated versions ask whether the respondent would pay $X to prevent the change or preserve the species. The answers reveal either an upper bound (in the case of a "no" answer) or a lower bound (in the case of a "yes" answer).

The major concern with the use of the contingent valuation method has been the potential for survey respondents to give biased answers. Four types of potential bias have been the focus of a large amount of research: (1) strategic bias, (2) information bias, (3) starting point bias, and (4) hypothetical bias.

Strategic bias arises when the respondent provides a biased answer in order to influence a particular outcome. If a decision to preserve a stretch of river for fishing, for example, depends on whether or not the survey produces a sufficiently large value for fishing, the respondents who enjoy fishing may be tempted to provide an answer that ensures a high value rather than a lower value that reflects their true valuation.

Information bias may arise whenever respondents are forced to value attributes with which they have little or no experience. For example, the valuation by a recreationist of a loss in water quality in one body of water may be based on the ease of substituting recreation on another body of water. If the respondent has no experience using the second body of water, the valuation will be based on an entirely false perception.

Starting-point bias may arise in those survey instruments in which a respondent is asked to check off his or her answers from a predefined range of possibilities. How that range is defined by the designer of the survey may affect the resulting answers. A range of $0 to $100 may produce a different valuation by respondents, for example, from a range of $10 to $100, even if no bids are in the $0 to $10 range.

The final source of bias, hypothetical bias, can enter the picture because the respondent is being confronted by a contrived, rather than an actual, set of choices. Since he or she will not

---

Example 3.1

Valuing the Northern Spotted Owl

The Northern Spotted Owl lives in an area of the Pacific Northwest where its habitat is threatened by logging. Its significance derives not only from its designation under the Endangered Species Act as a threatened species, but also from its role as an indicator of the overall health of the Pacific Northwest's old growth forest.

In 1990 an interagency scientific committee presented a plan to withdraw certain forested areas from harvesting and preserve them as "habitat conservation areas." Would preserving these areas represent an efficient choice?

To answer this question, a national contingent valuation survey (this technique is described below) was conducted to estimate the nonuse value of preservation in this case. Conducted by mail, the survey went to 1,000 households.

The results suggested that the benefits of preservation outweighed the costs by at least three to one, regardless of the assumptions necessitated by the need to resolve such issues as how to treat the nonresponding households. (One calculation, for example, included them all as a zero nonuse value.) Under the assumptions most favorable to preservation, the ratio of benefits to costs was 43 to one. In this example the nonuse values were large enough to indicate that preservation was the preferred choice.

The authors also point out, however, that the distributional implications of this choice should not be ignored. While the benefits of preservation are distributed widely throughout the entire population, the costs are concentrated on a relatively small group of people in one geographic region. Perhaps the public should be willing to share some of the preservation benefits by allocating tax dollars to this area to facilitate the transition and to reduce the hardship. This is ultimately what happened.

Source: Daniel A. Hagen, James W. Vincent and Patrick G. Welle. "Benefits of Preserving Old-Growth Forests and the Spotted Owl," *Contemporary Policy Issues*, Vol. 10 (April, 1992): 13–26.

---

have actually to pay the estimated value, the respondent may treat the survey casually, providing ill-considered answers. One survey of the field (Hanemann, 1994) found that 10 studies have directly compared willingness-to-pay estimates derived from surveys with actual expenditures. Though some of the studies found that the willingness-to-pay estimates derived from surveys exceeded actual expenditures, the majority of those found that the differences were not statistically significant.[2]

Much experimental work has been done on contingent valuation to determine how serious a problem these biases may present. One recent survey (Carson, et. al., 1994) uncovered 1,672 contingent valuation studies. Are the results from these surveys reliable enough for the policy process?

---

[2]For a much more skeptical view of this evidence, see Diamond, Peter A. and Jerry A. Hausman. "Contingent Valuation. Is Some Number Better than No Number?" *Journal of Economic Perspectives* Vol. 8, No. 4 (Fall, 1994): 45–64.

Faced with the need to answer this question in order to compute damages from oil spills, the National Oceanic and Atmospheric Administration (NOAA) convened a panel of independent economic experts (including two Nobel Prize laureates) to evaluate the use of contingent valuation methods for determining nonuse values. Their report, issued on January 15, 1993 (58 FR 4602) was cautiously supportive.

The committee made clear that it had several concerns with the technique. Among those concerns, the panel listed: (1) the tendency for contingent valuation willingness-to-pay estimates to seem unreasonably large; (2) the difficulty in assuring the respondents have understood and absorbed the issues in the survey; and (3) the difficulty in assuring that respondents are responding to the specific issues in the survey rather than reflecting general warm feelings about public-spiritedness or the "warm glow" of giving.

But the panel also made clear its conclusion that suitably designed surveys could eliminate or reduce these biases to acceptable levels and it provided in an appendix specific guidelines for determining whether a particular study was suitably designed.

The panel concluded that following the guidelines:

> can produce estimates reliable enough to be the starting point of a judicial process of damage assessment, including lost passive-use values.... [A well-constructed contingent valuation study] contains information that judges and juries will wish to use, in combination with other estimates, including the testimony of expert witnesses.

The NOAA panel report has created an interesting dilemma. Although it has legitimized the use of contingent valuation for estimating passive-use nonuse values, the panel has also set some rather rigid guidelines that reliable studies should follow. The cost of completing an "acceptable" contingent valuation study will be sufficiently high that they will only be useful for incidents where the damages are high enough to justify their use. Yet due to the paucity of other techniques, the failure to use contingent valuation may, by default, result in passive-use values of zero, which isn't right either.

One key to resolving this dilemma may be provided by a technique called meta-analysis. In this context meta-analysis would use a cross section of contingent valuation studies as a basis for isolating the determinants of nonuse value. Once these determinants have been isolated and related to specific policy contexts, it may be possible to transfer estimates from one context to another without incurring the time and expense of conducting new surveys each time.

The third category is indirect observable methods, which are "observable" because they involve actual (as opposed to hypothetical) behavior, and "indirect" because they infer a value rather than estimate it directly. Suppose, for example, a particular sport fishery is being threatened by pollution, and one of the damages caused by that pollution is a reduction in sport fishing. How is this loss to be valued when access to the fishery is free?

One way is through travel-cost methods. Travel-cost methods may infer the value of a recreational resource (such as a sport fishery, a park, or a wildlife preserve where visitors hunt with a camera) by using information on how much the visitors spent in getting to the site to construct a demand curve for willingness to pay for a "visitor day."

Freeman (1993) identifies two variants of this approach. In the first, analysts examine the number of trips visitors make to a site. In the second, the analysts examine whether people decide to visit a site and, if so, which site.

The first variant allows the construction of a travel-cost demand function. The value of the flow of services from that site is the area under the estimated demand curve for those services or for access to the site, aggregated over all who visit the site.

The second variant allows the analysis of how specific site characteristics influence choice and therefore indirectly how valuable those characteristics are. Knowledge of how the value of each site varies with respect to its characteristics allows the analyst to value how degradation of those characteristics (from pollution, e.g.) would lower the value of the site.

Two other indirect observable methods are known as the hedonic property value and hedonic wage approaches. They share the characteristic that they use a statistical technique known as multiple regression analysis to "tease out" the environmental component of value in a related market. Hedonic property value studies attempt to decompose the various attributes of value in property into their component parts. For example, it is possible to discover that, all other things being equal, property values are lower in polluted neighborhoods than in clean neighborhoods. (Property values fall in polluted neighborhoods because they are less desirable places to live.) And the multiple regression equations allow the analyst to separate out the relationship between property values and pollution. This relationship can then be used to produce a willingness to pay for pollution reduction.

Hedonic wage approaches are similar except that they attempt to isolate the component of wages which serves to compensate workers in risky occupations for taking on the risk. It is well known that workers in high-risk occupations demand higher wages in order to induce them to undertake the risks. When the risk is environmental (such as exposure to a toxic substance), the results of the multiple regression analysis can be used to construct a willingness to pay to avoid this kind of environmental risk.

A final example of an indirect observable method involves examining "averting or defensive expenditures." Averting expenditures are those designed to reduce the damage caused by pollution by taking some kind of averting or defensive action. An example would be to install indoor air purifiers in response to an influx of polluted air or to rely on bottled water as a response to the pollution of local drinking water supplies (Example 3.2). Since people would not normally spend more to prevent a problem than would be caused by the problem itself, averting expenditures can provide a lower-bound estimate of the damage caused by pollution.

The final category, indirect hypothetical methods, is illustrated by a technique known as contingent ranking. Respondents are given a set of hypothetical situations that differ in terms of the environmental amenity available and other characteristics the respondents are presumed to care about, and are asked to rank these situations in terms of their desirability (Example 3.3). These rankings can then be compared to see the implicit tradeoffs between more of the environmental amenity and less of the other characteristics. When one or more of these characteristics can be expressed in terms of a monetary value, it is possible to use this information and the rankings to impute a value to the environmental amenity.

Sometimes a valuation exercise may use more than one of these techniques simultaneously. In some cases that is necessary to capture the total economic value; in other cases it is done to provide independent estimates of the value being sought (Example 3.4).

Valuing Human Life. One fascinating public policy area where these various approaches have been applied is in the valuation of human life. Many government programs, from those controlling hazardous pollutants in the workplace or in drinking water to those improving

Example 3.2

Valuing Damage from Groundwater Contamination Using Averting Expenditures

How many resources should be allocated to the prevention of groundwater contamination? In part that depends on how serious a risk is posed by the contamination. How much damage would be caused? One way to obtain a lower-bound estimate on the damage caused is to discover how much people are willing to spend to defend themselves against the threat.

In late 1987 trichloroethylene (TCE) was detected in one of the town wells in Perkasie, a town in southeastern Pennsylvania. Concentrations of the chemical were seven times the EPA's safety standard. Since no temporary solution was available to reduce concentrations to safe levels, the county required the town to notify customers of the contamination.

Once notified, consumers took one or more of the following actions: (1) they purchased more bottled water; (2) they started using bottled water; (3) they installed home water treatment systems; (4) they hauled water from alternative sources; and (5) they boiled water. Through a survey analysts were able to discover the extent of each of these actions and combine that information with their associated costs.

The results indicated that residents spent from $61,313.29 to $131,334.06 over the 88-week period of the contamination. They further indicated that families with young children were more likely to take averting actions and, among those families who took averting actions, to spend more on those actions than childless families.

Source: Abdalla, Charles W., et al, "Valuing Environmental Quality Changes Using Averting Expenditures: An Application to Groundwater Contamination," *Land Economics* Vol. 68, No. 2 (1992): 163–169.

nuclear power plant safety, are designed to save human life as well as to reduce illness. How resources should be allocated among these programs depends crucially on the value of human life. How is life to be valued?

The simple answer, of course, is that life is priceless, but that turns out to be not very helpful. Because the resources used to prevent loss of life are scarce, choices must be made. The economic approach to valuing lifesaving reductions in environmental risk is to calculate the change in the probability of death resulting from the reduction in environmental risk and to place a value on the change. Thus, it is not life itself that is being valued but rather a reduction in the probability that some segment of the population could be expected to die earlier than otherwise.

It is possible to translate the value derived from this procedure in an "implied value of human life." This is accomplished by dividing the amount each individual is willing to pay for a specific reduction in the probability of death by the probability reduction. Suppose, for example, that a particular environmental policy could be expected to reduce the average concentra-

Example 3.3

Valuing Diesel Odor Reduction by Contingent Ranking

Emissions from diesel engines can adversely affect human health; they also produce an unpleasant odor. Reducing those emissions produces both a health benefit and reduction in odor. How much emission reduction is efficient therefore depends on how beneficial odor reduction is; if odor reduction is highly valued, more emission reduction is justified.

To discover whether odor reduction is valued sufficiently highly to make it an important component in diesel emission reduction decisions, a contingent ranking study was conducted in Philadelphia. Each respondent was required to smell two odors: odor A was a mild diesel smell, while odor B was a more intense smell. Respondents were then asked to rank the desirability of various options. Each option contained a level of exposure to odor and a level of annual transportation cost which was associated with reducing the number of exposures to the specified level. Higher transportation costs (reflecting the higher degree of control) were associated with lower exposure levels.

The analysis of these data revealed a willingness-to-pay of between $3.03 and $5.49 per year to avoid one weekly contact with odor A and between $14.57 and $18.50 to avoid one weekly contact with odor B. Combining this information with the average number of weekly exposures to each of these odor types produced an estimate of $75 per year to avoid completely all odor exposures. Since EPA programs to control diesel emissions are estimated to cost about $3.60 per household, the value of diesel odor reduction seems significant.

Source: Thomas J. Lareau and Douglas A. Rae, "Valuing WTP for Diesel Odor Reductions: An Application of Contingent Ranking Technique," *Southern Economic Journal* Vol. 55, No. 3 (1989): 728–742.

tion of a toxic substance to which one million people are exposed. Suppose further that this reduction in exposure could be expected to reduce the risk of death from 1 out of 100,000 to 1 out of 150,000. This implies that the number of expected deaths would fall from 10 to 6.67 in the exposed population as a result of this policy. If each of the one million persons exposed is willing to pay $5 for this risk reduction (for a total of $5 million), then the implied value of a life is approximately $1.5 million ($5 million divided by 3.33).

What actual values have been derived from these methods? A survey (Viscusi, 1996) of a large number of studies examining reductions in a number of life-threatening risks found that most implied values for human life (in 1986 dollars) were between $3 million and $7 million. This same survey went on to suggest that the most appropriate estimates were probably closer to the $5 million estimate. In other words, all government programs resulting in risk reductions costing less than $5 million would be justified in benefit-cost terms. Those costing more might or might not be justified, depending on the appropriate value of a life saved in the particular risk context being examined.

Example 3.4

The Value of Wildlife Viewing

One strategy we shall examine later in this book for preserving wildlife involves the use of ecotourism. Ecotourism tries to capture some of the willingness to pay for preserving wildlife as expressed by those who embark on safaris to view wildlife in their native habitat and uses that revenue to support wildlife preservation activities. How successful that strategy will be depends in part on how large that willingness to pay is.

One study attempted to find out how large it was for the Lake Nakuru National Park in Kenya. Originally established as a bird sanctuary in 1961, this park was expanded in 1969 and 1972. It is the home of some 1.4 million flamingos as well as some 360 other species of birds. Lately, however, the number of flamingos has diminished due to water pollution from increased farming activities.

Using both a travel-cost method and a contingent-valuation method, the authors calculated the use value of visits to the park to view wildlife. The travel-cost estimates indicated that the annual value of recreational viewing in this park in 1991 was ($US) 13.7 to 15.1 million. Of that, ($US) 3.6 to 4.5 million was from residents of Kenya; the rest (the majority) was from nonresidents. The total value estimated by contingent valuation was ($US) 7.5 million.

Several points are worth noting:

- According to the travel-cost results, the majority of the value comes from nonresidents, which is not surprising given that the average nonresident visitor had a much higher income than the average resident visitor.

- Despite the fact that this study examined only use values and ignored nonuse values, the resulting estimates are quite high. Apparently ecotourism (in this park at least) could bring in significant revenue.

- The calculated values of wildlife viewing were much higher than the prevailing fees charged at the time, implying that more revenue for protecting wildlife could be extracted. (Recognizing this fact, the government raised nonresident entrance fees by 310% in 1993.)

- While it is normally recognized that controlling pollution costs money, this study points out that *not* controlling pollution *also* costs money (by killing the valuable wildlife). Although this study did not actually examine the cost of controlling the pollution, that would be an obvious next step.

Source: Ståle Navrud and E.D. Mungatana, "Environmental Valuation in Developing Countries: The Recreational Viewing of Wildlife." *Ecological Economics* 11 (November, 1994): 135–151.

How have health, safety and environmental regulations lived up to this recommendation? As Table 3.2 suggests, not very well. A very large number of regulations listed in that table could be justified only if the value of a life saved were much higher than the upper value of $7 million.

TABLE 3.2 The Cost of Risk-Reducing Regulations

	Agency Year and Status	Initial Annual Risk	Annual Lives Saved	Cost Per Life Saved (Millions) of 1984 $)
Unvented Space Heaters	CPSC 1980 F	2.7 in 10^5	63.000	$ .10
Cabin Fire Protection	FAA 1985 F	6.5 in 10^8	15.000	.20
Passive Restraints/Belts	NHTSA 1984 F	9.1 in 10^5	1,850.000	.30
Seat Cushion Flammability	FAA 1984 F	1.6 in 10^7	37.000	.60
Floor Emergency Lighting	FAA 1984 F	2.2 in 10^8	5.000	.70
Concrete &Masonry Constr.	OSHA 1988 F	1.4 in 10^5	6.500	1.40
Hazard Communication	OSHA 1983 F	4.0 in 10^5	200.000	1.80
Benzene/Fugitive Emissions	EPA 1984 F	2.1 in 10^4	0.310	2.80
Radionuclides/Uranium Mines	EPA 1984 F	1.4 in 10^4	1.100	6.90
Benzene	OSHA 1987 F	8.8 in 10^4	3.800	17.10
Arsenic/Glass Plant	EPA 1986 F	8.0 in 10^4	0.110	19.20
Arsenic/Copper Smelter	EPA 1986 F	9.0 in 10^4	0.060	26.50
Uranium Mill Tailings Inactive	EPA 1983 F	4.3 in 10^4	2.100	27.60
Uranium Mill Tailings Active	EPA 1983 F	4.3 in 10^4	2.100	53.00
Asbestos	EPA 1989 F	2.9 in 10^5	10.000	104.20
Arsenic/Glass Manufacturing	EPA 1986 R	3.8 in 10^5	0.250	142.00
Benzene/Storage	EPA 1984 R	6.0 in 10^7	0.043	202.00
Radionuclides/DOE Facilities	EPA 1984 R	4.3 in 10^6	0.001	210.00
Radionuclides/Elem. Phos.	EPA 1984 R	1.4 in 10^5	0.046	270.00

(continued)

Table 3.2 (continued)

Benzene/Ethylbenzenol Styrene	EPA 1984 R	2.0 in 10^6	0.006	483.00
Arsenic/Low-Arsenic Copper	EPA 1986 R	2.6 in 10^4	0.090	764.00
Benzene/Maleic Anhydride	EPA 1984 R	1.1 in 10^6	0.029	820.00
Land Disposal	EPA 1988 F	2.3 in 10^8	2.520	3,500.00
Formaldehyde	OSHA 1987 F	6.8 in 10^4	0.010	72,000.00

"Initial Annual Risk" indicates annual deaths per exposed population, an exposed population of 10^3 is 1000. 10^4 is 10,000, etc. In the "Agency Year and Status" column, R and F represent Rejected and Final rule, respectively.

Sources: Adapted from W. Kip Viscusi, Economic Foundations of the Current Regulatory Reform Efforts." *The Journal of Economic Perspectives* 10 (No. 3 Summer,1996): Tables 1 and 2: 124–125.

Issues in Benefit Estimation[3]

The analyst charged with the responsibility for performing a benefit-cost analysis encounters many decision points requiring judgment. If we are to understand benefit-cost analysis, the nature of these judgments must be clear in our minds.

Primary Versus Secondary Effects. Environmental projects usually trigger both primary and secondary consequences. For example, the primary effect of cleaning a lake will be an increase in recreational uses of the lake. This primary effect will cause a further ripple effect on services provided to the increased number of users of the lake. Are these secondary benefits to be counted?

The answer depends upon the employment conditions in the surrounding area. If this increase in demand results in employment of previously unused resources, such as labor, the value of the increased employment should be counted. If, on the other hand, the increase in demand is met by a shift in previously employed resources from one use to another, this is a different story. In general, secondary employment benefits should be counted in high unemployment areas or when the particular skills demanded are underemployed at the time the project is commenced. This should not be counted when the project simply results in a rearrangement of productively employed resources.

Tangible Versus Intangible Benefits. *Tangible* benefits are those which can reasonably be assigned a monetary value. *Intangible* benefits are those which cannot be assigned a monetary value, either because data are not available or reliable enough or because it is not clear how to measure the value even with data.[4]

---

[3]This section relies heavily on Peskin, Henry M. and Eugene Seskin, *Cost-Benefit Analysis and Water-Pollution Control Policy* (Washington, D.C.: The Urban Institute, 1975).

[4]The division between tangible and intangible benefits changes as our techniques improve. Recreation benefits were, until the advent of the travel cost model, treated as intangible.

How are intangible benefits to be handled? One answer is perfectly clear: they should not be ignored. To ignore intangible benefits is to bias the results. That benefits are intangible does not mean they are unimportant.

Intangible benefits should be quantified to the fullest extent possible. One frequently used technique is to conduct a sensitivity analysis of the estimated benefit values derived from less than perfectly reliable data. We can determine, for example, whether or not the outcome is sensitive, within wide ranges, to the value of this benefit. If not, then very little time has to be spent on the problem. If the outcome is sensitive, the person or persons making the decision bear the ultimate responsibility for weighing the importance of that benefit.

Approaches to Cost Estimation

Estimating costs is generally easier than estimating benefits, but it is not easy. One major problem for both derives from the fact that benefit-cost analysis is forward-looking and thus requires an estimate of what a particular strategy *will* cost, which is much more difficult than tracking down what an existing strategy *does* cost.

Another frequent problem is posed by collecting cost information when availability of that information is controlled by a firm having an interest in the outcome. Pollution control is an obvious example. Two approaches have been used to deal with this problem.

The Survey Approach.   One way to discover the costs associated with a policy is to ask those who bear the costs, and presumably know the most about them, to reveal the magnitude of the costs to policymakers. Polluters, for example, could be asked to provide control-cost estimates to regulatory bodies. The problem with this approach is the strong incentive not to be truthful. An overestimate of t..he costs can trigger less stringent regulation; therefore, it is financially advantageous to provide overinflated estimates.

The Engineering Approach.   The engineering approach bypasses the source being regulated by using general engineering information to catalog the possible technologies which could be used to meet the objective and to estimate the costs of purchasing and using those technologies. The final step in the engineering approach is to assume that the sources would use technologies which minimize cost. This produces a cost estimate for a "typical," well-informed firm.

This approach has its own problems. These estimates may not approximate the actual cost of any particular firm. Unique circumstances may cause the costs of that firm to be higher, or lower, than estimated; the firm, in short, may not be typical.

The Combined Approach.   To circumvent these problems, analysts frequently use a combination of survey and engineering approaches. The survey approach collects information on possible technologies, as well as special circumstances facing the firm. Engineering approaches are used to derive the actual costs of those technologies, given the special circumstances. This combined approach attempts to balance information best supplied by the source with that best derived independently.

In the cases described so far, the costs are relatively easy to quantify and the problem is simply finding a way to acquire the best information. This is not always the case, however.

Some costs are not easy to quantify, though economists have developed some ingenious ways to secure monetary estimates even for those costs.

Take, for example, a policy designed to conserve energy by forcing more people to carpool. If the effect of this is simply to increase the average time of travel, how is this cost to be measured?

For some time transportation analysts have recognized that people do value their time, and quite a literature has now grown up to provide estimates of this valuation. The basis for this valuation is opportunity cost—how the time might be used if it weren't being consumed in travel. Although the results of these studies depend on the amount of time involved, individuals seem to value their time at a rate not more than half their wage rates.

The Treatment of Risk

For many environmental problems, it is not possible to state with certainty what consequences a particular policy will have, because scientific estimates themselves often are imprecise. Determining the efficient exposure to potentially toxic substances requires obtaining results at high doses and extrapolating to low doses, as well as extrapolating from animal studies to humans. It also requires relying upon epidemiological studies which infer a pollution-induced adverse human health impact from correlations between indicators of health in human populations and recorded pollution levels.

Another illustration of the significance of scientific uncertainty is afforded by the global warming problem. Certain gases, when emitted into the atmosphere, are suspected of causing the planetary temperature to rise. If this suspicion is correct, it could have very serious implications. Among others it could trigger a rise in the sea level and could result in the deaths of large numbers of plants no longer suited for the temperatures to which they would be subjected. The conjecture that increased emissions of carbon dioxide and other greenhouse gases are causing a rise in temperature is based upon a computer model which has only partially been validated. This is a prototypical example of a problem that is poorly understood but that, if the conjectures are true, could pose significant problems in the future.

The treatment of risk in the policy process involves two major dimensions: (1) identifying and quantifying the risks; and (2) deciding how much risk is acceptable. The former is primarily scientific and descriptive, while the latter is more evaluative or normative.

Benefit-cost analysis grapples with the evaluation of risk in several ways. Suppose, for example, that we have a range of policy options *A, B, C, D* and a range of possible outcomes *E, F, G* for each of these policies depending on how the economy evolves over the future. These outcomes, for example, might depend on whether the demand growth for the resource is low, medium, or high. Thus, if we choose policy *A*, we might end up with outcomes *AE, AF,* or *AG*. Each of the other policies has three possible outcomes as well, yielding a total of 12 possible outcomes.

We could conduct a separate benefit-cost analysis for each of the 12 possible outcomes. Unfortunately, the policy which maximizes net benefits for *E* may be different from that which maximizes net benefits for *F* or *G*. Thus, if we only knew which outcome would prevail, we could select the policy that maximized net benefits; the problem is that we don't. Furthermore, choosing the policy which is best if outcome *E* prevails may be disastrous if *G* results instead.

When a dominant policy emerges, this problem is avoided. A *dominant policy* is one which confers higher net benefits for every outcome. In this case, the existence of risk concerning the future is not relevant for the policy choice. Though this fortuitous circumstance is exceptional rather than common, it can occur.

Other options exist even when dominant solutions do not emerge. Suppose, for example, that we were able to assess the likelihood that each of the three possible outcomes would occur. Thus we might expect outcome E to occur with probability 0.5, F with probability 0.3, and G with probability 0.2. Armed with this information, we can estimate the expected present value of net benefits. The *expected present value of net benefits* for a particular policy is defined as the sum over outcomes of the present value of net benefits for that policy where each outcome is weighted by its probability of occurrence. Symbolically this is expressed as:

$$EPVNB_j = \sum_{i=1}^{I} P_i \, PVNB_{ij}, \qquad j = 1,\ldots,J,$$

where

$EPVNB_j$ = expected present value of net benefits for policy j

P_i = probability of the ith outcome occurring

$PVNB_{ij}$ = present value of net benefits for policy j if outcome i prevails

J = number of policies being considered

I = number of outcomes being considered

The final step is to select the policy with the highest expected present value of net benefits.

This approach has the substantial virtue that it weighs higher probability outcomes more heavily. It also, however, makes a specific assumption about society's preference for risk. This approach is appropriate if society is risk-neutral. *Risk-neutrality* can be defined most easily by the use of an example. Suppose you were allowed to choose between being given a definite $50 or entering a lottery in which you had a 50 percent chance of winning $100 and a 50 percent chance of winning nothing. (Notice that the expected value of this lottery is $50 = 0.5($100) + 0.5($0).) You would be said to be risk-neutral if you would be indifferent between these two choices. If you view the lottery as more attractive, you would be exhibiting *risk-loving* behavior, while a preference for the definite $50 would suggest *risk-averse* behavior. Using the expected present value of net benefits approach implies that society is risk-neutral.

Is that a valid assumption? The evidence is mixed. The existence of gambling suggests that at least some members of society are risk lovers while the existence of insurance suggests that at least for some risks others are risk-averse. Since the same people may gamble and own insurance policies, it's likely that the type of risk may be important.

Even if individuals were demonstrably risk-averse, this would not be a sufficient condition for the government to forsake risk neutrality in evaluating public investments. One famous article by Arrow and Lind (1970) argues that risk neutrality is appropriate since "when the risks of a public investment are publicly borne, the total cost of risk-bearing is insignificant and, therefore, the government should ignore uncertainty in evaluating public investments." The logic behind this result suggests that as the number of risk bearers (and the degree of diversification of risks) increases, the amount of risk borne by any individual diminishes to zero.

When the decision is irreversible, as demonstrated by Arrow and Fisher (1974), considerably more caution is appropriate. Irreversible decisions may subsequently be regretted, but the option to change course will be lost forever. Extra caution also affords an opportunity to learn more about alternatives to this decision and its consequences before acting. Isn't it comforting to know that procrastination can occasionally be optimal?

There is a movement in national policy in both the courts and the legislature to search for imaginative ways to define acceptable risk. In general, the policy approaches reflect a case-by-case approach. We shall see that current policy reflects a high degree of risk aversion toward a number of environmental problems.

Choosing the Discount Rate

In the previous chapter we discussed how the discount rate could be defined conceptually as the social opportunity cost of capital. This cost of capital can be divided further into two components: (1) the riskless cost of capital and (2) the risk premium.

As Example 3.5 indicates, this has been, and continues to be, an important issue. When the public sector uses a discount rate lower than that in the private sector, the public sector will find more projects with longer payoff periods worthy of authorization. And, as we have already seen, the discount rate is a major determinant of the allocation of resources among generations as well.

Traditionally, economists have used long-term interest rates on government bonds as one measure of the cost of capital, adjusted by a risk premium which would depend on the riskiness of the project considered. Unfortunately, the choice of how large an adjustment to make has been left to the discretion of the analysts. This ability to affect the desirability of a particular project or policy by the choice of discount rate led to a situation in which government agencies were using a variety of discount rates to justify programs or projects they supported. One set of hearings conducted by Congress during the 1960s discovered that, at one time, agencies were using discount rates ranging from 0 percent to 20 percent.[5]

During the early 1970s the Office of Management and Budget came out with a circular which required, with some exceptions, all government agencies to use a discount rate of 10 percent in their benefit-cost analysis. A revision issued in 1992 reduced the required discount rate to 7 percent. This standardization reduces biases by eliminating the agency's ability to choose a discount rate which justifies a predetermined conclusion. It also allows a project to be considered independently of fluctuations in the true social cost of capital due to cycles in the behavior of the economy. On the other hand, when the social opportunity cost of capital differs from this administratively determined level, the benefit-cost analysis will not, in general, define the efficient allocation.[6]

A Critical Appraisal

The approaches to benefit estimation are sophisticated, but most observers feel that the resulting estimates are not yet sufficiently reliable that they could be used to fine-tune policy.

---

[5]Senator William Proxmire, "PPB, The Agencies and the Congress," in *The Analysis and Evaluation of Public Expenditures: The PPB System.* U.S. Congress, Joint Economic Committee, Subcommittee on Economy in Government (Washington, D.C.: Government Printing Office, 1969): xiii.

[6]For a detailed treatment of current discounting practices in the U.S. government, see the special issue of the *Journal of Environmental Economics and Management* 18 (March 1990) which is devoted to this subject.

Example 3.5

The Importance of the Discount Rate

For years the United States and Canada had been discussing the possibility of constructing a tidal power project in the Passamaquoddy Bay between Maine and New Brunswick. This project would have heavy initial capital costs, but low operating costs which presumably would hold for a long time into the future. As part of their analysis of the situation, a complete inventory of costs and benefits was completed in 1959.

Using the same benefit and cost figures, Canada concluded that the project should not be built, while the United States concluded that it should. Because these conclusions were based on the same benefit-cost data, the differences can be attributed solely to the use of different discount rates. The United States used 2.5 percent while Canada used 4.125 percent. The higher discount rate makes the initial cost weigh much more heavily in the calculation, leading to the Canadian conclusion that the project yields a negative net benefit. Since the lower discount rate weights the lower future operating costs relatively more heavily, Americans saw the net benefit as positive.

There are a number of other examples, as well. During 1962, Congress authorized a number of water projects which had been justified by benefit-cost analysis using a discount rate of 2.63 percent. Upon examining these projects, economists Fox and Herfindahl (1964, p. 202) found that, at an 8% rate of discount, only 20 percent of the projects would have had favorable benefit-cost ratios.

The choice of the discount rate even played a major role following a highly publicized dispute between President Jimmy Carter and Congress. President Carter wanted to rescind authorization from many previously approved water projects that he viewed as wasteful. The President based his conclusions on a discount rate of 6.38 percent while Congress was using a lower one.

Far from being an esoteric subject, the choice of the discount rate is fundamentally important in defining the role of the public sector, the types of projects undertaken, and the allocation of resources across generations.

Sources: Edith Stokey and Richard Zeckhauser, A Primer for Policy Analysis (New York: W. W. Norton, 1978): 164–165; Raymond Mikesell, The Rate of Discount for Evaluating Public Projects (Washington, DC: The American Enterprise Institute for Public Policy Research, 1977): 3–5. Irving K. Fox and Orris C. Herfindahl, "Attainment of Efficiency in Satisfying Demands for Water Resources," American Economic Review 54 (May 1964): 202.

One well-known survey of the field (Freeman 1979), commissioned by the Council on Environmental Quality, a government body, concluded:

> This report makes two points quite clear. First, in spite of recent advances, the estimation of certain kinds of environmental benefits is still in need of much additional refinement....Second, where state-of-the-art analyses of environmental benefits have been undertaken—as exemplified by the studies in this report—they strongly suggest that environmental protection is good economics.

While the estimates are certainly good enough to tell us that the benefits from environmental control are large and worth pursuing, they may not be reliable enough to use in picking a single pollution level as the efficient one.

Similar concerns can be raised about costs. The Environmental Protection Agency (EPA) commissioned a study to examine just how accurate cost forecasts were. The study compared actual capital outlays by firms responding to the pollution control laws to the forecasts of those same costs made earlier by both the EPA and by affected industries. When issued in June 1980, the report found that "both EPA and industry forecasts tend to overestimate compliance costs more often than they underestimate these costs."[7] Further, the report found that some of these overestimates were substantial. For the oil-refining industry, for example, both EPA and the industry projected capital costs of $1.4 billion. The actual costs were around $590 million, less than half of the projected total.

We have seen that it is sometimes, though not always, difficult to estimate benefits and costs. When this estimation is difficult or unreliable, it limits the value of a benefit cost analysis. This problem would be particularly disturbing if biases tended to systematically increase or decrease net benefits. Do such biases exist?

In the early 1970s, economist Robert Haveman (1972) did a major study which sheds some light on this question. Focusing on Army Corps of Engineers water projects, such as flood control, navigation, and hydroelectric power generation, Haveman compared the *ex ante* (before the fact) estimate of benefits and costs with their *ex post* (after the fact) counterparts. Thus he was able to address the issues of accuracy and bias. He concluded that:

> In the empirical case studies presented, *ex post* estimates often showed little relationship to their *ex ante* counterparts. On the basis of the few cases and the *a priori* analysis presented here, one could conclude that there is a serious bias incorporated into agency *ex ante* evaluation procedures, resulting in persistent overstatement of expected benefits. Similarly in the analysis of project construction costs, enormous variance was found among projects in the relationship between estimated and realized costs. Although no persistent bias in estimation was apparent, nearly 50 percent of the projects displayed realized costs that deviated by more than plus or minus 20 percent from *ex ante* projected costs.[8]

In the cases examined by Haveman, at least, the notion that benefit cost analysis is purely a scientific exercise was clearly not consistent with the evidence; the biases of the analysts were merely translated into numbers.

Another shortcoming of benefit cost analysis is that it does not really address the question of who reaps the benefits and who pays the cost. It is quite possible for a particular course of action to yield high net benefits, but to have the benefits borne by one group of society and the costs borne by another. This admittedly extreme case does serve to illustrate a basic principle—ensuring that a particular policy is efficient provides an important, but not always the sole, basis for public policy. Other aspects, such as who reaps the benefit or bears the burden, are also important.

---

[7]Cited in "Antipollution Costs Were Overestimated by Government and Industry, Study Says," *Wall Street Journal* (June 19, 1980): 7.

[8]A more recent assessment of costs (Harrington, et al., 1999) found evidence of both overestimation and underestimation although overestimation was more common. The authors attributed the overestimation mainly to a failure to anticipate technical innovation.

In summary, on the positive side, benefit cost analysis is frequently a very useful part of the policy process. Even when the underlying data are not strictly reliable, the outcomes may not be sensitive to that unreliability. In other circumstances, the data may be reliable enough to give indications of the consequences of broad policy directions, even when they are not reliable enough to fine-tune those policies. Benefit-cost analysis, when done correctly, can provide a useful complement to the other influences on the political process by clarifying what choices yield the highest net benefits to society.

On the negative side, benefit cost analysis has been attacked as seeming to promise more than can actually be delivered, particularly in the absence of solid benefit information. There have been two responses to this kind of concern. First, regulatory processes have been developed which can be implemented with very little information and yet have desirable economic properties. The recent reforms in air pollution control, which we cover in Chapter 16, provide one powerful example.

The second approach involves techniques which supply useful information to the policy process without relying on controversial techniques to monetize environmental services which are difficult to value. The rest of this chapter deals with the two most prominent of these—cost effectiveness analysis and impact analysis.

Even when benefits are difficult or impossible to quantify, economic analysis has much to offer. Policy-makers should know, for example, how much various policy actions will cost and what their impacts on society will be, even if the efficient policy choice cannot be identified with any certainty. Cost-effectiveness analysis and impact analysis both respond to this need, albeit in different ways.

◆ COST-EFFECTIVENESS ANALYSIS

What can be done to guide policy when the requisite valuation for benefit-cost analysis is either unavailable or not sufficiently reliable? Without a good measure of benefits, making an efficient choice is no longer possible.

In such cases it frequently is possible, however, to set a policy target on some other basis other than a strict comparison of benefits and costs. One example is pollution control. What level of pollution should be established as the maximum acceptable level? In many countries, studies of the effects of a particular pollutant on human health have been used as the basis for establishing that pollutant's maximum acceptable concentration. Researchers attempt to find a threshold level below which no damage seems to occur. That threshold is then further lowered to provide a margin of safety and that becomes the pollution target.

Approaches could also be based upon expert opinion. Ecologists, for example, could be enlisted to define the critical numbers of certain species or the specific critical wetlands resources that should be preserved.

Once the policy target is specified, however, economic analysis can have a great deal to say about the cost consequences of choosing a means of achieving that objective. The cost consequences are important not only because eliminating wasteful expenditures is an appropriate goal in its own right, but also to assure that they do not trigger a political backlash.

Typically, several means of achieving the specified objective are available; some will be relatively inexpensive, while others turn out to be very expensive. The problems are frequently complicated enough that identifying the cheapest manner of achieving an objective cannot be accomplished without a rather detailed analysis of the choices.

Cost-effectiveness analysis frequently involves an *optimization procedure.* An optimization procedure, in this context, is merely a systematic method for finding the lowest cost means of accomplishing the objective. This procedure does not, in general, produce an efficient allocation because the predetermined objective may not be efficient. All efficient policies are cost-effective, but not all cost-effective policies are efficient.

In the preceding chapter we introduced the efficiency equimarginal principle. According to that principle, net benefits are maximized when the marginal benefit is equal to the marginal cost.

A similar, and equally important, equimarginal principle exists for cost-effectiveness:

Second Equimarginal Principle (the Cost-Effectiveness Equimarginal Principle): The least-cost means of achieving an environmental target will have been achieved when the marginal costs of all possible means of achievement are equal.

Suppose, for example, we want to achieve a specific emission reduction across a region, and several possible techniques for reducing emissions exist. How much of the control responsibility should each technique bear? The cost-effectiveness equimarginal principle suggests that the techniques should be used such that the desired reduction is achieved and the cost of achieving the last unit of emission reduction (in other words the marginal control cost) should be the same for all sources.

To demonstrate why this principle is valid, suppose that we have an allocation of control responsibility where marginal control costs are much higher for one set of techniques than for another. This cannot be the least cost allocation since we could lower cost while retaining the same amount of emission reduction. Costs could be lowered by allocating more control to the lower marginal cost sources and less to the high marginal cost sources. Since it is possible to find a way to lower cost, then clearly the initial allocation could not have minimized cost. Once marginal costs are equalized, it becomes impossible to find any lower-cost way of achieving the same degree of emissions reduction; therefore that allocation must be the allocation which minimizes costs.

In our pollution control example, cost-effectiveness can be used to find the least-cost means of meeting a particular standard and its associated cost. Using this cost as a benchmark case, we can estimate how much costs could be expected to increase from this minimum level if policies which are not cost-effective are implemented. Cost-effectiveness analysis can also be used to determine how much compliance costs can be expected to change if the EPA chooses a more stringent or less stringent standard. The case study presented in Example 3.6 not only illustrates the use of cost-effectiveness analysis, it also shows that costs can be very sensitive to the regulatory approach chosen by the EPA.

◆IMPACT ANALYSIS

What can be done when the information needed to perform a benefit-cost analysis or a cost-effectiveness analysis is not available? The analytical technique designed to deal with this problem is called *impact analysis*. An impact analysis, regardless of whether it focuses on economic impact or environmental impact or both, attempts to quantify the consequences of various actions.

Example 3.6

NO$_2$ Control in Chicago: An Example of Cost-Effectiveness Analysis

In order to compare compliance costs of meeting a predetermined ambient air quality standard in Chicago, Seskin, Anderson, and Reid (1983) gathered information on the cost of control for each of 797 stationary sources of nitrogen oxide emissions in the city of Chicago, along with measured air quality at 100 different locations within the city. The relationship between ambient air quality at those receptors and emissions from the 797 sources was then modeled using mathematical equations. Once these equations were estimated, the model was calibrated to ensure that it was capable of recreating the actual situation in Chicago. Following successful calibration, this model was used to simulate what would happen if EPA were to take various regulatory actions.

The results indicated that a cost-effective strategy would cost less than one-tenth as much as the traditional approach to control and less than one-seventh as much as a more sophisticated version of the traditional approach. In absolute terms, moving to a more cost-effective policy was estimated to save more than $100 million annually in the Chicago area alone. We shall examine in detail the current movement toward cost-effective polices, a movement triggered in part by studies such as this one.

In contrast to benefit-cost analysis, a pure impact analysis makes no attempt to convert all these consequences into a one-dimensional measure, such as dollars, to ensure comparability. In contrast to both benefit cost analysis and cost-effectiveness analysis, impact analysis does not necessarily attempt to optimize. Impact analysis places a large amount of relatively undigested information at the disposal of the policy-maker. It is up to the policy-maker to assess the importance of the various consequences and act accordingly.

On January 1, 1970, President Nixon signed the National Environmental Policy Act of 1969. This act, among other things, directed all agencies of the federal government to:

include in every recommendation or report on proposals for legislation and other major Federal actions significantly affecting the quality of the human environment, a detailed statement by the responsible official on—

(i)   the environmental impact of the proposed action.

(ii)   any adverse environmental effects which cannot be avoided should the proposal be implemented,

(iii)   alternatives to the proposed action,

(iv)   the relationships between local short-term uses of man's environment and the maintenance and enhancement of long-term productivity; and

(v)   any irreversible and irretrievable commitments of resources which would be involved in the proposed action should it be implemented.[9]

---

[9]83 Stat. 853.

This was the beginning of the environmental impact statement, which is now a familiar, if controversial, part of environmental policy-making.

Current environmental impact statements are more sophisticated than their early predecessors and may contain a benefit-cost analysis or a cost-effectiveness analysis in addition to other more traditional impact measurements. Historically, however, the tendency had been to issue huge environmental impact statements which are virtually impossible to comprehend in their entirety.

In response, the Council on Environmental Quality, which, by law, administers the environmental impact statement process, has set content standards that are now resulting in shorter, more concise statements. To the extent that they merely quantify consequences, statements can avoid the problem of "hidden value judgments" that sometimes plague benefit cost analysis, but they do so only by bombarding the policy-makers with masses of noncomparable information. All three of the techniques discussed in this chapter are useful, but none of them can stake a claim as being universally the "best" approach. The nature of the information which is available and its reliability make a difference.

SUMMARY

In this chapter we have examined the most prominent but certainly not the only techniques available to supply policy-makers with the information needed to implement efficient policy. Finding the total economic value of the service flows requires estimating three components of value: (1) use value, (2) option value, and (3) nonuse or passive value.

Our review of these various techniques included direct observation, contingent valuation, contingent ranking, travel cost, hedonic property and hedonic wage studies and averting or defensive expenditures. Examples of actual studies using these techniques were presented.

Because benefit-cost analysis is both very powerful and very controversial, in 1996 a group of economists of quite different political persuasions got together to attempt to reach some consensus on its proper role in environmental decision-making. Their conclusion is worth reproducing in its entirety:

> Benefit-cost analysis can play an important role in legislative and regulatory policy debates on protecting and improving health, safety and the natural environment. Although formal benefit-cost analysis should not be viewed as either necessary or sufficient for designing sensible policy, it can provide an exceptionally useful framework for consistently organizing disparate information, and in this way, it can greatly improve the process and, hence, the outcome of policy analysis. If properly done, benefit-cost analysis can be of great help to agencies participating in the development of environmental, health and safety regulations, and it can likewise be useful in evaluating agency decision-making and in shaping statutes.[10]

---

[10]Kenneth Arrow, et al., "Is There a Role for Benefit-Cost Analysis in Environmental, Health and Safety Regulation?" *Science* 272 (April 12, 1996): 221-222.

Even when benefits are difficult to calculate, however, economic analysis in the form of cost effectiveness can be valuable. This technique can establish the least expensive ways to accomplish predetermined policy goals and to assess the extra costs involved when policies other than the least-cost policy are chosen. What it cannot do is answer the question of whether those predetermined policy goals are efficient.

At the end of the spectrum is impact analysis, which merely identifies and quantifies the impacts of particular policies without any pretense of optimality or even comparability of the information generated. Impact analysis does not guarantee an efficient outcome.

FURTHER READING

Barde, Jean-Philippe, and David W. Pearce. *Valuing the Environment: Six Case Studies* (London: Earthscan Publications, 1991). A series of essays describing the use of economic valuation of environmental resources to inform public policy. Includes case studies from Germany, Italy, the Netherlands, Norway, the United Kingdom, and the United States.

Boardman, Anthony E., David H. Greemberg, Aiden R. Vining, and David L. Weimer. *Cost-Benefit Analysis: Concepts and Practice* (Upper Saddle River, NJ: Prentice-Hall, 1996). An excellent basic text on the use of cost-benefit analysis.

Costanza, R., et al. "The Value of the World's Ecosystem Services and Natural Capital" (Reprinted from *Nature,* Vol. 387, p. 253, 1997), *Ecological Economics* Vol. 25, No. 1 (1998): 3–15. An ambitious but ultimately flawed attempt to place an economic value on ecosystem services. This issue of *Ecological Economics* also contains a number of articles that demonstrate some of the flaws.

Cummings, Ronald G., David S. Brookshire, and William D. Schulze. *Valuing Environmental Goods: An Assessment of the Contingent Valuation Method* (Totowa, NJ: Rowman and Littlefield, 1986). A critical evaluation of the contingent valuation method by both practitioners and impartial reviewers.

Diamond, Peter A. and Jerry A. Hausman. "Contingent Valuation. Is Some Number Better than No Number?" *Journal of Economic Perspectives* Vol. 8, No. 4 (Fall, 1994): 45–64.

Dixon, John A. and Maynard M. Hufschmidt. *Economic Valuation Techniques for the Environment* (Baltimore: The Johns Hopkins University Press, 1986). Several case studies on the application of valuation techniques to environmental problems in less developed countries.

Glickman, Theodore S. and Michael Gough, eds. *Readings in Risk* (Washington, DC: Resources for the Future, Inc., 1990).

Hausman, Jerry A., ed. *Contingent Valuation: A Critical Assessment* (Amsterdam: North-Holland, 1993). The critics of contingent valuation weigh in.

Kneese, Allen V. *Measuring the Benefits of Clean Air and Water* (Washington, DC: Resources for the Future, 1984). An accessible introduction to a large number of studies attempting to quantify the benefits of cleaner air and water.

Kopp, Raymond J. and V. Kerry Smith, eds. *Valuing Natural Assets: The Economics of Natural Resource Damage Assessment* (Washington, D.C.: Resources for the Future, Inc., 1993). A comprehensive set of essays by some of the chief practitioners in the field evaluating both the legal framework for damage assessment and the validity and reliability of the methods currently being used.

Mitchell, Robert Cameron and Richard T. Carson. *Using Surveys to Value Public Goods: The Contingent Valuation Method* (Washington: Resources for the Future, 1989). A comprehensive examination of contingent valuation research with brief summaries of representative studies.

Viscusi, W. Kip. "Economic Foundations of the Current Regulatory Reform Efforts," *Journal of Economic Perspectives,* Vol. 10, No. 3 (Summer, 1996): 119–134.

ADDITIONAL REFERENCES

Arrow, Kenneth J. and Robert C. Lind. "Uncertainty and the Evaluation of Public Investment Decisions," *American Economic Review* Vol. 60, No. 3 (June, 1970): 364–378.

Arrow, K. J. and A. C. Fisher. "Preservation, Uncertainty, and Irreversibility," *Quarterly Journal of Economics* Vol. 87 (1974): 312–319.

Adger, W. N., et al. "Total Economic Value of Forests in Mexico," *Ambio* Vol. 24, No. 5 (1995): 286–296.

Brookshire, D. S. and M. McKee. "Is the Glass Half Empty, Is the Glass Half Full?—Compensable Damages and the Contingent Valuation Method," *Natural Resources Journal* Vol. 34, No. 1 (1994): 51–72.

Carson, Richard T., et al. *A Bibliography of Contingent Valuation Studies* (La Jolla, CA: Natural Resource Damage Assessment, Inc., 1994).

Carson, R. T., et al. "Contingent Valuation and Revealed Preference Methodologies: Comparing the Estimates for Quasi–Public Goods," *Land Economics* Vol. 72, No. 1 (1996): 80–99.

Castle, E. N., et al. "Natural Resource Damage Assessment—Speculations about a Missing Perspective," *Land Economics* Vol. 70, No. 3 (1994): 378–385.

Cummings, Ronald G., David S. Brookshire, and William D. Schulze. *Valuing Environmental Goods: An Assessment of the Contingent Value Method* (Towtowa, NJ: Rowman and Littlefield, 1986).

Cummings, Ronald G. and Glenn W. Harrison. "The Measurement and Decomposition of Nonuse Values: A Critical Review," *Environmental and Resource Economics* Vol. 5, No. 3 (1995): 225–247.

Dixon, John. *Economics of Protected Areas: A New Look at Benefits and Costs* (Washington, DC: Island Press, 1990).

Dixon, John A. and Maynard M. Hufschmidt. *Economic Valuation Techniques for the Environment* (Baltimore, MD: Johns Hopkins University Press, 1986).

Haneman, W. Michael, "Valuing the Environment Through Contingent Valuation," *Journal of Economic Perspectives* Vol. 8, No. 4 (Fall, 1994): 19–43.

Harrington, W., R. D. Morgenstern; and P. Nelson, "Predicting the Costs of Environmental Regulations: How Accurate Are Regulators' Estimates?" *Environment* 41(7): 10–14, 40–44.

Howarth, R. B. and R. B. Norgaard. "Environmental Valuation under Sustainable Development," *American Economic Review* Vol. 82, No. 2 (1992): 473–477.

Kosz, M. "Valuing Riverside Wetlands: The Case of the 'Donau-Auen' National Park," *Ecological Economics* Vol. 16, No. 2 (1996): 109–127.

Loehman, E. T., et al. "Willingness to Pay for Gains and Losses in Visibility and Health," *Land Economics* Vol. 70, No. 4 (1994): 478–498.

Loomis, J. B. "Measuring The Economic Benefits of Removing Dams and Restoring the Elwha River: Results of a Contingent Valuation Survey," *Water Resources Research* Vol. 32, No. 2 (1996): 441–447.

Navrud, S. and E. D. Mungatana. "Environmental Valuation in Developing Countries: The Recreational Value of Wildlife Viewing," *Ecological Economics* Vol. 11, No. 2 (1994): 135–151.

Orians, Gordon H., et al., ed. *The Preservation and Valuation of Biological Resources* (Seattle, WA: University of Washington Press, 1990).

Peters, C, et al. "Valuation of an Amazonian Rainforest," *Nature* Vol. 339 (1989): 655–56.

Siachoono, S. M. "Contingent Valuation as an Additional Tool for Evaluating Wildlife Utilization Management in Zambia: Mumbwa Game Management Area," *Ambio* Vol. 24, No. 4 (1995): 246–249.

Van Houten, George and Maureen L. Cropper. "When Is a Life Too Costly to Save? The Evidence from U.S. Environmental Regulations," *Journal of Environmental Economics and Management* Vol. 30, No. 3 (1996): 348–368.

Whitehead, J. C., et al. "Assessing the Validity and Reliability of Contingent Values: A Comparison of On-Site Users, Off-Site Users, and Non-Users," *Journal of Environmental Economics and Management* Vol. 29, No. 2 (1995): 238–251.

WEB SITES OF INTEREST

1. *http://www.rff.org/*
   The homepage for Resources for the Future, Inc., a leading environmental economics research organization. The section on Methods, Tools and Techniques is particularly relevant for this chapter.

2. *www.epa.gov/ORD/publications*
   Publications of the Office of Research and Development, many on risk assessment.

3. *www.epa.gov/ttnecas1/reg_doc.html*
   Examples of EPA publications on air pollution regulatory impact analysis.

DISCUSSION QUESTIONS

1. Is risk neutrality an appropriate assumption for cost-benefit analysis? Why or why not? Does it seem more appropriate for some environmental problems than others? If so, which ones? If you were evaluating the desirability of locating a hazardous waste incinerator in a particular town, would the Arrow-Lind rationale for risk neutrality be appropriate? Why or why not?

2. Was the executive order issued by President Reagan mandating a heavier use of cost-benefit analysis in regulatory rule making a step toward establishing a more rational regulatory structure, or was it a subversion of the environmental policy process? Why?

3. Certain environmental laws prohibit EPA from considering the costs of meeting various standards when the levels of the standards are set. Is this a good example of "putting first things first" or simply an unjustifiable waste of resources? Why?

4

Property Rights, Externalities, and Environmental Problems

The charming landscape which I saw this morning, is indubitably made up of some twenty or thirty farms. Miller owns this field, Locke that, and Manning the woodland beyond. But none of them owns the landscape. There is a property in the horizon which no man has but he whose eye can integrate all the parts, that is, the poet. This is the best part of these men's farms, yet to this their land deeds give them no title.

RALPH WALDO EMERSON, *NATURE* (1836)

◆ INTRODUCTION

In Chapter 2 we developed specific normative criteria for making rational choices about the relationship between the economic system and the environment. According to those criteria, an environmental problem exists when resource allocations are inefficient.

When would breaches of efficiency occur? Why would individual or group interests diverge from those of society at large? What circumstances give rise to this division of interests, and what can be done about it? One useful way to examine this question is based on the concept known as a *property right*. In this chapter we explore this concept and how it can be used to understand why the environmental asset can be undervalued by both the market and governmental policy. We also discuss how the government and the market can, on occasion, use knowledge of property rights and their effects on incentives to orchestrate a coordinated approach to resolving these difficulties.

◆ PROPERTY RIGHTS

Property Rights and Efficient Market Allocations

The manner in which producers and consumers use environmental resources depends on the property rights governing those resources. In economics, *property right* refers to a bundle of entitlements defining the owner's rights, privileges, and limitations for use of the resource. By examining such entitlements and how they affect human behavior, we will better understand how environmental problems arise from government and market allocations.

These property rights can be vested either with individuals, as in a capitalist economy, or with the state, as in a centrally planned socialist economy. It is not uncommon to hear that the source of environmental problems in a capitalist economy is the market system itself or, more specifically, the pursuit of profits. You may have heard this point of view expressed as, "Corporations are more interested in profits than in the needs of people." Those who espouse this view look longingly at centrally planned economies as a means of avoiding environmental excess.

Simple answers rarely suffice for complex problems; environmental and natural resource problems are not an exception. Centrally planned economies, such as the former Soviet Union, have not historically avoided pollution excesses (Example 4.1). On the other hand, the pursuit of profits is not inevitably inconsistent with fulfilling the needs of the people. Though the pursuit of profits may sometimes be inconsistent with fulfilling these needs, it is not always inconsistent. In fact, this pursuit is often the essential ingredient in meeting people's needs. How can we tell when the pursuit of profits is consistent with societal objectives, such as efficiency, and when it is not?

Efficient Property Right Structures

Let's begin by describing the structure of property rights that could produce efficient allocations in a well-functioning market economy. An efficient structure has three main characteristics:

1. *Exclusivity*—All benefits and costs accrued as a result of owning and using the resources should accrue to the owner, and only to the owner, either directly or indirectly by sale to others.
2. *Transferability*—All property rights should be transferable from one owner to another in a voluntary exchange.
3. *Enforceability*—Property rights should be secure from involuntary seizure or encroachment by others.

An owner of a resource with a well-defined property right (one exhibiting these three characteristics) has a powerful incentive to use that resource efficiently because a decline in the value of that resource represents a personal loss. Farmers who own the land have an incentive to fertilize and irrigate it because the resulting increased production raises income level. Similarly, they have an incentive to rotate crops when that raises the productivity of their land.

When well-defined property rights are exchanged, as in a market economy, this exchange facilitates efficiency. We can illustrate this point by examining the incentives consumers and producers face when a well-defined system of property rights is in place. Because the seller has the right to prevent the consumer from consuming the product in the absence of pay-

Example 4.1

Pollution In Centrally Planned Economies

Since environmental problems are thought to be caused by a divergence between individual incentives and collective incentives, it is not uncommon to hear that centrally planned economies avoid environmental problems. Centralizing power in the state, as occurs in a centrally planned economy, is believed to allow collective decisions to be made at the outset.

Studies of air and water pollution in the former Soviet Union and other Eastern European countries suggest that the problems found in market economies occur with equal intensity in the Eastern block. Copsa Mica, Romania, for example, is called Europe's most polluted urban area. Weakened by acid rain, monuments in Krakow, Poland, are crumbling. Women with newborn babies in Czechoslovakia have priority access to bottled water because tap water is considered injurious to infant health.

How can this be? Goldman suggests that the centralized planning system creates different, but no less potent, divergences between individual and collective incentives. For example, as of 1970, 65 percent of all factories in the largest Soviet republic, the Russian Soviet Federated Socialist Republic, discharged their waste into the water without any attempt to clean it up. They did this because the managers were being judged solely in terms of output, not in terms of the harm they caused to the environment. The central plans which set the priorities to be followed by the managers very simply emphasized economic growth over the environment.

In his summary Goldman states:

. . . not private enterprise but industrialization is the primary cause of environmental disruption. This suggests that state ownership of all the productive resources is no cure-all.

Source: Marshall I. Goldman, "Economics of Environmental and Renewable Resources in Socialist Systems," in Allen V. Kneese and James L. Sweeney, eds. *Handbook of Natural Resource and Energy Economics*, Vol. II (Amsterdam: North-Holland, 1985): 725–745; Louis Berney, "Black Town of Transylvania Is Called Europe's Most Polluted," *The Boston Globe* (March 28, 1990): 2, Hilary F. French, "Industrial Wasteland," *Worldwatch* (November/December 1988): 21–30; Vladimir Kotov and Elena Nikitina, "Russia in Transition: Obstacles to Environmental Protection," *Environment* 35 (December 1993): 10–19.

ment, the consumer must pay to receive the product. Given a market price, the consumer decides how much to purchase by choosing that amount which maximizes his or her individual net benefit (Figure 4.1).

The consumer's net benefit is the area under the demand curve minus the area representing cost. The cost to the consumer is the area under the price line, since that area represents the expenditure on the commodity. Obviously, for a given price P^*, consumer net benefit is maximized by choosing to purchase Q_d units. Area A is then the geometric representation of the net benefit received, known as *consumer surplus*. It is the area under the demand curve

FIGURE 4.1   The Consumer's Choice

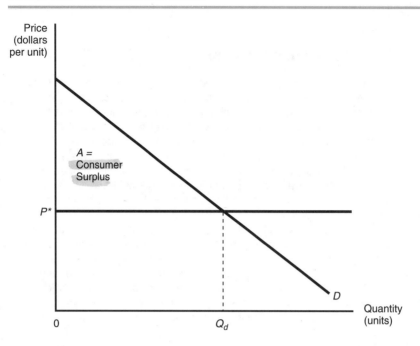

that lies above the price, bounded from the left by the vertical axis and from the right by the quantity of the good being considered.

Meanwhile, sellers face a similar choice (Figure 4.2). Given price P^*, the seller maximizes his or her own net benefits by choosing to sell Q_s units. The net benefit received (Area B) by the seller is called *producer surplus.* It is the area under the price line that lies over the marginal cost curve, bounded from the left by the vertical axis and the right by the quantity of the good being considered.

The price level which producers and consumers face will adjust until supply equals demand, as depicted in Figure 4.3. Given that price, consumers maximize their surplus, producers maximize their surplus, and the market clears.

Is this allocation efficient? According to our definition of static efficiency from the previous chapter, it is clear the answer is yes. The net benefit is maximized by the market allocation and, as seen in Figure 4.3, it is equal to the sum of consumer and producer surpluses. Thus, we have established a procedure for measuring net benefits, and a means of describing how the net benefits are distributed between consumers and producers.

This distribution is crucially significant. Efficiency is *not* achieved because consumers and producers are seeking efficiency. They aren't! In a system with well-defined property rights and competitive markets in which to sell those rights, producers try to maximize their surplus and consumers try to maximize their surplus. The price system, then, induces those self-interested parties to make choices which are efficient from the point of view of society as a whole. It channels the energy motivated by self-interest into socially productive paths.

FIGURE 4.2   The Producer's Choice

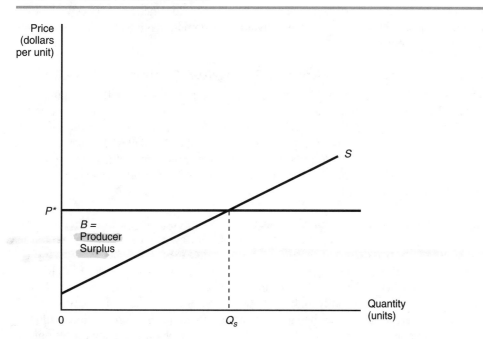

FIGURE 4.3   Market Equilibrium

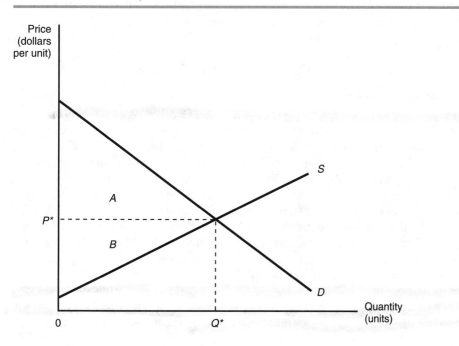

Though familiarity may have dulled our appreciation, it is noteworthy that a system designed to produce a harmonious and congenial outcome could function effectively while allowing consumers and producers so much individual freedom in making choices. This is truly a remarkable accomplishment.

Producer's Surplus, Scarcity Rent, and Long-Run Competitive Equilibrium

Since the area under the price line is total revenue, and the area under the marginal cost curve is total variable cost, producer's surplus is related to profits. In the short run when some costs are fixed, producer's surplus is equal to profits plus fixed cost. In the long run when all costs are variable, producer surplus is equal to profits plus rent, the return to scarce inputs owned by the producer. As long as new firms can enter into an industry where profits are earned without raising the prices of purchased inputs, long-run profits will equal zero and producer surplus will equal rent.

Scarcity Rent.   Most natural resource industries, however, do give rise to rent and, therefore, producer's surplus is not eliminated by competition, even with free entry. This producer's surplus which persists in long-run competitive equilibrium is called *scarcity rent*.

David Ricardo was the first economist to recognize the existence of scarcity rent. Ricardo suggested that the price of land was determined by the least fertile marginal unit of land. Since the price had to be sufficiently high to allow the poorer land to be brought into production, other, more fertile, land could be farmed at an economic profit. Competition could not erode that profit because the amount of land was limited and lower prices would serve only to reduce the supply of land below demand. The only way to expand production would be to bring additional, less fertile, land (more costly to farm) into production; consequently, additional production does not lower price, as it does in a constant-cost industry. As we shall see other circumstances also give rise to scarcity rent for natural resources.

◆ EXTERNALITIES AS A SOURCE OF MARKET FAILURE

The Concept Introduced

Exclusivity is one of the chief characteristics of an efficient property rights structure. This characteristic is frequently violated in practice. One broad class of violations occurs when an agent making a decision does not bear all of the consequences of his or her action.

Suppose two firms are located by a river. The first produces steel, while the second, somewhat downstream, operates a resort hotel. Both use the river, though in different ways. The steel firm uses it as a receptacle for its waste, while the second uses it to attract customers seeking water recreation. If these two facilities have different owners, an efficient use of the water is not likely to result. Because the steel plant does not bear the cost of reduced business at the resort resulting from waste being dumped into the river, it is not likely to be very sensitive to that cost in its decision making. As a result, it could be expected to dump too much waste into the river, and an efficient allocation of the river would not be attained.

This situation is called an externality. An *externality* exists whenever the welfare of some agent, either a firm or household, depends not only on his or her activities, but also on activities under the control of some other agent. In the example, the increased waste in the river

FIGURE 4.4 The Market for Steel

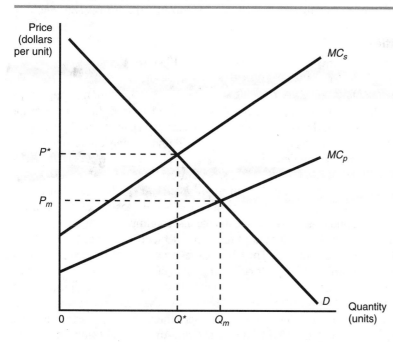

imposed an external cost on the resort, a cost the steel firm could not be counted upon to consider appropriately in deciding the amount of waste to dump.

The effects of this external cost on the steel industry can be seen in Figure 4.4, which depicts the market for steel. Steel production inevitably involves producing pollution as well as steel. The demand for steel is shown by the demand curve D, and the private marginal cost of producing the steel (exclusive of pollution control and damage) is depicted as MC_p. Because society considers both the cost of pollution and the cost of producing the steel, the social marginal cost function (MC_s) includes both of these costs as well.

If the steel industry faced no outside control on its emission levels, it would seek to produce Q_m. That choice, in a competitive setting, would maximize its private producer surplus. But that is clearly not efficient, since the net benefit is maximized at Q^* not Q_m.

With the assistance of Figure 4.4, we can draw a number of conclusions about market allocations of commodities causing pollution externalities:

1. The output of the commodity is too large.
2. Too much pollution is produced.
3. The prices of products responsible for pollution are too low.
4. As long as the costs are external, no incentives to search for ways to yield less pollution per unit of output are introduced by the market.
5. Recycling and reuse of the polluting substances are discouraged since release into the environment is so inefficiently cheap.

The effects of a market imperfection for one commodity end up affecting the demands for raw materials, labor, and so on. The ultimate effects are felt through the entire economy.

Types of Externalities

External effects can be either positive or negative. Historically, the terms *external diseconomy* and *external economy* have been used to refer, respectively, to circumstances in which the affected party is damaged or benefited by the externality. Clearly, the water-pollution example represents an external diseconomy. External economies are not hard to find, however. Private individuals who purchase a particularly scenic area provide an external economy to all who pass. Generally, when external economies are present, the market will undersupply the resources.

One other distinction is important. One class of externalities, known as *pecuniary externalities*, does not present the same kinds of problems as pollution does. Pecuniary externalities arise when the external effect is transmitted through higher prices. Suppose that a new firm moves into an area and drives up the rental price of land. That increase creates a negative effect on all those paying rent and, therefore, is an external diseconomy.

This pecuniary diseconomy, however, does not cause a market failure because the resulting higher rents are reflecting the scarcity of land. The land market provides a mechanism by which the parties can bid for land; the prices that result reflect the value of the land in its various uses. Without pecuniary externalities, the price signals would fail to sustain an efficient allocation.

The pollution example is *not* a pecuniary externality because the effect is not transmitted through prices. In this example, prices do not adjust to reflect the increasing waste load. The scarcity of the water resource is not signaled to the steel firm. An essential feedback mechanism that is present for pecuniary externalities is not present for the pollution case.

The externalities concept is a broad one covering a multitude of sources of market failure (Example 4.2). The next step is to investigate some other circumstances which can give rise to externalities.

◆ IMPROPERLY DESIGNED PROPERTY RIGHTS SYSTEMS

Other Property Rights Regimes[1]

Private property is, of course, not the only possible way of defining entitlements to resources use. Other possibilities include state-property regimes (where the government owns and controls the property), common-property regimes (where the property is jointly owned and managed by a specified group of co-owners) and *res nullius* regimes (in which no one owns or exercises control over the resources). All of these create rather different incentives for resource use.

State-property regimes exist not only in former communist countries (as in Example 4.1), but also to varying degrees in virtually all countries of the world. Parks and forests, for example, are frequently owned and managed by the government in capitalist as well as in socialist nations. As Example 4.1 indicates, problems with both efficiency and sustainability can

---

[1]This section relies on the classification system presented in Bromley, Daniel W. *Environment and Economy: Property Rights and Public Policy* (Oxford: Basil Blackwell, Inc., 1991). A detailed exploration of the property rights approach to environmental problems.

Example 4.2

Shrimp Farming Externalities in Thailand

In the Tha Po village on the coast of Surat Thani Province in Thailand, more than half of the 1,100 hectares of mangrove swamps have been cleared for commercial shrimp farms. Although harvesting shrimp is a lucrative undertaking, mangroves serve as nurseries for fish and as barriers for storms and soil erosion. Following the destruction of the local mangroves, Tha Po villagers experienced a decline in fish catch and suffered storm damage and water pollution. Can market forces be trusted to strike the efficient balance between preservation and development for the remaining mangroves?

Calculations by an economist, Dr. Sathirathai, demonstrated that the value of the ecological services that would be lost from further destruction of the mangrove swamps exceeded the value of the shrimp farms that would take their place. Preservation of the remaining mangrove swamps would be the efficient choice.

Would a potential shrimp-farming entrepreneur make the efficient choice? Unfortunately the answer is no. The private net benefits are maximized by further development. Whereas most of the benefits of preservation are borne by someone other than the entrepreneur (the majority of shrimp farms were owned by outsiders), most of the benefits of shrimp farming are received directly by the entrepreneur. In the absence of some sort of external control imposed by collective action, development would be the normal, if inefficient, result. The externalities associated with the ecological services provided by the mangroves support a biased decision that results in fewer social net benefits, but greater private net benefits.

Source: Suthawan Sathirathai, *Economic Valuation of Mangroves and the Roles of Local Communities in the Conservation of Natural Resources: Case Study of Surat Thani, South of Thailand*, Economy and Environmental Program for Southeast Asia Research Report, Singapore (January 1999).

arise in state-property regimes when the incentives of bureaucrats who implement and/or make the rules for resource use diverge from collective interests.

Common-property resources are those that are owned in common rather than privately. Entitlements to use common-property resources may be formal, protected by specific legal rules, or they may be informal, protected by tradition or custom. Common-property regimes exhibit varying degrees of efficiency and sustainability, depending on the rules which emerge from collective decision making. While some very successful examples of common-property regimes exist, unsuccessful examples are even more common.[2]

One successful example of a common-property regime involves the system of allocating grazing rights in Switzerland. Though agricultural land is normally treated as private property

---

[2]The two cases which follow and many others are discussed in Ostrom, Elinor. *Crafting Institutions for Self-Governing Irrigation Systems* (San Francisco: ICS Press, 1992). Argues that common-pool problems are sometimes solved by voluntary organizations rather than by a coercive state. Among the cases considered are communal tenure in meadows and forest, irrigation communities, and fisheries.

in Switzerland, grazing rights on the Alpine meadows have been treated as common property for centuries. Overgrazing is protected by specific rules, enacted by an association of users, which limit the amount of livestock permitted on the meadow. The families included on the membership list of the association have been stable over time as rights and responsibilities have passed from generation to generation. This stability has apparently facilitated reciprocity and trust, thereby providing a foundation for continued compliance with the rules.

Unfortunately, that kind of stability may be the exception rather than the rule, particularly in the face of heavy population pressure. The more common situation can be illustrated by the experience of Mawelle, a small fishing village in Sri Lanka. Initially, a complicated but effective rotating system of fishing rights was devised by villagers to assure equitable access to the best spots and best times while protecting the fish stocks. Over time, population pressure and the infusion of outsiders both raised demand and undermined the collective cohesion sufficiently that the traditional rules became unenforceable, producing overexploitation of the resource and lower incomes for all the participants.

Res nullius property resources, the main focus of this section, can be exploited on a first-come, first-served basis, because no individual or group has the legal power to restrict access. *Open-access resources*, as we shall henceforth call them, have given rise to what has become known popularly as the "tragedy of the commons."

The problems created by open-access resources can be illustrated by recalling the fate of the American bison. Bison are an example of "common pool" resources. Common-pool resources are characterized by nonexclusivity and divisibility. Nonexclusivity implies that they can be exploited by anyone while divisibility means that the capture of part of the resource by one group subtracts it from the amount available to the other groups. (Note the contrast between common-pool resources and public goods in the next section.) In the early history of the United States, bison were plentiful; unrestricted hunting access was not a problem. Frontier people who needed hides or meat could easily get whatever they needed; the aggressiveness of any one hunter did not affect the time and effort expended by other hunters. In the absence of scarcity, efficiency was not threatened by open access.

As the years slipped by, however, the demand for bison increased and scarcity became a factor. As the number of hunters increased, eventually every additional unit of hunting activity increased the amount of time and effort required to produce a given yield of bison. In Figure 4.5, we depict the social benefits and costs of bison hunting. Total benefits are calculated by multiplying, for each level of hunting activity, the (assumed constant) price of bison by the amount harvested. The marginal benefit curve is downward sloping because the greater the amount of hunting effort expended, the smaller the resulting population size. Smaller populations support smaller harvests per unit of effort expended.

The efficient level of hunting activity in this model (Q_1) is the level where the marginal benefit curve crosses the marginal cost curve. At this level of activity, the marginal benefit would be just equal to the marginal cost, implying that net benefits are maximized. This allocation would yield a scarcity rent equal to area A + C.

With all hunters having completely unrestricted access to the bison, the resulting allocation would not be efficient. No individual hunter would have an incentive to protect scarcity rent by restricting hunting effort. Individual hunters, without exclusive rights, would exploit the resource until their total benefit equaled total cost, implying a level of effort equal to (Q_2). Excessive exploitation of the herd occurs because individual hunters cannot appropriate the

FIGURE 4.5 Bison Harvesting

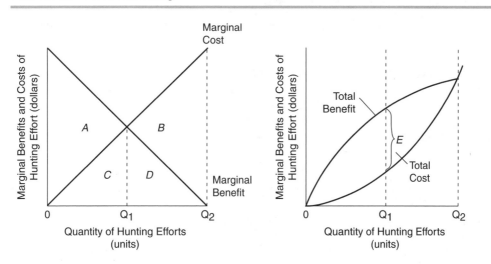

scarcity rent; therefore, they ignore it. One of the losses from further exploitation which could be avoided by exclusive owners—the opportunity cost of overexploitation—is not part of the decision-making process of open-access hunters.

Two characteristics of this formulation of the open-access allocation are worth noting: (1) In the presence of sufficient demand, unrestricted access will cause resources to be over-exploited; (2) the scarcity rent is dissipated; no one appropriates the rent, so it is lost.

Why does this happen? Unlimited access destroys the incentive to conserve. A hunter who can preclude others from hunting this stock has an incentive to keep the herd at an efficient level. This restraint results in lower costs in the form of less time and effort expended to produce a given yield of bison. On the other hand, a hunter exploiting an open-access resource would not have any incentive to conserve because the benefits derived from restraint would, to some extent, be captured by other hunters. Thus unrestricted access to resources promotes an inefficient allocation.

Public Goods

Public Goods, defined as those that exhibit both consumption indivisibilities and nonexcludability, present a particularly complex category of environmental resources. *Nonexcludability* refers to a circumstance where, once the resource is provided, even those who fail to pay for it cannot be excluded from enjoying the benefits it confers. Consumption is said to be *indivisible* when one person's consumption of a good does not diminish the amount available for others. Several common environmental resources are public goods, including not only the "charming landscape" referred to by Emerson, but also clean air, clean water, and biological diversity.[3]

Biological diversity includes two related concepts: (1) the amount of genetic variability among individuals within a single species, and (2) the number of species within a community

---

[3]Notice that public "bads," such as dirty air and dirty water, are also possible.

but...

of organisms. *Genetic diversity,* critical to species survival in the natural world, has also proved to be important in the development of new crops and livestock. It enhances the opportunities for crossbreeding and, thus, the development of superior strains. The availability of different strains was the key, for example, in developing a new, disease-resistant barley.

Because of the interdependence of species within ecological communities, any particular species may have a value to the community far beyond its intrinsic value. Certain species contribute balance and stability to their ecological communities by providing food sources or holding the population of the species in check.

The richness of diversity within and among species has provided new sources of food, energy, industrial chemicals, raw materials, and medicines. Yet there is considerable evidence that biological diversity is decreasing.

Can we rely on the private sector to produce the efficient amount of public goods such as biological diversity? Unfortunately, the answer is no! Suppose that in response to diminishing ecological diversity we decide to take up a collection to provide some means of preserving endangered species. Would the collection yield sufficient revenue to pay for an efficient level of ecological diversity? The general answer is no. Let's see why.

In Figure 4.6, individual-demand curves for preserving biodiversity have been presented for two consumers *A* and *B*. The market-demand curve is represented by the vertical summation of the two individual-demand curves. A vertical summation is necessary because everyone can simultaneously consume the same amount of biological diversity. We are therefore able to determine the market demand by finding the sum of the amounts of money they would be willing to pay for that level of diversity.

What is the efficient level of diversity? It can be determined by a direct application of our definition of efficiency. The efficient allocation maximizes net benefits. Net benefits, in turn, are represented geometrically by the portion of the area under the market–demand curve that lies above the marginal-cost curve. The allocation that maximizes net benefits is Q^*, the allocation where the demand curve crosses the marginal-cost curve.

Inefficiency results because each person is able to become a free rider on the other's contribution. A *free rider* is someone who derives the benefits from a commodity without contributing to its supply. Because of the consumption indivisibility and nonexcludability properties of the public good, consumers receive the benefits of any diversity purchased by other people. When this happens it tends to diminish incentives to contribute, and the contributions are not sufficiently large to finance the efficient amount of the public good; it would be undersupplied.

Notice, however, that the privately supplied amount is not zero. Some diversity would be privately supplied. Indeed, as suggested by Example 4.3, the privately supplied amount may be considerable.

What is the efficient level of diversity? It can be determined by a direct application of our definition of efficiency. The efficient allocation maximizes net benefits. On a graph, net benefits are represented geometrically by the portion of the market–demand curve that lies above the marginal-cost curve. The allocation that maximizes net benefits is Q^*, the allocation where the market–demand curve crosses the marginal-cost curve. Both consumers consume this amount. At this level of availability, the marginal net benefit to person *B* is OB whereas the marginal net benefit to person *A* is OA. Adding these together produces $OA + OB$, society's marginal net benefit, which is equated to marginal cost.

Would a private market supply this amount? In general, the answer is that it would not. The typical market will undersupply diversity.

FIGURE 4.6 Efficient Provision of Public Goods

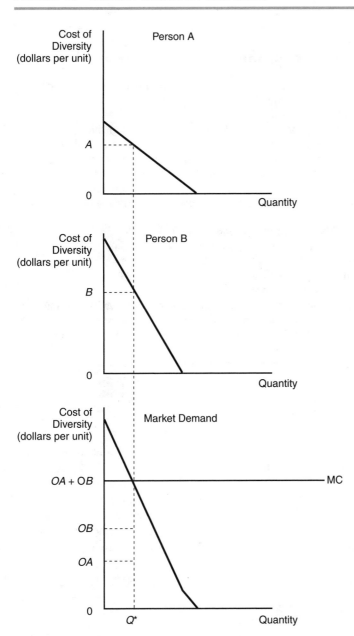

One further insight can be gained from Figure 4.6, and it is this insight that led to characterizing public-good problems as "complex" in the opening sentence of this section. The efficient market equilibrium for a public good requires different prices for each consumer. In Figure 4.6, if consumer A is charged price P_a (= OA), and consumer B is charged price P_b (= OB),

Example 4.3

Public Goods Privately Provided: The Nature Conservancy

Can a demand for a public good such as biological diversity be observed in practice? Would the market respond to that demand? Apparently so, according to the existence of an organization called The Nature Conservancy.

The Nature Conservancy was born of an older organization called the Ecologist Union on September 11, 1950, for the purpose of establishing natural area reserves to preserve or aid in the preservation of areas, objects, and fauna and flora which have scientific, educational, or aesthetic significance. This organization purchases, or accepts as donations, land which has some unique ecological or aesthetic significance, to keep it from being used for other purposes. In so doing they preserve many species by preserving the habitat.

From humble beginnings, The Nature Conservancy has, as of 1999, been responsible for the preservation of more than 11 million acres of forests, marshes, prairies, mounds, and islands. These areas serve as home to rare and endangered species of wildlife and plants. The Conservancy owns and manages some 1,600 preserves, the largest privately owned nature preserve system in the world.

This approach has considerable merit. A private organization can move more rapidly than the public sector. Because it has a limited budget, the Nature Conservancy sets priorities and concentrates on acquiring the most ecologically unique areas. Yet the theory of public goods reminds us that if this were to be the sole approach to the preservation of biological diversity, it would preserve a smaller than efficient amount.

Source: *The Nature Conservancy Magazine*, Vol. 49, No. 5 (1999).

---

then both consumers will be satisfied with the efficient allocation (the efficient allocation would have maximized their net benefits given the prices).

Furthermore, the revenue collected will be sufficient to finance the supply of the public good (because $P_b \times Q^* + P_a \times Q^* = MC \times Q^*$). Thus, although an efficient pricing system exists, it is very difficult to implement. The efficient pricing system requires charging a different price to each consumer; in the absence of excludability, consumers may not choose to reveal the strength of their preference for this commodity. Therefore, the producer could not possibly know what prices to charge.

◆ IMPERFECT MARKET STRUCTURES

Environmental problems also occur when one of the participants in an exchange of property rights is able to exercise an inordinate amount of power over the outcome. This can occur, for example, when a product is sold by a single seller, or *monopoly.*

It is easy to show that monopolies violate our definition of *efficiency* (Figure 4.7). According to our definition of *static efficiency* (Chapter 2), the efficient allocation would result when

FIGURE 4.7 Monopoly and Inefficiency

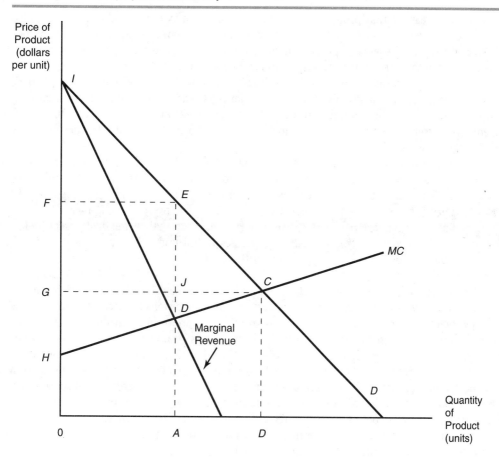

OB is supplied. This would yield net benefits represented by triangle *HIC*. The monopoly, however, would produce and sell O*A*, where marginal revenue equals marginal cost, and would charge price O*F*. At this point, the producer's surplus albeit maximized, is clearly inefficient, because this choice causes society to lose net benefits equal to triangle *EDC*.[4] Monopolies supply an inefficiently small amount of the good.

Imperfect markets clearly play some role in environmental problems. For example, the major oil-exporting countries have formed a cartel, resulting in higher-than-normal prices and lower-than-normal production. A *cartel* is a collusive agreement among producers to restrict production and raise prices. This collusive agreement allows the group to act as a monopolist.

---

[4]Producers would lose area *JDC* compared to the efficient allocation, but they would gain area *FEJG*, which is much larger. Meanwhile, consumers would be worse off, because they lose the area *FECJG*. Of these, *FEJG* is merely a transfer to the monopoly, whereas *EJC* is pure loss to society. The total pure loss *(EDC)* is called a *deadweight loss*.

◆ DIVERGENCE OF SOCIAL AND PRIVATE DISCOUNT RATES

We concluded earlier that producers, in their attempt to maximize producer surplus, also maximize the present value of net benefits under the "right" conditions, such as the absence of externalities, the presence of properly defined property rights, and the presence of competitive markets within which the property rights can be exchanged.

Now let's consider one more condition. If resources are to be allocated efficiently, firms must use the same rate to discount future net benefits as is appropriate for society at large. If firms were to use a higher rate, they would extract and sell resources faster than would be efficient. Conversely, if firms were to use a lower-than-appropriate discount rate, they would be excessively conservative.

Why might private and social rates differ? As stated in the previous chapter, the social discount rate is equal to the social opportunity cost of capital. This cost of capital can be separated into two components: risk-free cost of capital and the risk premium.[5] The *risk-free cost of capital* is the rate of return earned when there is absolutely no risk of earning more or less than the expected return. The *risk premium* is an additional cost of capital required to compensate the owners of this capital when the expected and actual returns may differ. Therefore, because of the risk premium, the cost of capital is higher in risky industries than in no-risk industries.

One difference between private and social discount rates may stem from a difference in social and private risk premiums. If the risk of certain private decisions is different from the risks faced by society as a whole, then the social and private risk premiums may differ. One obvious example is the risk *caused* by the government. If the firm is afraid its assets will be taken over by the government, it may choose a higher discount rate to make its profits before nationalization occurs.[6] From the point of view of society—as represented by government—this is not a risk and, therefore, a lower discount rate is appropriate. When private rates exceed social rates, current production is higher than is desirable to maximize the net benefits to society. Energy production and forestry both have been subject to this source of inefficiency.

Though private and social discount rates do not always diverge, they may. When those circumstances arise, market decisions are not efficient.

◆ GOVERNMENT FAILURE

Market processes are not the only sources of inefficiency. Political processes are fully as culpable. As will become clear in the chapters which follow, some environmental problems have arisen from a failure of political rather than economic institutions. To complete our study of the ability of institutions to allocate environmental resources, we must understand this source of inefficiency as well.

Government failure shares with market failure the characteristic that improper incentives are the root of the problem. Special interest groups use the political process to engage in

---

[5]This point is discussed in more detail in Joel D. Scheraga and Frances G. Sussman, "Discounting and Environmental Management" in T. Tietenberg and H. Folmer, eds., *The International Yearbook of Environmental and Resource Economics 1998/1999* (Cheltenham, UK): Edward Elgar, 1998): 1–32.

[6]This case is described in Griffin, James M. and Henry B. Steele. *Energy Economics and Policy* (New York: Academic Press, 1980): 85–86.

what has become known as *rent seeking*. Rent seeking is the use of resources in lobbying and other activities directed at securing protective legislation. Successful rent-seeking activity will increase the net benefits going to the special interest group, but it will also frequently lower net benefits to society as a whole. In these instances it is a classic case of the aggressive pursuit of a larger slice of the pie leading to a smaller pie.

Why don't the losers rise up to protect their interests? One main reason is voter ignorance. It is economically rational for voters to remain ignorant on many issues simply because of the high cost of keeping informed and the low probability that any single vote will be decisive. In addition, it is difficult for diffuse groups of individuals, each of whom is affected only to a small degree, to organize a coherent, unified opposition. Successful opposition is, in a sense, a public good, with its attendant tendency for free riding on the opposition of others. Opposition to special interests would normally be underfunded.

Rent seeking can take many forms. Producers can seek protection from competitive pressures brought by imports or can seek price floors to hold prices above their efficient levels. Consumer groups can seek price ceilings or special subsidies to transfer part of their costs to the general body of taxpayers. Whatever form it takes, the existence of rent seeking provides a direct challenge to the presumption that more direct intervention by the government automatically leads to greater efficiency.

These cases illustrate the general economic premise that environmental problems arise because of a divergence between individual and collective objectives. This is a powerful explanatory device because not only does it suggest why these problems arise, but it also suggests how they might be resolved—by realigning individual incentives to make them compatible with collective objectives. As self-evident as this approach may be, it is controversial (see Example 4.4). The controversy involves whether the problem is our improper values or the improper translation of our quite proper values into action.

Economists have always been reluctant to argue that values of consumers are warped, because that would necessitate dictating the "correct" set of values. Both capitalism and democracy are based on the presumption that the majority knows what it is doing, whether it is casting ballots for representatives or dollar votes for goods and services.

◆ THE PURSUIT OF EFFICIENCY

We have seen that environmental problems arise when property rights are ill defined, when these rights are exchanged under something other than competitive conditions, and when social and private discount rates diverge. We can now use our definition of efficiency to explore possible remedies, such as private negotiation, judicial remedies, and regulation by the legislative and executive branches of government.

Private Resolution through Negotiation

The simplest means to restore efficiency occurs when the number of affected parties is small, making negotiation feasible. Suppose, for example, we return to the case used earlier in this chapter to illustrate an externality—the conflict between the polluting steel company and the downstream resort.

Because the steel company does not exclusively bear all the costs of its actions, an inefficiency occurs and the firm produces too much output and too much pollution. Without

Example 4.4

Religion as the Source of Environmental Problems

One of the many alternative explanations of the source of environmental problems was advanced by historian Lynn White, Jr. His thesis, simply put, is that the environmental crisis is due to the teachings of Judaism and Christianity which in Western culture have created a warped view of the proper relationship between humans and their environment.

The basis for this thesis is to be found in the first book of the Old Testament:

Then God said, "Let us make man in our image, after our likeness; and let them have dominion over the fish of the sea, and over the birds of the air, and over the cattle, and over all the earth, and over every creeping thing that creeps upon the earth" [Gen. 1:26].

Two aspects of this passage are crucial to his argument: (1) God created man in His own image, and (2) man was given dominion over the other forms of life. Both of these aspects make man the dominant force on earth and, according to White, suggest that "it is God's will that man exploit nature for his proper ends." White also makes the point that, among the world's religions, this is a unique view of the human-environment relationship.

His policy solution follows directly:

More science and more technology are not going to get us out of the present ecological crisis until we find a new religion, or rethink our old one [p. 1205].

White believes that we must adopt new values which reject the primacy of humans and elevate the stature of nature.

This view provides a stark contrast to the economics approach, which suggests that the problem is neither the primacy of humans nor warped values but an imperfect translation of those values into practice.

Sources: Lynn White, Jr., "The Historical Roots of Ecologic Crisis," Science 155 (March 10, 1967): 1203–1207; E. F. Schumacher, "Buddhist Economics," in *Small is Beautiful* (New York: Harper Colophon Books, 1973): 50–58; Keith Thomas, *Man and the Natural World* (New York: Knopf, 1983): 17–25.

considering the resort's welfare, the steel company chooses an output level of Q_m, a choice dictated solely by the firm's maximization of its private net benefits (Figure 4.8).

Meanwhile the efficient level of output Q^* is the level which maximizes the net benefit for society as a whole because it takes into account all costs, not merely the subset born by the steel company. How can efficiency be restored in this nonmarket relationship? The first possibility is individual negotiation. The resort could bribe the steel company. Suppose, for example, the resort offered to pay an amount equal to the damages it would otherwise incur for every level of output the steel company would reduce. What level of output would the steel company choose?

The diagram reveals the answer. The steel company would cut its production to Q^*. Compensating the steel company for each unit reduced would produce a bribe of *ABCD*, while the net benefits lost from reduced production would only be *ACD*. The steel company would experience a gain of *ABC*, by accepting the bribe and cutting its production to Q^*.

Would the resort bribe the firm to cut back more than that? It would not. The bribe that the resort would offer for further reductions (which would certainly be no larger than the

FIGURE 4.8   Efficient Output with Pollution Damages

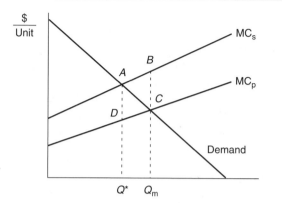

damage caused if the production were to occur) would necessarily be smaller than the firm's loss of net benefits from further production cutbacks. Can you see why?

Bribes are, of course, not the only means victims have at their disposal for lowering pollution. They can attempt to inflict costs on the polluter as well. When the victims also consume the products produced by the polluters, for example, consumer boycotts are possible. When the victims are employed by the producer, strikes or other forms of labor resistance are possible. We shall examine these approaches later in the book.

Our discussion of individual negotiations raises two questions: (1) Should the property right always belong to the party who gained or seized it first (in this case the steel company)? (2) How can environmental risks be handled when prior negotiation is clearly impractical? These questions are routinely answered by the court system.

The Courts: Property Rules and Liability Rules

The court system can respond to environmental conflicts by imposing either property rules or liability rules. Property rules specify the initial allocation of the entitlement. The entitlements at conflict in our example are, on the one hand, the right to add waste products to the river and, on the other, the right to an attractive river. In applying property rules, the court merely decides which right is preeminent and places an injunction against violating that right. The injunction is removed only upon obtaining the consent of the party whose right was violated. Consent is usually obtained in return for an out-of-court monetary settlement.

Notice that in the absence of a court decision the entitlement is naturally allocated to the party which can most easily seize it. In our example the natural allocation would give the entitlement to the steel company. The courts must decide whether to overturn this natural allocation.

How would they decide? And what difference would their decision make? The answer may surprise you.

In a classic article, economist Ronald Coase (1960) held that as long as negotiation costs are negligible and affected consumers can negotiate freely with each other (when the number of affected parties is small), the court could allocate the entitlement to *either* party, and an efficient allocation would result. The only effect of the court's decision would be to change the distribution of costs and benefits among the affected parties. This remarkable conclusion has come to be known as the Coase theorem.

Why is this so? We have already shown (in Figure 4.8) that if the steel company has the property right, it is in the resort's interest to offer a bribe which results in the desired level of output. Suppose, now, the resort had the property right instead. To pollute in this case, the steel company must bribe the resort. Suppose it could pollute only if it compensated the resort for all damages. (In other words, it would agree to pay the difference between the two marginal cost curves up to the level of output actually chosen.) As long as this compensation were required, the steel company would choose to produce Q^* since that is the level at which its private net benefits are maximized. (Notice that, due to the compensation, the curve the steel company uses to calculate its private net benefits is the MC_s curve.)

The difference between these two different ways of allocating property rights lies in how the cost of obtaining the efficient level of output is shared between the parties. When the property right is assigned to the steel company, the cost is borne by the resort (part of the cost is the damage and part is the bribe to reduce the level of damage). When the property right is assigned to the resort, the cost is borne by the steel company (it now must compensate for all damage). In either case the efficient level of production results. The Coase theorem shows that the very existence of an inefficiency triggers pressures for improvements. Furthermore, the existence of this pressure does not depend on the assignment of property rights.

This is an important point. As we shall see in succeeding chapters, private efforts triggered by inefficiency can frequently prevent the worst excesses of environmental degradation. Yet the importance of this theorem should not be overstated. Both theoretical and practical objections can be raised. The chief theoretical qualification concerns the implicit assumption that wealth effects do not matter. The decision to confer the property right on a particular party results in a transfer of wealth to that party. This transfer might shift the demand curve for either steel or resorts out, as long as higher incomes result in greater demand. Whenever wealth effects are significant, the type of property rule issued by the court affects the outcome by shifting the level of the marginal benefit curve.

Wealth effects normally are small, so the zero-wealth-effect assumption is probably not a fatal flaw. Some serious practical flaws, however, do mar the usefulness of the Coase theorem. The first involves the incentives for polluting that result when the property right is assigned to the polluter. Since pollution would become a profitable activity with this assignment, other polluters might be encouraged to increase production and pollution in order to earn the bribes. That certainly would not be efficient.

Negotiation is also difficult to apply when the number of people affected by the pollution is large. You may have already noticed that in the presence of several affected parties, pollution reduction is a public good. The free-rider problem would make it difficult for the group to act cohesively and effectively for the restoration of efficiency.

When individual negotiation is not practical for one reason or another, the courts can turn to liability rules. These are rules which award monetary damages, after the fact, to the injured party. The amount of the award is designed to correspond to the amount of damage inflicted. Thus, returning to Figure 4.8, a liability rule would force the steel company to compensate the resort for all damages incurred. In this case it could choose any production level it wanted, but it would have to pay the resort an amount of money equal to the area between the two marginal cost curves from the origin to the chosen level of output. In this case the steel plant would maximize its net benefits by choosing Q^*. (Why wouldn't the steel plant choose to produce more than that? Why wouldn't the steel plant choose to produce less than that?)

The moral of this story is that appropriately designed liability rules can also correct inefficiencies by forcing those who cause damage to bear the cost of that damage. Internalizing previously external costs causes profit-maximizing decisions to be compatible with efficiency.

Liability rules are interesting from an economics point of view because early decisions create precedents for later ones. Imagine, for example, how the incentives to prevent oil spills facing an oil company are transformed once it has a legal obligation to clean up after an oil spill and to compensate fishermen for reduced catches. It quickly becomes evident that accident prevention is cheaper than retrospectively dealing with the damage once it has occurred.

This approach, however, also has its limitations. It relies on a case-by-case determination based on the unique circumstances for each case. Administratively, such a determination is very expensive. Expenses, such as court time, lawyers' fees, and so on, fall into a category called *transaction costs* by economists. In the present context, these are the administrative costs incurred in attempting to correct the inefficiency. When the number of parties involved in a dispute is large and the circumstances are common, we are tempted to correct the inefficiency by statutes or regulations rather than court decisions.

Legislative and Executive Regulation

These remedies can take several forms. The legislature could dictate that no one produce more steel or pollution than Q^*. This dictum might then be backed up with sufficiently large jail sentences or fines to deter potential violators. Alternatively, the legislature could impose a tax on steel or on pollution. A per unit tax of $T = AD$, for example, would induce the steel company to reduce the output to Q^* (Figure 4.8).

Legislatures could also establish rules to permit greater flexibility and yet reduce damage. For example, zoning laws might establish separate areas for steel plants and resorts. This approach assumes that the damage is substantially smaller if nonconforming uses are kept apart.

They could also require the installation of particular pollution control equipment (as when catalytic converters were required on automobiles), or deny the use of a particular production ingredient (as when lead was removed from gasoline). In other words they can regulate outputs, inputs, production processes, emissions, and even the location of production in their attempt to produce an efficient outcome. In subsequent chapters we shall examine the various options policy makers have to show how they can modify environmentally destructive behavior, but also to establish the degree to which they can promote efficiency.

Bribes are, of course, not the only means victims have at their disposal for lowering pollution. When the victims also consume the products produced by the polluters, consumer boycotts are possible. When the victims are employed by the producer, strikes or other forms of labor resistance are possible. In Chapter 19 we shall examine how likely these approaches are to restore efficiency.

◆ AN EFFICIENT ROLE FOR GOVERNMENT

While the economic approach suggests that government action could well be used to restore efficiency, it also suggests that inefficiency is not a sufficient condition to justify government intervention. Any corrective mechanism involves transaction costs. If these transaction costs are high enough, and the benefit to be derived from correcting the inefficiency small enough, then it is best simply to live with the inefficiency.

Consider, for example, the pollution problem. Wood-burning stoves, which were widely used for cooking and heat in the late 1800s in the United States, were sources of pollution, but because of the enormous capacity of the air to absorb the emissions, no regulation resulted. In the 1980s, however, the resurgence of demand for wood-burning stoves precipitated in part by high oil prices resulted in strict regulations for wood-burning stove emissions.

As society has evolved, the scale of economic activity (and emissions) has expanded. For many air and water pollutants cities are experiencing severe problems because of the clustering of activities. Both the expansion and the clustering have increased the amount of emissions per unit volume of air or water. As a result, pollutant concentrations have caused perceptible problems with human health, vegetation growth, and aesthetics.

Historically, as incomes have risen, the demand for leisure activities has also risen. Many of these leisure activities, such as canoeing and backpacking, take place in unique, pristine environmental areas. With the number of these areas declining as a result of conversion to other uses, the value of remaining areas has increased. Thus, the benefits from protecting some areas have risen over time until they have exceeded the transaction costs of protecting them from pollution and/or development.

The level and concentration of economic activity, having increased pollution problems and driven up the demand for clean air and pristine areas, have created the preconditions for government action. Can government respond or will rent seeking prevent efficient political solutions? We devote much of this book to searching for the answer.

SUMMARY

How producers and consumers use the resources making up the environmental asset depends on the nature of the property rights governing resource use. When property right systems are exclusive, transferable, and enforceable, the owner of a resource has a powerful incentive to use that resource efficiently, since the failure to do so results in a personal loss.

The economic system will not always sustain efficient allocations, however. Specific circumstances which could lead to inefficient allocations include externalities, improperly defined property-right systems (such as common-pool resources and public goods), imperfect markets for trading the property rights to the resources (monopoly), and the divergence of social and private discount rates (under the threat of nationalization). When these circumstances arise, market allocations do not maximize the present value of the net benefit.

Due to rent-seeking behavior by special interest groups or the less than perfect implementation of efficient plans, the political system can produce inefficiencies as well. Voter ignorance on many issues coupled with the public-good nature of any results of political activity tend to create a situation in which private, but not social, net benefits are maximized.

The efficiency criterion can be used to assist in the identification of circumstances in which our political and economic institutions lead us astray. It can also assist in the search for remedies by facilitating the design of regulatory, judicial, or legislative solutions.

FURTHER READING

Bromley, Daniel W. *Environment and Economy: Property Rights and Public Policy* (Oxford: Basil Blackwell, Inc., 1991). A detailed exploration of the property rights approach to environmental problems.

Bromley, Daniel W., ed. *Making the Commons Work: Theory, Practice and Policy* (San Francisco: ICS Press, 1992). An excellent collection of 13 essays exploring various formal and informal approaches to controlling the use of common-property resources.

Ostrom, Elinor. *Crafting Institutions for Self-Governing Irrigation Systems* (San Francisco: ICS Press, 1992). Argues that common-pool problems are sometimes solved by voluntary organizations rather than by a coercive state. Among the cases considered are communal tenure in meadows and forest, irrigation communities, and fisheries.

Sandler, Todd. *Collective Action: Theory and Applications* (Ann Arbor: University of Michigan, 1992). A formal examination of the forces behind collective action's failures and successes.

Stavins, Robert N. "Harnessing Market Forces to Protect the Environment," *Environment* 31 (1989): 4–7, 28–35. An excellent, nontechnical review of the many ways in which the creative use of economic policies can produce superior environmental outcomes.

Several books of readings have recently been published that provide a wealth of additional material to interested readers. These include the following:

Bromley, Daniel W. *The Handbook of Environmental Economics* (Cambridge, MA: Blackwell, 1995).

Krishnan, Raharam, Jonathan M. Harris, and Neva Goodwin, eds. *A Survey of Ecological Economics* (Washington, DC: Island Press, 1995).

Markandya, Anil, and Julie Richardson, eds. *Environmental Economics: A Reader* (New York: St. Martin's Press, 1992).

Oates, Wallace E., ed. *The Economics of the Environment* (Brookfield, VT: Edward Elgar, 1992).

ADDITIONAL REFERENCES

Anderson, Terry L. and P. J. Hill. "The Evolution of Property Rights: A Study of the American West," *The Journal of Law and Economics* 18 (April 1975): 163–179.

Anderson, Terry L. and Randy T. Simmons, eds. *The Political Economy of Customs and Culture: Informal Solutions to the Commons Problem* (Lanham, MD: Rowman & Littlefield Publishers, Inc., 1993).

Bolotin, Frederic N. *International Public Policy Sourcebook.* Vol. 2, *Education and Environment* (Boulder, CO: Greenwood Press, 1989).

Bromley, Daniel W. *Economic Interests and Institutions: The Conceptual Foundations of Public Policy* (Oxford: Basil Blackwell, 1989).

Coase, Ronald. "The Problem of Social Cost," *The Journal of Law and Economics* 3 (October 1960): 1–44.

Gordon, H. Scott. "The Economic Theory of a Common Property Resource: The Fishery," *Journal of Political Economy* 62 (April 1954): 124–142.

Griffin, James M. and Henry B. Steele. *Energy Economics and Policy* (New York: Academic Press, 1980): 85–86.

Johnson, Stanley P. *The Environmental Policy of the European Communities* (London: Graham & Trotman, 1989).

McKenzie, Richard B. and Gordon Tullock, "Rent Seeking," in the *New World of Economics: Explorations into the Human Experience*, 3rd ed. (Homewood, IL: Richard D. Irwin, 1981): Chapter 15.

OECD. *Environment and Economics* (Paris: Organization for Economic Cooperation and Development, 1985).

Ostrom, Elinor. *Governing the Commons: The Evolution of Institutions for Collective Action* (Cambridge: Cambridge University Press, 1990).

Ross, Lester. *Environmental Policy in China* (Bloomington, IN: Indiana University Press, 1988).

Weitzman, M.L. "On the Environmental Discount Rate," *Journal of Environmental Economics and Management*. Vol. 26, No. 2 (1994): 200–09.

WEB SITES OF INTEREST

1. *http://www.worldbank.org/nipr/*
   A site that focuses on the use of economic incentives to improve pollution control in developing countries.

2. *http://www.aere.org/*
   The site of the Association of Environmental and Resource Economists. A good place to check out the addresses of web pages of members as well as the graduate program and discussion lists.

DISCUSSION QUESTIONS

1. In a well-known legal case, *Miller v. Schoene* (287 U.S. 272), a classic conflict of property rights was featured. Red cedar trees, used only for ornamental purposes, carried a disease that could destroy apple orchards within a radius of two miles. There was no known way of curing the disease except by destroying the cedar trees or by ensuring that apple orchards were at least two miles away from the cedar trees. Apply the Coase theorem to this situation. Does it make any difference to the outcome whether the cedar tree owners are entitled to retain their trees or the apple growers are entitled to be free of them? Why or why not?

2. In primitive societies the entitlements to use land were frequently possessory rights rather than ownership rights. Those on the land could use it as they wished, but they could not transfer it to anyone else. One could acquire a new plot by simply occupying and using it, leaving the old plot available for someone else. Would this type of entitlement system cause more or less incentive to conserve the land than an ownership entitlement? Why? Would a possessory entitlement system be more efficient in a modern society or a primitive society? Why?

5

Sustainable Development: Defining the Concept

We usually see only the things we are looking for—so much so that we sometimes see them where they are not.

ERIC HOFFER, THE PASSIONATE STATE OF MIND (1993)

◆ INTRODUCTION

In previous chapters we have developed two specific means for identifying environmental problems. The first, static efficiency, allows us to evaluate those circumstances where time is not a crucial aspect of the allocation problem. Typical examples might include allocating water or solar energy where next year's flow is independent of this year's choices. The second, more complicated criterion, dynamic efficiency, is suitable for those circumstances where time is a crucial aspect. Typical examples might include the allocation of depletable resources where resources used now are unavailable for use by future generations.

After defining these criteria and showing how they can be operationally invoked, we demonstrated how helpful they can be. They are useful not only in identifying environmental problems and ferreting out their behavioral sources, but also in providing a basis for identifying types of remedies and even for designing the various policy instruments which might restore some sense of balance.

But the fact that these are powerful and useful tools in the quest for a sense of harmony between the economy and the environment does not imply that they are the only criteria in which we should be interested. In a general sense the efficiency criteria are designed to prevent wasting environmental and natural resources. That is a desirable attribute, but it is not the only possible desirable attribute. We might care, for example, not only about the value of the environment (the size of the pie), but how this value is shared as well (the size of each piece to all recipients). In other words fairness or justice concerns should accompany efficiency considerations.

In this chapter we investigate one particular fairness concern—the treatment of future generations. We begin by considering a specific, ethically challenging situation—the allocation of a depletable resource over time. Using a numerical example, we shall trace out the temporal allocation of a depletable resource and show how this allocation is affected by changes in the discount rate. To lay the groundwork for our evaluation of whether this is a fair allocation, we then turn to the task of defining what we mean by a fair intertemporal allocation. Finally, we take this theoretical definition and consider how it can be made operationally measurable.

◆ A TWO-PERIOD MODEL

According to dynamic efficiency, the objective is to balance present and future uses of this resource by maximizing the present value of the net benefits derived from the use of those resources. This implies a particular allocation of the resource across time. We can investigate the properties of this allocation and the influence of such key parameters as the discount rate with the aid of a simple numerical example. We begin with the simplest of models—deriving the dynamic efficient allocation across two time periods. In subsequent chapters we show how these conclusions generalize to longer time periods and to more complicated situations.

Assume that we have a fixed supply of a depletable resource to allocate between two periods. Assume further that demand is constant in the two periods, the marginal willingness-to-pay is given by the formula $P = 8 - 0.4q$, and marginal cost is constant at $2 per unit (see Figure 5.1). Notice that if the total supply were 30 or greater, and we were concerned only with these two periods, an efficient allocation would produce 15 units in each period, *regardless of the discount rate*. The supply is sufficient to cover the demand in both periods; the production in Period 1 does not reduce the production in Period 2. In this case the static efficiency criterion is sufficient, since time is not an important part of the problem.

Examine, however, what happens when the available supply is less than 30. Suppose it is equal to 20. How do we determine the efficient allocation? According to the dynamic efficiency criterion, the efficient allocation is the one that maximizes the present value of the net benefit. The present value of the net benefit for both years is simply the sum of the present values in each of the two years. To take a concrete example, consider the present value of a particular allocation: 15 units in the first period and 5 in the second. How would we compute the present value of that allocation?

The present value in the first period would be that portion of the geometric area under the demand curve which is over the supply curve—45.00.[1] The present value in the second period is that portion of the area under the demand cure which is over the supply curve from

---

[1] The height of the triangle is $6 [$8 − $2] and the base is 15 units. The area is therefore $(\frac{1}{2})(\$6)/(15) = \$45$.

FIGURE 5.1 The Allocation of an Abundant Depletable Resource. (a) Period 1; (b) Period 2.

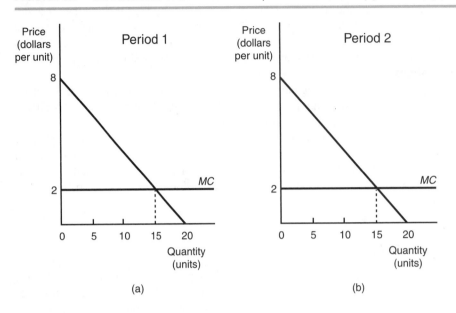

the origin to the 5 units produced multiplied by $1/(1 + r)$. If we use $r = 0.10$, then the present value of the net benefit received in the second period is $22.73,[2] and the present value of the net benefits for the two years is $67.73.

We now know how to find the present value of net benefits for any allocation. How does one find the allocation that maximizes present value? One way, with the aid of a computer, is to try all possible combinations of q_1 and q_2, which sum to 20. The one yielding the maximum present value of net benefits can then be selected. That is tedious and, for those who have the requisite mathematics, unnecessary.

The dynamically efficient allocation of this resource has to satisfy the condition that the present value of the marginal net benefit from the last unit in Period 1 equals the present value of the marginal net benefit in Period 2 (see appendix at the end of this chapter). Even without mathematics, this principle is easy to understand, as can be demonstrated with the use of a simple graphical representation of the two-period allocation problem.[3]

Figure 5.2 depicts the present value of the marginal net benefit for each of the two periods. The net benefit curve for Period 1 is to be read from left to right. The net benefit curve intersects the vertical axis at $6; demand would be zero at $8 and the marginal cost is $2, so the difference (marginal net benefit) is $6. The marginal net benefit for the first period goes to zero at 15 units because, at that quantity, the willingness to pay for that unit exactly equals its cost.

The only tricky aspect of drawing the graph involves constructing the curve for the present value of net benefits in Period 2. Two aspects are worth noting. First, the zero axis for the

---

[2]The undiscounted net benefit is $25.00 (Why?) The discounted net benefit is therefore $25/1.10 = 22.73$.

[3]This type of analysis first appeared in James McInerney, "The Simple Analytics of Natural Resource Economics," *Journal of Agricultural Economics* 27(1976): 31–52.

FIGURE 5.2   The Dynamically Efficient Allocation

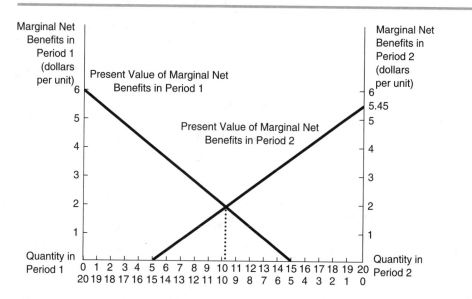

Period 2 net benefits is on the right, rather than the left, side. Therefore, increases in Period 2 are recorded from right to left. This way, any point along the horizontal axis yields a total of 20 units allocated between the two periods. Any point on that axis picks a unique allocation between the two periods.[4]

Second, the present value of the marginal benefit curve for Period 2 intersects the vertical axis at a different point than does the comparable curve in Period 1. (Why?) This intersection is lower because the marginal benefits in the second period are discounted. Thus with the 10 percent discount rate we are using, the marginal net benefit is $6 and the present value is $6/1.10 = $5.45. Notice that larger discount rates rotate the Period 2 marginal-benefit curve around the point of zero net benefit ($q_1 = 5, q_2 = 15$) toward the right-hand axis. We shall use this fact in a moment.

The efficient allocation is now readily identifiable as the point where the two curves representing present value of marginal net benefits cross. The total present value of net benefits is then the area under the marginal net-benefit curve for Period 1 up to the efficient allocation, plus the area under the present value of marginal net-benefit curve for Period 2 from the right-hand axis up to its efficient allocation. Because we have an efficient allocation, the sum of these two areas is maximized.[5]

Since we have developed our efficiency criteria independent of an institutional context, these criteria are equally appropriate for evaluating resource allocations generated by markets,

---

[4]Note that the sum of the two allocations in Figure 5.2 is always 20. The left-hand axis represents an allocation of all 20 units to Period 2, and the right-hand axis represents an allocation entirely to Period 1.

[5]Demonstrate by first allocating slightly more to Period 2 (and therefore less to Period 1) and showing that the total area decreases. Conclude by allocating slightly less to Period 2 and showing that, in this case as well, total area declines.

government rationing, or even the whims of a dictator. While *any* efficient allocation method must take scarcity into account, the details of precisely how that is done depends on the context.

Intemporal scarcity imposes an opportunity cost that we henceforth refer to as the *marginal user cost*. When resources are scarce, greater current use diminishes future opportunities. The marginal user cost is the present value of these forgone opportunities at the margin. To be more specific, uses of those resources which would have been appropriate in the absence of scarcity may no longer be appropriate once scarcity is present. Using large quantities of water to keep lawns lush and green may be wholly appropriate for an area with sufficiently large replenishable water supplies, but quite inappropriate when it denies drinking water to future generations. Failure to take the higher scarcity value of water into account in the present will lead to an inefficiency or an additional cost to society due to the additional scarcity imposed on the future. This additional marginal value that scarcity creates is the marginal user cost.

We can illustrate how this concept is used by returning to our numerical example. With 30 or more units, each period would be allocated 15 and the resource would not be scarce. With 30 or more units, therefore, the marginal user cost would be zero.

With 20 units, however, scarcity does exist. No longer can 15 units be allocated to each period; each period will have to be allocated less than would be the case without scarcity. The marginal user cost for this case is not zero. As can be seen from Figure 5.2, the present value of the marginal user cost, the additional value created by scarcity, is graphically represented by the vertical distance between the quantity axis and the intersection of the two present-value curves. It is identical to the present value of the marginal net benefit in each of the periods. This value can either be read off the graph or determined more precisely from the chapter appendix to be $1.905.

We can make this concept even more concrete by considering its use in a market context. An efficient market would have to consider not only the marginal cost of extraction for this resource, but the marginal user cost as well. Whereas in the absence of scarcity, the price would equal the marginal cost of extraction; with scarcity, the price would equal the sum of marginal extraction cost and marginal user cost.

To see this, solve for the prices that would prevail in an efficient market facing scarcity over time. Inserting the efficient quantities (10.238 and 9.762, respectively) into the willingness-to-pay function ($P = 8 - 0.4q$) yields $P_1 = 3.905$ and $P_2 = 4.095$. The corresponding supply and demand diagrams are given in Figure 5.3.

In an efficient market the marginal user cost for each period is the difference between the price and the marginal cost of extraction. Notice that it takes the value $1.905 in the first period and $2.095 in the second. In both years the present value of the marginal user cost is $1.905. In the second year the actual marginal user cost is $1.905(1 + r)$. Since $r = 0.10$ in this example, the marginal user cost for the second period is $2.095.[6] Thus, while the present value of marginal user cost is equal in both periods, the actual marginal user cost rises over time.

Both the size of the marginal user cost and the allocation of the resource between the two periods is affected by the discount rate. In Figure 5.2, because of discounting, the efficient allocation allocates somewhat more to Period 1 than to Period 2. A discount rate larger than 0.10 would be incorporated in this diagram by rotating the Period 2 curve an appropriate amount toward the right-hand axis, holding the point at which it intersects the horizontal

---

[6]You can verify this by taking the present value of $2.095 and showing it to be equal to $1.905.

FIGURE 5.3 The Efficient Market Allocation of a Depletable Resource: The Constant–Marginal–Cost Case. (a) Period 1; (b) Period 2.

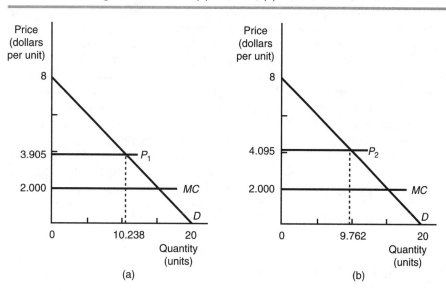

axis fixed. The larger the discount rate is, the greater the amount of rotation required. The amount allocated to the second period would be necessarily smaller with larger discount rates. The general conclusion, which holds for all models we consider, is that higher discount rates tend to skew resource extraction toward the present because they give the future less weight in balancing the relative value of present and future resource use.

◆ DEFINING INTERTEMPORAL FAIRNESS

While no generally accepted standards of fairness or justice exist, some have more prominent support than others. One such standard concerns the treatment of future generations. What legacy should earlier generations leave to later ones? This is a particularly difficult issue because, in contrast to other groups for which we may want to insure fair treatment, future generations cannot articulate their wishes, much less negotiate with current generations ("We'll take your radioactive wastes, if you leave us plentiful supplies of titanium").

One starting point for intergenerational equity is provided by philosopher John Rawls in his monumental work *A Theory of Justice*. Rawls suggests one way to derive general principles of justice is to place, hypothetically, every person in an original position behind a "veil of ignorance." This veil of ignorance would prevent them from knowing their eventual position in society. Once behind this veil, people would decide on rules to govern the society that they would, after the decision, be forced to live in.

In our context this approach would suggest a hypothetical meeting of all members of present and future generations to decide on rules for allocating resources among generations. Because these members are prevented by the veil of ignorance from knowing the generation to which they will belong, they will not be excessively conservationist (lest they turn out to be a member of an earlier generation) or excessively exploitative (lest they become a member of a later generation).

What kind of rule would emerge from such a meeting? One possibility is the sustainability criterion. The *sustainability criterion* suggests that, at a minimum, future generations should be left no worse off than current generations. Allocations that impoverish future generations, in order to enrich current generations, are, according to this criterion, patently unfair.

In essence, the sustainability criterion suggests that earlier generations are at liberty to use resources that would thereby be denied to future generations as long as the well-being of future generations remains just as high as that of all previous generations. On the other hand, diverting resources from future use would violate the sustainability criterion if it reduced the well-being of future generations below the level enjoyed by preceding generations.

One of the implications of this definition of sustainability is that it is possible to use resources (even depletable resources) as long as the interests of future generations could be protected. Do our institutions provide adequate protection for future generations? We begin with examining the conditions under which efficient allocations satisfy the sustainability criterion. Are all efficient allocations sustainable?

◆ ARE EFFICIENT ALLOCATIONS FAIR?

In the numerical example we have constructed, it certainly does not appear that particular efficient allocation satisfies the sustainable criterion. In the two-period example, more resources are allocated to the first period than to the second. Therefore, net benefits in the second period are lower than in the first. Sustainability does not allow earlier generations to profit at the expense of later generations, and this example certainly appears to be a case where that is happening.

Yet choosing this particular extraction path does not prevent those in the first period from saving some of the net benefits for those in the second period. If the allocation is dynamically efficient, it will always be possible to set aside sufficient net benefits accrued in the first period for those in the second period, so that those in the second period will be at least as well off as they would have been with any other extraction profile.

We can illustrate this point with a numerical example which compares a dynamic efficient allocation with sharing to an allocation where all resources are committed equally to each generation. Suppose, for example, you believe that setting aside half (10 units) of the available resources for each period would be a better allocation than the dynamic efficient allocation. The net benefits to each period from this alternative scheme would be $40.00 (can you see why?).

Now let's compare this to an allocation of net benefits that could be achieved with the dynamic efficient allocation. If the dynamic efficient allocation is to satisfy the sustainability criterion, we must be able to show that it can produce an outcome such that each generation would be at least as well off as it would be with the equal allocation. Can that be demonstrated?

In the dynamic efficient allocation the net benefits to the first period were 40.466, while those for the second period were 39.512.[7] Clearly, if no sharing between the periods took place, this example would violate the sustainability criterion; the second generation is worse off.

---

[7]The supporting calculations are $(1.905)(10.238) + 0.5(4.095)(10.238)$ for the first period and $(2.095)(9.762) + 0.5(3.095)(9.762)$ for the second period.

But suppose sharing took place. If the first generation keeps net benefits of $40.00 (thereby making it just as well off as if equal amounts were extracted in each period) and saves the extra 0.466 (the $40.466 net benefits earned during the first period in the dynamic efficient allocation minus the $40 reserved for itself) at 10 percent interest for those in the next period, this savings would grow to 0.513 by the second period [0.466(1.10)]. Add this to the net benefits received directly from the dynamic efficient allocation ($39.512), and the second generation would receive $40.025. Those in the second period would be better off by accepting the dynamic efficient allocation with sharing than they would if they demanded that resources be allocated equally between the two periods.

This example demonstrates that although dynamic efficient allocations do not automatically satisfy sustainability criteria, they can be perfectly consistent with sustainability, even in an economy relying heavily on depletable resources. The possibility that the second period will be better off is not a guarantee; the required degree of sharing must take place. In subsequent chapters we shall examine both the conditions under which we could expect the appropriate degree of sharing to take place and the conditions under which it would not.

◆ APPLYING THE SUSTAINABILITY CRITERION

One of the difficulties in assessing the fairness of intertemporal allocations using this version of the sustainability criterion is that it is so difficult to apply. Discovering whether the well-being of future generations is lower than that of current generations requires us to know not only something about the allocation of resources over time, but also something about the preferences of future generations (in order to establish how valuable various resource streams are to them). That is a tall (impossible?) order!

Is it possible to develop a version of the sustainability criterion that is more operational? Fortunately it is, thanks to what has become known as the "Hartwick Rule." In an early article, John Hartwick (1977) demonstrated that a constant level of consumption could be maintained perpetually if all the scarcity rent were invested in capital. Furthermore, that level of investment would be sufficient to assure that the value of the total capital stock (defined below) would not decline.

Two important insights flow from this reinterpretation of the sustainability criterion. First, with this version it is possible to judge the sustainability of an allocation by examining whether or not the value of the total capital stock is nondeclining. That test can be performed each year without knowing anything about future allocations or preferences. Second, this analysis suggests the specific degree of sharing that would be necessary to produce a sustainable outcome, namely all scarcity rent must be invested.

Let's pause a moment to make sure we understand what is being said here and why it is being said. Although we shall return to this subject later in the book, it is important now to have at least an intuitive understanding of the implications of this analysis. Consider an analogy. Suppose a grandparent left you an inheritance of $10,000, and you put it in a bank where it earns 10 percent interest.

What are the choices for allocating that money over time and what are the implications of those choices? If you spent exactly $1,000 per year, the amount in the bank would remain $10,000 and the income would last forever; you are spending only the interest, leaving the principal intact. If you spend more than $1,000 per year, the principal would necessarily decline over time and eventually the balance in the account would go to zero. In the language of this chapter, spending $1,000 per year or less would satisfy the sustainability criterion while spending more would violate the sustainability criterion.

What does the Hartwick Rule mean in this context? It suggests that one way to tell whether an allocation (spending pattern) is sustainable or not is to examine what is happening to the principal over time. If the principal is declining, the allocation (spending pattern) is not sustainable. If the principal is increasing or remaining constant, the allocation (spending pattern) is sustainable.

How do we apply this to the environment? In general, the Hartwick Rule suggests that the current generation has been given an endowment. Part of the endowment consists of environmental and natural resources (known as "natural capital") and physical capital (such as buildings, equipment, schools, roads, and so on). Sustainable use of this endowment implies that we should keep the principal (the value of the endowment) intact and live off only the flow of services provided. We should not, in other words, chop down all the trees and use up all the oil, leaving future generations to fend for themselves. Rather we need to assure that the value of the total capital stock is maintained, not depleted.

The desirability of this version of the sustainability criterion depends crucially on how substitutable the two forms of capital are. If physical capital can readily substitute for natural capital, then maintaining the value of the sum of the two is sufficient. If, however, physical capital cannot completely substitute for natural capital, investments in physical capital may not be enough to assure sustainability.

How strong is the assumption of complete substitutability between physical and natural capital? Clearly it is untenable for certain categories of environmental resources. Though we can contemplate the replacement of natural breathable air with universal air-conditioning in domed cites, both the expense and the artificiality of this approach make it an absurd compensation device. Obviously intergenerational compensation must be approached carefully (Example 5.1).

Recognizing the weakness of the constant total capital definition in the face of limited substitution possibilities has led some economists to propose a new definition—a sustainable allocation is one that maintains the value of the stock of *natural* capital. This definition assumes that it is natural capital that drives future well being, and further assumes that little or no substitution between physical and natural capital is possible. To differentiate these two definitions the maintenance of total capital is now known as the "weak substitutability" definition, while maintaining natural capital is known as the "strong sustainability" definition.

A final definition, known as "environmental sustainability" requires that certain *physical flows* of certain *individual* resources should be maintained. This definition suggests that it is not sufficient to maintain the value of an *aggregate*. For a fishery, for example, this definition would emphasize assuring that catch levels did not exceed the growth of the biomass for the fishery. For a wetland it would involve the preservation of the specific ecological functions.

◆ IMPLICATIONS FOR ENVIRONMENTAL POLICY

In order to be useful guides to policy, our sustainability and efficiency criteria must be neither synonymous nor incompatible. Do these criteria meet that test?

They do. As we shall see later in the book, not all efficient allocations are sustainable and not all sustainable allocations are efficient. Yet some sustainable allocations are efficient and

Example 5.1

Nauru: Weak Sustainability in the Extreme

The weak sustainability criterion is used to judge whether the depletion of natural capital is offset by sufficiently large increases in physical or financial capital as to prevent total capital from declining. It seems quite natural to suppose that a violation of that criterion does demonstrate *unsustainable* behavior. But does fulfillment of the weak sustainability criterion provide an adequate test of *sustainable* behavior? Consider the case of Nauru.

Nauru is a small Pacific island that lies some 3,000 kilometers northeast of Australia. It contains one of the highest grades of phosphate rock ever discovered. Phosphate is a prime ingredient in fertilizers.

Over the course of a century, first colonizers and then, after independence, the Nauruans decided to extract massive amounts of this rock. This decision has simultaneously enriched the remaining inhabitants (including the creation of a trust fund believed to contain over $1 billion) and destroyed most of the local ecosystems. Local needs are now mainly met by imports financed from the financial capital created by the sales of the phosphate.

However wise or unwise the choices made by the people of Nauru were, they could not be replicated globally. Everyone cannot subsist solely on imports financed with trust funds; every import must be exported by someone! The story of Nauru demonstrates the value of complementing the weak sustainability criterion with other, more demanding criteria. Satisfying the weak sustainability criterion may be a necessary condition for sustainability, but it is not always sufficient.

Source: Gowdy, J. W. and C. N. McDaniel. "The Physical Destruction of Nauru: An Example of Weak Sustainability," *Land Economics* 75(2)(1999): 333–338.

some efficient allocations are sustainable. Furthermore, market allocations may be either efficient or inefficient and either sustainable or unsustainable.

Do these differences have any policy implications? Indeed they do. In particular they suggest a specific strategy for policy. Among the possible uses for resources that fulfill the sustainability criterion, choose the one that maximizes either dynamic or static efficiency as appropriate. In this formulation the sustainability criterion acts as an overriding constraint on social decisions. Yet by itself, it is insufficient because it fails to provide any guidance on which of the infinite number of sustainable allocations should be chosen. That is where efficiency comes in. It provides a means for maximizing the wealth derived from all the possible sustainable allocations.

This combination of efficiency with sustainability turns out to be very helpful in guiding policy. Many unsustainable allocations are the result of inefficient behavior. Correcting the inefficiency can either restore sustainability or move the economy a long way in that direction. Furthermore, and this is important, correcting inefficiencies can frequently produce win-win situations. In win-win changes, the various parties affected by the change are all better off after the change than before. This contrasts sharply with changes in which the gains to the gainers are offset by losses to the losers.

Win-win situations are possible because removing an inefficiency increases net benefits. The increase in net benefits provides a means for compensating those who might otherwise lose from the change. Compensating losers reduces the opposition to change, thereby making change more likely. Do our economic and political institutions normally produce outcomes that are both efficient and sustainable? In future chapters we will provide explicit answers to this important question.

SUMMARY

Both efficiency and ethical considerations can guide the desirability of private and social choices involving the environment. Whereas the former is concerned mainly with eliminating waste in the use of resources, the latter is concerned with assuring the fair treatment of all parties.

Previous chapters have focused on the static and dynamic efficiency criteria. A subsequent chapter will focus on the environmental justice implications of environmental degradation and remediation for members of the current generation. This chapter examines one possible characterization of the obligation previous generations owe to those generations that follow and the policy implications that flow from acceptance of that obligation.

The specific obligation examined in this chapter—sustainable development—is based upon the notion that earlier generations should be free to pursue their own well-being as long as in so doing they do not diminish the welfare of future generations. This notion gives rise to three alternative definitions of sustainable allocations:

Weak Sustainability. Resource use by previous generations should not exceed a level that would prevent subsequent generations from achieving a level of well-being at least as great. One of the implications of this definition is that the value of the capital stock (natural plus physical capital) should not decline. Individual components of the aggregate could decline in value as long as other components were increased in value (normally through investment) sufficiently to leave the aggregate value unchanged.

Strong Substitutability. According to this interpretation, the value of the remaining stock of natural capital should not decrease. This definition places special emphasis on preserving natural (as opposed to total) capital under the assumption that natural and physical capital offer limited substitution possibilities. This definition retains the focus of the previous definition on preserving value (rather than a specific level of physical flow) and on preserving an aggregate of natural capital (rather than any specific component). This has become known as the "strong sustainability" definition.

Environmental Sustainability. Under this definition the physical flows of individual resources should be maintained, not merely the value of the aggregate. For a fishery, for example, this definition would emphasize maintaining a constant fish catch (referred to as a sustainable yield), rather than a constant value of the fishery. For wetland it would involve preserving its ecological functions, not merely its value.

It is possible to examine and compare the theoretical conditions that characterize various allocations (including market allocations and efficient allocations) to the necessary conditions for an allocation to be sustainable under these definitions. According to the theorem which is now known as the "Hartwick Rule," if all of the scarcity rent from the use of scarce resources is invested in capital, the resulting allocation will satisfy the first definition.

In general, not all efficient allocations are sustainable and not all sustainable allocations are efficient. Furthermore market allocations can be: (1) efficient, but not sustainable, (2) sustainable, but not efficient, (3) inefficient and unsustainable and (4) efficient and sustainable. One class of situations, known as "win-win" situations, provides an opportunity to increase simultaneously the welfare of both current and future generations.

We shall explore these themes much more intensively as we proceed through the book. In particular we shall inquire into when market allocations can be expected to produce allocations that satisfy the sustainability definitions and when they cannot. We shall also see how the skillful use of economic incentives can allow policy makers to exploit "win-win" situations to promote a transition onto a sustainable path for the future.

FURTHER READING

Atkinson, G. et al. *Measuring Sustainable Development: Macroeconomics and the Environment*. (Cheltenham, UK: Edward Elgar, 1997). This book tackles the tricky question of how one can tell whether development is sustainable or not.

Desimone, L. D. *Eco-Efficiency: The Business Link to Sustainable Development*. (Cambridge, MA: MIT Press, 1997). What is the role for the private sector in sustainable development? Is concern over the "bottom line" consistent with the desire to promote sustainable development?

Hartwick, J. M. "Intergenerational Equity and the Investing of Rents from Exhaustible Resources," *American Economic Review* Vol. 67 (1977): 972–974. The classic article which formulated the "Hartwick Rule."

May, P. and R. S. D. Motta, eds. *Pricing the Planet: Economic Analysis for Sustainable Development*. (New York: Columbia University Press, 1996). Ten essays dealing with how sustainable development might be implemented.

Perrings, C. *Sustainable Development and Poverty Alleviation in Sub-Saharan Africa: The Case of Botswana*. (New York, Macmillan, 1996). One of the leading practitioners in the field examines the problems and prospects for sustainable development in the African nation of Botswana.

Scheraga, J. and F. Sussman. "Discounting and Environmental Management," in *The International Yearbook of Environmental and Resource Economics 1998/1999*, T. Tietenberg and H. Folmer, ed.

(Cheltenham, UK, Edward Elgar: 1–31. A review of the state of the art on the role of discounting in environmental management.

Toman, M. A., J. Pezzey, et al. "Neoclassical Economic Growth Theory and 'Sustainability.'" *Handbook of Environmental Economics*. D. W. Bromley. (Oxford, UK, Blackwell, 1995): 139–165. An excellent survey of the economics literature on sustainable development.

ADDITIONAL REFERENCES

Chichilnisky, G. "What Is Sustainable Development?" *Land Economics* 73(4) (1997): 467–491.

Howarth, R. B. "Discount Rates and Sustainable Development," *Ecological Modeling* 92(2–3) (1996): 263–270.

Munda, G. "Environmental Economics, Ecological Economics, And the Concept of Sustainable Development," *Environmental Values* 6(2) (1997): 213–233.

Neumayer, Eric. *Weak Versus Strong Sustainability: Exploring the Limits of Two Opposing Paradigms* (Cheltenham, UK: Edward Elgar, 1999).

Pezzey, J. "Sustainability: An Interdisciplinary Guide," *Environmental Values* 1 (1992): 321–62.

Rawls, John. *A Theory of Justice.* (Cambridge, Ma.: Harvard University Press, 1971).

Stern, D. I., M. S. Common, et al. "Economic Growth and Environmental Degradation: The Environmental Kuznets Curve and Sustainable Development." *World Development* 24(7) (1996): 1151–1160.

Tilton, J. E. "Exhaustible Resources and Sustainable Development—Two Different Paradigms." *Resources Policy* 22(1-2) (1996): 91–97.

WEB SITES OF INTEREST

1. *http://www.class.csupomona.edu/earth.html*
   A site with lots of leads to other sites.

2. *http:/www.un.org/esa/sustdev/*
   This is the UN's sustainable development web site. It discusses Agenda 21 and the Commission on Sustainable Development.

3. *http://www.iisdl.iisd.ca/*
   This is the homepage of the International Institute for Sustainable Development.

4. *http://www.colby.edu/personal/thtieten/*
   The web site by the author of this text. Click on the Sustainable Development site that focuses on the relationship between economics and sustainable development. Includes bibliographies, case studies, and links to other related sites.

DISCUSSION QUESTION

1. The notion of sustainability is not the same in the natural sciences as in economics. In the natural sciences, sustainability frequently means maintaining a constant physical flow of each and every resource (e.g., fish from the sea or wood from the forest), while in economics it means maintaining the *value* of those service flows. When might the two criteria lead to different choices? Why?

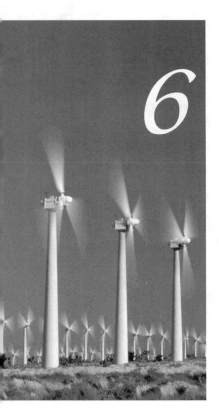

6

The Population Problem

The choices of the next ten years will decide the speed of population growth for much of the next century; . . . they will decide whether the pace of damage to the environment speeds up or slows down; . . . they may decide the future of the earth as habitation for humans.

Dr. Nafis Sadik, Executive Director of the UN Population Fund
The State of the World Population 1990

◆ INTRODUCTION

In the first chapter of this book we examined two strikingly different views of what the future holds for the world economic system. At the heart of those views lie rather divergent views of the world population problem. Meadows and her team see population growth as continuing relentlessly, putting enormous pressure on food and environmental resources. Simon, on the other hand, sees the world as being in a period of transition from high rates of natural increase to strikingly lower ones, culminating eventually in zero population growth. Because of abundant technological possibilities for satisfying the temporarily increasing, but eventually stable, population, Simon maintains an optimistic outlook.

These views are symptomatic of a debate that has deep historical roots. Thomas Malthus, a turn-of-the-century classical economist, concluded that population growth posed a trap for nations seeking to develop. Temporary increases in income were seen as triggering increases in population until the land could no longer supply adequate food. Cornell University Professor David Pimentel has brought this argument into the twentieth century by suggesting that

TABLE 6.1 Average Annual Population Change (percent), 1985–2010

	1985–90	*1995–2000*	*2005–10*
World	1.7	1.4	1.2
Africa	2.8	2.6	2.5
Asia	1.9	1.4	1.2
Europe	0.4	0.0	0.1
South America	1.9	1.5	1.3
United States	1.0	0.8	0.8

Source: From World Resources Institute, *World Resources 1998-99*: (New York, Oxford University Press): 244–245.

the *optimum global population,* defined as the largest population that could be supported sustainably in relative prosperity, is about 2 billion people. Since this is approximately one third of the current population, his analysis suggests the need for considerable reductions in current population *levels,* not merely growth.[1]

Contrasting views are held by representatives of third-world countries and some prominent population economists. Julian Simon, the author of the optimistic vision in Chapter 1, maintains that not only has Pimentel overstated the seriousness of the problem, but also that he fails to recognize that population growth in many of the developing countries is desirable. Clearly, no consensus exists.

In this chapter we examine the manner in which population affects and is affected by the development process, as well as the microeconomic issues dealing with economic determinants of fertility. This economic perspective provides one basis for understanding the causes and consequences of population growth and provides an approach for controlling population.

◆ HISTORICAL PERSPECTIVE

World Population Growth

It has been estimated that at the beginning of the Christian era, A.D. 1, world population stood at about 250 million people and was growing at 0.04 percent per year (not 4 percent!). Not long ago, the world's population passed 6 billion and was growing at an annual rate around 1.5 percent per year. If that 1.5 percent growth rate were to continue unabated, the world's population would double in only 35 years. Since the beginning of time, the population has grown to over 6 billion people; at a 2.0 percent growth rate, the next 5 billion could take only 35 years.

In recent years, with the notable exception of Africa, the average rate of population growth has declined (Table 6.1). This slowdown has been experienced in both developed and less developed countries, although rates remain higher in the less developed countries.

The World Fertility Survey, a multinational survey of some 400,000 women in 61 countries, revealed a significant downward trend in fertility rates and birthrates over the last decade. This tendency appears in both developing and developed nations, with only African

---

[1]David Pimentel, "Natural Resources and the Optimum Human Population," a paper presented at the annual meeting of the American Association for the Advancement of Science, San Francisco, 21 February 1994.

nations bucking the trend. The survey found several apparent causes, including increased use of contraception, a growing preference for fewer children, and couples marrying later.

Although the trend toward falling birthrates is pervasive, the fact remains that most developing countries still have, and can be expected to have in the future, substantial increases in their populations. Some 98 percent of the population growth between 1998 and 2025 is expected to occur in the poorer countries.

For example, in 1995–2000 Rwanda and Liberia had growth rates of 7.9 percent and 8.6 percent respectively. During the same period Italy and Portugal experienced annual average growth rates of less than one tenth of one percent. Hungary, Bulgaria, and Latvia all currently have declining populations.[2]

Population Growth in the United States

As seen in Table 6.1, population growth in the United States has followed the general declining pattern of most of the developed world, although in most periods U.S. growth rates have exceeded the average for Europe by a substantial margin. These large reductions in U.S. population growth rates have primarily been due to declines in the birthrate, which fell from a high of 30 live births per 1,000 population in 1909 to only 14.6 live births per 1,000 in 1975, the lowest recorded birthrate in the period covered by the data. By 1996 the birthrate had climbed a bit to 14.8 (Figure 6.1).

Birthrates provide a rather crude measure of the underlying population trends, however, primarily because they do not account for age structure. To understand the effect of age structure, let's separate the birthrate experience into two components: (1) the number of women in the childbearing years and (2) the number of children those women are bearing.

To quantify the second of these components, the Census Bureau uses a concept known as the *total fertility rate,* which is the number of live births an average woman has in her lifetime if, at each year of age, she experiences the average birthrate occurring in the general population of similarly aged women. The concept can be used to determine what level of fertility would, if continued, lead to a stationary population. A *stationary population* is one in which age- and sex-specific fertility rates yield a birthrate that is constant and equal to the death rate, so that the growth rate is zero. The level of the total fertility rate that is compatible with a stationary population is called the *replacement rate*. Total fertility rates higher than the replacement rate would lead to population growth; rates lower would lead to population declines. Once the replacement fertility rate is reached, the World Bank estimates that it takes approximately 25 years for the population to stabilize, because of the large numbers of families in the childbearing years. As the age structure reaches its older equilibrium, the growth rate declines until a stationary population is attained.

In the United States, the replacement rate is 2.11. The two children replace the mother and her mate, and the extra 0.11 is to compensate for those women who do not survive the childbearing years and for the fact that slightly more than 50 percent of births are males. The total U.S. fertility rate dropped below the replacement rate in 1972 and has remained below it ever since (Figure 6.2). In 1996 (the latest year for which data were available) the rate stood at 2.04.

---

[2]The comparative population-growth-rate figures can be found in World Resources Institute, *World Resources: 1998–99* (New York: Oxford University Press, 1999): 244–245.

FIGURE 6.1 U.S. Birthrates from 1909–1996

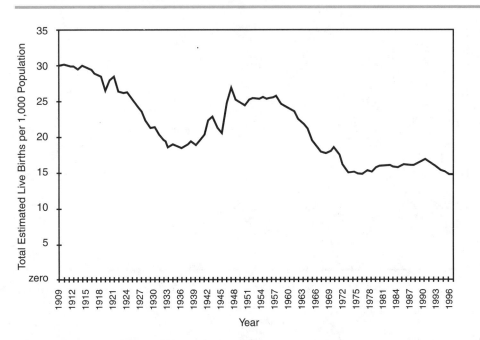

Note: Birthrates before 1959 are adjusted for underregistration.

Sources: *Vital Statistics of the United States* (1993), Vol. I, p. 1-2 for 1909–1992 and *U.S. Bureau of the Census, Statistical Abstract of the United States 1998*, 118 ed. Washington D.C. p. 77 for 1993–1995.

Two questions arise when we think about how population growth affects sustainability: (1) What is the relationship between population growth and economic growth? and (2) How can the rate of population growth be altered when alteration is appropriate? The first question lays the groundwork for considering the effect of population growth on quality of life, including the effects of a stationary population. The second allows us to consider public policies geared toward manipulating the rate of population growth, when it is desirable to do so.

◆ EFFECTS OF POPULATION GROWTH ON ECONOMIC DEVELOPMENT

A number of questions guide our inquiry. Does population growth enhance or inhibit the opportunities of a country's citizens? Does the answer depend on the stage of the nation's economic development? Given that several countries are now entering a period of declining population growth, what are the possible effects of this decline on economic development?

Population growth affects economic growth, and, as long as each person contributes something to the economy, those effects generally are positively correlated. As long as their marginal product is positive, additional people mean additional output. This is not a very restrictive condition; therefore it should usually hold true.

FIGURE 6.2   U.S. Total Fertility Rates from 1940–1996

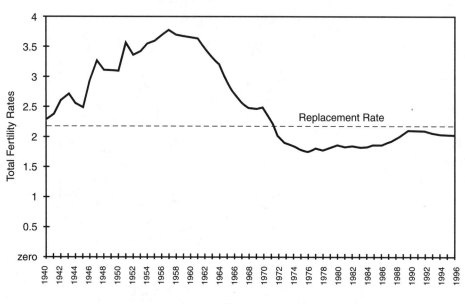

Note: Births before 1950 are adjusted for underregistration.

Sources: *The Statistical History of the United States, Colonial Times to the Present,* p. 50, *Vital Statistics of the United States* (1993), Vol. 1, p. 10 and *U.S. Bureau of the Census, Statistical Abstract of the United States 1998,* 118 ed. Washington D.C. p. 79.

However, the existence of a positive marginal product is not a very appropriate test of the desirability of population growth! Perhaps a better one is to ask whether population growth positively affects the average citizen. Whenever the marginal product of an additional person is lower than the average product, adding more people simply reduces the welfare level of the average citizen. Can you see why?

For a range of marginal productivities, between zero and the average product, economic growth measured in aggregate terms would increase; however, measured in per capita terms it would decrease. Similarly, for another range of marginal productivities—those greater than the average product—economic growth would increase regardless of whether it were measured in aggregate or per capita terms. Whether or not the material status of the average citizen is improved by population growth becomes a question of whether the marginal product of additional people is higher or lower than the average product.

To facilitate our examination of the population-related determinants of economic development, let's examine a rather simple definition of *output* as

$$O = LX$$

FIGURE 6.3   Age Structure of Two Populations for the year 2000

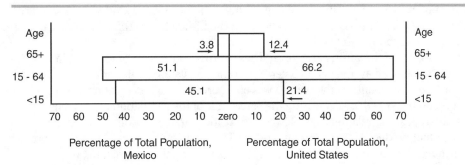

Percentage of Total Population, Mexico

Percentage of Total Population, United States

Source: *World Resources Institute, World Resources (1998-99)* (New York: Oxford University Press), p. 246-47.

where O is the output level, X is the output per worker, and L is the number of workers. This equation can be expressed in per capita terms by dividing both sides by population, denoted by P:

$$\frac{O}{P} = \frac{L}{P}X$$

This equation now states that output per capita is determined by the product of two factors: (1) the share of the population that is in the labor force and (2) the output per worker. Each of these two factors provides a channel through which population growth affects economic development.

The most direct effect of population growth on the percentage of the population employed, the *age structure effect,* results from induced changes in the age distribution. Suppose we were to compare two populations—one rapidly growing and one slowly growing. The one with the rapid growth would contain a much larger percentage of younger persons (Figure 6.3).

Because of its slow growth, the U.S. population is in general older. Whereas approximately 45 percent of Mexico's population is 15 years of age or younger, the comparable figure for the United States is 21.4 percent. This is reinforced at the other end of the age structure, where some 12.4 percent of the U.S. population is 65 or older as compared to only 3.8 percent in Mexico.

These differences in the age structure have mixed effects on the percentage of the labor force available to be employed. The abundance of youth in a rapidly growing population creates a large supply of people too young to work, a situation referred to as the *youth effect.* On the other hand, a country characterized by slow population growth has a rather larger percentage of persons who have reached, or are past, the traditional retirement age of 65, a situation referred to as the *retirement effect.* Some developing countries are experiencing both effects simultaneously as better public health policies reduce death rates while birthrates remain high. How do the youth and retirement effects interact to determine the percentage of the population in the labor force? Does the youth effect surpass the retirement effect?

Let's examine the percentage of population in the prime working ages, 15–64, for each country. As Figure 6.3 shows, this percentage is much higher for the United States. A larger percentage of the population is in the work force in the United States than is the case in Mexico. For Mexico the youth effect is the greater of the two.

This dominance of the youth effect generalizes to other countries. For example, in 2000 the African countries had an average of 53.8 percent of the population in the prime working ages, whereas for European countries the average was 65.5 percent.[3] High population growth retards per capita economic growth by decreasing the percentage of the population in the labor force.

How about possible relationships between population growth and the second factor, the amount of output produced by the average worker? The most common way to enhance productivity is through the accumulation of capital. As the capital stock is augmented (e.g., through the introduction of assembly lines or production machinery), workers become more productive. Can a connection between population growth and capital accumulation be established?

One main connection, originally explored by Coale and Hoover, involves the link between savings and capital accumulation in low-income countries.[4] The availability of savings affects the level of additions to the capital stock. Availability of savings, in turn, is affected in part by the age structure of the population. Older populations are presumed to save more because their direct spending on the care and nurturing of children is less. Therefore, all other things being equal, societies with rapidly growing populations could be expected to save proportionately less. This lowered availability of savings would lead to lower amounts of capital stock augmentation and lower productivity per worker. Apparently, the magnitude of the effect of demographic change on savings in the 1960s and 1970s was small, but that may be changing. A large study by Kelley and Schmidt found that population growth and demographic dependency exerted a sizable negative impact on savings in the 1980s.[5]

A final model suggesting a negative effect of population growth on economic development involves the presence of some fixed essential factor for which limited substitution possibilities exist (e.g., land or raw materials). In this case, the *law of diminishing marginal productivity* applies. This law states that in the presence of a fixed factor (land), successively larger additions of a variable factor (labor) will eventually lead to a decline in the marginal productivity of the variable factor. It suggests that in the presence of fixed factors, successive increases in labor will drive the marginal product down. When the marginal product falls below the average product, per capita income will decline with further increases in the population.

Not all arguments suggest that growth in output per capita will be restrained by population growth. Perhaps the most compelling arguments for the view that population growth enhances per capita growth are those involving technological progress and *economies of scale* (Figure 6.4).

The vertical axis shows marginal productivity measured in units of output. The horizontal axis describes various levels of labor L employed on a fixed amount of land. Population growth implies an increase in the labor force, which is recorded on the graph as a movement to the right on the horizontal axis.

---

[3]World Resources Institute, *World Resources: 1998–99* (New York: Oxford University Press, 1999): 246–47.

[4]Ansley J. Coale and Edgar M. Hoover, *Population Growth and Economic Development in Low Income Countries* (Princeton, NJ: Princeton University Press, 1958).

[5]Allen C. Kelley and Robert M. Schmidt, *Population and Income Change: Recent Evidence* (Washington, DC: World Bank, 1994). See also the evidence in Kenneth H. Kang, "Why Did Koreans Save So 'Little' and Why Do They Now Save So 'Much'?" *International Economic Journal* 8(1994): 99-111.

FIGURE 6.4 Technological Progress and the Law of Diminishing Returns

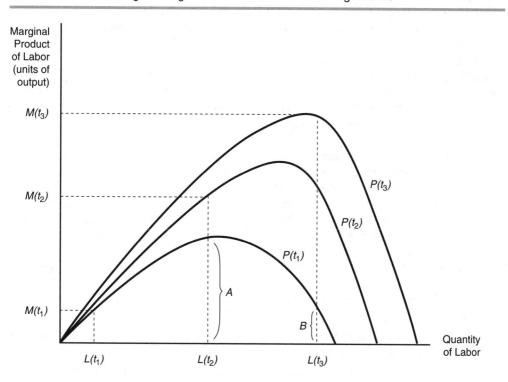

The curve labeled $P(t_1)$ shows the functional relationship between the marginal product of labor $M(t)_1$ and the amount of labor employed on a fixed plot of land at a particular point in time t_1. Different curves represent different points in time because in each period of time there exists a unique state of art in the knowledge of how to use the labor most effectively. Thus, as time passes, technological progress occurs, advancing the state of the art and shifting the productivity curves outward, as demonstrated by $P(t_2)$ and $P(t_3)$.

Three particular situations are demonstrated by Figure 6.4. At time t_1, an application of labor quantity $L(t_1)$ yields a marginal product of $M(t_1)$. At times t_2 and t_3, the application of $L(t_2)$ and $L(t_3)$ units of labor yield $M(t_2)$ and $M(t_3)$ marginal units of output, respectively. In other words, marginal products increased as larger amounts of labor were added.

Consider what would have happened, however, if the state of technical knowledge had not increased. The increase in labor from $L(t_2)$ to $L(t_3)$ would have been governed by the $P(t_1)$ curve, and the marginal product would have declined from A to B. This is precisely the result anticipated by the law of diminishing marginal productivity. Technological progress provides one means of escaping the law of diminishing marginal productivity.

The second source of increase in output per worker is *economies of scale*. Economies of scale occur when increases in inputs lead to a more than proportionate increase in output. By increasing demand for output, population growth allows these economies of scale to be exploited. In the United States, at least, this has been a potent source of growth. Edward Dennison, in a major study of U.S. economic growth, concluded that economies of scale accounted for slightly over 10 percent of the growth in total potential national income per unit input in the 1929–1969 period.[6] Although it seems clear that the population level in the United States is already sufficient to exploit economies of scale, the same is not necessarily true for all developing countries.

In the absence of trade restrictions, however, the relevant market now is the global market, not the domestic market. The level of domestic population has little to do with the ability to exploit economies of scale in the modern global economy unless tariffs, quotas, or other trade barriers prevent the exploitation of foreign markets. If trade restrictions are a significant barrier, the appropriate remedy is to reduce trade restrictions, not boost the local population.

Because these a priori arguments suggest that population growth could either enhance or retard economic growth, it is necessary to rely on empirical studies to sort out the relative importance of these effects. Several researchers have attempted to validate the premise that population growth inhibits per capita economic growth. Their attempts were based on the notion that if the premise were true, one should be able to observe lower growth in per capita income in countries with higher population growth rates, all other things being equal.

In a study for the National Research Council, researchers conducted an intensive review of the evidence.[7] Did the evidence support the expectations? Their major conclusions were:

1. Slower population growth raises the amount of capital per worker and, hence, the productivity per worker.

2. Slower population growth is unlikely to result in a net reduction in agricultural productivity and might well raise it.

3. National population density and economies of scale are not significantly related.

4. Rapid population growth puts more pressure on both depletable and renewable resources.

A subsequent study by Kelley and Schmidt found that "A statistically significant and quantitatively important negative impact of population growth on the rate of per capita output growth appears to have emerged in the 1980s."[8] This result is consistent with the belief that, although population growth may initially be advantageous, ultimately, as capacity constraints become binding, it becomes an inhibiting factor. Kelley and Schmidt also found that the net negative impact of demographic change diminishes with the level of economic development; the impact is larger in the relatively impoverished, less developed countries. According to this analysis, those most in need of higher living standards are the most adversely affected by population growth.

---

[6]Edward Dennison, *Accounting for United States Economic Growth, 1929–1969* (Washington, DC: Brookings Institution, 1974): 128–30.

[7]Working Group on Population Growth and Economic Development, National Research Council, *Population Growth and Economic Development: Policy Questions* (Washington, DC: National Academy Press, 1986).

[8]Allen C. Kelley and Robert M. Schmidt, *Population and Income Change: Recent Evidence* (Washington, DC: World Bank, 1994).

Rapid population growth may also increase the inequality of income. Perhaps the clearest statement of this argument comes from Peter Lindert[9] He believes that high population growth increases the degree of inequality for a variety of reasons, but the most important involve a depressing effect on the earning capacity of children and on wages.

The ability to provide for the education and training of children, given fixed budgets of time and money, is a function of the number of children in the family—the fewer the children, the higher the proportion of income (and wealth, such as land) available to develop each child's earning capacity. Because low-income families tend to have larger families than high-income families, the offspring from low-income families are usually more disadvantaged. The result is a growing gap between the rich and the poor.

Thomas Espenshade has provided some revealing estimates of parental expenditures on childbearing in the United States that tend to confirm certain key aspects of this argument.[10] The average expenditure to raise a child to age 18 depends crucially on income level and the size of the family, ranging from an expenditure of $239,600 (in constant 1997 dollars) for high-income families including two wage earners and only one child to $102,900 spent on the average child by a lower-income family including a single wage earner and three children. Adding in college expenditures where appropriate would boost these figures considerably.

Espenshade also examines the proportion of the typical family's income spent on child rearing as well as the sensitivity of this proportion to the number of children in the family. According to his analysis, families with only one child commit about 30 percent of total family expenditures to their child. This percentage rises to between 40 and 45 percent for two-child families and nearly 50 percent in three-child families. The detailed data in this study make clear that average expenditures per child consistently decline as the number of children in a family increases.

Another link between population growth and income inequality results from the effect of population growth on the labor supply. High population growth could increase the supply of labor faster than otherwise, depressing wage rates vis-à-vis profit rates. Because low-income groups have a higher relative reliance on wages for their income than do the rich, this effect would also increase the degree of inequality.

After an extensive review of the historical record for the United States, Lindert concludes:

> There seems to be good reason for believing that extra fertility affects the size and "quality" of the labor force in ways that raise income inequalities. Fertility, like immigration, tends to reduce the average "quality" of the labor force, by reducing the amounts of family and public school resources devoted to each child. The retardation in the historic improvement in labor force quality has in turn held back the rise in the incomes of the unskilled relative to those enjoyed by skilled labor and wealth-holders. [p. 258]

Lindert's interpretation of the U.S. historical record does seem to be valid for developing countries as well. The National Research Council study found that slower population growth

---

[9] Peter Lindert. *Fertility and Scarcity in America* (Princeton, NJ: Princeton University Press, 1978).

[10] Thomas J. Espenshade, *Investing in Children: New Estimates of Parental Expenditures* (Washington, DC: Urban Institute Press, 1984).

would decrease income inequality and raise the education and health levels of the children. This link between rapid population growth and income inequality provides an additional, powerful motivation for controlling population. Slower population growth reduces income inequality.

At the level of individual countries, some powerful evidence is beginning to emerge on the negative environmental effects of population density when coupled with poverty. In Africa, forestlands are declining as trees are cut down to provide fuel for cooking for an expanding population. Because of a shortage of land, peasants in Bangladesh settle on islands formed from the silt deposited by soil erosion. Several thousand were drowned when a cyclone hit the area in 1985. In Brazil and Southeast Asia, peasants are forced to farm marginal lands, which rapidly erode and lose their nutrients. Forced to sacrifice long-term objectives merely to survive, the poor are becoming both a major source of environmental problems and the major victims of them. Population growth bears some responsibility for both the degree of poverty and the intensity of the problems it triggers.

◆ EFFECTS OF ECONOMIC DEVELOPMENT ON POPULATION GROWTH

Up to the point, we have considered the effects of population growth on economic development. We have now to examine the converse relationship. Does economic development affect population growth? Table 6.1 suggests that it may, because the higher-income countries are characterized by lower population growth rates.

This suspicion is reinforced by some further evidence. Most of the industrialized countries have passed through three stages of population growth. The conceptual framework that organizes this evidence is called the *theory of demographic transition*. This theory suggests that as nations develop they eventually reach a point where birthrates fall (Figure 6.5).

According to this theory, during stage 1, the period immediately prior to industrialization, birthrates are stable and slightly higher than death rates, ensuring population growth. During stage 2, the period immediately following the initiation of industrialization, death rates fall dramatically, with no accompanying change in birthrates. This decline in mortality results in a marked increase in life expectancy and a rise in the population growth rate. In Western Europe, stage 2 is estimated to have lasted somewhere around 50 years.

Stage 3, the period of demographic transition, involves large declines in the birthrate that exceed the continued declines in the death rate. Thus, the period of demographic transition involves further increases in life expectancy but rather smaller population growth rates than those that characterize the second stage. The Chilean experience with such a demographic transition is illustrated in Figure 6.6. Can you identify the stages?

The theory of demographic transition is useful because it suggests that reductions in population growth might accompany rising standards of living, at least in the long run. However, it also leaves many questions unanswered. Why does the fall in birthrates occur? Can the process be speeded up? Will lower-income countries automatically experience demographic transition as living standards improve? Are better designed agricultural production systems or industrialization possible solutions to "the population problem"?

To answer these questions it is necessary to begin to look more deeply into the sources of change behind the demographic transition. Once these sources are identified and understood, they can be manipulated in such a way as to produce the maximum social benefit.

FIGURE 6.5   The Demographic Transition

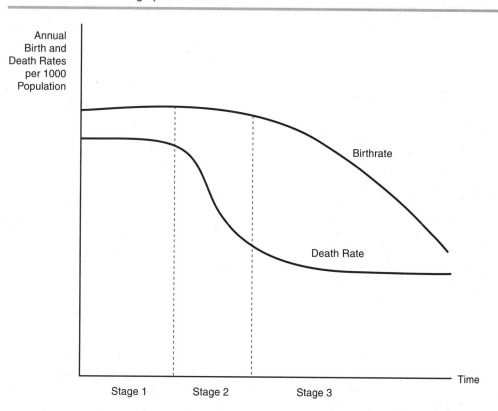

◆ THE ECONOMIC APPROACH TO POPULATION CONTROL

Is the current rate of population growth efficient? Is it sustainable? The issue of sustainability is most easily dealt with in specific resource settings (e.g., the ability to produce sufficient food); therefore, intensive consideration of that question will be deferred until succeeding chapters.

The efficiency question can be attacked in two ways. The first is to conduct a benefit-cost analysis of population control to see whether some government control would maximize efficiency. Such a study was conducted by Enke and Zind (Example 6.1). Focused purely on the effects of additional population on output per capita, the study found that intensified population control measures would increase net benefits.

The demonstration that population growth reduces per capita income, however, is not sufficient to prove that an inefficiency exists. If the reduced output is borne entirely by the families of the children, this reduction may represent a conscious choice by parents to sacrifice production in order to have more children. The net benefit gained from having more children (not measured by Enke and Zind) would exceed the net benefit lost as output per person declined.

To establish whether or not population control is efficient, we must discover whether or not there are potential behavioral biases toward overpopulation. Will parents always make efficient childbearing decisions?

FIGURE 6.6   Annual Birthrates, Death Rates, and Rates of Natural Population Increase in Chile, 1929–1996.

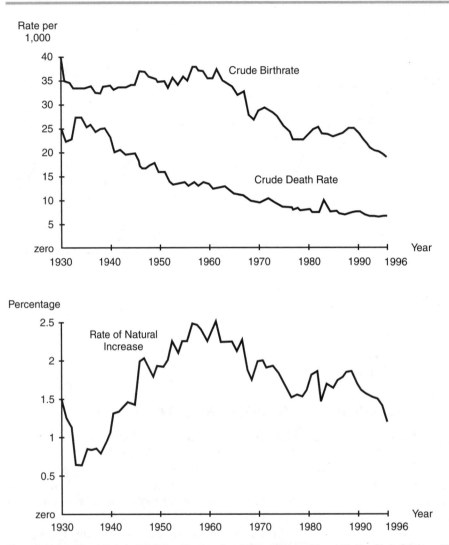

Sources: *International Historical Statistics: The Americas (1750–1988)*, pp. 76 and 78. New York: Stockton, 1993; *1993 Demographic Yearbook*, pp. 294 and 321. United Nations (1995); *1997 Demographic Yearbook*, pp. 373 and 403. United Nations (1999).

A negative response seems appropriate for three specific reasons. In the first place, child-bearing decisions impose external costs outside the family. Second, the prices of key commodities or services related to childbearing and/or child rearing may be inefficient, thereby sending the wrong signals. And, finally, parents may not be fully informed about, or may not have reasonable access to, adequate means for controlling births.

Example 6.1

The Value of an Averted Birth

If population growth tends to reduce average income, then the nation experiencing this population growth would have an incentive to spend money on population control. Determining how much money should be spent depends upon a comparison of the costs of the population control program with the value of an averted birth.

Enke and Zind developed a simulation model to assess the value of an averted birth. The model allowed for substitution among capital and labor, the restraining effect of a large number of dependent, nonproducing youths, and the effect of an age structure and income on savings. To obtain the value of averted births, they compared a scenario with no birth control to one in which a reduction in fertility over a 30-year period was compatible with 50 percent of all women in each age group practicing contraception. The implied terminal fertility rate was approximately 23 per 1,000.

On the basis of this simulation they concluded:

A modest birth control programme, costing perhaps 30 cents a year per head of national population, can raise average income over only 15 years by almost twice the percentage that it would rise without birth control. . . . The value of permanently preventing the birth of a marginal infant is about twice an LDC's [less developed country's] annual income per head. [p. 41]

This is a controversial finding. There is not uniform agreement that the simulated mechanisms approximate those that would actually prevail in developing countries, particularly if the population growth is moderate rather than rapid. Nonetheless, it does suggest that for those countries that are experiencing very rapid population growth, the potential payoff to instituting means of controlling that population growth could be substantial.

Sources: S. Enke and R. Zind, "Effect of Fewer Births on Average Income," *Journal of Biosocial Science* 1 (1969): 41–55; Julian L. Simon, *The Economics of Population Growth* (Princeton, NJ: Princeton University Press, 1977).

Some externalities can be identified immediately. Adding more people to a limited space gives rise to *congestion externalities*, higher costs resulting from the attempt to use resources at a higher than optimal capacity. Examples include too many people attempting to farm too little land and too many travelers attempting to use a specific roadway. These costs are intensified when the resource base is treated as free-access common property. And, as noted above, high population growth may exacerbate income inequality. Income equality is a public good. The population as a whole cannot be excluded from the degree of income equality that exists. Furthermore, it is indivisible, because, in a given society, the prevailing income distribution is the same for all the citizens of that country.

Why should individuals care about inequality per se as opposed to simply caring about their own income? Aside from a purely humane concern for others, particularly the poor, people care about inequality because it can create social tensions. When these social tensions exist, society is a less pleasant place to live.[11]

The demand to reduce income inequality clearly exists in modern society, as evidenced by the large number of private charitable organizations created to fulfill this demand. Because the reduction of income inequality is a public good, we also know that these organizations cannot be relied upon to reduce inequality as much as would be socially justified. Similarly, parents are not likely to take either the effect of more children on income inequality or the effect of congestion externalities into account when they make their family-size decisions. Decisions that may well be optimal for individual families will result in inefficiently large populations.

Excessively low prices on key commodities can create a bias toward inefficiently large populations as well. Two particularly important commodity prices are (1) the cost of food and (2) the cost of education. It is common for developing countries to subsidize food by holding prices below market levels. Lower than normal food prices artificially lower the cost of children as long as the quantities of food available are maintained by government subsidy (as discussed further in Chapter 9). As for the second area in which the costs of children are not fully borne by the parents, education, primary education is usually financed by the state with the funds collected by taxes. The point is *not* that parents do not pay these costs; in part they do. The point is rather that their level of contribution is not usually sensitive to the number of children they have. The school taxes paid are generally the same whether parents have two children, ten children, or even no children. Thus the marginal educational expenditure for a parent—the additional cost of education due to the birth of a child—is certainly lower than the true social cost of educating that child.

Unfortunately, very little has been accomplished toward assessing the empirical significance of these externalities. Despite this lack of evidence, the interest in controlling population is clear. The task is a difficult one. The right to bear children is considered in many countries, if not most, as an inalienable right, immune to influences outside the family. Indira Gandhi, a former prime minister of India, lost an election in the late 1970s principally because of her aggressive and direct approach to population control. Though she subsequently regained her position, political figures in other democratic countries are not likely to miss the message. Dictating that no family can have more than two children is not politically palatable at this time. Such a dictum is seen as an unethical infringement on the rights of those who are mentally, physically, and monetarily equipped to care for larger families. Yet the failure to control population growth can prove devastating to the quality of life, particularly in high-population-growth, low-income countries. Partha Dasgupta describes the pernicious, self-perpetuating process that can result.[12]

> Children are borne in poverty, and they are raised in poverty. A large proportion suffer from undernourishment. They remain illiterate, and are often both stunted and wasted. Undernourishment retards their cognitive (and often motor) development. [p. 361]

What, then, is a democratic country to do? How can it gain control over population growth while allowing individual families considerable flexibility in choosing their family size? Successful population control involves two components: (1) lowering the desired family size and

---

[11]See Linda Feldman, "Study Correlates Population Rise, Political Instability," *The Christian Science Monitor* (26 June 1989): 8.

[12]Partha Dasgupta, *An Inquiry into Well-Being and Destitution* (Oxford: Oxford University Press, 1993).

(2) providing sufficient access to contraceptive methods and family planning information to allow the family to realize its family-size choice.

The economic approach to population control *indirectly* controls population by lowering the desired family size. This is accomplished by identifying those factors that affect desired family size and changing them. In order to use the economic approach, we need to know how fertility decision making is affected by the economic environment experienced by the family.

The major model attempting to assess the determinants of childbirth decision making from an economic viewpoint is called the *microeconomic theory of fertility.* The point of departure for this theory is the view that children are "consumer durables." The key insight is that the demand for children will, as with more conventional commodities, be downward sloping. All other things being equal, as children become more expensive, the demand for them will lessen.

With this point of departure, childbearing decisions can be modeled with a traditional demand-and-supply framework (Figure 6.7). We shall designate the initial situation (prior to the

FIGURE 6.7 The Demand for Children

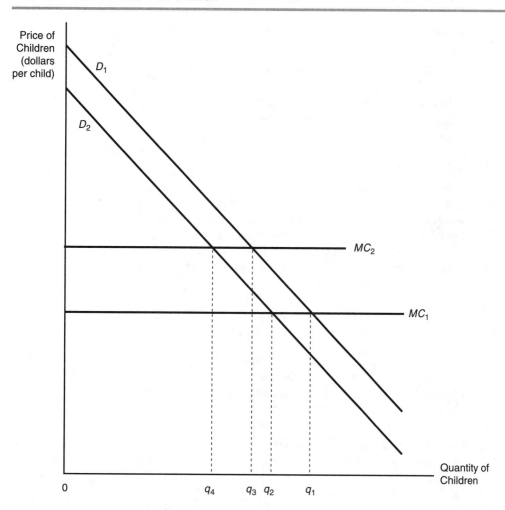

imposition of any controls) as the point where demand D_1 and marginal cost MC_1 are equal. The desired number of children at this point is given as q_1. Notice that, according to the analysis, the desired number of children can be reduced by an inward shift of the demand curve to D_2, or an upward shift in the marginal cost of children to MC_2, or both. What would cause these to shift?

Let's consider the demand curve. Why might it have shifted inward during the demographic transition? Several possible sources of this change have emerged:

1. The shift from an agricultural to an industrial economy reduces the productivity of children. In an agricultural economy, extra hands are useful, but in an industrial economy, child labor laws result in children's contributing substantially less to the family. Therefore, the investment demand for children is reduced.

2. In countries with primitive savings systems, one of the very few ways a person can provide for old-age security is to have plenty of children to provide for him or her in the twilight years. One would not, at first glance, think of children as social security systems, but in many societies they are precisely that. When alternative means of providing for old-age security are developed, the demand for children decreases.

3. In some countries a woman's status is almost exclusively defined in terms of the number of children she bears. If personal status is positively correlated with a large desired family size, this will increase the demand for children.

4. A decrease in infant mortality can also cause the demand curve to shift inward. When infant mortality is high, it takes a large number of births to produce the desired number of children at the ages when they are needed. Support for this argument was obtained during an attempt to reduce infant mortality in one of the southern states of India. Apparently, this program did have the side effect of reducing the birthrate.

5. Some evidence also suggests that the amount the demand curve shifts inward as a result of economic growth depends on the manner in which the increased employment associated with development is shared among the members of society. Those countries that have typically entered into a sustained-fertility-decline phase in spite of low levels of average per capita income levels are usually characterized by a relatively equal distribution of income and a relatively widespread participation in the benefits of development. (See Example 6.2)

Desired family size is also affected by changes in the cost of children. The costs of raising children can be changed as a means of controlling population.

1. One of the main components of the cost of children is the opportunity cost of the mother's time. By increasing the educational and labor market opportunities for women, the opportunity cost of raising children is increased. This can affect the observed fertility rate both by deferring the time of marriage and by causing a reduction in the number of children desired.

2. As societies urbanize and industrialize, housing space becomes more expensive because of the concentrated demands in specific locations. Thus, although the cost of extra space for children may be low in rural settings, it tends to be much higher in urban settings.

Example 6.2

Fertility Decline in Korea: A Case Study

The dramatic fertility decline in the Republic of Korea that occurred during the period from 1960 to 1974 has been one of the fastest ever recorded. Therefore, it provides a unique opportunity to study the forces that led to this decline and the extent to which they might be applicable to other countries.

The period prior to the dramatic decline encompassed a series of shattering events, including the Korean War. Culturally homogeneous to start with, Korea emerged from this period as a relatively egalitarian society. During the fertility decline, Korea experienced very rapid economic growth—stimulated, to a large extent, by imported capital and technology. Because the development approach focused on labor-intensive technologies, the fruits of this development were spread rather uniformly throughout the economy. Rising real wages and an expanded demand for labor served to preserve the relatively equal income distribution that had been inherited from the 1950s.

This combination of rapid economic growth and widespread participation in that growth among various sectors of the economy produced a dramatic fertility decline in almost all groups of society. Birthrates started to decline simultaneously in all regions, classes, and categories of households.

The changes in economic institutions that accompanied economic growth reinforced the tendency toward declining fertility rates. This period saw the rise, for example, of savings institutions, the widespread ownership of property (which permitted the accumulation of some wealth), and social insurance. These tended to provide alternative mechanisms for assuring old-age security.

A substantial increase also occurred in the percentage of females in the labor force, resulting in an increase in the age of marriage and a reduction in the fertility rate of married women. At the same time, education levels of women rose, which also contributed to the decline.

Though the degree of income and cultural equality in Korea was unusual, many of the other factors contributing to fertility decline, such as pursuing a development plan that reduced income inequality as the nation grew, providing alternative social security systems, and assuring expanding labor-market opportunities for women, are available to other nations.

Source: Robert Repetto, *Economic Equality and Fertility in Developing Countries* (Baltimore, MD: Johns Hopkins University Press, 1979): 69–120.

3. The cost of children to parents may also be affected to a large extent by the cost of education. As nations struggle to improve their literacy rates by universal compulsory education, they may simultaneously raise the cost of raising children. These costs rise not only because of direct additional parental expenditures on education but also because of the earnings that are forgone when the children are in school rather than working.

4. As development occurs, parents generally demand more and higher-quality education for their children. Depending on the system for financing education, providing this higher-quality education may raise the cost of every child, even if the cost of a given quality of education is not rising.

All of this provides a menu of opportunities for population control. The reasons listed here represent potent forces for change, yet these methods should be used with care. Inducing a family to have fewer children without assisting the family in satisfying the basic needs the children were fulfilling (such as old-age security) would be inequitable.

Policies in China illustrate just how far economic incentives can be carried. On the basis of announced regulations, one-child parents receive subsidized health expenditures; priority in education, health care and housing; and additional subsidized food. Meanwhile, parents who have more than two children receive a reduction of 5 percent in their total income for the third child, 6 percent for the fourth, and so on. Also, families are denied access to further subsidized grain beyond that which they already receive for their two previous children.

Initially these policies did bring about a rather dramatic fall in the birthrate in China. China's fertility rate had dropped from 5.97 in 1968 to 1.8 in 1995. However, the policies are so draconian as to have precipitated a degree of resistance sufficient to undermine the effort.

Countries seeking to reduce fertility do not have to resort to extreme measures. Policies such as enhancing the status of women, providing alternative sources of old-age security, and supplying employment opportunities that equalize income distribution are both humane and effective.

Vernon Ruttan has summarized some of the studies that have evaluated the effects of this type of approach: (1) Greater family wealth sustains higher education levels and better health; (2) a rise in the value of the mother's time has a positive effect on the demand for contraceptive services and a negative effect on fertility; (3) a rise in the value of the father's earnings has a positive effect on completed family size, child health, and child education; and (4) increases in mother's schooling has a negative effect on fertility and infant mortality and a positive effect on nurturing and children's schooling.[13]

One way to empower women is to increase their income-earning potential. The typical way to increase income-earning potential is through investment in either human capital (e.g., education and training) or physical capital (e.g., looms and agricultural equipment). Funds for investment are normally obtained from banks. In order to minimize their risk, banks usually require *collateral* (i.e., property that can be sold to cover the proceeds of the loan in a case of failure to repay). In many developing countries, women are not allowed to own property, so they have no collateral. As a result traditional credit facilities are closed to them and good investment opportunities are forgone.

One innovative solution to this problem was developed by the Grameen Bank in Bangladesh.[14] This bank uses peer pressure rather than collateral requirements to lower the

---

[13]Vernon W. Ruttan, "Perspectives on Population and Development," *Indian Journal of Agricultural Economics* 39, No. 4 (October/December 1984): 636. Ruttan in turn credits Robert E. Evenson, "Notes on the New Home Economics," in *Home Economics and Agriculture in Third World Countries*, Miriam Seltzer, ed. (St. Paul, MN: University of Minnesota College of Home Economics Center for Youth Development and Research, 1980).

[14]Abu N. Wahid, ed., *The Grameen Bank: Poverty Relief in Bangladesh* (Boulder, CO: Westview Press, 1993).

EXAMPLE 6.3

Income-Generating Activities as Fertility Control: Bangladesh

In Bangladesh the Grameen Bank and other organizations have begun to combine family planning programs with projects designed to generate income for women. Relying on peer pressure to encourage repayment of small loans designed to enable women to obtain either physical capital or human capital, the three programs have been successful. Loan recovery rates range between 96 percent and 100 percent. Results show that credit provision has been associated with productive self-employment, increase in income, accumulation of capital, and meeting basic needs of the poor borrowers.

A variety of income-generating activities are undertaken by participating women in order to pay back the loans. Such activities include paddy husking, poultry raising, weaving, goat raising, and horticulture. In addition, all three programs emphasize other, complementary government-financed social development activities such as sanitation, health care, nutrition, functional education, and population education. Family planning is actively and routinely promoted in group meetings, loan workshops, and training sessions which are financed by the agencies.

Results from this case study show that knowledge of contraceptive methods (through the population education component and group meetings with staff members) and the desire for no more children were higher among the beneficiaries of income-generating projects than the control group. About 60 percent of the beneficiaries were current users of contraceptives, compared to about 38 percent among the control group. Also, about 80 percent of the beneficiaries desired no more children, whereas only 63 percent of the control group shared that desire.

The income-generating projects led to an increase in contraceptive use, regardless of the particular population education components. Over 50 percent who did not participate in the population education components were current users of contraceptives, compared to 38.4 percent of the control group. This suggests that the income-generating projects have an independent effect on the demand for fertility regulation and contraceptive.

Sources: J. Chowdhury, Ruhul Amin, and A. U. Amhed, "Poor Women's Participation in Income Generating Projects and their Fertility Regulation in Rural Bangladesh: Evidence from a Recent Survey," *World Development,* April 1994: 555–64, and Web site: *http://www.colby.edu/personal/thtieten/pop-ban.html.*

risk of nonpayment. Small loans are made to individual women who belong to a group of five or so members. Upon complete repayment of all individual loans within the group, the members of the group become eligible for additional loans. If any member of the group fails to repay, all members remain ineligible until the full loan is repaid. Not only have repayment rates reportedly been very high, but the increasing income-earning capacity generated by these loans has enhanced the effect of family planning programs (Example 6.3).

In terms of population growth, child nutrition, and health, these studies indicate a large payoff for making women fuller partners in the quest for improved living standards in the third world. According to Lawrence Summers, who held the post of chief economist at the

World Bank, the rates of return on investments in power plants in developing countries (a common investment) averaged less than 4 percent, whereas investments in education for girls produced returns of 20 percent or more.[15]

In the words of Dr. Nafis Sadik, executive director of the United Nations Population Fund:[16]

> The extent to which women are free to make decisions affecting their lives may be the key to the future, not only of the poor countries, but the rich ones too. As mothers; producers or suppliers of food, fuel and water; traders and manufacturers; political and community leaders, women are at the centre of the process of change. [p. 3]

The desire to reduce family size, however, is not sufficient if access to birth control information and contraceptives is inadequate. Where access is very good, fertility tends to decline, particularly when access is coupled with better education and opportunities for women.

SUMMARY

World population growth has slowed considerably in recent years, with only African nations resisting the trend. Population declines are already occurring in some countries. The U.S. total fertility rate is now below the replacement level. If maintained for a number of years, this fertility behavior will usher in an era of zero or negative population growth for the United States.

Those countries experiencing declines in their population growth will also experience a rise in the average age of their population. This transition to an older population should boost income per capita growth by increasing the share of the population in the labor force and by allowing more family wealth to be concentrated on the nutrition, health, and education of the children.

All other things being equal, lower population growth should also help to reduce income inequality. Because lower-income families typically have larger families, on average they will feel this effect most strongly. This tendency for incomes of lower-income families to increase faster than those of higher-income families should be reinforced by the effects on labor supply. By preventing an excess supply of labor, which holds wages down, slower population growth benefits wage earners. Wages are a particularly important source of income for lower-income families.

Finally, although population growth is not the sole, or perhaps even the most important, source of nonsustainability, it is definitely a significant factor. If, as seems reasonable, there exists a maximum level of economic activity that can be sustained without undermining the resource base upon which it depends, population growth determines how the fruits of that activity are shared. Although a smaller global population could experience relatively high individual standards of living, a larger population would have to settle for less.

---

[15]Lawrence Summers, "The Most Influential Investment," *Scientific American* (August 1992): 132.

[16]Nafis Sadik, *The State of World Population 1989* (New York: UN Population Fund, 1989).

FURTHER READING

Dasgupta, Partha. *An Inquiry into Well-Being and Destitution* (Oxford: Oxford University Press, 1993). A seminal work that deals comprehensively with the forces (including population growth) that create and accentuate poverty.

Kelley, Allen C. "Economic Consequences of Population Change in the Third World," *Journal of Economic Literature* 26 (December 1988): 1685–728. Excellent review of a complex literature. Includes a detailed bibliography.

Kelley, Allen C., and Robert M. Schmidt. *Population and Income Change: Recent Evidence* (Washington, DC: World Bank, 1994). An excellent review of the theory and evidence underlying the relationship between population growth and economic development that is complemented by some original empirical studies that reveal distinct new emerging patterns.

Schultz, T. Paul. *Economics of Population* (Reading, MA: Addison-Wesley, 1981). Intended for undergraduates, an intensive introduction to the field. Gives a sense of the controversies existing in the field.

Simon, Julian L. *Population and Development in Poor Countries: Selected Essays* (Princeton, NJ: Princeton University Press, 1992). A collection of essays from the primary proponent of the idea that moderate (as opposed to zero or high) population growth may be helpful to developing countries.

ADDITIONAL REFERENCES

Becker, Gary. "An Economic Analysis of Fertility," in *Demographic and Economic Changes in Developed Countries* (Princeton, NJ: Princeton University Press, 1960): 209–31.

Caldwell, John C. "Fertility in Africa," in *Fertility Decline in the Less Developed Countries,* Nick Eberstadt, ed. (New York: Praeger, 1981): 97–118.

Commission on Population Growth and the American Future, *Research Reports*, Vols. I–VII, Elliot R. Morss and Richie H. Reed, eds. (Washington, DC: Government Printing Office, 1972).

Davis, Kingsley, et. al., *Below Replacement Fertility in Industrial Societies: Causes, Consequences, Policies* (New York: Cambridge University Press, 1987).

Easterlin, Richard A. *Population, Labor Force and Long Swings in Economic Growth* (New York: Columbia University Press, 1968).

Easterlin, Richard A. "The Economics and Sociology of Fertility: A Synthesis," in *Historical Studies of Changing Fertility,* Charles Tilly, ed. (Princeton, NJ: Princeton University Press, 1978): 57–133.

Easterlin, Richard A., ed. *Population and Economic Change in Developing Countries* (Chicago: University of Chicago Press, 1980).

Eberstadt, Nick. *Fertility Decline in the Less Developed Countries* (New York: Praeger, 1981).

Espenshade, Thomas J., *Investing in Children: New Estimates of Parental Expenditures* (Washington, DC: Urban Institute Press, 1984).

Goldberg, David. "Residential Location and Fertility," in *Population and Development: The Search for Selective Intervention,* Ronald Ridker, ed. (Baltimore, MD: Johns Hopkins University Press, 1976): 387–428.

Hardee-Cleaveland, Karen, and Judith Banister, "Fertility Policy and Implementation in China, 1986-88," *Population and Development Review* 14 (June 1988): 245–286.

Johnson, D. Gale, and Ronald D. Lee. *Population Growth and Economic Development: Issues and Evidence* (Madison: University of Wisconsin Press, 1987).

Kuznets, Simon. *Population, Capital, and Growth: Selected Essays* (New York: W. W. Norton, 1973).

Lapham, Robert J., and W. Parker Mauldin, "Contraceptive Prevalence: The Influence of Organized Family Programs," *Studies in Family Planning* 16 (1985).

Lee, Ronald D., et al., eds. *Population, Food, and Rural Development* (New York: Oxford University Press, 1988).

Lindert, Peter. *Fertility and Scarcity in America* (Princeton, NJ: Princeton University Press, 1978).

Mahadevan, K. *Fertility Policies of Asian Countries* (Newbury Park, CA: Sage, 1988).

Maudlin, W. Parker. "Patterns of Fertility Decline in Developing Countries, 1970-5" in *Fertility Decline in the Less Developed Countries,* Nick Eberstadt, ed. (New York: Praeger, 1981): 72–96.

National Research Council, *Population Growth and Economic Development: Policy Questions* (Washington, DC: National Academy Press, 1986).

Pimentel, David. "Natural Resources and the Optimum Human Population" (a paper presented at the annual meeting of the American Association for the Advancement of Science, San Francisco, 21 February 1994.)

Repetto, Robert. "The Effects of Income Distribution on Fertility in Developing Countries," in *Fertility Decline in the Less Developed Countries,* Nick Eberstadt, ed. (New York: Praeger, 1981): 254–273.

Ridker, Ronald, ed. *Population and Development: The Search for Selective Interventions* (Baltimore, MD: Johns Hopkins University Press, 1976).

Ruttan, Vernon W. "Perspectives on Population and Development," *Indian Journal of Agricultural Economics* 39 (October/December 1984).

Sadik, Nafis. *The State of World Population 1989* (New York: UN Population Fund, 1989).

Simmons, Ozzie C. *Perspectives on Development and Population* (New York: Plenum, 1988).

Summers, Lawrence. "The Most Influential Investment," *Scientific American* (August 1992): 132.

WEB SITES OF INTEREST

1. *www.popin.org*
   The UN Population Division web site. Contains world population estimates and projections by the UN, historical population levels, and so on.

2. *www.npg.org*
   The Negative Population Growth homepage. Contains world population facts, U.S. population facts, U.S. State population statistics, and U.S. and world population clock.

3. *www.worldwatch.org*
   Worldwatch Institute web site. It contains links to many population web sites as well as news briefs on population.

DISCUSSION QUESTIONS

1. Fertility rates vary widely among various ethnic groups in the United States. Black and Spanish-speaking Americans have above-average rates, for example, whereas Jews have below-average fertility rates. This may be due to different ethnicity-based beliefs, but it may also be due to economic factors. How could you use economics to explain these fertility rate differences? What tests could you devise to see whether this explanation has validity?

2. The microeconomic theory of fertility provides an opportunity to determine how public policies that were designed for quite different purposes could affect fertility rates. Identify some public policies (e.g., subsidies to people who own their own home, or subsidized day care) that could have an effect on fertility rates, and describe the relationship.

3. "According to the theory of the demographic transition, industrialization lowers population growth." Discuss.

Natural Resource Economics: An Overview

The whole machinery of our intelligence, our general ideas and laws, fixed and external objects, principles, persons, and gods, are so many symbolic, algebraic expressions. They stand for experience; experience which we are incapable of retaining and surveying in its multitudinous immediacy. We should flounder hopelessly, like the animals, did we not keep ourselves afloat and direct our course by these intellectual devices. Theory helps us to bear our ignorance of fact.

SANTAYANA, *THE SENSE OF BEAUTY* (1896)

◆ INTRODUCTION

In the *Beyond the Limits* vision of the future, society's demand for resources suddenly exceeds their availability. Rather than anticipating a smooth transition to a steady state, this vision estimates that the system will overshoot the resource base, precipitating a collapse. Is this realistic? Is profit maximization inconsistent with smooth adjustments to increasing scarcity?

We begin with the simple but useful *resource taxonomy* (classification system) that is used to distinguish various categories (measures) of resource availability. Confusing these categories and thereby using published information incorrectly can cause, and has caused, considerable mischief.

We then turn to the question of how markets allocate these resources over time. Whether or not the market is capable of yielding a dynamically efficient allocation in the presence or absence of a renewable substitute provides a focal point for the analysis. Succeeding chapters will use these principles both to examine the allocation of energy, food, and water resources and as a basis for developing more elaborate models of renewable biological populations such as fisheries and forests.

◆ A RESOURCE TAXONOMY

Three separate concepts are used to classify the stock of depletable resources: (1) *current reserves,* (2) *potential reserves,* and (3) *resource endowment.* In the United States the U.S. Geological Survey (USGS) has the official responsibility for keeping records of the U.S. resource base, and it has developed the classification system described in Figure 7.1.

Notice the two dimensions—one economic and one geological. A movement from top to bottom represents movement from cheaply extractable resources to those extracted at substantially higher prices. A movement from left to right represents increasing geological uncertainty about the size of the resource base.

Current reserves (white area in Figure 7.1) are defined as known resources that can profitably be extracted at current prices. The magnitude of these current reserves can be expressed as a number. *Potential reserves,* on the other hand, are most accurately defined as a function rather than a number. The amount of reserves potentially available depends upon the price people are willing to pay for those resources—the higher the price, the larger the potential reserves. For example, Congress conducted a study on the amount of additional oil that could be recovered from existing oil fields using enhanced recovery techniques such as injecting solvents or steam into the well to lower the density of the oil. These techniques, more expensive than conventional ones, allow greater amounts of oil to be recovered. As the price per barrel increases, the amount of oil that can be economically recovered also increases (Table 7.1).

The *resource endowment* represents the natural occurrence of resources in the earth's crust. Because prices have nothing to do with the size of the resource endowment, the latter is a geological rather than an economic concept. This concept is important because it represents an upper limit on the availability of terrestrial resources.

The distinctions among these three concepts are significant. One common mistake in failing to respect these distinctions is that of using data on current reserves as if it represented the maximum potential reserves. As Example 7.1 indicates, this fundamental error can lead to conclusions wide of the mark.

A second common mistake is to assume that the entire resource endowment can be made available as potential reserves at some price people would be willing to pay. Clearly, if an infinite price were possible, then the entire resource endowment could be exploited. However, an infinite price is not likely.

Certain mineral resources are so costly to extract that it is inconceivable that any current or future society would be willing to pay the price necessary to extract them. Thus, it seems likely that the maximum feasible size of the potential reserves is smaller than the resource endowment. Exactly how much smaller cannot yet be determined with any degree of certainty.

Other distinctions among resource categories are also useful. The first such category includes all depletable, recyclable resources, such as copper. A *depletable resource* is one for which the natural-replenishment feedback loop can safely be ignored. The rate of replenishment for these resources is so low that it does not offer a potential for augmenting the stock in any reasonable time frame.

A *recyclable resource* is one that, although currently being used for some particular purpose, exists in a form allowing its mass to be recovered once that purpose is no longer necessary or desirable. For example, copper wiring from an automobile can be recovered after the

FIGURE 7.1 A Categorization of Resources

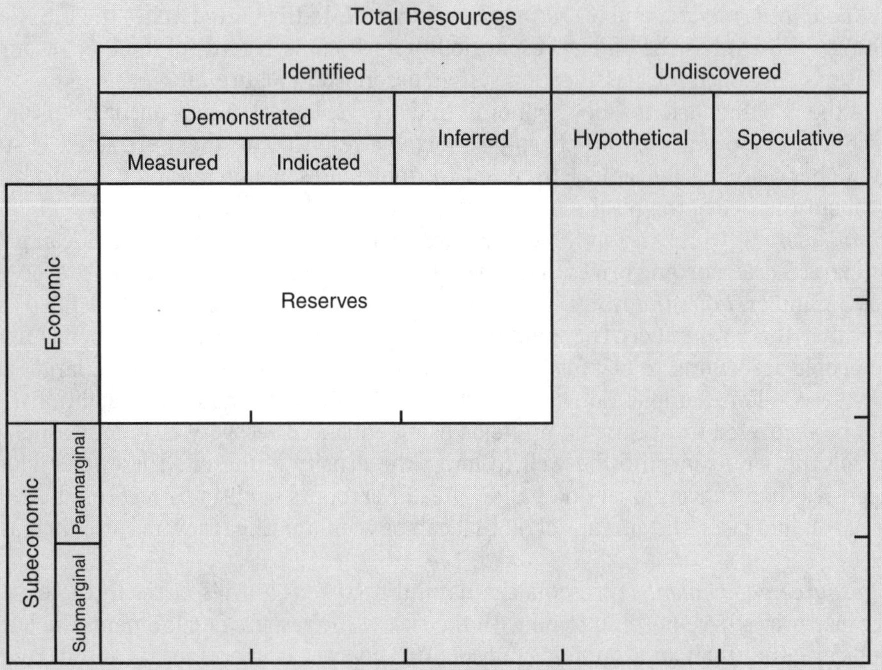

Total Resources

	Identified			Undiscovered	
	Demonstrated		Inferred	Hypothetical	Speculative
	Measured	Indicated			
Economic	Reserves				
Subeconomic — Paramarginal / Submarginal					

Terms

Identified resources: Specific bodies of mineral-bearing material whose location, quality, and quantity are known from geological evidence, supported by engineering measurements

Measured resources: Material for which quantity and quality estimates are within a margin of error of less than 20 percent, from geologically well-known sample sites

Indicated resources: Material for which quantity and quality have been estimated, partly from sample analyses and partly from reasonable geological projections

Inferred resources: Material in unexplored extensions of demonstrated resources based on geological projections

Undiscovered resources: Unspecified bodies of mineral-bearing material surmised to exist, on the basis of broad geological knowledge and theory

Hypothetical resources: Undiscovered materials reasonably expected to exist in a known mining district under known geological conditions

Speculative resources: Undiscovered materials that may occur either in known types of deposits in favorable geological settings where no discoveries have been made, or in yet unknown types of deposits that remain to be recognized

Source: U.S. Bureau of Mines and the U.S. Geological Survey. "Principle of the Mineral Resource Classification System of the U.S. Bureau of Mines and the U.S. Geological Survey," *Geological Survey Bulletin* 1450-A, 1976.

Example 7.1

The Pitfalls of Misusing Reserve Data

The number of years a given resource will last is commonly estimated by computing what is known as the *static reserve index,* the ratio of current reserves to current consumption. The result of the calculation is supposed to be interpreted as the number of years remaining until the resource is exhausted. This is a correct calculation of the time to exhaustion *if and only if* (1) the consumption of the resource remains at current levels until the time of exhaustion (i.e., it can neither increase nor decrease) and (2) no additions to the reserves occur in the intervening period (current reserves and potential reserves are assumed equal for the prices that can be expected to prevail).

These assumptions generally are not even approximately accurate. For example, in 1934 the static reserve index for copper was 40, indicating that the reserves would be exhausted in 40 years. In 1974, 40 years later, the index stood at 57. A similar calculation for crude oil, iron ore, and lead would reveal the same pattern: The static index tends to underestimate the time until exhaustion.

The *Beyond the Limits* study used an index called the *exponential reserve index,* which tends to underestimate the time to exhaustion by an even greater amount than does the static index. This exponential index assumes that consumption will grow over time at a constant rate of growth. No correction is made for additions to reserves or for the effects of higher prices on demand. It is therefore neither very surprising, nor very interesting, that the study team's time of exhaustion estimates are so proximate.

Sources: Paul R. Ehrlich and Anne H. Ehrlich, *Population Resources Environment,* 2nd ed. (San Francisco: W. H. Freeman, 1972), pp. 70–72; Earl Cook, "Limits to Exploitation of Nonrenewable Resources," *Science* 191 (20 February 1976): 667–82.

car has been shipped to the junkyard. The degree to which a resource is recycled is determined by economic conditions, a subject covered in subsequent chapters.

The current reserves of a depletable, recyclable resource can be augmented by economic replenishment as well as by recycling. Economic replenishment takes many forms,

TABLE 7.1 Estimates of Ultimately Recoverable Oil from Enhanced Oil Recovery with 10 Percent Minimum Rate of Return (price in constant 1997 dollars)

Price per Barrel	Ultimate Recovery (10^9 barrels)
$32.78	21.2
$38.79	29.4
$62.06	41.6
$84.62	49.2
More than $84.62	51.1

Source: U.S. Congress, Office of Technology Assessment (OTA), *Enhanced Oil Recovery Potential in the United States* (Washington, D.C.: OTA, 1978): p. 7. Updated to 1997 dollars using Consumer Price Index.

all sharing the characteristic that they turn previously unrecoverable resources into recoverable ones. One obvious stimulant for this replenishment is price. As price rises, producers find it profitable to explore more widely, dig more deeply, use lower-concentration ores, and so on.

Higher prices also stimulate technological progress. *Technological progress* simply means an advancement in the state of knowledge that allows us to do things we were not able to do before. One profound, if controversial, example can be found in the successful harnessing of nuclear power.

The other side of the coin for depletable, recyclable resources is that their potential reserves can be exhausted. The depletion rate is affected by the demand for and durability of the products built with the resource and by the ability to reuse the products. Except where demand is totally *price inelastic* (i.e., insensitive to price), higher prices tend to reduce the quantity demanded. Durable products last longer, reducing the need for newer ones. Reusable products provide a substitute for new products. In the commercial sector, reusable soft-drink bottles provide one example; flea markets (where secondhand items are sold) provide an example for the household sector.

For some resources, the size of the potential reserves depends explicitly on our ability to store the resource. For example, helium generally is found commingled with natural gas in common fields. Unless the helium is simultaneously captured and stored as the natural gas is extracted, it diffuses into the atmosphere. This results in such low concentrations that extraction of helium from the air is not economical at current or even likely future prices. Thus, the useful stock of helium depends crucially on how much we decide to store.

Not all depletable resources permit recycling or reuse. Depletable energy resources such as coal, oil, and gas are consumed as they are used. Once they are combusted and turned into heat energy, the heat dissipates into the atmosphere and becomes nonrecoverable.

The endowment of depletable resources is of finite size. Current use of depletable, noncyclable resources precludes future use; hence, the issue of how they should be shared among generations is raised in the starkest, least-forgiving form.

Depletable, recyclable resources raise this same issue, though somewhat less starkly. Recycling and reuse make the useful stock last longer, all other things being equal. It is tempting to suggest that depletable recyclable resources could last forever with 100 percent recycling, but unfortunately the physical theoretical upper limit on recycling is less than 100 percent—an implication of a version of the entropy law defined in Chapter 2. Some of the mass is always lost during recycling.

For example, copper pennies can be melted down to recover the copper, but the amount rubbed off during circulation would never be recovered. As long as less than 100 percent of the mass is recycled, the useful stock must eventually decline to zero. Even for recyclable depletable resources, the cumulative useful stock is finite, and current consumption patterns still have an effect on future generations.

Renewable resources are differentiated from depletable resources primarily by the fact that natural replenishment augments the flow of renewable resources at a nonnegligible rate. Solar energy, water, cereal grains, fish, forests, and animals are all examples of renewable resources. Thus it is possible, though not inevitable, that a flow of these resources could be maintained perpetually.[1]

For some renewable resources, the continuation and volume of their flow depend crucially on humans. Soil erosion and nutrient depletion reduce the flow of food. Excessive fishing reduces the stock of fish, which in turn reduces the rate of natural increase of the fish population. Newsprint can be recycled. Other examples abound. For other renewable resources, such as solar energy, the flow is independent of humans. The amount consumed by one generation does not reduce the amount that can be consumed by subsequent generations.

Some renewable resources can be stored; others cannot. For those that can, storage provides a valuable way to manage the allocation of the resource over time. We are not left simply at the mercy of natural ebbs and flows of the source. Without proper care, food perishes rapidly, but with storage, it can be used to feed the hungry in times of famine. Unstored solar energy radiates off the earth's surface and dissipates into the atmosphere. Although solar energy can be stored in many forms, the most common natural form of storage occurs when it is converted to biomass by photosynthesis.

Storage of renewable resources usually performs a different service than does storage of depletable resources. Storing depletable resources extends their economic life; storing renewable resources, on the other hand, can serve as a means of "smoothing out" the cyclical imbalances of supply and demand. Surpluses are stored for later time periods when deficits may occur. Food stockpiles and the use of dams to store hydropower are two familiar examples.

Managing renewable resources presents a different challenge than managing depletable resources, though an equally significant one. The challenge for depletable resources involves allocating dwindling stocks among generations while meeting the ultimate transition to renewable resources. In contrast, the challenge for managing renewable resources involves the maintenance of an efficient, sustainable flow. The next six chapters deal with how the economic and political sectors have responded to these challenges for particularly significant types of resources.

◆ EFFICIENT INTERTEMPORAL ALLOCATIONS

If we are to judge the adequacy of market allocations, we must define what is meant by *efficiency* in relation to the management of depletable and renewable resource allocations. Because allocation over time is the crucial issue, dynamic efficiency becomes the core concept. As we noted earlier, the dynamic-efficiency criterion assumes that society's objective is to maximize the present value of net benefits coming from the resource. For a depletable,

---

[1]Even renewable resources are ultimately finite, because their renewability is dependent on energy from the sun, and the sun is expected to serve as an energy source for only the next 5 or 6 billion years. That fact does not eliminate the need to manage resources effectively until that time. Furthermore, the finiteness of renewable resources is sufficiently far into the future to make the distinction useful.

nonrecyclable resource, this maximization requires a balancing of the current and subsequent uses of the resource. In order to review how the dynamic-efficiency criterion defines this balance, we shall elaborate on the very simple two-period model developed in Chapter 2. We shall show how these earlier conclusions can be generalized to accommodate longer planning horizons and more complicated situations.

The Two-Period Model Revisited

In Chapter 5 we defined a situation involving the allocation, over two periods, of a finite resource that could be extracted at a constant marginal cost. With a stable demand curve for the resource, an efficient allocation meant that more than half of the resource was allocated to the first period and less than half to the second period. This allocation was affected both by the marginal cost of extraction and by the marginal user cost. Because of the fixed and finite supplies of depletable resources, production of a unit today precludes production of that unit tomorrow. Therefore, production decisions today must take forgone future net benefits into account. Marginal user cost is the opportunity cost measure that allows balancing to take place.

The marginal cost of extraction is assumed to be constant, but the current value of the marginal user cost rises over time. In fact, as was demonstrated in Chapter 5, when the demand curve is stable over time and the marginal cost of extraction is constant, the rate of increase in the current value of the marginal user cost is equal to r, the discount rate. Thus, in period 2, the marginal user cost would be $1 + r$ times as large as it was in period 1.[2] In an efficient allocation, marginal user cost rises at rate r in order to preserve the balance between present and future production.

In summary, our two-period example suggests that an efficient allocation of a finite resource with a constant marginal cost of extraction involves rising marginal-user cost and falling quantities consumed. We can now generalize to longer time periods.

The N-Period Model

We begin this generalization by retaining the constant-marginal-extraction-cost assumption while extending the time horizon within which the resource is allocated. In the numerical example shown in Figures 7.2(a) and 7.2(b), the demand curves and the marginal-cost curves from the two-period case are retained. The only changes in this numerical example relative to the two-period case involve spreading the allocation over a larger number of years and increasing the total recoverable supply from 20 to 40.

Figure 7.2(a) demonstrates how the efficient quantity of the resource extracted varies over time, whereas Figure 7.2(b) shows the behavior of the marginal user cost and the marginal cost of extraction. *Total marginal cost* refers to the sum of the two costs. The marginal cost of extraction is represented by the lower line, and the marginal user cost is depicted as the vertical distance between the marginal extraction cost and the total marginal cost. To avoid confusion, note that the horizontal axis is defined in terms of time, not

---

[2]The condition that marginal user cost rises at rate r is true only when the marginal cost of extraction is constant. For the more complicated case see T. H. Tietenberg, *Environmental and Natural Resource Economics* (Reading, MA: Addison-Wesley, 2000): Chapter 7.

FIGURE 7.2 Constant Marginal Extraction Cost with No Substitute Resource. (a) Quantity Profile; (b) Marginal-Cost Profile

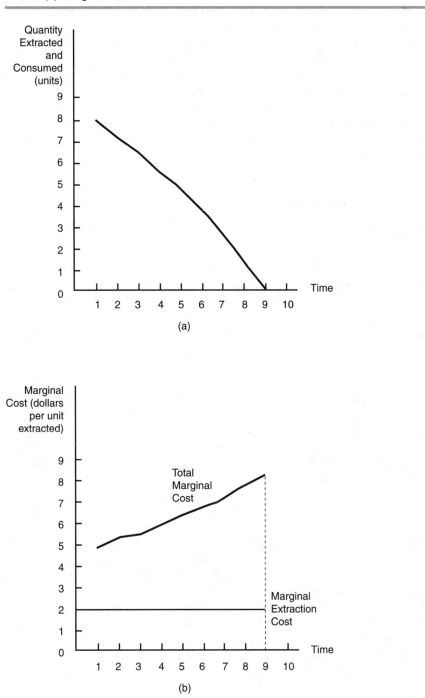

(a)

(b)

in terms of the more conventional designation, quantity, and the top figure has quantity on the vertical axis.

Several trends are worth noting. First of all, in this case (as in the two-period case), the efficient marginal user cost rises steadily despite the constancy of the marginal cost of extraction. This rise in the efficient marginal user cost reflects increasing scarcity and the accompanying rise in the opportunity cost of current consumption. In response to these rising costs over time, the quantity extracted falls over time until it finally reaches zero, which occurs precisely at the moment when the total marginal cost becomes $8. At this point, total marginal cost is equal to the highest price anyone is willing to pay, so that demand and supply simultaneously equal zero. Thus, even in this difficult case involving no increase in the marginal cost of extraction, an efficient allocation envisions a smooth transition to the exhaustion of a resource. The resource does not "suddenly" run out—although in this case it does eventually run out.

Transition to a Renewable Substitute

So far we have discussed the allocation of a depletable resource when no substitute is available to take its place. However, suppose we consider the nature of an efficient allocation when a substitute renewable resource is available at a constant marginal cost. This scenario could describe the efficient allocation of oil or natural gas with a solar substitute, for example, or the efficient allocation of exhaustible groundwater with a surface-water substitute. How could we define an efficient allocation in this circumstance?

Because this problem is very similar to the one already discussed, we can use what we have already learned as a foundation for mastering this new situation. The depletable resource would be exhausted in this case, just as it was in the previous case. However, that will be less of a problem in this case, because we will merely switch to the renewable resource at the appropriate time.

The total marginal cost for the depletable resource would never exceed the marginal cost of the substitute because society could always use the renewable resource instead, whenever it was cheaper to do so. Thus, although the maximum willingness to pay (the "choke price") sets the upper limit on total marginal cost when no substitute is available, the marginal cost of extraction of the substitute sets the upper limit when an alternative resource is available at a marginal cost that is lower than the choke price.

In this efficient allocation, the transition is once again smooth. Quantity extracted is gradually reduced as the marginal use cost rises until the switch is made to the substitute. No abrupt change is evident in either the marginal-cost or quantity profile.

Because the renewable resource is available, more of the depletable resource would be extracted in the earlier periods than would be the case without a renewable resource (as in our previous numerical example). As a result, the depletable resource would be exhausted sooner than it would have been without the renewable-resource substitute.

At the transition point, called the *switch point,* consumption of the renewable resource begins. Prior to the switch point, only the depletable resource is consumed, whereas after the switch point, only the renewable resource is consumed. This sequencing of consumption patterns results from the cost patterns. Prior to the switch point, the depletable resource is cheaper. At the switch point, the marginal cost of the depletable resource (including the marginal user cost) rises to meet the marginal cost of the substitute, and the transition occurs.

Exploration and Technological Progress

The search for new resources is expensive. As the more easily discovered resources are exhausted, we must search in less rewarding environments, such as the bottom of the ocean or locations deep within the earth. This suggests that the *marginal cost of exploration,* which is the marginal cost of finding additional units of the resource, should be expected to rise over time, just as the marginal cost of extraction does.

As the total marginal cost for a resource rises over time, society should actively explore possible new sources of that resource. The higher the expected rise in the marginal cost of extraction for known sources, the larger is the potential increase in net benefits from exploration.

Some of this exploration would be successful: New sources of the resource would be discovered. If the marginal extraction cost of the newly discovered resources is low enough, these discoveries could lower, or at least retard, the increase in the total marginal cost of production. As a result, the new finds would tend to encourage more consumption. Successful exploration would cause a smaller and slower decline in consumption while dampening the rise in total marginal cost.

It is also not difficult to expand our concept of efficient resource allocations to include consideration of technological progress. In the present context, technological progress would be manifested as reductions in the cost of extraction. For a resource that can be extracted at constant marginal cost, a one-time breakthrough lowering the future marginal cost of extraction but not the present marginal cost would move the time of transition further into the future.

The most pervasive effects of technological progress involve continuous downward shifts in the cost of extraction over some time period. The total marginal cost of the resource could actually fall over time if the cost-reducing nature of technological progress became so potent that, in spite of increasing reliance on inferior ore, the marginal cost of extraction decreased (Example 7.2). With a finite amount of this resource, the fall in total marginal cost would be transitory, because ultimately it would have to rise. This period of transition could last quite a long time, however.

◆ MARKET ALLOCATIONS

In the preceding sections we have examined in detail how the efficient allocation of substitutable depletable and renewable resources over time would be defined in a variety of circumstances. We must now address the question of whether actual markets can be expected to produce an efficient allocation. Can the private market—a market involving millions of consumers and producers each reacting to his or her own unique preferences—*ever* result in a dynamically efficient allocation? Is profit maximization compatible with dynamic efficiency?

Example 7.2

Technological Progress in the Iron Ore Industry

The term *technological progress* plays an important role in the economic analysis of mineral resources. Yet, at times, it can appear abstract, even mystical. It shouldn't! Far from being a "blind faith" assertion detached from reality, *technological progress* refers to a host of ingenious ways in which people have reacted to impending shortages with sufficient imagination that the available supply of resources has been greatly expanded at reasonable cost. To illustrate how concrete a notion technological progress is, let's discuss one example of how it has worked in the past.

In 1947 the president of Republic Steel, C. M. White, calculated the expected life of the Mesabi range of northern Minnesota (the source of some 60 percent of iron ore consumed during World War II) as being about five to seven years. By 1955, only eight years later, *U.S. News and World Report* was able to conclude that worry over the scarcity of iron ore could be forgotten. The source of this remarkable transformation of a problem of scarcity into one of abundance was the discovery of a new technique, called *pelletization,* for preparing iron ore.

Prior to pelletization, the standard ores from which iron was derived contained from 50 to more than 65 percent iron in crude form. There was a significant percentage of taconite ore available containing less than 30 percent iron in crude form, but no one knew how to prepare it at reasonable cost. Pelletization is a process by which these ores are processed and concentrated at the mine site prior to shipment to the blast furnaces. The advent of pelletization allowed the profitable use of the taconite ores.

While expanding the supply of iron ore, pelletization reduced its cost—in spite of the use of an inferior ore grade. There were several sources of the cost reduction. First, substantially *less* energy was used: The shift in ore technology toward pelletization produced net energy savings of 17 percent even though the pelletization process itself required more energy. The reduction came from the discovery that the blast furnaces could be operated much more efficiently using pelletization inputs. The process also reduced labor requirements per ton by some 8.2 percent while increasing the output of the blast furnaces. By 1960, a blast furnace owned by Armco Steel in Middletown, Ohio, which had a rated capacity of approximately 1,500 tons of molten iron per day, was able to achieve production levels of 2,700 and 2,800 tons per day when fired with 90 percent pellets. Pellets nearly doubled the blast furnace's productivity!

Sources: Peter J. Kakela, "Iron Ore: Energy Labor and Capital Changes with Technology," *Science* 202 (15 December 1978): 1151–57; "Iron Ore: From Depletion to Abundance," *Science* 212 (10 April 1981): 132–36.

Appropriate Property-Right Structures

The most common misconception of those who believe that even a perfect market could never achieve an efficient allocation is a belief that producers want to extract and sell the resources as fast as possible because that is how they derive the most value from the resource. This misconception makes people see markets as myopic and unconcerned about the future.

As long as the property-rights structures governing natural resources have the characteristics of exclusivity, universality, transferability, and enforceability (Chapter 4), the markets in which those resources are bought and sold will not necessarily lead to myoptic choices. When bearing the marginal user cost, the producer acts in an efficient manner. A resource in the ground has two potential sources of value to its owner: (1) a use value when it is sold (the only source considered by those diagnosing inevitable myopia) and (2) an asset value when it remains in the ground. As long as the price of a resource continues to rise, the resource in the ground is becoming more valuable. However, the owner of this resource accrues this capital gain only if the resource is conserved. A producer who sells all resources in the earlier periods loses the chance to take advantage of higher prices in the future.

A prescient, profit-maximizing producer attempts to balance present and future production in order to maximize the value of the resource. Because higher prices in the future provide an incentive to conserve, a producer who ignores this incentive would not be maximizing the value of the resource. We would expect the resource to then be bought by someone willing to conserve it and prepared to maximize its value. As long as social and private discount rates coincide, property-right structures are well-defined, and reliable information about future prices is available, a producer who selfishly pursues maximum profits simultaneously provides the maximum present value of net benefits for society.

The implication of this analysis is that, in prescient, competitive resource markets, the price of the resource equals the total marginal cost of extracting and using the resource.

Environmental Costs

One of the most important situations in which property-right structures may not be well-defined is that in which the extraction of a natural resource imposes an environmental cost on society that is not internalized by the producers. The aesthetic costs of strip mining, the health risks associated with uranium tailings, and the acids leached into streams from mine operations are all examples of associated environmental costs. Not only is the presence of environmental costs empirically important, it is also conceptually important. It forms one of the bridges between the traditionally separate fields of environmental economics and natural resource economics.

Suppose, for example, that the extraction of the depletable resource caused some damage to the environment not adequately reflected in the costs faced by the extracting firms. This would be an external cost. The cost of getting the resource out of the ground, as well as processing and shipping it, is borne by the resource owner and considered in the calculation of how much of the resource to extract. The environmental damage, however, is not borne by the owner and, in the absence of any outside attempt to internalize that cost, it will not be part of the extraction decision. How would the market allocation, based on only the former cost, differ from the efficient allocation, which is based on both?

The inclusion of environmental costs results in higher prices, which tend to dampen demand. This lowers the rate of consumption of the resource, which, all other things being equal, would make it last longer.

What can we learn about the allocation of depletable resources over time when environmental side effects are not borne by the agent determining the extraction rate? The price of the depletable resource would be too low and the resource would be extracted too rapidly.

This once again shows the interdependencies of the various decisions we have to make about the future. Environmental and natural resource decisions are intimately and inextricably linked.

SUMMARY

The efficient allocation of substitutable depletable and renewable resources depends on the circumstances. When the resource can be extracted at a constant marginal cost, the efficient quantity of the depletable resource extracted declines over time. If no substitute is available, the quantity declines smoothly to zero. If a renewable, constant-cost substitute is available, the quantity of the depletable resource extracted will decline smoothly to the quantity available from the renewable resource. In both cases, all of the available depletable resource would be eventually used up and marginal user cost would rise over time, reaching a maximum when the last unit of depletable resource was extracted.

Introducing technological progress and exploration activity tends to delay the transition to renewable resources. Exploration expands the size of current reserves; technological progress keeps marginal user cost from rising as much as it otherwise would. If these effects are sufficiently potent, marginal extraction cost could actually decline for some period of time, causing the quantity extracted to rise.

When property-right structures are properly defined, market allocations of depletable resources can be efficient. Self-interest and efficiency are not necessarily incompatible.

When the extraction of resources imposes an external environmental cost, however, market allocations will not generally be efficient. The market price of the depletable resource would be too low, and too much of the resource would be extracted too rapidly.

In an efficient market allocation, the transition from depletable to renewable resources is smooth and exhibits none of the overshoot and collapse characteristics of the *Beyond the Limits* view of the world. Whether the actual market allocations of these various types of resources are efficient remains to be seen. To the extent that they are efficient, a laissez-faire policy would represent an appropriate response by the government. On the other hand, if the market is not capable of yielding an efficient allocation, then some form of government intervention may be necessary. In the next few chapters we shall examine these questions for a number of different types of depletable and renewable resources.

FURTHER READING

Bohi, Douglas R., and Michael A. Toman. *Analyzing Nonrenewable Resource Supply* (Washington, DC: Resources for the Future, 1984). A reinterpretation and evaluation of existing research that attempts to weave together theoretical, empirical, and practical insights concerning the management of depletable resources.

Chapman, Duane. "Computation Techniques for Intertemporal Allocation of Natural Resources," *American Journal of Agricultural Economics* 69, No. 1 (February 1987): 134–42. Shows how to find numerical solutions for the types of depletable resource problems considered in this chapter.

Conrad, Jon M., and Colin W. Clark. *Natural Resource Economics: Notes and Problems* (Cambridge, UK: Cambridge University Press, 1987). Reviews techniques of dynamic optimization and shows how they can be applied to the management of various resource systems.

Fisher, Anthony C. *Resource and Environmental Economics* (Cambridge, UK: Cambridge University Press, 1981). This volume presents a careful heuristic development of the major mathematical results in optimal resource use for depletable and renewable resources. It also has chapters on preserving natural environments and on pollution. This text is written for graduate students or upper-level undergraduates.

Toman, Michael A. "'Depletion Effects' and Nonrenewable Resource Supply," *Land Economics* 62 (November 1986): 341–53. An excellent, nontechnical discussion of the increasing-cost case with and without exploration and additions to reserves.

ADDITIONAL REFERENCES

Anders, Gerhard, W. Philip Gramm, S. Charles Maurice, and Charles W. Smithson. *The Economics of Mineral Extraction* (New York: Praeger, 1980).

Dasgupta, P. S., and G. M. Heal. *Economic Theory and Exhaustible Resources* (Cambridge, UK: Cambridge University Press, 1979).

Dasgupta, Partha. *The Control of Resources* (Cambridge, MA: Harvard University Press, 1982).

Kneese, Allen V., and James L. Sweeney, eds. *Handbook of Natural Resource and Energy Economics: Vol. III* (Amsterdam: North-Holland, 1986).

Peterson, Frederick M., and Anthony C. Fisher. "The Exploitation of Extractive Resources: A Survey," *Economic Journal* 88 (December 1977): 681–721.

Scott, Anthony, ed. *Progress in Natural Resource Economics* (Oxford: Clarendon Press, 1985).

DISCUSSION QUESTIONS

1. Identify any external costs that might be associated with the following activities: (a) extracting timber from public lands, (b) extracting timber from one's own land, (c) harvesting fish from the ocean, and (d) taking water from a shared groundwater source. How would these external costs affect the extraction of these resources over time?

2. What causes technological progress? Can the rate of technological progress be influenced by the government? Why or why not?

8

Energy

If it ain't broke, don't fix it!

OLD MAINE PROVERB

◆ INTRODUCTION

Energy is one of our most critical resources; without it, life would cease. We derive energy from the food we eat. Through photosynthesis, the plant life we consume—both directly and indirectly when we eat meat—depends on energy from the sun. The materials we use to build our houses and produce the goods we consume are extracted from the earth's crust, then transformed into finished products through expenditures of energy.

Currently, most industrialized countries depend on oil and natural gas for most of their energy needs. In the United States, for example, these two resources together supply 67 percent of all energy consumed. Both are depletable, nonrecyclable sources of energy. Proven crude oil reserves peaked during the 1970s, natural gas peaked in the 1980s in the United States and in Europe. Since that time, the amount extracted has exceeded additions to reserves[1] (see Figures 8.1 and 8.2).

---

[1]In contrast, world reserves of oil and gas have continued to increase during the 1980s. See U.S. Energy Information Administration, *International Energy Annual* (Washington, DC: Government Printing Office): various issues.

FIGURE 8.1   Estimated Crude Oil Reserves for the United States and Western Europe Over Time

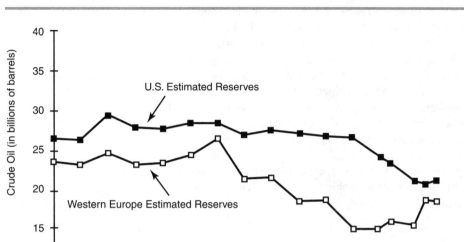

Source: U.S. Energy Information Administration, *International Energy Annual* (Washington, DC: Government Printing Office): various issues.

Note: 1994 data not published

FIGURE 8.2   Estimated Natural Gas Reserves for the United States and Western Europe Over Time

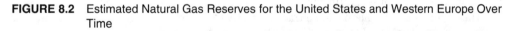

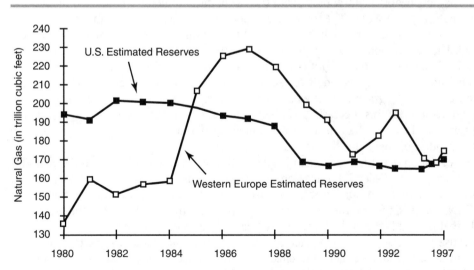

Source: U.S. Energy Information Administration, *International Energy Annual* (Washington, DC: Government Printing Office): various issues.

Because they are depletable resources, oil and natural gas would be transition fuels in an efficient allocation. They would be used until the marginal cost of further use exceeded the marginal cost of substitute resources—either more abundant depletable resources, such as coal, or renewable sources, such as solar energy.[2] In an efficient market path, the transition to these alternative sources would be smooth and harmonious. Have the allocations of the last several decades been efficient or not?

In a 1977 speech to the nation, U.S. President Jimmy Carter suggested that the resolve needed to solve our energy problems was "the moral equivalent of war." The existence of a crisis atmosphere suggests that the allocations have not been efficient. Why not? Is the market mechanism flawed in its allocation of depletable recyclable resources? If so, is the flaw fatal? If not, what caused the inefficient allocations? Is the problem correctable?

In this chapter we shall examine some of the major issues associated with the allocation of energy resources over time and see how economic analysis can clarify our understanding of both the sources of the problems and their solution. Because energy is too complex a subject to treat comprehensively in one chapter, however, additional references are provided.

◆ NATURAL GAS: PRICE CONTROLS

In the United States during the winter of late 1974 and early 1975, serious shortages of natural gas developed. Customers who had contracted and were willing to pay for natural gas were unable to get as much as they wanted. The shortage (or *curtailment* as the Federal Energy Regulatory Commission calls it) amounted to 2.0 trillion cubic feet of natural gas in 1974–1975, which represented roughly 10 percent of the marketed production in 1975. In an efficient allocation, shortages of that magnitude would never have happened. Why did they?

The source of the problem can be traced directly to government controls over natural gas prices. This story begins, oddly enough, with the rise of the automobile, which traditionally has not used natural gas as a fuel. The increasing importance of the automobile for transportation created a rising demand for gasoline, which in turn stimulated a search for new sources of crude oil. This exploration activity uncovered large quantities of natural gas (known as *associated gas*), in addition to large quantities of crude oil, which was the object of the search.

As natural gas was discovered, it replaced manufactured gas—and some coal—as an energy source in the geographic areas where it was found. Then, as a geographically dispersed demand developed for this increasingly available gas, a long-distance system of gas pipelines was designed and constructed. In the period following World War II, natural gas became an important source of energy for the United States.

The regulation of natural gas began in 1938 with the passage of the Natural Gas Act. This act transformed the Federal Power Commission (FPC) into a federal regulatory agency charged with maintaining "just" prices. In 1954, a Supreme Court decision in *Phillips Petroleum Co.* v. *Wisconsin* forced the FPC to extend its price control regulations to the producers. Prior to that time, it had merely limited its regulation to pipeline companies.

Because the process of setting price ceilings proved cumbersome, the hastily conceived initial ("interim") ceilings remained in effect for almost a decade before the commission was able to impose more carefully considered ceilings. What was the effect of this regulation?

---

[2]When used for other purposes, oil can be recycled. Waste lubricating oil is now routinely recycled.

The ceilings prevented prices from reaching their normal levels. Because price increases are the source of the incentive to conserve, the lower prices caused more of the resource to be used in earlier years. Consumption levels in those years were higher with price controls than without them. Attracted by artificially low prices, consumers would invest in equipment to use natural gas, only to discover—after the transition—that natural gas was no longer available.

Price controls may cause other problems as well. Up to this point, we have discussed permanent controls. Not all price controls are permanent; they can change at the whim of the political process, in unpredictable ways. The fact that prices can suddenly rise when the ceiling is lifted also creates unfortunate incentives. If producers expect a large price increase in the near future, they have an incentive to stop production and wait for the higher prices. Needless to say, this circumstance could cause severe problems for consumers.

For legal reasons the price controls on natural gas were placed solely on gas shipped across state lines. Gas consumed within the states where it was produced could be priced at what the market would bear. As a result, gas produced and sold within a given state received a higher price than that sold in other states. Consequently, the share of gas in the interstate market fell over time, as producers found it more profitable to commit reserve additions to the *intrastate,* rather than the *interstate,* market. In the 1964–1969 period, about 33 percent of the average annual reserve additions were committed to the interstate market. By 1970–1974, this commitment had fallen to a little less than 5 percent.

The practical effect of charging less for gas destined for the interstate market was to cause the shortages to be concentrated in states served by pipeline and dependent on the interstate shipment of gas. As a result, the damage caused was greater than it would have been if all consuming areas had shared somewhat more equitably in the shortfall. The price control system not only caused the damage, it intensified it!

Natural gas allocations not only hastened the time of transition to a substitute resource, they also caused a transition to an inefficient substitute. The reason for this substitution bias and its implications are explored in Example 8.1.

It seems fair to conclude that, by sapping the economic system of its ability to respond to changing conditions, price controls on natural gas created a significant amount of turmoil. If this kind of political control is likely to recur with some regularity, perhaps some of the *Beyond the Limits* concerns may be valid, though for different reasons. The overshoot-and-collapse syndrome in this case would be caused by government interference rather than by any pure market behavior. If so, the proverb that opens this chapter becomes particularly relevant!

Why did Congress embark on such a counterproductive policy? The answer is found in rent-seeking behavior that can be explained through the use of our consumer- and producer-surplus model. Let's examine the political incentives in a simple model.

Consider Figure 8.3. An efficient market allocation would result in quantity Q^* supplied at price P^*. The net benefits received by the country would be represented by the total geometric area encompassed by areas A and B. Of these net benefits, area A would be received by consumers as consumer surplus and B would be received by producers as producer surplus.

Now suppose that a price ceiling were established. From the preceding discussion we know that this ceiling would reduce the marginal user cost because higher future prices would no longer be possible. In Figure 8.3, this has the effect for current producers of lowering the perceived-supply curve, because of the lower marginal user cost. As a result of this shift in the perceived-supply curve, current production would expand to quantity Q_c and price would fall to P_c.

Example 8.1

Price Controls and Substitution Bias

Faced with shortages in the 1970s, pipeline companies looked for alternative sources of supply. Two that they discovered were liquid natural gas (LNG), sent from abroad in pressurized ships, and synthetic natural gas (SNG), manufactured from various petroleum products. These sources were both very expensive.

Pipeline companies induced consumers to use these substitutes by using average cost pricing. The artificially cheap natural gas was blended with the synthetic gas and sold at the average cost of the two—with the actual price depending on the proportions used. Thus, if a company used 90 percent natural gas at $1 per unit and 10 percent other sources at $5 per unit, the cost of the combined gas was $1.40 per unit (0.90 × $1 + 0.10 × $5). Thus, instead of paying the high marginal cost of the substitute for additional units consumed, as efficiency would dictate, consumers paid the much lower average cost. The pricing system sent them the wrong signal.

This system of pricing created a bias toward substitutes that could be blended with natural gas and away from substitutes that could not. In this case, the bias was particularly unfortunate; not only did it create additional demand for imported energy sources (e.g., LNG) at a time when the official policy was to discourage such imports, it also encouraged lower levels of thermodynamic efficiency in the use of our diminishing oil resources. The conversion to gas caused some of the potential energy to be lost. Substitutes rendered noneconomic in certain parts of the country by this pricing system included heat pumps and residential solar space heating.

Because this system of average cost pricing encouraged pipeline companies to accept high-cost sources of imported or synthetic gas that could be commingled with the artificially cheap natural gas during the 1970s, the price rise was especially rapid and sharp when natural gas prices began to be decontrolled in the early 1980s. The large base of artificially low-cost natural gas no longer provided a counterbalance to the very high cost of the new sources. Average residential prices for natural gas rose from $2.98 per thousand cubic feet in 1979 to $6.12 in 1984. Since that time prices have stabilized, with the 1998 price being $6.82; the excess demand in the natural gas market had been eliminated by higher prices.

Sources: Thomas H. Tietenberg, "Substitution Bias in a Depletable Resource Model with Administered Prices," in *Erschöpfbare Ressourcen* (Berlin: Duncker and Humlot, 1980): 522–29; U.S. Energy Information Administration, *Monthly Energy Review* (July 1999): 125.

Current consumers would unambiguously be better off, because consumer surplus would be area $A + B + C$ instead of area A. They would have gained a net benefit equal to $B + C$.

It may appear that producers could also gain if $D > B$, but that is not correct. Because producers would be overproducing, they would be giving up the scarcity rent they could have gotten without price controls. Area D measures only current profits, without considering scarcity rent. When the loss in scarcity rent is considered, producers unambiguously lose net benefits.

FIGURE 8.3 The Effect of Price Controls

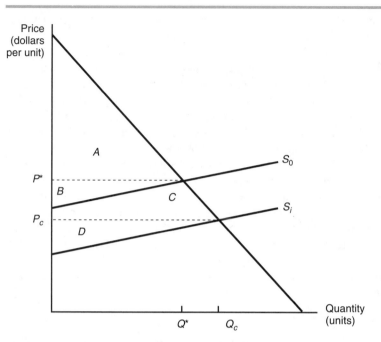

Meanwhile, some future consumers are also worse off. Because the supplies are used more rapidly, the point when the price to future consumers is higher than it would be otherwise will eventually be reached. The higher price implies lower consumer surplus.

Congress may view scarcity rent as a possible source of revenue to transfer from producers to consumers. As we have seen, however, scarcity rent is an opportunity cost that serves a distinct purpose—the protection of future consumers. When government attempts to reduce this scarcity rent through price controls, the result is an overallocation to current consumers and an underallocation to future consumers. Thus, what appears to be a transfer from producers to consumers is, in large part, also a transfer from future consumers to present consumers. Because current consumers mean current votes and future consumers may not know whom to blame by the time shortages appear, price controls are politically attractive. Unfortunately, they are also inefficient: The losses to future consumers and producers are greater than the gains to current consumers. Because they distort the allocation toward the present, controls are also unfair. Thus, markets in the presence of price controls are indeed myopic, but the problem lies with the controls, not with the market.

Over the long run, price controls end up harming consumers rather than helping them. Scarcity rent plays an important role in the allocation process, and attempts to eliminate it can create more problems than are solved. After long debating the price control issue, Congress passed the Natural Gas Policy Act on 9 November 1978. This act initiated the eventual phased decontrol of natural gas prices. Included among its other provisions was a movement away from the average cost pricing of substitute gas for industrial customers and the imposition of price controls for the first time on intrastate gas, until such time as all prices should be decontrolled. On 27 July 1989 President George Bush signed a bill removing in stages all remaining controls on natural gas. By January 1993, no sources of natural gas were subject to price controls.

◆ OIL: THE CARTEL PROBLEM

Inasmuch as we have considered similar effects on natural gas, we shall merely note that price controls have been responsible for much mischief in the oil market as well. A second source of misallocation in the oil market, however, deserves consideration. Most of the world's oil is produced by a cartel called the Organization of Petroleum Exporting Countries (OPEC). The members of this organization collude to exercise power over oil production and prices. Seller power over resources because of a lack of effective competition leads to an inefficient allocation. Sellers with market power can restrict supply and thus force prices higher than they would be otherwise.

A monopolist can extract more scarcity rent from a depletable resource base than competitive suppliers can, simply by restricting supply. The monopolistic transition results in slower production and higher prices. The monopolistic transition to a substitute therefore occurs later than a competitive transition. It also reduces the net benefit society receives from these resources.

The cartelization of the oil suppliers has been very effective. Why? Were the conditions that made it profitable unique to oil, or could oil cartelization be the harbinger of a wave of natural resource cartels? To answer these questions, we must isolate the factors that make cartelization possible. Though many factors are involved, four stand out: (1) the price elasticity of demand for OPEC oil in both the long run and the short run, (2) the income elasticity of demand for oil, (3) the supply responsiveness of the oil producers who are not OPEC members, and (4) the compatibility of interests among members of OPEC.

Price Elasticity of Demand

The price elasticity of oil demand is an important ingredient because it determines how responsive demand is to price. When demand elasticities are less than 1.0 (i.e., when the % quantity response is smaller than the % price change), price increases lead to increased revenue. Exactly how much the revenue would increase when prices increase depends on the price elasticity of demand. In general, the lower the price elasticity of demand, the larger the gains to be derived from forming a cartel.

The price elasticity of demand for oil depends on the opportunities for conservation as well as on the availability of substitutes. As storm windows cut heat losses, the same temperature can be maintained with less heating oil. Smaller automobiles reduce the amount of gasoline needed to travel a given distance. The larger the set of these opportunities and the smaller the cash outlays required to exploit them, the more price elastic the demand. This suggests that the price elasticity of demand in the long run (when sufficient time has passed to allow adjustments) will be greater, perhaps significantly, than in the short run.

The availability of substitutes is important because it limits the degree to which prices can be raised by a producer cartel. Abundant quantities of substitutes available at prices not far above competitive oil prices can set an upper limit on the cartel price. Unless OPEC controls those sources as well—and it doesn't—any attempts to raise prices above those limits would cause the consuming nations to simply switch to these alternative sources; OPEC would price itself out of the market.

Alternative sources clearly exist, although they are expensive and the time of transition is long. Although petroleum could be extracted from unconventional sources—such as deep offshore wells, wells in the polar seas, heavy oils, enhanced recovery techniques, oil shales, tar sands, and synthetic oils—these sources are very expensive. Although coal is clearly a substi-

Example 8.2

Are "Soft Energy" Paths Doomed?

In 1976 a young physicist named Amory Lovins published an article in *Foreign Affairs* that built an immediate following for him and his ideas. His thesis, boldly stated, was that we could follow two paths to our energy future. One, dubbed by Lovins the "hard path," consisted of an increasing reliance on large-scale, centralized technologies, whereas the second, the "soft path," relied more on smaller, decentralized technologies. The former is epitomized by nuclear plants, whereas solar home heating, windmills, and small dams provide examples of the latter. Furthermore, Lovins argued, these paths are mutually exclusive, and the existing system is biased toward the former. If valid, this argument would cast a dark shadow over any expectation that the transition to the soft path would be efficient and smooth.

Lovins suggests that the current system of relying upon centralized power has allowed the preeminence of parties having vested interests in maintaining the status quo. One way this dominance might be perpetuated is for the utilities to refuse to purchase excess power from the soft-path producers. With no market or distribution system, soft-path producers would have less incentive to produce power by these means.

Whatever validity that argument may have had at the time it was made, it seems to have been weakened by congressional action. In 1978 Congress passed the Public Utility Regulatory Policies Act to encourage the production of electricity from renewable resources and from cogeneration systems. *Cogeneration* is the combined production of electricity and useful thermal energy. Among other provisions, this act (1) requires utilities to purchase excess power at a price equal to what it would have cost the utilities to generate the power themselves, (2) requires utilities to provide backup power to those producers at average cost (usually lower than the price utilities pay the producers for excess power), and (3) stipulates that the qualifying small-production units cannot be owned by utilities. Though this is a controversial piece of legislation, undoubtedly it has spurred the development of small, renewable energy sources for producing electricity.

Source: Amory B. Lovins, "Energy Strategy: The Road Not Taken?" *Foreign Affairs* 60 (October 1976): 65–98. The importance of this act to potential investors in renewable resources is described in Colin Norman, "Renewable Power Sparks Financial Interest," *Science* 212 (26 June 1981): 1479–81.

tute for some uses and is available in large supplies, as we shall see in the next section, coal use triggers a number of environmental problems.

Clearly, the ultimate substitute is solar energy, and it is the cost of solar energy that will set the long-run upper limit on the ability of OPEC to raise its prices. Because in many parts of the United States solar energy for space and hot-water heating is currently cost competitive, that limit is probably not substantially higher than recent OPEC prices. Although it will take a significant amount of time for these new technologies to get all the bugs worked out and begin to penetrate the market on a massive scale, the transition seems to be proceeding smoothly. As Example 8.2 indicates, this transition has extended to electricity production as well, which some observers felt would resist that change.

Income Elasticity of Demand

The income elasticity of oil demand is important because it indicates how sensitive oil demand is to growth in the world economy. At constant prices, as income grows, oil demand should grow. This continual increase in demand fortifies the ability of OPEC to raise its prices. High income elasticities of demand support the cartelization of oil. All other things being equal, the higher the income elasticity of demand, the higher the price would have to rise to bring demand to zero (in the absence of substitutes) or the more rapidly it would have to rise to the level of substitute resource, when one is available.

The income elasticity of demand is also important because it registers how sensitive demand is to the business cycle. The higher the income elasticity of demand, the more sensitive demand is. This is a major source of the 1983 weakening of the cartel. A recession caused a large reduction in the demand for oil, putting new pressure on the cartel to absorb this demand reduction.

Non-OPEC Suppliers

Another key factor in the ability of producer nations to exercise power over a natural resource market is their ability to prevent new suppliers (i.e., those not part of the cartel) from entering the market and undercutting the price. OPEC current produces about two thirds of the world's oil. If the remaining producers were able, in the face of higher prices, to expand their supply dramatically, they would increase the amount of oil supplied and cause the prices to fall, decreasing OPEC's market share. If this response were large enough, the allocation of oil would approach the competitive allocation.

Currently, only Mexico appears to have large enough reserves to make an individual difference in the world oil market. However, because both the size of its reserves and its production profile are uncertain, it is difficult to assess Mexico's ultimate impact on the future world market.

This does not mean that non-OPEC members collectively do not have an impact on price. They do. The cartel must take the nonmembers into account when setting prices. The impact of this competitive fringe on OPEC behavior was dramatically illustrated by events in the 1985–1986 period. In 1979, OPEC accounted for approximately 50 percent of world oil production, but by 1986 this had fallen to approximately 30 percent. Total world oil production during this period was down over 10 percent for all producers, so the pressures on the cartel mounted, and prices ultimately fell. The real cost of crude oil imports in the United States fell from $34.95 per barrel in 1981 to $11.41 in 1986 (Figure 8.4). OPEC simply was not able to hold the line on prices. The necessary reductions in production were too large for the individual cartel members to sustain.

Compatibility of Member Interests

The final factor we shall consider in determining the potential for cartelization of natural resource markets is the internal cohesion of the cartel. When there is only one seller, the objective of that seller can be pursued without worrying about alienating others who could undermine the profitability of the enterprise. In a cartel composed of many sellers, that freedom is no longer as wide-ranging. The incentives of each member and the incentives of the group as a whole may diverge.

Cartel members have a strong incentive to cheat. A cheater, if undetected by the other members, could surreptitiously lower its oil price and steal part of the market away from the

FIGURE 8.4 Real Crude Oil Price (1973-1998)

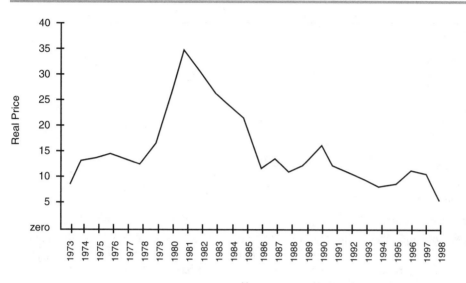

Source: Price of Crude Oil: monthly Energy Review Online (http://www.eia.doe.gove/emeu/mer/prices.html) CPI: Bureau of Labor Statistics (http://stats.bls.gov/epihome.htm)

others. Formally, the price elasticity of demand facing an individual member is substantially higher than that for the group as a whole, because some of the increase in individual sales at a lower price represents sales reductions for other members. With a higher price elasticity, lower prices maximize profits. Thus, successful cartelization presupposes a means for detecting cheating and enforcing the collusive agreement.[3]

In addition to cheating, however, there is another threat to the stability of cartels—the degree to which members fail to agree on pricing and output decisions. Oil provides an excellent example of how these dissensions can arise. Since the 1974 rise of OPEC as a world power, Saudi Arabia has exercised a moderating influence on the pricing decisions of OPEC. Why?

One highly significant reason is the size of Saudi Arabia's oil reserves (see Table 8.1). Saudi Arabia holds approximately 33 percent of the OPEC proven reserves; its reserves are larger than those of any other member. Because of this, Saudi Arabia has an incentive to preserve the value of those resources. It is worried about setting prices so high as to undercut the future demand for its oil. As was stated earlier, the demand for oil in the long run is more price elastic than in the short run. Meanwhile, the countries with smaller reserves know that in the long run their reserves will be gone, and they are more concerned about the near future. Because alternative sources of supply are not much of a threat in the near future because of long development times, other countries want to extract as much rent as possible now.

---

[3]During February, 1985, OPEC hired a large Dutch accounting firm to help it detect cheating among its members. See "Dutch Accountants Take on a Formidable Task: Ferreting Out 'Cheaters' in the Ranks of OPEC," *The Wall Street Journal* (26 February 1985): 39.

TABLE 8.1 The World's Largest Oil Reserves

Country	Reserves (in billions of barrels)
Saudi Arabia	261.5
Iraq	112.5
United Arab Emirates	97.8
Kuwait	96.5
Iran	93.0
Venezuela	71.7
Russia	48.6
Mexico	40.0
Libya	29.5
China	24.0
United States	22.5
Nigeria	16.8

Source: *Oil and Gas Journal,* (http://www.eia.doe.gov/emeu/iea/table81.htm).

The size of Saudi Arabia's production also gives it the potential to make its influence felt. Its capacity to produce is so large that it can unilaterally affect world prices. In January 1981, for example, it was producing approximately 10.3 million barrels of crude oil a day—representing about 41 percent of all OPEC production.

Cartelization is not an easy path for producers to pursue. However, when it is possible it can be very profitable. When the resource is a strategic and pervasive raw material, cartelization can be very costly for consuming nations.

Strategic-material cartelization also confers on the members political, as well as economic, power. Economic power can become political power when the revenue is used to purchase weapons or the capacity to produce weapons. The producer nations can also use an embargo of the material as a lever to cajole reluctant adversaries into foreign policy concessions.

◆ TRANSITION FUELS: ENVIRONMENTAL PROBLEMS

Currently the industrialized world depends on oil and gas for most of its energy. In the distant future we shall make a transition to renewable sources of energy. How about the intermediate time period?

Though some observers believe the transition to renewable sources will proceed so rapidly that no transition fuels will be necessary, most believe that transition fuels will probably play a significant role. Though other contenders, such as natural gas from deep wells, are clearly present, the fuels receiving the most attention as transition fuels are coal and uranium.

Domestic coal is abundantly available. On a heat-equivalent basis, coal resources are approximately 22 times as large as oil and gas resources combined. Neither availability nor dependency on foreign countries is an issue with coal.

Resource availability is a problem with uranium as long as we depend on conventional reactors. However, if the United States moves to the new generation of breeder reactors, which can use a wider range of fuels, availability will cease to be an important issue. On a heat-equivalent basis, if they are used in conventional reactors, domestic uranium resources are 4.2 times as great as domestic oil and gas resources. With breeder reactors, however, the U.S. uranium base is 252 times the size of its oil and gas base.

The main issue defining the role for these two fuels involves their environmental impact. Coal's main drawback is its contribution to air pollution. Its high sulfur content makes it a potentially large source of sulfur dioxide emissions, one of the chief culprits in the acid rain problem. It is also a major source of particulate emissions and carbon dioxide, one of the greenhouse gases implicated in global warming. Because a detailed analysis of these environmental problems follows in subsequent chapters, we shall not consider them any further here except to note that if those who burn coal fail to consider these environmental costs, the market will foster an excessive reliance on coal.

The other main transition fuel, uranium, used in nuclear electrical generation stations, has its own limitations, principally safety. Two sources of concern stand out: (1) nuclear accidents and (2) the storage of radioactive waste. Is the market likely to make the correct decisions on these questions? In both cases the answer is no, given the current decision-making environment. Let's consider these issues one by one.

The production of electricity by nuclear reactors requires radioactive elements. If these elements escape into the atmosphere (say, during a nuclear accident) and come in contact with humans in sufficient concentrations, they produce birth defects, cancer, and death. Some radioactive elements may also escape during the normal operation of a plant, but the greatest risk of nuclear power is still the threat of nuclear accidents.

Nuclear accidents may inject large doses of radioactivity into the environment. There are many possible ways in which this might happen. The most dangerous of these possibilities is the core meltdown. Unlike other types of electrical generation, nuclear processes continue to generate heat even after the reactor is turned off. This means that the nuclear fuel must be continuously cooled or the heat levels will escalate beyond the design capacity of the reactor shield. If, in this case, the reactor vessel should fracture, clouds of radioactive gases and particulates would be released into the atmosphere.

For some time, conventional wisdom had held that nuclear accidents involving a core meltdown were only a remote possibility. On 25 April 1986, however, a serious core meltdown occurred at the Chernobyl nuclear plant in the Soviet Union. Though safety standards are generally conceded to be much higher in the Western industrialized world than in the former Soviet Union, this incident has added yet another burden for an already troubled industry to bear.

Nuclear power has been beset by economic as well as political forces. New nuclear power plant construction has become much more expensive, in part because of the increasing regulatory requirements designed to provide a safer system. Its economic advantage over coal has dissipated, and the demand for new nuclear plants has been eliminated. In the United States, for example, in 1973, 219 nuclear power plants were either planned or in operation. By the end of 1998 that number had fallen to 104, the difference being explained by cancellations. No new applications for nuclear plants are pending.

Not all nations are making the same choice with respect to the nuclear option. Sweden not only has pledged not to build any new nuclear plants, but also plans to shut down those currently in operation by early in the twenty-first century. In France and Japan, however, standardized plant design and regulatory stability have resulted in electricity generating costs for nuclear power that are lower than those for coal-generated power. Both countries are expanding the role of nuclear power.

An additional concern relates to storing nuclear wastes. The waste storage issue relates to both ends of the nuclear fuel cycle—the disposal of uranium tailings from the mining process and of spent fuel from the reactors, though the latter receives most of the publicity. Uranium tailings contain several elements, the most prominent being thorium-230, which decays with a half-life of 78,000 years to a radioactive, chemically inert gas, radon-222. Once formed, this gas has a very short half-life (38 days).

The spend fuel from nuclear reactors contains a variety of radioactive elements with quite different half-lives. In the first few centuries, the dominant contributors to radioactivity are fission products, principally strontium-90 and cesium-137. After approximately 1,000 years, most of these elements will have decayed, leaving the transuranic elements having substantially longer half-lives. These remaining elements would remain a risk for up to 240,000 years. Thus, decisions made today affect not only the level of risk borne by the current generation—in the form of nuclear accidents—but also that borne by a host of succeeding generations (because of the longevity of radioactive risk from the disposal of spent fuel).

Can we expect the market to make the correct choice with respect to nuclear power and accident possibilities? Because this seems to be a clear case of externalities, we might expect the answer to be no. Third parties, those living near the reactor, would receive the brunt of the damage from a nuclear accident. Would the utility have an incentive to choose the efficient level of precaution?

If the utility had to compensate fully for all the damages caused, then the answer would be yes. In the United States full compensation is not paid by the individual utilities for two reasons: (1) the role of the government in sharing the risk and (2) the role of insurance in underwriting the risk.

When the government first allowed private industry to use atomic power to generate electricity, there were no takers. No utility could afford the damages if an accident occurred. No insurance company would underwrite the risk. Then, in 1957, with the passage of the Price-Anderson Act, the government underwrote the liability. That act provided for a liability ceiling of $560 million (i.e., once that amount had been paid out, no more claims would be honored), of which the government would bear $500 million. The industry would pick up the remaining $60 million. The Act was originally designed to expire in 10 years, at which time the industry would assume full responsibility for the liability.

The Act didn't expire, though over time a steady diminution of the government's share of the liability has occurred. Currently, the liability ceiling still exists, albeit at a higher level; the amount of private insurance has increased; and a system has been set up to assess all utilities by retrospective premium in the event an accident occurs.

The effect of the Price-Anderson Act is to reduce the expected cost of nuclear power to the utility choosing to use it. Both the liability ceiling and the portion of the liability borne by government reduce the potential compensation the utility would have to pay. As the industry assumes an increasing portion of the liability burden, the risk sharing embodied in the retrospective premium system (the means by which it assumes that burden) breaks the link between precautionary behavior by the individual utility and the compensation it might have to pay. Under this system, increased safety by the utility does not reduce its premiums.

The individual utilities pay into a fund that compensates victims. The important point is that the actual cost of an accident to the utility is not sensitive to the level of precautions it takes. The cost to all utilities, whether they have accidents or not, is the premium paid both before and after any accident. These premiums do not reflect the amount of precautionary measures taken by an individual plant; therefore, individual utilities have little incentive to provide an efficient amount of safety.[4]

In recognition of the utilities' lower-than-efficient concern for safety, the federal government has established the Nuclear Regulatory Commission (NRC), which is empowered to oversee the safety of nuclear reactors, among its other responsibilities. In the aftermath of the nuclear accident at Three Mile Island on 28 March 1979, a Presidential commission was established to provide an independent evaluation of this system of safety regulation. Its final report,[5] issued on 30 October 1979, was highly critical of the existing system and made a series of recommendations to improve it. Though the problem of nuclear accidents is manageable in principle, it may or may not be manageable in practice.

Both the operating safety issue and the nuclear waste storage issue can be viewed as a problem of determining appropriate compensation. Those who gain from nuclear power should be forced to compensate those who lose. If they can't, in the absence of externalities, the net benefits from adopting nuclear power are not positive. If nuclear power is efficient, by definition, the gains to the gainers will exceed the losses to the losers. Nonetheless, it is important that this compensation actually be paid, because without compensation, the losers can block the efficient allocation.

A compensation approach is already being taken in those countries still expanding the role of nuclear power. The French government, for example, has announced a policy of reducing electricity rates by roughly 15 percent for those living near nuclear stations. And in Japan during 1980, the Tohoku Electric Power Company paid the equivalent of $4.3 million to residents of Ojika, in northern Japan, to get them to withdraw their opposition to a nuclear power plant being built there.

This approach could also help resolve the current political controversy over the location of nuclear waste disposal sites. Most plans current focus on burying the waste in some geologically stable formation. Current and future generations of people living near the chosen sites would have a tendency to oppose nuclear power because the costs to them would appear to outweigh the benefits. To others, however, who might enjoy nuclear-produced electricity and might live far from the sites, the benefits might exceed the costs. This rationale prompted a number of states to pass laws permitting nuclear power but prohibiting the permanent storage of waste within their borders.

Under a compensation scheme, those consuming nuclear power should be taxed in order to compensate those who live in the areas of the disposal site. If the compensation is adequate to induce them to accept the site, then nuclear power is a viable option and the costs of disposal are ultimately borne by the consumers. Some towns, such as Naurita, Colorado, are actively seeking to become disposal sites. If taxes to obtain a sufficient number of disposal sites are so high that nuclear energy becomes noncompetitive, then nuclear energy is not an efficient source.

Are future generations adequately represented in the transaction? The quick answer is no, but that answer is not correct. Those living around the sites will experience declines in the

---

[4]For further discussion of this point, see Jeffrey A. Dubin and Geoffry S. Rothwell, "Subsidy to Nuclear Power Through Price-Anderson Liability Limit," *Contemporary Policy Issues* (July 1990).

[5]The President's Commission on the Accident at Three Mile Island, *The Need for Change: The Legacy of TMI* (New York: Pergamon Press, 1979).

market value of land, reflecting the increased risk of living or working there. The payment system is designed to compensate those who experience the reduction, the current generation. Future generations, should they decide to live near a disposal site, would be compensated by lower land values. If the land values were not cheap enough to compensate them, they would not have to live there. As long as full information on the risks posed is available, those who do bear the cost of locating near the sites do so only if they are willing to accept the risk in return for lower land values.[6]

◆ CONSERVATION AND LOAD MANAGEMENT

As the previous discussion indicated, environmental problems associated with transition fuels present particular difficulties for generating electrical power. Although alternative fuels and solar power will eventually play an increasingly important role, most experts seem to feel that they will penetrate the market slowly as they become more familiar and accessible. How, then, is the transition to these long-term solutions to be managed by the electrical utilities sector in light of the problems associated with transition fuels?

For a number of utilities, conservation has assumed an increasingly significant role. To a major extent, conservation has already been stimulated by market forces. High oil and natural gas prices, coupled with the rapidly increasing cost of both nuclear and coal-fired generating stations, have reduced electrical demand significantly. Yet many public utilities commissions, (the state bodies charged with regulating the production, transmission, and sale of electricity) are coming to the conclusion that more conservation is needed.

Perhaps the most significant role for conservation is its ability to defer capacity expansion. Each new electrical generating plant tends to cost more than the last, and frequently the cost increase is substantial. When the new plants come on line, rate increases to finance the new plant are necessary. By reducing the demand for electricity, conservation delays the date when the new capacity is needed to satisfy the higher demand. Delays in the need to construct new plants translate into delays in rate increases as well.

The dominant electricity pricing system is ill-designed to stimulate the efficient amount of conservation. Average cost pricing is common. This pricing system implies that the new, higher-cost sources are averaged in with the lower-cost sources, yielding a rate that is substantially lower than the true marginal cost of the power being generated. Thus, the consumer considering investing in conservation would save less money by conserving with average cost pricing than would be the case if the energy saved were priced at its true marginal cost. Less than an efficient amount of conservation would be the expected outcome.

Utilities are reacting to this situation in a number of ways. One is to consider investing in conservation, rather than in new plants, when conservation is the cheaper alternative. Typical programs have established systems of rebates for residential customers who install conservation measures in their homes, have provided free home weatherization to qualified low-income homeowners, have offered owners of multifamily residential buildings incentives for installing solar water-heating systems, and have provided subsidized energy audits to inform

---

[6]For further discussion of possible compensation schemes, see Robert Cameron Mitchell and Richard T. Carson, "Property Rights, Protest, and the Siting of Hazardous Waste Facilities," and Howard Kunreuther and Paul R. Kleindorfer, "A Sealed-Bid Auction Mechanism for Siting Noxious Facilities," *American Economic Review* 76, No. 2 (May 1986): 285–90, 295–99.

customers about money-saving conservation opportunities. Similar incentives have been provided to the commercial, agricultural, and industrial sectors. Though the costs of these investments must also be recovered from customers, most report that the savings have been dramatic and customer satisfaction has been high.[7] Less power consumed means available energy supplies last longer.

The total amount of electrical energy demanded in a given year is not the only concern utilities have. They are also concerned with how that energy demand is spread out over the year. The capacity of the system must be high enough to satisfy the demand during the periods when the energy demand is highest (called the peak period). During other periods, much of the capacity remains underutilized.

Demand during the peak period imposes two rather special costs on utilities. First, the peaking units, those generating facilities fired up only during the peak periods, produce electricity at a much higher marginal cost than do base-load plants, those fired up virtually all the time. Peaking units are typically cheaper to build than base-load plants, but they have higher operating costs. Second, it is the growth in peak demand that frequently triggers the need for capacity expansion. Slowing down the growth in peak demand may delay the need for new, expensive capacity expansion so that a higher proportion of the power needs can be met by the most efficient generating plants.

Utilities are responding to this problem by adopting load-management techniques to produce a more balanced use of this capacity over the year. One economic load-management technique is called *peak-load pricing*. Peak-load pricing attempts to impose the full (higher) marginal cost of supplying peak power on those consuming peak power by charging higher prices during the peak period.

Although many utilities have now begun to use simple versions of this approach, some are experimenting with very innovative ways of implementing rather refined versions of this system. One innovative system, for example, transmits electricity prices every five minutes over regular power lines. In a customer's household, the lines attached to one or more appliances can be controlled by switches that turn the power off any time the prevailing price exceeds a limit established by the customer. Other, less sophisticated pricing systems simply inform consumers in advance what prices will prevail in predetermined peak periods.

Studies by economists at the Rand Corporation in California[8] indicate that even the rudimentary versions of peak-load pricing work. Based on the actual experience with time-of-day rates by more than 6,000 commercial and industrial customers, Rand found that business customers saved themselves and utilities on average $1,000 per year for an added metering cost of only $50. Working with an additional sample of over 3,000, the authors found that residential customers also saved by shifting some of their demand to less expensive periods. The greatest shifts were registered by the largest residential customers and those with several electrical appliances.

Interestingly, this study found the gains from peak-load pricing in the United States to be somewhat lower than those reported for European customers, who have been exposed to

---

[7]For the contrary view that these programs are really quite costly, see Paul L. Joskow and Donald B. Matron, "What Does Utility-Subsidized Energy Efficiency Really Cost?" *Science* 260 (16 April 1993): 281, 370.

[8]Jean Paul Acton, et al., *Time-of-Day Electricity Rates for the United States*, Report R3086-HF (Santa Monica, CA: Rand Corporation, 1983), and Rolla Edward Park, et al., *Response to Time-of-Day Electricity Rates by Large Business Customers: Initial Analysis of Data from Ten U.S. Utilities*, Report R-3080-HF/MD/RC (Santa Monica, CA: Rand Corporation, 1983).

peak-load pricing for a longer period of time. Studies of the European experience have found that a significant proportion of the total amount of electricity consumed can be shifted to a period of excess capacity, particularly in the industrial sector.[9] Attributing the large European response in part to the longer time Europeans have had to adapt to this system, the authors speculate that the longer-term response by U.S. customers could turn out to be quite a bit greater than that already recorded.

A third innovation in the utility sector involves procedures for internalizing the environmental costs. Those who have typically been assigned the responsibility for regulating utility prices have focused almost exclusively on holding prices down by choosing the cheapest sources of power. Unfortunately, only generating and distribution costs were considered; the damage caused by emissions was ignored. The resulting choices turned out not to be the cheapest when all costs were considered.

To rectify this imbalance in the procedures for choosing generating sources, some states have begun explicitly incorporating environmental costs in their decision-making process. New York State, for example, adds 1.4 cents per kilowatt-hour to the estimated cost of electricity produced from fossil fuel sources to account for the various negative environmental effects. By creating a more level playing field for competing sources, this technique has increased the competitiveness of renewable power sources such as hydro, solar, and wind.

◆ THE LONG RUN

Ultimately, our energy needs will have to be fulfilled from renewable energy sources, either because the depletable energy sources have been exhausted or, as is more likely, because the environmental costs of using the depletable sources have become so high that renewable sources are cheaper.

Depending on how the scientific uncertainty is resolved, the most compelling case for the transition may well be made by the mounting evidence that the global climate is being jeopardized by current and prospective energy-consumption patterns. If the third world were to follow the energy-intensive, fossil-fuel-based path to development pioneered by the industrialized nations, the amount of carbon dioxide emissions injected into the air would be unprecedented. One half of all developing nations rely on imported oil for more than 75 percent of their commercial energy needs.[10] A transition away from fossil fuels to other energy forms in both the industrialized and the third-world nations would be an important ingredient in any strategy to reduce carbon dioxide emissions. Can our institutions manage that transition in a timely and effective manner?

Renewable energy comes in many different forms. Hydro power can be derived from flowing water; biomass can be burned; solar energy can be used to produce heat used to drive steam turbines or converted directly into electricity by means of photovoltaics; wind energy can drive turbines; hydrogen extracted from the air by solar energy can fuel cars or furnaces; and geothermal energy can be captured from the bowels of the earth and put to useful work.

[9]Bridger Mitchell, Willard G. Manning, Jr., Jan Paul Acton, *Peak-Load Pricing: European Lessons for U.S. Experience* (Cambridge, MA: Ballinger, 1978).

[10]U.S. Agency for International Development (AID), *Decentralized Hydropower in AID's Development Assistance Program* (Washington, DC: AID, 1986).

The extent to which these sources will penetrate the market will depend upon their relative cost and consumer acceptance. Relative cost will no doubt change over time as research uncovers better ways to harness the power of renewable sources. Perhaps the best example of how research can lower costs is provided by the experience with photovoltaics.

Photovoltaics involves the direct conversion of solar energy to electricity (as opposed to indirect conversions such as when steam energy is used to drive a turbine). Anticipating a huge potential market, private industry has been very interested in photovoltaics and has poured a lot of research dollars into improving its commercial viability. The research has paid off. In 1976, the average market price for a photovoltaic module was $44 per peak watt installed, and 0.5 megawatts were sold. By 1997 this had fallen to $4.06 per peak watt.[11] Rural electrification projects using photovoltaics are slowly spreading into the third world.

Windpower is also beginning to penetrate the market on a rather large scale. New turbine technology has reduced the cost and increased the reliability of wind-generated electricity to the point that it now can compete with conventional sources in favorable sites—even when environmental costs have not been internalized. (Favorable sites are those with sufficiently steady, strong winds). Although many unexploited favorable sites still exist around the world, the share of windpower in the total energy mix will ultimately be limited by the diminishing availability of those sites.

Somewhat lower down the scale in terms of commercial viability is using hydrogen as a fuel. If an electric current (e.g., produced by photovoltaics) is conducted through a reservoir of water, the liquid splits into its constituent elements—hydrogen and oxygen. When burned with oxygen, hydrogen creates a single by-product—drinkable water.

Hydrogen has many potential uses, including serving as a fuel for automobiles. Prototype cars that use this fuel have already been built. Although the costs of supplying and using this fuel have declined in response to recent research, the declines are not yet sufficiently large to make it a competitor in the near future.

Consumer acceptance is an important ingredient in the transition to any alternative source of energy. New systems are usually less reliable and more expensive than old systems. Once they become heavily used, their reliability normally increases and cost declines; experience is a good teacher. Because the early consumers, the pioneers, experience both lower reliability and higher costs, procrastination can be an optimal individual strategy. If every consumer procrastinates about switching, however, the industry will not be able to operate at a sufficient scale and will not be able to gain enough experience to produce the reliability and lower cost that will assure a large, stable market. How can this initial consumer reluctance be overcome?

One strategy, the one used in the United States, involves using tax dollars to subsidize purchases by the pioneers. Once the market is sufficiently large that it can begin to take advantage of economies of scale and can eliminate the initial sources of unreliability, the subsidies can be eliminated. The available empirical evidence suggests that the tax-credit approach has significantly increased the degree of market penetration of solar equipment in the United States.[12]

In the United States, substantial tax credits authorized at both the federal and the state levels were influential in inducing a number of independent producers to accept the

[11]http://www.eia.doe.gov/cneaf/solar.renewables/rea_data/html/chapter2.html#1 (accessed at 1/20/00).

[12]Catherine A. Durham, Bonnie G. Colby, and Molly Longstreth, "The Impact of State Tax Credits and Energy Prices on Adoption of Solar Energy Systems," *Land Economics* 64 (November 1988): 347–55; Gene R. Fry, "The Economics of Home Solar Water Heating and the Role of Solar Tax Credits," *Land Economics* 62 (May 1986): 134–44.

financial and engineering risks associated with developing wind power. Although the original federal tax credits expired in 1985, a 1.5 cents per kilowatt-hour production incentive for producers of wind-power-generated electricity was implemented in 1992. It expired in 1999.

In contrast with the on-again, off-again nature of the U.S. subsidies, European nations have been steadily increasing the economic incentives for encouraging wind power. As a result, Europe is expected to dominate the production of wind power by the beginning of the twenty-first century. England, Denmark, Germany, and the Netherlands are expected to lead the way.

The penetration by renewable energy resources would have been even greater if the cartel had been able to sustain the very high oil prices that were in effect at the beginning of the 1980s. As oil prices fell in real terms, both residential and commercial enthusiasm for making the transition to solar energy was undermined. Because saving money is a primary motivation for making the switch and low oil prices translate into relatively low or even negative savings, uncertainty associated with the path of future oil and natural gas prices could continue to be a barrier to the transition.

SUMMARY

We have seen that the relationship between government and the market is not always a harmonious and efficient one. In the past, price controls have tended to reduce energy conservation, to discourage exploration and supply, to cause biases in the substitution among fuel types, and to penalize future consumers. This important area makes a clear case for less, not more, regulation.

This is not universally true, however. Other dimensions of the energy problem suggest the need for some government role. The government should ensure that the costs of energy fully reflect the potentially large environmental costs and that fluctuating resource prices do not undermine the transition to appropriate renewable energy resources that make sense in the long run. Government should also oversee nuclear reactor safety and should ensure that communities forced to accept nuclear waste disposal sites are fully compensated. Given the environmental difficulties with both of the traditional transition fields (coal and uranium), conservation and load-management techniques are now playing and will continue to play a larger role in the electric utilities sector. Two economic measures that have been instrumental in ushering in this greater role are (1) subsidizing conservation where it is cheaper for the utility than capacity expansion and (2) peak-load pricing. The potential for an efficient allocation of energy resources by the economic and political institutions clearly exists, even if it has not always occurred in the past.

FURTHER READING

Goldemberg, J. "Solving the Energy Problems in Developing Countries," *Energy Journal* 11, No. 1 (1990): 19–24. The energy-development connection from a developing-country perspective.

International Energy Agency. *Taxing Energy: Why and How?* (Paris: OECD, 1993). Examines energy taxation in five OECD countries.

Johansson, Thomas B., et al., eds. *Renewable Energy: Sources for Fuels and Electricity* (Washington, DC: Island Press, 1993). The first comprehensive reference work on alternative energy sources to appear in more than a decade. This group of studies was commissioned to provide input to the 1992 United Nations Conference on Environment and Development (the "Earth Summit").

Kosmo, Mark. *Money to Burn? The High Cost of Energy Subsidies* (Washington, DC: World Resources Institute, 1987). An examination of the extent to which current energy choices have been biased by the existence of subsidies.

Shea, Cynthia Pollock. "Shifting to Renewable Energy," in *State of the World: 1988,* Lester R. Brown et al., eds. (New York: W. W. Norton, 1988): 62–82. A wealth of information on how the transition to renewable resources is shaping up around the world.

ADDITIONAL REFERENCES

Bhatia, Ramesh, and Armand Pereira. *Socioeconomic Aspects of Renewable Energy Technologies* (New York: Praeger, 1988).

Congressional Budget Office. "Cleaning Up the Department of Energy's Nuclear Weapons Complex" (Washington, DC: U.S. Congress, 1994).

Dubin, Jeffrey A., and Geoffrey S. Rothwell. "Subsidy to Nuclear Power through Price Anderson Liability Limit," *Contemporary Policy Issues* 8 (July 1990): 73–79.

Durham, Catherine A., Bonnie G. Colby, and Molly Longstreth. "The Impact of State Tax Credits and Energy Prices on Adoption of Solar Energy Systems," *Land Economics* 64 (November 1988): 347–55.

Folkens-Landau, E. "The Social Cost of Imported Oil," *Energy Journal* 5 (July 1984): 4158.

Fry, Gene R. "The Economics of Home Solar Water Heating and the Role of Solar Tax Credits," *Land Economics* 62 (May 1986): 134–44.

Griffin, James M. "OPEC Behavior: A Test of Alternative Hypotheses," *American Economic Review* 75 (December 1985): 954–63.

Griffin, James M., and Henry B. Steele. *Energy Economics and Policy,* 2nd ed. (New York: Academic Press, 1986).

Hall, Darwin C., ed. "Social and Private Costs of Alternative Energy Technologies," a special issue of *Contemporary Policy Issues* (July 1990).

Kunreuther, Howard, and Paul R. Kleindorfer. "A Sealed-Bid Auction Mechanism for Sitting Noxious Facilities," *American Economic Review* 76 (May 1986): 295–99.

Lee, Dwight R. "Price Controls, Binding Constraints, and Intertemporal Economic Decision Making," *Journal of Political Economy* 86 (1978): 293–301.

Lerner, A. P. "OPEC—A Plan—If You Can't Beat Them, Join Them," *Atlantic Economic Journal* 8 (September 1980): 1–3.

Lind, Robert C., et al. *Discounting for Time and Risk in Energy Policy* (Washington, DC: Resources for the Future, 1982).

Mitchell, Bridger M., Willard G. Manning, Jr., Jan Paul Acton, *Peak-Load Pricing: European Lessons for U. S. Experience* (Cambridge, MA: Ballinger, 1978).

Mitchell, Robert Cameron, and Richard T. Carson, "Property Rights, Protest, and the Siting of Hazardous Waste Facilities," *American Economic Review* 76 (May 1986): 285–90.

Moreira, J.R., and J. Goldemberg. "The Alcohol Program," *Energy Policy,* Vol. 27, No. 4 (1999): 229-245.

Nichols, A. L., and R. J. Zeckhauser. "Stockpiling Strategies and Cartel Prices," *Bell Journal of Economics* 7 (Spring 1976): 66–96.

Oliver, M., and T. Jackson. "The Market for Solar Photovoltaics," *Energy Policy,* Vol. 27, No. 7 (1999): 371-385.

Salant, S. W., "Exhaustible Resources and Industrial Structure: A Nash-Cournot Approach to the World Oil Market," *Journal of Political Economy* 84 (1976): 1079–93.

Teisberg, Thomas, "A Dynamic Programming Model of the U.S. Strategic Petroleum Reserve," *Bell Journal of Economics* 12 (autumn 1981): 526–46.

Toman, Michael, and Molly K. Macauley. "Risk Aversion and the Insurance Value of Strategic Oil Stockpiling," *Resources and Energy* 8 (1986): 151–65.

U.S. Agency for International Development (AID). *Decentralized Hydropower in AID's Development Assistance Program* (Washington, DC: AID, 1986).

West, Ronald E., and Frank Kreith. *Economic Analysis of Solar Thermal Energy Systems* (Cambridge, MA: MIT Press, 1988).

WEB SITES OF INTEREST

1. *www.eia.doe.gov/*

   U.S. Energy Information Administration. This is an excellent site on all aspects of energy; contains information on depletable and renewable energy sources as well as "transition fuels."

2. *www.doe.gov/*

   U.S. Department of Energy. Contains organizational chart, news and information (speeches, press releases), science education, people and places, field and operations offices, energy laboratories.

3. *www.eren.doe.gov/*

   Energy Efficiency and Renewable Energy Network (EREN). Contains informatin on energy efficiency, including new technologies, renewable energy information, access to 600 links and 80,000 documents; it also has a fuel economy section where you can compare specific car models.

4. *http://www.iea.org/homechoi.htm*

   International Energy Agency. A wealth of information (publications and statistics) on the international energy situation and the links between energy use and climate change.

DISCUSSION QUESTIONS

1. Should benefit-cost analysis play the dominant role in deciding the proportion of U.S. electrical energy to be supplied by nuclear power? Why or why not?

2. One economist (Lerner [1980]) proposed that the United States impose a tariff on oil imports equal to 100 percent of the import price. This tariff is designed to reduce dependence on foreign sources as well as to discourage OPEC from raising prices (because, as a result of the tariff, the delivered price would rise twice as much as the OPEC increase, causing a large subsequent reduction in consumption). Should this become public policy? Why or why not?

9

Water

You'll never miss the water
Til your well runs dry.

WILLIAM CHRISTOPHER HANDY, "JOE TURNER'S BLUES" (1915)

◆ INTRODUCTION

To the red country and part of the gray country of Oklahoma, the last rains came gently, and they did not cut the scarred earth. . . . The sun flared down on the growing corn day after day until a line of brown spread along the edge of each green bayonet. The clouds appeared and went away, and in awhile they did not try anymore.

With these words John Steinbeck sets the scene for his powerful novel *The Grapes of Wrath*. Drought and poor soil-conservation practices combined to destroy the agriculture institutions that had provided nourishment and livelihood to Oklahoma residents since settlement in that area had begun. In desperation, many of those who had worked that land were forced to abandon not only their possessions, but their past. Moving to California to seek employment, they were uprooted, only to be caught up in a web of exploitation and hopelessness.

Based on an actual situation, the novel demonstrates how the social fabric can tear when subject to tremendous stress, such as an inadequate availability of water, and how painful those tears can be. Clearly, problems such as these should be anticipated and prevented as much as possible.

Water is one of the essential elements of life. We humans depend not only on an intake of water to replace the continual loss of body fluids but also on food sources that themselves need water to survive. This resource deserves special attention.

In this chapter we shall examine how our economic and political institutions have allocated this important resource in the past and how they might improve on its allocation in the future. We initiate our inquiry by examining the likelihood and severity of water scarcity. Turning to the management of our water resources, we will define the efficient allocation of groundwater and surface water over time and compare these allocations to current practice, particularly in the United States. Finally, we will examine the menu of opportunities for meaningful institutional reform.

◆ THE POTENTIAL FOR WATER SCARCITY

The earth's renewable supply of water is governed by the hydrologic cycle, a system of continuous water circulation (Figure 9.1). Enormous quantities of water are cycled each year

FIGURE 9.1 The Hydrologic Cycle

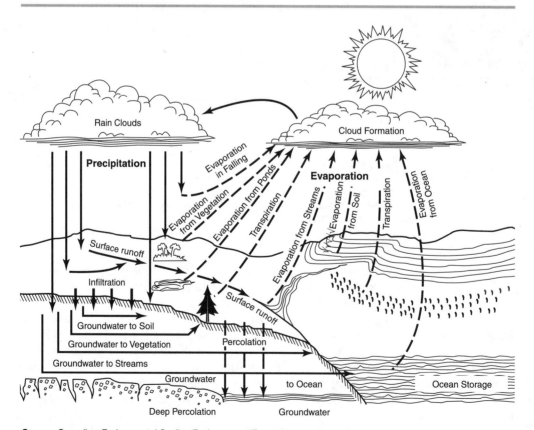

Source: Council on Environmental Quality, *Environmental Trends* (Washington, D.C.: Government Printing Office, 1981): 210

through this system, though only a fraction of circulated water is available each year for human use.

Available supplies are derived from two rather different sources—surface water and groundwater. As the name implies, *surface water* consists of the fresh water in rivers, lakes, and reservoirs that collects and flows on the earth's surface. By contrast, *groundwater* collects in porous layers of underground rock known as *aquifers*. Though some groundwater is renewed by percolation of rain or melted snow, most has been accumulated over geologic time and, because of its location, cannot be recharged once it is depleted. Of the 16,000 trillion gallons of groundwater estimated to be available for extraction in the United States, only about 400 trillion gallons are available on a renewable basis. The rest is a finite, depletable resource.

If we were simply to add up the available supply of fresh water (total runoff) on a global scale and compare it with the demand for it, we would discover that the supply is currently about 10 times demand. Though comforting, that statistic is also misleading, because it masks the impact of growing demand and the rather severe excess-demand situations that already exist in certain parts of the world. Taken together, these insights suggest that, in many parts of the world, water scarcity is already upon us, and that other areas, including several parts of the United States, can be expected to experience water scarcity in the next few decades.

The problem with groundwater is even more severe. Groundwater levels have been declining in some areas of the country as a result of intensive pumping, and significant depletion of groundwater supplies has occurred in three regions—southern Arizona, the High Plains (from Nebraska to Texas), and California.

Tucson, Arizona, demonstrates how western communities cope. Until the completion of the Central Arizona Project, which diverts water from the Colorado River, Tucson, which averages about 11 inches of rain a year, was the largest city in the United States to rely entirely on groundwater. The water levels in some wells in Tucson have dropped 100 feet in 10 years. Tucson annually pumped 5 times as much water out of the ground as nature put back in. At *current* consumption rates the aquifers supplying Tucson would have been exhausted in less than 100 years. Despite the rate at which its water supplies were being depleted, Tucson continued to grow at a rapid rate. To head off this looming gap between increasing water demand and declining supply the Central Arizona Project—a giant network of dams, pipelines, tunnels, and canals—was constructed to transfer water from the Colorado River to Tucson. Water diversion has been a common, but increasingly unavailable, policy response.

Though the discussion thus far has focused on the quantity of water, that is not the only problem. Quality is also a problem. Much of the available water is polluted with chemicals, radioactive materials, salt, or bacteria. Though we shall reserve for subsequent chapters a detailed look at the water pollution problem, it is important to keep in mind that water scarcity has an important qualitative dimension that further limits the supply of potable water.

This brief survey of the evidence suggests that in certain parts of the world groundwater supplies are being depleted to the potential detriment of future users. Supplies, which for all practical purposes will never be replenished, are being "mined" to satisfy current needs. Once used, they are gone. Is this allocation efficient, or are there demonstrable sources of inefficiency? In order to answer this question we must be quite clear about what is meant by an *efficient allocation* of surface water and groundwater.

◆ THE EFFICIENT ALLOCATION OF SCARCE WATER

What efficiency means for the allocation of water depends crucially on whether surface water or groundwater is being tapped. In the absence of storage, the problem with surface water is to allocate a renewable supply among competing users. Intergenerational effects are less important, as future supplies depend on natural phenomena (e.g., precipitation) rather than on current withdrawal practices. For groundwater, on the other hand, withdrawing water now does affect the resources available to future generations. In this case, the allocation over time is a crucial aspect of the analysis. Because it represents a somewhat simpler analytical case, we shall start by considering the efficient allocation of surface water.

Surface Water

An efficient allocation of surface water (1) must strike a balance among a host of competing users and (2) must supply an acceptable means of handling the year-to-year variability in surface water flow. The former issue is acute, because so many different potential users have legitimate competing claims: Some (e.g., municipal drinking water suppliers or farmers) withdraw the water for consumption; others (e.g., swimmers or boaters) use but do not consume the water. The latter challenge arises because surface water supplies are not constant from year to year or month to month. Because precipitation, runoff, and evaporation all change from year to year, less water will be available to be allocated in some years than in others. Not only must a system for allocating the average amount of water be in place, above-average and below-average flows must also be anticipated and allocated.

With respect to the first problem, the dictates of efficiency are quite clear—the water should be allocated so that the marginal net benefit is equalized for all uses. (Remember that the marginal net benefit is the vertical distance between the demand curve for water and the marginal cost of extracting and distributing that water for the last unit of water consumed.) To demonstrate why efficiency requires equal marginal net benefits, consider a situation in which the marginal net benefits are *not* equal. We shall show that in this situation it is always possible to find some reallocation of the water that increases net benefits. Because net benefits could be increased by this reallocation, the initial allocation could not have maximized net benefits. Inasmuch as an efficient allocation maximizes net benefits, the allocation through which net benefits are not equalized cannot be efficient.

If marginal net benefits have not been equalized, it is always possible to increase net benefits by transferring water from those uses with low net marginal benefits to those with higher net marginal benefits. By transferring water to the users who value the marginal water more, the net benefits of the water use are increased; those losing water are giving up less than those receiving the additional water are gaining. When the marginal net benefits are equalized, no such transfer is possible without lowering net benefits.

Marginal scarcity rent would be zero if water were not scarce. All users would get all they want. Their marginal net benefits would still be equal, but in this case they would be zero.

Groundwater

When withdrawals exceed recharge from a particular aquifer, the resource will be mined over time until supplies are exhausted or until the marginal cost of pumping additional water become prohibitive. The marginal extraction cost (the cost of pumping the last unit to the surface) would rise over time as the water table fell. Pumping would stop either (1) when the water table ran dry or (2) when the marginal cost of pumping was either greater than the marginal benefit of the water or greater than the marginal cost of acquiring water from some other source.

Abundant surface water in proximity to the location of the groundwater could serve as a substitute for groundwater, effectively setting an upper bound on the marginal cost of extraction. The user would not pay more to extract a unit of groundwater than it would cost to acquire surface water. Unfortunately, in many parts of the country where groundwater overdrafts are particularly severe, the competition for surface water is already keen; a cheap source of surface water doesn't exist.

In efficient groundwater markets, the water price would rise over time. The rise would continue until the point of exhaustion, the point at which the marginal pumping cost become prohibitive or the marginal cost of pumping becomes equal to the next-least-expensive source of water. At that point the marginal pumping cost and the price would be equal.

◆ THE CURRENT ALLOCATION SYSTEM

Riparian and Prior-Appropriation Doctrines

Within the United States the means of allocating water differ from one geographic area to the next, particularly with respect to the legal doctrines that govern conflicts. In this section we shall focus on the allocation systems that prevail in the arid Southwest, which must cope with the most potentially serious and imminent scarcity of water.

In the earliest days of European settlement in the U.S. Southwest and West, the government had a minimal presence. Residents were pretty much on their own in creating a sense of order. Property rights played a very important role in reducing conflicts in this potentially volatile situation.

As water was always a significant factor in the development of an area, the first settlements were usually oriented near bodies of water. The property rights that evolved, called *riparian rights,* allocated the right to use the water to the owner of the land adjacent to the water. This was a practical solution because, by virtue of their location, these owners had easy access to water. Furthermore, enough sites had access to water that virtually all who sought water could be accommodated.

With population growth and the consequent rise in the demand for land, this allocation system became less appropriate. As demand increased, the amount of land adjacent to water became scarce, forcing some spillover onto land that was not adjacent to water. The owners of this land began to seek means of acquiring water to make their land more productive.

About this time, with the discovery of gold in California, mining became an important source of employment. With the advent of mining came a need to divert water away from streams to other sites. Unfortunately, riparian property rights made no provision for water to be diverted to other locations. The rights to the water were tied to the land and could not be separately transferred.

This situation created a demand for a change in the property-right structure from riparian rights to one that was more concordant with the need for transferability. The waste resulting from the lack of transferability became so great that it outweighed any transition costs of changing the system of property rights. The evolution that took place in the mining camps became the forerunner of what has become known as the *prior-appropriation* doctrine.

The miners established the custom that the first person to arrive had the superior claim on the water. In practice, this severed the relationship that had existed under the riparian doctrine between the rights to land and the rights to the water. As this new doctrine became adopted in legislation, court rulings, and seven state constitutions, widespread diversion of water based on prior appropriation became possible. Stimulated by the profits that could be made in shifting water to more valuable uses, private companies were formed to construct irrigation systems, and to transport water from surplus to deficit areas. Agriculture flourished.

Although prior to 1860 the role of the government was rather minimal, after 1860 that began to change—slowly at first, but picking up momentum as the twentieth century began. The earliest incursion involved establishing the principle that the ownership of water properly belonged to the state. Claimants were accorded a right to use, known as a *usufruct right,* rather than an ownership right. The establishment of this principle of public ownership was followed in short order by the establishment of state control over the rates charged by the private irrigation companies, the imposition of restrictions on the ability to transfer water out of the district, and the creation of a centralized bureaucracy to administer the process.

This was only the beginning. The demand for land in the arid West and Southwest was still growing, creating a complementary demand for water to make the desert bloom. The tremendous profits to be made from large-scale water diversion created the political climate necessary for the federal government to get involved.

The federal role in water resources originated in the early 1800s, largely out of concern for the nation's regional development and economic growth. Toward these ends, the federal government built a network of inland waterways to provide transportation. Since 1902, the federal government has built almost 700 dams to provide water and power to help settle the West.

To promote growth and regional development, the federal government has paid an average of 70 percent of the combined construction and operating costs of such projects, leaving states, localities, and private users to carry the remaining 30 percent. Such subsidies have even been extended to cover some of the costs of providing marketable water services. For example, the federal government pays 81 percent of the cost of supplying irrigation water and 64 percent of municipal water costs.[1]

This, in a nutshell, is the current situation for water. Both the state and federal governments play a large role. Though the prior-appropriation doctrine stands as the foundation of this allocation system, it is heavily circumscribed by government regulations and direct government appropriation of a substantial amount of water.

Sources of Inefficiency

The current system is not efficient. The prime source of inefficiency involves restrictions that have been placed on water transfers, preventing their gravitation to the highest-valued use. Other sources, such as charging inefficiently low prices, must bear some of the responsibility.

---

[1]Kenneth Rubin, *Efficient Investments in Water Resources: Issues and Options* (Washington, DC: Congressional Budget Office, 1983): xii.

Restrictions on Transfers.   To achieve an efficient allocation of water, the marginal net benefits would have to be equalized across all uses of the water (including nonconsumptive instream uses). With a well-structured system of water property rights, efficiency can be a direct result of the transferability of the rights.[2] Users who were receiving low marginal net benefits from their current allocation would trade their rights to those who would receive higher net benefits. Both parties would be better off. The payment received by the seller would exceed the net benefits forgone, whereas the payment made by the buyer would be less than the value of the water acquired.

Unfortunately, the existing mixed system of prior-appropriation rights coupled with quite restrictive regulations has diminished the actual degree of transferability. Diminished transferability in turn reduces the market pressures toward equalization of the marginal net benefits. By itself this indictment is not sufficient to demonstrate that the existing system is inefficient. If it could be shown that this regulatory system were able to substitute some bureaucratic process for finding and maintaining this equalization, efficiency would still be possible. Unfortunately, that has not been the case, as can be seen by examining in more detail the specific nature of these restrictions. The allocation is inefficient.

One of the earliest restrictions required that users either fully exercise their water rights or lose them. It is not difficult to see what this "use it or lose it" principle does to the incentive to conserve. Particularly careful users who, at their own expense, find ways to use less water find their allocations reduced accordingly. The regulations strongly discourage conservation.

A second restriction, known as the *preferential-use* doctrine, attempts to establish bureaucratically a value hierarchy of uses. Under this doctrine, the government attempts to establish allocation priorities across categories of water. Within categories (e.g., irrigation for agriculture) the priority is determined by prior appropriation ("first in time—first in right"), but among categories, the preferential-use doctrine governs.

The preferential-use doctrine supports three rather different kinds of inefficiencies. First, it substitutes a bureaucratically determined set of priorities for market priorities, resulting in a lower likelihood that marginal net benefits will be equalized. Second, it reduces the incentive to make investments that complement water use in lower-preference categories for the simple reason that such water could be withdrawn as the needs in higher-level categories grow. Finally, it allocates the risk of shortfalls in an inefficient way.

Although the first two inefficiencies are rather self-evident, the third merits further explanation. Because water supplies fluctuate over time, unusual scarcities can occur in any particular year. With a well-specified system of property rights, damage caused by this risk would be minimized by allowing those most damaged by a shortfall to purchase a larger share of the diminished amount of water available during a drought from those less hurt by the increased shortfall.

Diminishing, and in some cases eliminating, the ability to transfer rights from so-called "high-preferential-use" categories to "lower-preferential-use" categories during times of acute need makes the damage caused by shortfalls higher than necessary. In essence, the preferential-use doctrine fails to adequately consider the marginal damage caused by temporary shortfalls, something a well-structured system of property rights would do automatically.

---

[2]Ronald C. Griffin and Shih-Hsun Hsu, "The Potential for Water Market Efficiency When Instream Flows Have Value," *American Journal of Agricultural Economics* 75 (May 1993): 292–303.

Inhibiting transfers has very practical implications. Because of low energy costs and the federal subsidies, agricultural irrigation has become the dominant use of water in the West. About 5 of every 6 gallons withdrawn and 9 out of every 10 gallons consumed go for the irrigation of nearly 50 million acres in 17 western states,[3] yet the marginal net benefits from agricultural uses are lower, sometimes substantially lower, than the marginal net benefits of water use by municipalities and industry.[4] A transfer of water from irrigated agriculture to these other uses would raise net benefits, but regulatory restrictions inhibit these transfers.[5]

Federal Reclamation Projects. By providing subsidies to approved projects, federal reclamation projects have diverted water to these projects—even when the net benefits were negative. Why was this done? What motivated the construction of inefficient projects?

Some work by Professor Chuck Howe of the University of Colorado provides a possible explanation.[6] He examined the benefits and costs of constructing the Big Thompson Project in northeastern Colorado. With this project the water is pumped to an elevation that allows it to flow through a tunnel to the eastern side of the mountains. On that side, electric power is produced at several points. At lower elevations, the water is channeled into natural streams and feeder canals for distribution.

Howe calculated that the *national* net benefits for this project, which include all benefits and costs, were either −$341.4 million or −$237.0 million, depending on the number of years used in the calculations. The project cost substantially more to construct than it returned in benefits. However, *regional* net benefits for the geographic region served by the facility were strongly positive ($766.9 million or $1,187 million, respectively). This facility was an extraordinary boon for the local area, because a very large proportion of the total cost had been passed on to national taxpayers despite the fact that the benefits were local. The local political pressure was able to secure project approval despite the project's inherent inefficiency.

Although the very existence of these facilities is one source of inefficiency, yet another is the manner in which the water is priced. The subsidies have been substantial. Ken Frederick has reported on some work done by the Natural Resources Defense Council to calculate the subsidies to irrigated agriculture in the Westlands Water District (one of the world's richest agricultural areas), located on the west side of California's San Joaquin Valley.[7] In recent years the Westlands Water District has paid about $10 to $12 per acre-foot, less than 10 percent of the unsubsidized cost of delivering water to the district. (An *acre-foot* is the amount of water

---

[3]Kenneth D. Frederick and Allen V. Kneese, "Competition for Water" in Ernest A. Engelbert with Ann Foley Scheuring, eds., *Water Scarcity* (Berkeley: University of California Press, 1984): 82.

[4]See the estimates in Diana C. Gibbons, *The Economic Value of Water* (Washington, DC: Resources for the Future, 1986).

[5]Although regulatory restrictions inhibit these transfers, they do not completely eliminate them. Several transfers from agricultural uses to municipalities have successfully overcome the regulatory hurdles. See Bonnie C. Saliba, "Do Water Markets 'Work'? Market Transfers and Trade-offs in the Southwestern States," *Water Resources Research* 23, No. 7 (July 1987): 1117.

[6]Charles W. Howe, "Project Benefits and Costs from National and Regional Viewpoints: Methodological Issues and Case Study of the Colorado–Big Thompson Project" *Natural Resources Journal* 26 (winter 1986).

[7]The estimates are in Kenneth Frederick, "Water Resource Management and the Environment: The Role of Economic Incentives" in Organization for Economic Co-operation and Development, *Renewable Natural Resources: Economic Incentives for Improved Management* (Paris: OECD, 1989): 33. The original NRDC report was Phillip E. LaVeen and Laura B. King, *Turning Off the Tap off Federal Water Subsidies: Volume 1, The Central Valley Project* (San Francisco: Natural Resources Defense Council, 1985).

it would take to flood an acre of level land to a depth of one foot). The resulting subsidy was estimated to be $217 per irrigated acre, or $500,000 per year for the average-size farm.

Water Pricing.   Restrictions on transfer are not the only source of inefficiency in the current allocation system. The prices charged by water distribution utilities do not promote efficiency of use either.

Both the level of prices and the rate structure are at fault. In general, the price level is too low, and the rate structure does not adequately reflect the costs of providing service to different types of customers.

In part, perhaps because water is considered an essential commodity, the prices charged by public water companies are too low. For surface water the rates are too low for two rather distinct reasons: (1) historic average costs are used to determine rates and (2) marginal scarcity rent is rarely included.

Efficient pricing requires the use of marginal cost, not average cost. To adequately balance conservation with use, the customer should be paying the marginal cost of supplying the last unit of water, yet these regulated utilities typically are allowed to charge prices just high enough to cover the costs of running the operation (as is revealed by figures from the recent past). Because average costs are now lower than marginal costs and historic costs are lower than current or prospective costs, prices are understated.

The second source of the problem is the failure of the regulators overseeing the operations of water distribution companies to allow a marginal user cost to be incorporated in the calculation of the appropriate price, a problem that is even more severe when groundwater is involved. One study by Martin and others found that, because of a failure to include a user cost, rates in Tucson, Arizona, were about 58 percent too low, despite some recent increases.[8]

Using average cost pricing and ignoring the marginal user cost leads to an excessive demand for water. Simple actions, such as fixing leaky faucets, are easy to overlook when water is excessively cheap. Yet, in a city such as New York, for example, leaky faucets can account for a significant amount of wasted water.

Common Property Problems.   The allocation of groundwater must confront one additional problem. When many users tap the same aquifer, that aquifer becomes a common-property resource. Tapping a common-property resource will tend to deplete it too rapidly; users lose the incentive to conserve. The marginal scarcity rent will be ignored.

The incentive to conserve a groundwater resource in an efficient market is created by the desire to prevent pumping costs from rising too rapidly and the desire to capitalize on the higher prices that could reasonably be expected in the future. With common-property resources, neither of these desires translates into conservation, for the simple reason that water conserved by one party may simply be used by someone else because the conserver has no exclusive right to the water that is saved. Water saved by one party to take advantage of higher prices can easily be pumped out by another user before the higher prices ever materialize.

For common-property resources, pumping costs would rise too rapidly, initial prices would be too low, and too much water would be consumed by the earliest users. The burden of this waste would not be shared uniformly. Because the typical aquifer is bowl-shaped, users

---

[8]William E. Martin, Helen M. Ingram, Nancy K. Laney, and Adrian H. Griffin, *Saving Water in a Desert City* (Washington, DC: Resources for the Future, 1984).

on the periphery of the aquifer tend to be particularly hard hit. When the water level declines, the edges go dry first, whereas the center can continue to supply water for substantially longer periods. Future users would also be hard hit relative to current users.

◆ POTENTIAL REMEDIES

Economic analysis points the way to a number of possible means of remedying the current water situation in the Southwestern United States. These reforms would promote efficiency of water use while affording more protection to the interests of future generations of water users.

The first reform would reduce the number of restrictions on water transfers. The "use it or lose it" component of the beneficial-use doctrine can promote the extravagant use of water and discourage conservation. Typically, water saved by conservation is forfeited.[9] Allowing users to capture the value of water saved by permitting them to sell it would stimulate water conservation and allow the water to flow to higher-valued uses (see Example 9.1).

One serious problem with the current water-use doctrine in the West and Southwest of the United States is that it fails to provide adequate protection for the instream uses of water, such as habitat for wildlife or for fishing and boating. As the competition for water increases, the pressure to allocate larger amounts of the stream for consumptive uses increases as well. Eventually, the water level becomes too low to support aquatic life and recreation activities.

Though they do exist (see Example 9.2), water rights for instream flow maintenance are few in number relative to rights for consumptive purposes. Those few instream rights that do exist typically have a low priority relative to the more senior consumptive rights. As a practical matter, this means that in periods of low water flow, the instream rights lose out and the water is withdrawn for consumptive uses. As long as the definition of *beneficial use* requires diversion, as it does in many states, water left for fish habitat or recreation is undervalued.

This undervaluation of instream uses is not inevitable, however, as some enterprising fisherman have discovered.[10] In the Yellowstone River Valley in Montana, several spring creeks are wholly contained within the boundaries of property owned by a single landowner. Because these creeks are not subject to the same legal restrictions that apply to waterways crossing property boundaries, landowners can sell the daily fishing rights. The revenues from these sales provide owners with an incentive to develop spawning beds, protect the fish habitat, and, in general, make the fishing experience as desirable as possible. By limiting the number of fishermen, the owners prevent overexploitation of the resource.

In England and Scotland, markets are relied upon to protect instream uses more than they are in the United States. Private angling associations have been formed to purchase fishing rights from landowners. Once these rights have been acquired, the associations charge for fishing, using some of the revenues to preserve and to improve the fish habitat. Because fishing rights in England sell for as much as $220,000, the holders of these rights have a substan-

---

[9]In *Salt River User's Association* v. *Kavocovich* [411 P.2d 201 (1966)], the Arizona Court of Appeals ruled that irrigators who lined their ditches could not apply "saved" water to adjacent land.

[10]These examples were drawn from Terry L. Anderson, *Water Crisis: Ending the Policy Drought* (Washington, DC: Cato Institute, 1983): 81–85.

Example 9.1

Using Economic Principles to Conserve Water in California

In 1977, when California governor Jerry Brown negotiated a deal to settle one of the state's perennial water fights by building a new water diversion project, environmental groups were opposed. The opposition was expected. What was not expected was the form it took. Rather than simply block every imaginable aspect of the plan, the Environmental Defense Fund (EDF) set out to show project supporters how the water needs could be better supplied by ways that put no additional pressure on the environment.

According to this strategy, if the owners of the agricultural lands to the west of the water district seeking the water could be convinced to reduce their water use by adopting new, water-saving irrigation techniques, the conserved water could be transferred to the district and the project rendered unnecessary. But the growers had no incentive to conserve, because conserving the water required the installation of costly new equipment and, as soon as the water was saved, it would be forfeited under the "use it, or lose it" regulations. What could be done?

On 17 January 1989, largely through the efforts of EDF, an historic agreement was negotiated between the growers association, a major user of irrigation water, and the Metropolitan Water District (MWD) of California, a public agency that supplies water to the Los Angeles area. Under that agreement, the MWD bears the capital and operating costs, as well as the indirect costs (e.g., reduced hydro power), of a huge program to reduce seepage losses as the water is transported to the growers and to install new water-conserving irrigation techniques in the fields. In return, they get all of the conserved water. Everyone gains. The district gets the water it needs at a reasonable price; the growers retain virtually the same amount of irrigation benefits without being forced to bear large additional expenditures.

Because the existing regulatory system created a very large inefficiency, moving to a more efficient allocation of water necessarily increased the net benefits. By using those additional net benefits in creative ways, it was possible to eliminate a serious environmental threat.

Source: Robert E. Taylor, *Ahead of the Curve: Shaping New Solutions to Environmental Problems* (New York: Environmental Defense Fund, 1990).

tial incentive to protect their investments. One of the forms this protection takes is illustrated by the Anglers Cooperative Association, which has taken on the responsibility of monitoring the streams for pollution and alerting the authorities to any potential problems.

Getting the prices right is another avenue for reform. Recognizing the inefficiencies associated with subsidizing the consumption of a scarce resource, the U.S. Congress passed the Central Valley Project Improvement Act in 1992. The act raises the prices that the federal government charges for irrigation water, though the full-cost rate is only imposed on the final 20

Example 9.2

Protecting Instream Uses Through Acquiring Water Rights

Attempts by environmental groups to protect instream water uses must confront two problems. First, any acquired rights are usually public goods, implying that others can free ride on their provision without contributing to the cause. Consequently, the demand for instream rights will be inefficiently low. This is not a sufficient remedy. Second, once the rights have been acquired, their use to protect instream flows may not be considered beneficial use (and therefore could be confiscated and granted to others for consumptive use) or may be so junior to other rights as to be completely ineffective in times of low flow, the times when they would most be needed.

Some movement toward protecting instream rights is occurring, however. In 1979, in what was then a precedent-setting action, the Nature Conservancy, an environmental public interest organization, applied to Arizona's Department of Water Resources for a permit for instream flow at the Ramsey Canyon Preserve, asking essentially for both the right to use a certain amount of water and the right to simply leave it in the stream. When the permit was approved in 1983, this was the first legal recognition in Arizona of the right to appropriate water for wildlife and recreational uses without diverting water from a streambed. As of mid-1987, over 25 minimum instream flow permit applications were pending and an Instream Task Force had been appointed to assist the Arizona authority in formulating new criteria and procedures for granting permits.

What worked at Ramsey Canyon was simple and straightforward, but it is not an adequate protection device in many places. Under the prior-appropriation doctrine, any rights that predate the 1983-granted instream flow right would have given the holder priority for the water.

Another approach has been followed in Colorado. Several years ago, a subsidiary of the Chevron Corporation gave the Nature Conservancy a gift entitling it to 300 cubic feet per second flow rate of water in the Black Canyon of Colorado's Gunnison River. Because Colorado law stipulates that instream flow rights can be held only by the state, the Conservancy was faced with the "use it, or lose it" rule under the prior-appropriation doctrine. Taking the only step available, the Conservancy negotiated a transfer of the instream flow rights to the state.

Sources: Ken Wiley, "Untying the Western Water Knot," *The Nature Conservancy* 40, No. 2 (March/April 1990): 5–13; Bonnie Colby Saliba and David B. Bush, *Water Markets in Theory and Practice: Market Transfers and Public Policy* (Boulder, CO: Westview Press, 1987): 74–77.

percent of water received.[11] Collected revenues will be placed in a fund to mitigate environmental damage in the Central Valley. The act also allows water transfers to new users.

For water distribution utilities, the traditional practice of recovering only the costs of distributing water and treating the water itself as a free good should be abandoned in favor of a marginal-cost-pricing system that includes a scarcity value for water in the price. Because

---

[11]An alternative approach would be to issue transferable coupons for the low-cost water. This system would have the further advantage that the low-cost water would not be squandered, because it could be sold to someone who valued it more. For a detailed analysis of this proposal see Robert A. Collinge, "Revenue Neutral Water Conservation: Marginal Cost Pricing with Discount Coupons," *Water Resources Research* 28 (March 1992): 617–22.

FIGURE 9.2 Increasing Block Rate Structure

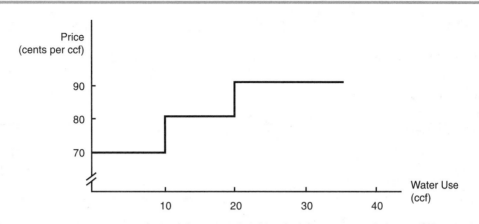

scarce water is not in any meaningful sense a free good, the user cost of that water must be imposed on current users. Only in this way will the proper incentive for conservation be created and the interests of future generations of users be preserved.

Including this user cost in water prices is rather more difficult than it may first appear. Water utilities are typically regulated because they have a monopoly in the local area. One typical requirement for the rate structure of a regulated monopoly is that it earn only a "fair" rate of return. Excess profits are not permitted. Charging a uniform price for water to all users that includes a user cost would generate profits for the seller. (Remember the discussion of scarcity rent?) The scarcity rent accruing to the seller as a result of incorporating the user cost would represent revenue in excess of operating and capital costs.

One way that water utilities are attempting to respect the rate of return requirement while promoting water conservation is through the use of an increasing-block rate. Under this system the price per unit of water consumed rises as the amount consumed rises (Figure 9.2).

In this example, the first 10 ccf of water cost $0.70 per ccf.[12] The next 10 ccf cost $0.80 per ccf, and the third cost $0.90 per ccf. A customer using 26 ccf would pay a bill for the month of $20.40 (10 × $0.70 + 10 × $0.80 + 6 × $0.90).

This type of structure encourages conservation by ensuring that the marginal cost of consuming additional water is high. At the margin, where the consumer decides how much extra water to use, quite a bit of money can be saved by being frugal with water use. However, it also holds revenue down by charging a lower price for the first units consumed. This has the added virtue that those who need some water, but cannot afford the marginal price paid by more extravagant users, can have access to water without placing their budget in as much jeopardy as would be the case with a uniform price.

How many U.S. utilities are using increasing-block pricing? As Table 9.1 indicates, almost one third, though decreasing block pricing is still more common. Some evidence from Europe suggests that except for Italy and Turkey increasing-block pricing is not common there either, although in individual cities like Zurich, Switzerland, it has made a considerable difference (Example 9.3).[13]

---

[12]A ccf is 100 cubic feet, or 748 gallons.

[13]Paul Harrington, *Household Water Pricing in OECD Countries* (Paris: Organization for Economic Co-operation and Development, 1999): 21.

TABLE 9.1 Pricing Structures for Public Water Systems in the United States (1982-1997)

	1982 %	1987 %	1991 %	1997 %
Flat Fee	1	—	3	2
Uniform Volume Charge	35	32	35	33
Decreasing Block	60	51	45	34
Increasing Block	4	17	17	31
Total	100	100	100	100

Source: Household Water Pricing in OECD Countries. Copyright OECD 1999.

Example 9.3

Water Pricing in Zurich, Switzerland

In 1975, largely in response to local groundwater pollution, Zurich instituted an excess charge that would be applied only if a customer exceeded a predefined consumption threshold. Households, for example, could consume up to 1000 litres/day at the basic price. Every unit over that threshold, however, would be changed the much higher (initially double) per unit rate. Other categories of consumers (such as commercial or industrial) faced a similar pricing system with unique thresholds and rates defined for each category.

Together with important changes in the wastewater pricing system, this rate structure seems to have quite an impact. From 1970 to 1997, despite population increases, total water consumption in Zurich fell by 23 percent. (During this same period Switzerland only achieved a 1 percent reduction.) In Zurich the amount of "excess" water consumed (the amount over the thresholds) fell from 7.3 percent to 3.7 percent of total consumption.

Source: Paul Harrington, *Household Water Pricing in OECD Countries* (Paris: Organization for Economic Co-operation and Development, 1999): 28–29.

A number of U.S. utilities are still using a flat fee, which from a scarcity point of view is the worst possible form of pricing. With a flat fee, the marginal cost of additional water consumption is zero. *Zero!* Water use by individual customers is not even metered.

Although more complicated versions of a flat fee system are certainly possible, they do not solve the incentive to conserve problem. At least until the late 1970s, Denver, Colorado, used eight different factors (including number of rooms, number of persons, and number of bathrooms) to calculate the monthly bill. Despite the complexity of this billing system, be-

---

Example 9.4

Politics and the Pricing of Scarce Water

Just as economics can make specific recommendations about the level and structure of water prices, politics can provide insights on the implementation of those recommendations. The implementation process is not always smooth or predictable, as the people of Tucson, Arizona, found out.

In 1976, the city of Tucson faced what it perceived as a water crisis. The development of its service capacity had not kept pace with rapid population growth, and artificially low prices reduced the incentive to conserve. The groundwater supplies on which the city depended were being depleted.

Assisted by a newly elected city council, the utility instituted a new rate structure involving higher water prices overall and more attention to the cost of service in determining the rate structure. An unexpectedly dry year (creating an abnormally high demand), coupled with a newly implemented increasing-block rate structure, conspired to ensure that water bills increased tremendously soon after the change. The resulting anger of the residents spawned a recall campaign in which the councilors responsible for the rate increase were retired from office.

Are major changes in prices politically infeasible? The authors of the Tucson study believe not, though they do believe that feasible increases also have to be implemented with greater care. In particular, they believe that local politicians must be willing to take risks, that local residents must be convinced that a real problem exists, and the burden of the increases must be distributed so that no one group is asked to bear too large a share.

Source: William E. Martin, Helen M. Ingram, Nancy K. Laney, and Adrian H. Griffin, *Saving Water in a Desert City* (Washington, DC: Resources for the Future, 1984).

---

cause the amount of the bill was unrelated to actual volume used (water use was not metered), the marginal cost of additional water consumed was still zero.

Declining-block pricing, another inefficient pricing system, is much more prevalent than is increasing-block pricing. By charging customers a higher marginal cost for low levels of water consumption and a lower marginal cost for higher levels, regulators are placing an undue financial burden on low-income people who consume little water and confronting high-income people with a marginal cost that is too low to provide adequate incentives to conserve.

Other aspects of the rate structure are important as well. Efficiency dictates that prices equal the marginal cost of provision (including the marginal user cost, when appropriate). Several practical corollaries follow from this theorem. First, prices during peak demand periods should exceed prices during off-peak periods. It is peak use that strains the capacity of the system and therefore triggers the needs for expansion. Therefore, peak users should pay the extra costs associated with system expansion by being charged higher rates. Few current water-pricing systems satisfy this condition in practice.

When it costs a water utility more to serve one class of customers than another, each class of customers should bear the costs associated with its service. Typically, this implies, for example, that those farther away from the source or at higher elevations (requiring more pumping) should pay higher rates. In practice, utility water rates make fewer distinctions among customer classes than is efficient. As a result, higher-cost water users are in effect subsidized; they receive too little incentive to conserve and too little incentive to locate in parts of the city that can be served at lower cost.

These principles suggest a much more complicated rate structure for water than merely charging everyone the same price. As Example 9.4 demonstrates, the political consequences of introducing these changes may be rather drastic.

SUMMARY

Though on a global scale the supply of available water exceeds demand, at particular times and in particular locations water scarcity is already a serious problem. In a number of locations, the current use of water exceeds replenishable supplies, implying that aquifers are being irreversibly drained.

Efficiency dictates that replenishable water be allocated so as to equalize the marginal net benefits of water use, even when supplies are higher or lower than normal. The efficient allocation of groundwater requires that the user cost of that depletable resource be considered. When marginal-cost pricing (including marginal user cost) is used, water consumption patterns strike an efficient balance between present and future uses. Typically, the marginal pumping cost would rise over time until it exceeded the marginal benefit received from that water or until the reservoir ran dry.

In earlier times in the United States, markets played the major role in allocating water, but in more recent times, governments have begun to play a much larger role in allocating this crucial resource.

Several sources of inefficiency are evident in the current system of water allocation in the southwestern United States. Transfers of water among various users are restricted so that the water remains in low-valued uses while high-valued uses are denied. Instream uses of water are actively discouraged in many western states. Prices charged for water by public suppliers typically do not cover costs, and the rate structures are not designed to promote efficient use of the resource. For groundwater, user cost is rarely included, and for all sources of water, the rate structure does not usually reflect the costs of services. These deficiencies combine to produce a situation in which we are not getting the most out of the water we are using and we are not conserving sufficient amounts for the future.

Reforms are possible. Allowing conservers to capture the value of water saved by selling it would stimulate conservation. Creating separate fishing rights that could be sold or allowing environmental groups to acquire and retain instream water rights would provide some incentive to protect streams as fish habitat. More utilities could adopt increasing-block pricing as a means of forcing users to realize and to consider all of the costs of supplying the water.

Water scarcity is not merely a problem to be faced at some distant time in the future. In many parts of the world it is already a serious problem, and unless preventive measures are taken, it will get worse. The problem is not insoluble, though to date the steps necessary to solve it have not yet been taken.

FURTHER READING

Anderson, Terry L. *Water Crisis: Ending the Policy Drought* (Washington, DC: Cato Institute, 1983). A provocative survey of the political economy of water, concluding that we have to rely more on the market to solve the crisis.

Dinar, Ariel, and David Zilberman, eds. *The Economics and Management of Water and Drainage in Agriculture* (Norwell, MA: Kluwer Academic Publishers, 1991). Examines the special issues associated with water use in agriculture.

Easter, K. William et. al. *Markets for Water: Potential and Performance* (Dordrecht: Kluwer Academic Publishers, 1998).

Gibbons, Diana. *The Economic Value of Water* (Washington, DC: Resources for the Future, 1986). A detailed survey and synthesis of existing studies on the economic value of water in various uses.

Harrington, Paul. *Pricing of Water Services* (Organization for Economic Co-operation and Development, 1987). An excellent survey of the water-pricing practices in OECD countries.

MacDonnell, L. J., and D. J. Guy, "Approaches to Groundwater Protection in the Western United States," *Water Resources Research* 27 (1991): 259–65. Discusses groundwater protection in practice.

Martin, William E., Helen M. Ingram, Nancy K. Laney, and Adrian H. Griffin. *Saving Water in a Desert City* (Washington, DC: Resources for the Future, 1984). A detailed look at the political and economic ramifications of an attempt by Tucson, Arizona, to improve the pricing of its diminishing supply of water.

Saliba, Bonnie Colby, and David B. Bush. *Water Markets in Theory and Practice: Market Transfers and Public Policy* (Boulder, CO: Westview Press, 1987): 74–77. A highly recommended, accessible study of the way western water markets work in practice in the United States.

Spulber, Nicholas, and Asghar Sabbaghi, *Economics of Water Resources: From Regulation to Privatization* (Hingham, MA: Kluwer Academic Publishers, 1993). Detailed analysis of the incentives structures created by alternative-water-management régimes.

ADDITIONAL REFERENCES

Anderson, Terry L., ed. *Water Rights: Scarce Resource Allocation, Bureaucracy, and the Environment* (Cambridge, MA: Ballinger, 1983).

Collinge, Robert A. "Revenue Neutral Water Conservation: Marginal Cost Pricing with Discount Coupons," *Water Resources Research* 28 (March 1992): 617–22.

Custodio, E., and A. Gurgui, eds. *Groundwater Economics: Selected Papers from a United Nations Symposium Held in Barcelona, Spain* (New York: Elsevier, 1989).

Frederick, K. D. "Water Supplies," in *Current Issues in Natural Resource Policy*, Paul R. Portney, ed. (Washington, DC: Resources for the Future, 1982): 216–52.

Frederick, K. D. *Scarce Water and Institutional Change* (Washington, DC: Resources for the Future, 1986).

Frederick, Kenneth. "Water Resource Management and the Environment: The Role of Economic Incentives," in *Renewable Natural Resources: Economic Incentives for Improved Management* (Paris: Organization for Economic Co-operation and Development, 1989).

Frederick, Kenneth D., and Allen V. Kneese. "Competition for Water," in *Water Scarcity*, Ernest A. Engelbert with Ann Foley Scheuring, eds. (Berkeley: University of California Press, 1984).

Griffin, Ronald C., and Shih-Hsun Hsu, "The Potential for Water Market Efficiency When Instream Flows Have Value," *American Journal of Agricultural Economics* 75 (May 1993): 292–303.

Howe, Charles W. "Project Benefits and Costs from National and Regional Viewpoints: Methodological Issues and Case Study of the Colorado–Big Thompson Project," *Natural Resources Journal* 26 (Winter 1986).

Kanazawa, M. "Pricing Subsidies and Economic Efficiency: The Bureau of Reclamation," *Journal of Law and Economics* 36 (1993): 205–34.

Livingston, Marie L., and Thomas A. Miller. "The Impact of Instream Water Rights on Choice Domains," *Land Economics* 62 (August 1986): 269–77.

Organization for Economic Co-operation and Development. *Renewable Natural Resources: Economic Incentives for Improved Management* (Paris: OECD, 1987).

Postel, Sandra. "Saving Water for Agriculture," in *State of the World: 1990*, Lester Brown et al. (New York: W. W. Norton, 1990).

Rubin, Kenneth. *Efficient Investments in Water Resources: Issues and Options* (Washington, DC: Congressional Budget Office, 1983).

Smith, Vernon L. "Water Deeds: A Proposed Solution to the Water Valuation Problem," *Arizona Review* 26 (January 1977): 7–10.

Saliba, Bonnie. "Do Water Markets 'Work'? Market Transfers and Trade-offs in the Southwestern States," *Water Resources Research* 23 (July 1987).

Steinbeck, John. *The Grapes of Wrath* (New York: Viking Press, 1939).

Torell, L. Allen, James D. Libbin, and Michael D. Miller. "The Market Value of Water in the Ogallala Aquifer," *Land Economics* 66 (May 1990): 163–75.

Wahl, Richard W. *Markets for Federal Water: Subsidies, Property Rights, and the Bureau of Reclamation* (Washington, DC: Resources for the Future, 1989).

Zamikau, J. "Spot Market Pricing of Water Resources and Efficient Means of Rationing Water During Scarcity," *Resources and Energy* 16 (August 1994): 189–210.

WEB SITES OF INTEREST

1. *http://www.epa.gov/OW/*
   USEPA's Office of Water. Contains information on publications, water laws and regulations and other web sites that link to state water issues.

2. *http://water.usgs.gov/*
   U.S. Geological Service. Good source of information on water resources of the United States.

3. *http://www.cnie.org/nle/crsh2o.html*
   U.S. Congressional Research Service Reports on water.

4. *http://www.worldbank.org/html/fpd/water/*
   Water Supply and Sanitation Program at the World Bank. Many reports on economic aspects of water use in developing countries.

DISCUSSION QUESTIONS

1. What pricing system identified in Table 9.1 best describes the pricing system used to price the water you use at your college or university? Does this pricing system affect your behavior about water use (length of showers, etc.)? How? Could you recommend a better pricing system in this circumstance? What would it be?

2. What system is used in your home town to price the publicly supplied water? Why was that pricing system chosen?

3. Suppose you come from a part of the world that is blessed with abundant water. Demand never comes close to the available amount. Should you be careful about the amount you use, or should you simply use whatever you want whenever you want it? Why?

Agriculture

The Commission's assessment of the future prospects for overcoming world hunger has led to one conclusion . . . the outcome of the war on hunger, by the year 2000 and beyond, will not be determined by forces beyond human control, but, rather, by decision and actions well within the capability of nations working individually and together.

PRESIDENTIAL COMMISSION ON WORLD HUNGER,
OVERCOMING WORLD HUNGER: THE CHALLENGE AHEAD (1980)

◆ INTRODUCTION

In Chapter 1, food was a point of contention between Simon and the *Beyond the Limits* team. The *Beyond the Limits* team foresaw the demand for food (driven by population growth) outstripping the supply (primarily because of a decline in the availability of arable land), suggesting a resulting famine as one source of societal collapse. Simon, on the other hand, foresaw population growth as diminishing, and a tremendous expansion in food supplies forthcoming from the applications of new technologies. Which vision seems more accurate?

Chronic malnourishment already exists on a large scale. The International Fund for Agricultural Development has reported that:[1]

- About 340 million people worldwide are currently chronically ill from malnutrition.

---

[1]International Fund for Agricultural Development, *The State of Rural World Poverty* (New York: New York University Press, 1992).

- Over 500 million do not get enough calories to do a full day's labor.
- At a time when enough grain is being produced to provide everyone in the world with twice the daily minimum caloric requirements, global hunger is at an all-time high.

Though some may quarrel with the specific numbers recognition that a substantial proportion of the world's population is currently malnourished seems universal.

Why has this situation arisen? Cereal grain, the world's chief supply of food, is a renewable private-property resource that, managed effectively, could be sustained as long as we receive energy from the sun. Are current agricultural practices sustainable? Are they efficient? Because land is typically not a common-property resource, farmers have an incentive to invest in irrigation and other means of increasing yield, because they can appropriate the additional revenues generated. On the surface, a flaw in the market process is not apparent. We must dig deeper to uncover the sources of the problem.

In this chapter we shall explore the validity of three common hypotheses used to explain widespread malnourishment: (1) a persistent global scarcity of food, (2) a maldistribution of that food both among nations and within nations, and (3) temporary shortages caused by weather or other natural causes. These hypotheses are not mutually exclusive; they could all be valid sources of a portion of the problem. As we shall see later in the chapter, it is important to distinguish among these sources and assess their relative importance, because each implies a different policy approach.

◆ GLOBAL SCARCITY

A number of commentators see the problem as an absolute global scarcity—a case of too many people chasing too little food.[2] Garrett Hardin, a human ecologist, has suggested the situation is so desperate that our conventional ethics, which involve sharing the available resources, are not only insufficient, they are counterproductive. He argues that we must replace these dated notions of sharing wealth with more-stern "lifeboat ethics."[3]

The allegory he invokes involves a lifeboat adrift in the sea that can safely hold 50 or, at most, 60 persons. Hundreds of other persons are swimming about, clamoring to get into the lifeboat, their only chance for survival. Hardin suggests that if passengers in the boat were to follow conventional ethics and allow swimmers into the boat, it would eventually sink, taking everyone to the bottom of the sea. In contrast, he argues, lifeboat ethics would suggest a better resolution of the dilemma; the 50 or 60 should row away, leaving the others to certain death, but saving those fortunate enough to gain entry to the lifeboat. The implication is that food sharing is counterproductive. It encourages more population growth and ultimately would cause inevitable and even more serious shortages in the future.

The existence of a global scarcity of food is the premise that underlies this view; when famine is inevitable, sharing is counterproductive. In the absence of global scarcity (i.e., when

---

[2]See, for example, Lester R. Brown, *In the Human Interest* (New York: W. W. Norton, 1974); and William Paddock and Paul Paddock, *Famine—1975!* (Boston, MA: Little, Brown, 1967).

[3]Garrett Hardin, "Living on a Lifeboat," *Bioscience* 24 (October 1974): 561–68.

the lifeboat has a large enough capacity for all), a worldwide famine can be avoided by a sharing of resources. How accurate is the premise of global scarcity?

Examining Global Scarcity

Most authorities seem to agree that an adequate amount of food is currently being produced. Studies made by the Food and Agricultural Organization of the United Nations, which report that the available supplies of food are more than adequate to supply the nutritional needs of all the world, are typical.

Because this evidence is limited to a single point in time, however, it provides no sense of whether scarcity is decreasing or increasing. If we are to identify and evaluate trends, we must develop more precise, measurable notions of how the market allocates food.

As a renewable resource, cereal grains could be produced indefinitely, if managed correctly. However, two facets of the world hunger problem have to be taken into account. First, although population growth has slowed down, it has not stopped. Therefore, it is reasonable to expect the rising demand for food to continue. Second, the primary input for growing food is land, and land is ultimately fixed in supply. Thus, our analysis must explain how a market reacts in the presence of rising demand for a renewable resource that is produced using a fixed factor of production!

A substantial and dominant proportion of the Western world's arable land is privately owned. Access to this land is restricted; the owners have the right to exclude others and can reap what they sow. The typical owner of farmland has sufficient control over the resource to prevent undue depreciation, but not enough control over the market as a whole to raise the specter of monopoly profits.

What kind of outcome could we expect from this market in the face of rising demand and a fixed supply of land? What do we mean by scarcity and how could we perceive its existence? The answer depends crucially on the nature of the supply curve (Figure 10.1).

Suppose the market is initially in equilibrium with quantity Q_0 supplied at price P_0. Let the passage of time be recorded as shifts outward in the demand curve so that D_1 = demand in the first period and D_6 = demand in the sixth period.

Consider what would happen in the fifth time period. If the supply curve were S_a, the quantity would rise to Q_{5a}. However, if the supply curve were S_b, the quantity supplied would only rise to Q_{5b}, but the price would rise P_{5b}.

This analysis sheds light on what is meant by *scarcity* in the world food market. It does not mean a shortage. Even under the relatively adverse supply circumstances pictured by the supply curve S_b, the amount of food supplied would equal the amount demanded. As prices rose, potential demand would be choked off and additional supplies would be called forth.

Some critics argue that the demand for food is not price sensitive. Because food is a necessary commodity for survival, they say, its demand is inflexible and doesn't respond to prices. Although it is a necessary commodity, not all food fits that category. We don't have to gaze very long at an average vending machine in a developed country to conclude that some food is far from a necessity.

Examples of food purchases being price responsive abound. One occurred during the 1960s, when the price of meat skyrocketed for what turned out to be a relatively short period. It wasn't long before hamburger substitute, made entirely out of soybean meal, appeared in

FIGURE 10.1. The Market for Food

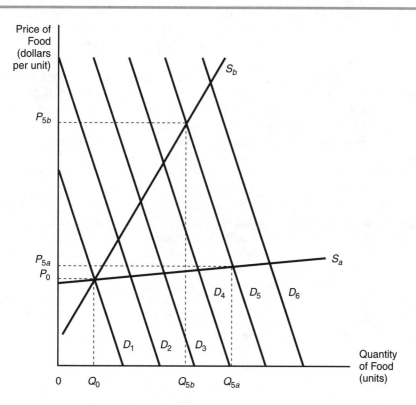

supermarkets. The result was a striking reduction in meat consumption. This is a particularly important example because the raising of livestock for meat in Western countries consumes an enormous amount of grain. This evidence suggests that the balance between the direct consumption of cereal grains and the indirect consumption through meat is affected by prices.

But enough about the demand side; what do we know of the supply side? What factors would determine whether S_a or S_b is a more adequate representation of the past and the future?

Although rising prices certainly stimulate a supply response, the question is, How much? As the demand for food rises, the supply can be increased either by expanding the amount of land under cultivation, by increasing the yields on the land already under cultivation, or by some combination of the two. Historically, both sources have been important.

Typically, the most fertile land is cultivated first. That land is then farmed more and more intensively until it is cheaper, at the margin, to bring additional, less-fertile land into production. Because it is less fertile, the additional land is brought into production only if prices rise high enough to make farming it profitable. Thus, the supply curve for arable land (and hence for food, as long as land remains an important factor of production) can be expected to slope upward.

Two forms of global scarcity can materialize. In the most serious case, per capita food production can decline. In terms of Figure 10.1, this could occur if the slope of the supply curve were sufficiently steep that production could not keep pace with increases in demand brought about by population growth. Declining per capita food consumption could provide some support for lifeboat ethics.

Even in the absence of declining per capita consumption, however, the global scarcity hypothesis can exist. If the supply curve is sufficiently steeply sloped that food prices increase more rapidly than other prices in general, the relative price of food can rise over time. Per capita welfare would decline, even if consumption were rising. This form of scarcity is related more to the cost of food than the availability of food; as supplies of food increase, the cost of food rises relative to the cost of other goods.

Have relative agricultural prices risen? Harold Barnett, a noted resource economist, published the results of a preliminary study on trends in resource prices, including agricultural prices.[4] Specifically, he examined the ratio of an index of agricultural prices to the general wholesale price index for a variety of countries over two different time periods (1950–1962 and 1961–1972). A total of 53 cases were examined. He discovered that for 23 of those cases agriculture prices rose at a statistically significant higher rate than wholesale prices in general. Using only the later time period (involving 31 countries), he found that some 15 countries experienced rises in agricultural prices that significantly exceed rises in wholesale prices.

According to the evidence, the supply curve for agricultural products is more steeply sloped than the supply curve for products in general in about half the countries. In those countries, at least, some global scarcity is apparent. Because not all market prices are efficient, as we shall see later in this chapter, we must not place too much faith in these numbers. Even so, the evidence suggests that agricultural supplies have increased faster than population, but at an increasingly relative cost.

Outlook for the Future

What factors will influence the future relative costs of food? A continuation of past trends would suggest an increasing role for the developing nations as they expand production to meet their increasing shares of population while the developed nations of the north continue their exports. The ability of developing nations to expand their role is considered in the next section as a part of the food-distribution problem. In this section, therefore, we shall deal with forces affecting productivity in the industrialized nations of the north to ascertain the sustainability of historic trends.

Rather dramatic historic increases in crop productivity were stimulated by improvement in machinery; increasing utilization of commercial fertilizers, pesticides, and herbicides; developments in plant and animal breeding; expanding use of irrigation water; and adjustments in location of crop production. In the United States the combined effect of these factors doubled average yield per acre from 1910 to 1977.[5] Will history repeat itself?

---

[4]Harold J. Barnett, "Scarcity and Growth Revisited," in *Scarcity and Growth Reconsidered,* V. Kerry Smith, ed. (Baltimore, MD: Johns Hopkins University Press, for Resources for the Future, 1979): 163–217.

[5]Melvin L. Cotner, Nelson L. Bills, and Robert F. Boxley, "An Economic Perspective of Land Use," in *Economics, Ethics, Ecology: Roots of Productive Conservation,* Walter E. Jeske, ed. (Ankeny, IA: Soil Conservation Society of America, 1981): 31.

Technological Progress.   Technological progress provides the main source of support for optimism about continued productivity increases. Three techniques appear particularly promising: (1) recombinant DNA, which permits genes from one species to be recombined with those of another; (2) tissue culture, which allows whole plants to be grown from single cells; and (3) cell fusion, which involves uniting the cells of species that would not normally mate in order to create new types of plants different from "parent" cells. One knowledgeable reviewer in the field suggested several applications for these genetic engineering techniques, including:

1. Making food crops more resistant to diseases and insect pests
2. Creating hardy new crop plants capable of surviving in marginal soils
3. Giving staple food crops such as corn, wheat, and rice the ability to make their own nitrogen-rich fertilizers by using solar energy to make ammonia from nitrogen in the air
4. Increasing crop yields by improving the way plants use the sun's energy during photosynthesis[6]

The World Bank has estimated that these techniques could increase yields at least 30 percent beyond those achieved with the best previously available seeds and technology.[7]

The outlook is not uniformly bright, however. Four concerns have arisen regarding the ability of the industrial nations to achieve further productivity gains: (1) the declining share of land allocated to agricultural use, (2) the rising cost of energy, (3) the rising environmental cost of traditional forms of agriculture, and (4) the role of price distortions in agricultural policy.[8] A close examination of these concerns reveals that current agricultural practices in the industrialized nations may be neither efficient nor sustainable and a transition to agriculture that satisfies both criteria could involve lower productivity levels.

Allocation of Agricultural Land.   During 1920 in the United States, 958 million acres were used for farming. By 1974 the comparable figure was 465 million acres.[9] Some 50 percent of the agricultural land in 1920 had been converted to nonagricultural purposes by 1974. A simple extrapolation of this trend would certainly raise questions about our ability to increase productivity at historical rates. Is a simple extrapolation reasonable? What determines the allocation of land between agricultural and nonagricultural uses?

Agricultural land will be converted to nonagricultural land when its profitability in nonagricultural uses is higher. If we are to explain the historical experience, we must be able to explain the decline of the relative value of land in agriculture.

Two factors stand out. First, an increasing urbanization and industrialization of society rapidly raised the value of nonagricultural land. Second, rising productivity of the remaining

---

[6]Robert Cooke, "Engineering a New Agriculture," *Technology Review* 85 (May/June 1982): 24–25.

[7]World Bank, *World Development Report, 1982* (Washington, DC: International Bank for Reconstruction and Development, 1982).

[8]See, for example, Lester R. Brown, "World Population Growth, Soil Erosion, and Food Security," *Science* (214 (27 November 1981): 995–1002.

[9]See Melvin L. Cotner, Nelson L. Bills, and Robert F. Boxley, op. cit.

land allowed the smaller amount of land to produce a lot more food. Less land was needed in agriculture to meet the demand for food.

It seems unlikely that simple extrapolation of the decline in agricultural land of the magnitude evidenced since 1920 would be accurate. Since the middle of the 1970s, the urbanization process has diminished to the point that many urban areas are experiencing declining population. This shift is not entirely explained by suburbia spilling beyond the boundaries of what was formerly considered urban. For the first time in our history, significant numbers of the population have moved from urban to rural areas.

Furthermore, as increases in food demand are accompanied by increased prices of food, the value of agricultural land should increase. Higher food prices would tend to slow conversion of agricultural land to nonagricultural uses and possibly even reverse the trend. To make this impact even greater, several states have now allowed agricultural land either to escape the property tax (until it is sold for some nonagricultural purpose) or to be taxed at lower rates. Confirming evidence for this generally optimistic assessment can be found in the fact that most of the conversion to nonagricultural uses actually occurred prior to World War II.[10]

Energy Costs. Agricultural production in the industrialized nations is very energy intensive. Some major portion of the productivity gains resulted from energy generated by using mechanization and by the increased use of pesticides and fertilizers, which are derived from petroleum feedstocks and natural gas. The costs of petroleum and natural gas have risen substantially and probably can be expected to continue to rise in real terms over the long run as the available supplies of fossil fuels are exhausted or as global warming concerns diminish their use. To the extent that energy-intensive producers cannot develop cheaper substitutes, the supply curve must shift to the left to reflect the increasing costs of doing business.

Ralph d'Arge, an economist investigating this question, notes that energy and capital are complements in agriculture.[11] Because of this complementary relationship, energy price increases could be expected to trigger some reduction in capital, as well as some reduction in energy on the typical energy-intensive farm, thereby reducing the yield per acre. Furthermore, because d'Arge found that farm wage rates have risen less rapidly than either energy costs or the costs of borrowing (as reflected by interest rates), he expects a readjustment of U.S. agriculture in the future, as labor is substituted for capital. A shift toward smaller, family-operated units would trigger a consequent reduction in the agricultural productivity growth rate.

Environmental Costs. Some of the past improvements in agricultural productivity have come from intensifying the environmental problems caused by agriculture. Not only has the use of land intensified in quality (with a resulting increase in the use of chemicals and fertilizers), but also in quantity, as grasslands and forests have been converted to farming.

Another source of environmental problems, soil erosion, has a different origin. Some soil erosion is natural, of course, and within certain tolerance limits does not harm productivity. The concern arises because some farm practices partially responsible for increasing produc-

---

[10]The decline in cropland since 1949 has involved only 13 of the more than 400 million acres converted since 1920. For more details on this, see Melvin L. Cotner, Nelson L. Bills, and Robert F. Boxley, op. cit.: 31–36.

[11]Ralph C. d'Arge, "The Energy Squeeze and Agricultural Growth," in *Economics, Ethics, Ecology: The Roots of Productive Conservation,* Walter E. Jeske, ed. (Ankeny, IA: Soil Conservation Society of America, 1981): 99–105.

tivity (e.g., continuous cropping rather than rotations with pasture or other soil-retaining crops) have tended to exacerbate soil erosion. The fears are further intensified by the belief that these losses are irreversible within one generation.

Given that increased soil erosion is taking place, why would a property owner allow this depletion? In the past, soil conservation simply did not pay. The techniques to avoid it were expensive, and the ready availability of cheap fertilizer to replace lost nutrients meant that the cost of soil depletion was low. Further, the damage caused to rivers and streams by this eroding soil was not borne by the farmers, who could best control it.

The barriers that prevented erosion from being checked are now disappearing. As the level of topsoil reaches lower tolerance limits, the fertility of the land is affected. Rising cost is making fertilizers a less desirable substitute for soil erosion, and public policy has begun to subsidize soil erosion techniques. In 1985, the U.S. Congress authorized the Conservation Reserve Program, which was designed to reduce soil erosion and stimulate tree planting. Acreage enrolled in the program peaked at 36.4 million acres in 1996. It is expected to reduce soil erosion by hundreds of millions of tons per year, to decrease sediment in reservoirs and streams, to increase the protection of recreational resources, and to preserve the long-term productivity of the land.[12] In the near future we may see more soil conservation techniques practiced because they are becoming profitable.

Some past agricultural practices have caused environmental damage, and continuing these would cause rising environmental costs. In recent years the frequency and quantity of agricultural chemicals used have increased dramatically.[13] Over the past 25 years, for example, nitrogenous fertilizer use increased by 150 percent in the Netherlands, by 225 percent in Denmark, and by 300 percent in the United States. Serious drinking water problems have emerged. In 1979 some 179 German water authorities were supplying drinking water with nitrate concentrations exceeding the standards. Four years later the number of communities violating the standards had increased 4 times, to 807. Some of the nutrients from fertilizers leak into lakes and stimulate the excessive growth of algae. Aside from the aesthetic cost to a body of water choked with plant life, this nutrient excess can deprive other aquatic life forms of the oxygen they need to survive.

Pesticide use has also increased. Since 1975, for example, the quantity of pesticides used in Germany has increased by 30 percent and in Denmark by 69 percent. A great deal of pest control in the past has relied upon pesticides. Many of these substances persist in the environment, and there is an increasing recognition that some toxicity extends to species other than the target population. The herbicides and pesticides can contaminate water supplies, rendering them unfit for drinking and for supporting normal populations of fish.

Throughout all OECD countries, "sustainable agriculture" is being increasingly associated with the reduced use of pesticides and mineral fertilizers, and policies have been established to facilitate the transition to low reliance on these substances. Denmark and Sweden are pursuing ambitious agricultural chemical reduction targets. In Austria, Finland, the Netherlands, and Sweden a variety of input taxes and input levies have recently been introduced.

---

[12]U.S. General Accounting Office, *1990 Farm Bill: Opportunities for Change* (Washington, DC: Government Printing Office, 1990): 23.

[13]The data in this section are from M. D. Young, *Agriculture and the Environment: OECD Policy Experiences and American Opportunities* (Washington, DC: U.S. Environmental Protection Agency, 1990).

The charges provide an incentive to use fewer agricultural chemicals, and the revenue is used to ease the transition by funding research on alternative approaches and the dissemination of information. Many OECD countries expect little effect on crop yields, though production levels are lower.[14]

Although most European countries are focusing on eliminating input subsidies (e.g., on pesticides or fertilizers), taxing inputs, or directly limiting input use, New Zealand has taken a more radical step by scrapping most of its agricultural supports. According to a study conducted for the New Zealand Ministry of Agriculture, the environmental consequences of this policy have been rather profound.[15] Fertilizer use has declined, farms have become more diversified, the most marginal land is now grazed less intensively, and the excessive conversion of land has stopped.

Irrigation, a traditional source of productivity growth, is also running into limits, particularly in the western United States. Some traditionally important underground sources of water supplies are not being replenished at a rate sufficient to offset the withdrawals. Encouraged by enormous subsidies that transfer the cost to the taxpayers, these water supplies are being exhausted. Those that remain are subject to rising levels of salt. Irrigation of soils with naturally occurring salts causes a concentration of the salts near the surface. This salty soil is less productive and, in extreme cases, kills the crops.

One sign that a transition is underway is the rise of organic farming. The number of organic farms in the European Union jumped from 6,300 in 1985 to more than 100,000 in 1998.[16] The transition will not be immediate or easy. It takes from 1 to 5 years to convert from conventional agriculture to organic farming. Studies comparing organic farms with comparable conventional farms have found that the organic farms had lower yields, but they also had lower costs, with the result that their income was about the same as that for comparable conventional agriculture farms.

A recent source of encouragement for organic farms has been the demonstrated willingness of consumers to pay a premium for organically grown fruits and vegetables. Because it would be relatively easy for producers to claim their produce was organically grown, even if it was not, organic growers need a reliable certification process to assure the consumers that they are indeed getting what they pay for. In some areas, growers associations handle the testing and labeling, but in others it is handled by new organizations that have sprung up specifically to provide this service.[17] In California, where labeling of organic produce has become routine, retail sales of organics grew from $1 million in 1979 to $50 million in 1987.

---

[14]Organization for Economic Co-operation and Development, *Agriculture and Environment: Opportunities for Integration* (Paris: OECD, 1988). See the most recent evidence on the retarding effects on food production in the industrialized countries in Lester R. Brown et al., *Vital Signs: 1992* (New York: W. W. Norton, 1992): 24, 40.

[15]Reynolds, Russ et al., "Impacts on the Environment of Reduced Agricultural Subsidies: A Case Study of New Zealand," Ministry of Agriculture Technical Paper, December 1993.

[16]This information came from a report to the European Union authored by Nicholas Lamkin and was cited by GREENWIRE (1/3/00).

[17]The first such organization, NutriClean, uses a complex evaluation procedure to establish whether the produce meets its "no detected residue" standard. If so, the produce is allowed to display the NutriClean label. The farmer pays for the service with a fee that is based on the sales volume.

The Role of Agricultural Policies

Past gains in agricultural productivity have come at a large environmental cost. Why? Part of the answer, of course, can be found in an examination of the externalities associated with agriculture. Many of the costs of farming are shifted to others. They are borne not by the farmers, who bear the responsibility for making the decisions that determine the size of the environmental cost, but by others—those subjected to the contaminated groundwater and polluted streams. But that is not the whole story. Government policies must bear some of the responsibility as well.

Government policies have completely subverted the normal functioning of the price system. Three types of agricultural policies are involved: (1) subsidies for specific farming inputs such as equipment, fertilizers, or pesticides; (2) guaranteed prices for outputs; and (3) trade barriers to protect against competition from imports.

Subsidies have helped to create a dependence on purchased inputs. One study examined whether the size of the farm subsidy (as measured by its proportion to total income) across countries was correlated with fertilizer use in those countries.[18] It was. Countries with the largest subsidies used considerably more fertilizer than those with few or no subsidies. The subsidies made it possible to use inefficient and unsustainable levels of fertilizer.

Guaranteed prices have the effect of increasing the profitability of agriculture, making it possible to convert formerly inappropriate land to agricultural purposes. New Zealand provides an interesting example. Frustrated with the high levels of subsidies that were being poured into the agricultural sector, the government in New Zealand eliminated most agricultural subsidies over a three-year period. Not only did fertilizer use fall 55 percent, but it turned out that the resulting shakeout in the agricultural sector resulted in a much higher proportion of smaller farms, which have a less adverse impact on the environment. The subsidies had propped up the larger farms.[19]

Other countries have not been eager to follow New Zealand's lead. The subsidies have become an important component of farm income, making them difficult to eliminate. Agricultural subsidies in the United States and the European Economic Community are responsible for about one third and one half of all farm income, respectively. In Japan farmers earn twice as much income from subsidies as from the practice of agriculture. In Switzerland the comparable figure is 4 times agricultural income.

Recently, however, governments have begun to encourage sustainable agriculture, not only by discouraging the harmful side effects of traditional agriculture, but by learning more about sustainable practices and disseminating the information derived from this research. In the United States, for example, the Food, Agriculture, Conservation, and Trade Act of 1990 expanded a program of research on sustainable agriculture first established under the Food Security Act of 1985.

---

[18]Richard Blackhurst and Kym Anderson, "The Greening of World Trade as cited in 'Agriculture Survey'," *The Economist* (12 December 1992): 17.

[19]It has been argued that these subsidies have been designed to help poor farmers, but this argument is not persuasive. Because they produced only one tenth of the output, poor farmers received only $1 from every $10 of subsidies paid. "*The Economist* Agriculture Survey," *The Economist* (12 December 1992): 7.

A Summing Up

Agricultural productivity in the industrialized countries can be expected to rise in the future, but at lower rates. The large historic increases in agricultural productivity were partly based upon unsustainable, inefficient, and environmentally destructive agricultural practices, which were supported and encouraged by agricultural subsidies. In the future we can expect that as farmers become less insulated from the energy and environmental costs of agriculture (i.e., as subsidies are removed), some of the expected gains from technological progress will be offset.

In addition to changes in the productivity of agriculture in the future, we can also expect changes in agricultural practices. A transition to alternative techniques of agriculture appears to be underway. What would be the effects of this transition if it were to penetrate deeply into traditional agriculture? According to a national study based upon a large model of U.S. agriculture, widespread adoption of organic farming methods in the United States would increase national net farm income, but would also increase consumer food costs and decrease agricultural export levels.[20]

◆ DISTRIBUTION OF FOOD RESOURCES

Imperfections in food distribution, particularly those associated with inadequate purchasing power, provide a second source of the malnourishment problem. According to this point of view, the basic problem is poverty. We would expect, therefore, that the poorest segments of society would be the most malnourished and that the poorest countries would contain the largest number of malnourished people.

If accurate, this representation suggests a very different policy orientation than that suggested by global scarcity. If the problem is maldistribution rather than shortage, the real issue is how to get the food to the poorest people. Eliminating poverty—thereby increasing the ability to pay for food—is a strategy that could alleviate the problem. If the problem were a lack of food, however, this strategy would be totally ineffectual.

Defining the Problem

Considerable and persuasive evidence suggests that the problem is one of distribution, as shown in Table 10.1. Though the data are far from perfect, a number of interesting conclusions can be drawn. Looking at the top line first, we find that the average citizen of a developing country has a sufficient caloric intake. This reinforces our conclusion that the problem is not currently one of global scarcity. It is also clear, however, that the food is not uniformly distributed among the world's peoples. For the least developed countries (LDCs), the average diet contains fewer calories than necessary to prevent nutritional deficiency.

Equally revealing, however, is the trend. Though clear progress has been made in the world as a whole in increasing per capita food production, production in the LDCs has failed to keep pace with the population growth. For the poorest countries, the average diet is woefully inadequate. Furthermore, their dependency on food imports has grown.

---

[20]Kent D. Olson, James Langley, and Earl O. Heady, "Widespread Adoption of Organic Farming Practices: Estimated Impacts on U.S. Agriculture," *Journal of Soil and Water Conservation* 37, No. 1 (January/February, 1982).

TABLE 10.1 Food Situation in Developing Countries

	Food Production 1988–90 (per capita index) (1989–91 = 100)	Daily calorie supply 1996 (per capita)
All Developing Countries	132	2,628
Least developed countries	115	2,095
Sub-Saharan Africa	116	2,205

Source: United Nations Development Programme, *Human Development Report 1993* (New York: Oxford University Press, 1999), Table 20, p. 214.

Poverty, population growth, and the sufficiency of food production are related problems, as we stated in the chapter on population growth. High poverty levels are generally conducive to high population growth, and high population growth rates may increase the degree of income inequality. Furthermore, excessive population levels and poverty together increase the difficulty of achieving food sufficiency. Because we have already examined population control strategies in Chapter 6, we shall now focus on strategies to increase the amount of food available to the poorest people. What can be done?

Domestic Production in LDCs

The first issue to be addressed concerns the relative merits of increasing domestic production in the less developed countries as opposed to importing more from abroad. There are several reasons for believing that many developing countries can profitably increase the percentage of their consumption that is domestically produced. One of the most important is that food imports use up precious foreign exchange.

Most developing countries cannot pay for imports with their own currencies. They must pay in an internationally accepted currency, such as the U.S. dollar, earned through the sale of exports. As more foreign exchange is used for agricultural imports, less is available for imports such as capital goods, which could raise the productivity (and, hence, incomes) of local workers.

The lack of foreign exchange has been exacerbated during periods of high oil prices. Many developing nations must spend large portions of export earnings merely to import energy. In 1993, for example, fuel imports made up one third of all imports for Kenya. That leaves little for capital goods or agricultural imports.

Although this pressure on foreign exchange supports a need for greater reliance on domestic agricultural production, it would be incorrect to carry that argument to its logical extreme by suggesting that all nations should become self-sufficient in food production. The reason why self-sufficiency is not always efficient is suggested by the *law of comparative advantage*.

Nations are better off specializing in those products for which they have a comparative advantage. If its comparative advantage is not in food but in textiles, for example, a given country would be better off producing and exporting textiles, and using the earnings to purchase food (Table 10.2). The opportunity costs of producing textiles and wheat (measured in hours of labor per unit of output) are given for a hypothetical LDC and a developed country (DC).

Suppose we are considering an eight-hour day in each country. If the average worker in each country were to spend four hours of each day on each activity, then 8 units of textile (4

TABLE 10.2 A Hypothetical Example of the Law of Comparative Advantage

	Hours to Produce 1 Unit of Textiles	*Hours to Produce 1 Unit of Wheat*
Less Developed Country	1	3
Developed Country	1	1

by the LDC and 4 by the DC) and $5^1/_3$ units of wheat ($1^1/_3$ by the LDC and 4 by the DC) would be produced by the two countries each day. (Be sure you can see how these numbers can be derived from the table).

Suppose, however, that the LDC in this case were to specialize in textiles (by allocating all eight hours to textile production), whereas the DC specialized in wheat. It is easy to verify that the total world production would now be 8 units of textiles and 8 units of wheat. *When countries specialize in those products in which they have a comparative advantage, total production can increase.*

Why did this happen in our example? It happened because the opportunity cost of making textiles in the LDC (in terms of forgone wheat) was lower than in the DC, whereas the opportunity cost of growing wheat in the DC (in terms of forgone textile production) was lower than that in the LDC. By freeing labor in the DC from making textiles, the LDC would be able to reap some of the benefits of the increased wheat production.

Although this example is hypothetical, the principle it conveys is real. Total self-sufficiency in food for all nations is not an appropriate goal. Those nations with a comparative advantage in agriculture because of climate, soil type, available land, and so on (e.g., United States) should be net exporters, whereas those nations (e.g., Japan) with comparative advantage in other commodities should remain net food importers. This balance should not be allowed to get out of line, however, by creating an excessive reliance on either domestic production or imports.

Because of price distortions and externalities in the agricultural sector, most developing countries have historically developed an excessive dependency on imports. What kind of progress has been made in reducing this dependency? According to the data in Table 10.1, dependency has increased, not fallen. And the lowest-income countries as a group are having trouble even keeping the level of dependency from increasing with population growth, much less making headway in reducing imports. Progress on this front is elusive, it seems.

The Undervaluation Bias

Why, for so many years has food production in the developing countries barely kept pace with population growth? Agriculture in the low-income countries has been undervalued, implying that the rate of return on investment in agriculture is well below what it would be if agricultural output were allowed to receive its full social value. As a result, investments in agriculture have been lower than they would otherwise have been and productivity has suffered.

Before investigating the sources and consequences of this problem, let's discuss one enduring myth that tends to distort thinking on the subject of agricultural incentives. According to the myth, peasant farmers do not respond to prices for cash crops because they are too ignorant, and they do not respond to prices for subsistence crops because they consume them rather than sell them. Therefore, the myth concludes, supply in peasant economies is not price elastic. Population-induced increases in demand would cause higher prices, but not in-

Example 10.1

The Price Responsiveness of Supply: Thailand

The market response to an increasing demand for food resulting from population growth is rising prices. This increase in prices is then presumed to call forth further increases in supply. The more price responsive is the supply, the smaller are the price increases needed to satisfy a given level of demand. Therefore, the question of agricultural-production responsiveness to prices is of major importance.

There is considerable debate about whether we should expect farmers to respond to prices. Those who believe that prices are important see even small-scale farmers as rational, calculating individuals seizing the opportunities presented to them in the form of higher prices. The other camp generally believes that small farmers are ignorant and so set in their ways as to be oblivious to what happens in the markets for their products.

Jere Behrman, an economist on the faculty of the University of Pennsylvania, has investigated this question. He published a major empirical study assessing the price responsiveness of four major annual crop supplies in Thailand over the period 1937–1963. Three (cassava, corn, and *kenaf**) were cash crops; the fourth (rice) was a subsistence crop where only the surplus was marketed.

Using sophisticated econometric models, Behrman found a substantial amount of price responsiveness in the supply of all four commodities. He found that the substantial price responses for kenaf are particularly noteworthy because this crop had been cultivated by near-subsistence farmers who previously were, at most, marginal participants in the national market. Behrman also discovered that Thai farmers were risk-averse; that is, production could be increased by lowering the risk—even if the expected price remained the same. In Thailand, at least, policies allowing prices to rise and reducing the risk have had a substantial impact. We should not sell small-scale peasant farmers short!

*Kenaf is a fiber used in the manufacture of gunny sacks and, to a lesser extent, rope and paper.

Source: Jere Behrman, *Supply Response in Underdeveloped Agriculture* (Amsterdam: North-Holland Publishing, 1968).

creased supplies. Typical of many studies, Example 10.1 indicates that this argument has one fatal flaw: It is just not true!

Governments have used many mechanisms that have the undesirable side effect of undervaluing agriculture and destroying incentives in the process. Two stand out—marketing boards and export taxes.

National *marketing boards* have been established to many developing countries to stabilize agricultural prices and hold food prices down in order to protect the poor from malnutrition. Typically, a marketing board sells food at subsidized prices. As the subsidy grows, the board looks around for ways to reduce the amount of the subsidy.

Two strategies regularly employed by marketing boards are (1) the wholesale importing of artificially cheap food from the United States (available under the food aid program originally designed to get rid of wheat surpluses) and (2) holding down prices paid to domestic farmers. Both, of course, have the long-term effect of disrupting local production. The perniciousness of this process is shown in Example 10.2.

The effects of holding prices down can be illustrated by what happened to farmers in Mali in 1979–1980. Although it cost Malian farmers 83 francs per kilo to produce their irrigated rice, the government paid them only 60 francs per kilo. During that period most Malian rice was smuggled across the border to Senegal, Niger, and Upper Volta, where it received market prices. A World Bank study during the period found that farmers in 13 surveyed countries received less than half of the value of their crops.[21]

Many developing countries depend on export taxes, levied on all goods shipped aboard, as a principal source of revenue. Some of these taxes fall on cash-crop food exports (bananas, cocoa beans, coffee, etc.). The impact of export taxes is to raise the cost to foreign purchasers, reducing the amount of demand. A reduction in demand generally means lower prices and lower incomes for the farmers. Thus, this strategy also impairs food production incentives.

Government policies in the third world affect not only the level of agricultural production, they affect the techniques employed as well. A 1987 study by the World Bank reported that, in nine developing countries, pesticide subsidies ranged from 15 to 90 percent of full retail cost, with a median of 44 percent.[22] Agricultural mechanization is another target for subsidies. As a result of this distortion of prices, farmers have been encouraged to rely heavily on pesticides and to embrace mechanization where possible. These strategies make little sense in the long run.

Having become dependent on the subsidies, it becomes difficult for these farmers to make the transition to sustainable agricultural practices. Nonetheless, some basis for optimism exists. Agricultural techniques that are both sustainable and profitable in a developing country can be identified. The World Resources Institute conducted a series of studies in India, the Philippines, and Chile to study the effects on farmer income of transitioning to a more sustainable form of agriculture.[23] Its conclusion was that sustainable agriculture could be profitable, but usually not without changing the current pricing structure to reflect the full environmental costs of production. Better means of diffusing information about sustainable agricultural techniques among farmers would also be needed.

Feeding the Poor

The undervaluation bias was caused by a misguided attempt to use price controls as the way to provide the poor with access to an adequate diet. It backfired because the price controls served to reduce the availability of food. Is there a way to reduce the nutritional gap among the poor while maintaining adequate supplies of food?

Some countries (e.g., Sri Lanka, Colombia, and the United States) are using food stamp programs to subsidize food purchases by the poor. In Colombia this is being accomplished by

---

[21]This information came from a study by agricultural economist Carl Eicher reported in Janet Raloff, "Africa's Famine: The Human Dimension, *Science News* 127 (11 May 1985): 300.

[22]World Bank Development Committee, *Environment, Growth and Development* (Washington, DC: World Bank, 1987): 20.

[23]Faeth, P., ed., *Agricultural Policy and Sustainability: Case Studies from India, Chile, the Philippines and the United States* (Washington: World Resources Institute, 1993).

Example 10.2

Perverse Government Intervention: The Case of Colombia

The failure of the market to increase productivity in the agricultural sector or to reduce the incidence of poverty sometimes has been due to government policies. The experience in Colombia is relatively typical.

Marketing of wheat in Colombia is controlled by the huge Colombia Institute for Agricultural Marketing, operated by the government. In 1951–1954, wheat production averaged 140,000 metric tons a year. By 1971, this production level had fallen to 49,000 tons. During this same period, consumption of wheat in Colombia rose from 179,000 tons to 434,000 tons. The difference, of course, had to be made up by imports.

Why did this happen? There seemed to be two reasons, both of which had the effect of lowering the real price of wheat received by the Colombian farmer—who, as expected, reacted by cutting production. The first reason was a massive inflow of surplus grain from the United States, which was subsidized by the U.S. government as part of our food aid program. This artificially cheap wheat simply stole much of the market normally supplied by domestic producers.

The second cause was a decision by the marketing institute to hold wheat prices constant in the 1968–1971 period—in spite of an annual inflation rate approaching 10 percent. The intended purpose, of course, was to hold prices down for consumers, which it temporarily did. The unintended side effect was to discourage domestic production and to increase the losses of the marketing institute, which had to pay the difference between what the imported wheat cost and the lower price at which it was offered to consumers.

Is there a moral to the story? Possibly. The supply side has to be kept continually in mind as governments attempt to raise the nutrition levels of their citizens.

Sources: Reed Hertford, "Government Price Policies for Wheat, Rice and Tractors in Colombia," in *Distortions of Agricultural Incentives,"* Theodore W. Schultz, ed. (Bloomington: Indiana University Press, 1978): 121–39; World Bank, *World Development Report, 1980* (Washington DC: International Bank for Reconstruction and Development, 1980): 87.

issuing food coupons to low-income women and children, who are particularly vulnerable to nutritional deficiency. The coupons can be used by recipients to purchase a number of high-nutrition, low-cost foods. About 200,000 households were reached by means of this program in 1980. By boosting the purchasing power of those with the greatest need, such programs provide access to food while protecting the incentives of farmers. In those countries lowering food prices to everyone, the government must make substantially higher payments in order to finance the programs. When governments look around for ways to finance these subsidies, they are tempted to try to reduce the subsidies by paying below-market prices to farmers or by relying more heavily on artificially low-cost imported food aid. In the long run, either of these strategies can be self-defeating.

Targeting the assistance to those who need it is one strategy that works. Another approach to feeding the poor is to attempt to ensure that the income distribution effects of agricultural policies benefit the poor. One great hope associated with the "green revolution" was that new varieties of seeds produced by scientific research would expand the supply of food, holding down prices and making a better diet accessible to the poor. It was also hoped that this strategy would provide expanding employment opportunities for the poor to supply more grain. How did it work out?

The green revolution started with maize hybrids adapted in the 1950s from the United States and Rhodesia and later spread across large parts of Central America and East Africa. Since the mid-1960s, short-stalk, fertilizer-responsive varieties of rice have spread throughout East Asia and comparable varieties of wheat have spread throughout Mexico and the Indian and Pakistan Punjabs.

In many areas with access to these hybrids, productivity has doubled or tripled over a 30-year period. Short-duration varieties have allowed many farmers to harvest two crops a year where only one was formerly possible. The transformation has been unprecedented.

The effects have been impressive.[24] In most areas with access to these modern varieties, small farmers have adopted them no less widely, intensively, or productively than have others. Labor use per acre has increased, with a consequent increase in the wage bill received by the poor. Poor people's consumption and nutrition are better with the new varieties than without them.

However, the adoption of these varieties has had a darker side as well. Reliance on a few species of hybrid cereal grains increases the risk from diseases and pests. Every Wall Street portfolio manager knows that risk can be lowered by holding a diverse collection of stocks. The security offered by diversity of agricultural species has diminished as larger and larger areas are planted with these new varieties. Other areas, those without access to the new varieties, have probably lost out as large quantities of new grain enter the market, eliminating by competition some of the more traditional sources. Small farmers are not always the beneficiaries of these new agricultural hybrids (see Example 10.3).

We are now in a position to define the role for aid from the developed nations. Temporary food aid is helpful when traditional sources are completely inadequate (e.g., as the result of natural disasters) or when the food aid does not interfere with the earnings of domestic producers. In the long run, developed nations could provide both appropriate technologies (e.g., solar-powered irrigation systems) and the financial capital to get farmer-owned local cooperatives off the ground. These cooperatives would then provide some of the advantages of scale (e.g., risk sharing and distribution) while maintaining the existing structure of small-scale farms. Coupled with effective population-control efforts and a balanced development program designed to raise the general standard of living, this approach could provide a solution to the distributional portion of the world food problem.

Industrialized nations could also open their markets to agricultural products from the developing countries by eliminating subsidies and by removing trade barriers. These acts would level the agricultural playing field, would remove some of the undervaluation bias that is due to external factors, and would provide a source of income to some of the poorest farmers in developing countries.

---

[24]For the evidence, see Michael Lipton and Richard Longhurst, *New Seeds and Poor People* (Baltimore, MD: Johns Hopkins University Press, 1989)

Example 10.3

The Distribution Dilemma: India's Green Revolution

India illustrates the trade-off between efficiency and equity sometimes faced by developing countries. India achieved substantial increases in its production of wheat (and, subsequently, of rice) through the introduction of new hybrid seed. Distributed through a limited-budget program, the new seed could either be given to small farmers in the poorer regions or to those in the richer Punjab area, where the preconditions for rapid-yield expansion were present. India chose the latter strategy.

Several barriers existed to substantially increased yields among the poorer farmers. The smaller farmers did not have the savings or the access to capital markets to put in the complementary inputs (principally, irrigation) required to gain the maximum productivity increase from the new seed. In addition, their land holdings were not typically large enough to utilize the optimum scale of the complementary inputs.

Two main developments resulted. Food products increased substantially, but the gains were captured by larger farms. Francine Frankel estimates that the majority of Indian farmers experienced a relative decline in their economic position (e.g., small rice farmers received 75 to 80 percent of the gains received by the larger farmers), and some smaller percentage of them actually experienced an absolute decline. For this latter category, the effect of the green revolution was to make them worse off, not better off.

Source: Francine Frankel, *India's Green Revolution: Economic Gains and Political Costs* (Princeton, NJ: Princeton University Press, 1971).

◆ FEAST AND FAMINE CYCLES

The remaining dimension of the world food problem concerns the year-to-year fluctuations in food availability caused by vagaries of weather and planting decisions. Even if the average level of food availability were appropriate, the fact that the average consists of a sequence of overproduction and underproduction years means that society as a whole can benefit from smoothing out the fluctuations.

The point is vividly depicted by an analogy. If a person were standing in two buckets of water—the first containing boiling-hot water, the second, ice-cold water—his misery would not be assuaged in the least by a friend's telling him that, on average, the temperature was perfect. The average does not tell the whole story.

The fluctuations of supplies for food seem to be rather large, and the swings in prices even larger. Why? One characteristic of the farming sector suggests that farmers' production decisions may actually make the fluctuations worse, or at least prolong them. This tendency is explored via the *cobweb model*.

Suppose, because of a weather-induced shortage, the price of a crop product rises. For the next growing season, farmers have to plant well in advance of harvest time. Their decisions about how much to plant will depend on the price they expect to receive. Let us suppose they use this year's price as their guess of what next year's price will be.

They will plan to supply a larger amount. Because the market cannot absorb that much of the commodity, the price falls. If farmers use this new, lower price to plan the following year's crop, they will produce less. This will cause the price to rise again, and so on.

The fluctuations that occur normally produce a damped oscillation. In the absence of further supply shocks, the amplitude of price and quantity fluctuations decreases over time until the equilibrium price and quantity are obtained.[25]

The demand for food tends to be price inelastic, particularly in developing countries. This has some important implications. The more price inelastic the demand curve, the higher the price has to go in order to bring the demand into line with supply when a weather-induced shortage occurs. One conclusion is immediately obvious—the more inelastic the demand curve, the more likely farmers as a group are to gain from the shortfall. As long as the demand curve is price inelastic in the relevant range (a condition commonly satisfied in the short run by food products), farmers as a group will be better off by supply shortfalls.[26]

On the consumer side of this issue, a quite different picture emerges. Consumers are unambiguously hurt by shortfalls and helped by situations with excess supply. The more price inelastic the demand curve, the greater is the loss in consumer surplus from shortfalls and the greater is the gain in consumer surplus from excess supply.

This creates some interesting (and, from the policy point of view, difficult) incentives. Producers as a group do not have any particular interest in protecting against supply shortfalls, but they have a substantial interest in protecting against excess supply. Consumers, on the other hand, have no quarrel with excess supply but want to guard against supply shortfalls.

Although society as a whole would gain from the stabilization of prices and quantities, the different segments of society have rather different views of how that stabilization should come about. Farmers will be delighted with price stabilization as long as the average price is high; consumers will be delighted if the average price is kept low.

The main means of attempting to stabilize prices and quantities is by creating stockpiles. These can be drawn upon during periods of scarcity and built up during periods of excess supply. Currently, two different types of food stockpiles exist. The first is a special internationally held emergency stockpile that would be used to alleviate the hunger caused by natural disasters (e.g., drought). Established in 1975 by the Seventh Special Session of the United Nations General Assembly, with an annual target of 500,000 tons, the World Emergency Stockpile has the potential to greatly reduce suffering without having any noticeable disruptive effect on the world grain market (involving some 70 million tons traded). Unfortunately, its full potential has not yet been reached. The bulk of accumulated reserves is distributed annually to needy nations, leaving little in reserve from year to year.

---

[25]Theoretically, *undamped oscillations,* which increase in amplitude over time, are possible under certain conditions, but this pattern does not seem to characterize existing food markets.

[26]This is not necessarily true for every farmer, of course. If the supply reduction is concentrated on a few, they will unambiguously be worse off, whereas the remaining farmers will be better off. The point is that the revenue gains received by the latter group will exceed the losses suffered by the former group.

The second kind of stockpile represents those held individually by the various countries. Although it was hoped that these stockpiles would be internationally coordinated, that has proven difficult to achieve. The Food and Agricultural Organization (FAO) Secretariat estimates the minimum safe level of world carryover stocks for cereals to be between 17 and 18 percent of world consumption. After a rather precipitous decline in 1973, by 1977 the stocks had been rebuilt to minimum safe levels. During the 1980s, they fell below safe levels again. Almost two thirds of the stockpile is controlled by the exporting countries.

The process has started to increase food security on a worldwide basis but has not yet reached the point of solving the problem. Significant, difficult political decisions on stockpile management, such as timing purchases and sales, have yet to be agreed upon. Until that time, because the interests of producer and consumer nations are no different, it is unlikely that any uncoordinated system will be fully effective.

SUMMARY

The world hunger problem is upon us, and it is real. Serious malnutrition is currently being experienced in many parts of the world. The root of the chronic problem is poverty—an inability to afford the rising costs of food, though solving the problem will become more difficult as past unsustainable agricultural practices are eliminated and food prices rise. The harm caused by poverty and rising food prices is intensified by fluctuations in the availability of food.

These problems are not insoluble. The FAO has concluded that developing countries *could* increase their food production well in excess of population growth. They conclude, however, that this will occur only if the developed nations share technology and provide the developing countries access to their markets and if the developing countries show a willingness to adopt pricing policies that do not restrict output. This can be accomplished without jeopardizing the poor by using direct food-purchase subsidies (e.g., a food-stamp program) rather than price controls.

Because a major part of the world hunger problem is poverty, it is not enough to simply produce more food. The ability of the poor to afford food has also to be improved. Reducing poverty can be accomplished by bolstering nonfarm employment opportunities as well as by enhancing the returns of smaller-scale farmers. Small-scale farmers can compete effectively, if given access to credit markets and new, improved technologies.

Food stockpiles—the key element in a program to provide food security—exist but are not yet fully effective. The emergency stockpile has not achieved its designed capacity and the system of national stockpiles is large but not effectively managed. The light is at the end of the tunnel and the train is moving, but the journey is distressingly slow.

FURTHER READING

Carlson, Gerald R., David Zilberman, and John A. Miranowski, eds. *Agricultural and Environmental Resource Economics* (New York: Oxford University Press, 1993). A textbook that provides considerably more detail about issues raised in this chapter.

Crosson, Pierre R., and Sterling Brubaker. *Resource and Environmental Effects of U.S. Agriculture* (Baltimore: Johns Hopkins University Press, for Resources for the Future, 1982). Identifies the environmental costs associated with future increases in production and suggests measures to deal with them.

Meier, Gerald M. *Leading Issues in Economic Development,* 5th ed. (New York: Oxford University Press, 1989). A highly regarded, extensive collection of integrated short articles on various aspects of the development process. Contains an excellent section on agricultural development, with an extensive bibliography.

Streeten, Paul. *What Price Food? Agricultural Policies in Developing Countries* (New York: St. Martin's Press, 1987). An excellent study of agricultural policies in developing countries.

Williams, Jeffrey C., and Brian D. Wright. *Storage and Commodity Markets* (Cambridge: Cambridge University Press, 1991). A primarily theoretical treatment of such issues as how large stockpiles should be, whether stockpiles are more useful in raw or in processed form, and how the existence of stockpiles affects commodity prices and production.

ADDITIONAL REFERENCES

Alexandros, Nikos, ed. *World Agriculture: Towards 2000* (New York: New York University Press, 1988).

Anderson, Kym, and Richard Blackhurst, eds. *The Greening of World Trade Issues* (Ann Arbor: University of Michigan Press, 1992).

Browder, John O., ed. *Fragile Lands of Latin America: Strategies for Sustainable Development* (Boulder, CO: Westview Press, 1988).

Cobia, David. *Cooperatives in Agriculture* (Englewood Cliffs, NJ: Prentice-Hall, 1988).

Collins, Robert A., and J. C. Headley. "Optimal Investment to Reduce the Decay of an Income Stream: The Case of Soil Conservation," *Journal of Environmental Economics and Management* 10 (March 1983): 60–71.

Crosson, Pierre R. *The Cropland Crisis: Myth or Reality?* (Washington, DC: Resources for the Future, 1982).

Crosson, Pierre R. *Productivity Effects of Cropland Erosion in the United States* (Washington, DC: Resources for the Future, 1983).

Gardner, B. L., "The Political Economy of Agricultural Pricing," *World Economy* 16 (1993): 611–19.

Hall, Darwin C., et al. "Organic Food and Sustainable Agriculture," *Contemporary Policy Issues* 7 (October 1989): 47–72.

Horowitz, J. K., and E. Lichtenberg. "Insurance, Moral Hazard, and Chemical Use in Agriculture," *American Journal of Agricultural Economics* 75 (1993): 926–35.

Madden, Patrick. "Can Sustainable Agriculture Be Profitable?," *Environment* 29 (May 1987): 19–34.

Paddock, William, and Paul Paddock. *Famine—1975!* (Boston: Little, Brown, 1967).

Presidential Commission on World Hunger. *Overcoming World Hunger: The Challenge Ahead* (Washington, DC: Government Printing Office, 1980).

Reganold, John P., et. al. "Soil Quality and Financial Performance of Biodynamic and Conventional Farms in New Zealand," *Science* 260 (16 April 1993): 344–49.

Regev, Uri, Halm Shalit, and A. P. Gutteirrez. "On the Optimal Allocation of Pesticides with Increasing Resistance: The Case of Alfalfa Weevil," *Journal of Environmental Economics and Management* 10 (March 1983): 86–100.

WEB SITES OF INTEREST

1. http://www.aphis.usda.gov/biotechnology/
   The U.S. Department Agriculture site for biotechnology.

2. *http://www.fao.org/*
   The Food and Agricultural Organization (FAO) of the United Nations, the main international organization dealing with agriculture.

3. *http://www.fao.org/waicent/search/default.htm*
   The FAO World Agricultural Information Center provides a search engine for agricultural topics.

DISCUSSION QUESTIONS

1. "By applying modern technology to agriculture, the United States has become the most productive food-producing nation in the world. The secret to solving the world food problem lies in transferring this technology to developing countries." Discuss.

2. Under Public Law 480, the United States sells surplus grains to developing countries, which pay in local currencies. Because the United States rarely spends all of these currencies, much of this grain transfer is *de facto* an outright gift. Is this an equitable and efficient way for the United States to dispose of surplus grain? Why or why not?

Biodiversity I:
Forest Habitat

There is nothing more difficult to carry out, nor more doubtful of success, nor more dangerous to handle, than to initiate a new order of things. For the reformer has enemies in all who profit by the old order, and only lukewarm defenders in all those who would profit from the new order. The lukewarmness arises partly from fear of their adversaries who have law in their favor; and partly from the incredulity of mankind, who do not truly believe in anything new until they have had actual experience of it.

MACHIAVELLI, *THE PRINCE* (1513)

◆ INTRODUCTION

Forests provide a variety of products and services. The raw materials for housing and many products made out of wood are extracted from the forest. In many parts of the world wood is an important fuel. Paper products are derived from wood fiber. Trees cleanse the air by absorbing carbon dioxide and adding oxygen. Forests provide shelter and sanctuary for wildlife, and they play an important role in the ecology of watersheds that supply much of our drinking water.

Although the contributions that trees make to our everyday life are easy to overlook, even the most rudimentary calculations indicate their significance. Slightly less than one third of the land in the United States is covered by forests, the largest category of land use with the exception of pasture and grazing land. In Maine, an example of a heavily forested state, 95 percent of the land area is covered by forest. In 1995 the comparable figure for the world was 31.7 percent.[1]

---

[1]OECD, *OECD Environmental Data: Compendium 1997* (Paris: Organization for European Co-operation and Development, 1997): 111.

A glance at some of the vital signs of the forest resource does not inspire confidence that it is being managed either efficiently or sustainably.[2] Deforestation is currently proceeding at an unprecedented rate. In 1998 the World Resources Institute reported that 185 million hectares of tropical forests, an area about the size of Mexico, were destroyed from 1980 through 1995, as trees were cut for timber and to clear land for agriculture and development.[3]

Deforestation poses a significant threat to biodiversity because it destroys forest habitat. Pressures on forest habitat come from logging activities and from the conversion of forested land to other uses (such as residential development or agriculture). Logging activities not only remove trees that serve as habitat, but the accompanying activities (such as road building) can degrade surrounding habitat as well. The threat posed by conversion involves a different, but no less significant, set of economic forces.

In the remainder of this chapter we show how economic forces can not only explain these high rates of deforestation, but can also provide some basis for protecting against this particular threat to biodiversity. We begin by characterizing what is meant by an "efficient allocation" of the forest resource when the value of the harvested timber is the only concern. Starting simply, we first model the efficient decision to cut a single stand (or cluster of trees) with a common age by superimposing economic considerations on a biological model of tree growth. This model is then expanded to demonstrate not only how the multiple values of the forest resource *should* influence the harvesting decision, but also why they currently do not. We then turn to the sources of the second threat—the conversion of forested land to other uses. A simple model of the allocation of land to competing uses is used both to explain current trends and to illustrate some possibilities for correction.

◆ DEFINING PROFIT-MAXIMIZING MANAGEMENT

Special Attributes of the Forest

Although forests share many characteristics with other living resources, they also have some unique aspects. Trees provide a saleable commodity when they are harvested. However, left standing, they are a capital asset, providing for increased growth the following year and a stream of environmental services such as watershed protection and wildlife habitat. Each year, the forest manager must decide whether to harvest a particular stand of trees or to wait. In contrast to many other living resources, however, the time period between initial investment (planting) and recovery of that investment (harvesting) is especially long. Intervals of 25 years or more are common in forestry, but not in many other industries.

---

[2]In this context, *sustainability* refers to harvesting no more than would be replaced by growth; sustainable harvest would preserve the interests of future generations by assuring that the volume of remaining timber was not declining over time. This is stronger than required by the criterion of weal sustainability, which only requires that future generations be as well off. It would conceivably be possible to make future generations better off even if the volume of wood were declining over time by providing a compensating amount of some commodity or service they value even more.

[3]World Resources Institute, *World Resources: 1998–99* (New York: Oxford University Press, 1998): 185.

FIGURE 11.1   Model of Tree Growth in a Stand of Douglas Fir

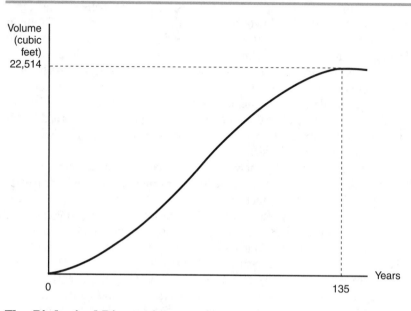

The Biological Dimension

Tree growth is measured on a volume basis, typically by cubic feet on a particular site. This measurement is taken of the trunks, exclusive of bark and limbs, between the stump and a 4-inch top. For larger trees, the stump is 24 inches from the ground. Only standing trees are measured; those toppled by wind or age are not included. In this sense the volume is measured in net rather than gross terms.

Based on this measurement of volume, the data reveal that even-aged tree stands go through distinct growth phases. Initially, when the trees are very young, growth is rather slow in volume terms, though the tree may experience a considerable increase in height. A period of sustained, rapid growth follows, with volume increasing considerably. Finally, slower growth sets in as the stand fully matures, until growth stops or even reverses.

The actual growth of a stand of trees depends on many factors, including the weather, the fertility of the soil, susceptibility to insects or disease, the type of tree, the amount of care devoted to the trees, and vulnerability to environmental factors or events, such as forest fire or air pollution. Thus, there is a tremendous amount of variability of tree growth from stand to stand. Some of these growth-enhancing or growth-retarding factors are under the influence of foresters; others are not.

Abstracting from these differences, it is possible to develop a hypothetical but realistic biological model of the growth of a stand of trees (Figure 11.1). In this case, our model is based on the growth of a stand of Douglas fir trees in the Pacific Northwest.[4]

---

[4]The numerical model in the text is based loosely on the data presented in Marion Clawson, "Decision Making in Timber Production, Harvest, and Marketing," Research Paper R-4 (Washington DC: Resources for the Future, 1977), Table 1, p. 13. The mathematical function relating volume to age of the stand in Figure 11.1 is a third-degree polynomial of the form $v = a + bt + ct^2 + dt^3$, where v = volume in cubic feet, t = age of the stand in years, and $a, b, c,$ and d are parameters that take on the values 0, 40, 3.1, and −0.016, respectively.

Notice that the figure is consistent with the growth phases mentioned earlier. Following an early period of limited growth, the stand experiences rapid growth in the middle ages, with growth ceasing after 135 years.

When should this stand be harvested? Foresters have come up with a calculation called the *mean annual increment* (MAI), which provides the basis for a biological approach to answering this question. Developing this concept provides a useful contrast to the economic approach, which is represented in subsequent sections.

The MAI is calculated by dividing the cumulative volume of the stand at the end of each decade by the cumulative number of years the stand has been growing up to that decade. For growth patterns like the ones represented by Figure 11.1, the MAI rises during the early ages and then falls during the later ages (Table 11.1).

According to the *biological decision rule*, the forest should be harvested at the age when the MAI is maximized. According to our Douglas fir example, this occurs when the stand is 100 years old. Column 4 in Table 11.1 helps us to understand what is special about this age. Annual incremental growth rises until the trees are about 70 years old, declining thereafter. The MAI rises for the first 100 years because the annual incremental growth is above the MAI during that period; it falls in the following years because the annual incremental growth is below the MAI.

The Economics of Forest Harvesting

It is possible to use the basic biological model of growth portrayed in Figure 11.1 as the basis for an economic model of the harvesting decision.

From the definition of *profit maximization*, the optimal time to harvest this stand would be the particular age that maximizes the present value of the net private benefits from the wood. The size of the net benefits from the wood depends on whether the land will be perpetually

TABLE 11.1 The Biological Harvesting Decision: Douglas Fir

Age (Years) (1)	Volume[a] (Cubic Feet) (2)	MAI[b] (Cubic Feet) (3)	Annual Incremental Growth[c] (Cubic Feet) (4)
10	694	6.9	6.9
20	1,912	95.6	121.8
30	3,558	118.6	164.6
40	5,536	138.4	198.8
50	7,750	155.0	221.4
60	10,104	168.0	235.4
70	12,502	178.6	239.8
80	14,848	185.6	234.6
90	17,046	189.4	219.8
100	19,000	190.0	195.4
110	20,614	187.4	161.4
120	21,792	184.6	117.8
130	22,438	172.6	64.4
135	22,514	166.8	11.6

[a] Calculated from the formula used to produce Figure 11.1. See footnote 4.

[b] Column 2 divided by column 1.

[c] Change over intervening period in column 1 divided by change in number of years in column 1.

committed to forestry or left to natural processes after harvest. We will assume that the stand will be harvested once and the land will be left as is following the harvest.

Two costs are presumed to be important in this decision: (1) planting costs and (2) harvesting costs. Apart form their magnitudes, these costs differ in one significant characteristic—the time at which they are borne. Planting costs are borne immediately, whereas harvesting costs are borne at the time of harvest. In a present-value calculation, harvesting costs are discounted (as is the value of the wood), because they are paid (received) in the future; however, planting costs are not discounted, because they are paid immediately. For the sake of our example, let's assume that planting this stand costs $1,000 and harvesting costs $0.30 per cubic foot of wood harvested.

With these additions to the model, it is now possible to calculate the present value of private net benefits that would be derived from harvesting this stand at various ages (Table 11.2). The net benefits are calculated by subtracting the present value of costs from the value of the timber at that age. Different discount rates are used to illustrate the influence of discounting on the harvesting decision. The undiscounted calculations ($r = 0.0$) simply indicate the actual values that would prevail at each age; the positive discount rates take the time value of money into account.

An interesting conclusion can be gleaned from Table 11.2. Discounting shortens the profit-maximizing age when the stand is harvested. Whereas the maximum undiscounted net benefits occur at 135 years, when a discount rate of only 0.02 is used, the maximum occurs at 68 years—roughly half the time of the undiscounted case. A higher discount rate yields an even shorter harvesting time, as shown in the table.

Higher discount rates imply shorter harvesting periods because they are less tolerant of the slow timber growth that occurs as the stand reaches maturity. The use of a positive discount rate implies a direct comparison between the increase in the value of the timber that occurs without harvesting and the increase in value that would occur if the forest were harvested and the money from the sale invested at rate r. In the undiscounted case, the opportunity cost of capital is zero; therefore, it pays to leave the money invested in trees as long as some growth is occurring. As long as r is positive, however, the trees will be harvested as soon as the growth rate declines sufficiently that more will be earned from financial investments. Notice, however, that high discount rates may destroy the incentive to replant. (This is the case when $r = 0.04$ in Table 11.2.)

◆ LAND CONVERSION

The previous section showed how high discount rates can increase the harvests (by shortening the age at harvest) and discourage replanting. In this section we deal with the deforestation that occurs when forested land is converted to other uses. In this section we examine the economics of land conversion in order to not only understand why it is occurring, but also to understand why the rate of conversion may be inefficiently high.

In general, as with other resources, land should be allocated to its highest valued use. Conversion from one use to another takes place when the relative values of the competing uses change.

Consider Figure 11.2, which graphs two hypothetical land uses—agriculture and forest. The left-hand side of the horizontal axis represents the location of the market. Moving to the right on that axis reflects an increasing distance away from the market.

TABLE 11.2 The Economic Harvesting Decision: Douglas Fir

Age (years)	10	20	30	40	50	60	68	70
Volume (cu. Ft.)	694	1,192	3,558	5,536	7,750	10,104	12,023	12,502
Undiscounted (*r* = 0.0)								
Value of timber ($)	694	1,192	3,558	5,536	7,750	10,104	12,023	12,502
Cost ($)	1,208	1,574	2,067	2,661	3,325	4,031	4,607	4,751
Net benefits ($)	-514	338	1,491	2,875	4,425	6,073	7,416	7,751
Discounted (*r* = 0.01)								
Value of timber ($)	628	1,567	2,640	3,718	4,712	5,562	6,112	6,230
Cost ($)	1,188	1,470	1,792	2,115	2,414	2,669	2,833	2,869
Net benefits ($)	-560	97	848	1,603	2,299	2,893	3,278	3,361
Discounted (*r* = 0.02)								
Value of timber ($)	567	1,288	1,964	2,507	2,879	3,080	3,128	3,126
Cost ($)	1,170	1,386	1,589	1,752	1,864	1,924	1,938	1,938
Net benefits ($)	-603	-98	375	755	1,015	1,156	1,190	1,188
Discounted (*r* = 0.04)								
Value of timber ($)	469	873	1,097	1,153	1,091	960	835	803
Cost ($)	1,141	1,262	1,329	1,346	1,327	1,288	1,251	1,241
Net benefits ($)	-672	-389	-232	-193	-237	-328	-415	-438

Age (years)	80	90	100	110	120	130	135
Volume (cu. Ft.)	14,848	17,046	19,000	20,614	21,792	22,438	22,514
Undiscounted (*r* = 0.0)							
Value of timber ($)	14,848	17,046	19,000	20,614	21,792	22,438	22,514
Cost ($)	5,454	6,114	6,700	7,084	7,538	7,731	7,754
Net benefits ($)	9,394	10,932	12,300	13,430	14,254	14,707	14,760
Discounted (*r* = 0.01)							
Value of timber ($)	6,698	6,961	7,025	6,899	6,603	6,155	5,876
Cost ($)	3,009	3,088	3,107	3,070	2,981	2,846	2,763
Net benefits ($)	3,689	3,873	3,917	3,830	3,622	3,308	3,113
Discounted (*r* = 0.02)							
Value of timber ($)	3,046	2,868	2,623	2,334	2,024	1,710	1,449
Cost ($)	1,914	1,860	1,787	1,700	1,607	1,513	1,435
Net benefits ($)	1,132	1,008	836	634	417	197	14
Discounted (*r* = 0.04)							
Value of timber ($)	644	500	376	276	197	137	113
Cost ($)	1,193	1,150	1,113	1,083	1,059	1,041	1,034
Net benefits ($)	-549	-650	-737	-807	-862	-904	-921

Volume of timber, from Table 11.1

Value of timber = price x volume/$(1 + r)^t$

Cost = $1,000 + $0.30 x volume/$(1 + r)^t$

Net benefits = value of timber - cost

The vertical axis represents net benefits per acre. Each of the two functions records the relationship between distance from the market and net benefits received for each type of land use. Both functions have a downward slope because transportation costs to the market lower profits per acre more for distant locations. According to this graph for this particular setting

FIGURE 11.2

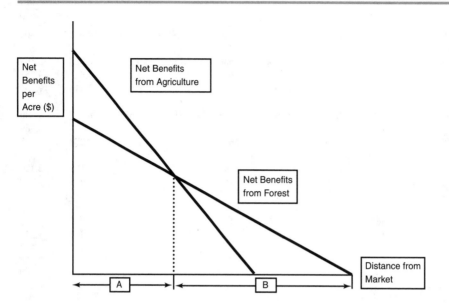

agricultural land has a higher value per acre close to the market, but forests have a higher value per acre farther away.

A market process that allocates land to its highest valued use would allocate the closest land to agriculture (a distance of A) and the other land to forest (from A to A + B). This allocation maximizes the net benefits received.

Conversion of land from one use to another would take place when these net benefit functions are changed. Conversion of forests to agricultural land would take place either when the net benefits function for agriculture shifted up and to the right or the net benefits function of forests shifted down and to the left.

Increases in the net benefits for agriculture could occur from:

- Domestic population increases that increase the domestic demand for food.
- Opening of export markets for agriculture that increase the foreign demand for local crops.
- Shifting from subsistence crops to cash crops (such as coffee or cocoa) for exports.
- The introduction of new crops that increase the yield per acre.
- New technologies that lower the costs and increase the profitability of producing crops.
- Lower agricultural transport costs due, for example, to the building of new roads into forested land.

Decreases in the net benefits for forests could result from a decline in the demand for forest products from either domestic or foreign markets.

◆ SOURCES OF INEFFICIENCY

The two previous sections demonstrated how profit-maximizing decisions can lead to defor-estation by promoting high rates of harvest, coupled with low rates of replanting, and by pro-moting the conversion of forest land to other uses. In this section we shall discover sources of inefficiency in those decisions. These inefficiencies have the effect of biasing profit-maximizing decisions toward excess rates of deforestation.

Perverse Incentives for the Landowner

Profit maximization does not produce efficient outcomes when the pattern of incentives fac-ing decision makers is perverse. Forestry provides an unfortunately large number of situa-tions where perverse incentives have produced very inefficient and unsustainable outcomes.

Privately owned forests are a significant force all over the world, but in some countries, such as the United States, they are the dominant force. Private forest decisions are plagued by externally generated costs of various types. Yields are adversely affected by externally imposed costs, such as air pollution. When heavy investments in forested lands can be wiped out by factors totally out of the control of the owners, the incentive to invest is undermined.

Providing a sustainable flow of timber is not the sole purpose of the forest, however. When the act of harvesting timber imposes costs on other valued aspects of the forest (e.g., watershed maintenance, prevention of soil erosion, and protection of biodiversity), these costs may not (and normally will not) be adequately considered in the decision.

The value of the standing forest as wildlife habitat or as a key element in the local ecosys-tem is one external cost that can lead to several inefficient decisions. Undervaluing the stand-ing forest provides an incentive to harvest an inefficiently large amount of timber and an incentive to harvest timber even when preservation is the preserved alternative. It also pro-vides an incentive to convert forest to other uses even when social net benefits are maximized by retaining the land as forest. The controversy that erupted in the Pacific Northwest of the United States between environmentalists concerned with the northern spotted owl and log-gers can, in part, be explained by the different values these two groups put on habitat destruc-tion. This region contains a number of old-growth Douglas firs, which can reach a height of 30 stories. These 200-year-old trees would be very valuable sources of timber, but they are also important components of the local ecosystem. (Among other ecosystem contributions, these trees provide a home for the endangered northern spotted owl.)

Perverse incentives can be created by governments as well. The rapid rate of deforestation in Brazil was in no small part due to perverse incentives created by the Brazilian government.[5]

The Brazilian government has reduced taxes on income derived from agriculture by as much as 90 percent. This tax discrimination overvalues agriculture and makes it profitable to cut down forests and convert the land to agriculture even when, in the absence of discrimina-tory tax relief, agriculture in these regions would not be profitable. In addition, land taxes dis-criminate against forests. A farm containing forests is taxed at a higher rate than one containing only pastures or cropland. This system of taxation encourages higher-than-efficient rates of conversion of land from forests to pasture or cropland and subsidizes an activity that,

---

[5]For further details on the Brazilian situation, see Hans P. Binswanger, "Brazilian Policies that Encourage Deforesta-tion in the Amazon," Working Paper No. 16 (Washington, DC: World Bank, 1989); and Dennis J. Mahar, *Government Policies and Deforestation on Brazil's Amazon Region* (Washington, DC: World Bank, 1989).

in the absence of tax discrimination, would not normally be economically viable. In essence, Brazilian taxpayers are subsidizing deforestation.

The system of property rights over land also is at fault. How do individuals establish a solid claim to unclaimed land in Brazil? Acquiring land by squatting has been formally recognized since 1850. A squatter acquires a *usufruct right* (the right to continue using the land) by (1) living on a plot of unclaimed public land and (2) using it "effectively" for at least a year and a day. If these two conditions are met for 5 years, the squatter acquires ownership of the land, including the right to transfer it to others. A claimant gets title for an amount of land up to three times the amount cleared of forest; hence, the more deforestation the squatter engages in, the larger the amount of land he or she acquires! In effect, deforestation was a necessary step in order for landless peasants to acquire land.

In the Far East and in the United States, perverse incentives take another form. Logging is the major source of deforestation in both regions. Why don't loggers act efficiently? The sources of inefficiency can be found in the concession agreements, which define the terms under which public forests can be harvested.

To loggers, existing forests have a substantial advantage over new forests: They can be harvested immediately. This advantage is reflected in the *economic rent* (called *"stumpage value"* in the industry) associated with a standing forest. In principle, governments have a variety of policy instruments at their disposal to extract this rent from the concessionaires, but they have typically given out the concessions to harvest this timber without capturing anywhere near all of the rent.[6] The result if that the cost of harvesting is artificially reduced and loggers can afford to harvest much more forestalled than is efficient. The failure of government to capture this rent also means that the wealth tied up in these forests has typically gone to a few; now wealthy, individuals and corporations rather than to the government to be used for the alleviation of poverty or other worthy social objectives.

Because forest concessions are typically awarded for limited terms, the concession holders have little incentive to replant, to exercise care in their logging procedures, or even to conserve younger trees until they reach the efficient harvest age. The future value of the forest will not be theirs to capture. The resulting logging practices destroy a multiple of the nubmer of trees represented by the high-value species because of the destruction of surrounding species by the construction of access roads, the felling and dragging of the trees, and the elimination of the protective canopy. Although sustainable forestry would be possible for many of these nations, concession agreements such as these make it unlikely.[7]

The list of losers from inefficient forestry practices frequently includes indigenous peoples who have lived in and derived their livelihood from these forests for a very long time. As the loggers and squatters push deeper and deeper into forests, the indigenous people,

---

[6]One way for the government to capture this rent would be to put timber concessions up for bid. Bidders would have an incentive to pay up to the stumpage value for these concessions. The more competitive the bidding was, the higher the likelihood that the government would capture all of the rent. In practice, many of the concessions have been given to those with influence in the government—at far below market rates. See Jeffrey R. Vincent, "Rent Capture and the Feasibility of Tropical Forest Management," *Land Economics* 66, No. 2 (May 1990): 212–23.

[7]Currently, foresters believe that the sustainable yield for closed tropical rain forests is zero, because they have not yet learned how to regenerate the species in a harvested area. Destroying the thick canopy, thereby allowing the light to penetrate, so changes the growing conditions and the nutrient levels of the soil that even replanting is unlikely to regenerate the types of trees included in the harvest.

who lack the power to stem the tide, are forced to relocate farther and farther away from their traditional lands.

Perverse Incentives for Nations

Another source of deforestation involves external costs that transcend national borders. Because the costs transcend national borders, it is unrealistic to expect national policy to solve the problem. Some international action would normally be necessary.

Biodiversity   Because of species extinction, the diversity of the forms of life that inhabit the planet is diminishing at an unprecedented rate. The extinction of species is an irreversible process. Deforestation, particularly the destruction of the tropical rain forests, is a major source of species extinction, because it destroys the most biologically active habitats. In particular, Amazonia has been characterized by Norman Myers as the "single richest region of the tropical biome."[8] The quantity of bird, fish, plant, and insect life that is unique to that region is unmatched anywhere else on the planet.

One of the tragic ironies of the situation is that these extinctions are occurring at precisely the moment in history when we would be most able to take advantage of the gene pool this biodiversity represents. Modern techniques now make it possible to transplant desirable genes from one species into another, creating species with new characteristics such as enhanced resistance to disease or pests. But the gene pool must be diverse if it is to serve as a useful source of donor genes. Tropical forests have already contributed genetic material to increase disease resistance of cash crops such as coffee and cocoa, and they have been the source of some entirely new foods. Approximately one quarter of all prescription drugs have been derived from substances found in tropical plants. Future discoveries, however, are threatened by deforestation's deleterious effect on habitats.

Global Warming   Deforestation also contributes to global warming. Because trees absorb carbon dioxide, a major greenhouse gas, deforestation eliminates a potentially significant means of ameliorating the rise in carbon dioxide emissions. Furthermore, burning trees, an activity commonly associated with agricultural land clearing, adds carbon dioxide to the air by liberating the carbon sequestered within the trees. Why is deforestation occurring so rapidly when the benefits conferred by a standing forest are so significant by virtually anyone's reckoning? The concept of externalities provides the key to resolving this paradox. Both the global warming and biodiversity benefits are largely external to the nation containing the forest, whereas the costs of preventing deforestation are largely internal. The loss of biodiversity precipitated by deforestation is perhaps most deeply felt by the industrialized world, not the countries that control the tropical forests. Currently, the technologies to exploit the gene pool this diversity represents are in widest use in the industrialized countries. Similarly, most of the damage from global warming would be felt outside the borders of the country being deforested, yet stopping deforestation means giving up the jobs and income derived from harvesting the wood or harvesting the land made available by clearing the forests. It is therefore not surprising that the most vociferous opposition to the loss of biodiversity is mounted in

---

[8]Norman Meyers, *The Primary Source: Tropical Forests and Our Future* (New York: W. W. Norton, 1984): 50.

the industrialized nations, not the tropical forest nations. Global externalities provide not only a clear rationale for market failure, but also a clear reason that the governments involved cannot be expected to solve the problem by themselves.

◆ POVERTY AND DEBT

Poverty and debt are also major sources of pressure on the forests. Peasants see unclaimed forestland as an opportunity to own land. Nations confronted with masses of peasants see un-owned or publicly owned forests as a politically more viable means of providing land for the landless than taking it forcibly from the rich. Without land, larger numbers of peasants descend upon the urban areas in search of jobs than can be accommodated by urban labor markets. Politically explosive tensions, created and nourished by the resulting atmosphere of frustration and hopelessness, force governments to open up forested lands to the peasants, or at least to look the other way as peasants stake their claims.

In eastern and southern Africa, positive feedback loops have created a downward cycle in which poverty and deforestation reinforce each other. Most natural forests have long since been cut down for timber, fuelwood, and cleared land for agricultural purposes. As forests disappear, the rural poor divert more time toward locating fuelwood. When fuelwood is no longer available, animal waste is burned, thereby eliminating it as a source of fertilizer to nourish depleted soils. The result, fewer trees, hastens soil erosion. Soil depletion leads to diminished nutrition, as does an inability to find or afford fuelwood or animal waste for cooking and for boiling unclean water. Lower nutrition saps energy, increases susceptibility to disease, and reduces productivity. Survival strategies may necessarily sacrifice long-term goals simply to ward off starvation or death; the forests are typically an early casualty.

Poverty at the national level takes the form of staggering levels of debt to service in comparison to the capacity to generate foreign exchange earnings. In periods of high real interest rates, servicing these debts commands most if not all foreign exchange earnings. Using these foreign exchange earnings to service the debt eliminates the possibility of using them to finance imports for sustainable activities to alleviate poverty.

The large debts owned by many developing countries also encourage these countries to overexploit their resource endowments in order to raise the necessary foreign exchange. Timber exports represent a case in point. As Gus Speth, the president of the World Resources Institute, points out, "By an accident of history and geography, half of the third-world external debt and over two-thirds of global deforestation occur in the same fourteen developing countries."

◆ SUSTAINABLE FORESTRY

We have examined two types of decisions by landowners—the harvesting decision and the conversion decision—that affect the rate of deforestation. The first type of decision involves how much timber to harvest, how often to harvest it, and whether to replant after a harvest. The second type of decision concerns whether and when to convert a forest to a different land use.

In both cases profit-maximizing decisions may not be efficient and these inefficiencies tend to create a bias toward higher rates of deforestation. In these cases correcting these inefficiencies can promote both efficiency and sustainability.

Does the restoration of efficiency guarantee sustainable outcomes? The answer depends on what is meant by *sustainable forestry*. If the possibility of compensation is entertained along with the "nondeclining welfare among generations" definition, then efficiency is fully compatible with sustainability as long as the economic gains from harvest are invested and shared with future generations. In this case, even when efficiency results in some deforestation, future generations will not suffer.

Let's suppose, however, that we consider sustainable forestry to be realized only when the forests are sufficiently protected that harvests can be realized perpetually. Under this definition, sustainable forestry would occur as long as harvests were limited to the growth of the forest, leaving the volume of wood unaffected over some specified period of time.

Efficiency is not necessarily compatible with this definition of sustainable forestry. Maximizing the present value involves an implicit comparison between the increase in value from delaying harvest (largely because of the growth in volume) and the increase in value from harvesting the timber and investing the earnings (largely a function of r, the interest rate earned on invested savings). With slow-growing species, the growth rate in volume is small; maximizing the present value may well involve harvest volumes higher than the net growth of the forest.

The search for sustainable forestry practices that are also economically sustainable has led to the development of rapidly growing tree species and plantation forestry. Rapidly growing species raise the attractiveness of replanting, because the invested funds are tied up for a shorter period of time. These species are raised in plantations, where they can be harvested and replanted at a low cost. Forest plantations have been established for such varied purposes as supplying fuelwood in developing countries to supplying pulp for paper mills in both the industrialized and developing countries.

Plantation forestry is controversial. Not only do plantation forests typically involve a single species of tree, which results in a poor wildlife habitat, they also require large inputs of fertilizer and pesticides.

In some parts of the world the natural resilience of the forest ecosystem is sufficiently high that sustainability is ultimately achieved, despite decades of unsustainable levels of harvest. In the United States, for example, sometime during the 1940s the net growth of the nation's timberlands exceeded timber removals. The four surveys conducted since that time confirm that net growth has exceeded harvests, in spite of a rather large and growing demand for timber. The total volume of forest in the United States has been growing since at least World War II; the harvests during that period have been sustainable in terms of forest volume, although the harvests of specific species in specific locations may not have been.

◆ PUBLIC POLICY

Does public ownership of the forests provide an answer? With the large amount of resources at its disposal, plus the ability to acquire land through eminent domain proceedings, the government can achieve the efficient scale rather easily. Furthermore, because it is not obligated to maximize profits, it can more easily take external effects on wildlife or recreation into account. Unfortunately, if the U.S. experience is typical, the potential to solve these problems by public ownership is more illusory than real.

Public ownership of lands in the United States started even before the fledgling nation had a constitution. The first public land, much of it forestland, was accepted as a donation by the Confederation of Congress on 29 October 1782. Though these lands were owned by the government, they were not managed by the government until more than a century later. The forest was treated as common property.

By the second half of the nineteenth century, a number of voices began to decry the apparent wanton destruction of the forests and to call for more enlightened use of the resource. The first piece of legislation designed to respond to this outcry was the Forest Reserve Act of 1891, which authorized the first permanent system of forest reserves. No provision for private harvesting of trees on the forest reserves was included. It was not until 1897, with the passage of a general administration bill, that Congress provided the funds and a process to manage this system. This act authorized private harvesting on forest reserves under other restrictive conditions.

The management for these reserves was transferred in 1905 to the U.S. Department of Agriculture's Forest Service. The Weeks Act, passed in 1911, enabled the Forest Service to acquire new forestland, which ultimately became a major part of the national forests in the eastern part of the United States.

The ambitious chief of the USDA Forest Service at that time, Gifford Pinchot, was to have an enormous influence over Forest Service management for several decades. Unlike other contemporaries—such as John Muir, who wanted to withdraw these lands from use—Pinchot vigorously pursued a philosophy that they should be used. Focusing first on timber production, his goal was the promotion of a sustainable level of harvest from the national forests. Concern over wildlife and recreation would come much later.

The desire to maintain a sustained level of harvest gave rise to the acceptance of a number of operational procedures by the Forest Service that were explicitly biologically based. Chief among these were the maximum average annual increment described earlier and the requirement to keep the allowable cut on the national forests steady through time to reduce the potential instability that would be faced by private forest owners if the market were flooded with timber from the public lands.

Although the Forest Service had, to some extent, followed a multiple-use philosophy since its inception, in the period following World War II public interest in nontimber uses grew sufficiently that the rather ad hoc methods of the Forest Service for achieving a balance were no longer deemed sufficient. During the 1960s and 1970s, a significant amount of new legislation was passed (Table 11.3).

In 1960, the Multiple Use–Sustained Yield Act mandated a multiple-use philosophy, without giving any guidance on how to implement that philosophy. In part, this act had been sought by the Forest Service to protect its multiple-use philosophy from attack by those seeking congressional or judicial support for single interests. However, subsequent legislation would force the Forest Service to be much more systematic in how it sought to define and implement a multiple-use philosophy.

The Wilderness Act of 1964 set aside specific forest areas to be preserved in their pristine state. No roads were permitted, and timber harvests were prohibited in wilderness areas. Although initially limited to designating specific areas that had by tradition not been harvested, the Act has in fact been the basis of a significant amount of judicial and agency interpretation, with the ultimate effect that it has ushered in much more wilderness land than was envisioned by those discussing it in Congress at the time the bill was passed.

TABLE 11.3 Major U.S. Forest Legislation

Date and Citation	Popular Name	Major Provisions
3 March 1891 26 STAT. 1095	Forest Reserve Act of 1891	Authorized first system of national, permanent forest reserves.
12 June 1960 74 STAT. 215	Multiple Use-Sustained Yield Act	Provided legislative mandate for multiple use of forestlands. No guidance on policy issues or management strategies.
3 Sept. 1964 78 STAT. 890	The Wilderness Act of 1964	Designated initial areas to be included as wilderness areas and set stringent rules governing use.
17 Aug. 1974 88 STAT. 476	Forest and Rangeland Renewable Resources Planning Act	A planning act, requiring an assessment of all renewable resources every 10 years and a program for the national forests every 5 years.

Though the management of public forests in the United States has been evolving since 1782, it has not yet reached the point where it yields efficient outcomes. Harvests from the public forests are subsidized by taxpayers.[9] The benefits of the forests to wildlife and recreation are inadequately protected.[10] Too many political pressures influence the process. Other policy approaches offer the prospect of a more rapid transition to efficiency.

One such approach involves restoring efficient incentives. Concessionaires should pay the full cost for their rights to harvest publicly controlled lands, including compensating for damage to the forests surrounding the trees of interest. The magnitude of land transferred to squatters should not be a multiple of the amount of cleared forest. The rights of indigenous peoples should be respected.

Another approach involves enlisting the power of consumers in the cause of sustainable forestry. The process typically involves the establishment of standards for sustainable forestry, employing independent certifiers to verify compliance with these standards, and allowing certified suppliers to display a label designating compliance (Example 11.1). The hope is that consumers will care enough to be willing to pay a sufficient premium for certified products so that certified firms can cover the extra costs of certification.

Most of these changes could be implemented by individual nations to protect their own forests, and to do so would be in their interests. By definition, inefficient practices cost more than the benefits received. The move to a more efficient set of policies would necessarily generate more net benefits, which could be shared in ways that build political support for the change. But what about the global inefficiencies? How can those be resolved?

---

[9]A review of several studies estimating the size of these subsidies can be found in Robert Repetto, *The Forest for the Trees? Government Policies and the Misuse of Forest Resources* (Washington, DC: World Resources Institute, 1988): 90–98.

[10]The below-cost sale of timber to harvesters is usually justified by the Forest Service in terms of the associated public benefits of harvesting (enhanced recreation opportunities and wildlife protection). This argument is difficult to accept because, as Robert Repetto puts it: "The supposed beneficiaries, including both environmental groups and fish and wildlife agencies in affected states, loudly oppose and are suing the Forest Service to stop it from providing the benefits they are allegedly receiving" (ibid, p. 97).

Example 11.1

Producing Sustainable Forestry Through Certification

The Forest Stewardship Council (FSC) is an international, not-for-profit organization headquartered in Oaxaca, Mexico. The FSC was conceived in large part by environmental groups, most notably the World Wide Fund for Nature (WWF). The goal of the FSC is to foster "environmentally appropriate, socially beneficial, and economically viable management of the world's forests." It pursues this goal through independent third-party certification of well-managed forests.

The FSC has developed standards to assess the performance of forestry operations. These standards address environmental, social, and economic issues. Forest assessments require one or more field visits by a team of specialists representing a variety of disciplines typically including forestry, ecology/wildlife, management/biology, and sociology/anthropology. In addition, the FSC requires that forest assessment reports be subject to independent peer review. Any FSC assessment may be challenged through a formal complaints procedure. FSC certified products are identified by an on-product label and/or off-product publicity materials.

Although the FSC is supported by a broad coalition of industry representatives, social justice organizations and environmental organizations, it is opposed by some mainstream industry groups, particularly in North America, and by some landowners associations in Europe. One unresolved issue is how to certify small- and medium-size landholdings.

Source: The ForestWorld Web Site; http:www.forestworld.com/. (Accessed 1/20/00.)

Several economic strategies exist. They share the characteristic of involving the compensation of the nations that confer external benefits so as to encourage conservation actions consistent with global efficiency.

Debt-Nature Swaps.   One strategy involves reducing the pressure on the forests caused by the international debt owed by many developing countries. Private banks hold most of the debt, and they are not typically motivated by a desire to protect biodiversity. Nonetheless, it is possible to find some common ground for negotiating strategies to reduce the debt. Banks realize that complete repayment of the loans is probably not possible. Rather than completely write off the loans, an action that not only causes harm to the income statement but also creates adverse incentives for repayment of future loans, they are willing to consider alternative strategies.

One of the most innovative policies that explores common ground in international arrangements has become known as the *debt-nature swap*. It is innovative in two senses: (1) the uniqueness of the policy instrument and (2) the direct involvement of nongovernmental organizations in implementing the policy. A debt-nature swap involves the purchase (at a discounted value in the secondary debt market) of a developing-country debt, usually by a nongovernmental environmental organization (NGO). The new holder of the debt, the NGO, offers to cancel the debt in return for an environmentally related action on the part of the debtor nation. In July 1987, for example, a U.S. environmental organization purchased $650,000 worth of Bolivia's foreign debt from a private bank at a discounted price of $100,000. It then swapped the face value of the debt with the government of Bolivia in return for an agreement to put together a public-private partnership. This partnership would develop a program that combines ecosystem conservation and regional development planning in 3.7 million acres of designated tropical forestland. The agreement also includes a $250,000 fund in local currency for establishing and administering a system for protecting the forest reserve.

Other arrangements involving different governments and different environmental organizations have since followed this lead. The main advantage of these arrangements to the debtor nation is that a significant foreign exchange obligation can be paid off with domestic currency. Debt-nature swaps offer a realistic possibility of turning what has been a major force for unsustainable economic activity (the debt crisis) into a force for resource conservation.

Extractive Reserves.   One strategy designed to protect the indigenous people of the forest as well as to prevent deforestation involves the establishment of *extractive reserves.* These areas would be reserved for the indigenous people to engage in their traditional hunting and gathering activities.

Extractive reserves have already been established in the Acre region of Brazil. Acre's main activity comes from the thousands of indigenous men who tap the rubber trees scattered throughout the forest, a practice dating back 100 years. Because of the activities of Chico Mendes, a leader of the tappers who was subsequently assassinated, the Brazilian government established four extractive reserves in June 1988 to protect the rubber tappers from encroaching development.

Establishing Conservation Easements.   A common global fund could be established to receive and dispense revenue raised in the industrialized nations for the purpose of protecting biodiversity. Controlled by representatives of these signatory nations, this fund could conceivably dispense monies for acquiring conservation easements for ecologically valuable sites. *Conservation easements* restrict the activities that can be permitted on the land. In the context of a tropical forest, a conservation easement would allow traditional uses of the forest by indigenous people, but clear-cutting would be prohibited. The easement could be granted in perpetuity or for a very long time.

One specific proposal on how this might be accomplished has been put forward by Katzman and Cale.[11] Five characteristics undergird their proposal:

1. Tropical nations would establish a legal distinction between conservation easements and other claims of ownership to forests in order to assure enforceability of the easement.

2. Industrialized nations would prioritize and evaluate habitats globally in order to assure that the expended funds achieved the maximum net benefits.

---

[11]Martin T. Katzman and William G. Cale, Jr., "Tropical Forest Preservation Using Economic Incentives," *Bioscience* 40, No. 11 (December 1990): 827–32.

3. Each tropical nation would establish an offering price for conservation easements on various habitats; in essence, each would compete for the limited funds.

4. Industrialized nations would agree to a budget for the acquisition of easements and for enforcement, and to a means for financing that budget.

5. A foundation would be established in each tropical nation to administer the financial transfer and to oversee the administration of the easement. (Unlike extractive reserves, where the easement is implicitly held by the tropical state, the conservation easement is granted to a foundation.)

One interesting precedent that shares some, but not all, of the elements of the Katzman and Cale proposal is that of the World Heritage Convention. This convention established the World Heritage Fund, which is used to protect environments of "outstanding universal value." Each signatory is required to contribute to the fund at least 1 percent of its contribution to the regular budget of UNESCO every two years. In practice, this means that the fund is financed almost entirely by the industrialized nations, but smaller nations can tap its resources. Some 57 natural sites are currently within this system, 25 of them in the Tropics.

Example 11.2

Success Stories in Conserving Tropical Forests

It is easy to lose sight of the positive steps that are being taken while concentrating on the problem of tropical deforestation, but some successes are apparent as well. These include:

- UNESCO's Man and Biosphere Program, which protects 244 "biosphere reserves" in 65 countries, 59 of them in 29 tropical countries
- Brazil's "protected-area system," which includes more than 12 million hectares of parks, biological reserves, forest reserves, hunting parks, game farms, and private reserves
- More than 500 conservation areas in Indonesia
- Peru's system of more than 20 parks and other protected areas, adding up to more than 4.3 million hectares, with four of the largest conservation areas in tropical forests
- Private reserve systems modeled after those in the developed countries (see Example 3.2) that are now beginning in several developing countries such as Venezuela, Indonesia, and Costa Rica

Source: Laural Tangley, "Saving Tropical Forests," *Bioscience* 36, No. 1 (January 1986): 4–8.

Some 90 nations have signed this agreement, which suggests that the fund arrangements have successfully exploited some common interests. Because subscribing to the agreement apparently confers benefits on the signatories, it is essentially self-enforcing. Other groups are pursuing similar objectives (see Example 11.2).

Debt-nature swaps, extractive reserves, and conservation easements all involve a recognition of the fact that resolving the global externalities component of deforestation requires a rather different approach than does resolving the other aspects of the deforestation problem. In general, this approach involves financial transfers from the industrialized nations to the tropical nations, transfers that are constructed so as to incorporate global interests into decisions about the future of tropical forests.

Sometimes these international funding efforts are combined with restrictive trade agreements. The objective is to apply pressure for sustainable harvesting by reducing the demand for any timber that has been harvested unsustainably (Example 11.3).

Recognizing the limited availability of international aid for the preservation of biodiversity habitat, nations have begun to tap other revenue sources. Tourist revenues have become an increasingly popular source, particularly where the tourism is specifically linked to the resources that are targeted for preservation. Rather than mixing these revenues with other public funds, nations are earmarking them for preservation (Example 11.4).

Example 11.3

The International Tropical Timber Agreement

International attempts to deal with the increasing rate of unsustainable deforestation in the Tropics resulted in the *International Tropical Timber Agreement* (ITTA). This agreement, which attempts to establish (in both the producing and consuming countries) the ground rules for trade in tropical timber, first came into force in 1983.

In 1990, the ITTA governments agreed to trade only in sustainably produced tropical timber after the year 2000. In the years following that commitment, however, the developing countries have increasingly pushed to have the same standards imposed on all internationally traded timber, including that produced in the Boreal and Temperate Zones, where most industrialized countries are located.

A new agreement reached in 1994 does not go so far as to require nontropical timber to be sustainably produced. It does, however, contain not only a pledge to adopt "appropriate guidelines and criteria for the sustainable management" of those forests, but also a pledge from the industrialized nations that they will provide "appropriate resources" for the forest conservation efforts initiated by developing countries.

Source: "New Tropical Timber Agreement Adopted," in *The Bulletin: Quarterly Review of Progress Towards Sustainable Development* (March 1994): 29.

Example 11.4

Trust Funds for Conservation

How can local governments finance biodiversity preservation when faced with limited availability of both international and domestic funds? One option, which is being aggressively pursued by the World Wildlife Fund, involves *trust funds*. Trust funds are moneys whose use is legally restricted to a specific purpose (as opposed to being placed in the general government treasury). They are administered by a trustees or board of trustees who are responsible for assuring compliance with the terms of the trust. Most, but not all, trust funds are *endowments,* meaning that the trustees can spend the interest and dividends from the funds, but not the principal. This assures the continuity of funds for an indefinite period.

Where does the money come from? Many nations that harbor biodiversity preserves can ill afford to spend the resources necessary to protect them. One possibility is to tap into foreign demands for preservation. In Belize the revenue comes from a "conservation fee" charged to all arriving foreign visitors. The initial fee, U.S.$ 3.75, was passed by Belize's parliament in January 1996. It is expected to raise $500,000 in revenues each year for the trust fund. Similar fees are being designed in Namibia and Papua, New Guinea.

Income from the trust funds can be used for many purposes, including training park rangers, developing biological information, paying the salaries of key personnel, and conducting environmental education programs, depending on the terms of the trust agreement.

Biodiversity preservation that depends on funds from the general treasury becomes subject to the vagaries of budgetary pressures. When the competition for funds intensifies, the funds may disappear or be severely diminished. The virtue of a trust fund is that it provides long-term sustained funding for the protection of biodiversity.

Source: Barry Spergel, "Trust Funds for Conservation," *FEEM Newsletter* 1 (April 1996): 13–16.

SUMMARY

Tree stands typically go through three distinct growth phases—slow growth in volume in the early stage, followed by rapid growth in the middle years and slower growth as the stand reaches full maturity. The owner who harvests the timber receives the income from its sale, but the owner who delays harvest will receive additional growth. The amount of growth depends on the part of the growth cycle the stand is in.

From an economic point of view, the efficient time to harvest a stand of timber is when the social net benefits are maximized. The net benefits are maximized when the marginal gain from delaying harvest one more year is equal to the marginal cost of the delay. For longer-then-efficient delays, the additional costs outweigh the increased benefits, whereas for earlier-than-efficient harvests, more benefits (in terms of the increased value of the timber) are given up than costs are saved. Typically, the efficient age of harvest is 25 years or older.

The harvest age depends on the circumstances. In general, the larger the discount rate the earlier the harvest. If standing timber provides amenity services (such as for recreation or wildlife management) in proportion to the volume of the standing timber, the efficient rotation will be longer than it would be in the absence of any amenity services.

Profit maximization can be compatible with both efficient and sustainable forest management under the right circumstances, but this is not always so. In particular, profit-maximizing private owners have an incentive to adopt the efficient rotation when amenity services are small and to undertake investments that increase the yield of the forest. Efficient harvest behavior is consistent with sustainability of a particular forest when the growth rate of the forest is larger than the discount rate.

In reality, not all private firms will follow efficient forest management practices because externalities may create inefficient incentives. When amenity values are large and not captured by the forest owner, the private rotation period may fail to consider these values, leading to an inefficiently short rotation period. Furthermore, these undervalued forests may be inefficiently converted to other land uses.

Inefficient deforestation has been encouraged by a failure to incorporate global benefits from standing forests; by concession agreements that provide incentives to harvest too much, too soon, and fail to provide adequate incentives to protect the interests of future generations; by land property-right systems that make the amount of land acquired by squatters a multiple of cleared forestland; and by tax systems that discriminate against standing forests.

Substantial strides toward restoring efficiency as well as sustainability can be achieved simply by recognizing and correcting the perverse incentives. Some corrective actions can be and should be taken by the tropical forest nations themselves as they are in their own interests. But these domestic actions will not, by themselves, provide adequate protection for the global interests in the tropical forests. Three schemes designed to internalize some of these benefits—debt-nature swaps, extractive reserves, and conservation easements—have already begun to be implemented.

FURTHER READING

Bowes, Michael D., and John V. Krutilla. "Multiple Use Management of Public Forestlands," in *Handbook of Natural Resource and Energy Economics,* Vol. 11, Allen V. Kneese and James L. Sweeney, eds. (Amsterdam: North-Holland, 1985). Excellent analytical treatment of the multiple-use strategy as it applies to U.S. forest policy. Somewhat mathematical.

Deacon, R. T. "The Simple Analytics of Forest Economics," in *Forestlands: Public and Private,* R. T. Deacon and M. B. Johnson, eds. (San Francisco: Pacific Institute for Public Policy Research, 1985). An especially accessible treatment of forestry economics.

Gregory, G. Robinson. *Resource Economics for Foresters* (New York: Wiley, 1987). An undergraduate text in forest economics that could be used to go beyond the material in this chapter.

Price, Colin. *The Theory and Application of Forest Economics* (Oxford: Basil Blackwell, 1989). A text aimed at "students of forestry and of natural resource management at both undergraduate and graduate levels."

Van Kooten, C., R. A. Sedjo, et al. "Tropical Deforestation: Issues and Policies." *The International Yearbook of Environmental and Resource Economics 1999/2000.* T. Tietenberg and H. Folmer, eds. (Cheltenham, UK, Edward Elgar, 1999): 198–249. A review of the economic research on tropical deforestation.

Wibe, Sören, and Tom Jones, eds. *Forests: Market and Intervention Failures* (London: Earthscan Publications, 1992). Case studies of forest policy in the United Kingdom, Sweden, Italy, Germany, and Spain.

ADDITIONAL REFERENCES

Berck, P. "Optimal Management of Renewable Resources with Growing Demand and Stock Externalities," *Journal of Environmental Economics and Management* 8 (1981): 105–17.

Clawson, Marion. *America's Land and Its Uses* (Washington, DC: Resources for the Future, 1972).

Clawson, Marion. *Forests for Whom and for What?* (Washington, DC: Resources for the Future, 1975).

Clawson, Marion. "Private Forests," in *Current Issues in Natural Resource Policy,* Paul R. Portney, ed. (Washington, DC: Resources for the Future, 1982): 283–92.

Clawson, Marion. *The Federal Lands Revisited* (Washington, DC: Resources for the Future, 1983).

Hartman, R. "The Harvesting Decision When a Standing Forest Has Value," *Economic Inquiry* 14 (1976): 52–58.

Howe, Charles W. *Natural Resource Economics: Issues, Analysis, Policy* (New York: Wiley, 1979).

Hyde, William F. *Timber Supply, Land Allocation, and Economic Efficiency* (Washington, DC: Resources for the Future, 1980).

Irland, Lloyd C. *Wilderness Economics and Policy* (Lexington, MA: Lexington Books, 1979).

Johansson, Per-Olov. *Economics of Forestry and Natural Resources* (New York: Basil Blackwell, 1985).

Merrifield, David E., and Richard W. Hayes. "The Adjustment of Product and Factor Markets: An Application to the Pacific Northwest Forest Products Industry," *American Journal of Agricultural Economics* 66 (February 1984): 79–87.

Repetto, R., and M. Gillis, eds. *Public Policy and the Misuse of Forest Resources* (Cambridge, UK: Cambridge University Press, 1988).

Samuelson, Paul A. "Economics of Forestry in an Evolving Society," *Economic Inquiry* 14 (1976): 466–492.

WEB SITES OF INTEREST

1. http://www.fs.fed.us/land/sustain_dev/welcome.htm
   The U.S. Forest Service's Sustainable Development Page.

2. *http://www.forestworld.com/*
   A site that has a considerable amount of information on forest certification programs.

3. *http://iisd1.iisd.ca/forests/*
   International Institute of Sustainable Development's International Forestry Policy Page.

DISCUSSION QUESTIONS

1. Should the U.S. national forests become "privatized" (i.e., sold to private owners)? Why or why not?

2. In his book *The Federal Lands Revisited,* Marion Clawson proposed what he called the "pullback concept":

   > Under the pullback concept any person or group could apply, under applicable law, for a tract of federal land, for any use they chose; but any other person or group would have a limited time between the filing of the initial application and granting of the lease or the making of the sale in which to "pull back" a part of the area applied for.... The user of the pullback provision would become the applicant for the area pulled back, required to meet the same terms applicable to the original application, ... but the use could be what the applicant chose, not necessarily the use proposed by the original applicant [p.216].

   Evaluate the pullback concept as a means for conservationists to prevent some mineral extraction or timber harvesting on federal lands.

Biodiversity II: Commercially Valuable Species

In an overpopulated (or overexploited) world, a system of the commons leads to ruin. . . . Even if an individual fully perceives the ultimate consequences of his actions he is most unlikely to act in any other way, for he cannot count on the restraint his conscience might dictate being matched by a similar restraint on the part of all others.

GARRETT HARDIN, *CARRYING CAPACITY AS AN ETHICAL CONCEPT* (1967)

◆ INTRODUCTION

Humans share the planet with many other living species. How those biological resources are treated depends on whether they are commercially valuable and the incentives of those who are best positioned to protect those species.

One major threat to wildlife is the destruction of its habitat. It follows that one important means of protecting wildlife is to protect the habitat in which it lives. We have seen in previous chapters how agricultural subsidies can cause excessive conversion of productive habitat to agriculture and how perverse incentives cause the destruction of forested ecosystems. Changing these perverse incentives can serve as a means of protecting wildlife habitat.

Protecting habitat is not enough, however, when the species becomes commercially valuable. Commercially valuable species are like a double-edged sword. On the one hand, the value of the species to humans provides a reason for human concern about its future. On the other hand, commercially exploited biological resources can also be depleted if not managed effectively. If, through human activities, the population is drawn down beyond a critical threshold, even commercially valuable species can become extinct.

Extinction, though important, is not the only critical renewable-resource-management issue. If it were, public policy could concentrate on avoiding extinction and not concern itself with any other outcome. Biological populations belong to a class of renewable resources we will call *interactive resources,* wherein the size of the resource stock (population) is determined jointly by biological considerations and by actions taken by society. The size of the population, in turn, determines the availability of resources for the future. Thus, humanity's actions determine the flow of these resources over time. Because this flow is not purely a natural phenomenon, a second crucial dimension is the optimum rate of use across time and across generations. What is the efficient rate of use of interactive renewable resources? In the absence of outside influences, can the market be relied upon to achieve and sustain this rate?

Using the fishery as a case study, we begin by defining what is meant by the *efficient level of harvest* from a fishery; we can then examine how well our economic and political institutions meet the efficiency test. We then consider how economic incentive systems can be used to assure sustainable harvests. Finally, we examine how another type of commercial opportunity, that associated with ecotourism, can be used for protection of certain specific types of wildlife.

◆ EFFICIENT HARVESTS

The Biological Dimension

Like many other studies, our characterization of the fishery rests on a biological model originally proposed by Schaefer.[1] The Schaefer model posits a particular average relationship between the growth of the fish population and the size of the fish population. This is an average relationship in the sense that it abstracts from such influences as water temperature and the age structure of the population. The model, therefore, does not attempt to characterize the fishery on a day-to-day basis, but rather in terms of some long-term average in which these various random influences tend to counterbalance each other (Figure 12.1).

The size of the population is represented on the horizontal axis and the growth of the population on the vertical axis. The graph suggests that there is a range of population sizes (S to S^*) where population growth increases as the population increases and a range (S^* to $\overline{S}$) where initial increases in population lead to eventual declines in growth.

We can shed further light on this relationship by examining more closely the two points S and $\overline{S}$ where the function intersects the horizontal axis and, therefore, growth in the stock is zero. $\overline{S}$ is known as the *natural equilibrium* because it is the population size that would persist in the absence of outside influences. Reductions in the stock because of mortality or out-migration would be exactly offset by increases in the stock because of births, growth of the fish in the remaining stock, and in-migration.

This natural equilibrium would persist because it is stable. A *stable equilibrium* is one in which movements away from this population level set forces in motion to restore it. If, for example, the stock temporarily exceeded $\overline{S}$, it would be exceeding the capacity of its habitat (called the *carrying capacity*). As a result, mortality rates or out-migration would

---

[1]M. D. Schaefer, "Some Considerations of Population Dynamics and Economics in Relation to the Management of Marine Fisheries," *Journal of the Fisheries Research Board of Canada* 14 (1957): 669–81.

FIGURE 12.1   The Relationship Between the Fish Stock and Growth

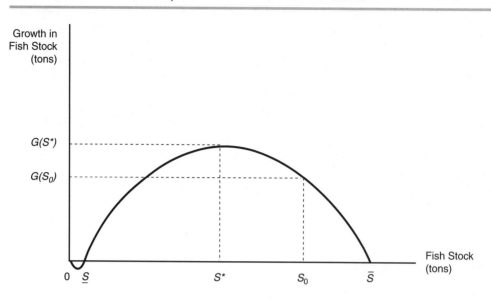

increase until the stock was once again within the confines of the carrying capacity of its habitat at $\bar{S}$.

This tendency for the population size to return to $\bar{S}$ works in the other direction as well. Suppose the population is temporarily reduced below $\bar{S}$. Because the stock is now smaller, growth would be positive and the size of the stock would increase. Over time, the fishery population would move along the curve to the right until $\bar{S}$ were reached again.

What about the other points on the curve? $\underline{S}$, known as the *minimum viable population*, represents the level of population below which growth in population is negative (i.e., deaths and out-migration exceed births and in-migration). In contrast to $\bar{S}$, this equilibrium is unstable. Population sizes to the right of $\underline{S}$ lead to positive growth and a movement along the curve to $\bar{S}$ and away from $\underline{S}$. When the population moves to the left of $\underline{S}$, the population declines until it eventually becomes extinct. In this region no forces act to return the population to a viable level.

A catch level is said to represent a *sustainable yield* whenever it equals the growth rate of the population, because it can then be maintained forever. As long as the population size remains constant, the growth rate (and, hence, the catch) will remain constant as well.

$S*$ is what is known in biology as the *maximum sustainable yield* population, defined as the population size that yields the maximum growth; hence, the maximum sustainable yield is equal to this maximum growth, and it represents the largest catch that can be perpetually sustained. If the catch is equal to the growth, the sustainable yield for any population size between $\underline{S}$ and $\bar{S}$ can be determined by drawing a vertical line from the stock size of interest on the horizontal axis to the point where it intersects the function and then drawing a horizontal line over to the vertical axis. The sustainable yield is the growth in the biomass defined by the intersection of this line with the vertical axis. Thus, in terms of Figure 12.1, $G(S_0)$ is the sustainable yield for population size S_0. Because the catch is equal to the growth, population size (and next year's growth) remains the same.

It should now be clear why $G(S^*)$ is the maximum sustainable yield. Larger catches would be possible in the short run, but these could not be sustained; they would lead to reduced population sizes and, eventually, if the population were drawn down to a level smaller than S, to the extinction of the species.

Static-Efficient Sustained Yield

Is the concept of maximum sustainable yield synonymous with that of efficiency? The answer is no. Efficiency, it may be remembered, is associated with maximizing the net benefit from the use of the resource. If we are to define the efficient allocation, we must include the costs of harvesting, as well as the benefits.

Let's begin by defining the *efficient sustainable yield* without worrying about discounting. The static-efficient sustainable yield is the catch level that, if maintained perpetually, would produce the largest annual net benefit. We shall refer to this as the *static-efficient* sustainable yield to distinguish it from the *dynamic-efficient* sustainable yield, which incorporates discounting. The initial use of this static concept enables us to fix the necessary relationships firmly in mind before dealing with the more difficult role discounting plays. Subsequently, we shall raise the question of whether or not efficiency always results in a sustainable yield as opposed to a catch that changes over time.

We shall condition our analysis on three assumptions that simplify the analysis without sacrificing too much realism: (1) The price of fish is constant and does not depend on the amount sold; (2) the marginal cost of a unit of fishing effort is constant; and (3) the amount of fish caught per unit of effort expended is proportional to the size of fish population (i.e., the smaller the population, the fewer fish caught per unit of effort).

In any sustainable yield, catches, population, effort levels, and net benefits remain constant over time. The static-efficient sustainable yield allocation maximizes the constant net benefit.

In Figure 12.2, the benefits (revenues) and costs are portrayed as a function of fishing effort and can be measured in vessel-years, hours of fishing, or some other convenient metric. The shape of the revenue function is dictated by the shape of the function in Figure 12.1, because the price of fish is assumed to be constant. To avoid confusion, notice that increasing fishing effort in Figure 12.1 would result in smaller population sizes and would be recorded as a movement from right to left. Because the variable on the horizontal axis in Figure 12.2 is effort, not population, an increase in fishing effort is recorded as a movement from left to right.

As sustained levels of effort are increased, eventually a point is reached (E^m) where further effort reduces the sustainable catch and revenue for all years. That point, of course, corresponds to the maximum sustainable yield in Figure 12.2, which involves identical population and growth levels. Every effort level portrayed in Figure 12.2 corresponds to a population level in Figure 12.1

The net benefit is presented in Figure 12.2 as the difference (vertical distance) between benefits (prices times the quantity caught) and costs (the constant marginal cost of effort times the units of effort expended). The efficient level of effort is E^e, that point in the diagram where the vertical distance between benefits and costs is maximized.

FIGURE 12.2 The Efficient Sustainable Yield for a Fishery

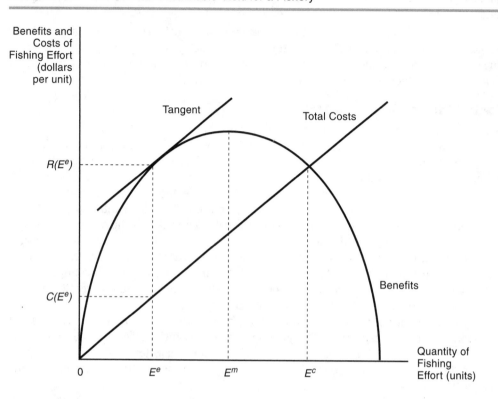

E^e is the efficient level of effort, because it is where marginal benefit (that graphically is the slope of the total-benefit curve) is equal to marginal cost (the *constant* slope of the total-cost curve). Levels of effort higher than E^e are inefficient, because the additional cost associated with them exceeds the value of the fish obtained. Can you see why lower levels of effort are inefficient?

Now we are armed with sufficient information to determine whether or not the maximum sustainable yield is efficient. The answer is clearly no. The maximum sustainable yield is efficient only if the marginal cost of additional effort is zero. Can you see why? (Hint: What is the marginal benefit at the maximum sustainable yield?) Because this is not the case, the efficient level of effort is *less* than that necessary to harvest the maximum sustainable yield. Thus, the static efficient level of effort leads to a *larger* fish population than does the maximum sustainable yield level of effort.

To fix these concepts firmly in mind, consider what would happen to the static efficient sustainable yield if a technological change (e.g., the use of sonar detection) were to occur, lowering the marginal cost of fishing. The lower marginal cost would result in a rotation of the total-cost curve to the right. With this new structure, the old level of effort is no longer efficient. The marginal cost of fishing (slope of the total-cost curve) is now lower than the marginal benefit (slope of the total-benefit curve). Because the marginal cost is constant, the equality of marginal cost and marginal benefit can only result from a decline in marginal benefits. This implies an increase in effort. The new static-efficient sustainable yield equilibrium implies more effort, a lower population level, a larger catch, and a higher net benefit for the fishery.

◆ APPROPRIABILITY AND MARKET SOLUTIONS

We have now defined an efficient allocation of the fishery. The next step is to characterize the normal market allocation and to contrast these two allocations. Where they differ, we can entertain the possibility of various public-policy corrective means.

Let's first consider the allocation resulting from a fishery managed by a competitive individual or sole owner. A sole owner would have a well-defined property right to the fish.

A sole owner would want to maximize his or her profits. Ignoring discounting for the moment, the owner can increase profits by increasing fishing effort until marginal revenue equals marginal cost. Clearly, this is effort level E^e, the static-efficient sustainable yield. This will yield positive profits equal to the difference between $R(E^e)$ and $C(E^e)$.

In ocean fisheries, however, sole owners are not normal. Ocean fisheries are typically common-property resources—no one exercises control over them. Because the property rights to the fishery are not conveyed to any single owner, no single fisherman can keep others from exploiting the fishery. Sometimes common-property resources can coexist in the same market as private-property fisheries (Example 12.1).

What problems arise when access to the fishery is completely unrestricted? Free-access resources create two kinds of externalities: (1) a *contemporaneous externality* and (2) an *intergenerational externality*. The contemporaneous externality, which is borne by the current generation, involves the overcommitment of resources to fishing—too many boats, too many fishermen, too much effort. As a result, current fishermen earn a substantially lower rate of return on their efforts. The intergenerational externality, borne by the future generations, occurs because overfishing reduces the stock, which in turn lowers future profits from fishing.[2]

Once too many fishermen have unlimited access to the same common-property fishery, the property rights to the fish are no longer efficiently defined. At the efficient level, each boat would receive a profit equal to its share of the scarcity rent. However, this rent serves as a stimulus for new fishermen to enter, drawing up costs and eliminating the rent. Hence, open access results in overexploitation.

The sole owner chooses not to expend more effort than E^e, because to do so would reduce the profits of the fishery, resulting in a personal loss. When access to the fishery is unrestricted, a decision to expend effort beyond E^e reduces profits to the fishery as a whole—but not to that individual fishermen. Most of the decline in profits falls on the other fishermen.

In a free-access resource, the individual fisherman has an incentive to expend further effort, until profits are zero. In Figure 12.2 that point is at effort level E^c, where net benefits are zero. It is now easy to see the contemporaneous externality—too much effort is being expended to catch too few fish, and the cost is substantially higher than it would be in an

---

[2]This will result in fewer fish for future generations as well as smaller profits if the resulting effort level exceeds that associated with the maximum sustainable yield. If the common-property effort level is lower than the maximum-sustainable-yield effort level (when extraction costs are very high), then reductions in stock would increase the growth in this stock, thus supplying more fish (albeit lower net benefits) to future generations.

Example 12.1

Property Rights and Fisheries: Oysters

The oyster industry provides a unique opportunity to study the effect of property-right structures on incentives, because it contains both private-property and common-property oyster beds. In some cases, these private-property and common-property beds compete with each other in the same market. This scenario allows us to compare the price and quantity behavior of markets supplied by fishermen operating under both property-right systems to markets that depend solely on one or the other.

What would we expect to find?

1. Common-property resources should be harvested earlier in the season, because there is less incentive to conserve common-property resources.

2. Common-property fishermen should earn lower average incomes, because the economic rent is dissipated.

3. The markets served purely by private-property fisheries should have higher prices, because private-property fishermen can respond to market conditions whereas common-property fishermen are driven to catch and sell as many fish as they can, as early as possible.

What was revealed by examining data from Maryland, Virginia, Louisiana, and Mississippi?

1. From 1945 to 1970 the ratio of the harvest in the earlier part of the harvesting season to that of the later part was 1.35 for the common-property resource state (Maryland) and 1.01 for the contiguous private-property state (Virginia).

2. Over the period 1950–1969 the average annual income of fishermen in Virginia was $2,453, whereas that for those of Maryland was $1,606. Another comparison revealed that fishermen in the private-property state of Louisiana earned $3,207, whereas their counterparts in the contiguous common-property state of Mississippi earned $870.

3. Over the period 1966–1969, the mean price per pound of oysters in markets served purely by private oyster beds was $0.94, whereas the mean price per pound for oysters from the common-property resource averaged only $0.73 per pound. In addition, in a comparison of contiguous private- and common-property states, the private-property states all experienced higher prices.

Though these results do not come from carefully controlled experiments and therefore cannot be regarded as definitive, they are completely compatible with our understanding of the way in which property-right structures influence decisions.

Source: Richard J. Agnello and Lawrence P. Donnelly, "Prices and Property Rights in the Fisheries," *Southern Economic Journal* 40 (October 1979): 253–62.

efficient allocation. If this point seems abstract, it shouldn't. Many fisheries are currently plagued by precisely these kinds of problems.

In a productive fishery in the Bering Sea and Aleutian Islands, for example, one study found significant overcapitalization.[3] Although the efficient number of "motherships" (used to take on and process the catch at sea so that the catch boats do not have to return to port as often) was estimated to be 9, the current level was 140. As a result, a significant amount of net benefits ($124 million a year) were lost. Had the fishery been harvested more slowly, the same catch could have been achieved with fewer boats used closer to their capacity.

An intergenerational externality occurs because the size of the population is reduced, causing future profits to be lower than would otherwise be the case. As the existing population is overexploited, the free-access catch initially is higher, but as growth rates are affected, the steady-state profit level, once attained, becomes lower.

When the resource owner has exclusive property rights, the use value of the resource is balanced against the asset value. When access to the resource is unrestricted, exclusivity is lost. As a result, it is rational for the individual fisherman to ignore the asset value, because he or she can never appropriate it, and simply maximize the use value. In the process, all the scarcity rent is dissipated.

Free-access resources do not automatically lead to a stock lower than that maximizing the sustained yield. We can draw a cost function with a slope sufficiently steep that it intersects the benefit curve at a point to the left of E^m. Nonetheless, it is not unusual for mature free-access common-property fisheries to be exploited well beyond the point of maximum sustainable yield.

Free-access fishing may or may not pose the threat of species extinction. It depends on the nature of the species and the benefits and costs of harvesting below the minimum viable population. Because the threat of extinction can only be determined in the context of empirical studies, it must be determined on a case-by-case basis (Example 12.2).

Are free-access resources and common-property resources synonymous concepts? They are not. On the one hand, governments can restrict entry, a topic we shall address in the next section. On the other hand, informal arrangements among those harvesting the common-property resource can also serve to limit access[4] (See Example 12.3).

Free access resources generally violate both the efficiency and sustainability criteria. If these criteria are to be fulfilled, some restructuring of the decision-making environment is necessary. How that could be done is the subject of the next section.

◆ PUBLIC POLICY TOWARD FISHERIES

What can be done? A variety of public policy responses are possible. Perhaps it is appropriate to start with the approach of simply allowing the market to work.

---

[3]Daniel D. Huppert, "Managing Alaska's Groundfish Fisheries: History and Prospects," Working Paper, University of Washington Institute for Marine Resources, May 1990.

[4]For other examples of these arrangements, see F. Berkes, D. Feeny, B. J. McCay, and J. M. Acheson, "The Benefits of the Commons," *Nature* 340, No. 6229 (July 1989): 91–93.

Example 12.2

Free-Access Harvesting of the Minke Whale

Amundsen, Bjørndal, and Conrad examined the effects of free-access fishing on the minke whale using an economic model that is very similar to the model developed in this chapter. Their model was designed to capture harvesting behavior, stock dynamics, and the response of the size of the fishing fleet relative to profitability. Their model was able to simulate both efficient and open-access equilibria.

Although the minke whale is found in both the northern and southern hemispheres, this study examined the North Atlantic stock that can be found in the areas around Spitsbergen (Norway), in the Barents Sea, along the Norwegian coast, and in the area around the British Isles.

The study results suggest that the efficient stock size is in the range of from 52,000 to 82,000 adult males, whereas the open-access stock level is in the 10,000–41,000 range. According to these results, free-access does cause substantial depletion of the stock, but it does not cause extinction. The benefits of further harvesting are lower than the costs.

Because the minke whale hunt went unregulated until 1973 (and was only loosely regulated for a while after that), it is possible for results from this simulation to be compared to the pre-regulation (open-access) historical experience with the fishery. In fact, the results of the model seem to conform rather well to that experience. Although it experienced a substantial increase after World War II, the harvest declined to a relatively stable level of 1,700 to 1,800 whales by 1973 and continued at approximately that level for some time, until effective regulation ultimately restricted fishing effort.

Source: E. S. Amundsen, T. Bjørndal, and J. M. Conrad, "Open Access Harvesting of the Northeast Atlantic Minke Whale," *Environmental and Resource Economics* 6, No. 2 (September 1995): 167–85.

Aquaculture

Having demonstrated that inefficient management of a fishery results from treating it as common, rather than private, property, we have one obvious solution—allowing some fisheries to be privately, rather than commonly, held. This approach can work when the fish are not very mobile (e.g., as lobsters), when they can be confined by artificial barriers, or when they instinctively return to their place of birth to spawn.

The advantages of such a move go well beyond the ability to preclude overfishing. The owners are encouraged to invest in the resource and undertake measures that will increase the productivity (yield) of the fishery.[5] This movement toward controlled raising and harvesting of fish is called *aquaculture,* and there are some noteworthy examples of its success.[6]

---

[5]For example, adding certain nutrients to the water or controlling the temperature can markedly increase the yields of some species.

[6]The examples of aquaculture in this chapter are drawn from John E. Bardach, John H. Ryther, and William O. McClarney, *Aquaculture: The Farming and Husbandry of Freshwater and Marine Organisms* (New York: Wiley Interscience, 1972).

Example 12.3

Harbor Gangs of Maine

Unlimited access to common-property resources reduces net benefits drastically, and this loss encourages those harvesting the resource to restrict access, if possible. The Maine fishery is one setting where informal arrangements have served to limit access.

Key among these arrangements is a system of territories that rely on informally established boundaries between fishing areas. These territories, particularly those near the offshore islands, tend to be exclusively harvested by close-knit, disciplined "gangs." Some gangs restrict access to their territory by various covert means, such as cutting the lines to lobster traps owned by new entrants, rendering them unretrievable. The income and catch levels achieved by the members of these gangs exceed those for comparable gangs lobstering less exclusive territories. Wilson (1977), for example, found that fishermen in the most restricted areas had 39 percent higher incomes and a 69 percent higher catch per trap haul.

Although it would be a mistake to assume that all common-property resources are characterized by unlimited access, it would also be a mistake to assume that these informal arrangements automatically provide sufficient social means for producing efficient harvests, thereby eliminating any need for public policy. The Maine lobster stock is also protected by regulations limiting the size of lobsters that can be taken and prohibiting the harvest of bearing females. Because estimates suggest that over 95 percent of legally harvestable lobsters are harvested, these regulations apparently afford significant protection to the stock. The main role of the informal arrangements has been to prevent the overcapitalization problem. When fewer fishermen harvest the available yield, income levels for those fishermen are higher.

Sources: James M. Acheson, *The Lobster Gangs of Maine* (Hanover, NH: University Press of New England, 1988), and J. A. Wilson, "A Test of the Tragedy of the Commons", in G. Hardin and J. Braden, eds., *Managing the Commons* (San Francisco: Freeman, 1977): 96–111.

Probably the highest yields ever attained through aquaculture resulted from using rafts to raise mussels. Some 300,000 kg/hectare (ha) of mussels, for example, have been raised in this manner in the Galician bays of Spain.[7] This productivity level approximates those achieved in poultry farming, widely regarded as one of the most successful attempts to increase the productivity of farm-produced animal protein.

In the United States aquaculture has been thwarted by a normal policy of treating bodies of water as common property. This need not be the case, of course. In Example 12.1 we saw that some oysters are raised in the United States in common-property beds and others are raised in private beds. As fish in the common-property resource become more scarce, triggering price increases, aquaculture probably becomes more profitable and prevalent.

---

[7]A *hectare* is a measure of surface area equal to 10,000 square meters, or 2.471 acres.

In some ways Japan, as a densely populated country depending heavily on fish for protein, has reached the point where merely harvesting what the sea offers is no longer sufficient to satisfy the market at low cost. Consequently, Japan has become a leader in aquaculture, undertaking some of the most advanced aquaculture ventures in the world. The government there has been supportive of these efforts, mainly by creating private-property rights for waters formerly held commonly. The governments of the prefectures (which are comparable to states in the United States) initiate the process by designating the areas to be used for aquaculture. The local fishermen's cooperative associations then partition these areas and allocate the subareas to individual fishermen for exclusive use. This exclusive control allows the individual owner to invest in the resource and to manage it effectively and efficiently.

Another market approach to aquaculture involves *fish ranching* rather than fish farming.[8] Whereas fish farming involves cultivating fish over their lifetime in a controlled environment, fish ranching involves holding them in captivity only for the first few years of their lives.

Fish ranching relies on the strong homing instincts in certain fish, such as Pacific salmon or ocean trout, which permits their ultimate capture. The young salmon or ocean trout are hatched and confined in a convenient catch area for approximately two years. When released, they migrate to the ocean. Upon reaching maturity, they return by instinct to the place of their births, where they are harvested. Brown estimates that 193,000 metric tons of salmon were harvested by the United States, the Soviet Union, and Japan in 1984.[9]

Aquaculture is certainly not the answer for all fish. Although it works well for shellfish, catfish, salmon, and some other species, some fish, such as tuna, will probably never be harvested domestically at a profit. Nonetheless, it is comforting to note that aquaculture can provide a safety valve in some regions and for some fish.[10]

Raising the Real Cost of Fishing

Perhaps one of the best ways to illustrate the virtues of using economic analysis to help design policies is to show the harsh effects of policy approaches that ignore it. Because the earliest approaches to fishery management had a single-minded focus on attaining the maximum sustainable yield with little or no thought given to maximizing the net benefit, they provide a useful contrast.

Perhaps the best concrete example is the set of policies originally designed to deal with overexploitation of the Pacific salmon fishery in the United States.[11] The Pacific salmon is particularly vulnerable to overexploitation, and even extinction, because of its migration pat-

---

[8]See R. L. Stokes, "The Economics of Salmon Ranching," *Land Economics* 58, No. 4 (November 1982): 464–77.

[9]Brown, Lester R., "Maintaining World Fisheries," in *State of the World: 1985,* Lester Brown et al. (New York: W. W. Norton, 1985): 90.

[10]In another example, Frederick Bell shows that the social welfare losses from the overexploitation of common-property wild crawfish were reduced by an estimated $1,068,933 in 1978 by the existence of private-property crawfish farms. Without them, social welfare losses would have been 4.16 times greater. See Frederick W. Bell, "Mitigating the Tragedy of the Commons," *Southern Economic Journal* 52, No. 3 (January 1986): 653–64.

[11]An excellent, detailed analysis of these policies can be found in J. A. Crutchfield and G. Pontecovo, *The Pacific Salmon Fisheries: A Study of Irrational Conservation* (Baltimore, MD: Johns Hopkins University Press, for Resources for the Future, 1969).

terns. Pacific salmon are spawned in the gravel beds of rivers. As juvenile fish they migrate to the ocean, only to return as adults to spawn in the rivers of their birth. After spawning, they die. When the adults swim upstream with an instinctual need to return to their native streams, they can easily be captured by traps, nets, or other catching devices.

Recognizing the urgency of the problem, the U.S. government took action. To reduce the catch, it raised the cost of fishing. Initially, this was accomplished by preventing the use of any barricades on the rivers and by prohibiting the use of traps (the most efficient catching devices) in the most productive areas. These measures proved insufficient, because mobile techniques (trolling, nets, etc.) proved quite capable, by themselves, of overexploiting the resource. Officials then began to close designated fishing areas and suspend fishing in other areas for certain periods of time. In Figure 12.3 these measures would be reflected as a rotation of the cost curve to the left until it intersected the benefits curve at a level of effort equal to E^e. The aggregate of all these regulations had the desired effect of curtailing the yield of salmon.

Were these policies efficient? They were not and would not have been even had they resulted in the efficient catch! This statement may seem inconsistent, but it is not. Efficiency implies both that the catch much be at the efficient level and that it must also be extracted at the lowest possible cost. This latter condition was violated by these policies (see Figure 12.3).

FIGURE 12.3 The Effect of Regulation

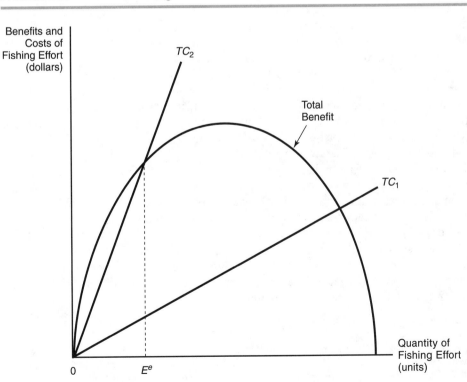

In Figure 12.3 are reflected the total cost in an efficient allocation (TC_1) and the total cost after these policies were imposed (TC_2). The net benefit received from an efficient policy is shown graphically as the vertical distance between total cost and total benefit. After the policy, however, the net benefit was reduced to zero; the net benefit (represented by vertical distance) was lost to society. Why?

The net benefit was wasted because of the use of excessively expensive means to catch the desired yield of fish. Traps would reduce the cost of catching the desired number of fish, but traps were prohibited, so that larger expenditures on capital and labor were required to catch the same number of fish. This additional capital and labor represents one source of the waste.

The limitations on fishing times had a similar effect on cost. Rather than allowing fishermen to spread their effort out over time so that the boats and equipment could be more productively utilized, fishermen were forced to buy larger boats that would allow them to take as much fish as possible during the shorter seasons.[12] Significant overcapitalization resulted.

Regulation imposed other costs as well. It was soon discovered that, although the preceding regulations were adequate to protect the depletion of the fish population, they had no effect on the incentive for individual fishermen to increase their share of the take. Even though the profits would be small because of high costs, new technological changes would allow those who adopted them to increase their share of the market and put others out of business. To protect themselves, the fishermen were successful in introducing bans on new technology. These restrictions took various forms, but two seem particularly noteworthy. The first was the banning of the use of thin-stranded monofilament net. The coarse-stranded net it would have replaced was visible to the salmon in the daytime and therefore could be avoided by them. As a result, it was useful only at night. By contrast, the thinner monofilament nets could be successfully used even during the daylight hours. The monofilament nets were banned in both Canada and the United States soon after they appeared.

The most flagrantly inefficient regulation was one in Alaska that barred gill-netters in Bristol Bay from using engines to propel their boats. This regulation lasted until the 1950s and heightened the public's awareness of the anachronistic nature of this regulatory approach. The world's most technologically advanced nation was reaping its harvest from the Bering Sea in sailboats while the rest of the world—particularly Japan and the Soviet Union—was modernizing its fishing fleets at a torrid pace!

Time-restriction regulations had a similar effect. Limiting fishing time provides an incentive to use that time as intensively as possible. Huge boats facilitate large harvests within the period and therefore are attractive, but they are very inefficient: The same harvest could have been achieved with fewer, smaller boats used to their optimum capacity.

Guided by a narrow focus on the maximum sustainable yield that ignored costs, these policies led to a substantial loss in the net benefit received from the fishery. Costs are an important dimension of the problem; when they are ignored, the incomes of fishermen suffer. When incomes suffer, further conservation measures become more difficult to implement, and incentives to violate the regulations are intensified.

---

[12]In one extreme example, the 1982 herring season in Prince William Sound lasted only four hours, and the catch still exceeded the area quota. This case is described in C. V. Tillion, "Fisheries Management in Alaska", *Papers Presented at the Expert Consultation on the Reduction of Fishing Effort (Fishing Mortality)*, FAO Fisheries Report 298, Supplement 3, (Rome: Food and Agriculture Organization, 1985): 291–97.

Taxes

Is it possible to provide incentives for cost reduction while assuring that the yield is reduced to the efficient level? Can a more efficient policy be devised? Economists who have studied the question believe that more efficient policies are possible.

Consider a tax on effort. In Figure 12.3 taxes on effort would be represented as a rotation of the *TC* line, and the after-tax cost to the fishermen would be adequately represented by line TC_2. Because the after-tax curve coincides with TC_2, the cost curve for all those inefficient regulations, doesn't this imply that the tax system is just as inefficient? No! The key to understanding the difference is the distinction between *transfer costs* and *real-resource costs*.

Under a regulation system of the type described earlier in this chapter, all of the costs included in TC_2 are real-resource costs, which involve utilization of resources. Transfer costs, by contrast, involve transfers of resources (from one part of society to another) rather than their use. Transfer costs apply to that part of society bearing them but are exactly offset by the gain received by the recipients. Resources are not used up; they are merely transferred. Thus, the calculation of the size of the net benefit should subtract real-resource costs, but not transfer costs, from benefits. For society as a whole, transfer costs are retained as part of the net benefit.

In Figure 12.3 the net benefit under a tax system is identical to that under an efficient allocation. The net benefit represents a transfer cost to the fisherman that is exactly offset by the revenues, received by the tax collector. This discussion should not obscure the fact that, as far as the individual fisherman is concerned, these are very real costs. Rent normally received by a sole owner is now received by the government. Because the tax revenues involved can be substantial (Example 12.4), fishermen wishing to have the fishery efficiently managed may object to this particular way of doing it. They would prefer a policy that restricts catches while allowing them to keep the rents. Is that possible?

Individual Transferable Quotas (ITQs)

One policy making it possible to obtain an efficient allocation is a properly designed quota on the number of fish that can be taken from the fishery. The "properly designed" caveat is important because there are many different types of quota schemes, and not all are of equal merit. An efficient quota system has three identifiable characteristics:

1. The quotas entitle the holder to catch a specified weight of a specified type of fish.
2. The total amount of fish authorized by the quotas held by all fishermen should be equal to the efficient catch for the fishery.
3. The quotas should be freely transferable among fishermen.

Each of these three characteristics plays an important role in obtaining an efficient allocation. Let's suppose, for example, the quota were defined in terms of the right to own and use a fishing boat rather than in terms of catch—not an uncommon type of quota. Such a quota is not efficient, because under this type of quota an inefficient incentive still remains for each boat owner to build larger boats, to place extra equipment on them, and to spend more time fishing. These actions would expand the capacity of each boat and cause the actual catch to exceed the target (efficient) catch. In a nutshell, the boat quota

Example 12.4

Efficient vs. Market Exploitation of Lobsters

Two economists, Henderson and Tugwell, set out to quantify the degree of overexploitation characterizing two particular Maritime Canadian common-property lobster fishing ports: Port Maitland and Miminegash. They estimated the relationship between effort and sustainable catch for each of the two fishing grounds and also the costs of various levels of fishing effort. Using these functions, they derived both the optimal and free-market solutions, which could then be compared to each other and to the maximum sustainable yield. These calculations could also be used to derive the tax required to force the market solution to converge with the efficient (optimal) solution.

| | PORT MAITLAND | | | MIMINEGASH | | |
	Optimal Solution	Actual Free Entry	Average 1959–63	Optimal Solution	Actual Free Entry	Average 1959–63
Lobster stock (1,000 lb.)	3,050	2,490	2,467	2,450	1,125	1,273
Lobster catch (1,000 lb.)	745	1,330	1,183	801	936	1,094
Effort (100 traps)	112	454	—	122	365	—
Ratio: catch/stock	0.25	0.53	0.48	0.33	0.83	0.86
Optimal tax/1,000 lb. catch	$270	NA	NA	$255	NA	NA
Annual resource savings: value of trap savings less value of reduced catch	$202,173	NA	NA	$180,470	NA	NA

	Port Maitland	Miminegash
Maximum sustainable yield stock	1,766	1,629
Lobster price/1,000 lb.	$485	$370
Opportunity cost/100 traps	$1,421	$950

Several features are noteworthy in these tables. The free-entry (or market) solutions for catch are remarkably close to the actual averages, in spite of the uncertainty of estimating the underlying equations. The free-entry catch levels are substantially greater than the optimal levels because of an inefficiently high level of effort (traps). The last line of entries in the first table indicates that the welfare losses (compared to the optimum level) run about $202,000 in Port Maitland and $180,000 in Miminegash *each year.* For Port Maitland this represents a loss of some 62 percent of the net benefits obtainable under an efficient program!

The first table also presents the optimum tax level that would cause the free-access and optimum solutions to converge. For Port Maitland this amounts to $270 per 1,000 pounds of lobster, approximately 56 percent of the current price ($485). If this tax were levied, some fishermen would exit and the catch would rise, but the remaining fishermen would not receive higher profits. The increased net benefits would be appropriated by the government. It is not difficult to understand why fishermen do not generally support tax policies, even though these policies could prevent overexploitation.

Source: J. V. Henderson and M. Tugwell, "Exploitation of the Lobster Fishery: Some Empirical Results," *Journal of Environmental Economics and Management* 6 (December 1979): 287–96.

limits the number of boats fishing but does not limit the amount of fish caught by each boat. If we are to reach and sustain an efficient allocation, it is the catch that must ultimately be limited.

Although the purpose of the second condition is obvious, the role of the third, transferability, deserves more consideration. With transferability, the entitlement to fish flows naturally to those gaining the most benefit from it because their costs are lower. Because it is valuable, the transferable quota commands a positive price. Those who have quotas but also have high costs find they make more money by selling the quotas than by using them. Meanwhile, those who have lower costs find they can purchase more quotas and still make money.

Transferable quotas also encourage technological progress. Adopters of new cost-reducing technologies can make more money on their existing quotas and profit from purchasing new quotas from others who have not adopted the technologies.

Therefore, in marked contrast to the earlier regulatory methods used to raise costs, both the tax system and the transferable quota system encourage low extraction rates.

How about the distribution of the rent? In a quota system the distribution of the rent depends crucially on how the quotas are initially allocated. There are many possibilities, each with different outcomes. The first possibility is for the government to auction these quotas off. But the government would then appropriate all the rent, and the outcome would be very similar to the outcome of the tax system. If the fishermen do not like the tax system, they would not like the auction system either.

In an alternative approach, the government could give the quotas to the fishermen—say, in proportion to their historical catch. The fishermen could then trade among themselves until a market equilibrium is reached. All the rent would be retained only by the *current* generation of fishermen. Fishermen who might want to enter the market would have to purchase the quotas from existing fishermen. Competition among the potential purchases would drive up the price of the transferable quotas until it reflected the market value of future rents, appropriately discounted.[13]

Thus, this type of quota system allows the rent to remain with the fishermen, but only with the current generation of fishermen. Future generations see little difference between this quota system and a tax system; in either case, they have to pay to enter the industry, whether it be through the tax system or by purchasing the quotas.

In 1983 a limited individual transferable quota (ITQ) system was established in New Zealand to protect its deepwater trawl fishery. Though this was far from being the only, or even the earliest, application of ITQs (Table 12.1), it provides an unusually rich opportunity to study how this approach works in practice.

Because this fishery was newly developed, allocating the quotas proved relatively easy. The total of allowable catches for the seven basic species was divided into ITQs and were allocated to existing firms on the basis of investment in harvesting equipment, investment in onshore production equipment, and recent onshore production. The rights to harvest were denominated in terms of a specific amount of fish, but were only granted for a 10-year period.

At the same time the deep-sea fishery policy was being considered, the inshore fisheries began to fall on hard times. Too many participants were chasing too many fish. Some particularly

---

[13]This occurs because the maximum bid any potential entrant would make is the value to be derived from owning that permit. This value is equal to the present value of future rents (the difference between price and marginal cost for each unit of fish sold). Competition will force the purchaser to bid near that maximum value, lest he or she lose the quota.

TABLE 12.1 Countries with Individual Transferable Quota Systems

Countries	Number of Species Covered
Australia	4
Canada	14
Chile	3
Iceland	16
Netherlands	4
New Zealand	33
United States	4

Sources: Information compiled from OECD, *Implementing Domestic Tradable Permits for Environmental Protection* (Paris: Organization for Economic Co-operation and Development, 1999):19, and P. Bernal and B. Aliaga, "ITQs in Chilean Fisheries," in A. Hatcher and K. Robinson, eds. *The Definition and Allocation of Use Rights in European Fisheries, Proceedings of the Second Concerted Workshop on Economics and the Common Fisheries Policy* (Brest, France, 5–7 May 1999), (published by the Center for the Economics and Management of Aquatic Resources, University of Portsmouth, UK): 117–130.

desirable fish species were being seriously overfished. Although the need to reduce the amount of pressure being put on the population was rather obvious, how to accomplish that reduction was not at all obvious. It was relatively easy to prevent new fishermen from entering the fisheries, but it was harder to figure out how to reduce the pressure from those who had been fishing in the areas for years or even decades. Because fishing is characterized by economies of scale, simply reducing everyone's catch proportionately wouldn't make much sense. That would simply place higher costs on everyone and waste a great deal of fishing capacity as all boats sat around idle for a significant proportion of time. A better solution would clearly be to have fewer boats harvesting the stock. That way, each boat could be used closer to its full capacity, without depleting the population. Which fishermen should be asked to give up their livelihood and leave the industry?

The economic incentive approach addressed this problem by having the government buy back catch quotas from those willing to sell them. Although initially this was financed out of general revenues, subsequently it was financed by a fee on catch quotas. Essentially, each fisherman stated the lowest price that he or she would accept for leaving the industry; the regulators selected those who could be induced to leave at the lowest price, paid the stipulated amount from the fee revenues, and retired their licenses to fish for this species. It wasn't long before a sufficient number of licenses had been retired, and the population was protected. Because the program was voluntary, those who left the industry only did so when they felt they had been adequately compensated.

Meanwhile, those who paid the fee realized that this small investment would benefit them greatly in the future as the population recovered. A difficult and potentially dangerous pressure on a valuable natural resource had been alleviated by the creative use of an approach that changed the economic incentives. Toward the end of 1987, however, a new problem emerged. The original stock of one species (orange roughy) turned out to have been seriously overestimated by biologists.

Because the total allocation of quotas was derived from this estimate, the practical implication was that an unsustainably high level of quotas had been issued; the stock was in jeopardy.

Faced with the unacceptably large budget implications of buying back a significant amount of the quota, the government ultimately shifted to a percentage share allocation of the quota. Under this system, instead of owning a quota defined in terms of a specific quantity of fish, fishermen own percentage shares of a *total allowable catch*. The total allowable catch is determined annually by the government. In this way, the government can annually adjust the total allowable catch, based on the latest stock assessment estimates, without having to buy back (or to sell) large amounts of the quota. This approach affords greater protection to the stock, but increases the financial risk to the fishermen.

Some other implementation problems have emerged as well. Fishing effort is frequently not very well targeted. Species other than those sought (known as "by-catch") may well end up as part of the catch. If those species are also regulated by quotas and the fishermen do not have sufficient ITQs to cover the by-catch, they are faced with the possibility of being fined when they land the unauthorized fish. Dumping the by-catch overboard allows them to avoid the fines. However, because the jettisoned fish frequently do not survive, this represents a double waste—not only is the stock reduced, but the harvested fish are wasted.

High-grading is another problem fisheries managers have had to deal with. High-grading can occur when quotas specify the catch in terms of weight of a certain species, but the value of the catch is affected greatly by the size of the individual fish. To maximize the value of the quota, fishermen have an incentive to throw back the less valuable (typically, smaller) fish, keeping only the most valuable individuals. As with by-catch, when release mortality is high, high-grading results in both smaller stocks and wasted harvests.

Some fisheries managers have successfully solved both problems by allowing fishermen to cover temporary overages with allowances subsequently purchased or leased from others. As long as the market value of the "extra" fish exceeds the cost of leasing the quota, the fishermen will have an incentive to land and market the fish, and the stock will not be placed in jeopardy.

The 200-Mile Limit

The final policy dimension concerns the international aspects of the fishery problem. Obviously, the various policy approaches to effective management of fisheries require that some governing body have jurisdiction over a fishery so that it can enforce the regulations.

This is not currently the case for many of the ocean fisheries. Much of the open water of the ocean is a common-property resource to governments as well as to individual fishermen. Therefore, no single body can exercise control over it. As long as that continues to be the case, the corrective action will be difficult to implement. In recognition of this fact, there is an evolving law of the sea, defined by international treaties. One of the concrete results of this law has been some limited restrictions on whaling. Whether or not this process ultimately yields a consistent and comprehensive system of management remains to be seen.

Countries bordering the sea have declared that their ownership rights extend some 200 miles out to sea. Within these areas, the countries have exclusive jurisdiction and can proceed to implement effective management policies. These declarations have been upheld and are now firmly entrenched in international law. Thus, very rich fisheries in coastal waters can be protected, whereas those in the open waters await the outcome of an international negotiations process.

Example 12.5

Local Approaches to Wildlife Protection: Zimbabwe

In 1989 an innovative program was initiated in Zimbabwe. It stands out as a success among other African wildlife protection schemes. The program transformed the role of wildlife from a state-owned treasure to be preserved into an active resource—one that is controlled and used by both commercial farmers and smallholders in communal lands. The transformation has been good for the economy and the wildlife.

The initiative is called the Communal Areas Management Program for Indigenous Resources, or CAMPFIRE. It was originally sponsored by several different agencies—including the University of Zimbabwe's Center for Applied Study, the Zimbabwe Trust, and the Worldwide Fund for Nature (WWF)—in cooperation with the Zimbabwe government.

Under the CAMPFIRE system, villagers collectively utilize local wildlife resources on a sustainable basis. Trophy hunting by foreigners is perhaps the most important source of revenue, because hunters require few facilities and are willing to pay substantial fees to kill a limited number of large animals. The government sets the prices of hunting permits, as well as quotas for the number of animals that can be taken per year in each locality. Individual communities sell the permits and contract with safari operators, who conduct photographic and hunting expeditions on the community lands.

The associated economic gains accrue to the villages, which then decide how the revenues should be used. The money may be paid out in one of two ways—(1) payments to households in the form of cash dividends, which may amount to 20 percent or more of an average family's income, or (2) payments to be used for capital investments in the community (e.g., schools, clinics, or laborsaving machines)—or some combination of the two methods. In at least one area, revenues compensate citizens who have suffered property loss because of wild animals. Households may also receive nonmonetary benefits, such as meat from problem animals or culled herds. By consistently meeting their needs from their own resources on a sustainable basis, local communities become self-reliant. This voluntary program has been steadily expanding since its inception and now includes about half of Zimbabwe's 55 districts.

Sources: Edward Barbier. "Community-Based Development in Africa" in Timothy Swanson, Edward Barbier, eds. *Economics for the Wilds: Wildlife, Diversity, and Development* (Washington, DC: Island Press, 1992): 107-118; Jan Bojö, "The Economics of Wildlife: Case Studies from Ghana, Kenya, Namibia and Zimbabwe," AFTES Working Paper No. 19, World Bank, February 1996, and the Web site: http://www.colby.edu/personal/ thtieten/end-zim.html.

◆ PREVENTING POACHING

A second type of threat to commercially valuable species comes from poaching. Poaching is the illegal harvest of the species.

One approach to poaching prevention involves providing appropriate incentives to local populations who are in a position to protect wildlife. One especially successful program has been established in Zimbabwe (Example 12.5).

Kenya, a country with large declines in its elephant population, has no such system. Whereas in Zimbabwe villagers have a very large stake in protecting the source of this income, the elephant herd, Kenyans have little stake in the elephants' protection. The potential revenue that could be used to institutionalize a protection system is enormous. Economists have estimated that some $25 million per year would be available in Kenya from tourists seeking to view and photograph elephants.[14]

One approach to the protection of biological species is to rearrange the economic incentives so that local groups have an economic interest in their preservation. Unlimited access to common-property resources undermines those incentives.

Although it is important to recognize that much of what we have covered in this chapter carries over from marine-based wildlife to land-based wildlife, it is equally important to recognize a significant difference. Land-based wildlife is threatened not only by the free-access problem we have been discussing, but also by competition for the land that provides their habitat, a subject covered in the previous chapter.

Hence, for land-based wildlife, preventing free-access overexploitation may be a necessary, but not sufficient, strategy. It is also necessary to complement strategies that limit access with strategies that prevent excessive conversion of habitat from other uses.[15]

SUMMARY

Unrestricted access to commercially valuable species will generally result in overexploitation. This overexploitation, in turn, results in overcapitalization, depressed incomes for harvesters, and depleted biological populations. Even extinction is possible, especially for species characterized by particularly low extraction costs (e.g., the Pacific salmon). Where extraction costs are higher, extinction is unlikely, even with unrestricted access.

Both the private and public sectors have moved to ameliorate the problems associated with past mismanagement of wildlife populations. For marine-based wildlife, Japan and other countries have stimulated the development of aquaculture by reasserting private-property rights. Governments in Canada and the United States have moved to limit overexploitation of the Pacific salmon. International agreements have been reached that place limits on whaling.

For land-based wildlife, countries such as Zimbabwe have initiated strategies to prevent excessive conversion of land currently used for habitat to uses such as agriculture, mining, and urbanization. In part, these strategies protect habitat by recognizing and capturing the value of that particular use of the land.

Creative strategies for sharing the gains from moving to an efficient level of use could prove to be a significant technique in the arsenal of weapons designed to protect a broad class of biological resources from overexploitation. An increasing reliance on individual transferable quotas (ITQs) offers the possibility to preserve stocks without jeopardizing the incomes

---

[14]Gardner Brown Jr. and Wes Henry, "The Economic Value of Elephants," Working Paper No. 89–12 (London Environmental Economics Centre, 1989).

[15]For an excellent treatment of this aspect of protecting wildlife, see Timothy Swanson, "The Economics of Extinction Revisited and Revised: A Generalized Framework for the Analysis of the Problems of Endangered Species and Biodiversity Losses," *Oxford Economic Papers,* Vol. 46 Supplement (1994): 822–40.

of those whose livelihoods depend on harvesting them. Furthermore, giving local communities a stake in preserving elephant herds has provided a vehicle for building political coalitions to prevent overexploitation of this resource.

It would be folly to ignore barriers to further action, such as the reluctance of individual fishermen to submit to many forms of regulation, the lack of a firm policy governing open ocean waters, and the difficulties of enforcing various approaches. Whether these barriers will fall before the pressing need for effective management remains to be seen.

FURTHER READING

Bjørndal, T. and G. R. Munro (1998). "The Economics of Fisheries Management: A Survey," *The International Yearbook of Environmental and Resource Economics 1998/1999.* T. Tietenberg and H. Folmer, eds. in (Cheltenham, UK, Edward Elgar):153-188. A review of current economic research on fisheries management.

Clark, Colin W. *Mathematical Bioeconomics: The Optimal Management of Renewable Resources,* 2nd ed. (New York: Wiley Interscience, 1990). Careful development of the mathematical models that underlie current understanding of the exploitation of renewable resources under a variety of property-rights regimes.

Schlager, Edella and Elinor Ostrom, "Property-Right Regimes and Natural Resources: A Conceptual Analysis," *Land Economics* 68 (1992): 249–62. The authors develop a conceptual framework for analyzing a number of property-rights regimes and use this framework to interpret findings from a number of empirical studies.

Townsend, Ralph E. "Entry Restrictions in the Fishery: A Survey of the Evidence," *Land Economics* 66 (1990): 361–78. Reviews the relevant experience with about 30 limited-entry programs around the world. Identifies those features of limited-entry programs that seem to contribute to success or to failure.

ADDITIONAL REFERENCES

Anderson, Lee G. *The Economics of Fisheries Management* (Baltimore: Johns Hopkins University Press, 1977).

Areason, R. "The Icelandic Individual Transferable Quota System: A Descriptive Account," *Marine Resource Economics* 8 (1993): 201–18.

Bell, Frederick W. *Food from the Sea: The Economics and Politics of Ocean Fisheries* (Boulder, CO: Westview Press, 1978).

Boyce, John R. "Individual Transferable Quotas and Production Externalities in a Fishery," *Natural Resource Modeling* 8 (1992): 385–408.

Brown, Lester. *In the Human Interest* (New York: W. W. Norton, 1974).

Campbell, H. F., and R. K. Lindner. "The Production of Fishing Effort and the Economic Performance of License Limitation Programs" *Land Economics* 66 (February 1990): 56–66.

Cheng, Juo-Shung, et al. "Analysis of Modified Model for Commercial Fishing with Possible Extinctive Fishery Resources," *Journal of Environmental Economics and Management* 8 (June 1981): 151–55.

Clark, C. W. "Profit Maximization and the Extinction of Animal Species," *Journal of Political Economy* 81 (August 1973): 950-60.

Clark, Colin W. *Mathematical Bioeconomics: The Optimal Management of Renewable Resources* (New York: Wiley Interscience, 1976).

Dupont, Diane P. "Rent Dissipation in Restricted Access Fisheries," *Journal of Environmental Economics and Management* 19 (July 1990): 26–44.

FAO, *The State of Food and Agriculture: 1992* (Rome: Food and Agriculture Organization of the United Nations, 1992).

Gallastegui, Carmen. "An Economic Analysis of Sardine Fishing in the Gulf of Valencia (Spain)," *Journal of Environmental Economics and Management* 10 (June 1983): 138–50.

Geen, Gerry, and Mark Nayar. "Individual Transferable Quotas in the Southern Bluefin Tuna Fishery: An Economic Appraisal," *Marine Resource Economics* 5 (1988): 365–88.

Gordon, H. Scott. 'The Economic Theory of a Common-Property Resource: The Fishery," *Journal of Political Economy* 62 (April 1954): 124–42.

Iudicello, Suzanne, et al. *Fish, Markets, and Fishermen: The Economics of Overfishing* (Washington, DC: Island Press, 1999).

Merrifield, J. "Implementation Issues: the Political Economy of Efficient Fishing," *Ecological Economics,* Vol. 30, No. 1 (July, 1999): 5–12.

Munro, G. R. "Fisheries, Extended Jurisdiction, and the Economics of Common-Property Resources," *Canadian Journal of Economics* 15 (August 1982): 405–25,

Muse, Ben, and Kurt Schelle. "New Zealands's ITQ Program," Alaska Commercial Fisheries Entry Commission Paper No. CFEC 88-3 (June 1988).

Muse, Ben and Kurt Schelle. "Individual Fisherman's Quotas: A Preliminary Review of Some Recent Programs," Alaska Commercial Fisheries Entry Commission Paper No. CFEC 89-1 (February 1989).

National Research Council Committee to Review Individual Fishing Quotas. *Sharing the Fish: Toward a National Policy on Fishing Quotas* (Washington: National Academy Press, 1999).

Simmons, Randy, T., and Urs P. Keuter. "Herd Mentality: Banning Ivory Sales Is No Way to Save the Elephant," *Policy Review* No. 50 (Fall 1989): 46–49

Sutinen, Jon G., and Peder Anderson. "The Economics of Fisheries Law Enforcement," *Land Economics* 61 (November 1985): 387–97.

Swanson, Timothy M. "International Regulation of the Ivory Trade," London Environmental Economics Centre Working Paper #89-04 (May 1989).

WEB SITES OF INTEREST

1. http://www.indiana.edu/~iascp/library.html
   The international Association for the Study of Common Property site. Contains a virtual library of sources on common property and common pool resources including links to other sites, reports, and bibliographies.

2. http://www.st.nmfs.gov/st1/index.html
   The Division of Fisheries Statistics & Economics in the National Marine Fisheries Ser-

vice. Contains fisheries data for the US, economic status reports and economic literature on fisheries. A link is also provided to some helpful related sites.

3. http://economics.iucn.org/
   IUCN-The World Conservation Union site on economics and the preservation of biodiversity.

DISCUSSION QUESTIONS

1. Is the establishment of the 200-mile limit a sufficient form of government intervention to ensure that the "tragedy of the commons" does not occur for fisheries within the 200-mile limit? Why or why not?

2. With discounting, it is possible for the efficient fish population to fall below the level required to produce the maximum sustained yield. Does this violate the sustainability criterion? Why or why not?

13

Environmental Economics: An Overview

Democracy is not a matter of sentiment, but of foresight. Any system that doesn't take the long run into account will burn itself out in the short run.

CHARLES YOST, *THE AGE OF TRIUMPH AND FRUSTRATION*

◆ INTRODUCTION

In the last few chapters we have dealt extensively with achieving a balanced set of mass and energy flows; it now remains to discuss how a balance can be achieved in the reverse flow of waste products back to the environment. Because the waste flows are inexorably intertwined with the flow of mass and energy into the economy, establishing a balance for waste flows will have feedback effects on the input flows as well.

Two questions must be addressed: (1) What is the appropriate level of waste flow? (2) How should the responsibility for achieving this flow level be allocated among the various sources of the pollutant when reductions are needed?

In this chapter we shall lay the foundation for understanding the policy approach to controlling pollution. We define efficient and cost-effective levels of control for a variety of pollutant types, compare these control levels with those achieved by market forces, and demonstrate how these insights can be used to design desirable policy responses. This overview is then followed by a series of chapters that show how these principles have been applied to the design of pollution control policies in various countries around the world.

◆ A POLLUTANT TAXONOMY

The amount of waste products emitted determines the load upon the environment. The damage done by this load depends on the capacity of the environment to assimilate the waste products (Figure 13.1). We shall refer to this ability of the environment to absorb pollutants as its *absorptive capacity*. If the emissions load exceeds the absorptive capacity, then the pollutant accumulates in the environment.

Pollutants for which the environment has little or no absorptive capacity are called *stock pollutants*. Stock pollutants accumulate over time as emissions enter the environment. Examples of stock pollutants include nonbiodegradable bottles tossed by the roadside; heavy metals, such as lead, that accumulate in the soils near the emission source; and persistent synthetic chemicals, such as dioxin and PCBs (polychlorinated biphenyls).

Pollutants for which the environment has some absorptive capacity are called *fund pollutants*. As long as the emission rate does not exceed the absorptive capacity of the environment, these pollutants do not accumulate. Examples of fund pollutants are easy to find. Many organic pollutants injected into an oxygen-rich stream will be transformed by the resident bacteria into less harmful inorganic matter. Carbon dioxide is absorbed by plant life and the oceans. The point is *not* that the mass is destroyed: The law of conservation of mass suggests this cannot be the case. Rather, when fund pollutants are injected into the air or water, they may be transformed into substances that are not considered harmful to people or to the ecological system, or they may be so diluted or dispersed that the resulting concentrations are not harmful.

Pollutants can also be classified by their zone of influence, defined both horizontally and vertically. The horizontal dimension deals with the domain over which damage from an emitted pollutant is experienced. The damage caused by *local* pollutants is experienced near the source of emission, whereas the damage from *regional* pollutants is experienced at greater distances from the source of emission. The local and regional categories are not mutually exclusive; it is possible for a pollutant to be both. Sulfur oxides and nitrogen oxides, for example, are both local and regional pollutants.

The vertical zone of influence describes whether the damage is caused mainly by ground-level concentrations of an air pollutant or by concentrations in the upper atmosphere. When

FIGURE 13.1   The Relationship Between Emissions and Pollution Damage

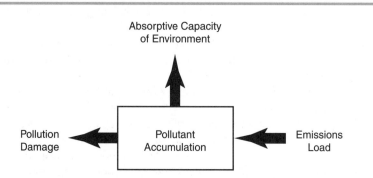

the damage caused by a pollutant is attributed mainly to concentrations of the pollutant near the earth's surface, it is called a *surface pollutant*. When the damage is related more to the pollutant's concentration in the upper atmosphere, the substance is called a *global pollutant*.

Water pollutants are obviously surface pollutants, but air pollutants can be surface pollutants, global pollutants, or both. One common global pollutant, carbon dioxide injected into the atmosphere as a product of fossil fuel combustion, has been implicated in rising world temperatures via the greenhouse effect. In addition, chlorofluorocarbon emissions are currently suspected of playing a role in the destruction of the ozone layer that protects the earth's surface from harmful solar radiation. As we shall see, the appropriate policy responses for global and surface pollutants are quite different.

This taxonomy will prove useful in designing policy responses to these various types of pollution problems. Each type of pollutant requires a unique policy response. The failure to recognize these distinctions leads to counterproductive policies.

◆ DEFINING THE EFFICIENT ALLOCATION OF POLLUTION

Pollutants are the residuals of production and consumption. These residuals must eventually be returned to the environment in one form or another. Because their presence in the environment may depreciate the service flows received, an efficient allocation of resources must take this cost into account. What, precisely, constitutes the efficient allocation of pollution depends on the nature of the pollutant.

Fund Pollutants

To the extent that the emission of fund pollutants exceeds the assimilative capacity of the environment, such pollutants accumulate. When the emission rate is low enough, however, the discharges can be assimilated by the environment, with the result that the link between present emissions and future damage may be broken.

When this happens, current emissions cause current damage and future emissions cause future damage, but the level of future damage is independent of current emissions. This independence of allocations among time periods allows us to explore the efficient allocation of fund pollutants using the concept of static, rather than dynamic, efficiency. Because the static concept is simpler, this affords us the opportunity to incorporate more dimensions of the problem without unnecessarily complicating the analysis.

The normal starting point for the analysis would be to maximize the net benefit from the waste flows. However, pollution is more easily understood if we deal with an equivalent formulation involving the minimization of two rather different types of costs: (1) damage costs and (2) control or avoidance costs.

In order to examine the efficient allocation graphically, we need to know something about how control costs vary with the degree of control and how the damages vary with the amount of pollution emitted. Though our knowledge in these areas is far from complete, economists generally agree on the shapes of these relationships.

Generally, the marginal damage caused by a unit of pollution increases with the amount emitted. When small amounts of the pollutant are emitted, the marginal damage is quite small. However, when large amounts are emitted, the marginal unit can cause significantly

FIGURE 13.2 The Efficient Allocation of a Fund Pollutant

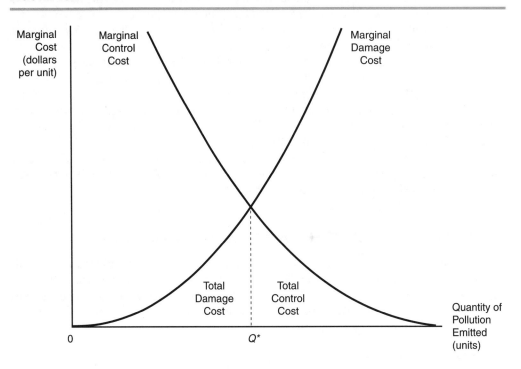

more damage. It is not hard to understand why. Small amounts of pollution are easily diluted in the environment, and the body can tolerate small quantities of substances. However, as the amount in the atmosphere increases, dilution is less effective and the body is less tolerant.

Marginal control costs commonly increase with the amount controlled. For example, suppose a source of pollution tries to cut down on its particulate emissions by purchasing an electrostatic precipitator that captures 80 percent of the particulates as they flow past in the stack. If the source wants further control, it can purchase another precipitator and place it in the stack above the first one. This second precipitator captures 80 percent of the remaining 20 percent, or 16 percent, of the uncontrolled emissions. Thus, the first precipitator would achieve an 80 percent reduction from uncontrolled emissions, whereas the second precipitator, which costs the same as the first, would achieve only a further 16 percent reduction. Obviously, each unit of emission reduction costs more for the second precipitator than for the first.

In Figure 13.2 we use these two pieces of information on the shapes of the relevant curves to derive the efficient allocation. A movement from right to left refers to greater control and less pollution emitted. The efficient allocation is represented by Q^*, the point at which the damage caused by the marginal unit of pollution is exactly equal to the marginal cost of avoiding it.[1]

---

[1]At this point, we can see why this formulation is equivalent to the net-benefit formulation. Because the benefit is damage reduction, another way of stating this proposition is to state that marginal benefit must equal marginal cost. That is, of course, the familiar proposition derived by maximizing net benefits.

Greater degrees of control (points to the left of Q^*) are inefficient, because the further increase in avoidance costs would exceed the reduction in damages. Hence, total costs would rise. Similarly, levels of control lower than Q^* would result in a lower cost of control, but the increase in damage costs would be even larger, yielding an increase in total cost. Either increasing or decreasing the amount controlled causes an increase in total costs. Hence, Q^* must be efficient.

The diagram suggests that, under the conditions presented, the optimal level of pollution is not zero. If you find this disturbing, remember that we confront this principle every day. Take the damage caused by automobile accidents, for example. Obviously, a considerable amount of damage is caused by automobile accidents. Yet we do not reduce that damage to zero, because the cost of doing so would be too high.

The point is *not* that we do not know how to stop automobile accidents. All we would have to do is eliminate automobiles! Rather, the point is because we value the benefits of automobiles, we take steps to reduce accidents (using speed limits) only to the extent that the costs of accident reduction are commensurate with the damage reduction achieved; that is, the efficient level of automobile accidents is not zero.

The second point to be made is that in some circumstances the optimal level of pollution *may* be zero, or close to it. This situation occurs when the damage caused by even the first unit of pollution is so severe that it is higher than the marginal cost of controlling the last unit of pollution. This would be reflected in Figure 13.2 as a leftward shift of the damage-cost curve of sufficient magnitude that its intersection with the vertical axis would lie above the point where the marginal-cost curve intersects the vertical axis. This circumstance seems to characterize the treatment of highly dangerous radioactive pollutants such as plutonium.

Insights besides the one that a zero level of pollution is not normally efficient are easily derived from our characterization of the efficient allocation. For example, it should be clear from Figure 13.2 that the optimal level of pollution generally is not the same for all parts of the country. Areas that have higher population levels or are particularly sensitive to pollution should have lower optimal pollution levels, whereas areas that have lower population levels or are less sensitive should have higher ones.

Examples of ecological sensitivity are not hard to find. For instance, some natural settings are less sensitive to acid rain than others because the local geological strata neutralize moderate amounts of the acid. Thus, the marginal damage caused by a unit of acid rain is lower in those fortunate regions than in others less tolerant. It can also be argued that pollutants affecting visibility are more damaging in national parks and other areas where visibility is an important part of the aesthetic experience than in other, more industrial, areas.

◆ MARKET ALLOCATION OF POLLUTION

Because air and water are treated in our legal system as free-access resources, it should surprise no one at this point in the book that the market misallocates them. Our general conclusion that free-access resources are overexploited certainly applies here. Air and water resources have been overexploited as waste repositories. However, this conclusion only scratches the surface of the issue; much more can be learned about market allocations of pollution.

When firms create products, rarely does the process of converting raw material into outputs use 100 percent of the mass. Some of the mass, called a *residual,* is left over. If the residual is valuable, it is simply reused. However, if it is not valuable, the firm has an incentive to deal with it in the cheapest manner possible.

The typical firm has several alternatives. It can control the amount of the residual by using inputs more completely so that less of the residual is left over. It can also produce less output, so that smaller amounts of the residual are generated. Recycling the residual is sometimes a viable option, as is removing the most damaging components of the waste stream and disposing of the rest.

Because damage costs are externalities but control costs are not, what is cheapest for the firm is not always cheapest for society as a whole. When pollutants are injected into watercourses or the atmosphere, they cause damages to those firms and consumers downstream or downwind of the source. These costs are *not* borne by the emitting source and, therefore, not considered by it, although they certainly are borne by society at large.[2] As with other services that are systematically undervalued, the disposal of wastes into the air or water becomes inefficiently attractive. As we saw in Chapter 4, inefficient pollution-control choices lead to further inefficiencies in product and input markets.

In the case of stock pollutants, the problem is particularly severe. Uncontrolled markets would lead to an excessive production of X, too few resources committed to pollution control, and an inefficiently large amount of the stock pollutant in the environment. Thus, the burden on future generations caused by the presence of this pollutant would be inefficiently large.

There are important differences between this case and the previously discussed inefficiencies associated with the extraction or production of minerals, energy, and food. For private-property resources, the market forces provide automatic signals of impending scarcity. These forces may be understated, but they operate in the correct direction. Even when some resources are treated as free-access resources (e.g., fisheries), the possibility for a private-property alternative (e.g., fish farming) is enhanced. As we saw with Example 12.1, when private-property and free-access resources sell in the same market, the private-property owners tend to ameliorate the excesses of those who exploit free-access properties. Efficient firms are rewarded with higher profits.

No comparable automatic amelioration mechanism is evident with pollution.[3] Because this cost is borne partially by consumers, rather than solely by producers, it does not find its way into product prices. Firms that attempt to control their pollution unilaterally are placed at a competitive disadvantage; because of the added expense, their costs of production are higher than those of their less conscientious competitors. Not only does the unimpeded market fail to generate the efficient level of pollution control, it penalizes those firms that might attempt to control an efficient amount. Hence, the case for some sort of government intervention is particularly strong for pollution control.

---

[2]Actually, the source certainly considers some of the costs—if only to avoid adverse public relations. The point, however, is that this consideration is likely to be incomplete; the source is unlikely to internalize all of the damage.

[3]Affected parties do have an incentive to negotiate among themselves, a topic covered in Chapter 3. As pointed out in that chapter, however, that approach only works well in cases where the number of affected parties is small.

◆ EFFICIENT POLICY RESPONSES

Our use of the efficiency criterion has helped in demonstrating why markets fail to produce an efficient level of pollution control and in tracing out the effects of this less-than-optimal degree of control on the markets for related commodities. It can also be used to define efficient policy responses.

Efficiency is achieved when the marginal cost of control is equal to the marginal damage caused by the pollution for each emitter. One way to achieve this equilibrium would be to impose a legal limit on the amount of pollution allowed by each emitter. If the limit were chosen precisely at the level of pollution where marginal control cost equals marginal damage (Q^* in Figure 13.2) efficiency would be achieved.

An alternative approach would be to internalize the marginal damage caused by each unit of emissions by means of a tax or charge on each unit of emissions (Example 13.1). This per unit charge could either increase with the level of pollution (following the marginal-damage

Example 13.1

Environmental Taxation in China

China's high pollution levels are causing considerable damage to human health. Traditional means of control have not been particularly effective. To combat this pollution China has instituted a wide-ranging system of environmental taxation with tax rates that are quite high by historical standards.

The program is expected to be phased in over a three-year period and will involve a two-rate tax system. Lower rates will be imposed on emissions below an official standard and higher rates on all emissions over that standard. The tax is expected not only to reduce pollution and the damage it causes, but also to provide needed revenue to local Environmental Protection Bureaus.

According to the World Bank (1997) this strategy makes good economic sense. Conducting detailed analysis of air pollution in two Chinese cities (Beijing and Zhengzhou) and relying on "back of the envelope" measurements of benefits, they found that the marginal cost of further abatement was significantly less than the marginal benefit for any reasonable value of human life. Indeed in Zhengzhou they found that achieving an efficient outcome (based upon an assumed value of a "statistical Life" of $8,000 per person) would require reducing current emissions by some 79 percent. According to their results, the current abatement level makes sense only if China's policy makers value the life of an average urban resident at approximately $270. It is hard to imagine that such a low value could be justified.

Source: Robert Bohm, et al. "Environmental Taxes: China's Bold Initiative," *Environment* Vol. 40, No. 7 (September, 1998): 10–13, 33–38; Susmita Dasgupta, Hua Wang, and David Wheeler, "Surviving Success: Policy Reform and the Future of Industrial Pollution in China." (Washington, DC: The World Bank, 1997), available on-line at http://www.worldbank.org/NIPR/work_paper/survive/china-htmp6.htm. (August 1998).

curve for each succeeding unit of emission) or be constant, as long as the rate is equal to the marginal social damage at the point where the marginal-social-damage and marginal-control costs cross (see Figure 13.2). Because the emitter is paying the marginal social damage when confronted by these fees, pollution costs would be internalized. The efficient choice would also be the cost-minimizing choice for the emitter.[4]

However, although the efficient levels of these policy instruments can be easily defined in principle, they are very difficult to implement in practice. To implement either of these policy instruments, it is necessary to know the level of pollution at which the two marginal-cost curves cross for every emitter. That is a tall order, one that imposes an unrealistically high information burden on control authorities. Control authorities typically have very poor information on control costs and little reliable information on marginal-damage functions.

How can environmental authorities allocate pollution control responsibility in a reasonable manner when the information burdens are apparently so unrealistically large? One approach, the approach now chosen by a number of countries (including the United States) is to select specific legal levels of pollution based upon some other criterion, such as providing adequate margins of safety for human or ecological health. Once these thresholds have been established, by whatever means, half of the problem has been resolved. The other half deals with deciding how to allocate the responsibility for meeting predetermined pollution levels among the large numbers of emitters.

This is precisely where the cost-effectiveness criterion comes in. Once the objective is stated in terms of meeting the predetermined pollution level at minimum cost, it is possible to derive the conditions that any cost-effective allocation of the responsibility must satisfy. These conditions can then be used as a basis for choosing among various kinds of policy instruments that impose more reasonable information burdens on control authorities.

◆ COST-EFFECTIVE POLICIES FOR EMISSION REDUCTION

Defining a Cost-Effective Allocation

Let's suppose that the regulatory authorities are interested in controlling the total weight of emissions in a manner that minimizes the cost of control. What can we say about the cost-effective allocation of control responsibility for reducing emissions by a predetermined amount?

Let's consider a simple example. We will assume that two emission sources are currently emitting a total of 30 units of emissions. We will assume further that the control authority determines that the environment can assimilate 15 units, making a reduction of 15 units necessary. How should this 15-unit reduction be allocated between the two sources in order to minimize the total cost of the reduction?

With the aid of Figure 13.3 we can demonstrate the answer. Figure 13.3 is drawn by measuring the marginal cost of control for the first source from the left-hand axis (MC_1) and the marginal cost of control for the second source from the right-hand axis (MC_2). Notice that a total of 15 units of reduction is achieved for every point on this graph; each point represents

---

[4]Another policy choice is to remove the people from the polluted area. The government has used this strategy for heavily contaminated toxic waste sites such as Times Beach, Missouri, and Love Canal, New York.

FIGURE 13.3 A Cost-Effective Reduction in Emissions

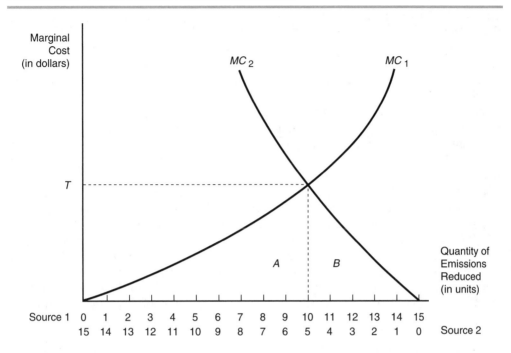

some different combination of reduction by the two sources. Drawn in this manner, the diagram represents all possible allocations of the 15-unit reduction between the two sources. The left-hand axis, for example, represents an allocation of the entire reduction to the second source; the right-hand axis represents a situation in which the first source bears the entire responsibility. All points in between represent different degrees of shared responsibility. What allocation minimizes the cost of control?

In the cost-effective allocation, the first source cleans up 10 units; the second source cleans up 5 units. The total variable cost of control of this particular assignment of the responsibility for the reduction is represented by area *A* plus area *B*. Area *A* is the cost of control for the first source, area *B* the cost of control for the second. Any other allocation would result in a higher total control cost (Convince yourself that this is true.).

Figure 13.3 also demonstrates one of the most important propositions in the economics of pollution control. *The cost of achieving a given reduction in emissions will be minimized if and only if the marginal costs of control are equalized for all emitters.*[5] This is demonstrated by the fact that the marginal-cost curves cross at the cost-effective allocation.

---

[5]This statement is true when marginal cost increases with the amount of emissions reduced (Figure 13.3). Suppose that, for some pollutants, the marginal cost were to decrease with the amount of emissions reduced. What would be the cost-effective allocation in this admittedly unusual situation?

Cost-Effective Pollution Control Policies

This proposition can be used as a basis for choosing among the various policy instruments that the control authority might use to achieve this allocation. Sources have a large menu of options for controlling the amount of pollution they inject into the environment. For example, they can change input mixes (low-sulfur vs. high-sulfur coal), output mixes, or the type of pollution (air, water, or solid waste); they can move the plant to a less vulnerable area; or they can isolate the population at risk by relocating it. The cheapest method of control will differ widely, not only among industries, but also among plants in the same industry. Selecting the cheapest method requires detailed information on the possible control techniques and their associated costs.

Plant managers are generally able to acquire this information for their plants when it is in their interest to do so. However, the government authorities responsible for meeting pollution targets are not likely to have this information. Because the degree to which these plants would be regulated depends on cost information, it is unrealistic to expect the plant managers to transfer unbiased information to the government. Plant managers have a strong incentive to overstate control costs in hopes of reducing their ultimate burden.

This situation poses a difficult dilemma for control authorities. The cost of incorrectly assigning the control responsibility among various polluters is likely to be large, yet the control authorities do not have the information at their disposal to make a correct allocation. Those who have the information—the plant managers—are not inclined to share it. Can the cost-effective allocation be found? The answer depends on the particular approach taken by the control authority.

Emission Standards

We start our investigation of this question by supposing that the control authority pursues a traditional legal approach by imposing a separate emission standard on each source. In the economics literature, this approach is referred to as the *command-and-control* (CAC) approach. An *emission standard* is a legal limit on the amount of the pollutant an individual source is allowed to emit. In our example, it is clear that the two standards should add up to the allowable 15 units. However, it is not clear how, in the absence of information on control costs, these 15 units are to be allocated between the two sources. The easiest method of resolving this dilemma—and the one chosen in the earliest days of pollution control—would be to allocate each source an equal reduction. As is clear from Figure 13.3, this strategy would not be cost effective. Although the first source would have lower costs, this cost reduction would be substantially smaller than the increase faced by the second source; compared to a cost-effective allocation, total costs would increase if both sources were forced to clean up the same amount.

When emission standards are used, there is no reason to believe that the authority will assign the responsibility for emission reduction in a cost-minimizing way. This is probably not surprising. Who would have believed otherwise?

Nonetheless, some policy instruments do allow the authority to allocate the emission reduction in a cost-effective manner even when it has no information on the magnitude of control costs. These policy approaches rely on economic incentives to produce the desired outcome. The two most common approaches are known as *emission charges* and *transferable emission permits.*

Emission Charges

An *emission charge* is a fee, collected by the government, levied on each unit of pollutant emitted into the air or water. The total payment any source would make to the government could be found by multiplying the fee times the amount of pollution emitted. The emission-charge approach reduces pollution because, under it, pollution costs the firm money. To save money, the source seeks ways to reduce its pollution.

How much pollution control would the firm choose to purchase? A profit-maximizing firm would control, rather than emit, pollution whenever it proved cheaper to do so. We can illustrate the firm's decision with Figure 13.4. The level of uncontrolled emission is 15 units, and the emission charge is *T*. Thus, if the firm were to decide against controlling any emissions, it would have to pay *T* times 15, represented by area *0TBC*.

Is this the best the firm can do? Obviously not, because it can control some pollution at a lower cost than paying the emission charge. It would pay the firm to reduce emissions until the marginal cost of reduction is equal to the emission charge. The firm would minimize its cost by choosing to clean up 10 units of pollution and emitting 5 units. At this allocation the firm would pay control costs equal to area *0AD* and total emission charge payments equal to area *ABCD*, for a total cost of *0ABC*. This is clearly less than *0TBC*, the amount the firm would pay if it chose not to clean up any pollution.

Let's carry this one step further. Suppose that we levied the same emission charge on both sources discussed in Figure 13.3. Each source would then control its emissions until its marginal-control cost equaled the emission charge. (Faced with an emission charge *T*,

FIGURE 13.4 Cost-Minimizing Control of Pollution with an Emission Charge

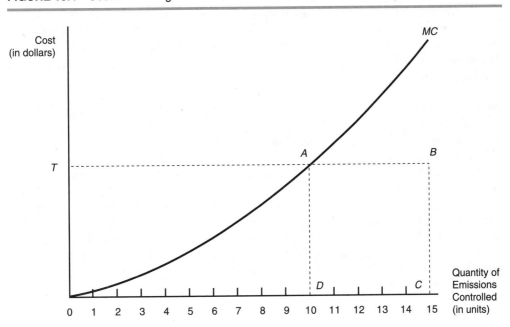

the second source would clean up 5 units.) Because they both are facing the same emission charge, they will *independently* choose levels of control consistent with equal marginal-control costs. This is precisely the condition that yields a cost-minimizing allocation.

This is a rather remarkable finding. We have shown that as long as the control authority imposes the same emission charge on all sources, the resulting reduction allocation *automatically* minimizes the costs of control. This is true in spite of the fact that the control authority may not have any knowledge of control costs.

However, we have not yet dealt with the issue of how the appropriate level of the emission charge is determined. Each level of a charge will result in *some* level of emission reduction. Furthermore, the responsibility for meeting that reduction will be allocated in a manner that minimizes control costs. How high should the charge be set in order to ensure that the resulting emission reduction is the *desired* level of emission reduction?

Without knowing the cost of control, the control authority cannot establish the correct tax rate on the first try. It is possible, however, to develop an iterative trial-and-error process to find the appropriate charge rate. This process is initiated by choosing an arbitrary charge rate and observing the amount of reduction that occurs when that charge is imposed. If the observed reduction is larger than desired, the charge should be lowered; if the reduction is smaller, the charge should be raised. The new reduction that results from the adjusted charge can then be observed and compared with the desired reduction. Further adjustments in the charge can be made as needed. This process can be repeated until the actual and desired reductions are equal. At that point, the correct emission charge would have been found.

The charge system not only causes sources to choose a cost-effective allocation on the control responsibility, it also stimulates the development of newer, cheaper means of controlling emissions, as well as promoting technological progress. This is illustrated in Figure 13.5.

The reason for this is rather straightforward. Control authorities base the emission standards on specific technologies. As new technologies are discovered by the control authority, the standards are tightened. These more strict standards force firms to bear higher costs. Therefore, with emissions standards, firms have an incentive to hide technological changes from the control authority.

With an emissions-charge system the firm saves money by adopting cheaper new technologies. As long as the firm can reduce its pollution at a marginal cost lower than T, it pays to adopt the new technology. In Figure 13.5 the firm saves A and B by adopting the new technology and voluntarily reduces its emissions from Q_0 to Q_1.

With an emissions charge, the minimum cost allocation of meeting a predetermined emission reduction can be found by a control authority even when it has no information on control costs. An emission charge also stimulates technological advances in emission reduction. Unfortunately, the process for finding the appropriate rate would take some experimentation. During the trial-and-error period of finding the appropriate rate, sources would be faced with a volatile emission charge. Changing emission charges would make planning for the future difficult. Investments that would make sense under a high emission charge might not make sense when it falls. From either a policymaker's or business manager's perspective, this process leaves much to be desired.

FIGURE 13.5   Cost Savings from Technological Change: Charges vs. Standards

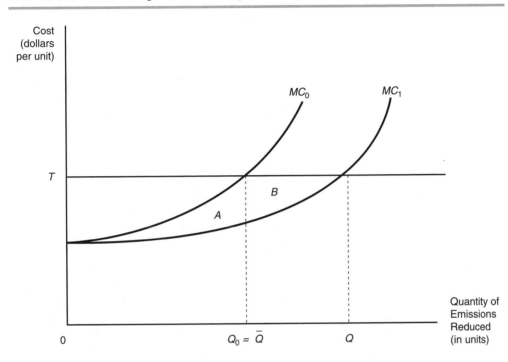

Transferable Emission Permits

Is it possible for the control authority to find the cost-minimizing allocation without going through a trial-and-error process? It is possible if a *transferable emission permit system* is used to control pollution. Under this system, all sources are required to have permits in order to emit. Each permit specifies exactly how much the firm is allowed to emit. The permits are freely transferable. The control authority issues exactly the number of permits needed to produce the desired emission level. Any emissions by a source in excess of those allowed by its permit would cause the source to face severe monetary sanctions.

Why this system automatically leads to a cost-effective allocation can be seen in Figure 13.6, which treats the same set of circumstances as in Figure 13.3. Suppose that somehow the first source found itself with 7 permits (each permit corresponds to 1 emission unit). Because it has 15 units of uncontrolled emissions, this would mean it must control 8 units. Similarly, suppose that the second source has the remaining 8 permits, meaning that it would have to clean up 7 units. Notice that both firms have an incentive to trade. The marginal cost of control for the second source (*C*) is substantially higher than that for the first (*A*). The second source could lower its cost if it could buy a permit from the first source at a price lower than *C*. Meanwhile, the first source would be better off if it could sell a permit for a price higher than *A*. Because *C* is greater than *A*, grounds for trade certainly exist.

FIGURE 13.6 Cost Effectiveness and the Emission Permit System

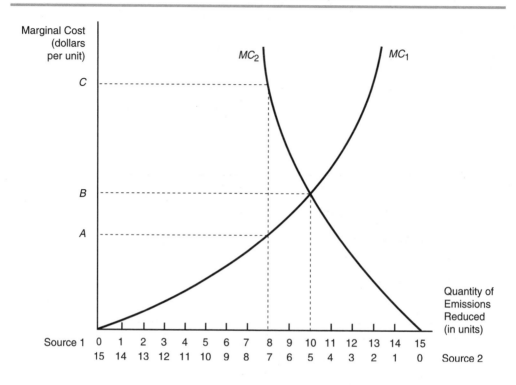

A transfer of permits would take place until the first source had only 5 permits left (and controlled 10 units), while the second source had 10 permits (and controlled 5 units). At this point, the permit price would equal *B*, because that is the marginal value of that permit to both sources, and neither source would have any incentive to trade further. The permit market would be in equilibrium.

Notice that the market equilibrium for an emission-permit system is the cost-effective allocation! Simply by issuing the appropriate number of permits (15) and letting the market do the rest, the control authority can achieve a cost-effective allocation without having even the slightest knowledge about control costs. This system allows the government to meet its policy objective while allowing greater flexibility in how that objective is met.

The incentives created by this system ensure that sources use this flexibility to achieve the objective at the lowest possible cost. As we shall see in the next two chapters, this remarkable property has been responsible for the prominence of this type of approach in current attempts to reform the regulatory process.

◆ OTHER POLICY DIMENSIONS

Two main pollution-control policy instruments rely on economic incentives—charges and transferable permits. Both of these allow the control authority to distribute the responsibility for control in a cost-effective manner. The major difference between them that we have discussed so far is that, for the charge approach, the appropriate charge can be determined only by an iterative trial-and-error process over time, whereas, for the transferable-permit approach, the permit price can be determined immediately by the market. Can other differences be identified?

One major additional difference concerns the manner in which these two systems react to changes in external circumstances in the absence of further decisions by the control authority. This is an important consideration, because bureaucratic procedures are notoriously sluggish and changes in policies are usually rendered rather slowly.[6] We shall consider three such circumstances—(1) growth in the number of sources, (2) inflation, and (3) technological progress.

In a graphical representation, if the number of sources were to increase in a permit market, the demand for permits would shift to the right. Given a fixed supply of permits, the price would rise, as would the control costs, but the amount of emissions would remain the same. If charges were being used, in the absence of additional action by the control authority, the charge level would remain the same. This implies that the existing sources would control only what they would control in the absence of growth. Therefore, the arrival of new sources would cause a deterioration of air or water quality in the region. The costs of abatement would rise, because the costs of control paid by the new sources must be considered; however, they would rise by a lesser amount than in a permit market because of the lower amount of pollution being controlled. If the choice is between a fixed fee and a fixed number of permits in a growing economy, the dominance of the permit system over the fixed-fee system increases over time.[7]

With a permit system, inflation in the cost of control would automatically result in higher permit prices, but with a charge system it would result in lower control. Essentially, the real charge (i.e., the nominal charge adjusted for inflation) declines with inflation if the nominal charge remains the same.

However, we should not conclude that, over time, charges always result in less control than permits do. Suppose, for example, that technological progress in designing pollution control equipment were to cause the marginal cost of abatement to fall. In a permit system, this would result in lower prices and lower abatement costs but the same aggregate degree of control. With a charge system, the amount controlled would actually increase and would therefore result in more control than a permit system that, prior to the fall in costs, controlled the same amount.

If the control authority were to adjust the charge in each of these cases appropriately, the outcome would be identical to that achieved by a permit market. The permit market reacts automatically to these changes in circumstances, whereas the charge system requires a conscious administrative act to achieve the same result.

The second major difference between permits and charges involves the cost of being wrong. Suppose that we have very imprecise information on damages caused and avoidance costs incurred by various levels of pollution, yet we have to choose either a charge level or a

---

[6]This is probably particularly true when the modification involves a change in the rate at which firms are charged for their emissions.

[7]See Richard V. Butler and Michael D. Maher, "The Control of Externalities in a Growing Economy," *Economic Inquiry* 20, No. 1 (January 1982): 155–63.

permit level and live with it. What can be said about the relative merits of permits versus charges in the face of this uncertainty?

The answer depends upon the circumstances.[8] Permits offer a great deal of certainty about the quantity of emissions; charges confer more certainty about the marginal cost of control. Therefore, an approach using permits is the only system that allows an ambient standard or an aggregate emission standard to be met with certainty. In other cases, however, when the objective is to minimize total costs (the sum of damage cost and control costs), permits would be preferred when the costs of being wrong are more sensitive to changes in the quantity of emission than to changes in the marginal cost of control. Charges would be preferred when control costs were more important. When would that be the case?

When the marginal-damage curve is steeply sloped and the marginal-cost curve is rather flat, certainty about emissions is more important than certainty about control costs. Smaller deviations of actual emissions from expected emissions can cause a rather large deviation in damage costs, whereas control costs would be relatively insensitive to the degree of control. Permits would prevent large fluctuations in these damage costs and would therefore yield a lower cost of being wrong than would charges.

Now suppose that the marginal-control-cost curve was steeply sloped, but the marginal-damage curve was flat. Small changes in the degree of control would have a large effect on abatement costs but would not affect damages very much. In this case, it makes sense to rely on charges to exercise more precise control over control costs, and to accept the less dire consequences of possible fluctuations in damage costs.

These cases suggest that a preference either for permits or for charges in the face of uncertainty is not to be predetermined, it depends on the circumstances. Theory is not strong enough to dictate a choice. Empirical studies are necessary in order to establish a preference in a particular situation. Example 13.2 discusses one such empirical study.

SUMMARY

In this chapter we developed the conceptual framework needed to evaluate current approaches to pollution control policy. The efficient amount of a fund pollutant was defined as the amount that minimizes the sum of damage and control costs. Using this definition, we were able to derive two propositions of interest: (1) The efficient level of pollution would vary from region to region, and (2) the efficient level of pollution would not generally be zero, though in some particular circumstances it might.

Because pollution is a classic externality, markets will generally produce more than the efficient amount of both fund pollutants and stock pollutants. For both types of pollutants, this will imply higher-than-efficient damages and lower-than-efficient control costs. For stock pollutants, an excessive amount of pollution would build up in the environment, imposing a detrimental externality on future generations as well as on current generations.

The market would not provide any automatic ameliorating response to the accumulation of pollution as it would in the case of natural-resource scarcity. Firms unilaterally attempting

---

[8]A more formal and mathematical treatment of this issue can be found in M. Weitzman, "Prices vs. Quantities," *Review of Economic Studies* 41 (1974): 447–91. A specific application to pollution control is presented in Z. Adar and J. M. Griffin, "Uncertainty and Choice in Pollution Control Instruments," *Journal of Environmental Economics and Management* 3 (1976): 178–88.

Example 13.2

Energy-Demand Uncertainty and the Cost of Being Wrong: Permits vs. Charges

The Four Corners area (where Utah, Arizona, New Mexico, and Colorado intersect) poses a classic confrontation between energy development and preserving the environment. Though sparsely populated, it is near several unique parks and wilderness areas and serves as the base for several large electrical generating stations, which provide power to a large number of southwestern and western states.

One of the uncertainties affecting the air quality of the region is the amount that electricity demand will grow over the next several years. The higher the growth in demand, the more uncontrolled emissions there will be. The higher the level of uncontrolled emissions, the more control that has to be placed on each source in order to preserve air quality. If, in incorrect anticipation of too high growth, the regulators impose too stringent a degree of control, then control costs will be excessively high. If controls are established at too low a level, damage costs would be too high. There are costs associated with each type of mistake.

In a doctoral dissertation submitted at Stanford, Charles Kolstad used this setting to investigate whether regulators would be better off using a permit system or an emission-charge system to protect air quality in the face of this uncertainty. Capturing the control-cost and damage functions in a computer simulation model, he calculated the cost of being wrong if regulators chose permits or if they chose charges. His findings were completely in accord with our analysis:

> For constant or declining marginal damage, emissions [charges] yield total costs (including damage) 5–10% lower than for [permits]. However, for even slightly upward sloping marginal damage, [permits] yield roughly 20% lower costs than emissions [charges]. [p. 206]

Because the increasing-marginal-damage case is probably the most likely for sulfur oxide emissions, the use of permits in the Four Corners would seem preferable.

Source: Charles Kolstad, *"Economic and Regulatory Efficiency,"* Report #LA-9458-T(Thesis) (Los Alamos, NM: Los Alamos National Laboratory, 1982).

to control their pollution are placed at a competitive disadvantage. Hence, the case for some sort of government intervention is particularly strong for pollution control.

Although policy instruments could, in principle, be defined in such a way as to achieve an efficient level of pollution for every emitter, in practice, it is very difficult, because the amount of information required by the control authorities is unrealistically high.

Cost-effectiveness analysis provides a way out of this dilemma. When the objective is defined in terms of reducing emissions by a predetermined amount, uniform emission charges or an emission-permit system could be used to attain the cost-effective allocation even when the control authority has no information whatsoever on either control costs or damage costs. Uniform emission standards would not, except by coincidence, be cost effective. In addition, reliance on either permits or charges would stimulate more technological progress in pollution control than would reliance on emission standards.

The permit approach and the charge approach respond differently to growth in the number of sources, to inflation, to technological change, and to uncertainty. As we shall see in the next few chapters, some countries (primarily in Europe) have chosen to rely on emission charges whereas others (primarily the United States) have chosen to rely on permits. We can now use this framework to evaluate the rather different policy approaches that have been taken toward the major sources of pollution.

FURTHER READING

Baumol, W. J. and W. E. Oates. *The Theory of Environmental Policy*, 2nd ed. (Cambridge, UK: Cambridge University Press, 1988). A classic on the economic analysis of externalities. Accessible only to those with a thorough familiarity with multivariate calculus.

Hahn, Robert W. "Economic Prescriptions for Environmental Problems: How the Patient Followed the Doctor's Orders," *Journal of Economic Perspectives* 3 (Spring 1989): 95–114. Chronicles the experience with both marketable permits and emission charges in the United States and Europe.

OECD. *Economic Instruments for Environmental Protection* (Paris: Organization for Economic Co-operation and Development, 1989). A survey of how economic incentive approaches to pollution control have been used in the industrialized nations that belong to the OECD.

OECD. *Environment and Taxation: The Cases of the Netherlands, Sweden and the United States* (Paris: Organization for Economic Co-operation and Development, 1994). Background case studies for a larger research project seeking to discover the extent to which fiscal and environmental policies could be made not only compatible, but mutually reinforcing.

Portney, Paul, ed. *Public Policies for Environmental Protection* (Washington, DC: Resources for the Future, 1990). A collection of essays reviewing problems of environmental regulation from the perspective of the late 1980s.

Tietenberg, T. H. *Emissions Trading: An Exercise in Reforming Pollution Policy* (Washington, DC: Resources for the Future, 1985). An examination of the use of marketable permits to control pollution in principle and in practice.

ADDITIONAL REFERENCES

Coltinge, R. A., and W. E. Oates. "Efficiency in Pollution Control in the Short and Long Runs: A System of Rental Emission Permits," *Canadian Journal of Economics* 15 (May 1982):347-54.

Dales, J. H. *Pollution, Property and Prices* (Toronto: Toronto University Press, 1968).

Jurado, J. and D. Southgate. "Dealing with Air Pollution in Latin America: The Case of Quito, Ecuador." *Environment and Development Economics* 4, (1999)(3): 375–87.

Kelman, Steven. *What Price Incentives? Economists and the Environment* (Westport, CT: Greenwood Publishing Group, 1981).

Kneese, Allen V., and Charles L. Schultz. *Pollution, Prices, and Public Policy* (Washington, DC: Brookings Institution, 1975).

Kraemer, A. and K. M. Banholzer. "Tradable Permits in Water Resource Management and Water Pollution Control," *Implementing Domestic Tradable Permits for Environmental Protection.* OECD, Organization for Economic Co-operation and Development(1999): 75–107.

Levinson, A. "Grandfather Regulations, New Source Bias, and State Air Toxics Regulations," *Ecological Economics* 28(1999)(2): 299–311.

Lyon, R. M. "Auctions and Alternative Procedures for Allocating Pollution Rights," *Land Economics* 58 (February 1982): 16–32.

Milliman, Scott R., and Raymond Prince. "Firm Incentives to Promote Technological Change in Pollution Control," *Journal of Environmental Economics and Management* 17 (November 1989): 247–65.

Montgomery, David W. "Markets in Licenses and Efficient Pollution Control Programs," *Journal of Economic Theory* 5 (December 1982): 395–418.

Orr, Lloyd. "Incentive for Innovation as the Basis for Effluent Charge Strategy," *American Economic Review* 66 (May 1976): 441–47.

Plourde, C. G. "A Model of Waste Accumulation and Disposal," *Canadian Journal of Economics* 5 (February 1982): 119–25.

Stavins, Robert N. "Harnessing Market Forces to Protect the Environment," *Environment* 31 (January/February 1989): 4–7, 28–35.

Soderholm, P. "Pollution Charges in a Transition Economy: The Case of Russia," *Journal of Economic Issues* 33(1999)(2): 403–410.

Tietenberg, T. "Lessons from Using Transferable Permits to Control Air Pollution in the United States," *Handbook of Environmental and Resource Economics. In* J. C. J. VandenBergh, eds. (Cheltenham, UK: Edward Elgar, 1999): 275–292.

Tietenberg, T. H. "Tradeable Permits for Pollution Control When Emission Location Matters: What Have We Learned?," *Environmental and Resource Economics* 5, No. 2 (1995): 95–113.

Tisato, Peter. "Pollution Standards vs. Charges Under Uncertainty," *Environmental and Resource Economics* 4 (1994): 295–304.

WEB SITES OF INTEREST

1. *http://www.epa.gov/docs/oppe/eaed/eedhmpg.htm*
   Home Page of USEPA's Economy and Environment Program.

2. *http://biff.econ.uoguelph.ca/~rmckit/epeq/polhome.html*
   Economic Performance and Environmental Quality Policy Page.

3. *http://www.worldbank.org/nipr/*
   The World Bank's New Ideas in Pollution Regulation Site.

DISCUSSION QUESTIONS

1. In his book *(What Price Incentives?)* Steven Kelman suggests that from an ethical point of view, the use of economic incentives (e.g., emission charges or emission permits) in environmental policy is undesirable. He argues that transforming our mental image of the environment from a sanctified preserve to a marketable commodity has detrimental effects not only on our use of the environment but also on our attitude toward it. His point is that applying economic incentives to environmental policy weakens and cheapens our traditional values with regard to the environment.

   a. Consider the effects of economic-incentive systems on prices paid by the poor, on employment, and on the speed of compliance with pollution control laws—as well as the Kelman arguments. Are economic-incentive systems more or less ethically justifiable than the traditional regulatory approach?

   b. Kelman seems to feel that because emission permits automatically prevent environmental degradation, they are more ethically desirable than emission charges. Do you agree? Why or why not?

Stationary-Source Local Air Pollution

When choosing between two evils, I always like to try the one I've never tried before.

MAE WEST, ACTRESS

◆ INTRODUCTION

Attaining and maintaining clear air is an exceedingly difficult policy task. In the United States, for example, an estimated 27,000 major stationary sources of air pollution, as well as hundreds of thousands of more minor sources, are subject to control. Many distinct production processes emit many different types of pollutants. The resulting damages range from minimal effects on plants and vegetation to the possible modification of the earth's climate.

The policy response to this problem has been continually evolving. The U.S. experience is not atypical. Congress enacted the first legislation to grapple with these problems in 1955. Called the Air Pollution Control Act of 1955, that law mainly subsidized research into air pollution problems. The following 14 years ushered in a period of vigorous legislative activity.

However, the amount of legislation is a misleading indicator of what was actually accomplished. It was not until 1967 that the federal government began to play much of a role other than subsidizing research, and even the 1967 Clean Air Act was mainly an attempt to cajole the states into action. The common thread woven by the federal air pollution statutes during this period was a reliance on cooperation from the states.

By 1970 the national government had discovered that this reliance was misplaced: State cooperation was not forthcoming. Fearing that the imposition of strict controls on industrial sources would place them at a competitive disadvantage in their quest for increases in employment and taxable industrial property, states were unwilling to take the lead in air pollution control policy.

In this atmosphere of frustration, the Clean Air Act Amendments of 1970 were passed. They set a bold new direction, which has been retained and refined by subsequent acts. By virtue of that act, the federal government assumed a much larger and much more vigorous direct role. The U.S. Environmental Protection Agency (EPA) was created to implement and oversee this massive attempt to control the injection of substances into our air. Individually tailored strategies were created to deal with mobile and stationary sources. These strategies depend, in part, on whether the type of pollutant being controlled is a "conventional" pollutant or a "hazardous" pollutant.

◆ CONVENTIONAL POLLUTANTS

Conventional pollutants are relatively common substances, found in almost all parts of the country, and are presumed to be dangerous only in high concentrations. In the United States these pollutants are called *criteria pollutants* because the Clean Air Act Amendments require that the EPA produce "criteria documents" to be used in setting acceptable standards for these pollutants. These documents summarize and evaluate all of the existing research on the various health and environmental effects associated with these pollutants. The central focus of air pollution control during the 1970s was on criteria pollutants.

The Command-and-Control Policy Framework

In the preceding chapter, several possible approaches to controlling pollution were described and analyzed in theoretical terms. The historical approach to air pollution control has been based primarily on emission standards. It has been a traditional command-and-control (CAC) approach. In this section we shall outline the specific nature of this approach, analyze it from both an efficiency and a cost-effectiveness perspective, and examine how a series of rather recent reforms based on economic incentives has worked to rectify some of these deficiencies.

For each of the conventional pollutants, the typical first step is to establish *ambient air quality standards.* These standards set legal ceilings on the allowable concentration of the pollutant in the outdoor air averaged over a specified time period. For many pollutants the standard is defined in terms of a long-term average (normally, as an annual average) and a short-term average (e.g., a three-hour average). These short-term averages can usually be exceeded no more than once a year. These standards have to be met everywhere, though as a practical matter they are monitored at a large number of specific locations. As Example 4.3 pointed out, control costs can be quite sensitive to the level of these short-term averages.

In the United States two ambient standards have been defined.[1] The *primary standard* is designed to protect human health. This is the first standard to have been determined, and it

---

[1] We shall discuss the U.S. approach in some detail to show how abstract command-and-control concepts can be translated into specific policy. Many industrialized countries have rather similar policies. For more detail on the environmental policies of some European countries and Japan, see Frederic N. Bolotin, ed., *International Public Policy Sourcebook: Volume 2, Education and Environment* (Westport, CT: Greenwood Press, 1989). The Japanese approach, which is rather different, will be treated in more detail subsequently in this chapter.

TABLE 14.1 National Primary and Secondary Ambient Air Quality Standards

Pollutant	Primary Standard[a]	Secondary Standard[a]
Sulfur oxides	a. 80 μg/m^3 (0.03 ppm) annual arithmetic mean b. 365 μg/m^3 (0.14 ppm) maximum 24-hour concentration not to be exceeded more than once a year	1,300 μg/m^3 (0.5 ppm) 3-hour concentration not to be exceeded more than once a year
Particulate matter[b]	a. 50 μg/m^3 annual arithmetic mean b. 150 μg/m^3 maximum 24-hour concentration not to be exceeded more than once per year	Same as primary standard
Carbon monoxide	a. 10 mg/m^3 (9 ppm) maximum 8-hour concentration not to be exceeded more than once per year b. 40 mg/m^3 (35 ppm) maximum 1-hour concentration not to be exceeded more than once per year	No secondary standard
Ozone	a. 235 μg/m^3 (0.12 ppm) average hourly concentration not to be exceeded more than once per year b. .08 ppm daily maximum 8-hour average	Same as primary standard Same as primary standard
Nitrogen dioxide	100 μg/m^3 (0.053 ppm) annual arithmetic mean	Same as primary standard
Lead	1.5 μg/m^3 arithmetic mean averaged over a calendar quarter	Same as primary standard

[a]Guide to measurements: μg/m^3 is micrograms per cubic meter; mg/m^3 is milligrams per cubic meter; and ppm is parts per million.

[b]TSP was the indicator pollutant for the original particulate matter standards. This standard was replaced with a new standard in 1987. The new standard tracks particles less than 10 μ in diameter as the new indicator pollutant.

Source: *Code of Federal Regulations,* Vol. 40, parts 50.4–50.6, 50.8–50.12 (1999).

has the earliest deadlines for compliance. All pollutants have a primary standard. The *secondary standard* has been designed to protect other aspects of human welfare from those pollutants having separate effects. Protection is afforded by the secondary standard for aesthetics (particularly visibility), physical objects (houses, monuments, etc.), and vegetation. When a separate secondary standard exists, both it and the primary standard must be met. The existing primary and secondary standards are given in Table 14.1.

The ambient standards are required by statute to be determined without any consideration given to the costs of meeting them. They are supposed to be set at a level sufficient to protect even the most sensitive members of the population.

Although the EPA is responsible for defining the ambient standards, the primary responsibility for ensuring that the ambient air quality standards are met falls on the state control agencies. They exercise this responsibility by developing and executing an acceptable *state implementation plan* (SIP), which must be approved by the EPA. This plan divides the state up into separate air quality control regions. There are special procedures for handling regions that cross state borders, such as the metropolitan New York area.

The SIP spells out for each control region the procedures and timetables for meeting local ambient standards and for abatement of the effects of locally emitted pollutants on other states. The degree of control required depends on the severity of the pollution problem in each of the control regions.

By 1975 it had become apparent that, despite some major gains in air quality, many areas had not met and would not meet the ambient standards by the statutory deadlines. Therefore, in the 1977 Amendments to the Clean Air Act, Congress extended the deadline for attainment of all primary (health-related) ambient standards to 1982, with further extensions to 1987 possible for ozone and carbon monoxide. The amendments also required the EPA to designate all areas not meeting the original deadlines as *nonattainment regions.*

The areas receiving this designation were subjected to particularly stringent controls. After the 1977 Amendments were passed, all portions of SIPs applying to nonattainment regions had to be revised by the state control authorities in order to ensure compliance with the new deadlines. To prod the states into action, Congress gave the EPA the power to halt the construction of major new or modified pollution sources and to deny federal sewage and transportation grants for any state not submitting a plan showing precisely how and when attainment would be reached.

State implementation plans in nonattainment regions must include a permit program for newly constructed large sources or large sources that have undergone some major modification. Permits cannot be granted to these sources unless the state can demonstrate that emissions resulting from commencing or expanding operations would not jeopardize the region's progress toward attainment. The state can satisfy this requirement by controlling existing sources to a sufficiently high degree that progress can be demonstrated even with the new sources in operation.

A second condition for the permit to be issued stipulates that all major new or modified sources in nonattainment areas must also control their own emissions to the *lowest achievable emission rate* (LAER). The LAER is defined as the lowest emission rate included in any SIP, *whether or not any source is currently achieving that rate.* This part of the law was designed to ensure that only the most stringent controls would be used by any source to be located in a nonattainment area. It is controversial because it implies that new sources could be forced to use technologies that have never been commercially tested.

Regions with air quality at least as high as the standards by the original deadline were subject to another set of controls known collectively as the *PSD policy.* This policy derives its name from its objective, namely the *prevention of significant deterioration* of the air in cleaner regions. The origin of this policy is found in the preamble to the 1970 Clean Air Act, which stated as an objective: "to protect and enhance the quality of the nation's air."

In 1972 the EPA was successfully sued by the Sierra Club for promulgating regulations that did not ensure that this objective would be met. The existing system of ambient standards prevented the deterioration of the air *beyond* the minimum level specified by the standard, but air significantly cleaner than the standard would normally have deteriorated until it reached the minimum standard. Following the court's decision, the EPA adopted a PSD program in 1974, and the 1977 Amendments to the Clean Air Act continued a modified version of that program.

The PSD regulations specify the maximum allowable increases or increments in pollution concentration beyond some baseline. To allow some variability in the size of these increments, Congress specified that PSD regions be subdivided into three types of areas, with each type allowed a different increment. Class I areas include national parks and wilderness areas. The increments for these regions are the smallest. Practically any degradation in these areas is considered significant and is disallowed.

All other areas were initially designated as Class II regions, where a modest increment is allowed. States may redesignate any Class II region as a Class I region (thus allowing less future deterioration) or as a Class III region (allowing more). Class III regions are allowed the largest increment. In no case, however, can pollutant concentrations in any PSD region rise above the governing ambient standard.

New sources seeking to locate in PSD regions must secure permits. As a condition of securing their permits, these sources must install the *best available control technology* (BACT). The specific technologies that satisfy their requirement are determined by states on a case-by-case basis. Each new permitted source consumes a portion of the allowable increment. Once the increment has been completely consumed, no further deterioration of the air is allowed in that area, even if the air is cleaner than required by the prevailing ambient standard. Thus, where the PSD increments are binding, for all practical purposes they define a tertiary standard varying in magnitude from region to region.

In addition to defining the ambient standards and requiring states to define BACT and LAER emission standards, the EPA itself has established national uniform emission standards for new sources of criteria pollutants or major modifications of existing sources.

The progress in defining those standards has been very slow. The standards governing new and modified sources of criteria pollutants are called the *New Source Performance Standards* (NSPS), and they were designed only to serve as a "floor" for BACT and LAER determinations by the states. Congress wanted to ensure that each source would have to meet a minimum standard, regardless of where it was located. This was seen as a way to prevent states from caving in to economic pressure as industry tried to play one state off against another in its attempt to seek the lowest possible emission standards. Neither LAER nor BACT can be lower than the new-source performance standards.

Simply stating the regulations is not enough. They must be enforced with appropriate sanctions whenever noncompliance occurs. Prior to the 1977 Amendments, noncompliance was a significant problem, with delays of up to six years being common. Because of this situation, in 1977 Congress established the *noncompliance penalty* as a means of reducing the profitability in delaying compliance.

Without sanctions, the source benefits from delaying compliance. The equipment purchases necessary to ensure compliance are expensive and add nothing to profits. In addition, court action is slow and sometimes sympathetic toward business. The noncompliance penalty is designed to harmonize these private incentives with the social objectives pursued by the Act.

Patterned after a system first used in Connecticut, the magnitude of the noncompliance penalty is determined by the economic value of delay to the source. Any economic gains received by the source as a result of noncompliance are included in the penalty and are transferred to the EPA; they no longer accrue to the source.

The final characteristic of the Clean Air Act that we shall discuss is that it rules out tailoring the degree of control to the prevailing meteorological conditions. All strategies must achieve better air quality through emission reductions stringent enough to ensure compliance in quite adverse conditions.

The Efficiency of the Command-and-Control Approach

Efficiency presumes that the ambient standards are set at efficient levels. To ascertain whether or not the current standards are efficient, it is necessary to inquire into five aspects of the standard-setting process: (1) the threshold concept on which the standards are based,

(2) the level of the standard, (3) the choice of uniform standards over standards more tailored to the regions involved, (4) the timing of emission flows, and (5) the failure to incorporate the degree of human exposure in the standard-setting process.

The Threshold Concept. Some basis is needed for setting the ambient standard. Because the Clean Air Act prohibits the balancing of costs and benefits, some alternative criterion must be used. For the primary (health-related) standard, this criterion is known as the *health threshold*. The standard is to be defined with a margin of safety sufficiently high that no adverse health effects would be suffered by any member of the population as long as the air quality is at least as good as that specified by the standards. This approach presumes the existence of a threshold such that concentrations above that level produce adverse health effects, but concentrations below it produce none.

If the threshold concept were valid, the marginal-damage function would be zero until the threshold were reached and would be positive at higher concentrations. The belief that the curve of the actual damage function has this shape is not consistent with the evidence. We are now learning that adverse health effects can occur at pollution levels lower than the ambient standards.[2] The standard that produces no adverse health effects among the general population (which, of course, includes especially susceptible groups) is probably zero or close to it. It is certainly lower than the established ambient standards. What the standards purport to accomplish and what they actually accomplish are rather different.

The Level of the Ambient Standard. The absence of a defensible threshold complicates the analysis (Example 14.1). Some other basis must be used for determining the level at which the standard should be established. Efficiency would dictate setting the standard in order to maximize the net benefit, which includes a consideration of costs as well as benefits.

The current policy explicitly excludes costs from consideration in setting the ambient standards. Costs are allowed to enter the process only when the policy instruments used to meet ambient standards are being defined. It is difficult to imagine that the process of setting the ambient standards would yield an efficient outcome when it is prohibited from considering one of the key elements of that outcome!

Unfortunately, for reasons that were discussed in some detail in Chapter 3, our current benefit measurements are not sufficiently reliable to permit the identification of the efficient level with any confidence. A 1990 EPA Report to Congress concludes that the total benefits (in 1990 dollars) derived from controlling stationary sources under the Clean Air Act from 1970 to 1990 lie somewhere in the interval from $5.6 trillion to $49.4 trillion, with a most likely point estimate of $22.2 trillion.[3] This can be compared to a total cost of stationary-source control of around $523 billion. These figures suggest that a high degree of confidence can be

---

[2]See, for example, Lester B. Lave and Eugene P. Seskin, *Air Pollution and Human Health* (Baltimore, MD: Johns Hopkins University Press, 1977), which discovered a positive association between pollution and mortality even in those cities meeting the primary standards.

[3]U.S. Environmental Protection Agency, Office of Air and Radiation, *The Benefits and Cost of the Clean Air Act, 1970 to 1990* (October 1997).

Example 14.1

The Particulate and Smog Ambient Standards Controversy

In proposing more stringent ambient standards for ozone and particulates the USEPA had concluded that 125 million Americans, including 35 million children, were not adequately protected by the existing standards. The new standards were estimated to prevent one million serious respiratory illnesses each year, and 15,000 premature deaths.

The proposed revisions were controversial because the cost of compliance would be very high. No health threshold existed at the chosen level (some health effects would be noticed at even more stringent levels than those proposed) and EPA was, by law, prohibited from using a benefit/cost justification. In the face of legal challenge EPA found it very difficult to defend the superiority of the chosen standards from slightly more stringent or slightly less stringent standards.

In a decision issued May 14, 1999 the United States Court of Appeals for the District of Columbia Circuit overturned the proposed revisions. In a 2-1 ruling the three-judge panel rejected EPA's approach to setting the level of those standards:

> "the construction of the Clean Air Act on which EPA relied in promulgating the NAAQS at issue here effects an unconstitutional delegation of legislative power. . . . Although the factors EPA uses in determining the degree of public health concern associated with different levels of ozone and PM are reasonable, EPA appears to have articulated no 'intelligible principle' to channel its application of these factors. . . . EPA's formulation of its policy judgment leaves it free to pick any point between zero and a hair below the concentrations yielding London's Killer Fog.

Regardless of how this case is ultimately resolved (it was appealed), it seems clear that the current process for setting ambient standards lacks a sufficiently definitive decision criterion.

---

attached to the belief that government intervention is justified, but they provide no evidence whatsoever on whether current policy is efficient.

Uniformity. The same primary and secondary standards apply to all parts of the country. No account is taken of the number of people exposed, the sensitivity of the local ecology, or the costs of compliance in various areas. All of these would have some effect on the efficient standard, and efficiency would therefore dictate different standards for different regions. In general, the evidence suggests that the inefficiencies associated with uniformity are greatest in rural areas, but we shall leave a full description and interpretation of that evidence for later in the book.

The PSD program does introduce some variability by establishing more stringent standards for regions with the cleanest air. If national parks and other Class I areas are especially sensitive to pollution, that portion of the program could represent a move toward efficiency. Because states have some flexibility in choosing which portions of their area would be designated as Class II and Class III regions, it is conceivable, but by no means obvious, that they would make efficient choices. Furthermore, it remains true that no area is allowed to experience air quality levels worse than the primary and secondary standards for any longer than is necessary to reach those standards.

Timing of Emission Flows.   Because concentrations are important for criteria pollutants, the timing of emissions is an important policy concern. Emissions clustered in time are as troublesome as emissions clustered in space. How do we handle those relatively rare but devastating occasions when thermal inversions prevent the normal dispersion and dilution of the pollutants? From an economic efficiency point of view, the most obvious approach is to tailor the degree of control to the circumstances. Stringent control would be exercised when meteorological conditions were relatively stagnant; less stringent control would be applied under normal circumstances. The strong stand against intermittent controls in the Clean Air Act, however, rules this approach out.

It turns out that a reliance on a constant degree of control, rather than allowing intermittent controls, raises compliance costs substantially, particularly when the required degree of control is high. In perhaps the earliest empirical study soundly based on economic theory, Azriel Teller examined the costs of controlling sulfur dioxide in Nashville, Tennessee, through fuel substitution.[4] He specifically examined two strategies: (1) constant abatement, which requires the same degree of control over time, and (2) forecasted abatement, which allows the degree of control to be tailored to forecasted weather conditions.

Both strategies achieve compliance with the ambient standards, but forecasted control requires less total emission reduction. Teller's results indicate that constant abatement would be 5 times more expensive than forecasted abatement.

Concentration versus Exposure.   Present ambient standards are defined in terms of pollutant concentrations in the outdoor air, yet health effects are more closely related to human exposure to pollutants. (Exposure is determined both by the concentrations of air pollutants in each of the places in which people spend time and by the amount of time spent in each place.) Because only about 10 percent of the population's person-hours are spent outdoors, indoor air becomes very important in designing strategies to improve the health risk of pollutants.[5] Some studies have suggested that exposure to pollutants is several times higher indoors than it is outdoors.[6] To date, despite its apparent importance, very little attention has been focused on controlling indoor air pollution.[7]

Cost-Effectiveness of the Command-and-Control Approach

Though the ambient standards are not efficient, determining the magnitude of the inefficiency is plagued by uncertainties. It is not possible to state definitively just how inefficient they are.

---

[4]Azriel Teller, "Air Pollution Abatement: Economic Rationality and Reality," in *America's Changing Environment,* Roger Revelle and Hans H. Landsberg, eds. (Boston, MA: Beacon Press, 1970).

[5]This estimate is for the United States.

[6]Kirk R. Smith, "Air Pollution: Assessing Total Exposure in the United States," *Environment* 30, No. 8 (October 1988): 10–15; 33–38.

[7]The one major policy response to indoor air pollution has been the large number of states which have passed legislation requiring "smoke-free" areas in public places to protect nonsmokers.

Cost-effectiveness is based on somewhat more solid evidence. Though it does not allow us to shed any light on whether a particular ambient standard is efficient or not, cost-effectiveness studies do allow us to see whether the command-and-control policy described earlier has resulted in the ambient standards' being met in the least costly manner possible.

As we have seen, the CAC strategy will normally not be cost effective, but general principles are not enough to establish the degree to which this strategy diverges from the least-cost ideal. If the divergence is small, the proponents of reform would not likely be able to overcome the inertia of the status quo. If the divergence is large, the case for reform is stronger.

The cost-effectiveness of the CAC approach depends on local circumstances such as prevailing meteorology, the locational configuration of sources, stack heights, and how costs vary with the amount controlled. Several simulation models capable of dealing with these complexities have now been constructed for a number of different pollutants for a variety of metropolitan areas (Table 14.2).

For a number of reasons, the estimated costs cannot be directly compared across studies; therefore, it is appropriate to develop a means of comparing them that minimizes the comparability problems. One such technique, the one we have chosen, involves calculating the ratio of the CAC allocation costs to the lowest cost of meeting the same objective for each study. A radio equal to 1.0 implies that the CAC allocation is cost effective. By subtracting 1.0 from the ratio in the table, it is possible to interpret the remainder as the percentage increase in cost from the least-cost ideal that results from relying on the CAC system.

Of the ten reported comparisons, eight find that the CAC policy costs at least 78 percent more than the least-cost allocation. If we omit the 1982 study by Hahn and Noll[8] (for reasons discussed in the next two paragraphs), the study involving the *smallest* cost savings (particulates in Santiago) finds that the CAC allocation results in abatement costs that are 31 percent higher than is necessary to meet the standards. In the Chicago study, the CAC costs are estimated to be 14 times as expensive as necessary, and, for particulates in the Lower Delaware Valley they are estimated to be 22 times more expensive than necessary.

The Hahn and Noll finding that the CAC strategy was close to being cost effective was somewhat unique in a couple of respects. Because we can learn something from this study about the conditions under which CAC policies may not be far off the mark, it is worth subjecting it to close scrutiny.

The city studied by Hahn and Noll, Los Angeles, has a large sulfate problem, necessitating a very high degree of control. In effect, virtually every source is forced to control as much as is economically feasible. All policies must ultimately arrive at this allocation.[9]

Does the degree of cost excess associated with the CAC approach depend on the stringency of the ambient standard being met? The evidence seems to suggest that it does depend on the stringency, but in rather well-defined ways. Atkinson and Lewis find, for example, that

---

8Robert W. Hahn and Roger G. Noll. "Designing a Market for Tradeable Emissions Permits," Reform of Environmental Regulation, Wesley A. Magat, ed. (Cambridge, MA: Ballinger, 1982).

9Hahn and Noll also suggest that the California Air Resources Board has specifically used its multimillion-dollar budget in part to promulgate cost-effective emission standards. Therefore, this board may be atypically cost effective in its approach to a CAC strategy because of both the amount of resources at its disposal and its inclination to use them to pursue cost-effective allocations of control responsibility.

TABLE 14.2   Empirical Studies of Air Pollution Control

Study and Year	Pollutants Covered	Geographic Area	CAC Benchmark	Assumed Pollutant Type	Ratio of CAC Cost to Least Cost
Atkinson and Lewis (1974)	Particulates	St. Louis metropolitan area	SIP regulations	Nonuniformly mixed	6.00
Roach et al. (1981)	Sulfur dioxide	Four Corners in Utah, Colorado, Arizona, and New Mexico	SIP regulations	Nonuniformly mixed	4.25
Hahn and Noll (1982)	Sulfates	Los Angeles	California emission standards	Nonuniformly mixed	1.07
Krupnick (1983)	Nitrogen dioxide	Baltimore	Proposed RACT regulations	Nonuniformly mixed	5.96
Seskin, Anderson, and Reid (1983)	Nitrogen dioxide	Chicago	Proposed RACT regulations	Nonuniformly mixed	14.40
McGartland (1984)	Particulates	Baltimore	SIP regulations	Nonuniformly mixed	4.18
Spofford (1984)	Sulfur dioxide	Lower Delaware Valley	Uniform percentage reduction	Nonuniformly mixed	1.78
	Particulates	Lower Delaware Valley	Uniform percentage reduction	Nonuniformly mixed	22.00
Maloney and Yandle (1984)	Hydrocarbons	All domestic Du Pont plants	Uniform percentage reduction	Uniformly mixed	4.15
O'Ryan (1995)	Particulates	Santiago, Chile	PER/APS	Nonuniformly mixed	1.31

Definitions: APS = Ambient permit system

CAC = Command and control, the traditional regulatory approach

PER = Percentage emisson reduction

SIP = State implementation plan

RACT = Reasonably available control technologies, a set of standards imposed on existing sources in nonattainment areas

within a middle range of possible ambient standards, the divergence between the CAC allocation and the least-cost allocation becomes larger as the ambient standard target becomes harder to meet.[10] However, two studies concentrating on the most stringent range of control (as opposed to the middle ranges of control examined by Atkinson and Lewis) have found that the relative divergence between the CAC and least-cost allocations declines as the ambient standard becomes tougher to meet. Spofford finds this to be the case for both particulates and

---

[10]S. E. Atkinson and D. H. Lewis, "A Cost-Effectiveness Analysis of Alternative Air Quality Control Strategies," *Journal of Environmental Economics and Management* 1, No. 3 (November 1974): 237–50.

sulfur oxides; Maloney and Yandle find it to be true for hydrocarbon control.[11] Apparently, the CAC air pollution policy approximates the least-cost allocation only at sufficiently high degrees of control that any control flexibility is effectively eliminated.

Air Quality

Despite the deficiencies of the CAC approach, it *has* produced better air quality in the United States. According to the U.S. EPA, during the period of 1970–1996, carbon monoxide emissions were reduced by 31 percent, sulfur dioxide emissions by 39 percent, and lead emissions by 98 percent. Particulate (e.g., dirt, soot) levels decreased 69 percent during the same period.

How typical has the U.S. experience been? Is pollution declining on a worldwide basis? The Global Environmental Monitoring System (GEMS), operating under the auspices of the World Health Organization and the United Nations Environment Program, monitors air quality around the globe. Scrutiny of its reports reveals that the U.S. experience is rather typical for the industrialized nations, which have generally reduced pollution (both in terms of emissions and ambient outdoor air quality).[12] Some of the reductions achieved in countries such as Japan and Norway have been spectacular. However, the air quality in most developing nations has steadily deteriorated, and the number of people exposed to unhealthy levels of pollution in those countries is frequently very high.[13] Because these countries typically are struggling merely to provide adequate employment and income to their citizens, they cannot afford to waste large sums of money on inefficient environmental policies, especially if the inefficiencies tend to subsidize the rich at the expense of the poor. Some cost-effective but fair means of improving air quality must be found.

◆ INNOVATIVE APPROACHES

Fortunately, some innovative approaches are available. Because various versions of these approaches have now been implemented around the world, we can learn from the experience gained from their implementation.

The Emissions Trading Program

Stripped to its essentials, the command-and-control approach toward stationary sources involves the specification of emission standards (legal ceilings) on all major emission sources. These standards are imposed on a large number of specific emission points such as stacks, vents, or storage tanks.

---

[11]See W. O. Spofford, Jr., "Efficiency Properties of Alternative Source Control Policies for Meeting Ambient Air Quality Standards: An Empirical Application to the Lower Delaware Valley," Discussion Paper D-118 (Washington, DC: Resources for the Future, 1984); and M. T. Maloney and B. Yandle, "Estimation of the Cost of Air Pollution Control Regulation," *Journal of Environmental Economics and Management* 11 (1984): 244–63.

[12]United Nations Environment Program and the World Health Organization, "Monitoring the Global Environment: An Assessment of Urban Air Quality," *Environment* 31, No. 8 (October 1989): 6–13, 26–37.

[13]For sulfur oxides, for example, the GEMS study estimates that only 30 to 35 percent of the world's population lives in areas where air is at least as clean as recommended by the World Health Organization guidelines.

The emissions trading program adopted in the United States attempts to inject more flexibility into the manner in which the clean air objectives are met. Sources are encouraged to change the mix of control technologies envisioned in the standards as long as air quality is improved or at least not adversely affected by the change. The program is implemented by means of four separate policies, linked by a common element known as the *emission reduction credit*. The emission reduction credit is the currency used in trading among emission points, whereas the other four policies—offset, bubble, emissions banking, and netting—govern how the currency can be spent or saved.[14]

The Emission Reduction Credit. Should any source decide to control any emission point to a higher degree than necessary to fulfill its legal obligations, it can apply to the control authority for certification of the excess control as an emission reduction credit (ERC). Certified credits can be banked or used in the bubble, offset, or netting programs. To receive certification, the emission reduction must be (1) surplus, (2) enforceable, (3) permanent, and (4) quantifiable.

The Offset Policy. The *offset policy* was established to resolve a conflict between economic growth and progress toward meeting the ambient standards in nonattainment areas. The dilemma posed by this conflict involved how new or expanded sources could be accommodated while meeting the statutory requirement that the ambient standards be met as expeditiously as possible. Because these sources would add emissions to the region, some means of offsetting them had to be found.

The offset policy allows qualified new or expanding sources to commence operations in a nonattainment area provided they acquire sufficient emission reduction credits from existing sources. Typically, they must acquire credits for 20 percent more reductions in emissions than would be added when the new facility commences operations. By buying the credits, new sources, in effect, finance emission controls undertaken by existing sources, thereby serving as a vehicle for improved air quality. Because regional emissions would be lower after the source began operations (counting the acquired ERCs) than before, economic growth becomes the means for achieving better air quality rather than the source of further deterioration.

Major new or modified sources are qualified to participate in this program only if (1) they control their own emissions to the degree required by the LAER standard and (2) all existing major sources owned or operated by the applicant in the same state as the proposed source are in compliance with their legal control responsibilities.

The Bubble Policy. The *bubble policy* allows existing sources to use emission reduction credits to satisfy their SIP control responsibilities. For example, existing sources in nonattainment areas can meet their assigned standards either by adopting the control technology used to define the standard or, if they adopt some technology that emits the pollutant at a somewhat higher rate, by making up the difference with acquired emission reduction credits. The sum of ERCs plus actual reductions must equal the assigned reduction.

---

[14]As described in the next chapter, these policies have recently been adopted for controlling acid rain and ozone-depleting chemicals as well.

Example 14.2

The Bubble and Offset Policies in Action

1. The Narraganset Electric Company has two generating stations in Providence, Rhode Island. Under the bubble policy it was allowed to use high-sulfur oil (2.2 percent sulfur) at one plant when the second plant was burning natural gas or was not operating, instead of being required to burn 1 percent sulfur oil at both plants. This action resulted in a saving of $3 million annually, reduced the use of imported oil by 600,000 barrels per year, and reduced sulfur emissions by 30 percent.

2. Manufacturers of cans have been allowed to comply with existing regulations for each individual can-coating line by averaging emissions of volatile organic compounds on a daily basis so long as the source did not exceed the total allowable plantwide emission per day. This is expected to save the industry $107 million in capital expenditures, $28 million per year in operating costs, and 4 trillion BTUs of natural gas per year, chiefly because expensive add-on pollution control equipment, which would have been energy-consuming, is no longer necessary.

3. A cement company in Texas entered into an agreement with another local company providing for that company to install dust collectors. The cement company paid for the equipment, and the other company agreed to accept the maintenance costs, which were negligible.

4. A company wanting to build an oil terminal to handle 40,000 barrels a day in Contra Costa County, California, was granted a permit when it acquired, for $250,000, an offset created when a local chemical company shut down.

Source: These examples were taken from the National Commission of Air Quality, *To Breathe Clean Air* (Washington, DC: Government Printing Office, 1981: 136–37; and Richard A. Liroff, *Air Pollution Offsets: Trading, Selling and Banking* (Washington, DC: Conservation Foundation, 1980): 13.

This policy derives its unusual name from its treatment of multiple emission points as if they were contained within an imaginary bubble; that is, this policy regulates only the amount leaving the bubble. These bubbles can be extended to include not only emission points within the same plant, but emission points in plants owned by other firms as well (Example 14.2).

Netting. *Netting* allows sources undergoing modification or expansion to escape the burden of new-source review requirements so long as any net increase (counting the emission reduction credits) in plantwide emissions is insignificant. Traditionally, the test of whether a source was subject to the new-source review process or not was applied by calculating the expected increases in emission occurring after modernization or expansion. When these increases passed predetermined thresholds, the source was subject to review. Netting allows ERCs earned elsewhere in the plant to offset the increases expected from the expanded, more modernized portion in order to determine whether the threshold had been exceeded. By "netting out" of review, the facility may be exempted from acquiring preconstruction permits as well as from meeting the associated requirements, such as modeling or monitoring the impact of the new source on air quality, installing BACT or LAER control technology, or meeting the offset requirement; it may also avoid any applicable bans on new construction. Those facilities satisfying the significant increase threshold must still meet emission limits established by the NSPS. Emission reduction credits cannot be used to avoid this national standard.

Banking. The banking component of the emissions trading program establishes procedures that allow firms to store emission reduction credits for subsequent use in the bubble, offset, or netting programs. States are authorized to design their own banking programs as long as the rules specify the ownership rights over the banked credits, the sources eligible to bank ERCs, and the conditions governing the certification, holding, and use of these credits.

Smog Trading

Although the original emissions trading program was initiated and promoted by the federal government, the newest programs have arisen from state initiatives. Faced with the need to reduce ozone concentrations considerably in order to come into compliance with the ozone ambient standard, states have chosen to use trading programs as a means of facilitating rather drastic reductions in precursor pollutants(those for which a part of the chemical reactions result in ozone).

One of the most ambitious of these programs is California's Regional Clean Air Incentives Market (RECLAIM) established by the South Coast Air Quality Management District, the district authority responsible for the greater Los Angeles area. Under RECLAIM, each of the almost 400 participating industrial polluters are allocated an annual pollution limit for nitrogen oxides and sulfur, which will decrease by 5 percent to 8 percent each year for the next decade. Polluters are allowed great flexibility in how they meet these limits, including approaches such as purchasing credits from other firms that have controlled more than their legal requirements.

The RECLAIM program departs from traditional practice in a couple of respects. First, it sets a cap on total emissions from this group rather than on emissions from each source; this cap assures that expansion must be accommodated within the cap by cutting back a compensating amount somewhere else rather than by allowing emissions to increase. Second, it changes the nature of the regulatory process. The burden of identifying the appropriate control strategies has been shifted from the control authority to the polluter. In part, this shift was a necessity (traditional processes were incapable of identifying enough appropriate technologies to produce sufficiently stringent reductions) and was, in part, motivated by a desire to make the process as flexible as possible.

As a result of this flexibility, many new control strategies are emerging. Instead of the traditional focus on "end-of-pipe" control technologies, this program gives pollution prevention an economic underpinning. All possible pollution-reduction strategies can, for the first time, compete on a level playing field.

The Effectiveness of Emissions Trading

Although comprehensive data on the effect of the natural emissions trading program do not exist, because substantial proportions of its are administered by local areas and no one collects information in a systematic way, some of the major aspects of experience are clear.[15]

The program has unquestionably and substantially reduced the cost of complying with the requirements of the Clean Air Act. Most estimates place the accumulated capital savings for all components of the program at over $10 billion. This does not include the recurring savings in operating cost. On the other hand, the program has not produced the magnitude of cost savings that was anticipated by most proponents at its inception.

The level of compliance with the basic provisions of the Clean Air Act has increased. The emissions trading program expanded the possible means for compliance, and sources have responded.

The vast majority of emissions trading transactions have involved large pollution sources trading ERCs either created by excess control of uniformly mixed pollutants (i.e., those for which the location of emission is not an important policy concern) or involving facilities in close proximity to one another. Emissions trading seems to work especially well for uniformly mixed pollutants. No diffusion modeling is necessary to establish effects on ambient concentrations, and regulators do not have to worry that trades will create "hot spots," or localized areas of high pollution concentration. Trades can be on a one-to-one basis.

Emissions trading integrates particularly smoothly into any policy structure that is based either directly (through emission standards) or indirectly (through mandated technology or input limitations) on regulating emissions. In this case, emission limitations embedded in the operating licenses can serve as the trading benchmark.

Because emissions trading allows the issue of who will pay for the control to be separated from who will install the control, it introduces an additional degree of flexibility. This flexibility is particularly important in nonattainment areas, because marginal control costs are so high. Sources that would not normally be controlled because they could not afford to implement the controls without going out of business can be controlled with emissions trading. The revenue derived from the sale of ERCs can be used to finance the controls, effectively preventing bankruptcy.

Because it is quantity-based, emissions trading also offers a unique possibility for leasing. The use of leasing credits is particularly valuable when the temporal pattern of emissions varies across sources. This appears to be the general case with utilities. In addition, when a firm plans to shut down one plant in the near future and to build a new one, the leasing-credits approach is a vastly superior alternative to temporarily installing equipment in the old plant that would be useless when the plant was retired. The useful life of this temporary control equipment would be wastefully short.

We have also learned that ERC transactions have higher transaction costs than we previously understood. Regulators must validate every trade. When nonuniformly mixed pollutants are involved, the transaction costs associated with estimating the air quality effects are particularly

---

[15]See the evaluations of this program in D. J. Dudek and J. Palmisano, "Emissions Trading: Why Is This Thoroughbred Hobbled?" *Columbia Journal of Environmental Law* 13, No. 2 (1988): 217–56; R. W. Hahn, "Economic Prescriptions for Environmental Problems: How the Patient Followed the Doctor's Orders," *Journal of Economics Perspectives* 3, No. 2 (spring 1989): 95–114; R. W. Hahn and G. L. Hester, "Where Did All the Markets Go? An Analysis of EPA's Emission Trading Program," *Yale Journal of Regulation* 6, No. 1 (winter 1989): 109–153; and T. H. Tietenberg, "Economic Instruments for Environmental Regulation," *Oxford Review of Economic Policy* 6, No. 1 (spring 1990): 17–33.

high. Delegating responsibility for trade approval to lower levels of government may, in principle, speed up the approval process, but unless the bureaucrats in the lower level of government support the program, the gain may be negligible.

Emissions trading places more importance on the operating permits and emissions inventories than other approaches. To the extent that these are deficient, the potential for trades that protect air quality may be lost. Firms that have actual levels of emissions substantially below allowable emissions find themselves with a trading opportunity which, if exploited, could degrade air quality. The trading benchmark has to be defined carefully.

One question that always arises about emissions trading is the degree to which market power could undermine its desirable properties. Hahn has examined the case where permits are allocated to emitters without charge (as is done in the emission trading program) rather than allocating them by an auction.[16] His most important finding was that this initial allocation could have an effect on both the final (posttrade) allocation of permits and the permit price in the presence of market power. This finding is in direct contrast to what would happen in competitive markets (as described in Chapter 12), where both the final price and the ultimate allocation of permits would be independent of the initial allocation.

It is not hard to obtain an intuitive understanding of why the initial allocation might have an effect on the potential for price-setting behavior. Whenever a single price-setting source receives an initial allocation that is either higher than or lower than its cost-effective allocation, an incentive for trading is created. When a price-setting source receives in an initial allocation fewer permits than its cost-effective allocation, it exercises power on the buyer's side of the market. If it receives more, it exercises power on the seller's side of the market. The farther the initial allocation diverges from the cost-effective allocation, the greater the potential for the price-setter to exercise power over the market.

Is the potential for price manipulation a serious potential flaw in permit markets? Existing simulation studies suggest that it is not. Hahn found in simulating the sulfate market in Los Angeles that the total-cost function was rather flat with respect to the initial allocation unless the price-setting firm received enough permits that it was able to become virtually a monopoly seller.

In another set of published data from the Du Pont Corporation involving some 52 plants and 548 sources of hydrocarbons, Maloney and Yandle investigated the effects of cartelization of plants on the permit market.[17] Assuming that all sources receive a proportional initial distribution of the permits based on their uncontrolled emissions, they calculated the effects on control costs if plants collude. According to their assumptions collusion may take place separately among buyers and sellers and the number of colluding plants may vary from 10 to 90 percent of the total number of plants buying or selling.

In general, these data support the notion that high degrees of cartelization are necessary before control costs are affected to any appreciable degree and that even high degrees of cartelization do not significantly erode the large savings to be achieved from permit

---

[16]Robert W. Hahn, "Market Power and Transferable Property Rights," *Quarterly Journal of Economics* 99, No. 4 (November 1984): 753–65.

[17]Michael T. Maloney and Bruce Yandle, "Estimation of the Cost of Air Pollution Control Regulation," *Journal of Environmental Economics and Management* 11, No. 3 (September 1984): 244–63.

markets. At the 90 percent credit monopoly (achieved when the cartel controls 90 percent of all credits sold), for example, yielding a 41 percent increase in control costs, Maloney and Yandle point out that the cost saving from this severe market-power situation, compared with CAC regulation, is still 66 (instead of 76) percent. The presence of market power does not seem to diminish the potential for cost savings very much. Even with market power, transferable permit systems seem to result in lower control costs than the CAC allocation does.

In summary, the current regulatory reforms embodying transferable permits represent a large, but incomplete, step toward cost effectiveness.

Emission Charges

Air pollution emission charges have been implemented by France and Japan. The French air pollution charge was designed to encourage the early adoption of pollution control equipment, with the revenues returned to those paying the charge as a subsidy for installing the equipment. In Japan the emission charge is designed to raise revenue to compensate victims of air pollution.

The French charge system has been in effect since 1985. Originally designed to operate only until 1990, it was renewed in that year. The change is levied on all industrial firms having a power-generating capacity of 50,000 watts or more, or industrial firms discharging over 2,500 tons of sulfur or nitrogen oxides per year. Only about 400 plants are affected. The charge is levied on the actual amount of sulfur oxides emitted. Some 90 percent of the charge revenue is recovered by charge payers as a subsidy for pollution control equipment; the remaining 10 percent is used for new technological developments.

Although data are limited, a few areas can be highlighted. The charge level is too low to have any incentive impact. Total revenues are estimated to be about one tenth of the revenue that would result from a charge sufficient to bring French industries in line with the air pollution control directions of the European Community.[18]

Economists typically envision two types of effluent or emissions charges. The first, an efficiency charge, is designed to produce an efficient outcome by forcing the polluter to compensate completely for all damage caused. The second, a cost-effective charge, is designed to achieve a predefined ambient standard at the lowest possible control cost. In practice, the French approach fits neither of these designs.

In Japan the charge takes on a rather different function. As a result of four important legal cases where Japanese industries were forced to compensate victims for pollution damages caused, in 1973 Japan passed the Law for the Compensation of Pollution-Related Health Injury. According to this law, upon certification by a council of medical, legal, and other experts, victims of designated diseases are eligible for medical expenses, lost earnings, and other expenses; they are not eligible for other losses, such as pain and suffering. Two classes of diseases are funded: (1) specific diseases, where the specific source is relatively clear, and (2) nonspecific respiratory diseases, where all polluters are presumed to have some responsibility.

---

[18]J. B. Opschoor and Hans B. Vos, *Economic Instruments For Environmental Protection* (Paris: Organization for Economic Co-operation and Development, 1989): 34–35.

This program is funded by an emissions charge on sulfur dioxides and from an automobile weight tax. The level of the tax is determined by the revenue needs of the compensation fund.

In contrast to emissions trading, where ERC prices respond automatically to changing market conditions, emission charges have to be determined by an administrative process. When the function of the charge is to raise revenue for a particular purpose, charge rates will be determined by the costs of achieving that purpose; when the costs of achieving that purpose rise, the level of the charge must rise in order to secure the additional revenue.[19]

Sometimes, that process produces an unintended dynamic. In Japan, for example, the charge is calculated on the basis of the amount of compensation paid to victims of air pollution in the previous year. Although the amount of compensation has been increasing, the amount of emissions (the base to which the charge is applied) has been decreasing. As a result, unexpectedly high charge rates are necessary in order to raise sufficient revenue for the compensation system.

Hazardous Pollutants

Hazardous pollutants are those that pose a localized risk of severe harm to human health. They are distinguished from criteria pollutants both by the degree of harm they pose to those exposed and by the fact that emission usually occurs only at a few key locations. In recognition of these unique characteristics, the Clean Air Act sets up a special process for dealing with hazardous pollutants.

The first step in the control process involves identifying those substances that are designated as hazardous and therefore must receive this special treatment. The Act requires the Administrator of the EPA to make and periodically update a list of hazardous pollutants. It allows a great deal of discretion in the choice of criteria to be used in distinguishing between hazardous and criteria pollutants and in the length of time necessary to decide whether a particular substance should be listed.

Once a substance is listed, the EPA must move with great speed (within 180 days) either to regulate emissions of the substance or to remove it from the list after finding that the evidence failed to support the tentative hazardous-substance designation. The decision to regulate a substance imposes on the EPA a requirement to establish a national emission standard or workplace standard for each regulated substance. These standards must be designed to protect human health with an adequate margin of safety.

The somewhat ambiguous language in this section of the Act has led to a great deal of controversy as well as litigation concerning the meaning of this mandate. It is generally conceded that there is no safe threshold level for airborne carcinogens. Therefore, environmentalists maintain that protecting the public with an adequate margin of safety requires eliminating all exposure to listed substances. Completely eliminating emissions would, at a minimum, be very expensive and in some cases may not be possible without shutting down the operation.

The EPA has reacted to this dilemma in two ways: (1) It has moved slowly in listing pollutants, and (2) it has chosen to balance costs and risks in deciding whether to list a substance

---

[19]Although it is theoretically possible (depending on the elasticity of demand for pollution abatement) for a rise in the tax to produce less revenue, this has typically not been the case.

or not. By 1999, the EPA had listed only seven pollutants: (1) asbestos (1971), (2) beryllium (1971), (3) mercury (1971), (4) vinyl chloride (1975), (5) benzene (1977), (6) radionuclides (1979), and (7) inorganic arsenic (1980).

In addition to moving very slowly in listing pollutants, the agency began to incorporate risk assessment and benefit-cost analysis into its decisions. The first step in this process is to decide whether the risk posed by the substance is "significant." Substances that are not found to be posing significant risks are not listed. The second step, taken only for listed pollutants, involves identifying the level of control that will be required. This entails comparing the costs of various control possibilities with the damages to health prevented by adopting the controls.

Based on the work of Haigh, Harrison, and Nichols, it is possible to see how this kind of economic analysis can be applied to regulating hazardous pollution.[20] In their study, the authors applied benefit-cost analysis to three hazardous pollutants: (1) benzene, (2) coke oven emissions, and (3) acrylonitrile. Benzene is a major industrial chemical, ranking among the top 15 in terms of production volume. Coke, produced by distilling coal in ovens, is essential to the production of steel. Acrylonitrile is an important industrial chemical used in the manufacture of a wide range of consumer products, including rugs, clothing, plastic pipe, and automobile hoses.

The analysis involved several steps. The amount and location of emission had to be identified for each substance. The number of people exposed to this risk and the amount of health risk they would experience had to be calculated. Finally, a dollar value had to be put on this risk so that it could be directly compared with the control costs. All of these steps had to be repeated for each considered regulatory option.

Three regulatory strategies were considered for each pollutant. The first strategy was the use of a rather stringent set of uniformly applied emission standards designed to require the use of the "best available technology," or BAT. (For benzene, the controls were applied to maleic anhydride plants, the largest source of emissions.) The second considered strategy involved a somewhat more relaxed version of the first strategy. Although the standards were still applied uniformly in this second case, the level of required control was lower. The final strategy involved differential controls based on exposure. The notion of uniform controls was dropped in this case in favor of placing heavier controls on those sources posing the greatest health risk.

The authors present their results in two main forms. The first calculates the value of human life that would be needed to justify a particular regulatory option. This form of presentation allows the reader to decide whether the regulatory option is a good idea or not by supplying his or her own sense of what the value of human life should be. The second uses a $1 million value of human life and calculates the net benefits of each option based on that assumption.

Using the $1 million figure for a human life, the results (Table 14.3) indicate that for all three pollutants the standard BAT strategy would yield negative net benefits. The combination of uniform standards with a very stringent level of control produces a situation where the costs exceed the benefits. A relaxed uniform standard reduces, but does not eliminate, the

---

[20]John A. Haigh, David Harrison, Jr., and Albert L. Nichols, "Benefits Assessment and Environmental Regulation: Case Studies of Hazardous Air Pollutants," Discussion Paper E-83-07, John F. Kennedy School of Government Energy and Environment Policy Center, Cambridge, MA, August 1983.

TABLE 14.3 Net Benefits ($Million/Year) of Alternative Strategies for a Value of Life Saved of $1 Million

Regulatory Strategy	Maleic Anhydride	Coke Oven Emissions	Acrylonitrile
Best available technology	-2.2	-8.7	-28.8
Relaxed uniform	-1.1	-3.2	-8.0
Differential	-0.6	-2.3	-4.9

Source: From "Benefits Assessment and Environmental Regulation: Case Studies of Hazardous Air Pollutants" by John A. Haigh, David Harrison, Jr., and Albert L. Nichols. John F. Kennedy School of Government Energy and Environment Policy Center Discussion Paper E-83-07 (August 1983). Reprinted by permission.

negative net benefits. Although lowering the uniform degree of control represents an improvement in the sense that costs are more commensurate with benefits, it still fails to target the reductions in the areas where they result in the most reduction in risk.

By configuring the controls so as to target the costs on those emitters posing the greatest risk to human health (the differential strategy), a dramatic improvement in net benefits is achieved for all three pollutants. However, for only one, coke oven emissions, are the net benefits positive. For the rest, even the differential strategy falls short of being justified by the benefits.

The significance of these data lies less in what they tell us about the correct regulatory option to choose for these specific pollutants than in the clues they provide concerning directions for policy movement in order to achieve greater efficiency in regulating hazardous pollutants in general. First, tailoring the strategy to the specific circumstances can produce significant reductions in cost while achieving the same risk, or it can achieve much larger risk reductions for the same cost. Uniformity, in short, imposes a large cost penalty. Second, the policies being pursued in regulating hazardous pollutants imply values for human life that differ by a factor of more than 100. This finding implies that by allocating more resources to the control of those substances that can be justified with even a lower value of life and less to those that can be justified only with a high value for life, more lives could be saved with the same expenditure of money.

How can these lessons be translated into policy? One answer is to consider the adoption of a charge levied not on emission, but rather on exposure (Example 14.3). By forcing those emitters exposing large numbers of people to a health risk to exert greater cleanup efforts than those emitters exposing fewer people to the same health risk, more lives can be saved, with the same expenditure of resources. In this context, uniform exposure charges have much to recommend them.

Emissions Fees

Recognizing that the bulk of enforcement activity falls on the states and wanting to provide increased funds for that endeavor without increasing the federal budget deficit, the U.S. Congress incorporated a system of fees on polluters in Title V of the Clean Air Act.[21] Just as economists would recommend, these fees are levied annually on emissions on a per unit basis; higher emission levels trigger higher payments. Some states are planning to further differ-

---

[21]Section 502(b)(3).

Example 14.3

Efficient Regulation of Hazardous Pollutants: the Benzene cCase

Regulatory approaches tend to emphasize uniform standards. As is clear from the discussion in the text, this can cause a particularly large deviation from efficiency when hazardous pollutants are involved, because both the control costs and damages are so localized.

Eight maleic anhydride plants in the United States emit more than half of the nation's benzene from chemical manufacturing. From Table 13.3 we know that BAT uniform standards yield negative net benefits. Is there a more efficient approach?

The damage caused by these emissions (primarily an increase in the risk of leukemia) is a function both of the concentration level and the exposed population. The highest economic-marginal-damage estimate found by a government agency was $1 for each person exposed continuously to a concentration of 1 part per billion (ppb) of benzene for one year. This corresponds to a risk of 3.4 ppb for one year and a value of $360,000 placed on each life lost.

The efficient solution would be to impose an emission charge of $1 per ppb person-year of exposure because this is the (high) estimate of marginal damage. Firms would respond by choosing that level of control where their marginal cost was equal to $1 per ppb person-year of exposure. Because this would guarantee the equivalence of marginal cost and marginal benefit, efficiency would be achieved.

The costs of the uniform standard were not justified by the benefits. The major problem with the proposed standard was that it did not take into account either the rather large differences among the plants in control costs and number of people exposed. Some plants in isolated areas exposed very few people, whereas others in more densely populated areas clearly put more people at risk. The $1 uniform *exposure* charge solves both of these problems simultaneously. A uniform *emission* charge takes into account the differences in costs, but not the differences in exposure. Uniform emission standards take neither costs nor exposure into account and, therefore, are doubly cursed.

Source: This example is based on Albert L. Nichols, "The Importance of Exposure in Evaluating and Designing Environmental Regulations: A Case Study," *American Economic Review* 72 (May 1982): 214–19.

entiate the fees based on the toxicity of the substances being emitted.[22] All polluters holding permits must pay the fees to the state enforcement agencies, and the revenues must be sufficient to cover the costs of administering the program. States are free to set their own fee schedule, although the Act creates a presumptive minimum annual fee of $25 per ton, adjusted each year by changes in the consumer price index. In essence, this program was designed to make polluters bear the financial responsibility for the monitoring and

---

[22]Differentiating by toxicity is a feature of the Maine Department of Environmental Protection's proposed regulation, for example.

enforcement system made necessary by their pollution. Though this fee system falls short of being fully efficient (because it is based on revenue needs, not damages), it is certainly a step in the right direction.

SUMMARY

Although air quality has improved in the industrialized nations, it has deteriorated in the developing nations. Because the historical approach to air pollution control has been a traditional command-and-control approach, it has been neither efficient nor cost effective.

The CAC policy has not been efficient, in part, because it has been based on a legal fiction, a threshold below which no health damages are inflicted on any member of the population. In fact, damages occur at levels lower than the ambient standards to especially sensitive members of the population, such as those with respiratory problems. This attempt to formulate standards without reference to control costs has been thwarted by the absence of a scientifically defensible health-based threshold. In addition, the policy fails to adequately consider the timing of emission flows. By failing to target the greatest amount of control on those periods when the greatest damage is inflicted, the current policy encourages too little control in high-damage periods and excessive control during low-damage periods. Current policy has also failed to pay sufficient attention to indoor air pollution, which may well pose larger health risks than are posed by outdoor pollution. Unfortunately, because the existing benefit estimates have large confidence intervals, the size of the inefficiency associated with these aspects of the policy has not been measured with any precision.

The policy is not cost-effective either. The allocation of responsibility among emitters for reducing pollution has resulted in control costs that are typically several times higher than necessary to achieve the air quality objective. This has been shown to be true for a variety of pollutants in a variety of geographic settings.

Recently, the EPA has initiated the Emissions Trading Program. The program is based on economic incentives designed to provide more flexibility in meeting the air quality goals while reducing the cost and the conflict between economic growth and the preservation of air quality. These reforms, known as the *bubble, offset, netting,* and *emissions banking programs,* also promise to stimulate more rapid development of new control technologies than was possible under the traditional system.

France and Japan have both introduced emission charges as part of their approach to pollution control, but neither application fits the textbook model very well. In France the charge level is too low to have the appropriate incentive effects. In Japan the charge is designed mainly to raise revenue with which to compensate victims of respiratory damage caused by pollution. Only sulfur oxides are taxed.

The program to control hazardous pollutants is inefficient both in the speed with which the process is operating and in the quality of the decisions being rendered. Faced with unrealistically short deadlines for publishing standards once a hazardous substance is listed, the EPA has reacted by taking an excessively cautious approach to listing hazardous substances. Past decisions have resulted in the application of stringent standards that are uniformly applied to emitters. The evidence suggests that strategies tailored more closely to the risk posed (with emissions posing the greatest risk being reduced more) produce substantially lower risks for the same expenditure as uniformly applied standards do. One reform proposal based on this analysis would impose an exposure (as opposed to an emission) charge on emitters that would take into account not only the concentration of the emission (and the resulting health risk to each exposed person), but also the number of people exposed.

FURTHER READING

Joeres, Erhard F., and Martin David, eds. *Buying a Better Environment: Cost Effective Regulation through Permit Trading* (Madison: University of Wisconsin Press, 1983). An excellent collection of essays on aspects of permit trading including permit design, distributional matters, and dealing with uncertainty.

Kosobud, Richard F., William A. Testa, and Donald A. Hanson, eds. *Cost Effective Control of Urban Smog* (Chicago: Federal Reserve Bank of Chicago, 1993). The proceedings of a conference providing background information for the Illinois smog-trading program.

Nichols, Albert L. *Targeting Economic Incentives for Environmental Protection* (Cambridge, MA: MIT Press, 1984). An excellent review of the use of economic incentives to control pollution, with a detailed treatment of the use of exposure charges to control airborne carcinogens.

ADDITIONAL REFERENCES

Anderson, Robert J., Jr., et al. "An Analysis of Alternative Policies for Attaining and Maintaining a Short-Term NO_2 Standard," a report prepared by MATHTECH, Inc., for the Council on Environmental Quality (September 17, 1979).

Krupnick, Alan J. "Costs of Alternative Policies for the Control of NO_2 in the Baltimore Region," *Journal of Environmental Economics and Management* 13 (June 1986): 189–97.

Marcus, Alfred A. "Japan," in *International Public Policy Sourcebook,* Vol. 2, *Education and Environment,* Frederic N. Bolotin, ed. (Westport, CT: Greenwood Press, 1989): 275–91.

McGartland, Albert M. "Marketable Permit Systems for Air Pollution Control: An Empirical Study," Ph.D. dissertation, University of Maryland, 1984.

Oates, Wallace E., Paul R. Portney, and Albert M. McGartland. "The Net Benefits of Incentive-Based Regulation: A Case Study of Environmental Standard-Setting," *American Economic Review* 79 (December 1989): 1233–42.

Portney, Paul R. "Air Pollution Policy," in *Public Policies for Environmental Protection,* Paul R. Pormey, ed. (Washington, DC: Resources for the Future, 1990): 27–96.

Roach, Fred, Charles Kolstad, Allen V. Kneese, Richard Tobin, and Michael Williams. "Alternative Air Quality Policy Options in the Four Corners Region," *Southwest Review* 1 (Summer 1981): 29–58.

Roumasset, James A. and Kirk R. Smith. "Exposure Trading: An Approach to More Efficient Air Pollution Control," *Journal of Environmental Economics and Management* 18 (May 1990): 276–91.

Schelling, Thomas C. ed. *Incentives for Environmental Protection* (Cambridge, MA: MIT Press, 1983).

Seskin, Eugene P., Robert J. Anderson, and Robert O. Reid. "An Empirical Analysis of Economic Strategies for Controlling Air Pollution," *Journal of Environmental Economics and Management* 10 (June 1983): 112–24.

WEB SITES OF INTEREST

1. *http://www.cfpa.org/issues/environment/etax/etmodleg.cfm*
   An Inventory of State Environmental Taxes.

2. *http://www.epa.gov/docs/oppe/eaed/eedhmpg.htm*
   Home Page of USEPA's Economy and Environment Program.

3. *http://www.worldbank.org/nipr/onthenet.htm*
   A large compilation of internet pollution control sites.

DISCUSSION QUESTIONS

1. As shown in Example 14.3, the efficient regulation of hazardous pollutants should take exposure into account—the more persons exposed to a given pollutant concentration, the larger is the damage caused by it and therefore the smaller is the efficient concentration level, all other things being equal. An alternative point of view would simply ensure that concentrations be held below a uniform threshold, regardless of the number of people exposed. From this latter point of view, the public policy goal is to expose any and all people to the same concentration level—exposure is not used to establish different concentrations for different settings. What are the advantages and disadvantages of each approach? Which do you think represents the best approach? Why?

2. European countries have relied to a much greater extent on emission charges than has the United States, which seems to be moving toward a greater reliance on transferable emission permits. From an efficiency point of view, should the United States follow Europe's lead and shift the emphasis toward emission charges? Why or why not?

15

Acid Rain
and Atmospheric
Modification

Everything should be made as simple as possible, but not simpler.

ALBERT EINSTEIN

◆ INTRODUCTION

As the zone of influence of pollutants extends beyond local boundaries, the political difficulties of implementing comprehensive, cost-effective control measures are compounded. Pollutants crossing boundaries impose external costs; neither the emitters nor the nations within which they emit have the proper incentives for controlling them.

Compounding the problem of improper incentives is the scientific uncertainty that limits our understanding of most of these problems. Our knowledge about various relationships that form the basis for our understanding of the magnitude of the problems and the effectiveness of various strategies to control them is far from complete. Unfortunately, the problems are so important and the potential consequences of inaction so drastic that procrastination is not usually an optimal strategy. To avoid having to act in the future under emergency conditions when the remaining choices are few in number, strategies that have desirable properties must be formulated now on the basis of the available information, as limited as it may be. As many future options as possible must be preserved.

The costs of inaction are not limited to the damages caused. International cooperation among such traditional allies as the United States, Mexico, and Canada and the countries of Europe has been undermined by disputes over the proper control of acid rain.

In this chapter we shall survey the scientific evidence on the severity of global and regional pollution and the potential effectiveness of policy strategies designed to alleviate these problems. We shall also consider difficulties confronted by the government in implementing solutions and the role of economic analysis in understanding how to circumvent these difficulties.

◆ REGIONAL POLLUTANTS

The primary difference between regional pollutants and local pollutants is the distance they are transported in the air. Although the damage caused by local pollutants occurs in the vicinity of emission, for regional pollutants the damage can occur at significant distances from the emission point.

The same substances can be both local pollutants and regional pollutants. Sulfur oxides, nitrogen oxides, and ozone, for example, have already been discussed as local pollutants, but they are regional pollutants as well. For example, sulfur emissions, the focal point for most acid rain legislation, have been known to travel some 200 to 600 miles from the point of emission before returning to the earth. As the substances are being transported by the winds, they undergo a complex series of chemical reactions. Under the right conditions, both sulfur and nitrogen oxides are transformed into sulfuric and nitric acids. Nitrogen oxides and hydrocarbons can combine in the presence of sunlight to produce ozone.

Acid Rain

"Acid rain," the popular term for atmospheric deposition of acidic substances, is actually a misnomer. Acidic substances are not only deposited by rain and other forms of moist air, they are also deposited as dry particles. In some parts of the world, such as the southwestern United States, dry deposition is a more important source of acidity than is wet deposition.

Precipitation is normally mildly acidic, with a global background pH of 5.0 (pH is the common measurement for acidity; the lower the number, the more acidic the substance, with 7.0 being the border between acidity and alkalinity). Industrialized areas commonly receive precipitation well in excess of the global background level. Rainfall in eastern North America, for example, has a typical pH of 4.4. Wheeling, West Virginia, once experienced a rainstorm with a pH of 1.5. The fact that battery acid has a pH of 1.0 may help put this event into perspective.

Though natural sources of acid deposition do exist, the evidence is quite clear that anthropogenic (human-made) sources have dominated deposition in recent years. An analysis of ice cores from Greenland, for example, covering the period from 1869 to 1984, indicates that anthropogenic sulfate has dominated sulfur deposition since the early twentieth century, and anthropogenic nitrate has dominated nitrogen deposition since about 1960.[1]

---

[1]P. A. Mayewski, et al., "A Detailed (1869–1984) Record of Sulfate and Nitrate Concentration from South Greenland," cited in World Resources Institute and International Institute for Environment and Development, *World Resources: 1986* (New York: Basic Books, 1986): 169.

In 1980 the U.S. Congress funded a 10-year study (called the National Acid Rain Precipitation Assessment Program) to determine the causes and effects of acid rain and to make recommendations concerning its control. The study concluded that damage from current and historic levels of acid rain ranged from negligible (on crops) to modest (on aquatic life in some lakes and streams). Specific findings included the following:[2]

1. Most species of sport fish can tolerate pH levels above 5.5, but relatively few species can sustain populations in water with a pH below 5.0. Some 9 percent of the lakes in the target population have a pH $\leq$ 5.0.

2. The regions of the United States estimated to have the highest percentage of acidified lakes are the Adirondacks in New York (Example 14.1), with 14 percent of 1,290 lakes acidified, and Florida, with 23 percent of 2,098 lakes acidified.

3. In many national parks in the East, fine sulfate particles, formed by chemical reactions of the sulfuric acid produced from emissions of SO_2, are responsible for a 50 to 60 percent degradation in visibility beyond that caused by natural influences.

4. No significant effect on crop growth was detected even at acidity levels 10 times the acidity level now observed in the eastern United States.

5. Acidic deposition and ozone appear to intensify the effects of natural stresses upon red spruce at eastern mountaintop locations. The cumulative effects of acidic deposition may alter the chemistry of some sensitive forest soils in the lower Midwest and the Southeast in the next 50 to 100 years, but the effect this will have on growth is unknown. The majority of U.S. forests appear healthy.

6. Acidic deposition can increase the rate of deterioration of some construction and culturally important materials and products such as galvanized steel, bronze, carbonate stone, and carbonate-based paints.

These findings were significantly less dire than expected and provide a rather sharp contrast with findings of higher levels of damage in Europe. Studies have documented that Sweden has some 4,000 highly acidified lakes; in southern Norway, lakes with a total surface area of 13,000 square kilometers support no fish at all; similar reports have been received from Germany, Scotland, and Canada.[3] Furthermore, as made clear by Example 12.1, acid deposition is one of the pollution sources implicated in the massive forest death taking place in Europe.

In many countries with a federal form of government, such as the United States, the policy focus in the past has been on treating all pollutants as if they were local pollutants, overlooking the adverse regional consequences in the process. By giving local jurisdictions a large amount of responsibility for achieving the desired air quality and by measuring progress at local monitors, the stage was set for making regional pollution worse rather than better.

---

[2]A concise summary of the findings can be found in National Acid Precipitation Assessment Program, *1989 Annual Report to the President and Congress* (Washington, DC: National Acid Rain Precipitation Assessment Program, 1990).

[3]See the review in World Resources Institute and International Institute for Environment and Development, *World Resources: 1986* (New York: Basic Books, 1986): 169–70.

Example 15.1

Adirondack Acidification

About 180 lakes in the Adirondack Mountains of New York State, mostly at higher altitudes, which had supported natural or stocked brook trout populations in the 1930s, no longer supported these populations by the 1970s. In some cases entire communities of six or more fish species had disappeared.

The location of these lakes, some distance east of any local emission sources, makes it quite clear that most of the acid deposition is coming from outside of the region. These lakes have relatively little capacity to neutralize deposited acid because they are in areas with little or no limestone or other forms of basic rock that might serve to buffer the acid.

This is a prime recreational area, particularly for fishing. Most of the sites are within the boundary of the 6-million acre Adirondack Park, the last substantially undeveloped area of its size in the northeastern United States. Its remoteness, mountainous terrain, and multitude of lakes provides an accessible outdoor recreation experience for the 55 million people who live within a day's traveling distance.

Acidification has substantially reduced the recreational value of the area. Using a version of the travel-cost method discussed in Chapter 4, Mullen and Menz conclude that the annual loss to New York resident anglers is in the neighborhood of at least $1 million in 1976 dollars.

One possibility for restoring these lakes would be to add lime (calcium carbonate) to buffer the effects of the acid. Would liming be efficient? In their investigation Menz and Driscoll found that a 5-year lake neutralization program would cost in the neighborhood of $2 to $4 million. Given the $1 million estimate of *annual* losses to recreational fishing, some neutralization would apparently be efficient. The exact number of lakes to be limed would have to be determined by comparing the marginal cost of liming each lake with the marginal gain to recreation that would result. The authors are quick to point out that although liming may be used to restore damaged lakes, it is not a substitute for controlling emissions.

Sources: U.S. General Accounting Office, *An Analysis of Issues Concerning "Acid Rain,"* Report No. GAO/RCED-85-13, 11 (December 1984): 13; John K. Mullen and Frederic C. Menz, "The Effect of Acidification Damages on the Economic Value of the Adirondack Fishery to New York Anglers," *American Journal of Agricultural Economics* 67, No. 1 (February 1985): 112–19; Frederic C. Menz and Charles T. Driscoll, "An Estimate of the Costs of Liming to Neutralize Acidic Adirondack Surface Waters," *Water Resources Research* 19, No. 5. (October 1983): 1139–1149.

In the early days of pollution control, local areas adopted the motto "Dilution is the solution." As implemented, this approach suggested that the way to control local pollutants was to emit them from tall stacks. By the time the pollutants hit the ground, according to this theory, the concentrations would be diluted, making it easier to meet the ambient standards at nearby monitors.

This approach had several consequences. First, it lowered the amount of emission reduction necessary to achieve ambient standards; with tall stacks, any given amount of emission would produce lower nearby ground-level concentrations than an equivalent level of emission from a shorter-stack source. Second, the ambient standards could be met at a lower cost. Using Cleveland as a case study, Scott Atkinson has shown that control costs would be approximately 30 percent lower but emissions would be 2.5 times higher if a local, rather than a regional, strategy were followed in a marketable-permit system.[4] In essence, local areas would be able to lower their own cost by exporting emissions to other areas. By focusing its attention on local pollution, the Clean Air Act actually made the regional pollution problem worse.

By the end of the 1980s, it had become painfully clear in the United States that the Clean Air Act was ill-suited to solving regional pollution problems. Revamping the legislation to do a better job of dealing with regional pollutants, such as acid rain, became a high priority.

Politically, that was a tall order. By virtue of the fact that these pollutants are transported long distances, the set of geographic areas receiving the damage is typically not the same as the set of geographic areas responsible for most of the emission causing the damage. In many cases, the recipients and the emitters are even in different countries! In this political milieu, it should not be surprising that those bearing the costs of damages should call for a large, rapid reduction in emissions, whereas those responsible for bearing the costs of that cleanup should want to proceed more slowly and with greater caution.

Economic analysis was helpful in finding a feasible path through this political thicket. In particular, a Congressional Budget Office (CBO) study helped to set the parameters of the debate by quantifying the consequences of various courses of action.[5] To analyze the economic and political consequences of various strategies designed to achieve reductions of SO_2 emissions from utilities anywhere from 8 to 12 million tons below the emission levels from those plants in 1980, the CBO used a computer-based simulation model that relates utility emissions, utility costs, and coal-market supply and demand levels to the strategies under consideration. The model, called the *National Coal Model,* is maintained by the Department of Energy.

The results of this modeling exercise will be presented in two segments. In the first segment we shall examine the basic available strategies, including both a traditional command-and-control strategy that simply allocates reductions on the basis of a specific formula and an emission charge strategy. This analysis will serve to show how sensitive costs are to various levels of emission reduction and to highlight some of the political consequences of implementing these strategies. The second segment of analysis then considers various strategies designed to mitigate the adverse political effects of the basic strategies as a means of ascertaining what is gained and lost by adopting these compromises.

In the proposed CAC strategies, the emission reductions were to be allocated to states on the basis of what is known as the "excess emissions" formula. For each plant, this formula subtracts from actual emissions the amount the plant would have been allowed to emit if it were forced to meet the 1979 NSPS sulfur standard for utilities. (Because that is a new-source standard, plants built before that date are not automatically required to meet it.) The amount left, the excess emissions, are then summed over all the excess-emission plants within each state and, finally, across states to get a national total. Each state would then be required to

[4]Scott E. Atkinson, "Marketable Pollution Permits and Acid Rain Externalities," *Canadian Journal of Economics* 16, No. 4 (November 1983): 704–22.

[5]U.S. Congress, Congressional Budget Office, *Curbing Acid Rain: Cost, Budget, and Coal-Market Effects* (Washington, DC: Government Printing Office, 1986).

TABLE 15.1 Costs Associated with Basic Strategies to Reduce Sulfur Emissions

Strategy	Total Program Cost[a] (Billions of $)	Annual Cost to Utilities[b] (Billions of $)	Cost-Effectiveness[c] ($ per ton)
8-million-ton rollback	$20.4	$1.9	$270
10-million-ton rollback	$34.5	$3.2	$360
12-million-ton rollback	$93.6	$8.8	$779
Emission charge	$37.5	$7.7	$327

[a]The present value (in 1985 dollars) of additional discounted utility costs incurred (over a current policy benchmark) from 1986 to 2015, using a real discount rate of 0.03. Any emission charges paid are not included.

[b]The additional cost to utilities of this strategy over the current policy benchmark in 1995 expressed in 1985 dollars. This value includes any emission charges paid.

[c]The discounted program cost divided by the annual discounted SO_2 reduction measured over the 1986–2015 period.

Source: U.S. Congress, Congressional Budget Office, *Curbing Acid Rain: Cost, Budget, and Coal-Market Effects* (Washington, D.C.: Government Printing Office, 1986): xx, xxii, 23, and 80.

meet the same share of the stipulated reduction (8, 10, or 12 million tons) that it has of the total excess emissions.

In the emission charge proposal each utility would be faced with a $600 per ton charge for all uncontrolled SO_2 emissions. The model assumes that utilities would minimize costs by cleaning up their emissions until the marginal cost of further cleanup were equal to $600 per ton. This results in a degree of emission reduction that is roughly comparable to the 10-million-ton CAC reduction.

The first implication of the analysis is that the marginal cost of additional control would rise rapidly, particularly after 10 million tons have been reduced (Table 15.1). The cost of reducing a ton of SO_2 would rise from $270 for an 8-million-ton reduction to $360 for a 10-million-ton reduction, and it would rise to a rather dramatic $779 per ton for a 12-million-ton reduction. Costs would rise much more steeply as the amount of required reduction was increased, because switching to low-sulfur coal—a relatively low-cost strategy—would be insufficient, by itself, to achieve the larger reductions. At stricter standards, reliance on the more expensive *scrubbers* would become necessary. (Scrubbers involve a chemical process to extract, or "scrub," sulfur gases before they escape into the atmosphere.)

The second insight, one that should be no surprise to readers of this book, is that the emission charge would be more cost effective than the comparable CAC strategy. Whereas the CAC strategy could secure a 10-million-ton reduction at about $360 a ton, the emission charge could do it for $327 a ton. The superiority of the emissions charge is due to the fact that it results in equalized marginal costs, a required condition for cost-effectiveness.[6]

It may seem a bit of a paradox that program costs are not minimized by an emission charge, because it is the most cost-effective strategy. The resolution of this paradox lies in the timing of the emission reductions achieved by an emission charge strategy. Because the au-

---

[6]Why, the alert reader might ask, isn't location of the emissions taken into account? Because the objective was stated as securing a reduction in emissions, not achieving an ambient standard, the cost-effective allocation is achieved when marginal control costs are equalized.

thors of this study chose in their analysis to impose the charge earlier than the CAC regulations would, the utilities secure the reductions earlier with an emission charge than with the CAC approach. Earlier reductions can only be achieved with earlier financial outlays, which, because all costs are discounted, cause higher program costs for the emission charge. Unlike the program cost calculation, which gives no credit for early emission reduction, the construction of the particular cost-effectiveness measure chosen by the CBO takes the timing of the emission reduction into account.

Though the emission charge approach may be the most cost-effective policy, it is not the most popular, particularly in states with a lot of excess emissions. With an emission charge approach, utilities not only have to pay the higher equipment and operating costs associated with the reductions, they also have to pay a charge on all uncontrolled emissions. As Table 15.1 indicates, the additional financial burden associated with controlling acid rain by means of an emission charge would be significant. Instead of paying the $3.2 billion for reducing 10 million tons under a CAC approach, utilities would be saddled with a $7.7 billion financial burden with an emission charge. The savings from lower equipment and operating costs achieved because the emission charge approach is more cost effective would be more than outweighed by the additional expense of paying the emission charges. What is least cost to society is not, in this case, least cost for the utilities.

The cost to utilities could be reduced, while retaining the cost-effectiveness properties of the straight emission charge, by instituting a sulfur-reduction emissions permit system. In such a system, the excess emissions formula would be used to allocate the initial control responsibility. Utilities would then be able to create emission reduction credits of surpassing their assigned control; other utilities could purchase these ERCs to help meet their own assigned control responsibilities. Compared to an emissions charge approach, this method would cut the cost to utilities almost in half by eliminating the charge on uncontrolled emissions. Another study, examining the cost savings that could be achieved within a single state (Illinois), concluded that the cost of control would be approximately one third lower if an emissions trading approach were instituted.[7]

A version of the emissions trading concept is an integral part of the revisions to the Clean Air Act signed in 1990. Known as the *sulfur allowance program,* this approach would complement, not replace, the traditional approach, which was geared to the attainment of local ambient air quality standards. As was the case with past acid rain proposals considered by Congress, under this innovative approach more stringent emissions controls would be placed on older plants emitting precursors of acid rain, as the first step. (Example 15.2)

Since its inception, the sulfur allowance market has become very active.[8] Transactions have increased steadily since 1994, and participants are developing innovative ways to structure allowance deals. Through the end of 1999, over 9,300 transfers moving 81.5 million allowances were reported to EPA's Allowance Tracking System. Approximately 62 percent of these allowances (50.4 million) were transferred within organizations. The remaining 31 million allowances were transferred between organizations.

---

[7]Stephen L. Feldman and Robert K. Raufer, *Emissions Trading and Acid Rain: Implementing a Market Approach to Pollution Control* (Totowa, NJ: Rowman & Littlefield, 1987).

[8]The information in this section was obtained from the EPA web page http://www.epa.gov/docs/acidrain/ats/qlyupd.html (June, 2000).

Example 15.2

The Sulfur Allowance Program

Under an innovative approach, known as the *Sulfur Allowance Program,* allowances to emit sulfur oxides have been allocated to older sulfur-emitting electricity-generating plants. The number of allowances has been restricted in order to assure a reduction of 10 million tons in emissions from 1980 levels by the year 2010.

These allowances, which provide a limited authorization to emit 1 ton of sulfur, are defined for a specific calendar year, but unused allowances can be carried forward into the next year. They are transferable among the affected sources. Any plants reducing emissions more than required by the allowances could transfer the unused allowances to other plants. Emissions in any plant may not legally exceed the levels permitted by the allowances (allocated plus acquired) held by the managers of that plant. An annual year-end audit balances emissions with allowances. Utilities that emit more than they are authorized to do by their holdings of allowances must pay a $2,000 a ton penalty and are required to forfeit an equivalent number of tons of emissions in the following year.

An important innovation in this program is that the availability of allowances is assured by the institution of an auction market. Each year the EPA withholds 2.24 percent of the allocated allowances; these go into the auction. These withheld permits are allocated to the highest bidders, with successful buyers paying their bid price. The proceeds are refunded to the utilities from whom the allowances were withheld, on a proportional basis.

Private allowance holders may also offer allowances for sale at these auctions. Potential sellers specify minimum acceptable prices. Once the withheld allowances have been disbursed, the EPA then matches the highest remaining bids with the lowest minimum acceptable prices on the private offerings and matches buyers and sellers until the sum of all remaining bids is less than that of the remaining minimum acceptable prices. Unfortunately, this auction design is not particularly efficient, because it provides incentives for inefficient strategic behavior.

Sources: Dallas Burtraw. "The SO_2 Emissions Trading Program: Cost Savings without Allowance Trades," *Contemporary Economic Policy* XIV, No. 2 (1996): 79–94; Nancy Kete, "The U.S. Acid Rain Control Allowance Trading System," in T. Jones and J. Corfee-Morlot, eds. *Climate Change: Designing a Tradeable Permit System* (Paris: Organization for Economic Co-operation and Development, 1992): 69–93; and Renee Rico, "The U.S. Allowance Trading System for Sulfur Dioxide: An Update on Market Experience," *Environmental and Resource Economics* 5, No. 2 (1995): 115–29.

Allowance prices have generally dropped, according to two different price indexes developed by allowance brokerage companies. In the first quarter of 2000 the average price was $136/ton, far below the $1,500/ton price expected by some observers before the program began.

Low allowance prices have apparently been due to larger-than-expected emission reductions, which have increased the supply of allowances and depressed prices. The availability of low-sulfur coal at lower-than-expected costs (including lower-than-expected rail transportation costs) has played a major role in these reductions.

Example 15.3

Why and How Do Environmentalists Buy Pollution?

Among the rather unique features of the sulfur allowance program, two have found particular favor with environmentalists. Not only does the program put a fixed upper limit on total annual sulfur emissions from the utilities sector, but it allows environmental groups to lower that limit by acquiring allowances.

In the auctions run by the Chicago Board of Trade, anyone (including environmental groups), can place a bid. Environmental group bids are typically financed by donations from individuals who want to reduce pollution. Successful bidders acquire allowances for whatever purpose they see fit—including "retiring" them so that they cannot be used to legitimize emissions. Every 1-ton sulfur oxide allowance that is retired represents an authorized ton of pollution that will not be emitted.

In the 1996 auction, one nonprofit organization known by the acronym *INHALE* purchased 454 allowances. The Maryland Environmental Law Society (MELS) bought and retired an allowance in the 1994 auction—the first student group to do so. Since then, a number of other schools have purchased and retired allowances.

Another organization that has raised funds to retire allowances is the Working Assets Funding Source. This nonprofit public-interest company regularly contributes 1 percent of its revenues to public-service organizations and uses its monthly bills to solicit charitable donations from customers for various featured causes. A summer 1993 campaign asked the 80,000 customers of its long-distance telephone service to add a small donation when paying their bills in order to support "our goal to reduce SO_2 emissions by 300 tons . . . and spark a movement to do much more." The result was $55,000 in donations, which enabled the group to purchase 289 allowances.

Allowances have also been retired through charitable donations. An agreement between Arizona Public Service Company and Niagara Mohawk Power Corporation, for example, resulted in the donation of 25,000 allowances to the Environmental Defense Fund. In another transaction, Northeast Utilities of Connecticut donated 10,000 allowances to the American Lung Association. The Lung Association has since contacted other utilities through its local chapters in an effort to receive further donations to be used to reduce pollution.

Source: http://www.epa.gov/acidrain/auctions/00index.html

Under the sulfur allowance program, anyone can purchase allowances. This option is increasingly being chosen by environmental groups as a means of producing fewer sulfur emissions than allowed by law (Example 15.3).

How tradeable emission allowances facilitate achieving the environmental goal at a lower cost is not difficult to understand. Achieving reductions of the magnitude envisioned by Congress would require some, but not all, utilities to adopt scrubbers. To force all older utilities to adopt scrubbers would be very expensive and unnecessary to achieve the desired reduction target. However, it is politically and legally difficult under the traditional system to isolate only a few utilities to bear this additional burden for the greater good.

Emissions-allowance trading would solve this problem by allowing some utilities to voluntarily accept greater control and by providing the proper incentive to assure that some do. The emissions standards would be stringent enough that some utilities would have to choose the use of scrubbers or some other form of overcontrol. Although all utilities would face similar, if not identical, allowable emissions standards, some utilities, presumably those for whom adopting scrubbers was the cheapest alternative, would voluntarily choose to install scrubbers. This action would automatically result in their exceeding their legal emissions control requirements.

By purchasing sufficient allowances to satisfy their own emissions standards in combination with any other additional control, the purchasing firms would eliminate the need to install scrubbers. The process would result in sufficient, but not excessive, control and would provide a market means of selecting those utilities that would install scrubbers. It would also provide a means of sharing the costs of installing scrubbers among all utilities. Those purchasing the emissions allowances would, in effect, be subsidizing a portion of the selling firm's installation of the pollution control device. Rather than isolating a few utilities to bear a disproportionate share of the control burden or requiring all utilities to bear the excessive burden of overcontrol in a misguided pursuit of fairness, emissions-allowance trading promotes voluntary cost-sharing. Fairness and efficiency can be compatible goals with the right choice of policy instruments.

It is not difficult to imagine a similar kind of scheme operating on a regional basis to control acid rain in Europe.[9] Many of the Western European nations are at the point where further control of their own emissions is very expensive. A disproportionate share of the remaining emissions affecting Western European nations are coming from Eastern European nations. However, because most of the Eastern European nations have troubled economies that can ill afford the shock of major new expenditures, they are not likely to undertake major pollution control reductions on their own in the near future.

One solution to this problem is to seek agreement that all nations implement some minimum level of control for all sources within their borders, allowing the Western industrialized nations to buy reductions above and beyond this minimum control level from the Eastern European nations.[10] In most Western countries, purchasing additional pollution control from Eastern Europe would represent the cheapest means of reducing acid rain, much cheaper than controlling their own emissions at an even higher level. The Eastern European nations would then use the revenue from the sale of emissions allowances to finance the installation of control equipment. In many cases, this equipment would probably be produced and sold by the Western nations, an additional inducement for them to participate in cost-sharing.

---

[9]This type of market has been simulated in Karl-Goran Mäler, "International Environmental Problems," *Oxford Review of Economic Policy* 6, No. 1 (spring 1990): 80–108. The benefits from cost-effective burden sharing across borders are apparently quite large.

[10]Sweden has already negotiated an agreement of this type with Poland.

◆ GLOBAL POLLUTANTS

Ozone Depletion

In the troposphere, the portion of the atmosphere closest to the earth, ozone (O_3) is a pollutant, and its presence has been linked to agricultural damage as well as to some adverse effects on human health. More will be said about this form of tropospheric pollution in the next chapter.

However, in the stratosphere, the portion of the atmosphere lying just above the troposphere, the rather small amounts of ozone present have a crucial positive role to pay in determining the quality of life on the planet. In particular, by absorbing the ultraviolet wavelengths, stratospheric ozone shields people, plants, and animals from harmful radiation, and by absorbing infrared radiation, it is a factor in determining the earth's climate.

Chlorofluorocarbons (CFCs) have been implicated in depleting this stratospheric ozone shield as a result of a complicated series of chemical reactions. These highly stable chemical compounds are used as aerosol propellants and in cushioning foams, packaging and insulating foams, industrial cleaning of metals and electronics components, food freezing, medical instrument sterilization, refrigeration for homes and food stores, and air conditioning of automobiles and commercial buildings.

The major known effect of the increase ultraviolet radiation resulting from ozone depletion is an increase in nonmelanoma skin cancer. Other potential effects, such as an increase in the more serious melanoma form of skin cancer, suppression of human immunological systems, damage to plants, eye cancer in cattle, and an acceleration of degradation in certain polymer materials, are suspected but are not as well established.

On 30 June 1978, the U.S. Environmental Protection Agency promulgated a regulation banning the manufacture, processing, and distribution of any "fully halogenated chlorofluoroalkane" for those aerosol propellant uses that are subject to the Toxic Substances Control Act (which is almost all aerosol uses).[11] This ban reduced the U.S. share from about one half to about one third of worldwide production. Nonetheless, worldwide release of the two principal chlorofluorocarbons—CFC-11 and CFC-12—continued to grow.

Because further progress on this issue was going to require instituting new controls on nonaerosol uses, a group of economists from the Rand Corporation was commissioned by the EPA to model the regulatory options.[12] The resulting study collected detailed information on the costs of controlling nonaerosol applications of these gases in the United States and constructed a 10-year simulation model to capture the effects of various regulatory approaches. Because chlorofluorocarbons accumulate in the atmosphere (they are expected to remain in the atmosphere for approximately a century), the desired reductions were defined in cumulative terms over the 10-year period.

In the study, a system of emissions standards for producers or users of these gases that would force them to adopt specific technologies was compared to a marketable permit system.

---

[11]This regulation can be found in 45 *Federal Register* 43721.

[12]A. R. Palmer, W. E. Mooz, T. H. Quinn, and K. A. Wolf, "Economic Implications of Regulating Chlorofluorocarbon Emissions from Nonaerosol Applications," Report No. R-2524-EPA, prepared for the U.S. Environmental Protection Agency by the Rand Corporation (June 1980).

In the simulation model, both approaches were constrained to yield roughly the same cumulative level of emissions reduction.

The magnitude of the superiority of the permit system in this case can be seen in Table 15.2. It could produce approximately the same amount of reduction as the mandatory controls at about one half the cost.

The Rand study also looked at the issue of *transfer costs* (the payments made to the government by the emitters for each unit of uncontrolled emissions). If the permits were auctioned off, firms would not only be faced with the cost of purchasing the control equipment or changing the production process, they would have to pay for the permits as well. Thus, depending on the relative magnitude of the cost savings from inducing cost-effective behavior and the additional cost imposed by the need to buy the permits, firms may or may not be better off under this type of economic incentive system than they would be under mandatory controls. This could only be determined by discovering the magnitude of the transfer costs.

The Rand study is quite clear that for this particular problem transfer costs are huge. On average, payments for permits would be some 15 times as large as the expenditures incurred in controlling emissions. Furthermore, they would be rather unequally distributed among the various industries responsible for reducing CFC emissions.

One aspect of this figure that is particularly noteworthy is the "other" category. This category contains some product areas (e.g., rigid insulating foams, liquid fast freezing, and sterilants) for which the authors found that no control methods would be introduced, even when marketable permits are used. For these product areas, the *only* expense is the cost of the permits, and it represents a huge outlay. The manufacturers of these product lines could be expected to be unusually vociferous in the support for a policy of no action or, if action is inevitable, of traditional regulation—an approach that in all likelihood would place no controls on them at all—or a "grandfathered" permits system, whereby they were given the permits free of charge.

Responding to the ozone depletion threat, 24 nations signed the Montreal Protocol during September 1988. According to this agreement, signatory nations were to restrict their

TABLE 15.2   Comparisons of Alternative Policies Having Similar Cumulative Emissions
Reductions

Policy Design	Emissions Reduction (millions of permit pounds)			Total Compliance Costs (millions of 1990 dollars)		
	1980	1990	Cumulative 1980–90	1980	1990	Cumulative 1980–90[a]
Mandatory controls	54.4	102.5	812.3	47.9	84.8	424.6
Permit system[b]	36.6	119.4	806.1	11.9	80.2	217.0

[a]Present value of annual compliance costs, discounted at 11 percent.

[b]Based on permit price rising from $0.25 in 1980 to $0.71 in 1990.

Source: A. R. Palmer, W. E. Mooz, T. H. Quinn, and K. A. Wolf, "Economic Implications of Regulating Chlorofluorocarbon Emissions from Nonaerosol Applications," Report No. R-2524-EPA, prepared for the U.S. Environmental Protection Agency by the Rand Corporation (June 1980): 225, Table 4.7.

production and consumption of the chief responsible gases to 50 percent of 1986 levels by 30 June 1998. Soon after the protocol was signed, new evidence suggested that it had not gone far enough; the damage was apparently increasing more rapidly than had been thought. In response, some 59 nations signed a new ozone agreement at a conference in London in July 1990. This agreement called for the complete phaseout of halons and CFCs by the end of the twentieth century. Moreover, two other destructive chemicals (carbon tetrachloride and methyl chloroform) were added to the protocol and being phased out.

An important component of this new agreement was the establishment of a special $240 million fund over the next three years to help poorer countries switch away from ozone-depleting chemicals to more expensive, but less harmful, substitutes.[13] This was an important breakthrough because, without this assistance, the use of ozone-depleting chemicals was expected to rise dramatically in the developing countries.[14]

The United States has chosen to use a tradeable permit system to implement its responsibilities under the protocols. This approach is discussed in Example 15.4.

Global Warming

Greenhouse gases, one class of global pollutants, absorb the long-wavelength (infrared) radiation from the earth's surface and atmosphere, trapping heat that would otherwise radiate out into space. The mix and distribution of these gases within the atmosphere is in no small part responsible for both the hospitable climate on the earth and the rather inhospitable climate on other planets. Changing the mix of these gases can modify the climate.

Though carbon dioxide is the most abundant and the most studied of these greenhouse gases, many others have similar thermal radiation properties. These include the chlorofluorocarbons, nitrous oxide, methane, and tropospheric ozone.

The current concern over the effect of this class of pollutants on climate arises because emissions of these gases are increasing over time, changing their mix in the atmosphere. Evidence is mounting that by burning fossil fuels, leveling tropical forests, and injecting more of the other greenhouse gases into the atmosphere, humans are creating a thermal blanket capable of trapping enough heat to raise the temperature of the earth's surface. The Intergovernmental Panel on Climate Change (IPCC), the official body of advisers to the Climate Change Convention, currently predicts an increase in global mean temperature of between 1°C and 3.5°C.[15] They expect the average rate of warming to be greater than any seen in the last 10,000 years. This is expected to trigger a sea level rise from 15 to 95 centimeters.

What are the likely consequences of temperature increases of this magnitude? Although a number of studies exist, most effort has gone into predicting the effects on agriculture. One group of economists has estimated that the damages in the United States would be small,

---

[13]A panel of experts from U.S. EPA has concluded that substitutes do exist, but they would cost between $1.25 and $4.00 a pound, compared to 60 to 70 cents for the traditional chemicals. *Science News* 131 (6 June 1987): 360.

[14]Daniel F. Kohler, John Haaga, and Frank Camm, "Projections of Consumption of Products Using Chlorofluorocarbons in Developing Countries," Report N-2458-EPA, Rand Corporation (January 1987). (Report prepared by Rand Corporation for the EPA.)

[15]J. T. Houghton, et. al., *Climate Change 1995: The Science of Climate Change* (Cambridge, UK: Cambridge University Press, 1996).

Example 15.4

Tradable Permits for Ozone-Depleting Chemicals

On 12 August 1988 the U.S. Environmental Protection Agency issued its first regulations implementing a tradeable permit system to achieve the targeted reductions in ozone-depleting substances. According to these regulations, all major U.S. producers and consumers of the controlled substances were allocated baseline production or consumption allowances using 1986 levels as the basis for the proration. Each producer and consumer was allowed 100 percent of this baseline allowance initially, with smaller allowances being granted after predefined deadlines. Following the London conference, these percent-of-baseline allocations were reduced in order to reflect the new, earlier deadlines and lower limits.

These allowances are transferable within producer and consumer categories, and allowances can be transferred across international borders to producers in other signatory nations if the transaction is approved by EPA and results in the appropriate adjustments in the buyer or seller allowances in their respective countries. Production allowances can be augmented by demonstrating the safe destruction of an equivalent amount of controlled substances by an approved means. Some interpollutant trading is even possible within categories of pollutants. (The categories are defined so as to group pollutants with similar environmental effects.) All information on trades is confidential (known only to the traders and the regulators) so that it is difficult to know how effective this program has been.

Since the demand for these allowances is quite inelastic, supply restrictions increase revenue. Because of the allocation of allowances to the seven major domestic producers of CFCs and halons, the EPA was concerned that its regulation would result in sizeable windfall profits (estimated to be in the billions of dollars) for those producers. The EPA handled this problem by imposing a tax on production in order to "soak up" the rents created by the regulation-induced scarcity.

This application was unique in two senses. It not only allowed international trading of allowances, but it involved the simultaneous application of permit and tax systems. Taxes on production, when coupled with allowances, have the effect of lowering permit prices. The combined policy, however, is no less cost effective than permits would be by themselves, and it does allow the government to acquire some of the rent that would otherwise go to permit holders.

Source: Tom Tietenberg, "Design Lessons from Existing Air Pollution Control Systems: The United States," in S. Hanna and M. Munasinghe, eds., *Property Rights in a Social and Ecological Context: Case Studies and Design Applications* (Washington, DC: World Bank, 1995): 15–32.

because higher valued crops could be substituted for the crops that are more vulnerable to the climate-induced increases in temperature.[16] Although these estimates are much more optimistic than others, Robert Mendelsohn and his coauthors attribute this to the fact that other studies fail to include all the possible adaptation strategies farmers could employ.

[16]Robert Mendelsohn et al., "The Impact of Global Warming on Agriculture: A Ricardian Analysis," *American Economic Review* 84 (1994): 753–71.

Others, with a more global focus, are less optimistic. Rosenzweig and Parry, for example, conclude that, although adaptability may be high in the industrialized countries, the limited opportunities for farmers in developing countries mean that they are likely to bear the brunt of the problem.[17] Because many of those countries are already producing too little food (see Chapter 9), global warming would only exacerbate the problem.

The implication of this analysis—that nations have different stakes in the international search for solutions to global warming—goes well beyond their differential ability to adapt. Regions with a characteristically cold climate, such as large portions of the former Soviet Union, may actually benefit from this warming trend, whereas others that are naturally somewhat arid may see marginal agricultural land become unproductive desert, triggering a diminished capacity to raise food. These differences (and the rather divergent senses of urgency they promote) could prove quite divisive in the search for cooperative solutions to the global warming problem.

Global warming poses a particularly difficult challenge for our economic and political institutions. The stratosphere is a public good. Its scarcity is not reflected in rising prices; it is not automatically rationed only to the highest valued uses. The damage caused by greenhouse pollutants is an externality in both space and time. Emitters impose costs not only on residents of other countries, but on subsequent generations as well. Free-rider problems can be expected to undermine unilateral national attempts to respond. Market allocations can certainly be expected to violate the efficiency criterion and may well violate the sustainability criterion as well (see Example 15.5).

What can be done? Four strategies have been considered: (1) climate engineering, (2) adaptation, (3) mitigation, and (4) prevention. *Climate engineering* envisions taking actions such as shooting particulate matter into the atmosphere in order to provide compensating cooling. *Adaptation* strategies would allow us to function effectively in warmer temperatures. *Mitigation* would attempt to moderate the temperature rise by using strategies designed to increase the planetary capacity to absorb greenhouse gases. *Prevention* strategies are designed to reduce emissions of greenhouse gases. Because only the last two of these have received serious attention in public policy arenas, we shall focus on them.

The most significant prevention strategy deals with our use of fossil fuel energy. Combustion of fossil fuel energy results in the creation of carbon dioxide. Carbon dioxide emissions can be reduced either by using less energy or by using alternative energy sources (e.g., wind, photovoltaics, or hydro) that produce no carbon dioxide. Because any serious reduction in carbon dioxide emissions would involve rather dramatic changes in our energy-consumption patterns and a high economic cost, how vigorously this strategy is to be followed is a controversial public policy issue.[18]

Because trees absorb carbon dioxide, reforestation is a commonly mentioned mitigation strategy. If the rate of deforestation were decreased and the rate of reforestation increased, greater amounts of carbon dioxide could be absorbed.

---

[17]Cynthia Rosenzweig and Martin L. Parry, "Potential Impact of Climate Change on World Food Supply," *Nature* 367 (January 1994): 133–38.

[18]According to research by William Nordhaus, a 10 to 20 percent reduction in carbon dioxide emissions could be achieved at a relatively low cost, but the marginal costs of larger reductions rise very rapidly. See "Greenhouse Economics: Count Before You Leap," *The Economist* (7 July 1990): 20–24.

Example 15.5

Ethics, Risk Aversion, and the Greenhouse Effect

Can benefit-cost analysis be trusted to reach an optimal decision about strategies to control the greenhouse effect? Two sources of concern are paramount: (1) the long time period before the damage would be felt and (2) the uncertainty about the ultimate size of the damage.

At current interest rates, a complete loss of the expected world GNP 100 years from now would have a present value of about $1 million. This is trivial in comparison to the present value of potential costs of controlling the greenhouse effect, because they would be spent in the near future. Because of discounting, events that happen so far in the future have little weight in decisions where costs are borne in the present. Although maximizing the present value of net benefits guarantees that the pie to be shared among generations is as large as possible, it does not automatically guarantee that the slices of pie are actually shared equitably among generations. The logical conclusion of this form of argument is that, from an ethical point of view, future generations may be inadequately protected by benefit-cost analysis.

A second concern deals with risk aversion. Conventional benefit-cost analysis assumes risk neutrality. Is risk neutrality a credible assumption in the face of a potential catastrophe? Common sense suggests that most people react to uncertainty by acting in a cautious, risk-averse manner. Should our governments act any differently?

Concluding that conventional benefit-cost analysis is ethically flawed when applied to the greenhouse problem, d'Arge, Schultze, and Brookshire have proposed a modest alternative. In particular, they proposed to establish whether the current generation would be willing to pay some amount of money to avoid climate modification. Relying on three samples of college students as a pilot study, they did find a willingness to spend current income to avoid an environmental catastrophe, even if such a disaster would occur, in all likelihood, after the respondent's death. Though these samples can hardly be called representative of the population at large, the amounts per person were sufficiently large that they would justify a much larger commitment of current resources to control the problem than would be justified by a conventional benefit-cost analysis.

Sources: Ralph C. d'Arge, William D. Schultze, and David S. Brookshire, "Benefit-Cost Valuation of Long-Term Effects: The Case of CO_2," a paper prepared for the Workshop on the Methodology for Economic Impact Analysis, April 24–25, 1980, Fort Lauderdale, FL; Ralph C. d'Arge, William D. Schultze, and David S. Brookshire, "Carbon Dioxide and Intergenerational Choice," *American Economic Review* 72, No. 2 (May 1982): 251–56.

What policy approaches are available to deal efficiently with the global warming problem? Although global warming and ozone depletion impose an environmental cost, currently that cost is not being borne, or even recognized, by those who ultimately control the magnitude of the problem. Furthermore, those choosing unilaterally to reduce their emissions expose themselves to the higher costs associated with prevention strategies.

A "carbon tax," which is currently being widely discussed in Europe and the United States, could be one component of this package.[19] Because carbon dioxide is only one of the greenhouse gases, however, taxes would necessarily be imposed on other gases as well. The appropriate level of this tax for each gas would depend upon its per unit contribution to the global warming problem; gases posing a larger per unit risk would bear higher tax rates.

Taxes on fossil fuels are not a radical concept.[20] Gasoline taxes have routinely been levied for years. Though gasoline taxes represent an input to combustion rather than an emissions rate, the administrative ease with which they can be implemented and the close relationship between the composition of the fuel and the composition of the emissions makes such taxes a popular candidate for use as one component in a package of corrective measures to reduce global warming.

Because gasoline taxes have already been implemented by nations for their own purposes, examining the degree to which these taxes deviate from the full-cost principle provides some indication of the complexity of the international negotiations to reform gasoline taxes so that they would conform to the principle. To the extent that the current system of taxes approximates the ideal, conditions would appear favorable to negotiating a transition. In fact, the gasoline taxes now in use around the world are not efficient.

Efficient carbon taxes would reflect the damage caused by emissions, thereby fostering a reduction in emissions. In contrast, current gasoline tax rates are commonly determined by the revenue needed to build more roads; added roadway capacity ultimately translates into more emissions, not fewer. Because they are driven by the need to finance capacity expansion rather than to account for the environmental effects of combustion, gasoline taxes are currently not efficient.

Although applying the full-cost principle for global warming also requires that the tax rates be uniformly applied, that condition is a far cry from actual experience. According to the International Energy Agency, the total U.S. tax rate on gasoline was around $0.38 in 1999. European tax rates were $2.48 per gallon in Germany, $3.54 in Britain, $2.87 in France, and $2.60 in Italy.[21] When the tax rates differ by a factor of 5 or more, the allocation of control responsibility for reducing gasoline-related emissions does not fulfill the uniformity requirement.

The transition to a more sustainable economic system in atmospheric terms will depend upon the development of new technologies and upon much greater levels of energy efficiency than are currently being achieved. Those transitions will not occur unless the prevailing economic incentives support and encourage them. Once the greenhouse gas and ozone-depletion taxes were in effect, the incentives would be changed: Greater energy efficiency and the development of new technologies would become top-priority objectives.

Because environmental taxes would generate revenue, a common global fund could be established to receive and dispense that revenue. Controlled by representatives of the signatory nations, this fund could conceivably dispense monies for projects as diverse as reforestation or

---

[19]As of 1989 two countries had already unilaterally levied carbon taxes. The Netherlands carbon tax was about $2.15 per ton of carbon whereas Finland's was about $5.00 per ton of carbon.

[20]T. Sterner et al., "Tax Policy, Carbon Emissions and the Global Environment," *Journal of Transport Economics and Policy* 26, No. 2 (1992): 109–19.

[21]www.iea.org/files/glance.htm

the promotion of solar-powered projects to provide income and subsistence to poor areas of the world. A fund financed by environmental taxes would help to reduce the twin causes of environmental problems: distorted market signals and poverty.[22]

Though not funded by environmental taxes, the Global Environmental Facility (GEF), housed in the World Bank, has begun to play an important role in funding deserving projects. Drawing from the Global Environmental Trust Fund, which is funded by direct contributions from some 26 countries, the GEF provides loans and grants to projects that have a global impact, including projects that reduce global warming.

The GEF uses a *marginal-external-cost rule* to determine the suitability of projects and the amount of funding provided. Recognizing that many projects have benefits that flow beyond national borders and that individual nations are unlikely to consider those global benefits, the GEF picks up the costs that cannot be justified domestically, but could be justified internationally. For example, suppose building a coal-fired power plant is the cheapest way for China to provide electricity to its people, but a slightly more expensive hydroelectric plant would result in substantially lower carbon dioxide emissions. Because the benefits from lower carbon dioxide emissions are largely global, not national, China has little incentive to consider them in its decision; therefore, it would choose the coal-fired plant. However, by picking up the extra cost from the hydroelectric facility, the GEF can increase the attractiveness of the alternative facility to China and thereby assure that China's decision makes sense both nationally and globally.

The 1992 United Nations Framework Convention on Climate Change (UNFCCC) recognized the principle of global cost-effectiveness of emission reduction and thus opened the way for flexibility. As it did not fix a binding emission target for any country, the need to invest in emission reduction either at home or abroad was not pressing, however.

In December 1997, though, industrial countries and countries with economies in transition agreed to legally binding emission targets at the Kyoto Conference and negotiated a legal framework as a protocol to the UNFCCC—the Kyoto Protocol. This Protocol will become effective if (and only if) it is ratified by at least 55 parties representing at least 55 percent of the total carbon dioxide (CO_2) emissions of Annex I countries (generally the industrialized countries and countries with economies in transition) in the year 1990.

The Kyoto Protocol defines a five-year commitment period (2008–2012) for meeting the individual country emission targets set out in Annex B. Collectively, if fulfilled, these targets would represent a 5 percent reduction in annual average emissions below 1990 levels.

This compliance target is defined as a weighted average of six greenhouse gases listed in Annex A: carbon dioxide, methane, nitrous oxide, HFCs, PFCs and sulfur hexafluoride. 100-year Global Warming Potentials are used to convert these six gases in the unidimensional metric that will be used to define compliance. Defining the target in terms of this

---

[22]By substituting environmental taxes for more traditional taxes, it would also be possible to eliminate the inefficiencies associated with the traditional taxes. Some estimates suggest that using carbon taxes to replace more distortion-producing revenue sources could reduce the cost of controlling greenhouse gases substantially. See I. Parry, R. C. Williams and L. H. Goulder. "When Can Carbon Abatement Policies Increase Welfare? The Fundamental Role of Distorted Factor Markets," *Journal of Environmental Economics and Management* 37(1)(1999): 52-84.

multi-gas index, rather than just carbon dioxide, has been estimated to reduce compliance costs by some 22 percent.[23]

The Kyoto Protocol identifies three possible cooperative mechanisms, but the most important (authorized by Article 17) involves a full international emissions trading system for greenhouse gases. The case for an emissions trading system is based on the advantages that it would offer compared to other politically feasible alternatives. In the short run it offers the possibility of reaching the environmental goals at a lower cost than would be possible if each country were limited to reduction options within its own borders.[24] Making it easier to reach the goals may allow more countries to join the Protocol and usually increases compliance with those goals.

Because it separates the issue of who pays for control from who implements control, it facilitates transboundary cost sharing (an item of particular importance to both the developing countries and the transition economies of Eastern Europe). Tradable permits also facilitate the mobilization of private capital for controlling global warming; private capital is likely to be a critically important component of any effective global warming strategy as long as public capital remains insufficient to do it alone.

Finally, and perhaps most importantly, emissions trading facilitates the development and implementation of innovative approaches to climate change control. By offering greater flexibility in how the emission reductions are achieved (as well as by providing economic incentives for the adoption and use of unconventional approaches), emissions trading can significantly lower the long-run cost. Lower long-run cost may be an important element in gaining greater international acceptance of the idea of limits and reducing the difficulties associated with assuring compliance. Furthermore if it becomes desirable to assure that participants cover the administrative costs of running the system, levying a low annual fee on each authorized ton of emission could raise revenue. This revenue could be used for financing technology transfers or for other worthy purposes without jeopardizing the cost-effectiveness of the system.

However, emissions trading is not without its problems. First, it will only achieve the goals of the Protocol if monitoring and enforcement is adequate. Monitoring and enforcing international agreements is much more difficult than enforcing domestic laws and regulations. Second, due to the way the goals of the Protocol were specified, some economies in transition (e. g., Russia and the Ukraine) have a lot of surplus allowances to sell. Since Protocol requirements are defined in terms of 1990 emissions levels and emissions in these countries are quite a bit lower than that due to the depressed state of their economies, the difference, known popularly as "hot air," can be traded to other countries. The presence of these surplus allowances naturally lowers prices and allows countries to take less domestic abatement than would otherwise be necessary.

How large should investments in the prevention of global warming be? In order to answer this question, we must first discover just how serious the problem is and then ascertain the

---

[23]J. Reilly, M. Mayer, and J. Harnisch, "Multiple Gas Control Under the Kyoto Agreement," Extended Abstract in the *Proceedings of the 2d International Symposium on Non-CO$_2$ Greenhouse Gases.* J. van Ham, et. al, eds. (Dordrecht, Netherlands: Kluwer Academic Publishers)

[24]Manne, A. S. and T. F. Rutherford, "International Trade in Oil, Gas and Carbon Emission Rights: An Intertemporal General Equilibrium Model," *Energy Journal* 15(1994)(1): 57–76.

costs of being wrong, either by acting too hastily or by procrastinating. Because of the rampant uncertainties in virtually every link in the logical chain from human activities to subsequent consequences, we cannot at this juncture, state unequivocally how serious the damage will be. We can, however, begin to elaborate the range of possibilities and see how sensitive the outcomes are to the choices before us.

The risks of being wrong are clearly asymmetric. If we control more than we must, current generations bear a larger than necessary cost. On the other hand, if the problem turns out to be as serious as the worst predictions indicate, catastrophic and largely irreversible damage to the planet would be inflicted on future generations. How can governments respond reasonably to this uncertainty? One familiar way is by acquiring some "insurance" against the potential harm—in this context, by undertaking prevention and mitigation strategies as a hedge against the consequences of global warming.

How much insurance should be purchased? One very interesting and provocative study was accomplished by William D. Nordhaus.[25] Based on a benefit-cost analysis of global warming, Nordhaus attempted to derive a reasonable level of carbon tax to deal with global warming. His estimates suggest that a tax of approximately $5 per ton of carbon (with equivalent taxes on other greenhouse gases) would be the most reasonable. A tax of this level would result in reductions of greenhouse gases of some 13 percent and net benefits of about $12 billion per year.

These results are controversial because many believe that benefit-cost analysis has limited applicability to global warming.[26] Because the present-value component of benefit-cost analysis emphasizes short-term over long-term consequences, the application of benefit-cost analysis will weight the current costs of controlling emissions more heavily than it will the distant future damages caused by global warming. Though this approach is not inherently biased against future generations, their interests will only be adequately protected if they would be willing to accept monetary compensation for a modified climate and if current generations were willing to set aside sufficient proceeds to provide this compensation. Because it is not obvious that either condition would be satisfied, the long lead times associated with this particular problem place the interests of future generations in maintaining a stable climate in jeopardy.

SUMMARY

Regional pollutants differ from local pollutants chiefly in the distance they are transported in the air. Whereas local pollutants damage the environment near the emission site, regional pollutants can cause damage far from the site of emission. Some substances, such as sulfur oxides, nitrogen oxides, and ozone, are both local and regional pollutants.

---

[25]William D. Nordhaus, "A Perspective on Costs and Benefits," *EPA Journal* 16, No. 2 (March/April 1990): 44–45; "The Economics of the Greenhouse Effect," paper presented at MIT Workshop on Energy and Environmental Modeling and Policy Analysis (July 1989); "Economic Policy in the Face of Global Warming," photocopy, 9 March 1990. The case for a much stronger policy response based upon lower discount rates and a longer planning horizon is made in William R. Cline, *The Economics of Global Warming* (Washington, DC: Institute for International Economics, 1992).

[26]See, for example, the discussion of this controversy in Nathan J. Rosenberg and Pierre R. Crosson, "RFF Workshop on Greenhouse Warming," *Resources* (Fall 1988): 16.

As the zone of influence of pollutants extends beyond local boundaries, the political difficulties of implementing comprehensive, cost-effective control measures increase. Pollutants crossing political boundaries impose external costs; neither the emitters nor the nations within which they emit have the proper incentives to institute efficient control measures.

Acid rain is a case in point. Sulfate and nitrate deposition has caused problems both between regions within countries and between countries. In the United States, the Clean Air Act has had a distinctly local focus. To control local pollution problems, state governments required the installation of tall stacks to dilute the pollution before it hit the ground level. In the process, a high proportion of the emissions were exported to other areas, reaching the ground hundreds of miles from the point of injection. A focus on local control made the regional problem worse.

Finding solutions to the acid rain problem has been very difficult, because those bearing the costs of further control are not those who will benefit from the control. In the United States, for example, opposition from the midwestern and Appalachian states had delayed action on acid rain legislation. Stumbling blocks included the higher electricity prices that would result from the control and the employment impacts on those states that would suffer losses of jobs in the high-sulfur coal-mining industry.

Economic analysis of the policy options indicates that the cost of reducing emissions rises dramatically as the amount of reduction is increased from 10 million to 12 million tons. It is therefore not surprising that the 10 million ton goal was adopted by the Clean Air Act Amendments of 1990. Those Amendments also instituted the sulfur allowance program, which placed a cap on total emissions from the utility sector. This approach has not only resulted in cost-effective control, but it also allows environmentalists to purchase allowances to keep them from being used to justify emissions.

Chlorofluorocarbons, the first of the discussed global pollutants, are a problem because they have been implicated in the destruction of the stratospheric ozone shield that protects the earth's surface from harmful ultraviolet radiation. Because this is an accumulating pollutant, an efficient response to this problem would involve reducing use over time. This could be accomplished either by an emission charge on CFCs that rises over time or a permit system that allows a fixed amount of emissions. Studies of nonaerosol uses of CFCs indicate that economic-incentive approaches such as these could achieve the emission target at about one-half the cost of regulatory standards. These studies also indicate, however, that emission charges would impose large additional financial burdens on the emitters. (The emission charge payments on uncontrolled emissions would be 15 times as large as the payments for controlling the pollution.) In part to avoid this financial burden, the United States has adopted a transferable allowance system, coupled with a tax on the additional profits generated by restricting the supply.

With regard to global warming, the emitters are separated in time from the consequences of their emissions. A doubling of carbon dioxide emissions is expected to occur well into the next century, when virtually all of the current decision makers will have passed away. The current generation bears the cost of control, whereas future generations would reap the benefits. Furthermore, international agreements are made more difficult by the fact that some countries may be benefited, not harmed, by global warming, diminishing even further their incentive control.

Economic analysis of this problem suggests that it makes sense to take some action to reduce emissions of greenhouse gases in order to provide insurance against the adverse, irreversible consequences if the damage tends to be higher than anticipated. Although the analysis suggests that drastic action is not called for yet, the next few years should be used fruitfully to assure that energy subsidies are removed, full costs are paid, and more knowledge about the problem is gained. The transition could be facilitated by either a system of taxes on greenhouse gases or a system of transferable emissions allowances for greenhouse gases. Some international cost-sharing is likely to be a necessary ingredient in a successful attack on the problem. During the next few decades, options must not only be preserved, they must be enhanced.

Responding in a timely and effective fashion to global and regional pollution problems will not be easy. Our political institutions are not configured in such a way to make decision making on a global scale easy. International organizations exist at the pleasure of the nations they serve. Only time will tell if the mechanisms of international agreements will prove equal to the task.

FURTHER READING

OECD. *Climate Change: Designing a Practical Tax System* (Paris: Organization for Economic Co-operation and Development, 1992). Fourteen essays grappling with the practical issues associated with designing a tax-based approach for controlling global warming.

OECD. *Climate Change: Designing a Tradeable Permit System* (Paris: Organization for Economic Co-operation and Development, 1992). Eleven essays grappling with the practical issues associated with designing a permit-based approach for controlling global warming.

Tietenberg, T. H. *The Economics of Global Warming* (Cheltenham, UK: Edward Elgar, 1996). A collection of 31 essays dealing with all economic aspects of dealing with global warming.

Van Ierland, Ekko, ed. *International Environmental Economics* (Amsterdam: Elsevier, 1994). Contains five essays on the economics of climate change.

ADDITIONAL REFERENCES

Adams, Donald D., and Walter P. Page. *Acid Deposition: Environmental, Economic, and Policy Issues* (New York: Plenum, 1985).

Barrett, S. "The Problem of Global Environmental Protection," *Oxford Review of Economic Policy* 6, No. 1 (spring 1990): 68–79.

Blackman, A., and W. Harrington. "The Use of Economic Incentives in Developing Countries: Lessons from International Experience." *Journal of Environment & Development* 9(1)(2000): 5–44.

Bohm, Peter. "Incomplete International Cooperation to Reduce CO_2 Emissions: Alternative Policies," *Journal of Environmental Economics and Management* 24, No. 3 (May 1993): 258–71.

Burtraw, D and E. Mansur. "Environmental Effects of SO_2 Trading and Banking." *Environmental Science & Technology* 33(20)(1999): 3489–3494.

Brown, Peter G. "Policy Analysis, Welfare Economics, and the Greenhouse Effect," *Journal of Policy Analysis and Management* 7 (spring 1988): 471–75.

Croker, Thomas D., ed. *Economic Perspectives on Acid Deposition Control* (Boston: Butterworth, 1984).

Grubb, M. *The Greenhouse Effect: Negotiating Targets* (London: Royal Institute of International Affairs, 1989).

ICF Resources. "Economic, Environmental, and Coal Market Impacts of SO_2 Emissions Trading under Alternative Acid Rain Control Proposals," a report prepared for the Regulatory Innovations Staff, U.S. Environmental Protection Agency (March 1989).

Jorgenson, D. W., and P. J. Wilcoxen. "Reducing U. S. Carbon Emissions: An Assessment of Different Instruments," *Journal of Policy Modeling* (October-December 1993): 491–520.

Lave, Lester B. "The Greenhouse Effect: What Government Actions Are Needed?," *Journal of Policy Analysis and Management* 7 (spring 1988): 460–70.

Manne, Alan S., and Richard G. Richels. *Buying Greenhouse Insurance: The Economic Costs of CO_2 Emission Limits* (Cambridge, MA: MIT Press, 1992): 89–99.

Meyer, Richard, and Bruce Yandle. "The Political Economy of Acid Rain," *Cato Journal* 7 (Fall 1987): 527–45.

National Research Council. *Changing Climate: Report of the Carbon Dioxide Assessment Committee* (Washington, DC: National Academy Press, 1983).

Nordhaus, William D., and Gary W. Yohe. "Future Paths of Energy and Carbon Dioxide Emissions," in National Research Council *Changing Climate: Report of the Carbon Dioxide Assessment Committee,* (Washington, DC: National Academy Press, 1983): 87–153.

Parry, I. W. H., R. C. Williams, et al. "When Can Carbon Abatement Policies Increase Welfare? The Fundamental Role of Distorted Factor Markets." *Journal of Environmental Economics and Management* 37(1)(1999): 52–84.

Pearce, David. "The Role of Carbon Taxes in Adjusting to Global Warming," *Economic Journal* 101 (July 1991): 938–48.

Piggott, J., et al. "How Large Are the Incentives to Join Subglobal Carbon-Reduction Initiatives?," *Journal of Policy Modeling* 15 (October-December 1993): 473–90.

Rosenberg, Nathan J., William E. Easterling III, Pierre R. Crosson, and Joel Darmstadler, eds. *Greenhouse Warming: Abatement and Adaptation* (Washington, DC: Resources for the Future, 1989).

Tietenberg, Tom. "Implementation Issues: A General Survey," in United Nations Conference on Trade and Development, ed., *Combating Global Warming: Study on a Global System of Tradeable Carbon Emission Entitlements* (New York: United Nations, 1992): 127–49.

Victor, D. G. "Limits of Market-Based Strategies for Slowing Global Warming: The Case of Tradeable Permits," *Policy Sciences,* 24, No. 2 (May 1991): 199–222.

Whalley, John, and Randall Wigle. "Cutting CO_2 Emissions: The Effects of Alternative Policy Approaches," *Energy Journal* 12 (1991): 109–24.

WEB SITES OF INTEREST

1. *http://www.epa.gov/docs/acidrain/trading.html*
   EPA's acid rain program.

2. *http://www.brixworth.demon.co.uk/acidrain2000/facts.htm*
   Acid rain in Europe.

3. *http://www.arb.ca.gov/pp/pp.htm*
   List of pollution prevention programs.

4. *http://www.epa.gov/docs/ozone/othlinks.html*
   Links to sites about ozone depletion.

5. *http://www.teap.org/*
   Web Site of the Technology and Economic Assessment Panel (TEAP) of the Montreal Protocol.

6. *http://www.iisd.ca/linkages/climate/index.html*
   Resources About the Framework Convention on Climate Change.

7. *http://www.weathervane.rff.org/*
   A Resources for the Future web site on climate change policy.

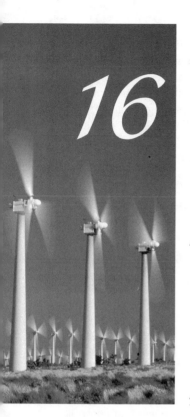

16

Transportation

There are two things you shouldn't watch being made, sausage and law.

ANONYMOUS

◆ INTRODUCTION

Though they emit many of the same pollutants as stationary sources, mobile sources require a different policy approach. These differences arise from the mobility of the source, the number of vehicles involved, and the role of the automobile in the U.S. lifestyle.

Mobility has two major impacts on policy. On the one hand, pollution is partly caused by the temporary location of the source—a case of being in the wrong place at the wrong time. This occurs, for example, during rush hour in metropolitan areas. Because the cars have to be where the people are, relocating them—as might be done with electric power plants—is not a viable strategy. On the other hand, it is more difficult to tailor vehicle emission rates to local pollution patterns because any particular vehicle may end up in many different urban and rural areas during the course of its useful life.

Mobile sources are also more numerous than stationary sources. Although there are only approximately 27,000 major stationary sources, well over 200 million vehicles travel on U.S. roadways. Enforcement is obviously more difficult the larger the number of sources being controlled.

Whereas stationary sources generally are large and run by professional managers, automobiles are small and run by amateurs. Their small size makes it more difficult to control emissions without affecting performance, and amateur ownership makes it more likely that emission control will deteriorate over time because of a lack of dependable maintenance and care.

These complications might lead us to conclude that perhaps we should ignore mobile sources and concentrate our control efforts solely on stationary sources. Unfortunately, that is not possible. Though each individual vehicle represents a minuscule part of the problem, mobile sources collectively represent a significant proportion of three criteria pollutants—ozone, carbon monoxide, and nitrogen dioxide. (Hydrocarbons and nitrogen dioxide are precursors of ozone.)

For two of these pollutants—ozone and nitrogen dioxide—the process of reaching attainment has been particularly slow. With the increased use of diesel engines, mobile sources are becoming responsible for a rising proportion of particulate emissions, and vehicles that burn leaded gasoline were until recently a major source of airborne lead.

Because it is necessary to control mobile sources, what policy options exist? What points of control are possible, and what are the advantages and disadvantages of each? In exercising control over these sources, the government must first specify the agent charged with the responsibility for the reduction. The obvious candidates are the manufacturer and the owner-driver. The balancing of this responsibility should depend on a comparative analysis of costs and benefits, with particular reference to such factors as (1) the number of agents to be regulated, (2) the rate of the sources' emission deterioration over time, (3) the life expectancy of automobiles, and (4) the availability, effectiveness, and cost of programs to reduce emissions at the point of production and at the point of use.

Although automobiles are numerous and ubiquitous, they are manufactured by a small number of firms. Because it is easier and less expensive to administer a system that controls relatively few sources, regulation at the point of production has considerable appeal.

Some problems are associated with limiting controls solely to the point of production, however. If the factory-controlled emission rate deteriorates during normal vehicle usage, control at the point of production may buy only temporary emission reduction. Though the deterioration of emission control can be combatted with warranty and recall provisions, the costs of these supporting programs have to be balanced against the costs of local control.

Because automobiles are durable, *new* vehicles make up only a relatively small percentage of the total fleet of vehicles. Therefore, control at the point of production, which affects only new equipment, takes longer to produce a given reduction in aggregate emissions, because newer, controlled cars replace old vehicles very slowly. Thus, a program of control at the point of production would produce emission reductions more slowly than would a program securing emission reductions from used as well as new vehicles.

Some possible means of reducing mobile-source pollution cannot be accomplished by regulating emissions at the point of production because they involve choices made by the owner-driver. The point-of-production strategy is oriented toward reducing the amount of emissions *per mile driven* in a particular type of car, but only the owner can decide what kind of car to drive, as well as when and where to drive it.

These are not trivial concerns. Diesel automobiles, buses, trucks, and motorcycles emit rather different amounts of pollutants than do gasoline-powered automobiles. By changing the mix of vehicles on the road, the amount and type of emissions can be affected, even if passenger miles are not changed.

Where and when the car (or other vehicle) is driven are also important. Because clustered emissions cause higher concentration levels than do dispersed emissions, driving in urban areas causes more environmental damage than driving in rural areas does. Local control strategies could internalize these location costs, whereas a uniform national strategy focusing solely on the point of production could not.

Timing of emissions is particularly important, because conventional commuting patterns lead to a clustering of emissions during the morning and evening rush hours. Indeed, plots of pollutant concentrations in urban areas during an average day typically produce a graph with two peaks, corresponding to the two rush hours.[1] Because high concentrations are more dangerous than low ones, some spreading over the 24-hour period could also prove beneficial.

◆ THE ECONOMICS OF MOBILE-SOURCE POLLUTION

Vehicles emit an inefficiently high level of pollution because they are not bearing the full cost of that pollution. This inefficiently low cost, in turn, has two sources: (1) implicit subsidies for road transport and (2) a failure to internalize external costs.

Implicit Subsidies

Several categories of the social costs associated with transporting goods and people over roads are related to mileage driven, but the private costs do not reflect that relationship. For example:

- The social costs associated with accidents are a function of vehicle-miles. The number of accidents rises as the number of miles driven rises. Generally, the costs associated with these accidents are paid for by insurance, but the premiums for these insurance policies rarely reflect the mileage-accident relationship. As a result, the additional private cost of insurance for additional miles driven is typically zero, though the social cost is certainly not zero.

- Road construction and maintenance costs, which are largely determined by vehicle-miles, are mostly funded out of tax dollars. The marginal private cost of an extra mile driven in terms of road construction and maintenance is zero, though the social cost is not.

- Despite the fact that building and maintaining parking space is expensive, parking is frequently supplied by employers at no marginal cost to the employee. The ability to park a car for free creates a bias toward private auto travel, because other modes receive no comparable subsidy.

---

[1]The exception is ozone formed by a chemical reaction involving hydrocarbons and nitrogen oxides in the presence of sunlight. For the evening rush-hour emissions, too few hours of sunlight remain for the chemical reactions to be completed, so graphs of daily ozone concentrations frequently exhibit a single peak.

Externalities

Road transport users also fail to bear the full cost of their choices, because many of the costs associated with those choices are actually borne by others. For example:

- Road transport is a major source of air pollution (Table 16.1). Major pollutants emitted include the precursors to ozone (particularly hydrocarbons and nitrogen oxides), carbon monoxide and dioxide, and particulates (largely from diesel engines).

- Road congestion creates externalities by increasing the amount of time required to travel a given distance.

To elaborate on the congestion point, let's consider Figure 16.1. As traffic volumes get closer to the design capacity of the roadway, traffic flow decreases; it takes more time to travel between two points. At this point the marginal social costs and marginal private costs begin to diverge. Although the driver entering a congested roadway will certainly consider the extra time it will take him or her to travel that route, he or she will not consider the extra time that his or her presence imposes on everyone else; it is an externality.

The efficient ratio of traffic volume to road capacity (V_e) occurs where the marginal benefits (as revealed by the demand curve) equal the marginal social cost. Because individual drivers do not internalize the external costs of their presence on this roadway, too many drivers will use the roadway, and traffic volume will be too high (V_p). The resulting efficiency losses would be represented by area *ACD* (the shaded area).

TABLE 16.1 Air Pollution from Road Transport, Selected Cities

Region	Year	Total Pollutants (thousand metric tons)	Percent Attributable to Road Transport
Mexico City	1987	5,027	80
São Paulo	1987	2,110	86
Ankara	1980	690	57
Manila	1987	500	71
Kuala Lumpur	1987	435	79
Athens[a]	1976	396	59
Gothenburg[a]	1980	124	78
London	1978	1,200	86
Los Angeles[a]	1982	3,391[b]	87
Munich	1974/5	213	73
Osaka	1982	141	59
Phoenix	1986	1,240[c]	28

[a]Percent shares apply to all transport. Motor vehicles account for 75 to 95 percent of the transport share.
[b]Excluding particulate matter.
[c]Includes 490,000 metric tons of dust from unpaved roads.

Source: Table constructed from data in Asif Fais, *Automobile Air Pollution: An Overview* (Washington, D.C.: World Bank, 1990), p. 12.

FIGURE 16.1   Congestion Inefficiency

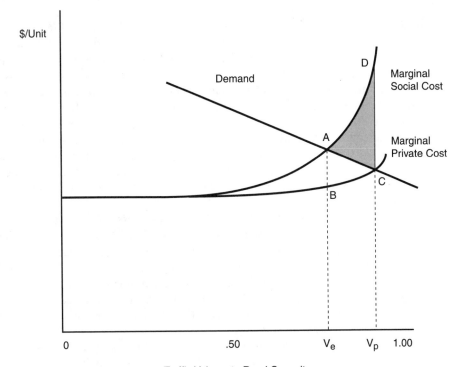

The Consequences

Understated road transport cost creates a number of perverse incentives. Too many vehicles use the roads. Too many miles are driven. Too many trips are taken. Transport energy use is too high. Pollution from transportation is excessive. Competitive modes of transportation—including mass transit, bicycles, and walking—all suffer from an inefficiently low demand.

Perhaps the most pernicious effect of understated transport costs, however, is its effect on land use. Low transport cost encourages dispersed settlement patterns. Residences can be located far from work and shopping because the costs of travel are so low. Unfortunately, this pattern of dispersal creates a tendency toward dependence that is hard to reverse. Once settlement patterns are dispersed, it is difficult to justify high-volume transportation alternatives (e.g., trains or buses). For example, both trains and buses need high-density travel corridors in order to generate the ridership necessary to pay the high fixed costs associated with building and running these systems. With dispersed settlement patterns, sufficiently high travel densities are difficult, if not impossible, to generate.

◆ POLICY TOWARD MOBILE SOURCES

Some History

Concern about mobile-source pollution originated in southern California in the early 1950s following a path-breaking study by Dr. A. J. Haagen-Smit of the California Institute of Technology. The study by Dr. Haagen-Smit identified motor vehicle emissions as a key culprit in forming the photochemical smog for which southern California was becoming infamous.

In the United States, the Clean Air Act Amendments of 1965 set national standards for hydrocarbon and carbon monoxide emissions from automobiles, which were to take effect during 1968. It is interesting to note that the impetus for the Act came not only from the scientific data on the effects of automobile pollution, but also from the automobile industry itself. The industry saw uniform federal standards as a way to avoid a situation in which every state passed its own unique set of emission standards, something the auto industry wanted to avoid. This pressure was successful in that the law prohibits all states except California from setting their own standards.

By 1970 there was general dissatisfaction with the slow progress being made on air pollution control in general and automobile pollution in particular. In a "get tough" mood as it developed the Clean Air Act amendments of 1970, Congress required new emissions standards that would reduce emissions by 90 percent below their uncontrolled levels. This reduction was to have been achieved by 1975 for hydrocarbon and carbon monoxide emissions and by 1976 for nitrogen dioxide. It was generally agreed at the time the Act was passed that the technology to meet the standards did not exist. By passing this tough law, Congress hoped to force the development of an appropriate technology.

It did not work out that way. The following years ushered in a series of deadline extensions. In 1972 the automobile manufacturers requested a one-year delay in the implementation of the standards. The administrator of the EPA denied the request and was taken to court. At the conclusion of the litigation in April 1973, the administrator granted a one-year delay in the 1975 deadline for the hydrocarbon and carbon monoxide standards. Subsequently, in July 1973, a one-year delay was granted for nitrogen oxides as well.[2] It was the first of many delayed deadlines.

Structure of the U.S. Approach

The current U.S. approach to mobile-source air pollution has served as a model for mobile-source control in many other countries (particularly in Europe). We shall therefore examine this approach in some detail.

The U.S. approach represents a blend of controlling emissions at the point of manufacture with controlling emissions from vehicles in use. New-car emission standards are administered through a certification program and an associated enforcement program.

Certification Program. The certification program tests prototypes of car models for conformity to federal standards. During the test, a prototype vehicle from each engine family is

---

[2]The only legal basis for granting an extension was technological infeasibility. Only shortly before the extension was granted, the Japanese Honda CVCC engine was certified as meeting the original standards. It is interesting to speculate on what the outcome would have been if the company meeting the standards had been American rather than Japanese.

driven 50,000 miles on a test track or a dynamometer. The vehicle follows a mandated strict pattern of fast and slow driving, idling, and hot-and-cold starts. The manufacturers run the tests and record emission levels at 5,000-mile intervals. If the vehicle satisfies the standards over the entire 50,000 miles, it passes the deterioration portion of the certification test.

The second step in the certification process is to apply less demanding (and less expensive) tests to three additional prototypes in the same engine family. Emission readings are taken at the 0- and 4,000-mile points and then, using the deterioration rate established in the first portion of the test, are projected to the 50,000-mile point. If those projected emission levels meet the standards, then that engine family is given a certificate of conformity. Only engine families with a certificate of conformity may be sold.

Associated Enforcement Programs. The certification program is complemented by an associated enforcement program, which contains assembly-line testing, as well as recall and anti-tampering procedures and warranty provisions. To ensure that the prototype vehicles are representative, the EPA tests a statistically representative sample of assembly-line vehicles. If these tests reveal that more than 40 percent of the cars do not conform with federal standards, the certificate may be suspended or revoked.

The EPA has also been given the power to require manufacturers to recall and remedy manufacturing defects that cause emissions to exceed federal standards. If the EPA uncovers a defect, it usually requests the manufacturer to recall vehicles for corrective action. If the manufacturer refuses, the EPA can order a recall.

The Clean Air Act also requires two separate types of warranty provisions. These warranty provisions are designed to ensure that a manufacturer will have an incentive to produce a vehicle that, properly maintained, will meet emission standards over its useful life. The first of these provisions requires the vehicle to be free of defects that could cause it to fail to meet the standards. Under this provision, any defects discovered by consumers would be fixed at the manufacturer's expense.

The second warranty provision requires the manufacturer to bring any car that fails an inspection and maintenance test (described below) during its first 24 months or 24,000 miles (whichever occurs first) into conformance with the standards. After the 24 months, or 24,000 miles, the warranty is limited solely to the replacement of devices specifically designed for emission control, such as catalytic converters. This further protection lasts 60 months.

The earliest control devices used to control pollution had two characteristics that rendered them susceptible to tampering: (1) They adversely affected vehicle performance, and (2) they were relatively easy to circumvent. As a result, the Clean Air Act Amendments of 1970 prohibited anyone from tampering with an emission control system prior to the sale of an automobile, but, curiously, prohibited only dealers and manufacturers from tampering after the sale. The 1977 amendments extended the coverage of the postsale-tampering prohibition to motor-vehicle repair facilities and fleet operators.

Lead. Section 211 of the Clean Air Act provides the EPA with the authority to regulate lead and any other fuel additives used in gasoline. Under this provision, gasoline suppliers are required to make unleaded gasoline available. By ensuring the availability of unleaded gasoline, this regulation sought to reduce the amount of airborne lead and to protect the effectiveness of the catalytic converter, which is poisoned by lead.[3] Penalties are assessed on distributors (but not individual owners) for supplying catalyst-equipped vehicles with leaded gasoline.

On 7 March 1985, the EPA issued regulations imposing strict new standards on the allowable lead content in refined gasoline. These regulations required further reductions from the then existing 1.10 grams per leaded gallon (gplg) to 0.50 gplg in July 1985 and to 0.10 gplg in January 1986.[4] These actions followed a highly publicized series of medical research findings on the rather severe health and developmental consequences, particularly to small children, of even rather low levels of atmospheric lead.

Local Responsibilities.   The Clean Air Act Amendments of 1977 recognized the existence of nonattainment areas. Special requirements were placed on control authorities to bring nonattainment areas into attainment. Because many of the nonattainment areas received that designation because of the presence of pollutants generated by mobile sources, local authorities in those areas were required to take further actions to reduce emissions from mobile sources.

Measures that local authorities are authorized to use include requiring new cars registered in that area to satisfy the more stringent California standard (with EPA approval) and the development of comprehensive transportation plans. These plans could include measures such as on-street parking controls, road charges, and measures to reduce the number of vehicle-miles traveled.

In nonattainment regions that could not meet the primary standard for photochemical oxidants, carbon monoxide, or both by 31 December 1982, control authorities could delay attainments until 31 December 1987, provided they agreed to a number of additional restrictions. For the purposes of this chapter, the most important of these is the requirement that each region gaining this extension must establish a vehicle *inspection and maintenance* (I&M) *program* for emissions.

The objective of the I&M program is to identify vehicles that are violating the standards and bring them into compliance, to deter tampering, and to encourage regular routine maintenance. Because the federal test procedure used in the certification process is much too expensive to use on a large number of vehicles, shorter, less expensive tests were developed specially for the I&M programs. Because of the expense and questionable effectiveness of these programs, they are one of the most controversial components of the policy package used to control mobile-source emissions.

Alternative Fuels and Vehicles.   In an attempt to foster the development of alternative vehicles and alternative fuels that would be less damaging to the environment, Congress and some states have passed legislation requiring their increased use. Title II of the Clean Air Act Amendments of 1990 mandates the sale of cleaner-burning reformulated gasoline in certain CO and severe ozone nonattainment regions. In the Energy Policy Act, passed in 1992, Congress requires the federal government (and some private fleet owners) to purchase alternative-fueled vehicles. The government also attempted to induce some regula-

---

[3] Three tankfuls of leaded gasoline used in a car equipped with a catalytic converter will produce a 50 percent reduction in the effectiveness of the catalytic converter.

[4] These can be found in 40 *Code of Federal Regulations* 80 (1990).

Example 16.1

Project XL—The Quest for Effective, Flexible Regulation

Project XL is a US pilot program that allows state and local governments, businesses and federal facilities to develop with USEPA innovative strategies to test better or more cost-effective ways of achieving environmental and public health protection. In exchange, the EPA authorizes sufficient regulatory flexibility to conduct the experiment. The objective is to produce both better environmental quality and lower compliance cost than would otherwise be possible with traditional "one-size-fits-all" regulation.

One example of a project involves the United States Postal Service (USPS), the State of Colorado, and the USEPA. The USPS wanted to replace some of its aging, high polluting vehicles in the Denver area. Denver is a nonattainment area for carbon monoxide. Colorado rules required that in the Denver area 50 percent of all new fleet vehicles purchased must be certified as low emitting vehicles (LEVs). Due to the special requirements for USPS vehicles the only bid that met the other USPS specifications was for Transitional Low-Emitting Vehicles (TLEVs), which could not meet the LEV requirement.

Rather than continue operating its aging fleet, the USPS applied for, and received, permission from both Colorado and USEPA to replace 512 aging postal vehicles in Denver with TLEVs. The new vehicles are able use up to 85% ethanol fuel. In addition USPS would relocate 282 1987–1991 vintage vehicles to areas with less need to reduce emissions.

The USPS proposal will result in lower emissions of carbon monoxide that would have been achieved even if compliance with the original Colorado rules were possible and will become part of the Denver's state implementation plan to reach attainment.

Source: http://www.epa.gov/projectxl/usps/index.htm.

tory flexibility designed to provide incentives for further adoptions (Example 16.1). California has "pushed the envelope" even further. In September 1990, the California Air Resources Board (CARB) passed its low-emission vehicle (LEV) and zero-emission vehicle (ZEV) regulations. The former requires increasingly stringent emissions standards over time for conventionally fueled vehicles. The latter mandates that at least 5 percent of new cars and light trucks sold by 2001 in the state must be zero emission vehicles (defined as vehicles that directly emit no VOCs, NOx, or CO; any indirect emissions from producing the electricity are not counted). This percentage rises to 10 percent by 2003.

European Approaches

By the late 1980s, emission standards patterned after the 1983 U.S. standards were introduced for all new cars in Austria, Sweden, Switzerland, Norway, and Finland. West Germany, Denmark, and the Netherlands have introduced tax incentives and lower registration fees for cleaner cars.

On 1 October 1989, the European Community's 12 member nations imposed U.S.-style emission standards on all new cars, starting with cars equipped with engines over 2 liters. Similar emission controls were to be extended to all engine sizes by 1993. The former Soviet Union, in principle, agreed to follow the example of Western Europe in introducing more stringent emission controls. Because unleaded gasoline is not widely available in the former Soviet Union, rapid change to catalytic converters is not expected.

The Netherlands, Norway, and Sweden are using differential tax rates to encourage consumers to purchase (and manufacturers to produce) low-emitting cars before regulations take effect requiring all cars to be low-emitting.[5] Tax differentiation confers a tax advantage (and, hence, an after-tax price advantage) on cleaner cars. The amount of the tax usually depends on (1) the emission characteristics of the car (heavier taxes being levied on heavily polluting cars), (2) the size of the car (e.g., in Germany, heavier cars qualify for larger tax advantages to offset the relatively high control requirements placed upon them), and (3) the year of purchase (the tax differential is declining because all cars will eventually have to meet the standards). It apparently works. In Sweden, 87 percent of the new cars sold have qualified for the tax advantage, and in Germany the comparable percentage has been over 90 percent.

Europe has also developed strategies to make better use of transportation capital. Its intercity rail system is better developed than in the United States and public transit ridership is typically higher within cities. Europe has also been a pioneer in the use of car sharing arrangements (Example 16.2).

◆ AN ECONOMIC AND POLITICAL ASSESSMENT

Perhaps the most glaring deficiency in the 1970 amendments occurred when an infeasible compliance schedule for meeting the ambient standards was established for mobile-source pollutants. The chief instruments to be used by local areas in meeting these standards were the new-car emission standards. Because these applied only to new cars, and because new cars make up such a small proportion of the total fleet, significant emission reductions were not experienced until well after the deadline for meeting the ambient standards. This created a very difficult situation for local areas, because they were forced to meet the ambient standards prior to the time that the emission standards (the chief sources of reduction) would have much of an impact.

All they could do was to develop local strategies to make up the difference. Recognizing the difficulties the states faced, the EPA granted an extension of the deadline for submitting the transportation plans that would spell out the manner in which the standards would be met. This extension was challenged in court by the Natural Resource Defense Council,[6] which successfully argued that the EPA did not have the authority to grant the extension. Faced with the court's decision, the EPA was forced to reject the implementation plans submitted by most states as inadequate because those plans could not ensure attainment by the deadlines.

---

[5]For the details on these approaches see J. B. Opschoor and Hans B. Vos, *Economic Instruments for Environmental Protection* (Paris: Organization for Economic Co-operation and Development, 1989): 69–71.

[6]475 F. 2d 968 (1973).

Example 16.2

Car Sharing: Better Use of Automotive Capital?

One of the threats to sustainable development is the growing number of vehicles on the road. Though great progress has been made since the 1970s in limiting the pollution each vehicle emits per mile of travel, as the number of vehicles and the number of miles increase, the resulting increases in pollution offset much of the gains from the cleaner vehicles.

How to limit the number of vehicles? One strategy that has become rather widespread in Europe and is just beginning to make a dent in America is car sharing. Car sharing recognizes that the typical automobile sits idle most of the time, a classic case of excess capacity. (Studies in Germany suggest the average vehicle use per day is one hour.) Therefore the car sharing strategy tries to spread ownership of a vehicle over several owners who share both the cost and the use.

The charges imposed by car-sharing clubs typically involve an upfront access fee plus fees based both on time of actual use and mileage. (Use during the peak periods usually costs more.) Some car-sharing clubs offer touch-tone automated booking, 24-hour dispatchers and such amenities as child-safety seats, bike racks, and roof carriers.

Swiss and German clubs started in the late 1980s. As of 1998 an estimated 25,000 Germans and 20,000 Swiss belonged to car-sharing groups.

What could the contribution of car-sharing be to air pollution control in those areas where it catches on? It probably does lower the number of vehicles and the resulting congestion. In addition peak-hour pricing probably encourages use at the less polluted periods. On the other hand, it does not necessarily lower the number of miles driven, which is one of the keys to lowering pollution. The contribution of this particular innovation remains to be clarified by some solid empirical research.

Source: Mary Williams Walsh, "Car-Sharing Holds the Road in German," *Los Angeles Times* (July 23, 1998): A1.

Because the law clearly states that the EPA must substitute its own plan for an inadequate plan, the EPA found itself thrust into the unfamiliar and unpleasant role of defining transportation control plans for states with rejected SIPs.

Two main problems with this development surfaced: (1) The EPA was not administratively equipped either in terms of staff or resources to design and implement these plans, and (2) because of the severity of the mismatch between deadline and implementation, the EPA could have done very little, even if the staff and resources had been available.

The EPA made a valiant but futile attempt to meet its statutory responsibilities. It concluded that the best way to resolve its dilemma was to work backward from the needs to the transportation plans and, once the plans were defined, to require states to implement and enforce them. To ensure state cooperation, it set up a system of civil penalties to be applied against states that failed to cooperate.

The resulting plans were virtually unenforceable because they were so severe. For example, in order to meet the ambient standard in Los Angeles by the deadline, the plan designed by the EPA called for an 82 percent reduction in gasoline consumption in the Los Angeles basin. The reduction was to be achieved through gasoline rationing during the six months of the year when the smog problem is most severe. In publishing the plan, EPA Administrator William Ruckelshaus acknowledged that it was infeasible and would effectively destroy the economy of the state if implemented, but argued that he had no other choice under the law.

The states raised a number of legal challenges to this approach, which were never really resolved in the courts by the time Congress revised the Act in 1977. The Clean Air Act Amendments of 1977 remedied the situation by extending the deadlines.

The lesson from this episode seems to be that tougher laws do not necessarily result in more rapid compliance. In this case, because the statutory requirement could not be met, virtually nothing was accomplished as the various parties attempted to fashion a resolution through the courts.

Technology Forcing and Sanctions

The lesson described above was underscored by the EPA's experience in gaining compliance with the national emission standards by the automobile manufacturers. The industry was able to obtain a number of delays in meeting those standards. The law was so tough that it was difficult to enforce within the time schedule envisioned by Congress.

This problem was intensified by the sanctions established by the act to ensure compliance. They were so brutal that the EPA was unwilling to use them; therefore, they did not represent a credible threat. For example, when an engine family failed the certification test, the law is quite specific in stating that vehicle classes not certified as conforming with the standards cannot be sold! Given the importance of the automobile industry in the U.S. economy, this sanction was not likely to be applied. As a result, there were considerable pressures on the EPA to avoid the sanctions by defining more easily satisfied procedures for certification and by setting sufficiently flexible deadlines that no manufacturer would fail to meet them.

Differentiated Regulation

In controlling the emissions of both mobile and stationary sources, the brunt of the reduction effort is borne by new sources. This raises the cost of the new sources and, from the purchaser's point of view, increases the attractiveness of used cars relative to new ones. The benefit from increased control is a public good and therefore cannot be appropriated exclusively by the new-car purchasers. One result of a strategy focusing on new sources would be to depress the demand for new cars while enhancing that for used cars.

Apparently, this is precisely what happened in the United States.[7] In response to the higher cost of new cars, people hold on to old automobiles longer. This has produced several unfortunate side effects. Because new cars are substantially cleaner than old cars, emission reductions have been delayed. In effect, this shift in fleet composition was equivalent to a set-

---

[7]See Howard K. Gruenspecht, "Differentiated Regulation: The Case of Auto Emission Standards," *American Economic Review* 72 (May 1982): 328–31.

back of three to four years in the timetable for reducing emissions.[8] Also, because older cars get worse gas mileage, gasoline consumption was higher than it would otherwise be. The focus on new sources is to some extent inevitable; the lesson to be drawn is that by ignoring these behavioral responses to differentiated regulation, the policymaker is likely to expect results to occur sooner than they are likely to.

Uniformity of Control

With the exception of the California standards, which are more stringent, the Clean Air Act requires the same emission standards on all cars. Example 16.3 shows how these standards were established. The calculations were designed to assure that required levels of control would be sufficient to meet the ambient standards in large cities such as Los Angeles or in high-altitude cities such as Denver. As a result, many of the costs borne by people in other parts of the country—particularly rural areas—do not yield much in the way of benefits.

This sounds like an inefficient policy, because the severity of control is not tailored to the geographic need, and, indeed, most of the studies that have been accomplished indicate that this is so. A report published by the National Academy of Sciences and the National Academy of Engineering estimated the discounted present value of benefits and costs over the period 1975–2101. It estimated the costs at \$126 billion and the benefits at \$137 billion.

Positive net benefits, of course, are not synonymous with efficiency, although negative net benefits do imply inefficiency. And other studies have found negative net benefits.[9]

The conclusion that the costs of control exceed the benefits for automobile pollution control seems to be generally shared.[10] Large uncertainties in the benefit estimations, a theme we have explored in several previous chapters, and the failure of any of these studies to consider the role of auto emissions of carbon in global warming force us to take these results with a grain of salt. It is nonetheless interesting that because the current policy forces manufacturers to operate on a very steep portion of the marginal-control-cost function, benefit uncertainty does not seem to affect the conclusion that the current standards are inefficiently strict.

The Deterioration of New-Car Emission Rates

As part of its investigation of the Clean Air Act, the National Commission on Air Quality investigated the emissions of vehicles in use and compared these emission levels to the standards. Its estimates were a blend of actual measured emissions for model years already in the fleet and forecasts for future model years based on a knowledge of the technologies to be used. Particularly for hydrocarbons and carbon monoxide, the deterioration of emission rates in use was pronounced.

The Commission also investigated the factors contributing to poor in-use emission performance. It found that the principal reason for the poor performance was improper mainte-

---

[8]Robert W. Crandall, Howard K. Gruenspecht, Theodore E. Keeler, and Lester B. Lave, *Regulating the Automobile* (Washington, DC: Brookings Institution, 1986), p. 96.

[9]Richard C. Schwing et al., "Benefit-Cost Analysis of Automotive Emission Reductions," *Journal of Environmental Economics and Management* 7 (1980): 57–58.

[10]See the discussion in Robert W. Crandall, Howard K. Gruenspecht, Theodore E. Keeler, and Lester B. Lave, op. cit., pp. 109–16.

Example 16.3

Setting the National Automobile Emission Standards

A set of national emission standards provides the backbone of the 1970 Clean Air Act Amendments. It is natural to imagine that these standards were set after a careful weighing of the benefits and costs of various levels, but the manner in which they were established was quite different. The analysis used to justify the standards could have been accomplished on the back of an envelope.

This basic approach was developed by D. S. Barth. His calculations relied on a rollback model that simply assumes that a linear relationship exists between emission reductions and reductions in pollutant concentrations. To initiate the analysis, he needed to pick a year in which the standards would be met—1990 was chosen. He then needed to calculate how much emissions would grow in the absence of controls and in the presence of more cars, more miles traveled, and so on. He assumed emissions would grow 2.18 times between 1967 and 1990. Finally, he needed to choose an actual air-quality level in 1967. For that, he chose the highest ambient pollution-concentration reading during the year in any city. These pieces of information he then combined in a formula:

$$DER = \left[1.00 - \frac{(2.18 \times 1967 \text{ max}) - DL}{(2.18 \times 1967 \text{ max}) - BL} \right] \times 1967 \text{ rate}$$

Here, DER is the desired emissions rate (in grams per mile), 1967 max is the maximum ambient concentration, DL is the desired ambient concentration, BL is the background concentration level, and 1967 rate is the actual emission rate (in grams per mile) that prevailed in 1967.

Source: This example was based on D. S. Barth, "Federal Motor Vehicle Emission Goals for CO, HC and NO_2. Based on Desired Air Quality Levels," *Air Pollution 1970, Part 5*, U.S. Senate Committee on Public Works (Washington, DC: Government Printing Office, 1970); and Eugene P. Seskin, "Automobile Air Pollution Policy," in *Current Issues in U.S. Environmental Policy*, Paul R. Portney, ed. (Baltimore, MD: Johns Hopkins University Press, 1978): 68–104.

nance. Carburetor and ignition-timing misadjustment were key factors. Component failure and tampering were also found to affect emission levels, though to a lesser degree.

Inspection and Maintenance Programs.   The policy response to emission rate deterioration was to require that there be I&M programs in nonattainment regions seeking extensions to the deadlines for reaching the ambient standards. There are reasons for concerns, however, as to whether this is a cost-effective response.

Apparently, the cost per ton of emission reduction from I&M programs turns out to be two to three times higher than that for securing an equivalent reduction from stationary sources. Because they reduce other pollutants, I&M programs do have merit; however, the current system provides little flexibility in how the program's objectives are met.

Do vehicle inspection programs yield positive net benefits? The evidence is mixed. A comparison of the EPA studies on the cost of the program ($645/ton) with other EPA studies of the benefits for automotive pollutants ($260 to $721/ton) reveals that, for some geographic areas, but not all, the programs are justified. A recent study of the Maryland inspection program, however, suggests that the EPA cost estimates may be understated by a large amount, because they do not include the costs of driver time and mileage to complete the inspection and comply with the findings. Including these costs yields a benefit-cost ratio in the neighborhood of 0.125 for Maryland.[11]

One strategy for making inspection and maintenance programs more cost effective is to target the maintenance at those cars for which the emissions reduction payoff is the highest. According to studies of on-road vehicles, fewer than 10 percent of the cars on the road produce half of the CO exhaust fumes. Identifying and fixing those high-polluting vehicles turns out to be remarkably cost effective. One study estimates the cost at about $100/ton of reduced CO,[12] which compares very favorably to the comparable costs for alternative sources of vehicle reduction.

Other Local Strategies. Another possible way to counter the effects of the deterioration rates of new-car emissions involves the implementation of local transportation controls, such as stimulating mass-transit usage. Such approaches allow the highly polluted areas to tailor the degree of control to their needs. The question of interest is whether or not these strategies are cost effective.

To examine this question and others, the National Science Foundation funded a multidisciplinary, multiuniversity study to examine the emissions payoffs and the costs of implementing various local strategies. The analysis was based on a computer model that was designed to simulate the transportation system of Boston, Massachusetts, and how that system would respond to various policies available to local authorities.

The model was based on a large amount of data on the origins and destinations of trips in the Boston area. It contained equations that simulated the choice of mode (e.g., bus or auto) as a function of such factors as travel time, cost, and so on. Once the travel patterns were simulated, the model projected the effects of these travel patterns on aggregate emissions and, finally, on the concentrations of pollutants expected in each of 123 different receptor locations in the city. With this model it was possible to keep track of both the size of the emission reductions and the areas in which pollutant concentrations were reduced. This latter information is important, because some parts of the city are more heavily polluted than others, and reductions in those areas would make a particularly valuable contribution to meeting the ambient air-quality standards.

As is generally true with simulation models of this sort, an enormous amount of information was generated. A small portion of this output is presented in Table 16.2. The Benchmark column represents the transportation and air quality situation in the Boston Air-Quality Control Region in 1970. For all other simulations, the population, income, and automobile fleet are assumed to be the same as for the benchmark case.

---

[11]Virginia D. McConnell, "Costs and Benefits of Vehicle Inspections: a Case Study of the Maryland Region," *Journal of Environmental Management* 30 (1990): 1–15.

[12]James E. Peterson and Donald H. Stedman, "Find and Fix the Polluters," *Chemtech* (January 1992): 42–53.

TABLE 16.2 Automobile Pollution Simulation

Statistic	Benchmark	Fare Reduction	Transit Extension	1980 Emission Standard
Annual vehicle-miles traveled (thousands)	19,818	19,510	19,799	19,818
Percentage of trips originating on mass transit	10.37	10.78	11.92	10.37
Average length of auto trip (mi)	9.91	9.80	10.06	9.91
Aggregate auto emissions (grams/sec)				
CO	19,609	19,343	19,497	4,022
HC	2,755	2,716	2,744	485
NO$_2$	934	919	933	401
Annual passenger-miles traveled on transit by auto users who switch to mass transit during trip	410,400	494,300	451,500	410,400
Annual dollar resource cost (thousands)	0	$11,517	$95,083	$120,000

Source: Copyright © 1975 The Trustees of Columbia University in the city of Ney York.

The Fare Reduction column portrays the effect of a 10 percent reduction in mass-transit fare, and the Transit Extension column gives the effect of a vigorous program of extending subway lines further into the suburbs. The 1980 Emission Standard column reflects the effect of having the degree of emission control on automobiles that should have been achieved by 1980.

The fare reduction clearly dominates the system extension on grounds of cost-effectiveness because it costs less and reduces pollution more, though neither strategy makes much of a difference. It is impossible to compare the other strategies, however, because the 1980 emission standards are both much more expensive and much more effective (in terms of reducing pollutants).

Most of the purely local strategies considered in this study are expensive and do not have a profound impact on air quality. Therefore, heavy reliance on traditional local strategies such as those covered in this study as a substitute for control over new-car emission rates would seem misguided. Yet, appropriately designed, more innovative local strategies can effectively complement new-car strategies, particularly as a means to achieve the additional control needed in those areas where the new-car standards are not sufficient to meet the ambient standards.

Lead Phaseout Program

Following the path established by the Emissions Trading Program, the government began applying the transferable-permit approach more widely. In the mid-1980s, prior to the issuance of new, more stringent regulations on lead in gasoline, the EPA announced the results of a cost-benefit analysis of their expected impact. The analysis concluded that the proposed 0.01 gplg standard would result in $36 billion (in 1983 dollars) in benefits (from reduced adverse health effects), at an estimated cost to the refining industry of $2.6 billion.

Although the regulation was unquestionably justified on efficiency grounds, the EPA wanted to allow flexibility in how the deadlines were met, without increasing the amount of lead used. Although some refiners could meet early deadlines with ease, others could do so only with a significant increase in cost. Recognizing that meeting the goal did not require that every refiner meet every deadline, the EPA initiated an innovative program to provide additional flexibility in meeting the regulations (Example 16.4).

Alternative Fuels

Although the possible availability of alternative fuels has incorporated another policy option into the control picture, how effective a strategy use of such fuels would be is not clear. One study examined the cost-effectiveness of methanol vehicles by projecting both costs and emissions reductions for the years 2000 and 2010 and calculating a cost per ton reduced.[13]

According to these calculations, flexible-fuel vehicles would be less cost effective than vehicles dedicated to burning either 85 percent methanol or 100 percent methanol. The cost per ton for flexible-fuel vehicles would be in the neighborhood of $66,000, whereas for the vehicle burning 85 percent methanol it would be $31,000.[14]

These numbers are very high, almost five times as high as alternative means of reducing hydrocarbon emissions. In 1989, the South Coast Air Quality Management District identified 120 options for reducing volatile hydrocarbons. The average cost-effectiveness of the 68 measures proposed was $12,250 per ton. Although early estimates such as these should not determine the outcome of the search for alternatives, they certainly do suggest that caution in proceeding too rapidly down this path would be appropriate.[15]

Air Quality

Have the policies we have examined improved air quality? In this section we shall examine the data on three pollutants for which mobile sources are very important—ozone, carbon monoxide, and lead.[16]

Ozone. Ozone continues to be the most pervasive ambient air-pollution problem in the United States, with 101 areas failing to meet the ozone ambient standard for 1986–1988. Some progress has been made, however. Emissions of volatile organic compounds, the precursors for

[13]Margaret A. Walls and Alan J. Krupnick, "Cost-Effectiveness of Methanol Vehicles," *Resources,* No. 100 (summer 1990).

[14]Vehicles burning 100 percent fuel are estimated to produce reductions at a cost of $51,000 per ton.

[15]Mandating fuel choices is less cost-effective than using economic incentives. For a specific comparison of the two approaches, see Robert A. Collinge and Anne Stevens, "Targeting Methanol or Other Alternative Fuels: How Intrusive Should Policy Be?," *Contemporary Policy Issues* 8 (January 1990): 54–61.

[16]In this section the data for the United States are from Office of Air Quality, *National Air Quality and Emissions Trends Report: 1991* (Raleigh: U.S. Environmental Protection Agency, 1992) and the international data are from World Resources Institute, *World Resources: 1992–1993* (New York: Oxford University Press, 1992).

Example 16.4

Getting the Lead Out: the Lead Phaseout Program

Under the *Lead Phaseout Program* a fixed number of "lead rights" (authorizing the use of a fixed amount of lead in gasoline produced during the period) were allocated to the 195 or so refineries. (Because of a loophole in the regulations, some new "alcohol-blender" refineries were created in order to take advantage of the program, but their impact was very small.) The number of issued rights declined over time. Refiners who did not need their full share of authorized rights could sell their rights to other refiners.

Initially, no banking of rights was allowed (i.e., rights had to be created and used in the same quarter), but the EPA subsequently allowed banking. Once banking was initiated, created rights could be used in that period or any subsequent period up to the end of the program in 1987. Prices of rights, which were initially about 0.75 cents per gram of lead, rose to 4 cents after banking was allowed.

Refiners had an incentive to eliminate the lead quickly, because early reductions freed up rights for sale. Acquiring these credits made it possible for other refiners to comply with the deadlines, even in the face of equipment failures or "Acts of God"; furthermore, fighting the deadlines in court, the traditional response, became unnecessary. Designed purely as a means of facilitating the transition to this new regime, the lead-banking program ended as scheduled on 31 December 1987.

Sources: Nussbaum, Barry D., "Phasing Down Lead in Gasoline in the U.S.: Mandates, Incentives, Trading and Banking" in T. Jones and J. Corfee-Morlot, eds. *Climate Change: Designing a Tradeable Permit System*, (Paris: Organization for Economic Co-operation and Development, 1992): 21–34; and Robert W. Hahn and Gordon L. Hester, "Marketable Permits: Lessons from Theory and Practice," *Ecology Law Quarterly* 16 (1989): 361–406.

ozone formation, have decreased some 11 percent from 1980 to 1995. Comparable data for other countries are not available.

Carbon Monoxide.　In the United States, carbon monoxide emissions declined by 30 percent over the 1980–1995 period, despite a dramatic increase in vehicle-miles traveled.

Although some Western European countries have experienced stabilized emissions or a gradual decline, others show increased emissions. In Iceland, emissions rose by 12 percent between 1980 and 1995. In both the Netherlands and the former West Germany, emissions declined 35 and 39 percent, respectively.

Data from Poland and Hungary suggest that CO emissions are also rising in some Eastern European countries. Experts also expect to find increasing emissions in industrializing Asian and South American countries, but current data are insufficient to confirm that conjecture.

Lead.　Declines in emissions of lead in the United States have been dramatic. From 1980 to 1996 emission of lead dropped 95 percent.

---

[17]Gasoline in Mexico City had the highest lead content in all sites in the global-monitoring network, and volunteers from that city had the highest reported levels of lead in their blood.

Although relatively few countries report lead emissions, the data indicate that lead in gasoline is generally being decreased in European and Asian countries, but not in Africa, or in South or Central America.[17]

◆ POSSIBLE REFORMS

We have seen that the current U.S. approaches have some salient weaknesses. Reliance on controlling emissions at the point of production has produced major improvements in cars leaving the assembly line, but emission rates deteriorate with use. The use of uniform standards has resulted in more control than necessary in rural areas and perhaps less than necessary in the most heavily polluted areas. Manufacturers have been able to delay implementation deadlines because the sanctions for noncompliance are so severe that the EPA has often been reluctant to deny a certificate of conformity.

As controls on manufacturers have become more common and vehicles have become cleaner, attention is increasingly turning to the user. Drivers have little incentive to drive or maintain their cars in a manner that minimizes emissions, because the full social costs of road transport have not been internalized by current policy. How far from a full internalization of cost are we? Table 16.3 looks at this issue from the point of view of fuel taxes. It provide estimates of how much higher current fuel taxes would have to be in selected countries in order to internalize the full social cost of road transport. The amount of increase would be quite large. Though it was not included in this study, the unusually low gasoline taxes in the United States seem to support a conjecture that large increases would be required for the United States, as well.

But fuel taxes are not the only way to begin to internalize costs and, by themselves, they would be only a blunt instrument, because they would typically not take into account when and where the emissions occurred. One way to focus on these temporal and spatial concerns is through *congestion pricing*, charging higher prices for access to congested roadways.

TABLE 16.3 Current Fuel Taxes as a Percentage of the Level Needed to Internalize the Social Costs of Road Transport (1992)

Country	Gasoline	Diesel
Austria	25	23
Denmark	40	30
France	39	23
Germany	50	33
Italy	59	44
The Netherlands	59	29
Norway[a]	52	—
Spain	52	39
Sweden[b]	60	40
Switzerland	27	31
United Kingdom	47	45

[a]In midst of raising diesel tax.
[b]1993

Source: Adapted from Table 10.4 in Per Kägerson, *Getting the Prices Right: A European Scheme for Making Transport Pay Its True Costs* (Stockholm: Katarinatryck AB, for the European Federation for Transport and Environment, 1993): 170.

Example 16.5

Innovative Mobile-Pollution Control Strategies: Singapore and Hong Kong

Mobile-source pollution is a function of the level of traffic congestion; the greater the congestion, the greater the resulting pollutant concentrations. Reducing the level of congestion is one strategy local areas can implement in order to reduce peak-hour concentration levels.

Singapore has successfully reduced congestion by forcing drivers to recognize the scarcity value of congested roadways. Since 1975, cars entering the city center during the morning rush hour with fewer than four people aboard have had to display a sticker. As of 1990, the sticker cost approximately $2.60 per day. Sanctions are imposed on cars found in the designated area without a sticker.

Initially, the scheme reduced the number of cars entering the restricted area by three quarters. Though that magnitude of reduction has not been maintained, city streets remain relatively uncongested, and pollution concentrations have been reduced.

To make further progress on reducing pollutant concentrations, Singapore authorities decided that they must not only limit access to certain areas during rush hours, but must also begin to reduce the total number of private vehicles. In 1990 the city adopted a system whereby motorists have to bid for the right to own new cars, with the licenses going to the highest bidders. Only 22,000 new vehicles—about 4.3 percent of the existing car population—were allowed on the roads in the first year of the program's operation.

Hong Kong recently experimented with another, more precise way of charging road users for the external costs associated with road congestion. There, cars were fitted with electronic number plates that identified them to various computers strategically located around the city. Based upon these computer readings, drivers were billed, according to the intensity, location, and time of their road use. Although the pilot scheme worked well, local politics prevented it from becoming permanent policy. Apparently, newly elected district councils were not satisfied with the disposition of the revenue.

Source: "Traffic Jams: The City, the Commuter and the Car," *The Economist* (February 1989): 19–22; and "Driving in Singapore," *The Wall Street Journal* (27 February 1990): A22.

Several Asian cities have undertaken some innovative approaches. Perhaps the most innovative can be found in Singapore and Hong Kong, where the price system is used to reduce congestion (Example 16.5). Bangkok bars vehicles from transporting goods from certain parts of the metropolitan area during various peak hours, leaving the roads available to buses, cars, and motorized tricycles.

Congestion tolls have existed for some time in Oslo, Norway, and Milan, Italy. In the United States, electronic toll collection systems are currently in place on the Santa Monica Freeway (California), the Oklahoma Turnpike, the Dallas North Tollway (Texas), and the Lake Pontchartrain Causeway (Louisiana). Reserved express bus lanes are also common in the United States. (Reserved lanes for express buses lower the relative travel time for bus com-

Example 16.6

Counterproductive Policy Design

As one response to unacceptably high levels of traffic congestion and air pollution, the Mexico City administration imposed a regulation that banned each car from driving on a specific day of the week. The specific day when a given car could not be driven was determined by the last digit of the license plate.

This approach appeared to offer the opportunity for considerable reductions in congestion and air pollution, at a relatively low cost. In this case, however, the appearance was deceptive, because of the way in which the population reacted to the ban.

An evaluation of the program by the World Bank found that, in the short run, the regulation was effective. Both pollution and congestion were reduced. However, in the long run the regulation was not only ineffective, it was counterproductive (paradoxically, it *increased* the level of congestion and pollution). The paradox resulted because a large number of residents reacted by buying an additional car (which would have a different license plate number and, therefore, be banned on a different day). Once the additional cars became available, total driving increased. Policies that are overly quick to anticipate and incorporate behavioral reactions run the risk that actual and expected outcomes may diverge considerably.

Source: Gunnar S. Eskeland and Tarhan Feyzioglu, "Rationing Can Backfire: The 'Day Without a Car Program' in Mexico City," World Bank Policy Research Working Paper 1554 (December 1995).

muters, thereby providing an incentive for passengers to switch from cars to buses.) Other possible policies focus on removing the parking subsidy. One proposal would require employers that currently supply parking to begin offering employees a choice between either free parking or the equivalent value in cash. Another would treat a parking subsidy as taxable income. A third approach would require employers to charge those using the service to pay the full cost of parking.

New policies are also beginning to consider how to assure that road users pay all the costs of maintaining the highways, rather than transferring that burden to taxpayers generally. One strategy, which has been implemented in Mexico and in Orange County, California, is to allow construction of new private toll roads. The tolls are set high enough to recover all consumption and maintenance costs and, in some cases, may include congestion pricing.

A final reform possibility involves the implementation of strategies to accelerate the retirement of older, more heavily polluting vehicles. This could be accomplished either by raising the cost of holding on to older vehicles (e.g., with higher registration fees for vehicles that pollute more) or by providing a bounty of some sort to those retiring heavily polluting vehicles early.

One version of the bounty program has become known as "cash for clunkers." Under this program, stationary sources are allowed to claim emission reduction credits (ERCs) for heavily polluting vehicles that are removed from service. In one version of the program, heavily polluting vehicles are identified either by inspection and maintenance programs or remote sensing. A vehicle owner can bring his or her vehicle up to code, usually an expensive proposition, or can sell it to the company running the cash for clunkers program. Purchased vehicles are usually disassembled for parts and the remainder of the hulk is recycled. The number of ERCs earned by the company running the program depends on such factors as the remaining useful life of the car and the estimated number of miles it would be driven, and this number is generally controlled so that the transaction results in a net increase in air quality.

Retirement strategies would tend to counteract the tendency for vehicles to be used longer as a result of the new-source focus of current automotive regulations. By eliminating these heavily polluting vehicles from the fleet earlier than would otherwise be the case, greater emission reductions could be achieved at an earlier date. This approach could be applied selectively in those local areas for which it could make a significant difference.

We also have learned some things about what doesn't work very well. One increasingly common strategy involves limiting the days any particular vehicle can be used in order to limit miles traveled. As Example 16.6 indicates, this strategy can backfire!

SUMMARY

The current U.S. policy toward motor vehicle emissions blends point-of-production control with point-of-use control, but the existing blend seems quite removed from what efficiency or cost-effectiveness would dictate. The history of legislation in this area has been a turbulent one, moving from a low federal profile (concerned mainly with studying the problem and assisting states) to a high federal profile (involving a preemptive responsibility for emission controls).

In a period of frustration, Congress wrote such a tough law that little was accomplished during the early years. The ambient standards could not be met by the deadlines. The sanctions used for noncompliance were so severe that the EPA was reluctant to use them. Because they were not a credible threat, the sanctions did little to alter behavior.

The focus on new source controls has caused the problem of people using older, more heavily polluting cars, and thereby has, in effect, delayed significant improvements in air quality. In addition, the technologies chosen by the manufacturers to meet their statutory responsibilities have failed to prevent a deterioration in operating-vehicle emission rates.

The U.S. national emission standards, which represent the core of the current approach in the United States and Europe, seem inefficient, for two rather different reasons: (1) According to benefit-cost calculations, they are too stringent; and (2) with the exception of California, they are uniform. These two inefficiencies are somewhat related. The controls are too stringent primarily because they require cars not contributing to nonattainment to bear the same cost of controls borne by those that do contribute. The current high standards cause these costs to be large. Thus, if uniform standards are to be retained, they probably should be lower.

Uniform emission standards, however, cannot be fully cost effective, whatever their stringency level. Cost-effectiveness requires that there be higher control costs in those areas that have real difficulty in meeting the ambient standards than in the rest of the country. Uniform emission standards do not make this crucial distinction.

Likewise, local approaches relying on inspection or maintenance are not generally cost effective. Some areas are currently required to establish these programs, whether doing so facilitates attainment or not. Other areas could find stationary-source control cheaper, but these areas, under current rules, are not allowed to substitute one for the other.

Despite the policy imperfections mobile-source pollutant concentrations and emissions (with the exception of ozone) have generally improved in the industrialized nations. The picture is bleaker in developing nations, where control levels are low and increases in vehicle ownership are rapid.

For many nonattainment areas, current policy has clearly not been enough to guarantee that the ambient standards are met. In part, the emissions standards themselves are at fault. Defined in terms of emissions per mile, they are powerless to prevent increases in emissions resulting from growth in the number of vehicles on the road or growth in the number of miles driven, or both. As the population expands, carrying with it an expansion in the number of vehicles on the road, air quality necessarily deteriorates—even if every car has met the standards. As suburban communities expand farther and farther from the urban center, the average number of miles driven per driver increases. Each mile driven contributes more emissions.

Appropriate regulation of emissions from mobile sources requires a great deal more effort and thought than does controlling emissions at the factory. Vehicle purchases, driving behavior, fuel choice, and even residential and employment locations must eventually be affected by the need to reduce mobile-source emissions. The historic low cost of auto travel has led to a very dispersed pattern of development. Because dispersed patterns of development make mass transit a less viable alternative, a downward spiral of population dispersal and the decline of mass transit occurs. In the long run, part of the strategy for meeting ambient standards will necessarily involve changing land-use patterns in order to create the kind of high-density travel corridors that are compatible with effective mass-transit use. That, of course, will only evolve over a long period of time, but ensuring that the true social costs of transportation are borne by those making residential location and transportation decisions will start the process moving in the right direction. The choices facing automobile owners can only be affected if the economic incentives associated with those choices are structured correctly.

Innovative policies aimed specifically at restructuring these incentives may fill the bill. A manufacturer's incentive to provide new types of vehicles would be greatly affected by the anticipated size of the market and the speed with which the new vehicles penetrate that market. In the absence of some kind of economic incentive, consumers will typically wait as long as possible to adopt new technologies because of fears about reliability and cost. Differential taxation, such as that used in Europe, can be used to speed up the rate of adoption.

Local approaches, such as those currently being implemented in many parts of the world, represent another point of departure. Using the price system to remove the parking subsidy, to allocate road maintenance costs to users, to internalize the costs of congestion and pollution, and to subside the removal of especially heavily polluting vehicles from the roadways can begin to internalize the full costs of road transport. Once that occurs, the playing field will have been leveled, and alternative modes of travel can compete effectively.

FURTHER READING

Button, Kenneth J. *Market and Government Failures in Environmental Management: The Case of Transport* (Paris: Organization for Economic Co-operation and Development, 1992). Analyzes and documents the types of government interventions—such as pricing, taxation and regulations—that often result in environmental degradation.

MacKenzie, James J., Roger C. Dower, and Donald D. T. Chen. *The Going Rate: What it Really Costs to Drive* (Washington, DC: World Resources Institute, 1992). Explores the full cost of a transportation system dominated by the automobile.

MacKenzie, James J. *The Keys to the Car: Electric and Hydrogen Vehicles for the Twenty-First Century* (Washington, DC: World Resources Institute, 1994). Surveys the environmental and economic costs and benefits of alternative fuels and alternative vehicles.

OECD. *Cars and Climate Change* (Paris: Organization for Economic Co-operation and Development and the International Energy Agency, 1993). Examines the possibilities, principally from enhanced energy efficiency and alternative fuels, for reducing greenhouse emissions from the transport sector.

ADDITIONAL REFERENCES

Dobes, L., "Kyoto: Tradeable Greenhouse Emission Permits in the Transport Sector." *Transport Reviews* 19(1)(1999): 81–97.

Forkenbrock, D. J., and L. A. Schweitzer. "Environmental Justice in Transportation Planning," *Journal of the American Planning Association* 65(1)(1999): 96–111.

Hahn, Robert W. and Gordon L. Hester. "Marketable Permits: Lessons for Theory and Practice," *Ecology Law Quarterly* 16 (1989): 380–91.

McConnell, Virginia D. "A Social Cost-Benefit Study of the Maryland Vehicle Emissions Inspection Program, Maryland Institute for Policy Analysis and Research (1986).

National Commission on Air Quality. *To Breathe Clean Air* (Washington, DC: Government Printing Office, 1981).

Reitze, Arnold W., Jr. "Controlling Automotive Air Pollution through Inspection and Maintenance Programs," *George Washington Law Review* 47 (May 1979): 724–36.

Walls, M., and J. Hanson. "Distributional Aspects of an Environmental Tax Shift: The Case of Motor Vehicle Emission Taxes," *National Tax Journal* 52(1)(1999): 53–65.

WEB SITES OF INTEREST

1. *http://www.hhh.umn.edu/centers/slp/conpric/conpric.htm*
   Congestion pricing home page.

2. *http://www.gov.sg/*
   Singapore's land transport authority.

3. *http://www.cnie.org/nle/air-25.html*
   A Report on vehicle retirement strategies.

DISCUSSION QUESTIONS

1. When a threshold concentration is used as the basis for pollution control as it is for air pollution, one possibility for meeting the threshold at minimum cost is to spread the emissions out over time. One way to accomplish this is to establish a peak-hour pricing system in which the charges for emissions during peak periods are higher.

   a. Would this represent a move toward efficiency or not? Why?

   b. What effects should this policy have on mass-transit usage, gasoline sales, downtown shopping, and travel patterns?

2. What are the advantages and disadvantages of using an increase in the gasoline tax to move transport decisions toward both efficiency and sustainability?

17

Water Pollution

It was the best of times, it was the worst of times, it was the age of wisdom, it was the age of foolishness, it was the epoch of belief, it was the epoch of incredulity. . . .

CHARLES DICKENS, *A TALE OF TWO CITIES* (1859)

◆ INTRODUCTION

Although various types of pollution have common attributes, important differences are apparent as well. These differences form the basis for the elements of policy unique to each pollutant. We have seen, for example, that although the types of pollutants emitted by mobile and stationary sources are often identical, the policy approaches differ considerably.

Water pollution control has its own unique characteristics as well. Two stand out as having particular relevance for policy:

1. Recreation benefits are much more important for water pollution control than for air pollution control.[1]

2. Large economies of scale in treating sewage and other wastes create the possibility for large, centralized treatment plants as one control strategy, whereas for air pollution, on-site control is the standard approach.

---

[1]See Daniel Feenberg and Edwin S. Mills, *Measuring the Benefits of Water Pollution Abatement* (New York: Academic Press, 1980): 164.

These characteristics create a need for yet another policy approach. In this chapter we shall explore the problems and prospects for controlling this unique and important form of pollution.

◆ THE NATURE OF WATER POLLUTION PROBLEMS

Types of Waste-Receiving Water

Two primary types of water are susceptible to contamination. The first, *surface water,* consists of the rivers, lakes, and oceans covering most of the earth's surface. In the past, policy makers have focused almost exclusively on preventing and cleaning up lake and river water pollution. Only recently has ocean pollution received the attention it deserves.

Groundwater, once considered a pristine resource, has been shown to be subject to considerable contamination from toxic chemicals. *Groundwater* is subsurface water that occurs beneath a water table in soils or rocks, or in geological formations that are fully saturated.

Groundwater is a vast natural resource. It has been estimated that the volume of groundwater is approximately 50 times the annual flow of surface water.[2] Though groundwater currently supplies only 25 percent of the freshwater used for all purposes in the United States, its use is increasing more rapidly than the use of surface water. Groundwater is used primarily for irrigation and as a source of drinking water.

Surface water also serves as a significant source of drinking water, but it has many other uses as well. Recreational benefits such as swimming, fishing, and boating are important determinants of surface-water policy in areas where the water is not used for drinking.

Sources of Contamination

Contamination of groundwater occurs when polluting substances leach into a water-saturated region. Many potential contaminants are removed by filtration and adsorption as the water moves slowly through the layers of rock and soil. Toxic organic chemicals are one major example of a type of pollutant that may not be filtered out during migration. Once these substances enter groundwater, very little, if any, further cleansing takes place. Moreover, because the rate of replenishment for many groundwater sources is small relative to the stock, very little mixing and dilution of the contaminants occurs (see Example 17.1).

Although some contamination has been accidental—the product of unintended and unexpected waste migration to water supplies—a portion of the contamination was deliberate. Watercourses were simply a convenient place to dump municipal or private sewage and industrial wastes. Along the shoreline of many lakes or rivers, pipes dumping human or industrial wastes directly into the water were a common occurrence before laws limiting this activity were enacted and enforced.

For lake and river pollution policy purposes it is useful to distinguish between two sources of contamination—point and nonpoint sources—even though the distinction is not always crystal clear. *Point sources* generally discharge into surface waters at a specific location through a pipe, an outfall, or a ditch, whereas *nonpoint sources* usually affect the water in a more indirect and diffuse way. From the policy point of view, nonpoint sources are more difficult to control and have received little legislative attention. As a result of the gains made

---

[2]Council on Environmental Quality, *Environmental Quality—1980* (Washington, DC: Government Printing Office, 1980): 83.

Example 17.1

Incidents of Groundwater Pollution

Traditional federal policies have paid little attention to groundwater, partly because of the high cost of testing and monitoring. Recent data, however, have shown that groundwater in many locations is contaminated by toxic chemicals. This may be posing unacceptable health risks for the public, because groundwater is widely used for drinking water. Many of the chemicals now being discovered in drinking water are either known or suspected carcinogens or mutagens.

Recently discovered incidents of groundwater contamination by toxic organic substances include the following:

1. In 1979 the Massachusetts Legislative Commission on Water Supply found that at least one third of the 351 communities in the commonwealth were affected by chemical contamination of drinking water, and wells were restricted or closed in 22 towns.

2. All wells in Groveland and Rowley, Massachusetts, were closed because of contamination by trichloroethylene (TCE), a known carcinogen in animals.

3. In January 1980, California public health officials closed 37 public wells that supplied water to 400,000 people in the San Gabriel Valley because of TCE contamination.

4. The New York Public Interest Research Group (NYPIRG) documented that all three major aquifers under Long Island were seriously contaminated with effluent from industrial wastes, municipal treatment plants, and runoff from highways. It also found evidence of mutagenic substances in 12 groundwater sites.

5. In 1993 arsenic was discovered in the city well serving Murray City, Utah. The city blamed a former mining site for the contamination.

Source: Council on Environmental Quality, *Environmental Quality—1980* (Washington, DC: U.S. Government Printing Office, 1980): 81–83 and World Resources Institute, *The 1994 Information Please Environmental Almanac* (Boston: Houghton Mifflin, 1994).

in controlling point sources, nonpoint sources now compose over half of the waste load borne by the nation's waters.

Rivers and Lakes. The most important nonpoint sources of pollution for rivers and lakes are agricultural activity, urban storm-water runoff, silviculture, and individual disposal systems. Contamination from agriculture has been attributed to eroded topsoil, pesticides, and fertilizer. Urban storm-water runoff contains a number of pollutants, including, typically, high quantities of lead. Forestry, if not carefully done, can contribute to soil erosion and, by removing shade cover, could have a large impact on the temperature of normally shaded streams. In the developing countries, more than 95 percent of urban sewage is discharged into surface waters without treatment.

The contamination of groundwater supplies usually results from the migration of harmful substances from sites where high concentrations of chemicals can be found. These include industrial waste storage sites, landfills, and farms.

The primary point sources are industries and municipalities. The primary nonpoint sources involve agricultural activities of one form or another.

Ocean Pollution.   The two primary sources of ocean pollution discussed in this chapter are oil spills and ocean dumping. Because a great deal of oil is transported over the oceans and is produced from platforms exploiting fields under the ocean, oil spills have become a more common occurrence (see Table 17.1). Various unwanted by-products of modern life have also been dumped in ocean waters based upon the mistaken belief that the vastness of the oceans allowed them to absorb large quantities of waste without suffering noticeable damage. Dumped materials have included sewage and sewage sludge, unwanted chemicals, trace metals, and even radioactive materials.

Types of Pollutants

For our purposes, the large number of water pollutants can be usefully classified by means of the taxonomy we developed earlier and review below.

Fund Pollutants.   *Fund pollutants* are those for which the environment has some assimilative capacity. If the absorptive capacity is high enough relative to the rate of injection, such pollutants may not accumulate at all. One type of fund water pollutants is called *degradable* because it degrades, or breaks into its component parts, within the water. Degradable wastes are normally organic residuals that are attacked and broken down by bacteria in the stream.

TABLE 17.1   Notable Oil Spills

Source and Location	Date	Tons Spilled
Ixtoc I oil well, southern Gulf of Mexico	3 June 1979	600,000
Nowruz oil field, Persian Gulf	February 1983	600,000 (est.)
Atlantic Express and *Aegean Captain,* off Trinidad & Tobago	19 July 1979	300,000
Castillo de Beliver, off Cape Town, South Africa	6 August 1983	250,000
Amoco Cadiz, near Portsall, France	16 March 1978	223,000
Torrey Canyon, off Land's End, England	18 March 1967	119,000
Sea Star, Gulf of Oman	19 December 1972	115,000
Urquiola, La Coruna, Spain	12 May 1976	100,000
Hawaiian Patriot, northern Pacific	25 February 1977	99,000
Othella, Tralhavet Bay, Sweden	20 March 1970	60,000–100,000
World Glory, off South Africa	13 June 1968	46,000
Burmah Agate, Galveston Bay, Texas	1 November 1979	36,400
Exxon Valdez, Prince William Sound, Alaska	24 March 1989	34,300

Source: Reprinted with permission from The World Almanac And Book of Facts 1990. Copyright © 1989 World Almanac Education Group. All rights reserved.

The process by which organic wastes are broken down into component parts consumes oxygen. The amount of oxygen consumed depends upon the magnitude of the waste load. All of the higher life forms in watercourses are *aerobic;* that is, they require oxygen for survival. As a stream's oxygen level falls, fish mortality increases, with the less tolerant fish becoming the first to succumb. The oxygen level can become low enough that even the aerobic bacteria die. When this happens, the stream becomes *anaerobic,* and the ecology changes drastically. This is an extremely unpleasant circumstance, because the stream takes on a dark hue and the stream water stinks!

To control these waste loads, two different types of monitoring are needed: (1) monitoring the ambient conditions in the watercourse, and (2) monitoring the magnitude of emissions. The measure commonly used to keep track of ambient conditions for these conventional fund pollutants is *dissolved oxygen* (DO). The amount of dissolved oxygen in a body of water is a function of ambient conditions, such as temperature, stream flow, and the waste load.[3] The measure of the oxygen demand placed on a stream by any particular volume of effluent is called the *biochemical oxygen demand* (BOD).

Using modeling techniques, emissions (measured as BOD) at a certain point can be translated into DO measures at various receptor locations along a stream. This step is necessary in order to tailor the degree of control to the amount of damage caused by the emissions.

If we were to develop a profile of DO readings in a stream where organic effluent is being injected, that profile would typically exhibit one or more minimum points called *oxygen sags*. These oxygen sags represent locations along the stream where the DO content is lower than at other points. An ambient permit or ambient charge system would be designed to reach a desired DO level at those sag points, whereas an emission permit or emission charge system would simply try to hit a particular BOD reduction target. The former would take the location of the emitter into account; the latter would not. Later in this chapter we will examine studies that model these systems on particular watercourses.

A second type of fund pollutant, *thermal pollution,* is caused by the injection of heat into a watercourse. Typically, thermal pollution is caused when an industrial plant or electric utility uses surface water as a coolant, returning the heated water to the watercourse. This heat is dissipated in the receiving waters by evaporation. By raising the temperature of the water near the outfall, thermal pollution lowers the DO content and can result in dramatic ecological changes in that area.

Yet another example if provided by a class of pollutants, such as nitrogen and phosphorus, that are plant nutrients. These pollutants stimulate the growth of aquatic plant life, such as algae and water weeds. In excess, these plants can produce odor, taste, and aesthetic problems. A lake with an excessive supply of nutrients is called *eutrophic.*

The various types of fund pollutants could be ordered on a spectrum. On one end of the spectrum would be pollutants for which the environment has a very large absorptive capacity, on the other end pollutants for which the absorptive capacity is virtually nil. The limiting case—those for which the environment has no absorptive capacity—are *stock pollutants.*

---

[3]The danger of anaerobic conditions is highest in the late summer and early fall, when temperatures are high and the stream flow is low.

Near the end of that spectrum is a class of inorganic synthetic chemicals called *persistent pollutants.* These substances are so-named because their complex molecular structures are not effectively broken down in the stream. Some degradation takes place, but so slowly that these pollutants can travel long distances in water in a virtually unchanged form.

These persistent pollutants accumulate, not only in the watercourses, but in the food chain as well. The concentration levels in the tissues of living organisms rise with the order of the species. Concentrations in lower life forms such as plankton may be relatively small, but, because small fish eat a lot of plankton and do not excrete the inorganic synthetic chemicals, the concentrations in small fish would be higher. The magnification continues as large fish consume small fish; concentration levels in the larger fish would be even higher.

Because they accumulate in the food chain, persistent pollutants present an interesting monitoring challenge. The traditional approach involves measurements of pollutant concentration in the water, but that is not the only variable of interest. The damage is related not only to its concentration in the water, but its concentration in the food chain as well. Although monitoring the environmental effects of these pollutants may be more compelling than monitoring other pollutants, it is also more difficult.

A final type of fund pollutant, comprising infectious organisms such as bacteria and viruses, is carried into surface and groundwater by domestic and animal wastes and by wastes from such industries as tanning and meat packing. These live organisms may thrive and multiply in water, or their population may decline over time, depending upon how hospitable or hostile the watercourse is for continued growth.

Accumulating Pollutants. The most troublesome cases result when pollutants accumulate in the environment. No natural process removes or transforms stock pollutants; the watercourse cannot cleanse itself of them.

Inorganic chemicals and minerals comprise the main examples of stock pollutants. Perhaps the most notorious members of this group are the heavy metals, such as lead, cadmium, and mercury. Extreme examples of poisoning by these metals have occurred in Japan. One ocean-dumping case was responsible for *Minamata disease,* named for the location where it occurred. Some 52 people died and 150 others suffered serious brain and nerve damage. Scientists puzzled for years over the source of the ailments, until it was traced to an organic form of mercury that had accumulated in the tissues of fish eaten three times a day by local residents.

In another case in Japan, involving the *Itai Itai* (literally, "ouch-ouch") *disease,* scientists traced the source of a previously undiagnosed, extremely painful bone disease to the ingestion of cadmium. Nearby mines were the source of the cadmium, which apparently was ingested by eating contaminated rice and soybeans.

As is typical with persistent pollutants, some of the stock pollutants are difficult to monitor. Those accumulated in the food chains give rise to the same problem as is presented by persistent pollutants. Ambient sampling must be supplemented by sampling tissues from members of the food chain. To further complicate matters, the heavy metals may sink rapidly to the bottom of the water body, remaining in the sediment. Although they could be detected in sediment samples, merely drawing samples from the water itself would allow these pollutants to escape detection.

◆ WATER POLLUTION CONTROL POLICY

Traditional Water Pollution Control Policy

Water pollution control policies vary around the world. In this section we begin with a somewhat detailed discussion of U.S. policy that provides a rather rich example of a typical legal approach to regulation. This is followed by a discussion of the European approach, which depends more heavily on economic incentives.

U.S. policy for water pollution control predates federal air pollution control. We might suppose that the policy for water pollution control would, therefore, be superior, because authorities have had more time to profit from earlier mistakes. Unfortunately, that is not the case.

Early Legislation

The first federal legislation dealing with discharge into the nation's waterways occurred when Congress passed the 1899 Refuse Act. Designed primarily to protect navigation, this act focused on preventing any discharge that would interfere with using rivers as transport links. All discharges into a river were prohibited unless approved by a permit from the Chief of the U.S. Engineers. Most permits were issued to contractors dredging the rivers, and they dealt mainly with the disposal of the removed material. This act was virtually unenforced for other pollutants until 1970, when the permit program was "rediscovered" and used briefly (with little success) as the basis for federal enforcement actions.

The Water Pollution Control Act of 1948 represented the first attempt by the federal government to exercise some direct influence over what previously had been a state and local function. A hesitant move, because it reaffirmed that the primary responsibility for water pollution control rested with the states, it did initiate the authority of the federal government to conduct investigations, research, and surveys.

The first hints of the current approach are found in the Amendments to the Water Pollution Control Act, which were passed in 1956. Two provisions of this act were especially important: (1) federal financial support for the construction of waste treatment plants and (2) direct federal regulation of waste discharges via a mechanism known as the *enforcement conference*.

The first of these provisions envisioned a control strategy based on subsidizing the construction of a particular control activity—waste treatment plants. Municipalities could receive federal grants to cover up to 55 percent of the construction of municipal sewage treatment plants. This approach not only lowered the cost to the local government of constructing these facilities, it also lowered the cost to users. Because the federal government contribution was a grant, rather than a loan, the fees charged users did not reflect the federally subsidized construction portion of the cost. The user fees were set at a lower rate, one that was only high enough to cover the unsubsidized portion of the construction cost as well as the operating and maintenance costs.

The 1956 amendments envisioned a relatively narrow federal role in the regulation of discharges. Initially, only polluters contributing to interstate pollution were included, but subsequent laws have broadened the coverage. By 1961 discharges into all navigable water were covered.

The mechanism created by the Amendments of 1956 to enforce the regulation of discharges was the enforcement conference. Under this approach, the designated federal control authority could call for a conference to deal with any interstate water pollution problem or could be requested to do so by the governor of an affected state. Because this authority was discretionary (not mandatory) and the control authority had very few means of enforcing any decisions reached, the conferences did not achieve the intended results.

The Water Quality Act of 1965 attempted to improve the process by establishing ambient water quality standards for interstate watercourses and by requiring states to file implementation plans. This sounds like the approach currently being used in air pollution control, but there are important differences. The plans forthcoming from states in response to the 1965 act were vague and did not attempt to link specific effluent standards on discharge to the ambient standards. They generally took the easy way out and called for secondary treatment, which removes 80 to 90 percent of BOD and 85 percent of suspended solids. The fact that these standards bore no particular relationship to ambient quality made them difficult to enforce in the courts, because the legal authority for them was based on this relationship.

Subsequent Legislation

Point Sources.   As discussed in the preceding chapters, an air of frustration regarding pollution control pervaded Washington in the 1970s. In terms of water pollution legislation, as with air pollution legislation, this frustration led to the enactment of a very tough Clean Water Act. The tone of the act is established immediately in the preamble, which calls for the achievement of two goals: (1) "that the discharge of pollutants into the navigable waters by eliminated by 1985"; and (2) "that wherever attainable, an interim goal of water quality which provides for the protection and propagation of fish, shellfish, and wildlife and provides for recreation in and on the water be achieved by June 1, 1983." The stringency of these goals represented a major departure from past policy.

This act also introduced new procedures for implementing the law. Permits were required of all dischargers (replacing the 1899 Refuse Act, which, because of its navigation focus, was difficult to enforce). The permits would be granted only when the dischargers met certain technology-based effluent standards. The ambient standards were completely bypassed, as these effluent standards were uniformly imposed and so could not depend upon local water conditions.[4]

According to the 1972 Amendments, the effluent standards were to be implemented in two stages. By 1977, industrial dischargers, as a condition of their permits, were required to meet effluent limitations based on the "best practicable control technology currently available" (BPT). In setting these national standards, the EPA was required to consider the total costs of these technologies and their relation to the benefits received, but not to consider the conditions of the individual source or the particular waters into which it was discharged. In addition, all publicly owned treatment plants were to have achieved secondary treatment by 1977. By 1983, industrial discharges were required to meet effluent limitations based on the presumably more stringent "best available technology economically achievable" (BAT) and publicly owned treatment plants were required to meet effluent limitations that depended upon the "best practicable waste treatment technology."

---

[4]Actually the ambient standards were not completely bypassed. If the uniform controls were not sufficient to meet the desired standard, the effluent limitation would have to be tightened accordingly.

The program of subsidizing municipal water treatment plants, begun in 1956, was continued in a slightly modified form by the 1972 Act. Whereas the 1965 Act allowed the federal government to subsidize up to 55 percent of the cost of construction of waste treatment plants, the 1972 Act raised the ceiling to 75 percent. The 1972 Act also increased the funds available for this program. In 1981 the federal share was reduced to 55 percent.

The 1977 Amendments continued this regulatory approach, but with some major modifications. This legislation drew a more careful distinction between the conventional and toxic pollutants, with more stringent requirements placed on the latter, and it extended virtually all of the deadlines in the 1972 Act.

For conventional pollutants a new treatment standard was created to replace the BAT standards. The effluent limitations for these pollutants were to be based on the "best conventional technology," and the deadline for these standards was set at 1 July 1984. In setting these standards, the EPA was required to consider whether the costs of adding the pollution control equipment were reasonable when compared with the improvement in water quality. For unconventional pollutants and toxics (i.e., any pollutant not specifically included on the list of conventional pollutants), the BAT requirement was retained, but the deadline was shifted to 1984.

Other deadlines were also extended. The year by which municipalities had to meet the secondary treatment deadline was moved from 1977 to 1983. Industrial compliance with the BPT standards was delayed until 1983, or whenever the contemplated system had the potential for application throughout the industry.

The final modification made by the 1977 Amendments involved the introduction of pretreatment standards for waste being sent to a publicly owned treatment system. These standards were designed to prevent the discharges that could inhibit the treatment process and to prevent the introduction of toxic pollutants that would not be removed by the waste treatment facility. Existing facilities were required to meet the standards three years after their date of publication, and facilities constructed later would be required to meet the pretreatment regulations upon commencement of operations.

Nonpoint Sources.   In contrast to the control of point sources, the EPA was given no specific authority to regulate nonpoint sources. This type of pollution was seen by Congress as a state responsibility.

Section 208 of the Act authorized federal grants for state-initiated planning that would provide implementable plans for areawide waste treatment management. Section 208 further specified that this areawide plan must identify significant nonpoint sources of pollution, as well as procedures and methods for controlling them. The reauthorization of the Clean Water Act, passed over President Reagan's veto during February 1987, authorized an additional $400 million for a new program to help states control runoff, but it still left the chief responsibility for controlling nonpoint sources to the states.

One federal role for controlling nonpoint sources has been the Conservation Reserve Program. Designed to remove some 40 to 45 million acres of highly erodible land from cultivation, this act provides subsidies to farmers for planting grass or trees. The subsidies are designed to produce a nationwide reduction of total erosion and a reduction in nitrogen, phosphorus, and total suspended solid loadings.

The TDML Program

In 1999, recognizing the problems with both the technology-based national effluent standards and the growing importance of nonpoint pollution control, the USEPA proposed new rules designed to breathe fresh life into the previously unenforced Total Maximum Daily Load (TMDL) provisions of the Clean Water Act. A TMDL is a calculation of the maximum amount of a pollutant that a water body can receive and still meet water quality standards as well as an allocation of that amount to the pollutant's sources. The calculation must include a margin of safety to ensure that the water body can be used for its designated purpose. The calculation must also account for seasonable variation in water quality.

The TDML program moves water pollution control toward the ambient standard approach long used to control air pollution. Under this program water quality standards are promulgated by states, territories, and/or tribes. The promulgated standards are tailored to the designated uses for each water body (such as drinking water supply or recreation (swimming and/or fishing). The states must then undertake strategies for achieving the standards, including significantly bringing nonpoint source pollutants under control.

The Safe Drinking Water Act

The 1972 policy focused on achieving water quality sufficiently high for fishing and swimming. Because that quality is not high enough for drinking water, the Safe Drinking Water Act of 1974 issued more stringent standards for community water systems. The primary drinking water regulations set maximum allowable concentration levels for bacteria, turbidity (muddiness), and chemical or radiological contaminants. National secondary drinking water regulations were also established to protect "public welfare" from odor and aesthetic problems that might cause a substantial number of people to stop using the affected water system. The secondary standards are advisory for the states; they cannot be enforced by the EPA.

The 1986 Amendments required the EPA (1) to issue primary standards within three years for 83 contaminants and by 1991 for at least 25 more, (2) to set standards based on the BAT, and (3) to monitor public water systems for both regulated and unregulated chemical contaminants. Approximately 60,000 public water systems are subject to these regulations. Civil and criminal penalties for any violations of the standards were also increased by the Amendments.

Ocean Pollution

Oil Spills. The Clean Water Act prohibits discharges of "harmful quantities" of oil into navigable waters. Because the EPA regulations define *harmful* to include all discharges that "violate applicable water quality standards or cause a film or sheen upon the surface of the water," virtually all discharges are prohibited.

Industry responsibilities include complying with Coast Guard regulations (which deal with contingency planning in case of a spill and various accident avoidance requirements) and assuming the financial liability for any accident. If a spill does occur, it must be immediately reported to the Coast Guard or the EPA. Failure to report a spill can result in a fine of up to $10,000, imprisonment for not more than one year, or both.

In addition to giving notice, the discharger must either contain the spill or pay the cost of cleanup by a responsible government agency. The discharger's liability for the government's actual removal cost is limited to $50 million, unless willful negligence or willful misconduct can be proved. Successful proof of willful negligence or willful misconduct eliminates the liability limit. In addition to cleanup costs, removal costs also include compensation for damages to the natural resources. (*Natural resource damages* are defined as "any costs or expenses incurred by the federal government or any state government in the restoration or replacement of natural resources damaged or destroyed as a result of a discharge of oil.")

Ocean Dumping.   Except for oil spills, which are covered by the Clean Water Act, discharges to the ocean are covered by the Marine Protection Research and Sanctuaries Act of 1972. This act governs all discharges of wastes to ocean waters within U.S. territorial limits and discharges of wastes in ocean waters by U.S. vessels or persons, no matter where the dumping occurs. With only a few exceptions, no ocean dumping of industrial wastes or sewer sludge is now permitted.[5] Radiological, chemical, and biological warfare agents and high-level radioactive wastes are specifically prohibited by the statute. Under the amended statute, the only ocean-dumping activities permitted are the disposal of dredged soil. This dumping is subject to specific regulations and is approved on a case-by-case basis.

Private Enforcement

The degree to which environmental quality is improved by public policy depends not only on the types of policies, but also on how well those policies are enforced. Policies that seem to offer promise may prove unsuitable if enforcement is difficult or lax.

The enforcement of the environmental statutes has long been the responsibility of state and federal environmental agencies. Enforcement at the state and federal level occurs through administrative proceedings or through civil and criminal judicial action. Because limited staff and resources do not enable these government agencies to fully enforce all of the environmental statutes, these methods alone do not provide the necessary level of enforcement.

During the early 1970s, a pervasive recognition that the federal government had neither the time nor resources to provide sufficient enforcement led Congress to create a private alternative—*citizen suits.* Though citizen suits are now authorized by a number of different environmental statutes, the program has been particularly successful in enforcing the Clean Water Act.

Empowered as private attorneys general, citizens are authorized to exercise oversight over government actions and to initiate civil proceedings against any private or public polluter violating the terms of its effluent standard. Environmental groups such as the Natural Resources Defense Council and the Sierra Club have become active participants in the process. Citizens may sue for an injunction (a court order requiring the illegal discharge to cease); they are also given the power to "apply any appropriate civil penalties."[6] The amount of penalty can vary between $10,000 and $25,000 per day, per violation.

---

[5]Sewer sludge from New York City and its environs was the major exception, but the statute established a 1991 deadline for stopping this dumping.

[6]Clean Water Act, Section 505, U.S.C. 1365.

◆ EFFICIENCY AND COST-EFFECTIVENESS

Ambient Standards and the Zero Discharge Goal

The 1956 Amendments defined ambient standards as a means of quantifying the objective being sought. A system of ambient standards allows the control authority to tailor the quality of a particular body of water to its use. Water used for drinking would be subject to the highest standards, for swimming, the next highest, and so on. Once the ambient standards are defined, the control responsibility can be allocated among sources. Greater efforts to control pollution would be expended where the gap between desired and actual water quality was the largest.

Unfortunately, the early experience with ambient standards for water was not reassuring. Rather than strengthening the legal basis for the effluent standards while retaining their connection to the ambient standards, Congress chose to downgrade the importance of ambient standards by specifying a zero discharge goal. Additionally, the effluent standards were given their own legal status apart from any connection with ambient standards. The wrong inference was drawn from the early lack of legislative success. In his own inimitable style, Mark Twain put the essential point rather well:

> We should be careful to get out of an experience only the wisdom that is in it—and stop there; lest we be like the cat that sits down on a hot stove lid. She will never sit down on a hot stove lid again—and that is well; but also she will never sit down on a cold one anymore.[7]

The most fundamental problem with the current approach is that it rests on the faulty assumption that the tougher the law, the more that is accomplished. The zero discharge goal provides one example of a case in which passing a tough standard, in the hopes of actually achieving a weaker one, can backfire. Kneese and Schultze point out that in the late 1960s the French experimented with a law that required zero discharge and imposed severe penalties for violations.[8] The result was that the law was never enforced because it was universally viewed as unreasonable. Less control was accomplished under this law than would have been accomplished with a less stringent law that could have been enforced.

Is the U.S. case comparable? It appears to be. In 1972 the EPA published an estimate of the costs of meeting a zero discharge goal, assuming that it is feasible. They concluded that over the decade from 1971 to 1981, removing 85 to 90 percent of the pollutants from all industrial and municipal effluents would cost $62 billion. Removing all of the pollutants would cost $317 billion, more than 5 times as much, and this figure probably understates the true cost.[9]

Is this cost justified? Probably not for *all* pollutants, though for some it may be. Unfortunately, the zero discharge goal makes no distinction among pollutant types. For some fund pollutants it seems extreme. Perhaps the legislators realized this, because when the legislation

---

[7]Mark Twain, *Pudd'nhead Wilson* (New York: Harper, 1897): 125.

[8]Allen V. Kneese, and Charles L. Schultze, *Pollution, Prices, and Public Policy* (Washington, DC: Brookings Institution, 1975).

[9]Ibid., p. 78.

was drafted, no specific timetables or procedures were established to ensure that the zero discharge goal would be met by 1985 or, for that matter, anytime.

National Effluent Standards

The first prong in the two-pronged congressional attack on water pollution was the national effluent standards (the other being subsidies for the construction of publicly owned waste treatment facilities). Deciding on the appropriate levels for these standards for each of the estimated 60,000 sources is not a trivial task. It is not surprising that difficulties arose.

Enforcement Problems.   Soon after passage of the 1972 Amendments, the EPA geared up to assume its awesome responsibility. Relying on a battery of consultants, it began to study the technologies of pollution control available to each industry in order to establish reasonable effluent limits. In establishing the guidelines, the EPA is required to take into account "the age of the equipment and facilities involved, the process employed, the engineering aspects of the application of various types of control techniques, process changes, nonwater quality environmental impact (including energy requirements) and such factors as the Administrator deems appropriate."

It is not clear whether this provision means that individual standards should be specified for each source, or general standards for broad categories of sources. Cost-effectiveness would require the former, but in a system relying on effluent standards (however, not one relying on emission charges or permits), the transaction costs associated with that approach would be prohibitively high and the delay unacceptably long. Therefore, the EPA chose the only feasible interpretation available and established general standards for broad categories of sources. Although the standards could differ among categories, they were uniformly applied to the large number of sources within each category.

The EPA inevitably fell behind the congressional deadlines. In fact, not one effluent standard was published within the one-year deadline. As the standards were published, they were immediately challenged in the courts. By 1977 some 250 cases challenging the published standards were already pending.[10] Some of the challenges were successful, requiring the EPA to revise the standards. All of this took time.

By 1977 the EPA was having so much trouble defining the BPT standards that it became evident that the deadlines for the BAT standards were completely unreasonable. Furthermore, for conventional pollutants, not only the deadlines but the standards themselves were irrational. Many bodies of water would have met the ambient standards without the BAT standard, whereas for others the effluent standards were not sufficient, particularly in areas with large nonpoint pollution problems. In addition, in some cases the technologies required by BPT would not be compatible (or even necessary) once the BAT standards were in effect. The situation was in a shambles.

The 1977 Amendments changed both the timing of the BAT standards (delaying the deadlines) and their focus (toward toxic pollutants and away from conventional pollutants). As a result of these amendments, the EPA was required to develop industry effluent standards based on the BAT guidelines for control of 65 classes of toxic priority pollutants. In a 1979 survey, the EPA discovered that all primary industries regularly discharge one or more of

---

[10]A. Myrick Freeman III, "Air and Water Pollution Policy," in *Current Issues in U.S. Environmental Policy,* Paul R. Portney, ed. (Baltimore, MD: Johns Hopkins University Press, for Resources for the Future, 1978): 46.

these toxic pollutants. As of 1980 the EPA had proposed BAT effluent limitations for control of toxic priority pollutants for nine primary industries.

The 1977 Amendments certainly improved the situation. Because toxics represent a more serious problem, it makes sense to set stricter standards for those pollutants. Extension of the deadlines was absolutely necessary; there was no alternative. However, these amendments have not resulted in a cost-effective strategy. In particular, they tend to retard technological progress and to assign the responsibility for control in an unnecessarily expensive manner.

Allocating Control Responsibility. Because the effluent standards established by the EPA are based upon specific technologies, these technologies are known to the industries. Therefore, in spite of the fact that the industry can choose any technology that keeps emissions under the limitation stated in the standard, in practice, industries tend to choose the specific equipment cited by the EPA when it established the standard. This, they reason, minimizes their risk. If anything goes wrong and they are hauled into court, they can simply argue they did precisely what the EPA had in mind when it set the standard.

The problem with this reaction is that it focuses too narrowly on a particular technology rather than on the real objective, emission reduction. The focus should be less on the purchase of a specific technology and more on doing what is necessary to hold emissions down, such as maintenance, process changes, and so on. In a field undergoing rapid technological change, tying all control efforts to a particular technology (which may become obsolete well before the standards are revised) is a poor strategy. Unfortunately, and to the detriment of securing clean water, technological stagnation has become a routine side effect of the current policy.

In allocating the control responsibility among various sources, the EPA was constrained by the inherent difficulty of making unique determinations for each source and by limitations in the Act itself, such as the need to apply relatively uniform standards. We know that uniform effluent standards are not cost effective, but it remains an open question whether or not the resulting increases in cost are sufficiently large to recommend an alternative approach, such as effluent charges or permits. The fact that the cost increases are large in the control of stationary-source air pollution does not automatically imply that they are large for water pollution control as well.

A number of empirical studies have investigated how closely the national effluent standards approximate the least-cost allocation (Table 17.2). These studies support the contention that the EPA standards are not cost effective, though the degree of cost-ineffectiveness is typically smaller than that associated with the standards used to control air pollution.

TABLE 17.2 Cost of Treatment Under Alternative Programs: The Delaware Estuary

	Program	
Dissolved Oxygen Objective (ppm)	*Least Cost ($ million/yr)*	*Uniform Treatment ($ million/yr)*
2	1.6	5.0
3–4	7.0	20.0

Source: From *Economics and the Environment* by Allen V. Kneese. Copyright © 1977 Allen V. Kneese. Reproduced by permission of Penguin Books, Ltd. and the author.

Perhaps the most famous study examining the cost-effectiveness of uniform standards was conducted on the Delaware Estuary.[11] This river basin, though small by the standards of the Mississippi or other major basins, drains an area serving a population in excess of 6 million people. It is a highly industrial, densely populated area.

In the study a simulation model was constructed to capture the effect on ambient DO content of a variety of pollutants discharged by a large number of polluters into the river at numerous locations. In addition, this model was capable of simulating the cost consequences of various methods used to allocate the responsibility for controlling effluent to meet DO standards.

The traditional approach was compared with the least-cost (LC) approach. Under the *uniform treatment* (UT) strategy, all discharges were faced with an effluent standard requiring them to remove a given percentage of their waste before discharging the remainder into the river. This method mirrors, in a crude way, the current EPA strategy. The LC strategy simply allocated the responsibility cost effectively.

For control of water pollution, this evidence suggests that the UT strategy does increase the cost substantially. For either DO objective, the costs are roughly three times higher.

Despite this evidence, the regulatory reform movement that played such an important role for air pollution control has not had anywhere near the same impact on water pollution control. Aside from the Fox River in Wisconsin (see Example 17.2), few examples exist.

The European Experience.   Economic incentives have been important in water pollution control in Europe, where effluent charges play a prominent role in a number of countries.[12] These charge systems take a number of forms. One common approach is illustrated by Czechoslovakia, which uses charges to achieve predetermined ambient standards. Others, such as the former West Germany, use charges mainly to encourage firms to control more than their legal requirements.

Czechoslovakia has used effluent charges to maintain water quality at predetermined levels for several decades. A basic charge is placed on BOD and suspended solids and is complemented by a surface ranging from 10 to 100 percent, depending upon the contribution of the individual discharge to ambient pollutant concentrations. The basic rates can be adjusted to reflect the quality of the receiving water. This system is conceptually very close to the ambient emission charge system, which is known to be cost effective.

The West German charge system was announced in 1976 and implemented in 1981. Under this system, the level of charge is related to the degree of compliance with the standards. Firms failing to meet their required standards pay a charge on all actual emissions. If, according to the issued permit, federal emission standards (which are separately defined for each industrial sector) are met, the charge is lowered to 50 percent of the base rate and is ap-

---

[11]This study is described in some detail in Allen V. Kneese and Blair T. Bower, *Managing Water Quality: Economics, Technology, Institutions* (Baltimore, MD: Johns Hopkins University Press, 1968): Chapter 11; and Allen V. Kneese, *Economics and the Environment* (New York: Penguin Books, 1977).

[12]For a summary of this experience, see Frederick R. Anderson et al., *Environmental Improvement Through Economic Incentives* (Baltimore, MD: Johns Hopkins University Press, for Resources for the Future, 1977): 59–68; and J. B. Opschoor and Hans B. Vos, *Economic Instruments for Environmental Protection* (Paris: Organization for Economic Co-operation and Development, 1989).

Example 17.2

Marketable Emission Permits on the Fox River

With the advent of the bubble and offset policies, marketable emission permits have become the centerpiece of the regulatory reform movement in air pollution control. Though no comparable scale of reform exists for control of water pollution, one attempt has been initiated in northern Wisconsin.

The Lower Fox River flows from Lake Winnebago to Green Bay, Wisconsin. Lining the banks of a key 22-mile segment of this river are 10 pulp and paper mills and 4 municipalities that discharge effluent into the river. During the summer the desired DO targets are not reached at two critical sag points, even when the industrial polluters are in compliance with BPT standards and the municipal polluters are providing secondary treatment.

The Wisconsin Department of Natural Resources was faced with meeting the standards in the face of industrial resistance. To assist in choosing a policy strategy, it funded a simulation model of the river to compare traditional regulatory rules with a marketable-permit system.

This model revealed significant differences among dischargers, a precondition if the market approach is to reach the environmental goals at a significantly lower cost. Under traditional abatement rules, marginal abatement costs differed by a factor of 4. The study concluded that the control costs would be some 40 percent higher if the department were to rely on traditional abatement rules. The potential annual saving realized from a permit approach was estimated at $6.7 million.

In March 1981 the department approved regulations allowing dischargers on the Lower Fox River to transfer permits by approved contracts. By 1982 the first trade had already taken place, but that also proved to be the only trade prior to 1990. The system clearly has not lived up to expectations, an experience that probably will inhibit any expansion of the concept to other geographic areas.

Source: This example was drawn from William B. O'Neill, "Pollution Permits, and Markets for Water Quality," an unpublished Ph.D. dissertation completed at the University of Wisconsin–Madison, 1980, and subsequent conversations with the author.

plied to the level of discharge implied by the minimum standard. If the firm can prove the discharge to be lower than 75 percent of minimum standards, one half of the base rate is applied to the (lower) actual discharge level. The charge is waived for three years prior to the installation of new pollution control equipment promising further reductions of at least 20 percent. Revenues from the charges can be used by the administering authorities for covering administrative costs and for financial assistance to public and private pollution-abatement activities.

Though these European approaches differ from one to another and are not all cost effective, their existence suggests that effluent charge systems are possible and practical. The German Council of Experts on Environmental Questions estimated the German effluent charge policy to be about one-third cheaper for the polluters as a group than an otherwise comparable uniform treatment policy. Furthermore, the policy encouraged firms to go beyond the uniform standards when the cost of such effort was justified.

Municipal Waste Treatment Subsidies

The second phase of the two-pronged water pollution control program involves subsidies for waste treatment plants. This program has run into problems as well, ranging from deficiencies in the allocation of the subsidies to the incentives created by the program.

The Allocation of Funds.   Because the available funds were initially allocated on a first-come, first-served basis, it is not surprising that the funds were not spent in areas having the greatest impact. It was not uncommon, for example, for completed treatment plants to dump effluent that was significantly cleaner than the receiving water. Also, federal funds have traditionally been concentrated on smaller, largely suburban communities rather than the larger cities with the most serious pollution problems.

The 1977 Amendments attempted to deal with this problem by requiring states to set priorities for funding treatment works while giving the EPA the right, after holding public hearings, not only to veto a state's priority list but to request a revised list. This tendency to ensure that the funds are allocated to projects having the highest priority was reinforced with the passage of the Municipal Wastewater Treatment Construction Grant Amendments of 1981. Under this act, states are required to establish project priorities that target funds to projects with the most significant water quality and public health consequences.

Operation and Maintenance.   The current approach subsidizes the *construction* of treatment facilities but provides no incentive for *operating* them effectively. The existence of a municipal waste treatment plant does not, by itself, guarantee cleaner water. The EPA's annual inspection surveys of operating plants in 1976 and 1977 found only about half of the plants performing satisfactorily. More recent surveys have found that the general levels of waste treatment performance has remained substantially unchanged from previous years.

When sewage treatment plants chronically or critically malfunction, the EPA may take a city to court in order to force compliance with a direct order or a fine. Because of various constitutional legal barriers, it is very difficult to force a city to pay a fine to the federal treasury. Without an effective and credible sanction, the EPA is in a difficult position when dealing with municipalities. Therefore, the resolution of the treatment plant malfunction problem cannot yet be pronounced with any assurance.

Capital Costs.   Because of the federal subsidies, local areas ended up paying only a fraction of the true cost of constructing these facilities. Because much of the money came from federal taxpayers, local communities had less incentive to hold construction costs down. One study estimated that substantially increasing the local share could reduce capital costs by as much as 30 percent.[13] Local areas are more careful with their own money.

---

[13]Congressional Budget Office, *Efficient Investments in Wastewater Treatment Plants* (Washington, DC: U.S. Congress, 1985).

Pretreatment Standards

To deal with hazardous wastes entering municipal waste treatment plants that cannot be treated or removed by those plants, the EPA has defined *pretreatment standards* regulating the quality of the wastewater flowing into the plants. These standards suffer the same deficiencies as other effluent standards; they are not cost effective (see Example 17.3). The control over wastewater flows into treatment plants provides one more example of an environmental policy area where economic-incentive approaches offer an opportunity to achieve equivalent results at a lower cost.

Nonpoint Pollution

The current law does little to control nonpoint pollution, which in many areas is a significant part of the total problem. In some ways, the government has tried to compensate for this uneven coverage by placing more intensive controls on point sources. Is this emphasis efficient?

It could conceivably be justified on two grounds. First, if the marginal damages caused by nonpoint sources are significantly smaller than those of point sources, then a lower level of control could well be justified. Because in many cases nonpoint-source pollutants are not the same as point-source pollutants, this is a logical possibility. Or, second, if the costs of controlling nonpoint sources even to a small degree are very high, this could justify benign neglect as well. Are either of these conditions met in practice?

Costs. Because research is in its infancy, cost information is scarce. Of the small amount of literature available, one study can give us a sense of the economic analysis. Palmini conducted an analysis of the potential effects of agricultural nonpoint policies on two small rural counties in Illinois.[14] The specific policies he examined were designed to control nitrogen (which can cause eutrophication), sediment (soil erosion), and pesticides. His model relates these policies to the choice of various farming practices, the effects of these choices on costs, and the financial return to farmers after covering variable costs.

His results indicated that a rather dramatic reduction (74 percent) in soil erosion could be achieved at a cost of less than 1 percent of the earnings after variable costs were covered. A ban on selected pesticides was predicted to cause a switch to other, less damaging pesticides, which would reduce the return to farmers by 0.7 percent.

The major estimated economic impact came from policies designed to reduce nitrogen use. Palmini considered the effects of quantity restrictions (ceilings on amount used per acre) and the impact of taxes on nitrogen use. Quantity restrictions necessary to reduce pollution also substantially reduced revenues and projections. Because the demand for nitrogen is price inelastic, if nitrogen taxes were used, very high rates would be needed to reduce nitrogen use very much.

The extra expense of nitrogen control would represent a large financial burden on farmers, which they could only pass on in higher prices if all farmers were subjected to similar controls. This would make unilateral state control difficult, because it would place the farmers in that state in jeopardy.

---

[14]Dennis J. Palmini, "The Secondary Impact of Nonpoint Pollution Controls: A Linear Programming–Input/Output Analysis," *Journal of Environmental Economics and Management* 9 (September 1982): 263–78.

Example 17.3

Cost-Effective Pretreatment Standards

The electroplating operations of the Rhode Island jewelry industry produce high concentrations of cyanide, copper, nickel, and zinc, which are routinely discharged into municipal sewer systems. Because the treatment plants are not designed to remove these hazardous substances, the EPA has defined pretreatment standards to prohibit excessive concentrations of these metals from entering the plants. These standards are financially burdensome, with some estimates suggesting that some 30 to 60 percent of the small firms could go out of business if the standards were imposed.

An economic analysis by Opaluch and Kashmanian (1985) of the alternative for meeting the EPA concentration objectives concludes that the EPA pretreatment standards achieve the objective at a cost almost 50 percent greater than the least-cost means of achieving the same concentration objectives. An emission permit system with a permit price of $40 per pound would, after trading, achieve the target at a cost of $12.5 million. Compared to the $19.3 million the EPA proposal would cost, this represents a considerable saving.

If the permits were auctioned off, the government would collect some $5.0 million from the sale. Although the financial burden of this auction system for allocating permits would be lower on the jewelry industry as a whole than complying with the EPA proposal, even considering this $5.0 million transfer, not every segment of the industry would be better off with this auction. In particular, the permit fees paid by large firms would be sufficiently high that they would bear more financial burden under the auction scheme than with the EPA proposal. If the permits were "grandfathered" (allocated free of charge) rather than auctioned off, however, all existing firms would be better off under the permit system than under the EPA proposal.

Source: James J. Opaluch and Richard M. Kashmanian, "Assessing the Viability of Marketable Permit Systems: An Application in Hazardous Waste Management," *Land Economics* 61, No. 3 (August 1985): 263–71.

This study suggests that some nonpoint control can probably be reasonably undertaken, because the costs seem low. However, it also suggests that the conclusion that all nonpoint sources can be cheaply controlled is not correct. As in other areas of environmental policy, the form and intensity of government intervention would have to be tailored to the specific problem.

The fact that point and nonpoint sources have received such different treatment from the EPA suggests the possibility that costs could be lowered by a more careful balancing of these control options. One study of phosphorus control in the Dillon Reservoir in Colorado by Industrial Economics, Inc., supports the validity of this suspicion.[15]

---

[15]Industrial Economics, *Case Studies on the Trading of Effluent Loads: Dillon Reservoir Final Report* (Cambridge, MA: Industrial Economics, 1984).

In this reservoir, four municipalities constitute the only point sources of phosphorus, whereas there are numerous uncontrolled nonpoint sources in the area. The combined phosphorus load on the reservoir from point and nonpoint sources is projected to exceed its assimilative capacity.

The traditional way to reduce the projected phosphorus load would be to impose even more stringent controls on the point sources. The study found, however, that by following a balanced program to control both point and nonpoint sources, the desired phosphorus target could be achieved at a cost of approximately $1 million a year less than would be spent if only point sources were controlled more stringently. The more general point that should be carried away from this study is that, as point sources are controlled to higher and higher degrees, rising marginal-control costs will begin to make controlling nonpoint sources increasingly attractive.

Oil Spills

One of the chief characteristics of the current approach to oil spills is that it depends heavily on the ability of the legal system to internalize the costs of a spill through liability law. In principle, the approach is straightforward. By forcing the owner of a vessel to pay for the costs of cleaning up the spill, including compensating for natural resource damages, a powerful incentive to exercise care is created. But is the outcome likely to be efficient in practice?

One problem with legal remedies is their high administrative cost. As Example 17.4 points out, assigning the appropriate penalties is no trivial matter. Even if the court were able to act expeditiously, the doctrines it imposes are not necessarily efficient, because the financial liability for cleaning up spills is limited by statute. The owner will minimize costs by choosing the level of precaution that equates the marginal cost of additional precaution with the resulting reduction in the marginal expected penalty. The marginal reduction in expected penalty is a function of two factors—the likelihood of a spill and the magnitude of the financial obligation it would trigger.

As long as the imposed penalty equaled the actual damage and the probability of having to pay the damage, once an accident occurred, was 1.0, this outcome would normally be efficient. The external costs would be internalized. The owner's private costs would be minimized by taking all possible cost-justified precaution measures to reduce both the likelihood and the seriousness of any resulting spill; taking precaution would simply be cheaper than paying for the cleanup.

Limited liability produces a different outcome, however. Lower levels of precaution imply damages that exceed the limit, but the vessel owner would not have to pay anything above the limit. (The only benefit to the vessel owner faced with limited liability that is offered by increasing precaution at lower levels of precaution is the reduction in the likelihood of a spill; in this range, increasing precaution does not reduce the magnitude of the financial payment should a spill occur.)

What is the effect of limited liability on the vessel owner's choice of precaution levels? As long as the liability limit is binding (which appears to routinely be the case with recent spills), the owner will choose too little precaution. Therefore, both the number and magnitude of resulting spills will be inefficiently large.

Example 17.4

Anatomy of an Oil Spill Suit: The *Amoco Cadiz*

On 17 March 1978, the *Amoco Cadiz,* an oil transport ship traveling in a bad storm, lost steering control and, after unsuccessful towing attempts, drifted onto the rocks off the shore of Portsall, France, on the Brittany coast. Ultimately, the ship broke in two and discharged 220,000 tons of crude oil and 4,000 tons of bunker fuels along the cost of a resort area, two months prior to the opening of the tourist season.

Before the end of the year of the grounding, a mountain of claims had been filed involving France, a consortium of resort owners and fishermen, Amoco (the owner of the vessel), Bugsier (the owner of the tug), Shell Oil (the owner of the oil being carried at the time), and Astilleros Españoles (the Spanish company that built the *Amoco Cadiz*). After extensive and expensive preparations by all parties, the trial began in May 1982.

During March 1984 a preliminary opinion was issued finding Amoco and the shipbuilder jointly liable. The process then turned to the separate issue of the magnitude of the damages to be awarded. On 21 February 1989, a judgment of 670 million francs (approximately $120 million) was levied against Amoco and Astilleros. The verdict was immediately appealed.

The trial judge, now retired from the bench, summed up the situation:

So here we are, twelve years after the accident, eleven years after the suit was filed, with the plaintiffs in possession of an enormous judgment and subject to enormous legal fees without one cent having changed hands. The case marches onward to the Court of Appeals with each principal party expected to appeal those aspects of the final judgment with which they disagree. This raises the possibility, almost unimaginable, but very real, that the whole case could have to be tried again.

Source: Frank J. McGarr, "Inadequacy of Federal Forum for Resolution of Oil Spill Damages," a talk given at a conference on oil spills at Newport, Rhode Island, on 16 May 1990. Judge McGarr was the trial judge for the *Amoco Cadiz* case.

Citizen Suits

As noted earlier, citizen suits add a private enforcement alternative to public enforcement in correcting environmental market failures.[16] Public and private enforcement are partial substitutes. If government enforcement were complete, all polluters would be in compliance, and citizen suits would have no role to play. Noncompliance is a necessary condition for a successful suit. In the early 1980s when public enforcement decreased, private enforcement—citizen

---

[16]For more details on this approach, see Wendy Naysnerski and Tom Tietenberg, "Private Enforcement," in T. H. Tietenberg ed., *Innovation in Environmental Policy* (Cheltenham, UK: Edward Elgar, 1992): 109–136.

suits—increased to take up the slack. Lax public enforcement appears to have played a significant role in the rise of citizen suits.

All attorneys' fees incurred by the citizen group in any successful action under the Clean Water Act must be reimbursed by the defendants. Reimbursement of attorneys' fees has affected both the level and focus of litigation activity. By lowering the costs of bringing citizen suits, attorney fee reimbursement has allowed citizen groups to participate far more often in the enforcement process than otherwise would have been possible. Because courts only reimburse for appropriate claims (noncompliance claims that are upheld by the court), citizen groups are encouraged to litigate only appropriate cases.

The existence of citizen suits should affect the decision-making process of the polluting firm. Adding citizen suits to the enforcement arena increases the expected penalty to the non-complying firm by increasing the likelihood that the firm will face an enforcement action. This can be expected to increase the amount of precaution taken by the firm, but the unavailability of compliance data makes it impossible to confirm this expectation, though participants believe compliance has increased.

Although citizen suits probably do lead to greater compliance, greater compliance is not necessarily efficient. Complete compliance is not necessarily efficient if the defendant polluters face inefficiently harsh standards. If the standards are excessively high, citizen suits have the potential to promote inefficiency by forcing firms to meet standards where the marginal benefits are significantly lower than the marginal costs. However, if the effluent standards are either inefficiently low or efficient, the existence of citizen suits will necessarily create a more efficient outcome. In these cases, increasing compliance is perfectly compatible with efficiency.

An Overall Assessment

Though the benefit estimates from water pollution control are subject to much uncertainty, they do exist. Although we must be careful not to place too much reliance on them, we can see what information can be gleaned from the studies in existence.

A. Myrick Freeman has summarized these studies, focusing on 1985 as a target year.[17] His survey of the field suggests that the 1985 benefit (in 1984 dollars) from conventional water pollution control policy could be as low as $5.7 billion or as high as $27.7 billion, with a more likely point estimate of $14.0 billion. This compares to estimated 1985 annual costs (in 1978 dollars) ranging from a low of $25 billion to a high of $30 billion. Thus, Freeman estimates that the net benefit from conventional control is probably negative.

A more recent study, using a different methodology, concludes that the current net benefits are positive, but are likely to become negative as costs escalate in the future. Relying on benefits estimates derived from contingent valuation, Carson and Mitchell estimate that aggregate benefits in 1990 exceeded aggregate costs by $6.4 billion.[18] They also found, however,

[17]A. Myrick Freeman, III, "Water Pollution Policy," in *Public Policies for Environmental Protection,* Paul R. Portney, ed., (Washington, DC: Resources for the Future, 1990): 122–26.

[18]R. T. Carson and R. C. Mitchell, "The Value of Clean Water: The Public's Willingness to Pay for Boatable, Fishable, and Swimmable Quality Water," *Water Resources Research* 29 (1993): 2445–54.

that projected aggregate costs would exceed aggregate benefits because of the high marginal costs and the low marginal benefits associated with bringing the remaining bodies of water up to swimmable quality.

Using cost-effective policies rather than the current approach, it would be possible to reduce costs substantially without affecting the benefits. Cost-effectiveness would require developing better strategies for point-source control and for achieving a better balance between point- and nonpoint-source control. The resulting reduction in costs probably would cause net benefits to become positive. That result would not necessarily make the policy efficient, however, because the level of control might still be too high or too low. Unfortunately, the evidence is not rich enough to prove whether or not the overall level of control maximizes the net benefit.

In addition to promoting current cost-effectiveness, economic-incentive approaches would stimulate and facilitate change better than would a system of rigid, technology-based standards. Clifford Russell has attempted to assess the importance of the facilitating role by simulating the effects on the allocation of pollution control responsibility in response to regional economic growth, changing technology, and changing product mix.[19] Focusing on the steel, paper, and petroleum-refining industries in the 11-county Delaware Estuary Region, his study estimated the change in permit use for three water pollutants (BOD, total suspended solids, and ammonia) that would have resulted if a marketable-permit system were in place over the 1940–1978 period. The calculations assume that the plants existing in 1940 would have been allocated permits in order to legitimize their emissions at that time, that new sources would have had to purchase permits, and that plant shutdowns or contractions would free up permits for others to purchase.

This study found that, for almost every decade and pollutant, a substantial number of permits would have been made available by plant closings, capacity contractions, product-mix changes, and the availability of new technologies. In the absence of a marketable-permit program, a control authority would not only have to keep abreast of all technological developments so that emission standards could be adjusted accordingly, but it would also have to assure an overall balance between effluent increases and decreases so as to preserve water quality. This tough assignment is handled completely by the market in a marketable-permit system, thereby facilitating the evolution of the economy by responding flexibly and predictably to change.

Marketable permits encourage, as well as facilitate, this evolution. Because permits have value, in order to minimize costs, firms must continually be looking for new opportunities to control emissions at lower cost. This search eventually results in the adoption of new technologies and in the initiation of changes in the production mix that result in lower amounts of emissions. The pressure on sources to continually search for better ways to control pollution is a distinct advantage that economic-incentive systems have over bureaucratically defined standards.

---

[19]Clifford O. Russell, "Controlled Trading of Pollution Permits," *Environmental Science and Technology* 15, No. 1 (January 1981): 1–5.

SUMMARY

Historically, policies for controlling water pollution have been concerned with conventional pollutants discharged into surface waters. More recently, concerns have shifted toward toxic pollutants, which apparently are more prevalent than previously believed; toward groundwater, which traditionally was thought to be an invulnerable pristine resource, and toward the oceans, which were mistakenly considered immune from most pollution problems, because of their vast size.

Early attempts at controlling water pollution followed a path similar to that of air pollution control. Legislation prior to the 1970s had little impact on the problem. Frustration then led to the enactment of a tough federal law that was so ambitious and unrealistic that little progress resulted.

There the similarity ends. Whereas in air pollution a wave of recent reforms has improved the process by making it more cost effective, no parallel exists for control of water pollution. Historic policy toward cleaning up rivers and lakes was based upon two approaches: (1) the subsidization of municipal waste treatment facilities and (2) the imposition of national effluent standards on industrial sources. Recently this has been complemented by the introduction of the Total Maximum Daily Load Program. This moves water pollution control away from national effluent standards and toward ambient standards tailored to the desired use of the water body.

The historic approach has been hampered by delays, by problems in allocating funds, and by the fact that about half of the constructed plants are not performing satisfactorily. In addition, effluent standards have assigned the control responsibility among point sources in a way that excessively raises cost. Nonpoint pollution sources have, until recently, been virtually ignored. Technological progress is inhibited rather than stimulated by the current approach. Benefit-cost analyses show the net benefit from the current approach was positive up to 1990, but may become negative as more expensive controls are imposed.

This lack of progress could have been avoided. It did not result from a lack of toughness but from a reliance on direct regulation rather than on emission charges or emission permits, which are more flexible and cost effective in both the dynamic and static sense. In this respect, the United States can perhaps take some lessons from the European experience.

The court system has assumed most of the responsibility for controlling oil spills. Those responsible for the spills are assessed the financial liability for cleaning the site up and compensating for any resulting damages to natural resources. Although, in principle, this approach can be efficient, in practice, it has been hampered by liability limitations and the huge administrative burden an oil spill trial entails.

Enforcement is always a key to successful environmental and natural resource policy. One rather recent innovation in enforcement involves giving private citizen groups the power to bring noncomplying firms into court. By raising the likelihood that noncomplying firms would be brought before the court and assessed penalties for noncompliance, this new system can be expected to increase compliance.

FURTHER READING

Braden, John B., and Stephen B. Lovejoy, eds. *Agriculture and Water Quality: International Perspectives* (Boulder, CO: Lynne Rienner, 1990). Ten papers consider public policies designed to reduce water pollution from agriculture in Sweden, Denmark, Australia, and the United States.

Letson, D. "Point/Nonpoint Source Pollution Reduction Trading: An Interpretive Survey," *Natural Resources Journal* 32 (1992): 219–32. Considers a host of implementation details that must be resolved if point-nonpoint source trading is to live up to its potential.

Russell, Clifford, and Jason Shogren, eds. *Theory, Modeling and Experience in the Management of Nonpoint-Source Pollution* (Hingham, MA: Kluwer Academic Publishers, 1993). A collection of 12 essays providing a state-of-the-art review of the economic perspective on nonpoint source pollution.

ADDITIONAL REFERENCES

Andreasson, I. M. "A Cost-Efficient Reduction of the Nitrogen Load to Laholm Bay," in A. Bubgard and A. Nielson, eds., *Economic Aspects of Environmental Regulations in Agriculture* (Kiel, Germany: Wissenschaftsverlag Vauk, 1989).

Ashworth, John, Ivy Papps, and David Storey. "Assessing the Impact upon the British Chlor-Alkali Industry of the EEC Directive on Discharges of Mercury into Waterways," *Land Economics* 63 (February 1987): 72–78.

Bockstael, N. E., et al. "Measuring the Benefits of Improvements in Water Quality: The Chesapeake Bay," *Marine Resources Economics* 6 (1989): 1–18.

Bressers, H. "A Comparison of the Effectiveness of Incentives and Directives: The Case of Dutch Water Quality Policy," *Policy Studies Review* 7 (1988): 500–518.

Bressers, H. "The Role of Effluent Charges in Dutch Water Quality Policy," in P. Downing and K. Hanf, eds. *International Comparisons in Implementing Pollution Laws* (Boston: Kluwer Nijhoff, 1983).

Brown, G. M. Jr., and R. W. Johnson. "Pollution Control by Effluent Charges: It Works in the Federal Republic of Germany, Why Not in the U.S.?," *Natural Resources Journal* 24 (1984): 929–966.

Eheart, J. Wayland, E. Downey Brill, Jr., and Randolph M. Lyon. "Transferable Discharge Permits for Control of BOD: An Overview," in *Buying a Better Environment: Cost-Effective Regulation through Permit Trading*, Erhard F. Joeres and Martin H. David, eds. (Madison: University of Wisconsin Press, 1983): 163–195.

Freeman, A. Myrick III. *Air and Water Pollution Control: A Benefit-Cost Assessment* (New York: Wiley, 1982).

Griffin, Ronald C. "Environmental Policy for Spatial and Persistent Pollutants," *Journal of Environmental Economics and Management* 14 (March 1987): 41–53.

Hanley, N., and D. Oglethorpe. "Emerging Policies on Externalities from Agriculture: An Analysis for the European Union." *American Journal of Agricultural Economics* 81 (1984)(5): 1222–1227.

Johnsen, F. H. "Economic Analyses of Measures to Control Phosphorous Run-Off from Nonpoint Agricultural Sources," *European Review of Agricultural Economics* 20 (1993): 399–418.

Johnson, Edwin L. "A Study in the Economics of Water Quality Management," *Water Resources Research* 3 (second quarter 1967): 291–305.

Koch, C. James, and Robert A. Leone. "The Clean Water Act: Unexpected Impacts on Industry," *Harvard Environmental Law Review* 3 (1979): 84–111.

Kraemer, A., and K. M. Banholzer. "Tradable Permits in Water Resource Management and Water Pollution Control." *Implementing Domestic Tradable Permits for Environmental Protection* (Washington, DC: OECD, Organization for Economic Co-operation and Development, 1999): 75–107.

Leone, Robert A., and John E. Jackson. "The Political Economy of Federal Regulatory Activity: The Case of Water Pollution Controls," in *Studies in Public Regulation,* Gary Fromm, ed. (Cambridge, MA: MIT Press, 1981).

Letson, David. "Investment Decisions and Transferable Discharge Permits: An Empirical Study of Water Quality Management under Policy Uncertainty," *Environmental and Resource Economics* 2 (1992): 441–458.

Magat, Wesley A., and W. Kip Viscusi. "Effectiveness of the EPA's Regulatory Enforcement: The Case of Industrial Effluent Standards," *Journal of Law and Economics* 33 (1990): 331–360.

Malik, A. S., et al. "Point/Nonpoint Source Trading of Pollution Abatement: Choosing the Right Trading Ratio," *American Journal of Agricultural Economics* 75 (1993): 959–967.

McConnell, Virginia D., John H. Cumberland, and Patrice L. Gordon. "Regional Marginal Costs and Cost Savings from Economies of Scale in Municipal Waste Treatment: An Application to the Chesapeake Bay," *Growth and Change* 19 (fall 1988): 1–13.

Naysnerski, Wendy, and Tom Tietenberg. "Private Enforcement of Environmental Law," *Land Economics* 68 (1992): 28–48.

Opaluch, James J., and Thomas A. Grigalunas. "Controlling Stochastic Pollution Events with Liability Rules: Some Evidence from OCS Leasing," *Rand Journal of Economics* 15 (1984): 142–151.

Peskin, Henry M., and Eugene P. Seskin. *Cost-Benefit Analysis and Water Pollution Control Policy* (Washington, DC: Urban Institute, 1975).

Raucher, Robert L. "The Benefits and Costs of Policies Related to Groundwater Contamination," *Land Economics* 62 (February 1986): 33–45.

Ribaudo, Marc O. "Targeting the Conservation Reserve Program to Maximize Water Quality Benefits," *Land Economics* 65 (November 1989): 320–332.

Segerson, Kathleen. "Liability for Groundwater Contamination from Pesticides," *Journal of Environmental Economics and Management* 19 (1990): 227–243.

Segerson, Kathleen. "Uncertainty and Incentives for Nonpoint Pollution Control," *Journal of Environmental Economics and Management* 15 (March 1988): 87–98.

Shortle, I., and J. Dunn, "The Relative Efficiency of Agricultural Source Water Pollution Control Policies," *American Journal of Agricultural Economics* (1986): 668–677.

Spurlock, S. R., and I. D. Clifton. "Efficiency and Equity Aspects of Nonpoint Source Pollution Controls," *Southern Journal of Agricultural Economics* 14 (December 1982): 123–129.

Wetzstein, M. E., and T. J. Centner, "Regulating Agricultural Contamination of Groundwater through Strict Liability and Negligence Legislation," *Journal of Environmental Economics and Management* 22 (1992): 1–11.

WEB SITES OF INTEREST

1. *http://www.epa.gov/owow/tmdl/*
   USEPA's total maximum daily load program.

2. *http://www.cciw.ca/gems/intro.html*
   United Nations Environment Program's Global Environmental Monitoring System for Water.

DISCUSSION QUESTIONS

1. "The only permanent solution to water pollution control will occur when *all* production by-products are routinely recycled. The zero discharge goal recognizes this reality and forces all dischargers to work steadily toward this solution. Less stringent policies are, at best, temporary palliatives." Discuss.

2. "In exercising its responsibility to protect the nation's drinking water, the government needs to intervene only in the case of public water supplies. Private water suppliers will be adequately protected without any government intervention." Discuss.

18

Solid Waste and Recycling

Man is endowed with reason and creative powers to increase and multiply his inheritance; yet up to now he has created nothing, only destroyed. The forests grow ever fewer; the rivers parch; the wildlife is gone; the climate is ruined; and with every passing day the earth becomes uglier and poorer.

ANTON CHEKHOV *UNCLE VANYA*, ACT I (1896)

◆ INTRODUCTION

As the level of waste rises and the amount of space available to store it safely without contaminating groundwater declines, what can be done? The traditional answer involves the three R's: reduce, reuse, recycle.

How can economics help to assure that the three R's play an appropriate role in alleviating the solid waste problem? Is the waste level inefficiently high? Why? What measures can be taken to reduce the level of waste? What is an efficient amount of recycling? Will the market automatically generate this amount in the absence of government intervention? How does the efficient allocation over time differ between recyclable and nonrecyclable resources? The phrase *planned obsolescence* is sometimes used to suggest that industries have an incentive to produce products with a short life span. Does the market produce an efficient level of product durability? What impact does product durability have on the allocation of virgin and recycled materials?

We shall begin our investigation by describing how an efficient market in recyclable, depletable resources would work. We then use this as a benchmark to examine recycling in some detail. We close by relating our findings back to the central questions of growth in a finite environment.

◆ EFFICIENT RECYCLING

Extraction and Disposal Costs

What determines the recycling rate? Historically, reliance has generally been on the natural inputs, because they have been cheaper. As the natural inputs have become scarce relative to the demand for them, industry has begun to search for other sources.

At the same time, the costs of disposing of the products have risen as the world has experienced a large increase in the geographic concentration of people. The attraction of cities and the exodus from rural areas led an increasingly large number of people to live in urban or near-urban environments.

This concentration creates waste-disposal problems. When land was plentiful and the waste stream was less hazardous, waste could be buried in landfills. But, as land has become scarce, burial has become increasingly expensive. In addition, concerns over environmental effects on water supplies and economic effects on the value of surrounding land have made buried waste less acceptable.

The rising costs of virgin materials and of waste disposal have increased the attractiveness of recycling. By recovering and reintroducing materials into the system, recycling provides an alternative to virgin ores and also reduces the waste-disposal load (see Example 18.1).

Consumers as well as manufacturers play a role on both the demand and supply side of the market. On the demand side, consumers would find that products depending exclusively on virgin raw materials are subject to higher prices than those relying on recycled materials. Consequently, consumers would have a tendency to switch to products made with the cheaper, recycled raw materials, as long as quality is not adversely affected. This powerful incentive is called the *composition-of-demand effect.*

As long as consumers bear the cost of disposal, they have the additional incentive to return their used recyclable products to collection centers. By doing so, they avoid disposal costs while reaping financial rewards for supplying a product someone wants.

For the cycle to be complete, the demand for the recycled products must be sufficiently high to justify making them available. New markets may ultimately emerge, but the transition may prove somewhat turbulent. Simply returning recycled products to the collection centers accomplishes little if they are simply dumped into a nearby landfill or if the supply is increased so much by mandatory recycling laws that prices for recycled materials fall through the floor. The purity of the recycled products also plays a key role in explaining the strength of demand for them. One of the reasons for the high rate of aluminum recycling and much lower rate of plastics recycling is the differential difficulty of producing a high-quality product from scrap. Whereas bundles of aluminum cans have a relatively uniform quality, waste plastics tend to be highly contaminated with nonplastic substances, and the plastics manufacturing process has little tolerance for impurities. Remaining contaminants in metals can frequently be eliminated by high-temperature combustion, but plastics are destroyed by high temperatures.

For some materials, having consumers do the separation and recovery is more costly, so that it is more efficient for municipal agencies to accomplish recycling. One example is currently operating in Saugus, Massachusetts, a North Shore suburb of Boston; it processes up to 1,500 tons of Boston refuse per day. From this waste, the facility annually recovers some 25,000 tons of ferrous metals and 40,000 tons of other materials suitable for use in construction. In addition, the plant is capable of producing 2 billion pounds of steam annually, which it sells to a nearby General Electric plant.

Example 18.1

Population Density and Recycling: The Japanese Experience

Because Japan has much greater population density than many of the other industrialized nations, it has been forced to come to grips with its solid waste disposal problems somewhat earlier. For the Japanese the solution of choice is recycling. In Tokyo enterprising firms have begun touring neighborhoods, collecting newspapers, magazines, and rags in exchange for new bathroom and facial tissue. People who want quick disposal of old refrigerators or TV sets need only make a special call to the sanitation department for a special pickup. And although a few years ago no Japanese would touch used goods, the latest trend is garage sales and flea markets, which give secondhand wares new life.

About 40 percent of solid waste is recycled, including about half the paper, 55 percent of glass bottles, and 66 percent of food and beverage cans.

Since the early 1970s, citizens have been forced to separate combustible from noncombustible trash. Burnable waste, which comprises some 72 percent of the total after recycling, is trucked to incinerators, which reduce its weight and volume. Every Japanese community has its own incinerator, totaling some 1,899 garbage-burning plants (compared with 155 large garbage-burning plants in the United States). Nonburnable garbage is separated, melted, and refabricated; ferrous metals are reclaimed. What's left, about 9 percent of the total initial waste, is deposited in a landfill.

Some problems still exist. Concern about the toxins within the trash that escape into the air from combustion and the water from landfills is mounting. Recycling peaked at about 50 percent and even declined somewhat during the 1980s.

Sources: "Teeing Off on Japan's Garbage," *Newsweek* (27 November 1989): 70; "The Good News: Japan Gives Trash a Second Chance," *Time* (2 January 1989): 47.

Recycling: A Closer Look

The model in the preceding section would lead us to expect that recycling would increase over time as virgin ore and disposal costs rose. This seems to be the case. Take copper, for example. During 1910, recycled copper accounted for about 18 percent of the total production of refined copper in the United States. By 1997, this figure had risen to 37 percent.

Though these percentages may seem low, in most cases recycling is not cheap. Transport and processing costs are usually significant. The sources of scrap are usually concentrated around cities, where the products are used, whereas the production facilities are concentrated near the sources of the virgin materials. Scrap materials must first be transported to the production facility; then there are additional expenses in collecting, separating, and processing them. Even when there is acute scarcity, nowhere near 100 percent of the materials are recycled; costs don't permit it!

As recycling becomes cost competitive, rather dramatic changes occur in the manufacturing process. Not only do manufacturers rely more heavily on recycled inputs; they also begin to design their products in order to facilitate recycling. Facilitating recycling through product design

Example 18.2

Lead Recycling

The domestic demand for lead has changed significantly over the last 25 years. In 1972, dissipative, non-recyclable uses of lead (primarily gasoline additives, pigments in paint, and ammunition) accounted for about 30 percent of reported consumption. Only about 30 percent of all produced lead came from recycled material.

Over the last two and a half decades, however, Congressional recognition of lead's negative health effects on children have led to a series of laws limiting the amount of allowable lead in gasoline and paints. Not only has this resulted in a decline in the total amount of lead used, but the decline has been most dramatic for the dissipative uses (which, as of 1997, had fallen to only 13 percent of total demand). A declining role for dissipative uses implies an increasing proportion of the production is available to be recycled. And, in fact, more was. By 1997, 77 percent of the domestic supply of lead was being recycled.

Old scrap accounts for some 96 percent of the total lead scrap recovered. Used batteries supply about 90 percent of that old scrap. Battery manufacturers have begun entering buyback arrangements with retail outlets, both as a marketing tool for new batteries and as a means of ensuring a supply of inputs to their downstream manufacturing operations.

Source: U.S. Department of the Interior. *Minerals Yearbook: 1997* (Washington, DC: Government Printing Office, 1997): 493–497.

is already important in industries where the connection between the manufacturer and disposal agent is particularly close. Aircraft manufacturers, which often are asked to scrap old aircraft, may stamp the alloy composition on parts during manufacturing to facilitate recycling. The idea is beginning to spread to other industries. For example, ski boot manufacturers in Switzerland have begun to stamp all component parts with a code to identify their composition.

An efficient economic system will orchestrate a balance between the consumption of depletable and recycled materials, between disposing of used products and recycling, and between imports and domestic production. Example 18.2 shows the market at work.

How close are we to efficiency? Have we achieved an efficient balance between imports and domestic production? Is the common pejorative notion that we are a "throwaway society" an accurate one? If so, is the market behaving efficiently—in the sense that the time for recycling has not yet come—or are there clearly identified sources of market failure, implying that the wrong price signals are being sent? The next few sections investigate these issues.

◆ WASTE DISPOSAL AND POLLUTION DAMAGE

The treatment of waste by producers and consumers can lead to biases in the market balance between recycling and the use of virgin materials. Because disposal cost is a key ingredient in determining the efficient amount of recycling, the failure of an economic agent to bear the full cost of disposal implies a bias toward virgin materials and away from recycling. We begin by considering how the method of financing the disposal of potentially recyclable waste affects the level of recycling.

Disposal Costs and Efficiency

We begin by being clear about the relationship of the marginal disposal cost to the efficient level of recycling. Suppose, for example, it costs a community $20/ton to recycle a particular waste product that can ultimately be sold to a local manufacturer for $10/ton. Can we conclude that this is an inefficient recycling venture because it is losing money?

No, we can't! In addition to earning the $10/ton from selling the recycled product, the town is avoiding the cost of disposing of the product. This avoided marginal cost is appropriately considered a marginal benefit from recycling. Suppose the marginal avoided disposal cost were $20/ton. In this case, the benefits to the town from recycling would be $30/ton ($20/ton avoided cost plus $10/ton resale value) and the cost would be $20/ton; this would be an efficient recycling venture. Both marginal disposal costs and the prices of recycled materials directly affect the efficient level of recycling.

The Disposal Decision

Potentially recyclable waste can be divided into two types of scrap: (1) new scrap and (2) old scrap. *New scrap* is composed of the residual materials generated during production. For example, as steel beams are formed, the small remnants of steel left over are new scrap. *Old scrap* is recovered from products used by consumers.

To illustrate the relative importance of new scrap and old scrap, consider the aluminum industry. In 1997, a total of 3,690,000 metric tons of aluminum were recovered from scrap of both kinds.[1] Of this, 2,160,000 metric tons came from new scrap, whereas the rest came from old, including the recycling of some 66.8 billion aluminum cans. About 55 percent of the aluminum used to make aluminum cans in the United States was being derived from scrap.

Recycling new scrap is significantly less difficult than recycling old scrap. New scrap is already at the place of production, and with most processes it can simply be reentered into the input stream without transportation costs. Transport costs tend to be an important part of the cost of using old scrap.

Equally important are the incentives involved. Because new scrap never leaves the factory, it remains under the complete control of the manufacturer. Having the joint responsibility of creating a product and dealing with the scrap, the manufacturer now has an incentive to design the product with the use of the scrap in mind. It would, therefore, be advantageous to establish procedures guaranteeing the homogeneity of the scrap and minimizing the amount of processing necessary to recycle it. For all these reasons, it is likely that the market for new scrap will work efficiently and effectively.

Unfortunately, the same is not true for old scrap. The market works inefficiently because the product users do not bear the full marginal social costs of disposing of their product. As a result, the market is biased away from recycling old scrap and toward the use of virgin materials.

---

[1]U.S. Department of Interior. *Minerals Yearbook: 1997* (Washington, DC: Government Printing Office, 1997): 62.1, 62.11.

TABLE 18.1   Description of User Charges on Municipal Waste, Selected Countries

Country	Charge Calculation	Target
Australia	Flat rate	Households, firms
Belgium	Flat rate or volume	Households
Canada	Flat rate	Households
	Flat rate + volume over threshold	Firms
Denmark	Flat rate	Households
	Waste volume	Firms
Finland	Waste volume	Households
	Volume + type + transport distance	Firms
France	Dwelling size (80% of population) *or*	Households, firms
	Waste volume (4% of population) *or*	Households, firms
	(None: Waste collection paid for from public budget)	
Italy	Dwelling size	Households, firms
The Netherlands	Flat rate	Households, firms
Norway	Flat rate	Households, firms
Sweden	Flat rate (53% of municipalities)	Households, firms
	Collection structure (45% of municipalities) *or*	Households, firms
United Kingdom	Flat rate	Households, firms
	Waste volume	

Source: Economic Instruments for Environmental Protection. Copyright OECD, 1989.

The key to understanding why these costs are not internalized lies in the incentives facing individual product users. Suppose you had some small aluminum products that were no longer useful to you. You could either recycle them, which usually means driving to a recycling center, or you could toss them into your trash. In comparing these two alternatives, notice that recycling imposes one cost on you (transport cost) whereas the second imposes another (disposal cost).

It is difficult for consumers to make this comparison accurately because of the way trash collection has traditionally been financed (Table 18.1). Urban areas have generally financed trash collection with taxes, if publicly provided, or user fees, if privately provided. Neither of these approaches directly relates the size of an individual's payment to the amount of waste. The *marginal* cost to the homeowner of throwing out one more unit of trash is negligible, even when the cost to society is not.

This point can be reinforced by a numerical example. Suppose your city provides trash pickup for which you pay $150 a year in taxes. Your cost will be $150 regardless (within reasonable limits) of how much you throw out. In a given year your additional (marginal) cost from throwing out these items is *zero*. Certainly, the marginal cost to society is *not* zero, so that the balance between these alternatives as seen by the individual homeowner is biased in favor of throwing things out.[2]

---

[2]The problem is not that $150 is too low; indeed, it may be too high! The point is that the cost of waste disposal does not increase with the amount of waste to be disposed of.

Littering is an extreme example of what we have been talking about. In the absence of some kind of government intervention, the cost to society of littering is the aesthetic loss plus the risk of damage to automobile tires and pedestrians caused by sharp edges of discarded cans or glass. Tossing used containers outside the car is relatively costless for the individual but costly for society.[3]

Disposal Costs and the Scrap Market

How would the market respond to a policy forcing product users to bear the true marginal disposal cost? The major effect would be on the supply of materials to be recycled. Consumers would now be able to avoid disposal costs and might even be paid for discarded products. This would cause the diversion of some materials to recycling centers, where they could be reintegrated into the materials process. If this expanded supply allows dealers to take advantage of previously unexploited economies of scale, it could well result in a lower average cost of processing, as well as more recycled materials.

The effect on the market is now clearly evident. The total consumption of recycled inputs increases because the price falls.

Public Policies

The current level of recycling in the United States is rather low, particularly when judged by the standards of Japan (refer back to Example 18.1). No doubt some of the responsibility for this lies in improper incentives created by inappropriate pricing. Can this misallocation resulting from the problem of inefficiently low disposal cost be corrected?

One approach, volume pricing, would impose disposal charges reflecting the true social cost of disposal.[4] (Example 18.3).

One preimplementation concern about the program was that it might impose a hardship on the poor residents of the area. Strategies based on higher prices always raise the specter that they will end up placing an intolerable burden on the poor.

That concern apparently was misplaced. Under the old system of financing trash collection, every household pays the same fee—regardless of how much trash was produced. Because elderly (and other low-income) households produce less trash, they are, in effect, subsidizing wealthier households under the old system.

Another suggestion now being applied in many areas is the *refundable deposit*. Already widely accepted for beverage containers, such deposits could become a remedy for many other products.

A refundable deposit system is designed to accomplish two purposes: (1) the initial charge reflects the cost of disposal and produces the desired composition-of-demand effect, and (2) the refund, attainable upon turning the product in for recycling, helps conserve virgin materials. Such a system already is employed in Sweden and Norway to counter the problem of abandoned automobiles.

---

[3]Using economic analysis, would you expect transients or residents to have a higher propensity to litter? Why?

[4]Robert Hanley, "Pay-by-Bag Trash Disposal Really Pays, Town Learns," *The New York Times* (24 November 1988): B1, B7.

Example 18.3

Pricing Trash in Marietta, Georgia

In 1994 the people of Marietta, Georgia, participated in a demonstration project that changed the way in which waste was priced. The traditional $15 monthly fee for trash pickup was cut to $8 per month. In addition half of the residents faced a per-bag price on waste ($.75 per bag), while the rest faced a monthly fee for pickup that depended on the maximum of cans per month that the customer wished to have picked up per month. This number was contracted in advance by the customer and did not vary from month to month. The fee was $3 or $4 per can (depending upon the number).

Economic theory suggests that while both plans should reduce waste and increase recycling, the per-bag fee should promote more. (Can you see why?)

And indeed that is what happened. The can program reduced nonrecycled waste by about 20 percent, whereas the bag program reduced it by as much as 51 percent. Both programs had an equally strong effect on encouraging households to recycle. The combined weights of waste and recyclables were reduced 36 percent under the bag program and 14 percent under the can program. Both programs not only diverted waste into recycling, they also reduced the amount of waste generated.

Could the costs associated with the program be justified in cost-benefit terms? According to the economists who conducted the study, they were. The net benefits for the city were estimated to be $586 per day for the bag program and $234 per day for the can program.

Source: G. L. Van Houtven, and G. E. Morris, "Household Behavior Under Alternative Pay-as-You-Throw Systems for Solid Waste Disposal," Land Economics, Vol. 75, No. 4 (November, 1999): 515–537.

The recycling of aluminum beverage cans has been one clear beneficiary of deposit-refund schemes.[5] Although not all states have passed "bottle bills," over 50 percent of aluminum beverage cans are now recycled in the United States. As a result, scrap aluminum has become an increasingly significant component of total aluminum supplies.

Recycling aluminum saves about 95 percent of the energy that is needed to make new aluminum from ore. In 1987 alone, recycling aluminum cans saved more than 10 billion kilowatt-hours of electricity, enough to supply the residential electricity needs of New York City for more than six months. The magnitude of these energy savings has had a significant influence on the demand for recycled aluminum as cost-conscious producers search for new ways to reduce energy costs.

Beverage can recycling also reduces littering, because an incentive is created to bring the can to a recycling center. In some cities scavenging and returning these cans has provided a significant source of income to the homeless. One Canadian study found that recycling creates six times as many jobs as landfilling does.

---

[5]A very strong demand for aluminum scrap was also influential. In fact the price for aluminum scrap went so high in 1988 that pilferers were stealing highway signs and guardrails for their aluminum content.

Deposit-refund systems are also being used for batteries and tires. New Hampshire and Maine place a surcharge on new-car batteries. Consumers in these states receive a rebate if they trade in their used battery for a new one. Oklahoma places a $1.00 fee on each new tire sold and then returns 50 cents to certified processing facilities for each tire handled.

Some states in the United States, as well as some developing countries, use deposit-refund systems to assure that pesticide containers are returned after use. Because these containers, after use, usually contain residues that can contaminate water and soil, collecting the containers and either reusing them or properly decontaminating them can eliminate this threat.

The tax system can also be used to promote recycling by taxing virgin materials and by subsidizing recycling activities. The European approach to waste-oil recycling, reinforced by the high cost of imported crude oil, has been to require both residential and commercial users to recycle all waste oil they generate. Virgin lubricating oils are taxed, and the resulting income is used to subsidize the recycling industry. As a result, many countries collect up to 65 percent of the available waste oil.

In the United States, which does not subsidize waste-oil recycling, the waste-oil market has been rather less successful. Currently, only about 15 percent of waste oil is recovered. The waste-oil industry has been in a relative decline since World War II, with the exception of the period immediately following the oil crisis during the 1970s, when oil prices rose dramatically.

Many areas are now using tax policy to subsidize the acquisition of recycling equipment in both the public and private sectors. Frequently taking the form of sales tax exemptions or investment tax credits to private industries or of loans or grants to local communities, these approaches are designed to get recycling programs off the ground with the expectation that such programs will ultimately be self-sustaining. The pioneers are being subsidized.

Examining Oregon's program can serve to illustrate how a tax approach works. From 1981 to 1987, in order to reduce energy consumption as well as to promote recycling, the Oregon Department of Energy granted tax credits to 163 projects. Being granted this credit allowed companies a five-year period in which to deduct from their taxes an amount equal to 35 percent of the cost of any equipment used solely for recycling. Oregon also offers a broader tax credit that covers equipment land, and building purchases. Paper companies, the major recipients of both types of credits, have used them to produce the capacity to use recycled newsprint and cardboard in the papermaking process. As a result, Oregon's newspaper-recycling rate (65%) is twice the national average.[6]

Any long-run solution to the solid waste problem must not only influence consumer choices about purchasing, packaging, and disposal, it must also influence producer choices about product design (to increase their recyclability), product packaging, and the use of recycled (as opposed to virgin materials) in the production process. In 1991 Germany took a new approach to orienting the market in this direction by implementing a law embodying the "take-back" principle (Example 18.4).

Pollution Damage

One other situation influences the use of recycled and virgin ores. When environmental damage results from extracting and using virgin materials and not from the use of recycled materials,

---

[6]Cynthia Pollock Shea, "Building a Market for Recyclables," *Worldwatch* (May/June 1988): 12–18.

Example 18.4

Implementing the "Take-Back" Principle

According to the "take-back" principle, all producers should be required to accept responsibility for their products (including packaging) from cradle to grave. This includes the responsibility for taking them back once the products have outlived their useful lives. In theory, this requirement was designed to encourage the elimination of inessential packaging, to stimulate the search for products and packaging that are easier to recycle, and to support the substitution of recycled inputs for virgin inputs in the production process.

Germany has required producers (and retailers, as intermediaries) to accept all packaging associated with products, including such different types of packaging as the cardboard boxes used for shipping hundreds of toothbrushes to retailers to the tube that toothpaste is sold in. Consumers are encouraged to return the packaging by means of a combination of convenient drop-off centers, refundable deposits on some packages, and high disposal costs for packaging that is thrown away.

Producers responded by setting up a new, private, nonprofit corporation, the *Duales System Deutschland* (DSD), to collect the packaging and to recycle the collected materials. This corporation is funded by fees levied on producers. The fees are based on the number of kilograms of packaging the producers use. The DSD only accepts packaging that it has certified as recyclable. Once certification is received, producers are allowed to display a green dot on their product, which signals to consumers that this product is accepted by the DSD system. Any other packaging must be returned directly to the producer or to the retailer, who returns it to the producer.

The law has apparently reduced the amount of packaging produced and has diverted a significant amount of packaging away from incineration and landfills. However, the law's most noteworthy failure was the inability of the DSD system to find markets for the recycled materials it has collected. Some German packaging even ended up in neighboring countries, causing some international backlash. The circumstance where the supply of recycled materials far exceeds the demand for them is so common—not only in Germany, but in the rest of the world as well—that further efforts to increase the degree of recycling will likely flounder unless new markets for recycled materials are forthcoming.

Despite the initial difficulties with implementing the take-back principle, the idea that manufacturers should have ultimate responsibility for their products has a sufficiently powerful appeal that it has moved beyond an exclusive focus on packaging and is now expanding to include the products themselves. According to a new law that took effect in 1996 (known popularly as the "materials recirculation law"), manufacturers in Germany will now have a legal obligation to design goods in such a manner that waste is minimized both in production and use. Early targets for applying the take-back principle to products include automobiles, computers, and large appliances.

Sources: A. S. Rousso and S. P. Shah, "Packaging Taxes and Recycling Incentives: The German Green Dot Program" *National Tax Journal* 47, No. 3 (September 1994): 689–701; Megan Ryan, "Packaging a Revolution," *World Watch* (September-October 1993):28–34: and Christopher Boerner and Kenneth Chilton, "False Economy: The Folly of Demand-Side Recycling," *Environment* 36 (January/February 1994): 6–15, 32–33.

the market allocation will be biased away from recycling. The damage might be experienced at the mine, such as the erosion and aesthetic costs of strip mining, or at the point of processing, where the ore is processed into a usable resource.

Suppose the mining industry were forced to bear the cost of this environmental damage. What difference would the inclusion of this cost have on the scrap market? The internalizing of this cost results in a leftward shift in the supply curve for the virgin ore (S_d). This would, in turn, cause a leftward shift in the total-supply curve. The market would be using less of the resource—because of higher price—while recycling more. Thus, the correct treatment of these environmental costs would share with disposal costs a tendency to increase the role for recycling.

One study by Spofford examines the significance of this cost in the context of the paper industry, which, in spite of the fact that it is based on a renewable resource, does rely on the recycling of used paper.[7] In his study (summarized in Figure 18.1), Spofford considers four costs: (1) acquiring and processing virgin pulp, (2) using scrap paper, (3) treatment and disposal of resulting pollutants, and (4) the external damage caused by untreated pollutants. Graphed as a function of the reuse ratio, the external damages and treatment costs are much higher with lower reuse ratios; the use of virgin materials generates most of these costs.

Spofford also differentiates the costs to society as a whole from the costs to the paper-making firm. These differ because society bears all the costs, whereas the firm bears only the costs of acquiring and processing virgin pulp and the costs of using scrap paper. The private costs do not include either the treatment costs (in the absence of government control, the firm would not choose to treat the pollutants) or the external damages. The major conclusion to be drawn is that the efficient reuse ration (0.8) is significantly higher than what the market would automatically provide (0.55), because of the undervaluation of environmental damage by the market.

◆ PRODUCT DURABILITY

In a memorable passage from *Death of a Salesman,* Willy Loman, the title character, laments:

> Once in my life I would like to own something outright before it's broken! I'm always in a race with the junkyard! I just finish paying for the car and it's on its last legs. The refrigerator consumes belts like a goddamn maniac. They time those things. They time them so when you've finally paid for them, they're used up.[8]

Willy is not alone in his anguish. In the early 1960s popular author Vance Packard came out with a book called *The Waste Makers,* in which he suggested that Willy's plight was the product of a conscious marketing strategy by corporations. If products wear out faster, the argument goes, consumers have to buy them more often and sales are increased. Is this a valid

---

[7]W. O. Spofford, "Solid Residual Management: Some Economic Considerations," *Natural Resource Journal* 11 (July 1971): 561–89.

[8]Arthur Miller, "Death of a Salesman," Act II, in *Arthur Miller's Collected Plays* 1 (New York: Viking Press, 1957): 174.

FIGURE 18.1   Optimal Reuse Ratio for Paper Residuals in the Production of Newsprint

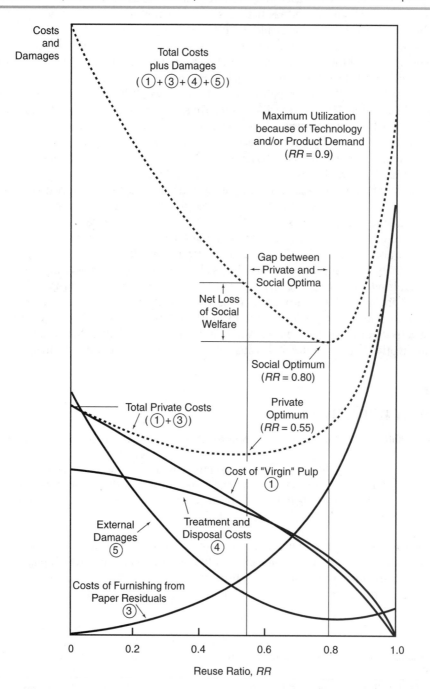

argument? If it is, the drain on the resource base is artificially high, and we have another reason for corrective measures.

Packard identifies three possible types of product obsolescence. *Functional obsolescence* occurs when a new product can perform the function in a superior manner to an older product. The vacuum tube became functionally obsolescent when it was replaced by the transistor. *Fashion obsolescence* occurs when consumers prefer a new product for reasons of taste. Wide ties and short skirts become obsolete when tastes shift to narrow ties and long skirts. *Durability obsolescence* occurs when the product can no longer perform its function because of wear and tear. A refrigerator becomes obsolete when it can no longer keep its inside temperature stable and cool. The economic implications of these three types of obsolescence are quite different.

Functional Obsolescence

Because functional obsolescence is not really a problem, we will spend little time on it. A vigorous amount of inventive activity is a natural and desirable consequence of a market economy. Those who find better ways of doing things can become wealthy from the sales of their product, whether it be a tastier way to fry chicken or a cheaper, higher-quality method of copying documents. Far from representing a problem, functional obsolescence is the natural consequence of the successful search for better products.

Fashion Obsolescence

Fashion obsolescence is trickier. On the one hand, if fashion is a valued characteristic for consumers, then it is possible to conceive fashion obsolescence as merely a special case of functional obsolescence. New fashions replace old because they are more satisfying to the consumer. In this view, there is no problem with fashion obsolescence, because it is merely the result of the market continually doing a superior job of satisfying consumer preference.

The opposite point of view starts from the premise that those consumer preferences being satisfied by the market are in fact *created* by the market. If consumer preferences are created by producers, then it is appropriate to question whether consumers are legitimately being made better off or are merely being manipulated into believing they are better off.

The apparel industry is certainly one where fashion obsolescence plays a strong role. However, it is not clear that fashion obsolescence is as important for other products. The automobile has certainly had its share of fashion obsolescence, perhaps best epitomized by the era in the 1950s when pronounced tailfins were in vogue. Yet, clearly, the auto industry can go only so far in promoting new fashions. It would be very difficult, for example, to explain the shift in consumer buying toward small imported automobiles in the late 1970s and early 1980s as reflecting a shift in what was fashionable.

Indeed, some observers believe that a significant portion of the malaise of the domestic auto industry in the 1980s was caused by its inability to anticipate and respond to consumer preferences. That is important, because the automobile market is one in which consumer preferences were thought to be dominated by the "Big Three" U.S. automakers. This is not the case.

Even when fashion influences consumer preferences, it is not clear that taste is dictated by the manufacturer or that it relates solely to new products. Antique furniture and antique cars are fashionable, but these fashions certainly are not created by manufacturers and do not help sell new cars or new furniture.

In looking at the totality of consumer decisions, we cannot conclude that consumer tastes are systematically manipulated by industry. Markets do exist for which a strong case can be made, but they seem to be isolated examples, rather than typical.

Durability Obsolescence

We come then to the final category, the one that triggered Willy Loman's lament. For this category, we must begin to answer two questions: (1) What is an efficient level of durability, and (2) will the market supply that level?

The *efficient level of durability* is the one that maximizes the net benefit from the product. Products that last longer confer more benefits on society, but they also cost more. Therefore, it is not obvious that the most durable product is also the most efficient one. Can we trust the market to find the efficient level of durability? To examine that issue, let's look at both the demand and supply sides of the market.

On the demand side, the consumer makes his or her choices by discounting benefits and costs. The capital costs of consumer durables are borne immediately (although payments can be spread out by borrowing money), whereas the benefits (flow of services), as well as operating and maintenance costs, are accrued as a flow over time. The consumer will purchase the commodity only if the net benefit is maximized by that level of durability (i.e., if the additional cost of making a more durable commodity is justified by the additional benefit received). In performing this balancing between cost and durability, will the consumer make efficient choices or, because of lack of information or some other market imperfection, will durability be undervalued or overvalued?

One way to test this is to examine a case in which the benefits and costs are relatively easy to quantify, thereby allowing a comparison of the discount rate implied by consumer purchases of durable goods with market rates. If their individual discount rates are higher than the social opportunity cost of capital (as measured by interest rates), consumers are undervaluing durability. If they use lower discount rates, they are overvaluing it.

Jerry Hausman of MIT conducted a fascinating study that relates to this issue.[9] He was able to acquire data on individual purchases of energy-suing consumer durables (room air conditioners). For each of these purchases, he could calculate the benefits (longer life plus energy savings resulting from higher energy efficiency) and cost (purchase price as well as expected operating and maintenance costs). From this information he could calculate the discount rates implied by the purchase made by the average consumer. High discount rates indicate a special sensitivity to the initial cost.

In his sample, the implied discount rates were higher than the market rates. Furthermore, Hausman found that discount rates were highest for the people with the lowest income, whereas they approximated the efficient rates for higher-income classes. This suggests that

---

[9]Jerry Hausman, "Individual Discount Rates and the Purchase and Utilization of Energy-Using Durables," *Bell Journal of Economics* 10 (Spring 1979): 33–54.

consumers—particularly low-income consumers—purchase less durability and less energy efficiency than are dictated by the dynamic-efficiency criterion.[10]

To be able to structure the appropriate policy response, however, the government would have to know more about the reasons for the higher implied discount rates. If the reason is inadequate consumer information, then the appropriate policy might well be increasing the flow of reliable information through testing, labeling requirements, and so on. If it is purely that the market rate of interest is higher for low-income consumers because they have a higher probability of defaulting on loan repayments, then some means of providing easier access to capital markets might be called for. In other cases, measures such as tax subsidies or enforced standards might be appropriate.

We must also consider the supply side of the market. If they can get away with it, producers as a group have an incentive to reduce product durability below the efficient level. By doing so, they would reduce their cost per unit and they would sell many more units over time. For example, a household could satisfy its demand over a 10-year period with one appliance lasting 10 years, but would have to purchase two if the appliance only lasted 5 years. As long as the profit was higher on the sale of two, rather than one (the presumption), firms would be better off with planned obsolescence.

But the key question is whether or not they can get away with it. As long as competitive suppliers, or even potential competitive suppliers, could enter the market to supply more-durable goods, the consumer could turn to these alternative suppliers instead. In a normal market process, competition prevents individual firms from producing insufficiently durable products. Those who sell products that don't last find their markets drying up.

This market process may not work efficiently in two different cases. The first case occurs when consumers are not well informed about the differences in durability and so do not have enough information to make efficient decisions. This, remember, was one possible interpretation of the Hausman study. To the extent that they face ignorant consumers, producers would have an incentive to position themselves in the lower initial price portion of the market by lowering the durability of their products.

In recognition of the importance of this information, organizations have been set up to supply it. Consumers' Union, the publisher of *Consumer Reports,* is one such organization. It performs its own independent testing and evaluating, a service that can rectify this lack of information at reasonable cost. Its chief limitation probably relates to products undergoing rapid technological change.

For rapidly changing products, by the time the testing lab acquires the product, tests it, and reports the results, other untested but potentially superior products are already on the market. This flaw, however, is not fatal; it merely means that the rate of adoption would be rather more sluggish than would be dictated by efficiency.

The second case where a firm could profit by producing a good with an inefficiently low durability is when it does not face competition. This would require either a monopoly—which

---

[10]These results were subsequently corroborated by a number of other authors. For a description of these, see Malcolm Gladwell, "Consumer's Choices About Money Consistently Defy Common Sense," *The Washington Post* (12 February 1990): A3.

is, of course, very rare—or explicit collusion in order to cut corners by all the members of the industry. Because competition comes from foreign firms as well as domestic ones and from potential entrants as well as existing firms, this must be a relatively rare circumstance.

The U.S. automobile industry provides an interesting case to examine the hypothesis that increased competition can increase durability, because that industry has faced increasingly intense foreign competition. The share of the U.S. market captured by imports rose from 14.8 percent in 1976 to 29.2 percent in 1988.[11] Did this lead to increased durability?

According to two possible measures, it did. Durable cars should last longer and be safer. The average age of passenger cars increased from 6.2 years in 1976 to 7.6 years in 1988, and the deaths per 100 million vehicle-miles traveled decreased from 3.33 in 1976 to 2.46 in 1988. Though other factors were certainly also at work, competition probably did play a major role in increasing durability.

SUMMARY

Market mechanisms typically create pressures for recycling and reuse that are generally in the right direction, though rarely of the correct intensity. Higher disposal costs and increasing scarcity of virgin materials do create a larger demand for recycling. For some products, such as copper and aluminum, this process is already in full swing.

However, a number of imperfections in the market suggest that the degree of recycling we are currently experiencing is less than the efficient amount. The expectation that virgin prices are steadily increasing is not always valid (Example 18.5). Coupled with artificially low disposal costs, these depressed prices contribute to depressed markets for recycled materials.

One imperfection, the supposed tendency of U.S. manufacturers to produce products less durable than efficient, seems overstated. However, the Hausman study indicates that some people do purchase products less durable than efficient, implying that the market penetration of more-energy-efficient devices may be lower than efficient. This is a more limited view of product durability problems than is usually espoused by writers such as Vance Packard, but a troubling one nonetheless.

One cannot help but notice that many of these problems result from government actions. It therefore appears, in this area, that the appropriate role for government is selective disengagement complemented by some fine-tuning adjustments.

The most important of these fine-tuning adjustments relates to the adoption of pricing strategies for waste disposal that impose the true marginal cost on the disposers. Two elements of appropriate pricing strategies are important: (1) assuring that prices are on a per unit volume basis, and (2) incorporating the costs of environmental damage.

The commonly heard ideological prescriptions suggesting that environmental problems can be solved either by ending government interference or by increasing the amount of government control are both inaccurate. The efficient role for government in achieving a balance between the economic and environmental systems requires less control in some areas and more in others.

---

[11]The data in this paragraph and the one that follows it came from Motor Vehicles Manufacturing Association, *Motor Vehicle Facts and Figures, 1989* (Detroit: MI: Motor Vehicles Manufacturing Association, 1989): 16, 26, and 90.

Example 18.5

The Bet

In 1980, each of two distinguished protagonists in the scarcity debate "put his money where his mouth was." Paul Ehrlich, an ecologist with a strong belief in impending scarcity, answered a challenge from Julian Simon, an economist known for his equally strong belief that concerns about impending scarcity were groundless.

According to the terms of the bet, Ehrlich would hypothetically invest $200 in each of any five commodities he selected. (He picked copper, chrome, nickel, tin, and tungsten.) Ten years later, the aggregate value of the same amounts of those five commodities would be calculated in real terms (after accounting for normal inflation). If the value increased, Simon would send Ehrlich a check for the difference. If it decreased, Ehrlich would send Simon a check for the difference.

In 1990, Ehrlich performed the calculations and sent Simon a check for $576.07. Not only were real prices lower for each of the five commodities, but some were less than half their former levels. New sources of the minerals had been discovered, substitutions away from these minerals had occurred in many of their uses (particularly computers), and the tin cartel, which had been holding up tin prices, collapsed.

Does this evidence provide a lesson for the future? You be the judge.

Source: John Tierney, "Betting the Planet," *New York Times Magazine* (December 2, 1990): 52–53, 74, 76, 78, and 80–81.

FURTHER READING

Bohm, Peter. *Deposit-Refund System: Theory and Application to Environmental, Conservation, and Consumer Policy* (Baltimore, MD: Johns Hopkins University Press, for Resources for the Future, 1981). A highly readable and analytically sound exploration of the experience with and potential applications for deposit-refund systems.

Curlee, T. Randall. *The Economic Feasibility of Recycling: A Case Study of Plastic Wastes* (New York: Praeger, 1986). Analyzes in nontechnical language the incentives for, and barriers to, recycling plastic.

Dinan, Terry. "Economic Efficiency Aspects of Alternative Policies for Reducing Waste Disposal," *Journal of Environmental Economics and Management* 25 (1993): 242–256. Argues that a tax on virgin materials is not enough to produce efficiency; a subsidy on reuse is also required.

Jenkins, Robin R. *The Economics of Solid Waste Reduction: The Impact of User Fees* (Cheltenham, UK: Edward Elgar, 1993). An analysis that examines whether user fees do, in fact, encourage people to recycle waste. Using evidence derived from nine U.S. communities, the author concludes that they do.

Kinnaman, T. C., and D. Fullerton. The Economics of Residential Solid Waste Management," in *The International Yearbook of Environmental and Resource Economics 2000/2001*. T. Tietenberg and H. Folmer, eds. (Cheltenham, UK, Edward Elgar, 2000): 100–147. A survey of the economics literature that reviews trends in residential solid waste and the effectiveness of policies designed to combat inefficiencies.

Repetto, Robert, et al. *Green Fees: How a Tax Shift Can Work for the Environment and the Economy* (Washington, DC: World Resources Institute, 1992). One of the case studies involves an examination of pay-by-the-bag disposal pricing.

Reschovsky, J. D., and S. E. Stone. "Market Incentives to Encourage Household Waste Recycling: Paying for What You Throw Away," *Journal of Policy Analysis and Management* 13 (1994): 120–39. An examination of ways to change the zero-marginal-cost-of-disposal characteristic of many current disposal programs.

Roxburgh, Nigel. *Policy Responses to Resource Depletion: The Case of Mercury* (Greenwich, CT: JAI Press, 1980). An intensive examination of the depletion experience with one particular material—mercury. Includes chapters on the resource base, extractive and scrap metal industries, and various industries that are heavy users of mercury.

Tilton, John E., ed. *Mineral Wealth and Economic Development* (Washington, DC: Resources for the Future, 1992). Explores why a number of mineral-exporting countries have seen their per capita incomes decline or their standards of living stagnate over the last several decades.

ADDITIONAL REFERENCES

Allen, J., et al. "Using Coupon Incentives in Recycling Aluminum: A Market Approach to Energy Conservation Policy," *Journal of Consumer Affairs* 27 (1993): 300–318.

Banks, Ferdinand E. *Bauxite and Aluminum: An Introduction to the Economics of Nonfuel Minerals* (Lexington, MA: Lexington Books, 1979).

Conrad, K. "Resource and Waste Taxation in the Theory of the Firm with Recycling Activities," *Environmental and Resource Economics* 14(1999)(2): 217–242.

Foley, Patricia T., and Joel P. Clark. "The Effects of State Taxation on United States Copper Supply," Land Economics 58 (May 1982): 153–180.

Gulley, D. A. "Severance Taxes and Market Failure," *Natural Resources Journal* 22 (July 1982): 597–617.

Harris, DeVerle P. *Mineral Resources Appraisal* (New York: Oxford University Press, 1984).

Hazilla, Michael, and Raymond J. Kopp. "Assessing U.S. Vulnerability to Raw Material Supply Disruptions: An Application to Nonfuel Minerals," *Southern Economic Journal* 52 (October 1984): 341–355.

Hong, S., and R. M. Adams. "Household Responses to Price Incentives for Recycling: Some Further Evidence," *Land Economics* 75(1999)(4): 505–514.

Kakela, Peter J. "Iron Ore: From Depletion to Abundance," *Science* 212 (April 10, 1981): 132–136.

Lee, D. R., P. E. Graves, and R. L. Sexton. "On Mandatory Deposits, Fines, and the Control of Litter," *Natural Resources Journal* 28 (fall 1988): 837–847.

McClure, Charles, and Peter Mieszkowski, eds. *Fiscal Federalism and the Taxation of Natural Resources* (Lexington, MA: Lexington Books, 1983).

Mikesell, Raymond F. *Nonfuel Minerals: Foreign Dependence and National Security* (Ann Arbor: University of Michigan Press, 1987).

Page, Talbott. *Conservation and Economic Efficiency: An Approach to Materials Policy* (Baltimore, MD: Johns Hopkins University Press, for Resources for the Future, 1977).

Peck, Merton J., ed. *The World Aluminum Industry in a Changing Energy Era* (Washington, DC: Resources for the Future, 1988).

Stollery, Kenneth R. "Mineral Depletion with Cost as the Extraction Limit: A Model Applied to the Behavior of Prices in the Nickel Industry," *Journal of Environmental Economics and Management* 10 (June 1983): 151–165.

Tilton, John E. ed. *Material Substitution: Lessons from Tin-Using Industries* (Washington, DC: Resources for the Future, 1985).

Tilton, John E., Roderick G. Eggert, and Hans H. Landsberg, eds. *World Mineral Exploration: Trends and Economic Issues* (Washington, DC: Resources for the Future, 1988).

VanHoutven, G. L., and G. E. Morris. "Household Behavior Under Alternative Pay-as-You-Throw Systems for Solid Waste Disposal," *Land Economics* 75(1999)(4): 515–537.

Versteege, Hetty M. "Variable Rates for the Collection of Household Waste," *Warmer Bulletin* 43 (November 1994): 7.

WEB SITES OF INTEREST

1. *http://www.obviously.com/recycle/*
   The Internet Consumer Recycling guide.

2. *http://www.epa.gov/epaoswer/non-hw/payt/index.htm*
   EPA's Pay-as-You-Throw web site.

3. *http://195.126.62.227/en/*
   The German "Green Dot" System web page (English version).

DISCUSSION QUESTIONS

1. Glass bottles can be either recycled (crushed and remelted) or reused. The market will tend to choose the cheapest path. What factors will tend to affect the relative cost of these options? Is the market likely to make the efficient choice? Are the "bottle bills" passed by many of the states requiring deposits on bottles a move toward efficiency or not? Why?

2. Many areas have attempted to increase the amount of recycled waste lubricating oil by requiring service stations to serve as collection centers or by instituting deposit-refund systems. On what grounds, if any, is government intervention called for? In terms of the effects on the waste-lubrication-oil market, what differences should be noticed among those states that do nothing, those that require all service stations to serve as collection centers, and those implementing deposit-refund systems? Why?

3. What are the income distribution consequences of "fashion"? Can the need to be seen driving a new car by the rich be a boon to those with lower incomes who will ultimately purchase a better, lower-priced used car as a result?

4. "As society's cost of disposing of trash increases over time, recycling rates should automatically increase as well." Discuss.

Toxic Substances and Hazardous Wastes

The fact that a problem will certainly take a long time to solve, and that it will demand the attention of many minds for several generations, is no justification for postponing the study. Our difficulties of the moment must always be dealt with somehow, but our permanent difficulties are difficulties of every moment.

T. S. ELIOT, *CHRISTIANITY AND CULTURE* (1949)

◆ INTRODUCTION

In one of the interesting ironies of history, the place that focused public attention in the United States on hazardous waste is called the Love Canal. *Love* is not a word any impartial observer would choose to describe the relationships among the parties to that incident.

The Love Canal typifies in many ways the dilemma posed by the creation and disposal of toxic substances. Until 1953, Hooker Electrochemical (now Hooker Chemical, a subsidiary of Occidental Petroleum Corporation) dumped waste chemicals into an old abandoned waterway known as the Love Canal, near Niagara Falls, New York.[1] At the time it seemed a reasonable solution, because the chemicals were buried in what was then considered to be impermeable clay.

In 1953 Hooker deeded the Love Canal property for one dollar to the Niagara Falls Board of Education, which then built an elementary school on the site. The deed specifically excused Hooker from any damages that might be caused by the chemicals. Residential development of the area around the school soon followed.

---

[1]Hooker was acquired by Occidental Petroleum in 1968.

The site became the center of controversy when, in 1978, residents complained of chemicals leaking to the surface. News reports emanating from the area included stories of spontaneous fires and vapors in basements. Medical reports suggested that the residents had experienced abnormally high rates of miscarriage, birth defects, and diseases of the liver.

Similar experiences befell sites in Europe and Asia. In 1976 an accident at an F. Hoffman–La Roche & Co. plant in Sevesco spewed dioxin over the Italian countryside. More recently, explosions in a Union Carbide plant in Bhopal, India, spread deadly gases over nearby residential neighborhoods with significant loss of life, and water used to quell a warehouse fire at a Sandoz warehouse near Basel, Switzerland, carried an estimated 30 tons of toxic chemicals into the Rhine River, a source of drinking water for a number of towns in the former Federal Republic of Germany.

In previous chapters we touched on a few of the policy instruments used to combat toxic-substance problems. Emission standards govern the types and amounts of substances that can be injected into the air. Effluent standards regulate what can be discharged directly into water sources, and pretreatment standards control the flow of toxics into waste treatment plants. Maximum concentration levels have been established for many substances in drinking water.

This impressive array of policies is not sufficient to resolve the Love Canal problem or others having similar characteristics. When violations of the standards for drinking water are detected, for example, the water is already contaminated. Specifying maximum contaminant levels helps to identify when a problem exists, but it does nothing to prevent or contain the problem. The various standards for air and water emission that do protect against pollution by *point* sources do little to prevent contamination by *nonpoint* sources. Furthermore, most waterborne toxic pollutants are stock pollutants, not fund pollutants; they cannot be absorbed by the receiving waters. Therefore, temporally constant controls on emissions (a traditional method used for fund pollutants) is inappropriate for these toxic substances because such controls would allow a steady rise in the concentration over time. Some additional form of control is necessary to curb toxic-substance pollution.

In this chapter we shall describe and evaluate the policies that deal specifically with the creation, use, transportation, and disposal of toxic substances. Many dimensions will be considered. What are appropriate ways to dispose of hazardous materials? How can the government ensure that all waste is appropriately disposed of? How do we prevent surreptitious dumping? Who should clean up old sites? Should victims be compensated for damages caused by toxic substances under the control of someone else? If so, by whom? What are the appropriate roles for the legislature and the judiciary in creating the proper set of incentives?

◆ THE NATURE OF TOXIC SUBSTANCE POLLUTION

The main objective of the current legal system for controlling toxic substances is to protect human health, though protecting other forms of life is a secondary objective. The potential health danger depends upon the toxicity of a substance to humans and their exposure to the substance. *Toxicity* occurs when a living organism experiences detrimental effects on being exposed to a substance. In normal concentrations most chemicals are not toxic. Others, such as pesticides, are toxic by design. Yet, in excess concentrations, even a benign substance such as table salt can be toxic.

A degree of risk is involved when using any chemical substance. There are benefits as well. The task for public policy is to define an acceptable risk by balancing the costs and benefits of controlling the use of chemical substances.

Health Effects

The two main health concerns associated with toxic substances are (1) risk of cancer and (2) effects on reproduction.

Cancer. Since the 1900s, mortality rates have fallen for most of the major causes of death. The most conspicuous exception is cancer. Even the mortality rate for heart disease, the number one killer, has declined in recent decades. Meanwhile, the mortality rate for cancer, currently the second most common cause of death, has increased steadily through this century.

Although many suspect that this increased mortality rate for cancer may be related to increased exposure to carcinogens, proving or disproving this link is very difficult because of the latency of the disease. In this context, *latency* refers to the state of being concealed during the period between exposure to the carcinogen and the detection of cancer. Latency periods for cancer can run from 15 to 40 years in length, but have been known to run as long as 75 years.[2]

In the United States, part of the increase in cancer has been convincingly linked to smoking, particularly among women. The proportion of women who smoke has increased, and the incidence of lung cancer has increased as well. Smoking does not account for all of the increase in cancer, however. A smaller percentage of men smoke today than in earlier decades, and modern cigarettes contain less tar. Despite this, the incidence of lung cancer among men has increased.[3]

Though it is not entirely clear what other agents may be responsible, one cause that has been suggested is the rise in the manufacture and use of synthetic chemicals since World War II.[4] A number of these chemicals have been shown in the laboratory to be carcinogenic. That does not necessarily implicate them in the rise of cancer, however, because it does not take exposure into account. The laboratory can reveal, through animal tests, the relationship between dosage and resulting effects. To track down the significance of any chemical in causing cancer in the general population would require an estimate of how large a segment of the population was exposed to various doses. Currently, our data are not extensive enough to allow these kinds of calculations to be done with any confidence.

Reproductive Effects.[5] Tracing the influence of environmental effects on human reproduction is still a new science. A growing body of scientific evidence, however, suggests that exposure to smoking, alcohol, and synthetic chemicals may contribute to infertility, may affect the

---

[2]Paul R. Portney, "Toxic Substance Policy and the Protection of Human Health," in *Current Issues in U.S. Environmental Policy,* Paul R. Portney, ed. (Baltimore, MD: Johns Hopkins University Press, 1978): 100.

[3]Council on Environmental Quality, *Environmental Quality—1980* (Washington, DC: Government Printing Office, 1980): 194.

[4]Davis and Magee raise this possibility but also conclude that, because of the latency period, it is too early to tell how much, if any, of the responsibility can be assigned to the increased exposure to synthetic chemicals. See Devra Lee Davis and Brian H. Magee, "Cancer and Industrial Chemical Production," *Science* 206 (21 December 1979): 1356–1358.

[5]For an excellent study of the literature, see Council on Environmental Quality, op. cit.: 199–205.

viability of the fetus and the health of the infant after birth, and may cause genetic defects that can be passed on for generations.

Problems exist for both men and women. In men, exposure to toxic substances has resulted in lower sperm counts, malformed sperm, and genetic damage. In women, exposure can result in genetic change, in sterility, or in birth defects in their children.

Policy Issues

Many aspects of the toxic substance problem make it difficult to resolve. Three important aspects are (1) the numbers of substances involved, (2) latency, and (3) uncertainty.

Number of Substances. Of the 2 million or so known chemical compounds, approximately 55,000 are actively used in commerce. More than 30,000 of these are in substantial use. Many exhibit little or no toxicity, and even a very toxic substance represents little risk as long as it is isolated. The trick is to identify problem substances and design appropriate policies as responses. The massive number of substances involved makes that a difficult assignment. The geographic location of industrial hazardous wastes, a major component of the hazardous waste problem, is given in Table 19.1.

TABLE 19.1   Toxic Releases in 1997, by State (in thousands of tons)

State	Quantity	State	Quantity
Texas	261.7	Washington	31.8
Louisiana	186.0	Arizona	31.4
Ohio	158.7	Oregon	31.0
Pennsylvania	143.2	Kansas	26.7
Illinois	127.6	Oklahoma	24.8
Indiana	122.6	West Virginia	24.8
Tennessee	106.9	New Jersey	20.7
Utah	103.7	Minnesota	20.2
Florida	95.4	Nebraska	18.0
Alabama	94.7	Idaho	17.7
Michigan	85.3	Maryland	13.7
North Carolina	85.1	Maine	9.8
Georgia	71.9	Conneticut	9.7
Mississippi	66.2	Wyoming	9.4
Missouri	62.8	Massachusetts	7.1
Arkansas	59.7	Colorado	5.1
South Carolina	58.4	Alaska	4.6
Virginia	58.0	Nevada	4.4
Wisconsin	50.6	South Dakota	4.2
Kentucky	47.3	Delaware	3.5
California	45.2	New Hampshire	2.8
Montana	43.4	North Dakota	2.4
New York	38.6	Rhode Island	2.2
Iowa	34.2	Vermont	0.6
New Mexico	34.2	Hawii	0.5
		Total	2,577.60

Source: U.S. EPA, *1997 Toxics Release Inventory, State Fact Sheets.*

Latency.   The period of latency exhibited by many of these exposure-effect relationships compounds the problem. Two kinds of toxicity are exhibited—acute and chronic. *Acute toxicity* is present when a short-term exposure to the substance produces a detrimental effect on the exposed organisms. *Chronic toxicity* is present when the detrimental effect arises from exposure of a continued or prolonged nature.

The process of screening chemicals as potentially serious causes of chronic illness is even more complicated than that of screening them as causes of acute illness. The traditional technique for determining acute toxicity is the *lethal-dose determination,* a relatively quick test performed on animals that calculates the dose that results in the death of 50 percent of the animal population. This test is less well suited for screening substances that exhibit chronic toxicity.

The appropriate tests for discovering chronic toxicity have typically involved subjecting animal populations to sustained low-level doses of the substance over an extended period of time. These tests are very expensive and time-consuming.[6] If all proposed chemicals were subjected to such long and detailed tests, the process itself would preclude the introduction of many new chemicals. If the EPA were to do the tests, given its limited resources, it could only test a few of the estimated 500 new chemicals introduced each year. If the industries were to do the tests, the expense could preclude the introduction of many potentially valuable new chemicals that have limited, specialized markets.

The EPA has attempted to respond by developing a series of screening tests that can be accomplished in a shorter period of time and at less expense. The chemicals identified by those screening tests as posing an unacceptable risk can be subjected to more expensive tests. As long as the short tests are sufficiently reliable for screening, the testing problem can be reduced to manageable proportions.

One particularly promising class of screening tests involves adding a chemical substance to a bacteria culture no longer capable of growth. If the substance is a mutagen, and therefore a likely carcinogen, the bacteria resume growth. Although these tests are considerably cheaper to perform, the correlation between mutagens and carcinogens is not perfect. For example, benzene, a known carcinogen, is not a mutagen. Some carcinogens could slip through the screening process undetected.

Uncertainty.   Another dilemma inhibiting policymakers is the uncertainty surrounding the scientific evidence on which regulation is based. Effects uncovered by laboratory studies on animals are not perfectly correlated with effects on humans. Large doses administered over a 3-year period may not produce the same effects as an equivalent amount spread over a 20-year period. Some of the effects are *synergistic*—that is, their effects are compounded by other variable factors. They are either more serious or less serious in the presence of other substances or conditions than they would be in the absence of those substances or conditions.[7] Once cancer is detected, in most cases it does not bear the imprint of a particular source. Policy makers have to act in the face of limited information.

---

[6]A two-year bioassay for carcinogenic effects of a single chemical would cost $1.25 million, according to R. C. Evans, J. Bakst, and M. Dreyfus, *An Analysis of TCSA Reauthorization Proposals* (Washington, DC: EPA Office of Pesticides and Toxic Substances, 1985).

[7]Asbestos workers who smoke are 30 times more likely to get lung cancer than their nonsmoking fellow workers, for example.

From an economic point of view, how the policy process reacts to this dilemma should depend on how well the market handles toxic substance problems. To the extent that the market generates the correct information and provides the appropriate incentives, policy may not be needed. On the other hand, when the government can best generate information or create the appropriate incentive, intervention may be called for. As the following pages demonstrate, the nature of the most appropriate policy response may depend crucially on the type of relationship existing between the polluter and the affected party or parties.

◆ MARKET ALLOCATIONS AND TOXIC SUBSTANCES

Toxic substance contamination can arise in a variety of settings. To define the efficient policy response, we must examine what responses would be forthcoming in the normal operation of the market. Let's look at three possible relationships between the source of the contamination and the victim: (1) employer-employee, (2) producer-consumer, and (3) producer-third party. The first two of these involve normal contractual relations among the parties; the latter involves noncontracting parties whose connection is defined solely by the contamination.

Occupational Hazards

Many occupations involve risk, including, for some people, exposure to toxic substances. Do employers and employees have sufficient incentives to act in concert toward achieving safety in the workplace?

The caricature of the market used by the most ardent proponents of regulation suggests not. In this view, the employer's desire to maximize profits precludes spending money on safety. Sick workers can simply be replaced. Therefore, the workers are powerless to do anything about it; if they complain, they are fired and replaced with others who are less vocal.

The most ardent opponents of regulation respond that this caricature omits significant market pressures and is not a particularly accurate guide. They argue that it fails to take into account employee incentives and the feedback effects of those incentives on employers.

If employees are to accept work in a potentially hazardous environment, they will do so only if appropriately compensated. Riskier occupations should call forth higher wages. The increase in wages should be sufficient to compensate the workers for the increased risk. These higher wages represent a real cost of the hazardous situation to the employer. They also produce an incentive to create a safer work environment, because greater safety would result in lower wages. One cost could be balanced against the other. What was spent on safety could be recovered in lower wages.

When the marginal increased wages accurately reflect marginal damages, market equilibria are efficient. As long as this stylized view of the world is correct, the market will tailor the appropriate degree of precaution to the situation.

Proponents point out that this allocation would also allow more choices for workers than would, for example, a system requiring all workplaces to be equally safe. With varying occupational risk, those occupations with more risk (e.g., working with radioactive materials) would attract people who were less averse to risk. These workers would receive higher than average wages (to compensate them for the increased risk), but paying these higher wages would be cheaper to the firm (and hence, consumers) than producing a workplace safe enough for the average worker. The risk-averse workers would be free to choose less risky occupations.

Existing empirical studies make clear that wages in risky occupations do contain a risk premium. Two conclusions about these risk premiums seem clear from these studies: (1) The willingness to pay for apparently similar risk reductions varies significantly across individuals; and (2) the revealed willingness to pay for risk reduction is substantial.[8]

What is the appropriate role for the public sector in controlling contamination in the workplace? One point raised by the court system is whether or not market solutions always satisfy ethical norms. For example, if the employee is a pregnant woman and the occupational hazard involves potential damage to the fetus, does the expectant mother have the right to risk the unborn child, or is some added protection for the fetus needed? Furthermore, if the lowest-cost solution is to ban pregnant—or even fertile—women from a workplace that poses a risk to a fetus, is that an acceptable solution, or is it unfair discrimination against women? As Example 19.1 suggests, these are not idle concerns.

Ethical concerns are not the only challenges for market solutions. The ability of the worker to respond to a hazardous situation depends upon his or her knowledge of the seriousness of the danger. With toxic substances, that knowledge is likely to be incomplete. Consequently, the marginal-increased-wages function may be artificially rotated toward the origin: The employer would choose too little precaution. Having access to the health records of all employees, the employer may be in the best position to assess the degree of risk posed, but the employer also has an incentive to suppress that information. To publicize risk would mean demands for higher compensatory wages and possible lawsuits.

Information on the dangers posed by exposure to a particular toxic substance is a public good to employees; each employee has an incentive to be a *free rider* on the discoveries of others. Individual employees do not have an incentive to bear the cost of doing the necessary research to uncover the degree of risk, either. Thus, it seems neither employers nor employees can be expected to produce the efficient amount of information on the magnitude of risk.[9]

As a result, the government may play a substantial role in setting the boundaries on ethical responses, in stimulating research on the nature of hazards, and in providing for the dissemination of information to affected parties. It does not necessarily follow, however, that the government should be responsible for determining the level of safety in the workplace once this information is available and the ethical boundaries are determined.

Our analysis suggesting that the market will not provide an efficient level of information on occupational risk is consistent with the enactment of "Right-to-Know" laws in several states. These laws require businesses to disclose to their employees and to the public any potential health hazards associated with toxic substances used on the job. Generally, employers are required to (1) label toxic substance containers, (2) inventory all toxic substances used in the workplace, and (3) provide adequate training on the handling of these substances to all affected employees. Significantly, proponents of these laws suggest that the targets are not the

---

[8]See the survey of this evidence in W. Kip Viscusi, *Risk by Choice: Regulating Health and Safety in the Workplace* (Cambridge, MA: Harvard University Press, 1983), pp. 93–113.

[9]Unions would be expected to produce more efficient information flows because they represent many workers and can take advantage of economies of scale in the collection, interpretation, and dissemination of risk information. Available evidence suggests that the preponderance of wage premiums for risk have been derived from unionized workers. See W. Kip Viscusi, op. cit.: 55.

Example 19.1

Susceptible Populations in the Hazardous Workplace

Some employees are especially susceptible to occupational hazards. Pregnant women and women in the childbearing years are particularly vulnerable. When an employer attempts to manage a work situation that poses a hazardous threat, either the susceptible population can be separated from the hazard or the hazard can be controlled to a sufficient level that its risk is acceptable to even the most susceptible employees.

The economic aspects of this choice are easily deduced. Removal of the susceptible population results in lower marginal risk to the workers, lower costs to the firm, and less precaution taken. But is it fair to those who are removed from their jobs?

This issue came to a head in 1978 when American Cyanamid decided to respond to an occupational risk by banning all fertile women from jobs in the section manufacturing lead chromate pigment at Willow Island, West Virginia. After reviewing the decision, the Occupational Safety and Health Administration (OSHA) cited the company under the general-duty clause of the Occupational Safety and Health Act, which requires an employer to provide a workplace free of hazards, and fined it $10,000. That was not the last of it. In early 1980, the Oil, Chemical and Atomic Workers Union sued the company under the 1964 Civil Rights Act on the grounds that the company has discriminated unfairly against women.

Source: This example was taken from Council on Environmental Quality, *Environmental Quality—1980* (Washington, DC: Government Printing Office, 1980): 205.

large chemical companies, which generally have excellent disclosure programs, but the smaller, largely nonunion, plants.

Product Safety

Exposure to a hazardous or potentially hazardous substance can also occur as a result of using a product, as when eating food containing chemical additives or when using pesticides. Does the market efficiently supply safe products?

One view holds that the market pressures on both parties are sufficient to yield an efficient level of safety. Safer products are generally more expensive to produce and carry a higher price tag. If consumers feel that the additional safety justifies the cost, they will purchase the safer product. Otherwise, they won't. Producers supplying excessively risky products will find their market drying up because consumers will switch to competing brands that are more expensive, but safer. Similarly, producers selling excessively safe products (meaning they eliminate, at great cost, risks consumers are perfectly willing to take in return for a lower purchase price) find their markets drying up as well. Consumers will choose the cheaper, riskier product.

Economic logic suggests that the market will not (and should not) yield a uniform level of safety for all products. Different consumers will have different degrees of risk aversion. Although some consumers might purchase riskier, but cheaper, products, others might prefer safer, but more expensive, products.[10] Thus, it would be common to find products with various safety levels supplied simultaneously, reflecting and satisfying different consumer preferences for risk. Forcing all similar products to conform to a single level of risk would not be efficient. Uniform product safety is no more efficient than uniform occupational safety.

If this view of the market were completely accurate, government intervention to protect consumers would not be necessary to assure the efficient level of risk. By the force of their collective buying habits, consumers would protect themselves.

The problem with the market's ability to provide such self-regulation is the availability of information on product safety. The consumer generally acquires his or her information on a product from personal experience. With toxic substances, the latency period may be so long as to preclude any effective market reaction. Even when some damage results, it is difficult for the consumer to associate it with a particular source. Although an examination of the relationships between purchasing patterns of a large number of consumers and their subsequent health might well reveal some suggesting correlations, it would be difficult for any individual consumer to deduce this correlation.

Although the government may need to assure that consumers receive adequate information on product risks, the need to dictate a prevailing level of safety is much less clear, particularly if the dictated level is uniformly applied. In situations where adequate information is available on the risks, consumers should have a substantial role in choosing the acceptable level of risk through their purchases.

Third Parties

The final case involves *third parties,* victims who have no contractual relationship to the source. When groundwater is contaminated by a neighboring waste treatment facility, by surreptitious dumping of toxic wastes, or by the improper applications of a pesticide, the victims would be third parties. In any of these situations, the affected party cannot bring any direct market pressure to bear on the source. Because these nonpoint sources are generally not controlled by the air and water regulations, the case for additional government intervention is strongest for third-party situations.

This does not necessarily imply that executive or legislative remedies are appropriate. The most appropriate response may well come from simply requiring better information on the risk or, as discussed in Chapter 3, from using the court system to impose liability.

California's Proposition 65, enacted by voter initiative on 4 November 1986, provides an example of the "better information" approach.[11] If a California business exposes anyone to a hazardous substance (other than through drinking water, which is handled separately), the

---

[10]A classic example is provided by the manner in which Americans choose their automobiles. It is quite clear that many of the larger domestic cars are safer and more expensive than smaller, cheaper foreign cars. Some consumers are willing to pay for the safety and others are not.

[11]David Roe, "Barking Up the Right Tree: Recent Progress in Focusing the Toxics Issue," *Columbia Journal of Environmental Law* 13, No. 2 (1988): 277–280.

business must provide a "clear and reasonable warning," unless the exposure poses "no significant risk." (Generally, the courts have interpreted "no significant risk" as occurring when the business is complying with an applicable standard.) Interestingly, one of the effects of this program has been for industry to encourage the adoption of standards. Prior to this approach the incentives were to try to delay the setting of standards as long as possible. Here the emphasis is on educating consumers and allowing them to make the choice about the amount of risk they will accept when no applicable standard has been developed.

Liability law provides one judicial avenue for internalizing the external costs in third-party situations. If the court finds that damage occurred, that it was caused by a toxic substance, and that a particular source was responsible for the presence of the substance, the source can be forced to compensate the victim for the damages caused. Unlike regulations that are uniformly (and hence, inefficiently) applied, a court decision can be tailored to the exact circumstances involved in the suit. Furthermore, the impact of any particular liability assignment can go well beyond the parties to that case. A decision for the plaintiff can remind other sources that they should take the efficient level of precaution now to avoid paying future damages.

In principle, liability law can force sources, including nonpoint sources, to choose efficient levels of precaution. Unlike regulation, liability law can provide compensation to the victims. We will see how well it functions in practice in the rest of the chapter. Example 19.2 shows how a judicial response to one spill has transformed the way one company handles its environmental responsibilities.

◆ CURRENT POLICY

Common Law

The common-law system is an extremely complicated approach to controlling risks. When a victim seeks recourse through the court system, a number of legal grounds can be used to pursue a claim. Not all of these may be available to every plaintiff (the person initiating the suit), because the appropriate doctrine depends partially on the legal tradition in the jurisdiction where the suit is filed. Not all jurisdictions allow a plaintiff to file on all grounds. Two of the more common legal grounds are (1) *negligence* and (2) *strict liability*.

Negligence.   Probably the most common legal theory used by plaintiffs to pursue claims is negligence. This body of law suggests that the defendant (the party allegedly responsible for the contamination) owes a duty to the plaintiff to exercise due care. If that duty has been breached, the defendant is found negligent and is forced to compensate the victim for damages caused. If the defendant is found to have exercised due care and to have performed that duty to the plaintiff, no liability is assessed. Under negligence law, the victim bears the liability unless it can be proved that the defendant was negligent.

The test conventionally applied by the courts in deciding whether or not the defendant has exercised due care, the *Learned Hand formula,* is fundamentally an economic one. Named after the judge (*yes*, Learned Hand!) who initially formulated it, this test suggests that the defendant is guilty of negligence if the loss caused by the contamination, multiplied by the probability of

Example 19.2

Judicial Remedies in Toxic Substance Control: The Kepone Case

Kepone is a highly toxic substance used in the manufacture of pesticides. Kepone was produced at Hopewell, Virginia, by Life Science Products Company, a company started by former employees of Allied Chemical Corporation. The kepone produced by Life Science was sold to Allied Chemical.

Conditions at the plant and spills into the James River resulted in high contamination levels, which affected workers and people eating fish taken from the river. Allied Chemical Corporation was indicted by a grand jury on criminal charges during May 1976 and was subsequently sued by various injured parties. Eventually, it paid more than $20 million in compensation, penalties, and legal fees.

As a result of the suit, Allied and a number of other companies have begun to dramatically increase expenditures on prevention. In 1977 Allied hired Arthur D. Little, a consulting firm, to develop a broad program to anticipate and prevent further accidents. By 1981 Allied had over 400 employees whose jobs involved environmental control concerns.

The staff has discovered that pollution control sometimes yields unexpected benefits. In the past, Allied treated its waste, including calcium chloride, from its Baton Rouge plant and discharged it into the river. New regulations from the EPA would have raised the costs of treating the waste. Allied decided to look for a market for the calcium chloride and found one, turning a liability into an asset.

The kepone suit changed this corporation's behavior as well as the behavior of other chemical companies. Such companies have found that anticipating can be much less costly than reacting.

Source: This example is based upon Georgette Jasen, "Like Other New-Breed Environmental Managers, Hillman of Allied Isn't Merely a Trouble Shooter," *The Wall Street Journal* (30 July 1981): 50.

contamination, exceeds the cost of preventing the contamination.[12] When correctly applied, this is simply a version of the expected-net-benefit formula developed earlier.[13] The maximization of expected net benefits is efficient as long as society is risk-neutral. Therefore, the common-law approach embodied in negligence law is, in principle, compatible with efficiency.

Sometimes, the plaintiff can prove negligence on the part of the defendant by showing that the defendant violated a statute. In many states, any related statutory violation is taken as sufficient proof of negligence.

---

[12]For a detailed discussion of this formula, see Richard A. Posner, "A Theory of Negligence," *Journal of Legal Studies"* 1 (1972): 29–96.

[13]For a description of necessary conditions for the formula to be applied, see J. P. Brown, "Toward an Economic Theory of Liability," *Journal of Legal Studies* 2 (June 1973): 323–339.

Strict Liability. Strict liability can be used by plaintiffs in some states and in some circumstances. Under this doctrine the plaintiff does not have to prove negligence. As long as the activity causes damage, the defendant is declared liable, even if the activity is completely legal and complies with all relevant laws.

Strict liability is usually applied in circumstances where the activity in question is inherently hazardous. Because the disposal of toxic substances is frequently considered such an activity, states are increasingly allowing toxic substance suits to be brought to court under this doctrine. In contrast to negligence, strict liability transfers liability for damages to the source—whether or not the source has exercised much care.

Strict liability can also be compatible with efficiency.[14] The agent dealing with toxic wastes must balance the costs of taking precautions with the likelihood of, and expected costs of, lawsuits. In cases where the precautionary expenditures are particularly high and the damages low, only limited precaution is likely to be taken. However, for truly dangerous substances, it is advantageous to take extraordinary precautions and avoid large damages.

Criminal Law

Strict liability and negligence are civil law doctrines, applied when one private party sues another. Increasingly, in environmental policy, the civil law approach is being complemented by the use of criminal law, in which the government serves as prosecutor, presumably acting as an agent of the people. The Kepone case, described in Example 19.2, involved both civil and criminal law.

Criminal law affords regulators a menu of remedies that differ from those available from civil law. Financial penalties imposed under criminal law cannot be covered by insurance as civil penalties can. Jail sentences may be handed out to those found breaking the law. Corporate executives, for example, could spend up to five years in jail for particularly onerous violations of the law. Fines could also be levied against guilty parties.

Several important aspects other than remedies also differentiate the civil and criminal judicial approaches to pollution control. Criminal charges can be brought against only those charged with breaking one or more specific laws, whereas civil suits can be brought against those causing damage, whether or not a law has been violated. The burden of proof is higher in a criminal trial. To convict a person, the state must prove the defendant is guilty "beyond a reasonable doubt," whereas in civil trials, the decision is based merely upon the "preponderance of evidence." The presumption of innocence, an important part of criminal trials, has no counterpart in civil trials. Civil trials create no presumption in favor of either party.

The final major difference between civil liability law and criminal law is that *civil liability law compensates victims directly, whereas criminal law does not.* Criminal law focuses on punishing the perpetrator rather than on compensating the victim.[15] Though the severity of punishment can be tailored to the amount of damage caused, the correspondence between the

---

[14]One well-known case where strict liability will not be efficient is when the victims can influence the likelihood of contamination and the magnitude of the damage caused. With full compensation, the victim's incentive to take precautions is undermined. In most toxic substance cases, the role of the victim is minimal, so this potential source of inefficiency is not important.

[15]Criminal law remedies forcing restitution do compensate the victim, but they are the exception rather than the rule. With restitution the guilty party is forced to pay a stipulated amount of money to the victim as part of the punishment.

length of a jail sentence and the damage caused is much less direct than forcing the defendant to pay exact monetary damages. By breaking the link between the monetary damage caused and the punishment received—the cornerstone of liability law—criminal law would be less likely than civil law to result in efficient resolutions of toxic chemical contamination problems.[16] Efficiency could result, but it would be more of a coincidence than an inherent characteristic of the process.

Statutory Law

Civil and criminal common-law remedies to toxic chemical problems have been accompanied by a host of legislative remedies. The statutes have evolved over time in response to particular toxic substance problems. Each time a new problem surfaced and people were able to get legislators aroused, a new law was passed to deal with it. The result is a collage of laws on the books, each with its own unique focus. We shall cover only the main ones here.

Federal Food, Drug, and Cosmetic Act.   The first concerns with toxic substances arose with *food additives,* because these are ingested and potentially pose a serious and immediate threat to health. Food and drug additives are regulated under the Federal Food, Drug, and Cosmetic Act of 1938, as amended in 1958. The organization administering this act is the Food and Drug Administration (FDA).

The 1938 Act contained a general safety provision authorizing the FDA to prohibit the sale of any food that "contains any poisonous or deleterious substance which may render it injurious to health." This provision was complemented in 1958 by a provision known as the "Delaney clause" after its legislative sponsor, which states that no additive should be deemed safe if it is found to induce cancer in humans or animals. Coupled with the first provision, this addition prohibits any food additive determined by the FDA to be a carcinogen in any dosage.

Manufacturers wishing to introduce new food additives or drugs must demonstrate the safety of their products through premarket testing. For cosmetics, no premarket testing is required. For the FDA to take any action on cosmetics, it must bear the burden of proof of demonstrating the product is unsafe. The burden is on the manufacturer to prove the safety of food additives and drugs.

Occupational Safety and Health Act.   This 1970 act created the Occupational Safety and Health Administration (OSHA) and charged the agency with the regulatory responsibility for protecting workers from hazards in the workplace. The Act also created the National Institute for Occupational Safety and Health (NIOSH), which, among its other responsibilities, must make recommendations for the OSHA regulatory standards.

In 1974, OSHA promulgated the first regulation establishing levels of pollutants that would be acceptable in the workplace atmosphere. The statute required the standards to be established at a level sufficiently stringent that no employee would suffer material impairment of health, even if that employee were exposed to the substance on a regular basis throughout his

---

[16]This does not imply, however, that criminal law has no efficient role to play in enforcement. For example, falsifying official reports to the EPA is, appropriately, a criminal offense. Without accurate reports, the entire enforcement function could be undermined. However, it would be difficult to determine the economic value of the damage caused by falsified reports, a prerequisite for assessing a financial civil penalty.

or her working life. In addition, occupational standards requiring special precautions and/or protective devices have been adopted or proposed for a number of workplace contaminants.

Carcinogens are handled more severely. Once any substance is confirmed as a carcinogen, ambient workplace standards are set, rapidly followed by the imposition of special handling requirements, protective devices, and minimum-contact regulations.

The approach taken by OSHA was to specify, often in excruciating detail, acceptable contaminant levels, as well as the approaches to be taken by employers to ensure the attainment of those contaminant levels.[17] In response to adverse public opinion about silly regulations, in 1978 OSHA revoked 928 previously promulgated regulations as unnecessary.

Federal Environmental Pesticide Control Act. This 1972 act amended the Federal Insecticide, Fungicide, and Rodenticide Act. (Congress has a flair for titles!) The thrust of the legislation is to provide for the registration of all pesticides, the certification of individuals applying these pesticides, and the premarket testing of all new pesticides.

All pesticide registrations automatically expire every five years. To secure a new registration, the manufacturer must prove that the benefits derived from that pesticide will outweigh its social costs. When the evidence permits, the EPA has the power to prohibit the sale of a pesticide or to restrict its use to specific applications. The EPA has used this power to dramatically decrease the use of a number of pesticides, with DDT being the earliest and most publicized example.

Certification procedures for individuals applying the pesticides represent a recognition that the danger posed depends to a large extent on how the substances are applied. With this procedure, the EPA can ensure proper training for commercial applicators, and, by threatening the withdrawal of certification (and the livelihood of the applicators), the EPA can influence their behavior.

Resource Conservation and Recovery Act. To counteract the unsafe dumping of toxic wastes, Congress passed Subtitle C of the Resource Conservation and Recovery Act of 1976. This act imposes standards for handling, shipping, and disposing of toxic wastes.

The regulations implementing this act define hazardous waste and establish a cradle-to-grave management system, including standards for generators of hazardous wastes, standards for its transporters, and standards and permit requirements for owners and operators of facilities that treat, store, or dispose of hazardous wastes.

The centerpiece of this rather large regulatory system is a manifest system for keeping track of the fate of the substances from their creation to their disposal. Waste generators are required to prepare a manifest for all controlled substances. If the substance is on the EPA list, it must be properly packaged and labeled, and must be delivered only to a permitted waste-disposal site. Through this recording system, the EPA hopes to monitor all hazardous substances and detect any surreptitious dumping. Failure to comply with the act is punishable by civil penalties and, in certain cases, by fines and imprisonment.

In 1984 this act was amended by the Hazardous and Solid Waste Amendments of 1984. The 1984 Amendments contain three major categories of changes: (1) They expanded the

---

[17]The humor in the situation was nicely illustrated by an ad for a political candidate opposed to OSHA. A cowboy is pictured riding off to the prairie. On the back of his horse is strapped a plastic toilet required by an OSHA regulation setting the maximum distance any employee could be from a comfort station.

amount of waste covered by the regulations; (2) they limited or, in some cases, banned the use of land disposal for certain kinds of waste; and (3) they brought under regulation some activities not previously controlled, such as underground storage tanks for certain chemicals.

Toxic Substances Control Act.   This 1976 act was passed as a complement to the Resource Conservation and Recovery Act. Whereas the Resource Conservation and Recovery Act was designed to ensure safe handling and disposal of existing substances, the Toxic Substances Control Act was designed to provide a firmer basis for deciding which of the chemical substances not controlled by the existing acts should be allowed to be commercially produced.

This act requires the EPA to inventory the approximately 55,000 chemical substances in commerce, to require premanufacture notice to the EPA of all new chemical substances, and to enforce record-keeping, testing, and reporting requirements so that the EPA can assess and regulate the relative risks of chemicals. At least 90 days before manufacturing or importing a new chemical, a firm must submit test results or other information to the EPA showing that the chemical will not present "an unreasonable risk" to human health or the environment.

On the basis of the information in the premanufacture notification, the EPA can limit the manufacture, use, or disposal of the substance. The Act is significant in that it represents one of the few instances where the burden of proof is on the manufacturer who must prove that the product should be marketed, rather than forcing the EPA to show why it should not be marketed.

Comprehensive Environmental Response, Compensation, and Liability Act.   Known popularly as the "Superfund Act," the Comprehensive Environmental Response, Compensation, and Liability Act of 1980 created a $1.6-billion fund to be used over a five-year period to clean up existing toxic waste sites. The revenue was derived mainly from taxes on chemical industries. The Act offers compensation for the loss or destruction of natural resources controlled by the state or federal government, but it does not provide any compensation for injured individuals. A $9-billion reauthorization bill passed in 1986 significantly increased the amount of money dedicated to the cleanup of these sites.

As amended, this act authorized federal and state government to respond quickly to incidents such as occurred in Times Beach, Missouri. Times Beach, a town of 2800 residents located about 30 miles southwest of St. Louis, had been contaminated by dioxin. Dioxin is a waste by-product created during the production of certain chemicals. One such chemical is Agent Orange, the defoliant used during the Vietnam War. The contamination occurred when a state oil hauler bought about 55 pounds of dioxin in 1971 from a now defunct manufacturer, mixed it with oil, and, under contract with the local government, spread it on unpaved roads as a dust control measure. On 23 December 1982, after soil tests revealed dangerous levels of dioxin, the Centers for Disease Control recommended total evacuation of the town.

By 22 February 1983, the federal government had authorized a transfer of some $33 million from the Superfund to cover the cost of buying out all businesses and residents and relocating them. For its part, the State of Missouri agreed to pay 10 percent of the cost— $3.3 million—into the Superfund, and fund representatives could attempt to recover damages from the responsible parties. The town is now totally vacant, an eerie reminder of the tragically high human cost that can result from the improper disposal of hazardous wastes.

The existence of the Superfund allows the governments involved to move rapidly. They are not forced to wait until the outcome of court suits against those responsible in order to raise the money nor are they forced to face the uncertainty associated with suits' ultimate success or failure.

This formidable list of statutory and common-law remedies embodies a variety of approaches to the resolution of toxic substance problems. The question is whether or not these approaches are efficient or cost effective.

International Agreements

One of the toxic substances issues erupting during the 1980s concerns the efficiency and morality of exporting hazardous waste to areas that are willing to accept it in return for suitably large compensation. A number of areas, particularly in poor countries, appear ready to accept hazardous waste under the "right conditions." The right conditions usually involve alleviating safety concerns and providing adequate compensation (e.g., in employment opportunities, money, and public services) so as to make acceptance of the wastes desirable from the receiving community's point of view. Generally, the compensation required is less than the costs of dealing in other ways with the hazardous waste, so that the exporting nations find these agreements attractive as well.

A strong backlash against these arrangements arose when opponents argued that communities receiving hazardous waste were poorly informed about the risks they faced and were not equipped to handle safely the volumes of material that could be expected to cross international boundaries. In extreme cases, the communities were completely uninformed, as sites were secretly located by individuals with no public participation in the process at all.

The Basel Convention on the Control of Transboundary Movements of Hazardous Wastes and Their Disposal was developed in 1989 in order to provide a satisfactory response to these concerns. Under the Basel Convention, the 24 nations that belong to the Organization for Economic Co-operation and Development (OECD) were required to obtain written permission from the government of any developing country before sending toxic waste there for disposal or recycling. This was followed in 1994 by an additional agreement on the part of most, but not all, industrialized nations that completely prohibited the export of toxic wastes from any OECD country to any non-OECD country. As of 1994, the United States was the only OECD member that had not signed either the basic Basel Convention or the 1994 agreement.

◆ AN ASSESSMENT OF THE LEGAL REMEDIES

The Common Law

Judicial-Legislative Complementarity. Common law provides a potentially useful complement to statutory law for occupational, consumer product, and third-party hazards. For all three types of toxic-substance problems, the market may create pressures preventing the flow of information about the dangers of these substances. Those employers or producers in the best position to transmit the information to parties who can best assess the risk (employees, consumers, or third parties) are not always willing to seek or relay the information. In a market where liability for damages is not placed on the source, sources have little incentive to uncover potential problems. Uncovering health problems will only lower sales or increase wages.

Legislative remedies such as the Right-to-Know laws described earlier are not sufficient if there is too little information to be shared. Because court actions that subject sources to liability for their damages make health damage information useful to the firm, they create incentives to keep good records and to analyze the results. The failure to accurately perceive a health risk could cause an enormous financial burden on the company.[18] It is cheaper to anticipate and prevent damages before the cost becomes prohibitive.

Even premarket testing of consumer products by the government is not an adequate substitute for the judicial approach. Government has neither the staff nor the financial resources to serve as the sole source of health damage information. Some substances inevitably slip through the safety net provided by government testing. It is essential that the prime responsibility for testing fall on the producer, with the costs being passed on to the consumer as part of the price of the product. The government would then bear the responsibility for ensuring the validity of the testing process.

Judicial remedies are especially important in handling third-party contamination. Without liability, the incentive to exercise due care by the manufacturers, transporters, users, and disposers of these substances would be inefficiently low. The use of the court system to control the third-party problem was enhanced by the passage of the Resource Conservation and Recovery Act of 1976.

Because of the manifest system created by this act, good information is available to the courts on the types and quantities of substances that are sold or transported. The Act also assists in tracing responsibility so that the sources can be identified and confronted with the evidence. This record-keeping system is immensely costly, however, and may turn out, in the glare of hindsight, to be excessively ambitious. Furthermore, hazardous wastes that do not leave the facility where they were created constitute an overwhelming percentage of the total hazardous wastes, but these are not covered by the manifest system.[19] With experience, the system may evolve toward a harmonious balance between the gains from this monitoring system and the administrative burden it imposes.

Two additional features of judicial remedies make them a useful complement to legislative remedies. First, liability law usually provides the only way the victim of a toxic substance accident can get compensated.[20] Even the Superfund bill does not compensate individuals for health-related damages. It only compensates for property damage.

The second attractive feature of judicial remedies is the degree to which they can be tailored to individual circumstances. We have seen (in the chapters on air and water pollution), the strong tendency for legislative remedies to be applied uniformly. We have also seen that uniform remedies are rarely efficient and that often the resulting loss of net benefit is sub-

---

[18]During 1982, for example, the Manville Corporation faced up to $5 billion in lawsuits resulting from worker exposure to asbestos. During that same year, Monsanto was fighting a $4.7-billion class action suit for alleged prolonged worker exposure to a hazardous substance in a West Virginia plant.

[19]Roger C. Dower, "Hazardous Waste," in *Public Policies for Environmental Protection,* Paul R. Portney, ed. (Washington, DC: Resources for the Future, 1990): 163.

[20]Normally, workers' compensation insurance provides for claims arising from proven occupational hazards. However, a study conducted by the Labor Department during 1981 found that, of the 2 million Americans who were partially or severely disabled as a result of an occupational disease, only 5 percent received workers' compensation. Many states have disallowed claims against workers' compensation for maladies that can take 30 years to show up.

stantial. When the courts impose damage remedies correctly, an efficient allocation of precaution would automatically be tailored to the specific circumstances involved.

Limitations of Judicial Remedies. The common law is far from a panacea, however. It does not cope with the largest or most complex problems, such as the emission of hazardous substances by large numbers of sources affecting large numbers of people. This was illustrated nicely in *Roger J. Diamond* v. *General Motors,* a California case in which the judge ruled that the court system was not the appropriate forum to resolve the Los Angeles problem of air pollution.[21] The problem was so complex and involved so many parties that it had to be resolved by the legislature.[22] Court remedies are administratively expensive and can be used efficiently only when they are used sparingly.

The common law also currently places a large, difficult-to-meet burden of proof on the plaintiff. Generally, a plaintiff must be able to (1) identify the harmful substances, (2) demonstrate that the defendant was the source of this substance, and (3) prove that identifiable damages occurred as a result of the presence of that substance. The last two steps may be difficult to establish in practice.

Suppose, for example, that a well owner who discovered a harmful substance in the well simultaneously experienced a series of illnesses for which he or she had no medical history. The owner might have discovered a source emitting the same chemical nearby, but that is not enough evidence to win a lawsuit. The court would have to be convinced not only that the substance traveled from the source to the well, but also that any documented illnesses were caused by the substance and not by unrelated causes. The frequent failure to establish these links can undermine the incentive properties of common law.[23]

Japan's court system has reacted to this problem by shifting the burden of proof from the injured plaintiff to the industry. The plaintiffs in those cases have to establish the nature and cause of their diseases and the mechanism by which they were affected. To establish the link to the defendant, they are able to introduce a high statistical correlation between the defendant's activity and the incidence of the disease. Once these elements have been established, a rebuttable presumption is created that shifts the burden of proof to the defendant. The defendant is then liable unless it can be proven that its activities are not responsible for the damage.

If the U.S. court system were to move in this direction, it would represent a radical departure from current practice.[24] The statistical approach lacks the rigor usually required by U.S. courts, because establishing a positive correlation between activity levels and the incidence of

---

[21]97 Cal. Report. 639.

[22]Even when the number of sources is small, the courts can be overwhelmed if the number of plaintiffs is large. It has been estimated that asbestos suits against the Manville Corporation were being filed at the rate of 500 per month during 1982. (See "Manville May Drive Congress to Action," *Business Week* [13 September 1982], p. 35.)

[23]If it becomes too easy to prove these links, the defendant will be forced to pay liability even when the substance produced by the defendant did not cause the plaintiff's problem. In this case, efficiency would be lost, because too much precaution would be taken.

[24]Some movement in this direction is now evident. A plaintiff with asbestosis, for example, may be required to prove only that the disease is more probably than not caused by several asbestos manufacturers. Having met this burden of proof, the plaintiff shifts the burden to the individual manufacturer to prove, if it can, that it did not cause the plaintiff's disease. See *Abel* v. *Eli Lilly & Co.,* 343 N.W. 2d 164 (1984).

the disease does not establish causation. Other factors correlated with the activities of the defendant may be responsible.

The Japanese system does effectively raise the question of who should bear the burden of proof. If the source were to bear it, nuisance suits could arise. Nuisance suits are filed mainly to harass defendants by making them spend a lot of money on defense. Such suits are without merit. As we have seen, however, if the plaintiff bears the burden of proof, the burden is particularly difficult, because the defendant generally knows so much more about the contaminating activities.

The Japanese approach gets around this problem by placing a sequential burden of proof on each party. The plaintiff is required to bear a burden sufficiently large that nuisance cases are eliminated. On the other hand, for serious cases where the plaintiff has been able to bear this initial burden of proof, the defendant (who, presumably, is the most knowledgeable about the subject) must then gather the information at his or her disposal.

We can quibble about whether the initial burden on the plaintiff is too low or too high under the Japanese system, but with its inherent shared responsibility, this system reduces the likelihood of nuisance suits while providing incentive for the most knowledgeable party to supply the necessary information to reach a decision.

One final concern about judicial remedies should be noted. Sometimes the source of the toxic substance problem is "judgment-proof" in the sense that it has no assets (or too few assets) to pay the damages. The marginal cost of additional damages to the source is zero, and profit-maximizing behavior leads the source to exercise too little precaution.

This problem is more serious for toxic substances than for conventional pollutants because the latency of the effects means the suits must be filed much later. By this time, the source may have gone out of business or have been transformed into a different corporate entity and, therefore, have become somewhat immune from past transgressions.

Joint and Several Liability Doctrine.   In interpreting the Superfund Act, the courts have allowed the government to sue "potentially responsible parties" (i.e., disposal site owners and operators, waste generators and transporters) for damages and site-recovery costs under the *joint and several liability doctrine.*[25] Reduced to its essence, the joint and several liability doctrine makes each successfully sued defendant potentially liable for an amount up to the entire damage caused, regardless of the magnitude of its individual contribution. Because of this doctrine, the government can elect to sue only a few of the wealthiest responsible parties, thereby avoiding the higher litigation costs associated with hauling everyone into court. In one case the EPA elected to sue only 10 percent of the responsible parties, letting the others off the hook.

Successfully sued defendants retain the *right of contribution,* which allows parties that have made payments (either by settling out of court or in response to a court decision) to seek reimbursement from other potentially responsible parties (PRPs) that have not. This right of contribution can be exercised by those settling out of court, as well as by those assessed damages following a trial. Once a party signs a consent decree of either type, however, it cannot be sued for contribution by other parties.

---

[25]Hooker Chemical, for example, was found liable for response costs at the Love Canal under the joint and several liability doctrine. See *United States* v. *Hooker Chemical and Plastics Corporation,* 18 ELR 20580.

The government enforces this act by seeking to encourage PRPs to initiate cleaning up the site on their own. However, it is prepared to initiate the investigation and even to clean up identified hazardous waste sites on its own, if necessary, financing the effort from the several-billion-dollar Hazardous Substance Response Trust Fund created by the Act. It then seeks reimbursement from parties who are potentially responsible for the conditions at each particular site. The potentially responsible parties are liable for any costs of restoring the site to a safe status as well as "damages for injury to, destruction of, or loss of natural resources, including the reasonable costs of assessing such injury, destruction, or loss resulting from such a release."[26]

Any liable party who "fails without sufficient cause to properly provide removal or remedial action," may be assessed punitive damages of "three times the amount of any costs incurred by the Fund as a result of such failure to take proper action."[27]

Designed primarily as a means of raising private funds to clean up hazardous waste sites, joint and several liability has not exactly worked as smoothly as expected, even as a means of collecting revenue. Between 1986 and the end of 1988, the EPA recovered only $166 million from private parties, or roughly 7 percent of the $2.4 billion spent on Superfund cleanups during the same period.[28] Even when the suits are successful, the litigation expenses are extremely high. In one study the Rand Institute for Civil Justice in Santa Monica, California, found that nearly 90 percent of the money spent by insurers on Superfund claims went for legal and related costs rather than site cleanup.[29]

Joint and several liability has also created some perverse incentive.[30] Under the joint and several liability doctrine, the expected liability a potentially responsible party faces is very uncertain: anywhere from 0 to 100 percent of the cleanup costs, regardless of the degree of precaution undertaken. Because larger firms are usually targeted by the EPA for Superfund suits, they have an incentive to take more than the efficient amount of precaution.[31] Meanwhile, smaller firms, who may expect to "get off the hook" because the expense of suing them exceeds the potential recovery, have little or no incentive to take appropriate precautions.

The uncertainty associated with expected damage payments has also wreaked havoc with the insurance market. Insurance companies have no idea how to set premiums, and many have left the market for environmental risks entirely. Without insurance, the probability of bankruptcy increases. Bankrupt firms contribute very little to the cleanup.

The Statutory Law

A commendable virtue of common law is that remedies can be tailored to the unique circumstances the parties find themselves in. But common-law remedies are also expensive to

---

[26]42 U. S. C. §9607c.

[27]42 U. S. C. §9607c3.

[28]Roger C. Dower, op. cit.: 185.

[29]Reported in Jonathan M. Moses, "Insurer Payouts Over Superfund Flow to Lawyers," *The Wall Street Journal* (24 April 1992): B1, B9.

[30]A formal analysis of these incentives can be found in T. H. Tietenberg, "Indivisible Toxic Torts: The Economics of Joint and Several Liability," *Land Economics* 65, No. 4 (November 1989): 305–319.

[31]Cleanup and litigation costs have become so high for large companies that some of the larger chemical companies have begun voluntarily cleaning up abandoned sites. See "Environmental, Industry Groups Tackle Hazardous Waste Disposal Sites," *Chemecology* (July/August): 2.

impose, and they are ill-suited to solving widespread problems affecting large numbers of people. Thus, statutory law has a complementary role to play as well.

Balancing the Costs.   As currently structured, statutory law does not efficiently fulfill its potential as a complement to the common law, because of the failure of current law to balance compliance costs with the damages being protected against.

The Delaney clause, the most flagrant example, precludes any balancing of costs whatsoever in food additives. A substance that has been known to be carcinogenic in any dose cannot be used as a food additive even if the risk is counterbalanced by a considerable compensating benefit.[32] As Example 19.3 illustrates, a rule this stringent can lead to considerable political mischief as attempts are made to circumvent it.

The Delaney clause is not the only culprit; other laws also fail to balance costs. The Resource Conservation and Recovery Act requires the standards imposed on waste generators, transporters, and disposal site operators to be high enough to protect human health and the environment. No mention is made of costs.

Even in less extreme cases, policymakers must face the question of how to balance costs. The Occupational Safety and Health Act (OSHA), for example, requires standards that ensure "to the extent feasible that no employee will suffer material impairment of health or functional capacity." In changing the standard for the occupational exposure to benzene from 10 ppm to 1 ppm, the EPA had presented no data to show that even a 10 ppm standard causes leukemia. Rather, the EPA based its decision on a series of assumptions indicating that some leukemia might result from 10 ppm, and that, therefore, even fewer cases might result from 1 ppm.

In a case receiving a great deal of attention, the Supreme Court set aside the new benzene standard, largely on the grounds that it was based on inadequate evidence.[33] In rendering their opinion the justices stated:

> ". . . the Secretary must make a finding that the workplaces in question are not safe. But "safe" is not the equivalent of "risk-free." A workplace can hardly be considered "unsafe" unless it threatens the workers with a significant risk of harm. [100 S. Ct. 2847]

In a concurring opinion that did not bind future decisions, because it did not have sufficient support among the remaining justices, Justice Powell went even further:

> ". . . the statute also requires the agency to determine that the economic effects of its standard bear a reasonable relationship to the expected benefits. [100 S. Ct. 2848]

It seems clear that the notion of a risk-free environment has been repudiated by the high court, as it should have been. But what is meant by an *acceptable risk?* Efficiency clearly dictates that an acceptable risk is one that maximizes the net benefit. Thus, the efficiency criterion would support Justice Powell in his approach to the benzene standard.

---

[32]It is interesting to note that a number of common foods contain natural substances that, in large enough doses, are carcinogenic. Radishes, for example, could probably not be licensed as a food additive, because of the Delaney clause.

[33]*Industrial Union Department, AFL-CIO v. American Petroleum Institute, et al.,* 100 S. Ct. 2844 (1980).

Example 19.3

Weighing the Risks: Saccharin

Saccharin is an artificial sweetener that has been used since the early part of the twentieth century. By the 1970s, it had become the staple of the diet food industry, particularly in soft drinks.

In the late 1960s a researcher at the University of Wisconsin reported that combinations of cholesterol and saccharin injected in the urinary bladders of mice resulted in a high incidence of bladder cancer. A special research group of the National Academy of Sciences convened to investigate the safety of saccharin and a year later declared it safe.

In January 1972, however, the FDA removed saccharin from its list of additives "generally recognized as safe." This action forced food processors to list saccharin on the ingredient label and to conform to maximum recommended dosages. Following some additional Canadian tests showing a link between bladder cancer and saccharin, in 1977 the FDA proposed a ban on the use of saccharin in all foods and beverages, citing the Delaney clause.

Because saccharin was the only approved artificial sweetener at that time, reaction was swift and vehement. Diabetics attacked the move as denying them access to any sweetener. Groups concerned with weight gain charged that this decision increased the risk of heart attacks. In April 1977 the FDA modified its proposed ban to the extent of allowing saccharin to be labeled as an over-the-counter drug (thus escaping the Delaney clause) and sold in tablets, powder, or liquid form. It still proposed to ban saccharin from commercially prepared foods and beverages.

Since then a number of studies have appeared, some upholding the link to cancer, others disputing it. Congress reacted by passing a series of moratoriums on the banning of saccharin, thus preventing the Delaney clause from having its intended effect.

These actions strongly suggest that zero risk is usually not an appropriate policy goal. The objective should be to balance the risks. Provisions (e.g., the Delaney clause) that prevent the balancing process are simply bad policy.

It is important to allay a possible source of confusion. The fact that it is difficult to set a precise standard using benefit-cost analysis because of the imprecision of the underlying data does not imply that some balancing of costs and benefits cannot, or should not, take place. It can and it should. Although benefit-cost analysis may not be sufficiently precise and reliable to suggest, for example, that a standard of 8 ppm is efficient, it usually is reliable enough to indicate clearly that 1 ppm and 15 ppm are inefficient. By failing to consider compliance cost in defining acceptable risk, statutes are probably attempting more and achieving less than we might hope for.

Degree and Form of Intervention.   The second criticism of the current statutory approach concerns both the degree of intervention and the form that intervention should take. The former issue relates to how deeply the government controls go; the latter relates to the manner in which the regulations work.

The analysis in the second section of this chapter suggested that consumer products and labor markets require less government intervention than do third-party cases. The main problem in those two areas was seen as the lack of sufficient information to allow producers, consumers, employees, and employers to make informed choices. With the Delaney clause as an obvious exception, most consumer-product-safety statutes deal mainly with research and labeling. They are broadly consistent with the results of our analysis.

This is not the case with occupational exposure, however. Government regulations have had a major—and not always beneficial—effect on the workplace. By covering such a large number of potential problems, OSHA has spread itself too thin and has had too little impact on problems that really count. Selective intervention, targeted at those areas where OSHA efforts could really make a difference, would get more results.

The form the OSHA regulations have taken also causes inflexibility. Not content merely to specify exposure limits, the regulations also specify the exact precautions to be taken. The contrast between this approach and the marketable-permit approach in air pollution is striking.

Under the bubble policy (as discussed in an earlier chapter), the EPA specifies the emission limit but allows the source great flexibility in meeting that limit. By dictating the specific activities to be engaged in or to be avoided, OSHA regulations deny this kind of flexibility. In the face of rapid technological change, inflexibility can lead to inefficiency, even if the specified activities were efficient when first required. Furthermore, having so many detailed regulations makes enforcement more difficult and probably less effective.

A serious flaw in the current approach to controlling hazardous wastes is in the insufficient emphasis placed on reducing the generation and recycling of these wastes. In order to provide additional revenue to fund the cleanups, for example, the 1980 Superfund bill imposed a tax on petroleum and chemical feedstocks. Because this tax is imposed on the front end of the production process and is not calibrated by toxicity, it does not provide the appropriate incentives to switch to less hazardous substances or to recycle the wastes.

An alternative, which is widely regarded as a superior means of raising revenue, involves the imposition of variable-unit taxes (called "waste-end" taxes) on waste generated or disposed of. Waste-end taxes would not only spur industry to switch to less toxic substances and to reduce the quantity of these substances used, it would also encourage consumers to switch away from products using large amounts of hazardous materials in the production process, because higher production costs would be translated into higher product prices. As of 1985, some 20 states had already adopted some form of waste-end taxation. Unfortunately, the Superfund Amendments and the Reauthorization Act of 1986 chose to replenish the Superfund with broad-based taxes rather than taxes specifically designed to reduce the generation of toxic wastes.

Scale. The size of the hazardous waste problem dwarfs the size of the EPA staff and budget assigned to control it. The Superfund process for cleaning up existing hazardous waste sites is a good case in point. Since its inceptin in 1980, the Superfund program placed 1,405 sites on the National Priorities List for extensive cleanup. As of 1997, 498 of the 1,405 sites had completed all construction work related to the cleanup. One comprehensive study suggests that the best estimate for cleaning up currently identified sites would be $750 billion (including outlays already made).[34]

Controlling the introduction and use of chemicals under the Toxic Substance Control Act presents similar problems. As of June 1991, the EPA had completed its review of test results for 16 of the 22 chemicals for which industry had met the data submission requirements. The average time required for testing the 16 chemicals from their nomination for testing through the completion of the testing was 8 years.

The huge scale of this undertaking has important implications for both the bureaucracy and the citizens it serves. Priorities must be established and the most serious problems attacked first. It is a fact of life that an exclusive reliance on the bureaucracy to provide complete safety is infeasible. Citizens should not abdicate their own responsibilities after being lulled into a false sense of security by the mistaken impression that the bureaucracy can and should provide adequate protection.

The scale of the problem also suggests that prevention makes excellent economic sense. Spending resources now to prevent the problem can, in the long run, be cheaper than attempting to clean up the mess once it has been allowed to happen.

Assurance Bonds: An Innovative Proposal

The current control system must cope with a great deal of uncertainty about the magnitude of future environmental costs associated with the disposal of hazardous waste. The costs associated with collecting funds from responsible parties through litigation are very high. Many potentially responsible parties declare bankruptcy when it is time to collect cleanup costs, thereby isolating themselves from their normal responsibility.

One proposed solution would require the posting of a *dated assurance bond* as a necessary condition for disposing of hazardous waste.[35] The amount of the required bond would be a function of the environmental authority's estimate of the costs of environmental repair or rehabilitation if the worst-case scenario were to come true between the posting date and the refund date. In case any site ultimately required restoration as a result of a hazardous waste leak, the funds tied up in the bond could be used to finance the work. Any unused proceeds would be redeemable at specified dates if the environmental costs turned out to be lower than were predicted by the worse case. As Example 19.4 points out, performance bonds may also be applied to producers of potentially toxic substances.

This kind of system would create incentives for precaution; lower actual environmental costs would trigger larger refunds. Every dollar of environmental damage prevented would be a dollar earned. Assurance bonds would also make sure that the money for cleanup was readily available as soon as needed and that no lengthy and costly legal process would be necessary to secure it.

---

[34]Milton Russell, E. William Colglazier, and Mary R. English, *Hazardous Waste Remediation: The Task Ahead* (Knoxville: Waste Management Research and Education Institute at the University of Tennessee, 1991): iv.

[35]Robert Costanza and Charles Perrings, "A Flexible Assurance Bonding System for Improved Environmental Management," *Ecological Economics* 2 (1990): 57–75. A similar proposal was advanced in Clifford S. Russell, "Economic Incentives in the Management of Hazardous Waste," *Columbia Journal of Environmental Law* 13, No. 2 (1988): 257–274.

Example 19.4

Performance Bonds for Brominated Flame Retardants

Brominated flame retardants (BFRs) are organic compounds used as additives to reduce the flammability of plastics and textiles. Their use was stimulated not only by government regulations attempting to reduce the risk posed by flammability, but also by the lower bromine prices that resulted from banning bromine (and, thereby lowering demand) in a few uses such as fumigants for agriculture. (Lower bromine prices made BFRs cheaper to make, thereby increasing their attractiveness to plastics producers.) Though a large and growing number of BFRs exist, considerable uncertainty exists about the environmental fate and long-run toxicity of many of the compounds.

Traditional remedies, such as banning particular compounds, seem insufficient, because some of the substitutes for banned substances may turn out to be worse than the original substances. The government is not in a position to pick winners and losers at this early stage, and the very real risk posed by flammability suggests that some BFR compounds should be used, at least until demonstrably safer compounds are developed.

Performance bonds have been suggested as one way to resolve this dilemma. Producers of flame retardants would be required to put up a pool of deposits sufficient to cover possible future damages. To the extent that those damages did not materialize, the deposits (plus accumulated interest) would be refunded.

The performance-bond approach shifts the financial risk of damage from the victims to the producers and, in so doing, provides incentives to assure product safety. Internalizing the costs of toxicity would sensitize producers not only to the risks posed by particular BFRs (or substitutes), but also to the amounts used. Performance bonds also provide incentives for the firms to monitor the consequences of their choices, because they bear the *ex post* burden of proving that the product is safe (in order to support claims for unused funds). Though similar to liability law in their ability to internalize damage costs, performance bonds are different in that they require that the money for damages be available up front.

Performance bonds are not without their problems, however. Calculating the right pool of deposits requires some understanding of the magnitude of potential damages. Furthermore, establishing causality between BFRs and any resulting damages is still necessary in order to make payments to victims as well as to establish the amount of the pool that should be returned.

Sources: Molly K. Macauley, Michael D. Bowes, and Karen L. Palmer, *Using Economic Incentives to Regulate Toxic Substances* (Washington, DC: Johns Hopkins University Press, for Resources for the Future, Inc., 1992); J. F. Shogren, J. A. Herriges, and R. Govindasamy, "Limits to Environmental Bonds," *Ecological Economics* 8, No. 2 (1993): 109–133.

SUMMARY

The potential for contamination of the environmental asset by toxic substances is one of the most complex environmental problems. Substances that could prove toxic number in the millions. Some 55,000 of these are in active use.

The market provides considerable pressure toward resolving toxic substance problems as they affect employees and consumers. With reliable information at their disposal, all parties have an incentive to reduce hazards to acceptable levels. However, this pressure is absent in cases involving third parties. Here, the problem frequently takes the form of an external cost imposed on innocent bystanders.

The efficient role of government can range from assuring the provision of sufficient information (so that participants in the market can make informed choices) to setting exposure limits on hazardous substances. Unfortunately, the scientific basis for decision making is weak. Only limited information on the effects of these substances is available, and the cost of acquiring complete information is prohibitive. Therefore, priorities must be established and tests developed to screen substances so that efforts can be concentrated on those that seem most dangerous.

In contrast to air and water pollution, the toxic substance problem is one in which the courts may play a particularly important role. Although screening tests will probably never be foolproof, and therefore some substances may slip through, they do provide a reasonable means for setting priorities. Liability law not only creates a market pressure for more and better information on potential damages associated with chemical substances, it also provides some incentives for manufacturers of substances, the generators of waste, the transporters of waste, and those who dispose of it to take precautions. Judicial remedies also allow the level of precaution to vary with the occupational circumstances and provide a means of compensating victims.

Judicial remedies are not sufficient, however. They are expensive and ill-suited for dealing with problems affecting large numbers of people. The burden of proof under the current U.S. system is difficult to surmount, though in Japan some radical new approaches have been developed to deal with this problem. The joint and several liability doctrine has created some perverse incentives and has wreaked havoc on the market for environmental insurance.

Though they are clearly a positive step, the statutory responses seem to have gone too far in regulating behavior. The exposure standards in many cases seem excessively stringent, having been set without balancing the costs involved. Furthermore, OSHA and the EPA have gone well beyond the setting of exposure limits by dictating specific activities that should be engaged in or avoided. The enforcement of these standards has proved difficult and has probably spread the available resources too thin.

Reinhold Niebuhr once said, "Democracy is finding proximate solutions to insoluble problems." That seems an apt description of the institutional response to the toxic substance problem. Our political institutions have created a staggering array of legislative and judicial responses to these problems that are neither efficient nor complete. They do, however, represent a positive first step in what must be an evolutionary process.

FURTHER READING

Crandall, Robert W. and Lester B. Lave. *The Scientific Basis of Health and Safety Regulation* (Washington, DC: Brookings Institution, 1981). For each of five health and safety regulatory actions, this book juxtaposes the views of a scientist, an economist, and a regulator on the scientific basis for the regulation and the desirability of the resulting decision. Cases considered are passive restraints in automobiles, cotton dust, saccharin, waterborne carcinogens, and sulfur dioxide.

Graham, Jon D., Laura C. Green, and Marc J. Roberts. *In Search of Safety: Chemicals and Cancer Risk* (Cambridge, MA: Harvard University Press, 1988). A detailed examination of the attempts to regulate two suspected carcinogens, benzene and formaldehyde.

Magat, Wesley A., and W. Kip Viscusi, *Information Approaches to Regulation* (Cambridge, MA: MIT Press, 1992). Draws from several empirical studies to assess the effectiveness of information strategies for controlling environmental risk.

Shapiro, Michael. "Toxic Substances Policy," in Paul R. Portney, ed., *Public Policies for Environmental Protection* (Washington, DC: Resources for the Future, 1990): 195–242. A comprehensive analysis of the U.S. statutes and implementation procedures used to combat environmental risks posed by toxic substances.

ADDITIONAL REFERENCES

Alberini, A. "Strict Liability as a Deterrent in Toxic Waste Management: Empirical Evidence from Accident and Spill Data," *Journal of Environmental Economics and Management* 38(1999)(1): 20–48.

Anderson, Frederick R. "Natural Resource Damages, Superfund, and the Courts," *Boston College Environmental Affairs Law Review* 16 (Spring 1989): 405–457.

Congressional Budget Office, *The Total Cost of Cleaning Up Nonfederal Superfund Sites* (Washington, DC: Government Printing Office, 1994).

Davis, Dechert W., and James L. Smith. "Environmental Liability and Economic Incentives for Hazardous Waste Management," *Houston Law Review* 25 (1988): 935–942.

Doniger, David D. *The Law and Policy of Toxic Substance Control: A Case Study of Vinyl Chloride* (Baltimore, MD: Johns Hopkins University Press, for Resources for the Future, 1978).

General Accounting Office, *Toxic Substances: Status of EPA's Reviews of Chemicals Under the Chemical Testing Program* (Washington, DC: GPO, 1991).

General Accounting Office, *Toxic Substances Control Act: EPA's Limited Progress in Regulating Toxic Chemicals* (Washington, DC: GPO, 1994).

Grigalunas, Thomas A., and James J. Opaluch. "Assessing Liability for Damages Under CERCLA: A New Approach for Providing Incentives for Pollution Avoidance," *Natural Resources Journal* 28 (1988): 509–533.

Johnson, Gary V., and Thomas S. Ulen. "Designing Public Policy Toward Hazardous Wastes: The Role of Administrative Regulations and Legal Liability Rules," *American Journal of Agricultural Economics* 68 (1986): 1266–1271.

Khanna, M., and L. A. Damon. "EPA's Voluntary 33/50 Program: Impact on Toxic Releases and Economic Performance of Firms," *Journal of Environmental Economics and Management* 37(1999)(1): 1–25.

Kopp, Raymond J., and V. Kerry Smith. "Benefit Estimation Goes to Court: The Case of Natural Resource Damage Assessments," *Journal of Policy Analysis and Management* 8 (Fall 1989): 593–612.

Lave, Lester B., ed. *Quantitative Risk Assessment in Regulation* (Washington, DC: Brookings Institution, 1982).

Levinson, A. "Grandfather Regulations, New Source Bias, and State Air Toxics Regulations." *Ecological Economics* 28(1999)(2): 299–311.

Mendeloff, John M. *The Dilemma of Toxic Substance Regulation* (Cambridge, MA: MIT Press, 1988).

Nichols, Albert L. "The Importance of Exposure in Evaluating and Designing Environmental Regulations: A Case Study," *The American Economic Review* 72 (May 1982): 214–219.

Segerson, Kathleen. "Risk and Incentives in the Financing of Hazardous Waste Cleanup," *Journal of Environmental Economics and Management* 16 (January 1989): 1–8.

Segerson, Kathleen, and Tom Tietenberg, "The Structure of Penalties in Environmental Enforcement: An Economic Analysis," *Journal of Environmental Economics and Management* 23 (1992): 179–200.

Sullivan, Arthur M. "Liability Rules for Toxics Cleanup," *Journal of Urban Economics* 20 (1986), 191–204.

WEB SITES OF INTEREST

1. *http://www.unep.ch/basel/*
   Basel Convention web site.

2. *http://www.unep.org/unep/ministry.htm*
   Links to various national environmental protection ministries or agencies.

3.. *http://europa.eu.int/comm/environment/*
   European Commission's Environment web site.

DISCUSSION QUESTIONS

1. How should the courts resolve the dilemma posed in Example 19.1? Why?

2. Over the last several decades in product liability law, there has been a movement in the court system from *caveat emptor* ("buyer beware") to *caveat venditor* ("seller beware"). The liability for using and consuming risky products has been shifted from buyers to sellers. Does this shift represent a movement toward or away from an efficient allocation of risk? Why?

3. Should it be illegal for the industrialized countries to ship their hazardous waste to the developing countries for disposal? Why or why not?

4. How should the public sector handle a toxic gas such as radon that occurs naturally and seeps into some houses through the basement or the water supply? Is this a case of an externality or not? Does the homeowner have the appropriate incentives to take an efficient level of precaution?

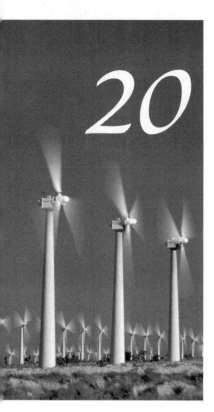

20

Development, Poverty, and the Environment

If there is any period one would desire to be born in, is it not the age of revolution when the old and the new stand side by side and admit of being compared? When the energies of all men are searched by fear, and by hope? When the historic glories of the old can be compensated by the rich possibilities of the new era? This time, like all times, is a very good one, if we but know what to do with it.

RALPH WALDO EMERSON, *THE AMERICAN SCHOLAR* (1873)

◆ INTRODUCTION

In previous chapters we invested a considerable amount of time and effort in investigating individual environmental and natural resource problems and the policy responses that have been, and could have been, taken to solve them. In general, solutions are possible, and our economic and political institutions, with some exceptions, seem to be muddling through.

Our next step must be a consideration of the global economic system and the scale of the challenges it will face in the twenty-first century. Perhaps the major challenge is finding a way to deal effectively with global poverty without jeopardizing the environment or degrading the resource base passed on to future generations.

Poverty has emerged as a significant cause of environmental problems. The worst recorded air pollution is not found, as might be expected, in the highly industrialized cities of the high-income countries, but rather in the major cities of lower-income countries. Deforestation is caused, in part, by the migration of landless peasants into the forests, seeking a plot of land to work. Soil erosion is caused, in part, when the poor are driven to farm highly erodible land to try to survive. Dealing effectively with these environmental problems and the human suffering that lies behind them will require raising living standards.

Traditionally, this has been accomplished through economic development.[1] One model for the development of the less industrialized countries is the path for rapid economic growth followed by the industrialized countries. How appropriate a model is this?

The two visions in Chapter 1 suggest two different answers to this question. The *Beyond the Limits* view holds that exponential economic growth on a global scale will continue unabated until the physical limits are reached. At that time the global economy will overshoot its resource base and collapse. In this view economic growth is the source of the problem, not the solution. The only rational policy is to exercise direct control over the growth process itself. No other course, including the collection of individual policies discussed in the preceding chapters, would avoid the collapse.

Simon, however, envisions the prospect for continued development. Far from being detrimental, in this view economic growth provides the vehicle for improving the welfare of future generations. As Simon sees it, to deny the growth would consign the members of poor third-world countries to perpetual poverty. Which view of the future is correct?

Examining the appropriateness of the traditional economic growth approach to development should start by understanding that approach and its success or lack of success as a means of eliminating poverty. We will begin by defining how economic growth takes place and how the growth process is affected by increasing resource scarcity and rising environmental costs. This understanding will then be used to characterize what changes in the growth process in the industrialized nations can be expected in the future.

The relationship between growth and development in the industrialized countries is then explored. Has growth increased the well-being of the average citizen in the developed countries? Or has the evident elevated consumption of material goods made possible by economic growth merely masked large offsetting problems that would cause an appropriately measured standard of living to go down, not up?

The fate of the average citizen, of course, does not always shed light on the fate of the poor. How have the poor fared in periods of rapid economic growth? Is John Kennedy's metaphor "A rising tide lifts all ships" apt, or does a rising tide leave more people treading water?

Although the historical experience in the industrialized countries is revealing, the transferability of this experience into a third-world context is by no means obvious. To what extent can economic growth provide an answer to the crushing problems of poverty that infect the third world? What are the barriers to achieving increased standards of living for the poor in third-world countries in a finite world?

---

[1] Herman Daly's useful distinction between growth and development is employed here. *Development* refers to a qualitative increase in well-being, whereas *growth* refers to a physical expansion in physical output of goods and services. They are related, but by no means synonymous, concepts. It is conceptually possible to have growth without development and development without growth, but historically the two have been inextricably entwined. See Herman E. Daly and John B. Cobb, Jr., *For the Common Good* (Boston, MA: Beacon Press, 1989).

◆ THE GROWTH PROCESS

The Nature of the Process

How does economic growth occur? It occurs in two main ways: (1) through increases in inputs (e.g., capital, labor, energy, and other resources) and (2) through increases in the productivity of those inputs, (or resources) as a result of technological progress. The former source of growth involves increasingly greater outputs, given the state of the art in production, whereas the latter source involves improvements in the state of the art.

Increases in Inputs.   The amount of growth occurring from increases in inputs is governed by two important economic concepts: (1) economies of scale and (2) the law of diminishing returns. The term *economies of scale* refers to the amount of increase in output obtained when all inputs are increased in the same proportion. The *law of diminishing returns* governs the relationship between inputs and output when some inputs are increased and others are held fixed.

The law of diminishing returns governs what happens when some, but not all, of the inputs are increased. Suppose, for example, that all the inputs are held fixed except for capital, which increases. As constant and successive increments of capital are added to the other fixed resources, the law of diminishing returns implies that eventually a point will be reached where each increment of input will produce smaller and smaller increments of output.

Technological Progress.   The other major source of growth, technological progress, involves the implementation of better, less wasteful ways of doing things. With technological progress, growth can occur even in the absence of increases in inputs simply because the inputs available are used more effectively. For example, with a new production technique, less energy might be wasted or fewer resources used to make a particular product.

Potential Sources of Reduced Growth

Historically, increases in factor inputs and technological progress were both important sources of growth. This does not automatically mean that they will continue to provide growth at historic levels in the future, however. A number of reasons suggest caution in extrapolating historically valid arguments into the future.

Reduced Input Flows.   Not all input flows are continuing at historic levels. Population growth has slowed considerably in most countries, which causes the growth in the labor force to slow and possibly stop. The growth fed by increasing labor is diminishing and will continue to diminish in the future.

The cost of energy and of raw materials seems to be rising, even in real terms. Producers respond to higher relative prices by cutting back on the use of these inputs, which diminishes their contribution to the growth process.

Capital formation has played a pivotal role in the past and is likely to continue doing so.[2] As workers were given more sophisticated capital equipment to work with, their productivity increased.

---

[2]One of the most sophisticated studies to date on the determinants of U.S. economic growth during the period 1948–1979 finds capital formation to be the dominant force. See D. W. Jorgenson, F. M. Gollop, and B. Fraumeni, *Productivity and U.S. Economic Growth* (Cambridge, MA: Harvard University Press, 1988).

Capital has broken down the barriers imposed by human limitations. With the advent of bulldozers, earth moving, once limited by the strength and endurance of workers, is limited no more. The size of the market, once limited by the time and effort required to transport commodities in a horse and buggy, expanded with the advent of the railroad, the truck, and the airplane. Limits on corporate controllability imposed by the size and competence of record-keeping staffs—as they attempted to stay on top of the information and paper flows—have expanded in the face of computers that can provide instant access to important information compiled in the most useful format.

Although capital is a reproducible asset, some indirect limits may diminish its role in the future. These include limitations on capital's substitutability for other factors, on the productivity of future investment, and on the incentive to invest.

The ability of capital to promote historical growth rates lies, in part, in its ability to substitute for those factor inputs that are experiencing limits. When substitution is easy, scarcity of particular inputs should not inhibit growth, but when substitution is difficult, scarcity imposes a drag on growth.

The first substitution possibility to be considered is between capital and labor. As population growth dwindles, the growth rate in the supply of labor diminishes as well. Historically, the economic growth rate has exceeded the growth rate of labor supply, as capital was continually substituted for labor. Most studies of production have found capital and labor to be quite strong substitutes for one another. When we think about the modern manufacturing sector, this seems quite reasonable. Therefore, dwindling population, by itself, doesn't seem a particularly large barrier.

Describing the substitution possibilities for other resources, however, becomes more complex. Studies of the capital-energy relationship over time in the United States have found that capital and energy are complements, rather than substitutes.[3] Thus, capital and energy have together substituted for labor and other resources—but not for each other. If one thinks of the tractor, the bulldozer, and the airplane, this seems like a natural finding.

The question of interest is whether capital and energy will remain complements in the future or whether substitution of capital for energy might be possible. This is an especially important question in light of the links between fossil fuel energy use and global warming. If the attack on global warming includes a reduction in the use of fossil fuel energy and capital is a complement of energy, global-warming strategies would have the side effect of reducing the rate of capital formation.

In some energy uses, substitution of capital for energy is clearly feasible, because energy-saving equipment, such as computer-controlled heating and cooling, already exists. Furthermore, some capital investments will clearly hasten the transition to passive solar energy, which conserves energy by making better use of what is available.

In other sectors, such as transportation, the substitution possibilities are not quite as obvious, but that does not mean they do not exist. One obvious substitute for personal transportation is the bicycle (heavily used in many European countries), as are cars powered by solar energy. To some extent, communication can even substitute for transportation, as more people use home-based computer terminals and phone lines to do their jobs without leaving

---

[3]Ernst R. Berndt and D. Wood, "Technology, Prices, and the Derived Demand for Energy," *Review of Economics and Statistics* 57 (August 1975): 259–268.

home. Although our historical experience would suggest limited substitution possibilities, it is not at all clear that this experience is relevant for the future. Some drag on economic growth from higher energy prices appears likely.

The second possible source of growth drag relates to the future productivity of capital. As pollution concentrations rise, the amount of resources committed to combating pollution also rise. A substantial proportion of new-plant and new-equipment expenditures is being allocated to pollution control. Unlike conventional investments, however, these investments do not cause more goods to be produced; they produce a cleaner environment. Because the value of this cleaner environment is not usually recorded in the conventional measures of economic output, conventionally measured output should rise more slowly as a large proportion of inputs is diverted from productivity enhancement to environment enhancement.

The final source of drag concerns the incentive to invest. The amount of capital investment should depend upon the rate of return on that investment. The more profitable the investment is, the larger the amount undertaken. Yet, we have already identified two related factors that reduce the rate of return on investments—the regulatory bias against new sources and the composition of investment. By focusing on new sources, the regulatory system diminishes the relative profitability of new investment while enhancing the profitability of existing capital stock. This new-source bias diminishes the incentive to invest in new capital. Meanwhile, the large proportion of new-plant and new-equipment expenditures going for pollution control tends to diminish the profitability of those expenditures being made, because improvements in the environment do not, in general, add to profits.

In sum, it appears that expecting increases in capital to completely compensate for reduced flows of other inputs would be risky. Some important transitions are occurring. Although they do not imply a cessation of growth catastrophically or otherwise in the near future, these transitions certainly suggest some diminution in the rate of economic growth resulting from reduced factor-input flows.

Limits on Technological Progress.   Can technological progress take up the slack? If technological progress is to compensate for declining input flows, an increase in the rate of technological progress must occur. Is that likely?

Some observers are beginning to suggest that the degree to which technological progress can continue to play its historic role as a growth stimulant may be limited. Some of these limits are perceived as institutional and a matter of choice; others are perceived as natural and inexorable.

The new-source regulatory bias in pollution control policy provides an example of an institutional limit. Because most technological progress bears fruit when it is embodied in new or modified production facilities, this new-source bias inhibits technological progress by reducing the number of these facilities.

Another institutional barrier is the decreasing commitment of resources to basic research, particularly by the public sector. Because basic research is frequently a precursor for technological progress, this trend could also diminish the rate of technological progress.

During the 1970s economic growth fell below that of earlier periods. The average rates of growth in manufacturing output were down markedly, as were growth rates in labor productivity (output divided by labor input) and technological progress. Does this dramatic decline reflect the beginning of a new era?

A number of economists have tried to isolate the sources of this decline—an assignment made difficult because so many interacting variables are involved. Nonetheless, some progress has been made and is worthy of our attention. We begin with an analysis of the effects of environmental policy on growth.

Environmental Policy

We have seen that pollution control laws impose large compliance costs on industry. These costs should have some effect on inflation (by boosting output prices) and employment, as well as on growth. The questions of interest are (1) how large those impacts have been and (2) how large they could be expected to be in the future.

Generally, studies suggest that the impact of environmental policy on the rate of inflation (measured by using the urban consumer price index) is very small, less than one half of a percentage point. This should not be surprising, since pollution control expenditures make up only a small proportion of costs.

The effect on employment is particularly interesting because it requires balancing the losses experienced by firms that have become technologically obsolete with the gains to firms that are now producing for new markets (e.g., the market for pollution control equipment). The evidence suggests that the gains to those producing the equipment more than offset the losses to those installing the equipment, resulting in more, not less, employment in the economy as a whole.

Economist Robert Haveman has surveyed the results of a range of studies conducted around the world on the effect of pollution control expenditures on employment.[4] These studies go beyond aggregate employment effects and delve into the types of workers affected, as well as into the effects of alternative ways of financing investments in pollution control. He concludes:

1. The employment demands of public sector spending for pollution control are greater than equivalent government spending for alternative purposes. About 60,000 to 70,000 jobs are created for each $1 billion of pollution control spending. For purposes of comparison, each $1 billion of GDP generates approximately 50,000 jobs, on the average.

2. Changes in the composition of employment triggered by environmental policy are likely to adversely affect low-skill, low-wage workers relative to high-skill, high-wage workers.

3. In a limited number of countries, environmental policy has been employed as a demand-inducing antirecession instrument—apparently, with some success. This result is, in part, due to the deficit public financing of the expenditures or subsidies.

4. Available evidence suggests that the adverse employment effects from plant closing attributable to environmental policy are very limited.

---

[4]Robert H. Haveman, "The Results and the Significance of the Employment Studies," Organization for Economic Co-operation and Development, *Employment and Environment* (Paris, France: OECD, 1978): 48–53.

While internationally comprehensive, this survey is now somewhat dated. Would more recent studies involving more stringent regulation reach the same conclusion? Apparently so, according to a recent survey of the literature.[5]

It even seems to be true for those areas facing the most stringent requirements to reduce pollution. At least in the Los Angeles area the evidence seems to suggest that strict environmental policy has not triggered increases in unemployment (Example 20.1).

However, this generally positive prognosis for the impact of environmental policy on employment should not obscure the problems. Gains in employment generally benefit a different set of workers than losses do. New jobs are rarely in the same location as those lost and, as Haveman points out, rarely involve the same skill levels. Even when overall employment effects are positive, the rising costs of environmental control could cause severe localized problems.

How much responsibility for the slowdown in productivity can be attributed to environmental policy? Using comparative data from the United States, Canada, and the former West Germany, Conrad and Morrison found that only a small part was the result of diverting investments toward environmental control.[6] In fact, some government requirements to install cleaner equipment may have raised productivity by forcing firms to invest in newer and more efficient equipment. For industries in the United States, a common finding seems to be that somewhere in the neighborhood of 12 percent of the responsibility of the productivity slowdown can be attributed to environmental regulations.[7] If these conclusions are at all accurate, environmental policy does not bear responsibility for much of the decline in the economic growth rate in the late 1970s.

Energy

A second possible source of growth drag is energy. Because large price increases occurred during 1973–1974, this period provides a unique opportunity to study the magnitude of the growth-inhibiting effects of energy.

What should we expect to find? Because energy and capital historically have been complements, we should find that price increases would slow down capital formation. At the same time, the fact that energy and labor are substitutes would suggest that the use of labor should be rising, which, in turn, would cause the average productivity of labor to fall.

On a general level, the evidence is consistent with this set of expectations. Investment is lower, and the average productivity of labor has fallen. Work by Jorgenson and others, such as Uri and Hassanein, confirms this impression.[8]

---

[5]Goodstein, E. "Jobs and the Environment—an Overview," *Environmental Management* 20(1996)(3): 313–321.

[6] Klause Conrad and Catherine Morrison, "The Impact of Pollution Abatement Investment on Productivity Change: An Empirical Comparison of the United States, Germany and Canada," *Southern Economic Journal* 55 (January 1989): 684–698.

[7] Anthony J. Barbera and Virginia D. McConnell, "The Impact of Environmental Regulations on Industry Productivity: Direct and Indirect Effects," *Journal of Environmental Economics and Management* 18 (January 1990): 50–65; Wayne B. Gray, "The Cost of Regulation: OSHA, EPA, and the Productivity Slowdown," *American Economic Review* 77 (December 1987): 998–1006; Gregory B. Christiansen and Robert H. Haveman, "The Contribution of Environmental Regulations to the Slowdown in Productivity Growth," *Journal of Environmental Economics and Management* 8 (1981): 381–390; and J. R. Norsworthy, Michael J. Harper, and Kent Kunze, "The Slowdown in Productivity Growth: Analysis of Some Contributing Factors," *Brookings Papers in Economic Activity* (2, 1979): 387–421.

[8]Dale W. Jorgenson, "Energy Prices and Productivity Growth," *Scandinavian Journal of Economics* 83 (1981): 165–179; Noel D. Uri and Saad A. Hassanein, "Energy Prices, Labour Productivity, and Causality: An Empirical Examination," *Energy Economics* 4 (April 1982): 98–104.

Example 20.1

Jobs versus The Environment: What is the Evidence?

The employment effects of environmental regulation are a hot political topic. Public opinion surveys show strong support for measures intended to produce a cleaner environment, but workers often feel that these measures threaten their jobs.

Is their anxiety justified? Theory tells us that regulation can reduce employment by raising marginal costs and decreasing sales; it also tells us that environmental regulation can increase employment by creating a demand for workers to monitor and maintain pollution control equipment. How important are these conflicting tendencies?

One particularly interesting way to gather evidence on this subject would be to examine the employment consequences of regulation in a geographic area that has experienced particularly stringent regulation. One study that did precisely that focused on the regulation of air pollution in manufacturing plants in the Los Angeles region. Because this area has some of the worst air quality in the nation, the South Coast Air Quality Management District has been forced to adopt regulations of unprecedented stringency to comply with national air quality standards. The study examines employment growth in the Los Angeles region in plants subject to these regulations, and compares growth at these plants to employment growth at similar plants in Texas and Louisiana, areas that had no significant increase in local air quality regulation.

The results indicate that in the 1979–91 period in the Los Angeles Basin increases in air quality regulation involving substantial increases in cost did not appreciably affect employment. In fact the study found very small *increases* in employment. Although the increases were not statistically significant, they were sufficient to rule out the possibility that the regulation had led to large decreases in employment.

Source: Eli Berman, and Linda T. M. Bui, "Cleaning the Air: The Impact of Air Quality Regulation on Jobs" (Washington, DC: Economic Policy Institute, 1997).

Focusing on the period 1973–1976, a time characterized by rapidly increasing energy prices, Jorgenson first examined the question of whether the decline in growth was due to declines in input growth or to declines in productivity. He found that input declines were much less significant than declines in productivity. He then attempted to discover the sources of this productivity decline by looking at the specific experience of 35 different industries.

Though a decline in economywide productivity could conceivably be caused either by a shift in resources from high-productivity industries to low-productivity industries or by a decline in productivity within each industry, Jorgenson found the latter to be far more important than the former. His analysis of the causes of these declines revealed that, in 29 of the 35 sectors examined, technological change was biased toward the use of energy. This result suggests that from 1973 to 1976, productivity growth resulting from technological progress declined as energy prices rose.

One puzzle to be explained by those who believe energy prices have already played a significant role in productivity declines is how that could be so when the energy cost share is so small. Factors with small cost shares should, in general, have rather small effects on output.

One resolution to this puzzle seems consistent with the evidence.[9] Berndt and Wood suggest that, in the short run, the capital services provided by the capital stock are largely fixed, as are its operating characteristics. Once the capital stock is in place, the ratio of energy to capital services actually utilized is therefore fixed. Dramatic changes in energy prices therefore affect the degree to which this capital is used, with the most energy-inefficient vintages being used least. By lowering the utilization of the existing capital stock, higher energy prices reduce total factor productivity.

In this story, the lower productivity does not necessarily persist. As long as new capital that uses less energy can be purchased, utilization rates rise, and productivity is restored as these new machines are installed. Once the stock of capital adjusts to the new regime of higher energy prices, productivity growth rebounds.

The key to thinking about the long run is to keep straight the differences between *ex post* and *ex ante* substitution possibilities. *Ex ante* refers to the time period prior to investment, whereas *ex post* refers to the time period after the equipment is installed. Limited *ex post* substitution possibilities, which seem to have played a significant role in the slowdown of productivity growth after the major energy price increases in the 1970s and in the early 1980s, do not automatically indicate that *ex ante* substitution possibilities will be small. It is the *ex ante* substitution possibilities that will determine the future of economic growth over the long run.

Most visions of sustainable development suggest the need for increasing the efficiency with which energy is used. In practice, this means investing in energy conservation in order to make better use of a smaller fossil fuel energy flow. What employment and income effects can be expected from investments in energy conservation? Geller et al. have investigated this question by constructing two quantitative scenarios: (1) a business-as-usual scenario and (2) a high-energy-efficiency scenario.[10] The high-energy-efficiency scenario involves an additional annual investment of about $49 billion in energy efficiency. They conclude that in addition to producing some rather dramatic reductions in pollutants (e.g., a 24 percent reduction in carbon dioxide), the high-energy-efficiency scenario results in both a rise in personal income (0.5% by 2010) and a net increase in jobs (an additional 1.1 million by 2010). The largest increases in jobs were estimated to occur in the construction, retail trade, and service industries, whereas the largest decreases were in the traditional energy-supply sectors. Other studies have found that transitioning from depletable to renewable energy sources is also likely to increase, rather than decrease, employment.[11]

---

[9]Ernst R. Berndt and David O. Wood, "Energy Price Shocks and Productivity Growth: A Survey," in *Energy: Markets and Regulation,* Richard L. Gordon, Henry D. Jacoby, and Martin B. Zimmerman, eds. (Cambridge, MA: MIT Press, 1987): 305–342.

[10] Howard Geller, John De Cicco, and Skip Laitner, *Energy Efficiency and Job Creation: The Employment and Income Benefits from Investing in Energy-Conserving Technologies* (Washington, DC: American Council for an Energy-Efficient Economy, 1992).

[11]Michael Renner, "Jobs in a Sustainable Economy," Paper No. 104 (Washington, DC: Worldwatch Institute, 1991): 25.

◆ OUTLOOK FOR THE NEAR FUTURE

Some of what the future holds for the United States and other developed countries is becoming clear. Because we are in a period of transition, some striking differences between our experiences in the recent past and what we will encounter in the near future are emerging. Though a detailed examination would be beyond the scope of this study, the following discussion will highlight some of the emerging changes.

Population Impacts

The dramatic fall in fertility rates experienced by most countries of the world will have a profound impact on productivity and well-being. Inevitably, the average age of the population will rise, putting pressure on social security systems. Because the United States relies on an unfunded social security system, current payments to retirees are financed out of current payments by workers. As long as the population is growing, the ratio of workers to retirees remains high enough to provide adequate benefit levels for retirees without putting excessive strain on current workers. When population growth declines, however, as is now happening, the ratio of workers to retirees declines as well. To keep the system solvent, benefit growth has to decline and/or worker payments have to increase.

Some studies by economists and demographers suggest that labor-market implications of declining population growth will be significant. One very positive effect will be a reduction in the unemployment rates of young adults. Because fewer young, inexperienced workers will be entering the labor market, it will be easier to absorb those that do so.

As a result of declines in population growth, the labor force will not grow as much as it has historically; this will create some upward pressure on wages. These higher wages should reinforce and support the rising participation rates for women and should entice older workers to stay in the workforce longer. In turn, these enhanced job opportunities for women should keep the fertility low, reinforcing the tendency for low rates of population growth.

The work by Lindert, studied in the population chapter, suggested that periods of tight labor markets have an equalizing effect on the income distribution. If this model is accurate, and no countervailing tendencies develop, we should witness a trend toward greater income equality in the future as the rewards to labor rise relative to other factors.

The Information Economy

The importance of capital and resources in the U.S. economy is a product of the industrial revolution. The industrial revolution ushered in an era of mass production where manufacturing replaced agriculture as the dominant source of employment and earnings. This transformation depended upon massive amounts of capital investment, and the scale of operations it brought about consumed large amounts of resources.

It now seems clear that the economy is in the midst of an equally important transformation from an industrial society to what Daniel Bell has labeled the *post-industrial society*.[12]

---

[12]Daniel Bell, *The Coming of the Post-Industrial Society: A Venture in Social Forecasting* (New York: Basic Books, 1973).

The key elements of this transformation are a change from a goods-producing to a service economy, a rise in the importance of theoretical knowledge as a source of growth, and an increasing reliance on information processing.

Until 1905, agricultural workers outnumbered industrial, service, and information workers. Industrial workers became the dominant force for the next 50 years. By 1955, information workers made up the largest category.

This transformation has profound implications for our society. Computer-controlled robots will step in to fill the slots vacated by lower population growth in a direct substitution of capital for labor. Working at home will become possible for larger numbers of people as computer communication provides a substitute for transportation. Such changes will boost productivity while reducing pollution and our dependence on raw materials and energy. Intelligence will replace oil as the prime mover of the system.

This vision suggests that in the future the demand for skilled labor will rise more rapidly than the demand for unskilled labor. Education will therefore grow in importance, not only as the means of providing that skilled labor, but also as the wellspring of ideas that fuel the new growth.

◆ THE GROWTH-DEVELOPMENT RELATIONSHIP

Has economic growth historically served as a vehicle for development? Has growth really made the average person better off? Would the lowest-income members of the United States and the world fare better with economic growth or without it?

These turn out to be difficult questions to answer in a way that satisfies everyone, but we must start somewhere. One appropriate point of departure is clarifying what we mean by *growth*. Some of the disenchantment with growth can be traced to how growth is measured. It is not so much that all growth is bad, but rather that increases in conventional indicators of growth are not always good. Some of the enthusiasm for zero economic growth stems from the fact that economic growth, as currently measured, can be shown to have several undesirable characteristics.

Conventional Measures

A true measure of development would increase whenever we, as a nation or as a world, were better off and decrease whenever we were worse off. Such a measure is called a *welfare measure,* and no conventional existing measure is designed to be a welfare measure.

What we currently have are *output measures,* which attempt to indicate how many goods and services have been produced, not how well-off we are. Measuring output sounds fairly simple, but in fact it is not. The measure of economic growth with which most are familiar is based upon the GDP, or gross domestic product. This number represents the sum of the outputs of goods and services in any year produced by the economy. Prices are used to weigh the importance of these goods and services in GDP. Conceptually, this is accomplished by totaling up the value added by each sector of the production process until the product is sold.

Why weight by prices? Some means of comparing the value of extremely dissimilar commodities is needed. Prices provide a readily available system of weights that takes into account the value of those commodities to consumers. From earlier chapters, we know that prices should reflect both the marginal benefit to the consumer and the marginal cost to the producer.

GDP is not a measure of welfare and was never meant to be one. One limitation of this indicator as a measure of welfare is that it includes the value of new machines that are replacing worn-out ones rather than increasing the size of the capital stock. To compensate for the fact that some investment merely replaces old machines and does not add to the size of capital stock, a new concept known as *net domestic product* (NDP) was introduced. *NDP is defined as the gross domestic product minus depreciation.*

NDP and GDP share a deficiency in that they are both influenced by inflation. If the flow of all goods and services were to remain the same while prices doubled, both NDP and GDP would also double. Because neither welfare nor output would have increased, an accurate indicator should reflect that fact.

To resolve this problem, national income accountants present data on *constant-dollar GDP* and *constant-dollar NDP.* These numbers are derived by "cleansing" the actual GDP and NDP data to take out the effects of price rises. Conceptually, this is accomplished by defining a market basket of goods that stays the same over time. Each year, this same basket is repriced. If the cost of the goods in the basket went up 10 percent, then, because the quantities are held constant, we know that prices went up by 10 percent. This information is used to remove the effects of prices on the indicators; remaining increases should be due to an increased production of goods and services.

However, this correction does not solve all problems. For one thing, not all components of GDP contribute equally to welfare. Probably the closest component we could use in the existing system of accounts would be *consumption,* the amount of goods and services consumed by households. It leaves out government expenditures, investments, exports, and imports.

The final correction that could easily be made to the existing accounts would involve dividing real consumption by the population in order to get *real consumption per capita.* This correction allows us to differentiate between rises in output needed to maintain the standard of living for an increasing population and rises indicating that more goods and services were consumed by the average member of that population.

Real consumption per capita is about as close as we can get to a welfare-oriented output measure using readily available data, but it is a far cry from being an ideal welfare indicator.

In particular, changes in real consumption per capita fail to distinguish between economic growth resulting from a true increase in income and economic growth resulting from a depreciation in what economists have come to call "natural capital" that is, the stock of environmentally provided assets such as the soil, the atmosphere, the forests, wildlife, and water.

The traditional definition of *income* was articulated by Sir John Hicks:

> The purpose of income calculations in practical affairs is to give people an indication of the amount they can consume without impoverishing themselves. Following out this idea, it would seem that we ought to define a man's income as the maximum value which he can consume during a week, and still expect to be as well off at the end of the week as he was at the beginning.[13]

---

[13]J. R. Hicks, *Value and Capital,* 2nd ed. (Oxford, UK: Oxford University Press, 1947): 172.

Although human-created capital (e.g., buildings, bridges) is treated in a manner consistent with this definition, natural capital is not. As human-created capital wears out, the accounts set aside an amount, called *depreciation,* to compensate for the decline in value. No increase in economic activity is recorded as an increase in income until depreciation has been subtracted from gross returns. That portion of the gains that merely serves to replace worn-out capital is not appropriately considered income.

No such adjustment is made for natural capital in the standard national income accounting system. Depreciation of the stock of natural capital is incorrectly counted as income. Development strategies that "cash in" the endowment of natural resources are, in these accounts, indistinguishable from development strategies that do not depreciate the natural capital stock; the returns from both are treated as income.

Consider an analogy. Many high-quality private educational institutions in the United States have large financial endowments. In considering their budgets for the year, these institutions take the revenue from tuition and other fees and add in some proportion of the interest and capital gains earned from the endowment. Except in extraordinary circumstances, however, standard financial practice does not allow the institution to attack the principal. Drawing down the endowment and treating this increase in financial resources as income is not allowed.

However, that is precisely what the traditional national accounts allow us to do in terms of natural resources. We can deplete our soils, cut down our forests, and douse ocean coves with oil, and the resulting economic activity is treated as income, not as a decline in the endowment of natural capital.

Because the Hicksian definition is violated for natural capital, policymakers are misled. By relying upon misleading information, policy makers are more likely to undertake unsustainable development strategies.

Adjusting the national income accounts to apply the Hicksian definition uniformly to human-made and natural capital could make quite a difference in resource-dependent countries. For example, Robert Repetto and colleagues of the World Resources Institute studied the growth rates of gross domestic product in Indonesia using both conventional unadjusted figures and figures adjusted to account for the depreciation of natural capital. Their study found that, whereas the unadjusted GDP increased at an average annual rate of 7.1 percent from 1971 to 1984, the adjusted estimates rose by only 4.0 percent per year.[14]

Motivated by a recognition of these serious flaws in the current system of accounts, a number of industrialized countries have now proposed (or, in a few cases, have already set up) systems of adjusted accounts. Included among these countries are Norway, France, Canada, Japan, the Netherlands, Germany, and the United States. Significant differences of opinion on such issues as whether the changes should be incorporated in a complementary system of accounts or in a complete revision of the standard accounts remain to be resolved.

In the United States the Bureau of Economic Analysis has published its initial estimates of the value of the U.S. stock of minerals—oil, gas, and coal, as well as nonfuel minerals—and how the value of that stock (in constant dollars) has changed over time.[15] The objective was to

---

[14]Robert Repetto, "Nature's Resources as Productive Assets," *Challenge* 32, No. 5 (September/October 1989): 16–20.

[15] Bureau of Economic Analysis, "Accounting for Mineral Resources: Issues and BEA's Initial Estimates," *Survey of Current Business* (April 1994): 50–72.

determine whether current use patterns are consistent with the constant-value version of the sustainability criterion. Declining values would indicate a violation of the criterion, whereas constant or increasing values would be compatible with it. In general, it found that the value of additions just about offset the value of the depletion; for the period 1958–1991, its estimates suggest that the criterion was not violated.

Alternative Measures

Because revised accounts are not yet available, we cannot use them to assess the relationship between growth and economic well-being. But the question won't go away, so we have to do the best we can with what information is available.

Several studies have attempted to adjust real consumption per capita figures on an ad hoc basis in order to come up with a measure that is closer to being a welfare measure. One of the first was by Nordhaus and Tobin.[16] Their first adjustment involves an attempt to account for the amount of welfare-reducing environmental damage being inflicted by pollution. Reasoning that part of the increased wages of urban workers represents compensation for having been exposed to the higher pollution concentrations, they used a portion of the income differential between urban and rural families as their measure of the monetary value of the damage caused. This estimate is then subtracted from the real consumption data.

They then adjust the data to treat consumer durables in a different way. In conventional accounts, consumer durables are incorporated by adding in their full cost at the time of purchase, in spite of the fact that services from those durable goods are received throughout their useful life. Nordhaus and Tobin subtract these durable good *purchases* and add back in an estimate of the annual *services* they provide.

The final subtraction from the conventional accounts involves excluding consumer expenditures that do not seem to raise welfare. The major expenditure they excluded was the cost of commuting to and from work. Although such expenditures are necessary, they do not themselves raise welfare.

Nordhaus and Tobin also correct for omissions that tend to bias the conventional accounts downward when interpreted in welfare terms. These include the value of leisure time and household production, neither of which is valued in conventional accounts. One benefit of growth is that productivity increases have resulted in a decline in the average workweek. This increased leisure is valued by Nordhaus and Tobin at the market wage rate that could have been earned if the time were spent working rather than in leisure activities. Household production involves the many services performed around the house. Unless there are hired servants, household production activities do not enter the conventional accounts.

The problem with the manner in which the conventional approach treats household production is nicely illustrated by an example. When a single person marries his or her housekeeper, GDP goes down, because an activity that was formerly a market activity is no longer such. Yet, we presume, because marriage is a voluntary arrangement, that welfare was increased. The change in the indicator sends the wrong signal. Nordhaus and Tobin correct this conventional approach by adding in an imputed value for nonmarketed household production.

---

[16]William D. Nordhaus and James Tobin, "Is Growth Obsolete?" in *Economic Growth, Fiftieth Anniversary Colloquium, Volume 5* (New York: National Bureau of Economic Research, 1972): 4–17.

Their final correction involves adding into personal consumption expenditures a value for the government services provided. Traditionally, the government sector is treated separately in the GDP, and its output is valued at cost. By including this measure, Nordhaus and Tobin are correcting two problems: (1) the omission of government services from the personal consumption expenditures, and (2) valuing these services as received rather than (in the case of government durables, such as roads) at the time of purchase.

After making all these adjustments, they arrive at an indicator they call the *measure of economic welfare* (MEW). The MEW per capita rose by about 42 percent between 1929 and 1965. This increase was only about one half of the 87.5 percent increase in real NDP per capita over the same period. According to Nordhaus and Tobin, real NDP per capita does overstate growth in economic well-being, but their estimate leaves no doubt that they believe correctly measured economic well-being has increased substantially since 1929.

Others have attempted to make different adjustments. In particular, Usher has adjusted the conventional accounts to incorporate the value of increased life expectancy and finds that this adjustment boosts the growth rate of the adjusted measure above the conventional measure.[17]

Zolotas performed a similar, but somewhat more detailed, set of calculations for the particular purpose of discovering whether the growth in well-being had declined over time.[18] The trends in his measure of welfare suggest that the additional increases in well-being are becoming smaller and smaller as growth continues. Similar results were subsequently obtained by Daly and Cobb.[19] They found that per capita welfare had increased 20 percent from 1951 to 1986 in the United States, but that increase was the net result of two offsetting trends. Per capita welfare had started to decline between 1970 and 1980. (Note that this is a decline in welfare, not a decline in the growth of welfare!) The estimated average annual decline during the 1970s was 0.14 percent, whereas the average annual decline during the 1980s was estimated to be 1.26 percent. If this evidence were ultimately confirmed by better designed accounts, it would show that the effects of economic growth on per capita well-being have in the past been positive but recently have turned negative. According to Daly and Cobb, further growth in the United States not only would not improve well-being, it would decrease it.

One source of dissatisfaction with all of these measures of well-being is their focus on an average. To the extent that the most serious problems of deprivation are not experienced by the average member of society, this focus may leave a highly misleading impression about well-being. To rectify this problem, in 1990 the United Nations Development Program (UNDP) constructed an alternative measure, *the human development index* (HDI). This index has three major components: (1) longevity, (2) knowledge, and (3) income. Though highly controversial (because both the measures to be included in this index and the weights assigned to each component are rather arbitrary), the UNDP has drawn some interesting conclusions from the results of comparing HDIs among countries.[20]

- The link between per capita national income and human development is not automatic; it depends on how the income is spent. Some relatively high-income countries

[17]Dan Usher, *The Measurement of Economic Growth* (New York: Columbia University Press, 1980).

[18]Xenophon Zolotas, *Economic Growth and Declining Social Welfare* (New York: New York University, 1981).

[19]Herman E. Daly and John B. Cobb, Jr., *For the Common Good* (Boston: Beacon Press, 1989): 401–455.

[20]United Nations Development Program, *Human Development Report: 1993* (New York: Oxford University Press, 1993).

(e.g., South Africa and the Persian Gulf states) do not fare as well as expected in human development terms, whereas some low-income countries (e.g., Sri Lanka and China) were able to achieve a higher level of human development than would be expected, given their income level.

- Nonetheless, income is a major determinant of the capacity to improve human development. It is not a coincidence that the top five countries in terms of HDI (Japan, Canada, Norway, Switzerland, Sweden) are all very-high-income countries.

◆ GROWTH AND POVERTY: THE INDUSTRIALIZED NATIONS

Conceiving of the growth-development relationship only in terms of the effects on the average citizen obscures a great deal of what may be happening in a society. Two societies may have the same per capita growth in average well-being, but if the fruits of this growth are shared uniformly in one and unequally in the second, it seems overly simplistic to argue that the increase in welfare levels would be the same in the two countries. As Example 20.2 indicates, relative income levels seems to make a difference in how well-off people feel.

Although the evidence suggests that economic growth has improved the lot of the average citizen in the developed world, it tells us nothing about how the poorest members of society fared. To determine whether the poorest citizens also benefit from growth, we must dig deeper into the nature of the growth process.

One source of information about this relationship is history. To exploit that source, we shall examine the data for a period of particularly high economic growth in the United States. Did it benefit the poor, or were they left behind?

The Effects on Income Inequality

Growth can help the poor in two main ways. First, it can provide more opportunity to earn income either by increasing the number of available jobs, by increasing the wages paid, or some combination of the two. Second, it is generally believed that income transfers are easier when the amount to be shared is growing. The donors can give up some of their gains and still be better off, whereas in a no-growth situation, any sharing must come from a reduction in the real income of the donors.

The experience from the United States suggests that periods of economic growth have reduced the degree of poverty. Although growth itself has been a factor, government transfers have made the most difference. Economic growth, in the absence of transfers, would not have lifted many persons from below to above the poverty threshold.[21] The linkage between growth and the poor depends more upon its effect on the willingness to transfer than on direct market effects. Although growth cannot be seen as a vehicle that inevitably creates equality of income among the rich and poor, the evidence shows that, in the United States at least, the quality of life experienced by the poor has been improved by it. This improvement has come both from a general rising standard of living and a rise in transfers from the rich to the poor.

---

[21]Eugene Smolensky, "Poverty in the United States: Where Do We Stand?," *University of Wisconsin—Madison, Institute for Research on Poverty Focus 5* (winter 1981–82).

Example 20.2

Does Money Buy Happiness?

In a highly subjective but interesting study, economist Richard Easterlin (1973) collected data from 30 surveys conducted in 19 developed and less-developed countries that analyze the relationship between happiness and income. In every one of these surveys, the respondents were asked to rate how happy they were feeling on a scale: "very happy," "mildly happy," "mildly unhappy," and "very unhappy." Information on respondent income levels were also collected.

In analyzing these data he found:

1. At any point in time, a larger portion of high-income people are happier than low-income people—for all countries and all years.
2. The proportion of happy and unhappy in each group remained relatively constant over time, in spite of generally rising incomes. For example, in the United States, roughly the same percentage of wealthy people and poor people said they were very happy in 1940 as in 1970.

The first finding suggests that higher income is positively correlated with happiness; the second suggests, that despite large increases in income, the percentage saying they were very happy did not increase. How are these apparently contradictory findings to be explained?

Easterlin explains them by suggesting that one of the components of happiness for people is their relative income. Thus, a person at the top of the heap in any particular country may be happier than he or she would be if that same income were earned in a richer country where lots of people earned that income. If this hypothesis is correct, it suggests that the average level of welfare in an economic system is an inadequate indicator of the total welfare in the society. The distribution of the fruits of economic growth makes a difference.

Source: Richard A. Easterlin, "Does Money Buy Happiness?" *The Public Interest* (Winter 1973): 3–10.

◆ POVERTY IN THE LESS INDUSTRIALIZED NATIONS

Economic growth can be a vehicle for development, and this form of development can benefit the poor as well as the rich, according to the historical experience in the industrialized nations. Though the relationship between economic growth and poverty is neither inevitable nor universally effective, it does provide one possible path for dealing with poverty.

How relevant is this experience for the third world? Can and should the traditional approach to economic growth serve as a model for those nations struggling to free themselves from the grip of poverty?

It would be delightful to find that the poverty problem is solving itself, but that is certainly not the case. Many of the world's poor are caught in a seamless web of deteriorating conditions.[22] According to a 1988 address by World Bank President Barber Conable: "Poverty on today's scale prevents a billion people from having even minimally acceptable standards of living. . . . In sub-Sahara Africa more than 100 million people—one in four—do not get enough to eat. Agricultural productivity per capita has been declining in Africa since 1967 and in Latin American since 1981. The World Bank reports that from 1980 to 1997 life expectancy fell in 11 African countries. In Zambia twice as many children died from malnutrition in 1984 as in 1980. In its 1989 annual report, the United Nations Children's Fund (UNICEF) concluded that "at least half a million young children have died in the last 12 months as a result of slowing down or the reversal of progress in the development world."

What are the trends in incomes? Many developing countries are actually losing ground. As Inter-American Development Bank President Enrique Iglesias said in September 1988, "The per capita income of the average Latin American is 9 percent lower today than it was in 1980. This is average. In some countries the standard of living has slipped back to where it was 20 years ago."

The picture is not totally bleak. Success against poverty is possible. Some Asian countries have done well in the 1980s, for example. Thailand has reported a 50 percent decrease in its poverty rate since 1960. The Republic of Korea, Taiwan, and Singapore have all experienced rapid industrialization and a rising standard of living.

The Appropriateness of the Traditional Model

How appropriate is the traditional economic growth model for these countries? Does it point the way out of poverty?

Scale. One of the first indicators that traditional models may be inappropriate derives from the ecological effects of the proposed global scale of economic activity necessary to eradicate poverty if the model of development followed by the industrialized nations of Asia, Europe, and Africa were adopted by the rest of the world. As Jim MacNeill, the former director of the World Commission on Environment and Development, has stated, "If current forms of development were employed, a five- to ten-fold increase in economic activity would be required over the next fifty years to meet the needs and aspirations of a population twice the size of today's 6.0 billion, as well as to begin to reduce mass poverty." Whether increases of this magnitude could be accomplished while still respecting the atmospheric and ecological systems on which all economic activity ultimately depends is not at all obvious.

Increased energy consumption to support new industry would add greenhouse gases. Increased refrigeration would add more of the gases depleting the stratospheric ozone level. The industrialized nations have freely used the very large capacity of the atmosphere to absorb these gases. Little absorptive capacity is left. Most observers seem to believe that in order to meet the challenge, we need to take an activist stance by controlling population,

---

[22]The information in this paragraph and the two that follow were obtained from Alan B. Durning, "Poverty and the Environment: Reversing the Downward Spiral," Paper No. 92 (Washington, DC: Worldwatch Institute, 1989): 15–18.

severely reducing emissions of these gases in the industrialized world, and discovering new forms of development that are sustainable.

Forms of Development. Economics can assist in the process of characterizing how the forms should differ. Appropriate development should capitalize on local strengths and stay away from weaknesses; it should be sensitive to factor prices.

Many, if not most, of the developing nations, are labor-surplus economies. It follows that their strategy for development, at least in the beginning stages, should be labor-intensive. Labor-intensive processes serve the twin purposes of capitalizing on an abundant resource and providing a source of income to large numbers of people.[23]

Although the forms of development in the industrialized nations are increasingly going to rely on a highly skilled labor force, that is inappropriate for countries where the educational systems may not currently be able to supply sufficient numbers of skilled workers to fill the need. By effectively utilizing the low-skilled workforce, developing countries can increase their incomes, decrease population growth, and ultimately create the wealth needed to support strong education systems.

Development in the industrialized countries has also been very fossil-fuel-dependent. Although this may be appropriate when supplies of fossil fuels are plentiful and the remaining capacity of the environment to accept the by-product gases is unlimited, it is certainly less appropriate for a future plagued by diminishing supplies and global warming.

Barriers to Development

What are the barriers to raising standards of living in the third world? Rising populations face increasingly limited access to land, health services, education, and financial resources. Many of these problems are intensified by the current international economy. Heavy debt burdens, falling prices for exports, and the flight of capital that could be used to create jobs and income are all significant barriers to sustainable development.

Population Growth. Poverty begets poverty. The positive feedback loop between population growth and poverty is one powerful example. Population growth rates are typically higher—substantially higher—in low-income populations. High infant mortality causes parents to compensate with large numbers of births. Children provide one of the few available means of old-age security. Knowledge about birth control techniques is sparse, and the availability of contraceptives is limited. Women frequently have low levels of education, and in some cultures large families are the only possible way for women to achieve status. Larger populations, in turn, tend to increase the degree of poverty by lowering wages and by spreading the resources allocated to children over a larger number.

Population growth also puts increased pressure on the natural resource base. Pushing larger numbers of people onto marginal land increases soil erosion and deforestation. Increasing population density can cause the carrying capacity of the land to be exceeded. In parts of Africa where nomadic tribes have coexisted for centuries with a fragile ecosystem, larger populations and reduced mobility have resulted in such a serious deterioration of the ecosystem that it is no longer able to satisfy basic human needs.

---

[23]Contrast this with capital-intensive processes, which use much less labor and distribute more of the returns to the owners of capital, who are typically well-off.

Land Ownership Patterns.   Pressures on the land arising from population growth are exacerbated by patterns of land ownership in many of the lower-income countries. In agricultural economies, access to land is a key ingredient in any attempt to eradicate poverty, but land ownership is frequently highly concentrated among a few extremely wealthy owners. Much of the undeveloped land that exists is ecologically valuable in its preserved state. Improvements in agricultural techniques can do little to raise living standards if peasants do not have access to their own land.

One common measure of the degree of inequality in land ownership is the *Gini coefficient*. The Gini coefficient can take on values of 0.0 (which would indicate perfect equality) to 1.0 (which would indicate perfect inequality). *Perfect equality* would occur if every farmer owned exactly the same amount of land. *Perfect inequality* would imply that all land was owned by a single farmer.

In Latin America, Gini coefficients in excess of 0.75 are common.[24] This region has the most skewed land-ownership patterns on the globe, a legacy of colonial times when colonial rulers accumulated vast amounts of land. Asian nations are somewhat better, with Gini coefficients ranging from 0.51 to 0.64 and in Africa, where collective tribal land ownership is common, the coefficients fall between 0.36 and 0.55.[25]

Trade Policies.   Some of the barriers faced by third-world countries as they attempt to raise living standards have been erected by the industrialized nations. Trade policies are one example. The terms of trade for many third-world countries have deteriorated in the recent past.[26]

Some of the reasons for this deterioration are natural effects of markets rather than misguided policies. Included in this category are the import substitutions in the industrialized world (e.g., when optical fibers are substituted for copper in phone lines) and lower demand for third-world exports triggered by lower economic growth in the industrialized countries.

Political factors are also important. When political forces in the developed countries conspire to eliminate or substantially reduce natural markets for the developing countries, these policies not only exacerbate the poverty in the developing nations, they have a direct degrading effect on the environment.[27]

The Multi-Fiber Arrangement, originally implemented in 1974, is a case in point. Its effect has been to severely reduce developing-country exports of textiles and other products made from fibers. In developing countries, fiber products are produced by labor-intensive techniques, causing the employment impact to be high. For local sustainable agriculture, the opportunity to provide the fiber raw materials is another source of employment. By artificially reducing the markets for these products and the fibers from which these products are manufactured, the

---

[24]The land ownership data are from Alan B. Durning, "Poverty and the Environment: Reversing the Downward Spiral," Paper No. 92 (Washington, DC: Worldwatch Institute, 1989): 25.

[25]To provide one, admittedly imperfect, basis for comparison, the 1986 U.S. Gini coefficient for the distribution of income among families was 0.389.

[26]The terms of trade determine international purchasing power. When the terms of trade deteriorate, third-world exports purchase fewer imports. Evidence on the deteriorating terms of trade can be found in World Bank, *World Development Report 1989* (Washington, DC: Oxford University Press, 1989), Table 14: 190–191.

[27]A study by the World Bank Staff shows that lowering tariff barriers in the European Economic Community, the United States, and Japan would permit exports from the highly indebted developing countries to increase by some $6.5 billion. World Bank, *World Debt Tables, 1988–89* (Washington, DC: World Bank, 1988): xxvii.

agreement has forced some nations to substitute resource-intensive economic activities, such as timber exports, for the more environmentally congenial fiber-based manufacturing in order to earn foreign exchange.

Agricultural trade flows not only demonstrate how price distortions can be translated into unsustainable development but also show how they can exacerbate poverty. In general, price distortions and artificially supported exchange rates have resulted in a pattern of trade that involves excessive agricultural production in the developed world and too little in the developing world. Agriculture in the developed world is supported by a number of different subsidies. In the developing world, the bias operates to promote underproduction rather than overproduction. Overvalued exchange rates increase the attractiveness of importing food and decrease the attractiveness of exporting food.

By discouraging small-scale agriculture in developing countries, an activity that would provide income to a segment of the population faced with the most severe forms of poverty, biased trade flows exacerbate the poverty problem. Furthermore, because income increases targeted on this particular group typically lead to slower population growth, even some of the population pressures on the environment could ultimately be related to biases in current trade patterns.

One common stereotype of the difference between developed and less-developed countries involves their respective supplies of minerals. According to this stereotype, less-developed countries control most of the world's mineral resources, and the developed world creates the demand for them. If accurate, this view would suggest that rising mineral prices would eventually create favorable terms of trade for most developing countries.

Unfortunately, upon closer inspection this stereotype represents, at best, an oversimplification. Although exports of minerals have increased from less developed to developed countries, not all less developed countries share these higher export levels. A few have large reserves of petroleum or nonfuel minerals, but most do not. The benefits from increasing mineral prices tend to bypass most less developed countries.

Debt.   Many third-world countries have staggering levels of debt to service. The World Bank has estimated that the total external debt of all developing countries reached $2 trillion in 1997. In 1989 poor nations sent $51.6 billion more to the industrialized nations in interest and principal repayment than they received in new capital.[28] External debt in 1997 was 92.3 percent of the gross national product of the severely indebted low-income countries. These percentages reach as high as 236.0 percent for Guyana and 305.6 percent for Nicaragua.[29]

Unfortunately, even private capital is flowing out of the capital-poor countries, where it is desperately needed, and into the capital-rich countries. The World Bank estimates that the stock of "flight" capital held abroad by citizens of severely indebted countries equals a significant fraction of those countries' external debt.

In periods of high real interest rates, servicing these debts puts a significant drain on foreign exchange of earnings. Using these foreign exchange earnings to service the debt eliminates the possibility of using them to finance imports for sustainable activities to alleviate

---

[28]Even if all official development assistance and private capital flows to the developing countries were included in the total, the net outflow would still be $9.8 billion. This evidence on the debt comes from the World Bank, *World Debt Tables 1989–90, Volume 1* (Washington, DC: World Bank, 1989): 1–9.

[29]United Nations, *Human Development Report 1999* (New York: Oxford Press).

poverty. One study found that, in all but one of the most indebted countries, the ratio of investment to GDP was substantially lower in the 1982–1988 period (when the debt burden was heaviest) than in the previous six years.[30] In Argentina the ratio fell from 25 percent to 15 percent, whereas comparable figures for Venezuela indicate a fall from 33 percent to 18 percent. This fall in investment has, in turn, reduced the growth of output and exports in debtor nations and, thereby, further undermined their ability to repay their debts.

With the notable exception of a relatively few oil-rich nations, most developing countries import a great deal of energy. Because this demand is relatively price inelastic, their expenditures on imports have risen tremendously, without similar compensating increases in receipts from the sale of exports.

The situation is reversed in many of the oil-exporting countries, which are commanding abnormally high prices for their oil. Their favorable terms of trade, however, have not always insulated them from development difficulties. Nigeria is a classic example. Buoyed by oil exports, the local wage structure and exchange rates ended up severely harming agricultural production. Resources flowed out of agricultural production and into oil production. Even the income distribution was adversely affected, becoming much more unequal.[31]

The evidence suggests that, although growth is no panacea for the problems of the developing world, it is probably better than no growth. However, the traditional form of growth experienced in the industrialized countries is not likely to be the most appropriate form for the less developed countries in the future. Circumstances have changed since the industrial revolution. Furthermore, the factor endowments in third-world countries are not the same as those in the industrialized countries. Changing circumstances call for changing approaches.

SUMMARY

Historically, increases in inputs and technological progress were important sources of economic growth in the industrialized nations. In the future, some factors of production, such as labor, will not increase as rapidly as they have in the past. The effect of this decline on growth depends on the interplay among the law of diminishing marginal productivity, substitution possibilities, and technological progress. The law of diminishing marginal productivity suggests slower growth rates, but technological progress and the availability of substitution possibilities counteract this drag.

Our examination of empirical evidence suggests that increased environmental control has not currently had a large impact on the economy as a whole, although certain industries have been hit quite hard. Environmental policy has triggered only a small rise in the rate of inflation and a mild reduction in growth. Environmental policy has apparently contributed more jobs than it has cost.

The situation is similar for energy. Though rather large increases in energy prices have occurred, the portion of the slowdown in economic growth during the 1970s attributed to these increases is not large. Some diminution of growth has certainly occurred, but it seems

---

[30]"Debtors' Hangover," *The Economist* (20 May 1989): 73.

[31]Jan S. Hogendorn, *Economic Development,* 2nd ed. (New York: HarperCollins, 1992).

premature to suggest that rising energy prices have already forced a transition to a period of substantially lower growth rates.

This is not to say, however, that the economy is not being transformed. It is. Two particularly important aspects of this transformation are (1) the decline in population growth and (2) the rise in the importance of information as a driving economic force. Both aspects tend to reduce the degree to which physical limits constrain economic growth and increase the degree to which current welfare levels are sustainable.

Some crude attempts have been made to assess whether or not growth in the industrialized countries has made the citizens of those countries better off. Results of these studies suggest that because growth has ultimately generated more leisure, longer life expectancy, and more goods and services, it has been beneficial. However, more recent studies suggest that the benefits from growth have been steadily diminishing over time. One study found that further growth in the United States now lowers economic well-being of the average U.S. citizen; at this stage of affluence the negative aspects were estimated to outweigh the positive aspects.

Our examination of the evidence suggests that the notion that all of the world's people are automatically benefited by economic growth is naive. Growth has demonstrably benefited the poor in the developed countries, mainly through transfers from more well-off members of society.

The outlook for the less industrialized nations is, at best, mixed. Solving many of their future environmental problems will require raising the standards of living. However, it is probably not possible for them to follow the path of development pioneered by the industrialized nations without triggering severe global environmental problems; the solution would become the problem. New forms of development will be necessary.

The less industrialized countries must overcome a number of significant barriers if development is to become a reality. At the local level, rising populations face increasingly limited access to land or productive assets. At the national level, corruption and development policies discriminate against the poor. Globally, their situation is worsened by rising debt burdens, falling export prices for the products they sell, and the flight of capital that could be used to create jobs and income.

How can the barriers be overcome? What new forms of development can be introduced? By what means can they be introduced? We shall deal with these questions in the next chapter.

FURTHER READING

Dasgupta, Partha. *An Inquiry into Well-Being and Destitution* (Oxford: Oxford University Press, 1993). A seminal work that deals comprehensively with the forces that create and accentuate poverty and their interaction with economic growth.

ADDITIONAL REFERENCES

Ahlburg, Dennis A., ed. *The Impact of Population Growth on Well-Being in Developing Countries* (Berlin: Springer, 1996).

Bartelmus, P. "Green Accounting for a Sustainable Economy—Policy Use and Analysis of Environmental Accounts in the Philippines." *Ecological Economics* 29(1999)(1): 155–170.

Brown, Gardiner Jr., and Barry Field. "The Adequacy of Measures for Signaling the Scarcity of Natural Resources," in *Scarcity and Growth Considered,* V. Kerry Smith, ed. (Baltimore, MD: Johns Hopkins University Press, 1979).

Carraro, C., M. Galeotti, et al. "Environmental Taxation and Unemployment: Some Evidence on the 'Double Dividend Hypothesis' in Europe," *Journal of Public Economics* 62(1996)(1–2): 141–181.

Cobb, Clifford W., and John B. Cobb Jr., eds. *The Green National Product: A Proposed Index of Sustainable Economic Welfare* (Lanham, MD: University Press of America, 1994).

Dasgupta, Ajit K. *Growth, Development and Welfare: An Essay on Levels of Living* (Oxford, UK: Basil Blackwell, 1988).

Goodstein, E. "Jobs and the Environment—an Overview," *Environmental Management* 20(1996)(3): 313–321.

Hansen, Stein. "Macroeconomic Policies and Sustainable Development in the Third World," *Journal of International Development* 2 (1990).

Lintott, J. "Environmental Accounting: Useful to Whom and for What?," *Ecological Economics* 16, No. 3 (1996): 179–90.

Markandya, A. "Employment and Environmental Protection—The Trade-offs in an Economy in Transition," *Environmental & Resource Economics* 15(2000)(4): 297–322.

Mellor, John W. "The Intertwining of Environmental Problems and Poverty," *Environment* 30 (1988): 8–13.

Neary, J. Peter, and Sweder Van Wijnbergen, eds. *Natural Resources and the Macroeconomy* (Cambridge, MA: MIT Press, 1986).

Perrings, Charles. *Economy and Environment: A Theoretical Essay on the Interdependence of Economic and Environmental Systems* (Cambridge, UK: Cambridge University Press, 1987).

Van Dieren, Wouter, ed. *Taking Nature Into Account: A Report to the Club of Rome* (New York: Springer-Verlag, 1995).

Van Ierland, Ekko C. *Macroeconomic Analysis of Environmental Policy* (Amsterdam: Elsevier, 1993).

WEB SITES OF INTEREST

1. *http://www.econet.apc.org/envjustice/*
   Economic Justice Network web site.

2. *http://www-esd.worldbank.org/eei/*
   The World Bank's Environmental Economics and Indicators site.

DISCUSSION QUESTIONS

1. "Economic growth has historically provided a valuable vehicle for raising the standard of living. Now that the standard of living is so high, however, further economic growth is unnecessary. When the undesirable side effects are considered, it is probably counterproductive. Economic growth is a process that has outlived its usefulness." Discuss.

2. Is affluence part of the problem or part of the solution when it comes to environmental problems? Why?

The Quest
for Sustainable
Development

The challenge of finding sustainable development paths ought to provide the impetus—indeed the imperative—for a renewed search for multilateral solutions and a restructured international economic system of co-operation. These challenges cut across the divides of national sovereignty, of limited strategies for economic gain, and of separated disciplines of science.

GRO HARLEM BRUNDTLAND, FORMER PRIME MINISTER OF NORWAY,
OUR COMMON FUTURE (1987)

◆ INTRODUCTION

Delegations from 178 countries met in Rio de Janeiro during the first two weeks of June 1992 to begin the process of charting a sustainable development course for the future global economy. Billed by its organizers as the largest summit ever held, the United Nations Conference on Environment and Development (known popularly as the "Earth Summit") sought to lay the groundwork for solving global environmental problems. The central focus for this meeting was *sustainable development*.

What is sustainable development? According to the "Brundtland report" which is widely credited with raising the concept to its current level of importance, "Sustainable development is development that meets the needs of the present without compromising the ability of future generations to meet their own needs."[1] However, that is far from the only possible

[1]World Commission on Environment and Development, *Our Common Future* (Oxford, UK: Oxford University Press, 1987): 43.

definition.[2] A nascent concept, sustainable development is still in the process of being re-fined and clarified.

Part of the widespread appeal of the concept, according to critics, is due to its vagueness. Being all things to all people can build a large following, but it also has a rather substantial disadvantage: Close inspection may reveal that the concept is vacuous. As the emperor discov-ered about his new clothes, things are not always what they seem.

In this chapter we shall take a hard look at the concept of sustainable development and whether or not it is useful as a guide to the future. What are the basic principles of sustainable development? What does sustainable development imply about changes in the way our system operates? How could the transition to sustainable development be managed? Will the global economic system automatically produce sustainable development, or will policy changes be needed? What policy changes?

◆ SUSTAINABILITY AND DEVELOPMENT

Suppose we were to map out possible future trends in the long-term welfare of the average citizen. Using a time scale measured in centuries on the horizontal axis (Figure 21.1), four ba-sic culture trends (labeled *A, B, C,* and *D*) emerge, with t_0 representing the present. Scenario *D* portrays continued exponential growth in which the future becomes a simple repetition of the past. In this scenario, not only would current welfare levels be sustainable, but growth in welfare would be sustainable. Our concern for intergenerational justice would lead us to favor current generations because they would be the poorest. Worrying about future generations would be unnecessary.

The second scenario (*C*) envisions slowly diminished growth culminating in a steady state where growth diminishes to zero. Each future generation is at least as well off as all previous generations. Current welfare levels are sustainable, though current levels of welfare growth would not be. Because the level of welfare of each generation is sustainable, artificial con-straints on the process would be unnecessary. To constrain growth would injure all subse-quent generations.

The third scenario (*B*) is similar in that it envisions initial growth followed by a steady state, but with an important different—those generations between time t_1 and time t_2 are worse off than the generations preceding them. This is the type of scenario anticipated by Meadows and her colleagues. Neither growth nor welfare levels are sustainable at current lev-els, and the sustainability criterion would call for an immediate transition to sustainable wel-fare levels.

The final scenario (*A*) denies the existence of sustainable per capita welfare levels, sug-gesting that the only possible sustainable level is zero. All consumption by the current gener-ation serves simply to hasten the end of civilization.

These scenarios suggest that three dimensions of the sustainability issue are important: (1) the existence of a positive sustainable level of welfare, (2) the magnitude of the ultimate

---

[2]One search for definitions produced 61, though many were very similar. See John Pezzey, "Economic Analysis of Sustainable Growth and Sustainable Development," Working Paper No. 15 (Washington, DC: World Bank Environ-mental Department, 1989).

FIGURE 21.1   Possible Alternative Futures

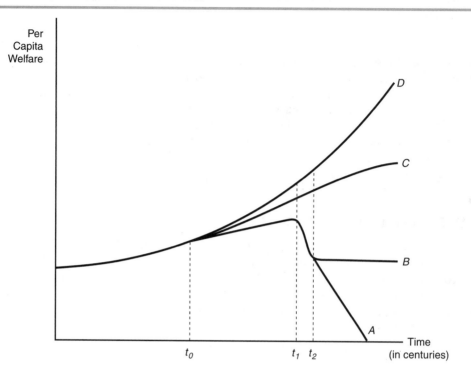

sustainable level of welfare vis-à-vis current welfare levels, and (3) the sensitivity of the future level of welfare to actions by previous generations. The first dimension is important because, if positive sustainable levels of welfare are possible, scenario *A*, which in some ways is the most philosophically difficult, is ruled out. The second is important because, if the ultimately sustainable welfare level is higher than the current level, radical surgery to cut current living standards is not necessary. The final dimension raises the issue of whether the ultimate sustainable level of welfare can be increased or reduced by the actions of current generations. If it can be affected, the sustainability criterion would suggest taking these impacts into account, lest future generations by unnecessarily impoverished by involuntary wealth transfers to previous generations.

The first dimension is relatively easy to dispense with. The existence of positive sustainable welfare levels is guaranteed by the existence of renewable resources, particularly solar energy, as well as by nature's ability to assimilate a certain amount of waste.[3] Therefore, we can rule out scenario *A*.

---

[3]One study has estimated that humans are currently using approximately 19 to 25 percent of the renewable energy available from photosynthesis. On land the estimate is more like 40 percent. See Peter M. Vitousek et al., "Human Appropriation of the Products of Photosynthesis," *BioScience* 36, No. 6 (June 1986): 368–373.

No one knows exactly what level of economic activity can ultimately be sustained, but the prediction of early societal collapse certainly seems grossly exaggerated. Because growth is slowing as a natural process, the most serious excesses of unregulated growth (e.g., pollution) are being mitigated, and solar energy is abundant, scenario *C* seems more likely, though with current levels of information no one can completely rule out *B*.

Current generations can affect the sustainable welfare levels of future generations both positively and negatively. We could use our resources to accumulate a capital stock, providing future generations with shelter, productivity, and transportation, but our decaying inner cities illustrate that machines and buildings do not last forever. Even capital that physically stands the test of time may become economically obsolete by being ill-suited to the needs of subsequent generations.

Our most lasting contribution to future generations would probably come from what economists call *human capital*—investments in people. Though the people who receive education and training are mortal, the ideas they bring forth are not. Knowledge endures.[4]

Current actions could also reduce future welfare levels, however. Fossil fuel combustion could modify the climate to the detriment of future agriculture. By depleting the atmosphere's ozone, current chlorofluorocarbon emissions might raise the incidence of skin cancer. The storage of radioactive wastes could increase the likelihood of genetic damage in the future. The reduction of genetic diversity in the stock of plants and animals could well reduce the number of medical discoveries in the future.

Suppose that high levels of sustainable welfare are feasible. Would our economic system automatically choose a growth path that produces sustainable welfare levels, or could it choose one that enriches current generations at the expense of future generations?

Market Allocations

Market imperfections—including intertemporal externalities, free-access resources, and market power—play havoc with the ability of a market to achieve sustainable outcomes. They create incentives that can interfere in important ways with the quest for sustainable development.

Allowing free access to resources promotes unsustainable allocations. Because free-access resources are overexploited by current generations, diminished stocks are left for the future. In the extreme, it is even possible that the species would become extinct.

Intertemporal externalities also undermine the ability of the market to produce sustainable outcomes. Emissions of greenhouse gases impose a cost on future generations that is external to current generations. Current actions to reduce the gases will cost this generation money, but the benefits would not be felt until significantly later. Economic theory clearly forecasts that too many greenhouse gas emissions would be forthcoming for the sustainability criterion to be satisfied.

The general conclusion that market imperfections exacerbate the problem of unsustainability, however, would not be correct. For example, the existence of an oil cartel holding up prices serves to retard demand and conserve more for future generations than would otherwise be the case.

---

[4]Although it is true that ideas can last forever, the value of those ideas may decline with time as they are supplanted by new ones. The person who conceived of horseshoes made an enormous contribution to society at the time, but the value of that insight to society has diminished, along with our reliance on horses for transportation.

Markets can sometimes provide a safety valve to ensure sustainability when the supply of a renewable resource is threatened. Fish farming is one example where declining supplies of a renewable resource trigger the availability of an alternative, renewable substitute. Even when the government intervenes detrimentally in a way that benefits current generations at the expense of future generations, as it did with natural gas, the market can limit the damage. The market for solar energy still exists as a substitute for natural gas, so that the effect of government regulation was to make the transition significantly less smooth than it might have been, rather than preventing the transition.

The notion that left to their own devices markets would automatically provide for the future is naive, despite their apparent success in providing for generations in the past.

Efficiency and Sustainability

Suppose future governments were able to eliminate all market imperfections, restoring efficiency to the global economic system. In this idealized world, intertemporal and contemporaneous externalities would be reduced to efficient levels. Access to common resources would be restricted to efficient levels, and harvesting excess capacity would be eliminated. Competition would be restored to previously cartelized natural resource markets. Would this package of policies be sufficient to achieve sustainability, or is something more required?

One way to examine this question is to consider a number of different models that capture the essence of intertemporal resource allocation. For each model, the question becomes, "Will efficient markets automatically produce sustainable development?" The conclusion to be drawn from these models is very clear: Restoring efficiency is not sufficient to produce sustainability.

Take the allocation of depletable resources over time. Imagine a simple economy where the only activity is the extraction and consumption of a single, depletable resource. Even when the population is constant and the demand curves are stable, the efficient-quality profiles show declining consumption over time. In this hypothetical world, later generations would be unambiguously worse off unless current generations transferred some of the net benefits into the future. Even an efficient market allocation would not be sustainable in the absence of transfers.

The existence of an abundant, renewable resource to serve as a backstop (e.g., solar energy) would not solve the problem; even in this more congenial set of circumstances, the quantity profile of the depletable resource would still involve declining consumption until the backstop was reached. In the absence of compensating transfers, even efficient markets would use the depletable resources to support a higher current standard of living than could be supported indefinitely.

Dasgupta and Heal find a similar result for a slightly more realistic model.[5] They examine an economy where a single consumption good is produced by combining capital with a depletable resource. The finite supply of the depletable resource can be used both to produce capital and in combination with capital to produce the consumption good. The more capital produced, the higher is the marginal product of the remaining depletable resource.

---

[5]P.S. Dasgupta and G. M. Heal, *Economic Theory and Exhaustible Resources* (Cambridge, UK: Cambridge University Press, 1979): 299.

They prove that a sustainable constant consumption level exists in this model. The rising capital stock (implying a rising marginal product for the depletable resource) would compensate for the declining availability of the depletable resource. They also prove, however, that the use of any positive discount rate would necessarily result in declining consumption levels, a violation of the sustainability criterion. Discounting, of course, is an inherent component of dynamically efficient allocations.

In all of these models, sustainable development is possible, but it is not the choice made by efficient markets. Why not? What would it take to assure sustainable allocations? Hartwick shows that the achievement of a constant per capita consumption path (which would satisfy our definition of *sustainability*) results when all scarcity rent is invested in capital. None of it should be consumed by current generations.[6]

Would all scarcity rent be invested? With a positive discount rate, some of the scarcity rent is consumed by the current generation, violating the Hartwick rule. The point is profound. Restoring efficiency will typically represent a move toward sustainability, but it will not, by itself, be sufficient. Further policies must be implemented in order to guarantee sustainable outcomes.

In Chapter 4 we pointed out that maintaining a nondeclining value of the capital stock (both physical and natural) provided an observable means of checking on the sustainability of current activity. If the value of the capital stock is declining, the activity is unsustainable (Example 21.1). How about the converse case? Can we automatically conclude that a nondeclining value of the capital stock implies the sustainability of current consumption levels? According to work undertaken by Asheim and elaborated on by Pezzey, we cannot.[7] Rising net wealth can coincide with unsustainability when the capital stock is being valued at the wrong (i.e., unsustainable) prices. When nonrenewable resources are being used up too rapidly, this drives prices down. Using these prices can create the false impression that the value of the depletion is less than the value of the additional investment and, therefore, that the value of the capital stock is rising. In fact, at the correct prices, it may be falling.

How about renewable resources? At least in principle, renewable resource flows could endure forever. Are efficient market allocations of renewable resources compatible with sustainable development? John Pezzey has examined the sustainability of an allocation of a single renewable resource (e.g., corn) over time.[8] Sustained growth of welfare can occur in this model, but only if two conditions both hold: (1) The resource growth rate exceeds the sum of both the discount rate and the population growth, and (2) the initial food supply is sufficient for the existing population. The first condition is sometimes difficult to meet, particularly with rapid population growth and slow-growing biological resources. Sustainable development of renewable resources is very much harder in the presence of rapid population growth rates because the pressure to exceed sustainable harvest rates becomes irresistible.

---

[6]J. M. Hartwick, "Intergenerational Equity and the Investing of Rents from Exhaustible Resources," *American Economic Review* 67 (December 1977): 972–974.

[7]Geir B. Asheim, "Net National Product as an Indicator of Sustainability," *Scandanavian Journal of Economics* 55 (1994): 257–65; and John Pezzey, "The Optimal Sustainable Depletion of Non-Renewable Resources," a paper presented at the Association of Environmental and Natural Resource Economists Workshop at Boulder, CO, June 5–6, 1994.

[8]John Pezzey, "Economic Analysis of Sustainable Growth and Sustainable Development," Working Paper No. 15 (Washington, DC: World Bank Environment Department, 1989): 43–46.

Example 21.1

Resource Depletion and Economic Sustainability: Malaysia

The historical record suggests, oddly enough, that countries with abundant natural resources tend to suffer a disadvantage in economic development. Why? One possible explanation for the apparent "natural resource curse" is that resource-rich countries have not invested enough of the scarcity rent in reproducible capital to offset resource depletion. Natural resources are a form of capital, which, if depleted, must be either replenished or substituted for if countries are to expand their asset base and sustain their consumption levels.

Malaysia is a particularly interesting country for examining this issue. Although it is one of the most resource-rich countries in the world, its per capita GDP growth rate during the last three decades has been among the highest in the world. But the very extraordinariness of Malaysia's resource-richness raises a troubling question: Is the country indeed on a sustainable growth path, or has it managed to keep growing simply by developing new resources?

In the Vincent (1997) study net investment (gross investment minus depreciation of physical and natural capital) and net domestic product (NDP; GDP minus depreciation of the two types of capital) were estimated for Malaysia and its three constituent regions (Peninsular Malaysia, Sabah, Sarawak) for all years during 1970–1990. The estimates reflected depreciation of two categories of natural resources, mineral and timber, which were the most important ones in the country.

At the national level, per capita net investment was found to be positive in all years but one. Hence, per capita total capital stocks increased in Malaysia during the 1970s and 1980s, despite the depletion of the country's mineral and timber resources. This was not the case in all three regions, however. Per capita net investment was positive in Peninsular Malaysia in all years, but it was negative in every year after 1975 in Sabah and in every year but one after 1983 in Sarawak.

The lesson for other resource-rich countries is to emulate Peninsular Malaysia's example, by adopting economic policies that result in the productive reinvestment of a substantial portion of resource rents. Sabah and Sarawak have instead grown by simply raising their natural resource output and consuming much of the rents thus generated. Although Malaysia's development appears to be sustainable at the national level, it might not be so in all subnational regions.

Source: Jeffrey R. Vincent, "Resource Depletion and Sustainability in Malaysia," *Environment and Development Economics*, Vol. 2, Part 1 (February, 1997): 19–37.

The second condition raises a more general—and a more difficult—concern. It implies the distinct possibility that, if the starting conditions are sufficiently far from a sustainable path, sustainable outcomes may not be achievable without outside intervention. The simplest way to see this point is to note that a country that is so poor that it is reduced to eating all of its seed corn sacrifices its future in order to survive in the present. The double message that can be derived from these results is that (1) it is important to assure that conditions do not deteriorate to this extent by acting quickly and (2) foreign aid is probably an essential part of sustainability policies for the poorest nations.

Global climate change presents a rather different example—one in which efficiency may not be sufficient for sustainability. Because the present-value component of dynamic efficiency emphasizes short-term over long-term consequences, the current costs of controlling emissions would be weighted more heavily than the distant future damages caused by global warming. Though this approach is not inherently biased against future generations, their interests would only be adequately protected (1) if they would be willing to accept monetary compensation for a modified climate and (2) if current generations would be willing to set aside sufficient proceeds to provide this compensation. Because it is not obvious that either condition would be satisfied in practice, the long lead times associated with this particular problem place in jeopardy the interests of future generations in maintaining a stable climate.

Efficient allocations can also violate the notion of sustainability in a deeper sense. Because the definition of *sustainability* that we have used in the immediately preceding analysis is based upon nondeclining average welfare levels, it does not require the preservation of individual resources. Harvesting fish stocks to extinction, for example, would be compatible with this concept of sustainability as long as future generations were sufficiently compensated.

However, we don't really know how much they would value the continued existence of those fish stocks. Not only is our knowledge about the ultimate ecosystem effects of the extinction of any species extremely limited, we have no idea how valuable those fish would be to future generations. It is possible that they would value the continued existence of the population substantially more than we. Not only would the appropriate amount of the compensation be difficult to determine (because we don't know their preferences), but making compensation would be silly if they were to value the continued existence of the population more than they would any compensation (including accrued interest) we would be willing to pay.

One rather straightforward way to deal with this uncertainty is to include in the definition of *sustainability* some protection of the resources themselves. According to this logic, because it is impossible to know the value future generations place on specific renewable resources, we can only preserve their options by guaranteeing access to the resources. Efficiency would certainly not guarantee this outcome, but preserving resources would.

We must be careful to distinguish between what has been said and what has not been said. Restoring efficiency will generally result in an improvement in sustainability, but it may not be necessary or sufficient. Three different cases can emerge. In the first case, the private inefficient outcome is sustainable, and the efficient outcome is also sustainable. In this case, restoring efficiency will raise well-being, but it is not necessary for sustainability. This case might prevail when resources are extraordinarily abundant relative to the use of them. In the second case, the private inefficient equilibrium is unsustainable, but the efficient outcome is sustainable. In this case, restoring efficiency not only increases current well-being, but is sufficient to assure sustainability. In the final case, neither the private inefficient outcome nor the efficient outcome are sustainable. In this case, restoring efficiency will not be enough to produce a sustainable outcome. Some sacrifice by current generations would be necessary in order to assure adequate protection for the well-being of future generations.

Although efficient markets cannot always achieve sustainable development paths, this does not mean that such markets would not normally result in sustainable allocations! Indeed, the historical record suggests that the incompatibility of the efficiency criterion and the sustainability criterion has been the exception, not the rule. Capital accumulation and technological progress have expanded the ways in which resources can be used and have increased subsequent welfare levels—in spite of a declining resource base. Nonetheless, the two criteria are not inevitably compatible. As resource bases diminish and global externalities increase, the conflict can be expected to become more intense.

◆ TRADE AND THE ENVIRONMENT

One of the traditional paths to development involves opening up the economy to trade. Freer international markets provide lower prices for consumer goods (because of competition from foreign producers) and the opportunity for domestic producers to exploit foreign markets. Recently, however, concerns have been raised about the environmental consequences of promoting a freer flow of capital and products across international borders. Prominent among these fears is the "pollution havens" hypothesis. According to the pollution havens hypothesis, stricter environmental regulations in one country either encourages domestic production facilities to move to countries with less stringent environmental regulations or encourages increasing imports from those countries. To the extent the pollution havens hypothesis is valid, it provides a reason for local areas to accept lower environmental standards as a means of protecting the jobs that would be lost if production moved to countries with less stringent regulations.

What is the evidence? Dean surveys a very large number of studies and finds absolutely no support for the pollution havens hypothesis.[9] Another survey reaches the same conclusion in terms of the effects of environmental regulations on U.S. competitiveness.[10] Actually, these results should not be surprising. Because pollution control costs constitute a relatively small part of the costs of production, it would be surprising if they were a major determinant of either firm-location decisions or the direction of trade.

A distinctly different point of view has been articulated by Michael Porter.[11] Now known as the "Porter hypothesis," this view suggests that firms in areas with the most stringent regulations derive a competitive *advantage* rather than a competitive disadvantage. Under this view, strict environmental regulations force firms to innovate, and innovative firms are more competitive. This advantage is particularly pronounced for firms that produce pollution control equipment (which can then be exported to firms in other countries, subsequently raising their environmental standards), but it might also be present for firms that, when forced to change their production processes, find that their costs are lower, not higher.

Some instances of regulation-induced lower production costs have been recorded in the literature[12], but few studies have attempted to examine the Porter hypothesis in its entirety. One study, undertaken by Stephen Meyer, examines whether those states in the United States that have stricter environmental standards show better or poorer economic performance.[13] In

---

[9] Judith M. Dean, "Trade and the Environment: A Survey of the Literature," in Patrick Low, ed., *International Trade and the Environment* (Washington, DC: World Bank, 1992): 15–28.

[10] Adam B. Jaffe et al., "Environmental Regulation and the Competitiveness of U.S. Manufacturing: What Does the Evidence Tell Us?," *Journal of Economic Literature* 33, No. 1 (1995): 132–163.

[11] Michael E. Porter and Claas van der Linde, "Toward a New Conception of the Environment-Competitiveness Relationship," *Journal of Economic Perspectives* 9, No. 4 (1995): 97–118.

[12] Anthony J. Barbera and Virginia D. McConnell, "The Impact of Environmental Regulations on Industry Productivity: Direct and Indirect Effects," *Journal of Environmental Economics and Management* 18 (1990): 50–65.

[13] Stephen M. Meyer, "Environmentalism and Economic Prosperity: Testing the Environmental Impact Hypothesis," M.I.T. Working Paper, Cambridge, MA., 1993.

general, he finds that states with the more stringent standards have experienced the best economic performance. Unfortunately, it is difficult to tell whether the results of Meyer's study reflect the Porter hypothesis at work or something as simple as the fact that stagnant states do not enact stringent regulations.

Taken in its entirety, this evidence suggests that environmental regulations are not a major determinant of either firm-location decisions or the direction of trade. This implies that reasonable environmental regulations should not be held hostage to threats that polluters will leave the area, taking their jobs with them. With few exceptions, firms that are going to move will move anyway, whereas firms that are not going to move will tend to stay where they are—whatever the regulatory environment.

Although the foregoing argument suggests that the starkest claims against the environmental effects of free trade do not bear up under close scrutiny, it would be equally wrong to suggest that opening borders to freer trade always produces a gain in efficiency and/or sustainability. One example of how freer trade intensifies environmental problems involves the effect of removing trade barriers when some nations (presumably, those in the less developed south) have poorly defined property rights, whereas others (primarily in the industrialized north) seek to import their resources or products made from those resources. Chichilnisky has shown that, in this kind of situation, the "tragedy of the commons" can become greatly intensified by freer trade.[14] Because of the poorly defined property rights in the exporting nations, the importing nations are encouraged (by artificially low prices) to greatly expand their consumption of the underpriced resources. In this scenario, trade intensifies environmental problems by increasing the pressure on common-property resources and hastening their degradation. The most desirable solution in this case is not to prevent trade, but rather to assure that the resources are protected by adequate property-rights regimes. On the other hand, if establishing appropriate property-rights regimes is not politically feasible, other means of protecting the resources must be found.

◆ A MENU OF OPPORTUNITIES

Is sustainable development just an unrealistic attempt to provide false hope in the face of a rather bleak future? Human nature being what it is, we need to have hope. When the situation is hopeless, the natural human tendency is to create scenarios that offer the illusion of hope. Is sustainable development one of those scenarios? Or can reasonable, skeptical people find grounds for believing in the existence of new forms of development that can raise living standards while respecting both the environment and the rights of future generations?

Although it is not possible in the space we have to go into detail about the various techniques that fulfill this vision, it is possible to convey a flavor[15]—with the hope that this flavor

---

[14]Graciela Chichilnisky, "North-South Trade and the Global Environment," *American Economic Review* 84 (1994): 851–874.

[15]The material in this section comes mainly from three excellent articles: Pierre R. Crosson and Norman J. Rosenberg, "Strategies for Agriculture"; John H. Gibbons, Peter D. Blair, and Holly L. Gwin, "Strategies for Energy Use"; and Robert A. Frosch and Nicholas E. Gallopoulos, "Strategies for Manufacturing." All can be found in *Scientific American* 261, No. 3 (September 1989). Readers interested in more detail should consult those articles and the references cited at the end of each article.

will be sufficient to demonstrate that sustainable development is a pragmatic possibility, not merely an illusion.

Agriculture

Most experts believe that food supply can be expanded to meet the forecasted increases in population, but sustainable development requires this expansion to take place in a way that does not destroy the natural environment. What are the prospects?

Multiple cropping—which includes crop rotations, intercropping (sometimes with trees and annual crops sharing the same fields), overseeding legumes into cereals, and double cropping—is one technique that offers the potential for reduced use of agricultural chemicals, increased productivity, less soil erosion, and more effective use of water. The concept is not new. A system employed in Central America since pre-Columbian times intermixes maize, beans, and squash. The maize provides a trellis for the beans; the beans enrich the soil with nitrogen; and the squash provides ground cover, reducing erosion, soil compaction, and weed growth.

Trees can be used in multiple cropping. In West Africa, leaf litter from the *Acacia alba* enriches the soil for the benefit of various grain and vegetable crops grown between them. In the U.S. Midwest, farmers are experimenting with growing corn with other, low-growing plants. In one experiment in Nebraska, two-row corn windbreaks were spaced every 15 rows through a field of sugar beets. The wind shelter provided by the corn increased sugar production by 11 percent. The greater access to sunlight and carbon dioxide increased corn yields by 150 percent.

In Montana, tall wheatgrass, a perennial, has been used to protect winter wheat. In winter, wheatgrass barriers capture snow, forming a uniform layer that insulates dormant plants from the effects of extremely low temperatures. In spring the snow melts, providing the moisture winter wheat needs for early growth. Once the winter wheat begins to grow, the wheatgrass serves as a wind barrier.

Multiple cropping can reduce the need for pesticides. In fields where crops are rotated regularly, pests (e.g., weeds, insects, and pathogens) cannot adapt themselves to a single set of environmental conditions and, therefore, do not increase as quickly.

Biotechnology and new irrigation techniques also offer prospects for reduced fertilizer and water use. Developing plants that "fix" nitrogen in the soil would lessen the demand for nitrogen fertilizer, and incorporating genes from pest-resistant plants into commercial crops could reduce the need for pesticides. Trickle (or drip) irrigation systems would reduce the amount of water needed by increasing the efficiency of the water used. Already widely used in Israel and part of the United States, trickle irrigation can also reduce the problems associated with salt buildup.

Energy

Prior to the 1970s, increases in the gross domestic product (GDP) were always accompanied by proportionate increases in energy consumption. This relationship proved so stable that it was used for forecasting energy consumption. Some observers at the time took this relationship as evidence that proportionate increases in energy would be a necessary condition for growth.

Following the oil embargo and the accompanying increases in prices during the 1970s, it became clear that growth and energy consumption did not have to move in lockstep. The industrialized world's *energy intensity*—the amount of energy used to produce one unit of GDP—fell by 36 percent between 1973 and 1998. In the United States, GDP grew 93 percent, whereas energy consumption per capita remained nearly constant.

Energy efficiency is the short-run key to sustainable development because it offers the opportunity to increase living standards without increasing energy consumption. Enhanced energy efficiency—which can stretch energy supplies, slow climate changes, and buy time to develop alternative energy resources—can be achieved in a variety of ways. Some of the possibilities are presented in Table 21.1.

Consider one possibility in more detail. Advanced building materials can sharply reduce loss of heat through windows, doors, and walls. In "superinsulated" homes, where normal insulation is doubled and a liner forms an airtight seal in walls, heat radiating from people, light, stoves, and other appliances alone can warm the house. In comparison with the average home built in the United States, some superinsulated homes in Minnesota require 68 percent less heat; for some residences in Sweden, the saving is higher. Similar savings would be possible in lighting, transportation, and manufacturing.

Waste Reduction

Sustainable development involves a more integrated approach to production than has traditionally been practiced in order to reduce raw material demands and waste discharge. In such an integrated system (1) the consumption of energy and materials is optimized, (2) waste generation is minimized, and (3) the effluent of one process—whether they are spent catalysts from petroleum refining, fly and bottom ash from electric-power generators, or discarded plastic containers from consumer products—serve as raw materials for another process.

As the costs of waste disposal rise and the regulations dealing with hazardous waste disposal become more strict, examples of industries adopting this type of integrated approach become more prevalent. Meridian National, a midwestern steel-processing company, now reprocesses the sulfuric acid with which it removes scale from steel sheets and slabs, reuses the acid, and sells ferrous sulfate compounds to magnetic tape manufacturers.

At the Atlantic Richfield Company's Los Angeles refinery complex, a series of relatively low-cost changes reduced waste volumes from about 12,000 tons a year during the early 1980s to about 3,400 tons a year by the end of the decade. Because disposal costs were about $300 a ton, the company saved over $2 million a year in disposal costs alone.

TABLE 21.1 Opportunities for Greater Energy Efficiency

	Car (mi/gal)	Home (1,000J/m²)	Refrigerator (kWh/day)	Gas Furnace (million J/day)	Air Conditioner (kWh/day)
Model average	18	190	4	210	10
New model	27	110	3	180	7
Best model	50	68	2	140	5
Best prototype	77	11	1	110	3

Source: "Opportunities for Greater Energy Efficiency," adapted from John H. Gibbons, Peter D. Blair, and Holly L. Gwin, "Strategies for Energy Use," *Scientific American* 261, No. 3 (September 1989): 141. Copyright © 1989 by Scientific American, Inc. Reprinted with the permission of *Scientific American*.

Example 21.2

Sustainable Development: Three Success Stories

In Kenya, 83 percent of the urban population and 17 percent of rural households use charcoal stoves known as *jikos*. A household in Nairobi with one wage earner typically spends more than one fifth of its income on charcoal. The typical *jiko* is very energy inefficient; it represents an unnecessary drain on both income and the forests that supply the wood for charcoal.

In 1981 the government of Kenya and a local nongovernmental organization began a project disseminating a new, more energy-efficient stove. By 1985 the new stove had captured 10 percent of the market. Nationwide savings on fuel were in the neighborhood of $2 million annually.

Much of Central America is faced with declining soil fertility because of soil erosion and monocropping. Guinope, Honduras, was not an exception. Farmers were migrating out of the area, and those remaining were plagued by low incomes.

In 1981, World Neighbors, a private voluntary organization, introduced a sustainable agriculture program that relied on soil conservation practices in use elsewhere in Central America. The program included constructing drainage ditches, planting grass barriers, erecting rock walls, training farmers in fertilizing methods using chicken manure, intercropping leguminous plants, and using some chemical fertilizers. Significantly, no subsidies were involved at all. All costs were borne by the farmers.

In the first year the yields tripled and in some cases quadrupled. Nearby villages have requested training and the program is spreading rapidly.

In Brazil, some 500,000 rubber tappers (*seringueiros*) have made their living from the Amazon since the late 1800s. Beginning in the 1970s, their livelihood was threatened by the migration of large numbers of people to the forests seeking land. Encouraged by government subsidies, these migrants ultimately discovered the land to be unsuitable for agriculture once the forest canopy has been removed. One sustainable form of land use was being jeopardized by another, unsustainable land use.

On 30 June 1987, the Brazilian government created an extractive reserve for the rubber tappers and, in the process, provided protection for the countless genetic species found in the forest. The extractive reserve allows continued extraction of rubber (as well as nuts and other renewable products) but protects the forest and its people from the ravages of deforestation.

Source: Walter V. C. Reid, "Sustainable Development: Lessons From Success," *Environment* 31, No. 4 (May 1989): 7–9, 29–35.

Markets have been found for much of Atlantic Richfield's former waste, adding further revenue. The company sells its spent alumina catalysts to Allied Chemical and its spent silica catalysts to cement makers. Alkaline carbonate sludge from a water-softening operation at the refinery goes to a sulfuric acid manufacturer a few miles away, where it is used to neutralize acidic wastewater.

Sustainable development frequently requires changes in how economic activities are conducted. Some of those changes are already occurring (see Example 21.2); others await additional policy changes.

◆ MANAGING THE TRANSITION

If sustainable development is, in fact, possible and unfettered markets are not capable, by themselves, of managing the transition, what can be done? How can the transition to sustainable development be accomplished?

Our situation is similar to that of the thoroughly disoriented tourist, a central character in Maine folklore. Enticed by unusually brilliant fall foliage, a tourist forsook the security of the well-marked main highways for some less traveled country roads. After an hour of driving, he was no longer sure he was even headed in the right direction. Seeing a Maine native mending a fence, he pulled over to the side of the road to seek assistance. After hearing the tourist's destination, the native sadly shook his head and, in his best Maine accent, responded "If I was goin' they-uh, I sure wouldn't start from he-uh!"

Had we known long ago that human activities could seriously impact environmental life-support systems and could deny future generations the quality of life to which our generation has become accustomed, we might have chosen a different, more sustainable, path for improving human welfare. The fact that we did not have that knowledge and, therefore, did not make that choice years ago means that current generations are faced with making more difficult choices, with fewer options. These choices will test the creativity of our solutions and the resilience of our social institutions.

The task of managing the transition to sustainable development is made more difficult by the fact that some entrenched development paths are not only unsustainable themselves, they have so dominated sustainable strategies that switching from one to the other has become very difficult.

Southern California represents a case in point. In the Los Angeles air basin, the ambient air quality standards, designed to protect human health, are currently violated on the order of several times a year. Because of the way the city has developed, regulators in Los Angeles now face a very difficult problem. As a prime example of an automobile-centered city, population growth in Los Angeles has spawned land-use patterns that accommodate the automobile and are, in turn, accommodated by the automobile. Responding to a massive program of highway construction and low gasoline prices, the city has become very spread out, with highly dispersed residential and employment locations. Because the efficient use of mass transit requires the existence of high-density travel corridors, an effective public transit alternative is now difficult to implement, though it could have been quite possible before the highly dispersed land-use patterns became so firmly entrenched. The options left open to these regulators have steadily diminished over time. The entire fabric of life in the Los Angeles area is so interwoven with automobile access that the problem cannot be solved without envisioning fairly radical changes in lifestyle.

In addition to the problem of reversing historic land use patterns that seem inconsistent with the goal of sustainable development, we face the problem of how to prevent more inefficient development from occurring in the future. Local officials across the country are pushing

Example 21.3

Controlling Land Use Development with TDRs

How can unique environmental sites be preserved from the threat of development? One way, of course, is for them to be purchased as a preserve either by the government or by a private group committed to preservation such as the Nature Conservancy. The considerable amount of financial resources needed to implement this approach, however, has limited its impact.

An alternative approach, which mobilizes private funds for preservation, involves the use of transferable development rights (TDRs). Pioneered by New York City in the 1970s as a means of protecting historic buildings, this approach severs, for some particularly unique land, the historic connection between the ownership of land and the right to develop it.

Owners of land that should be preserved are typically opposed to preservation because they bear all the costs while society as a whole bears the benefits. Transferable development rights change that dynamic by allowing the owners of preserved land to sell their development rights to developers. The revenue from selling these rights compensates the owners for their inability to develop their land.

How it works can be illustrated with an example. The New Jersey Pinelands is a largely undeveloped, marshy area in the south eastern part of the State encompassing approximately one million acres. It provides habitat for several endangered species. In an effort to direct development to the least environmentally sensitive areas, the Pinelands Development Commission created Pineland Development Credits (PDCs), a form of transferable development rights.

Landowners in environmentally sensitive areas receive PDCs in exchange for limiting development at the rate of 1 PDC for every 39 acres of existing farmland, 1 PDC for every 39 acres of preserved upland, and 0.2 PDCs for every 39 acres of wetlands. To create a demand for these credits, developers seeking to increase the standard density on land zoned for development are required to acquire one PDC for each four units of increase.

The Commission also established a Pinelands Development Credit Bank to act as a purchaser of last resort for PDCs at the statutory price of $10,000 per credit. In 1990 the Bank auctioned its inventory at the price of $20,200 per PDC. By 1997, developers had used well over 100 PDCs.

Source: Robert C. Anderson and Andrew Q. Lohof, "The United States Experience with Economic Incentives in Environmental Pollution Control Policy" (Washington, DC: Environmental Law Institute, 1997).

a variety of measures to preserve open space. Here too the market may be enlisted as part of the preservation strategy (Example 21.3).

To meet the challenges of the next century, it will be necessary to foster and support institutional change by being somewhat more creative in how we deal with environmental policy. One key to exploiting these opportunities involves harnessing the power of the marketplace and focusing that power on the reduction, or even eradication, of poverty in an environmentally sound manner.

Prospects for International Cooperation

As the scale of economic activity has proceeded steadily upward, the scope of environmental problems triggered by that activity has transcended both geographic and generational boundaries. Whereas the nation-state used to be a sufficient form of political organization for resolving environmental problems, that may no longer be the case. Whereas the earliest generations of humans had the luxury of being able to satisfy its own needs without worrying about the needs of those generations to come, that is no longer the case, either. Solving problems such as poverty, global warming, ozone depletion, and the loss of biodiversity requires international cooperation. Ideally, the search for solutions would also involve intergenerational cooperation, but, of course, that is not possible. Future generations cannot speak for themselves; we must speak for them. Our policies must incorporate our obligation to future generations, however difficult or imperfect that incorporation might prove to be.

International cooperation is by no means a foregone conclusion. Global environmental problems can trigger very different effects on the countries that will sit around the negotiating table. Whereas low-lying countries could be completely submerged by the sea-level rise predicted by some global-warming models or arid nations could see their marginal agricultural lands succumb to desertification, other nations may see agricultural productivity rise, as warmer climates support longer growing seasons in traditionally intemperate climates.

Countries that unilaterally set out to improve the global environmental situation run the risk of making their businesses vulnerable to competition from less conscientious nations. Industrialized countries that undertake stringent environmental policies may not suffer greatly at the national level (because of offsetting employment and income increases in the industries that produce pollution control equipment), but some individual industries confronting the stringent regulations will face higher costs than their competitors and can be expected to suffer accordingly. Declining market share and employment in industries confronted by especially stringent regulations are powerful political weapons that can be used to derail efforts to implement an aggressive environmental policy. The search for solutions must accommodate these concerns.

Forging new international agreements is not enough. To produce the desired effect, the agreements must be enforceable. Enforceability will be a difficult criterion to satisfy as long as the agreements infringe upon significant segments of society with legitimate claims to an alternative future. The most legitimate such claim is perhaps advanced by those currently in abject poverty.

Many individuals and institutions currently have a large stake in maintaining the status quo. Fisherman harvesting their catch from an overexploited fishery are loath to undertake any reduction in harvests, even if the reduction is necessary to conserve the stock and to return the population to a healthy level. Farmers who have come to depend on fertilizer and pesticide subsidies will be reluctant to give them up. The principle of inertia applies to political as fully as to physical bodies: A body at rest will tend to stay at rest unless a significant outside force is introduced. Changing economic incentives can provide that force.

Opportunities for Cooperation

This list of barriers to international cooperation is certainly imposing, but the new global environmental problems also offer new opportunities for cooperation, opportunities that in some ways are unprecedented. Although the degrees to which various nations are affected by these problems differs, a point made earlier, it is also true that some potential common ground exists.

One important foundation for this common ground is the inefficiency of many current economic activities. In many cases, these inefficiencies are very large indeed; resources are being wasted. Whenever resources are wasted, much more environmental improvement could be obtained for current expenditures, or the same improvement could be realized with a much smaller commitment of resources. By definition, moving from an inefficient policy to an efficient one creates gains to be shared. Agreements on how these gains should be shared among the cooperating parties can be used to build coalitions.

The natural reluctance of nations to impose increasingly stringent environmental policies within their borders can be diminished by assuring that the policies imposed are cost effective. We live in an age when the call for tighter environmental controls intensifies with each new discovery of yet another injury modern society is inflicting on the planet, but resistance to additional controls is growing with the recognition that the cost of compliance is also growing, as all the "easy" techniques become used up. Choosing cost-effective and flexible policy instruments can reduce the potential for backlash.[16]

The choice of policy instruments can also affect enforceability. In developing countries, local communities typically have the greatest accessibility to and knowledge about local biological resources. As these countries have undergone a centralization of political power, including the power to control these resources, some of the local commitment to them has been lost. Policy instruments that reestablish this commitment by offering these local communities a stake in the preservation of the resources can enhance enforceability.

With creative design of policy instruments, the incentives of local and global communities can become compatible. In some cases, being creative requires the use of conventional economic instruments in unconventional ways; in others, it requires the use of unconventional instruments in unconventional ways.

Unconventional approaches are not pipe dreams. Most of them have been successfully employed in one form or another in local communities around the globe. The experience with these instruments in their current setting provides a model for their use on an international level. How well this model fits remains an open question, but it is better to sit down for a dinner with a full menu offering some novel, but interesting, choices than one offering only a limited selection of familiar, unappetizing fare.

Restructuring Incentives

How can economic incentives be used to provide the kinds of signals that will make sustainable development possible? Perhaps the best way to begin to answer this question is to recall a few examples of how this approach has worked in practice, focusing this time on how they fit into the quest for sustainable development.

---

[16]Nations that impose stringent environmental regulations on themselves may even end up gaining a competitive advantage in international markets. Using Germany and Japan to illustrate his point, Michael Porter concludes that being the first to develop new production techniques provides significant market opportunities when others subsequently adopt similar regulations and firms begin searching for the means of meeting them. See Michael E. Porter, "America's Green Strategy," *Scientific American* 264, No. 4 (April): 168.

Recall how the use of economic incentives was able to reduce the stress on an already over-exploited New Zealand fishery. Because of their desirability and the traditional open access to the fishery, the populations of several species of fish off the coast of New Zealand were being depleted. Although the need to reduce the amount of pressure being put on the population was rather obvious, how to accomplish that reduction was not at all clear. It was relatively easy to prevent new fishermen from entering the fisheries, but it was harder to figure out how to reduce the pressure from those who had been fishing in the area for years or even decades. Because fishing is characterized by economies of scale, simply reducing everyone's catch proportionately wouldn't make much sense. That would simply place higher costs on everyone and waste a great deal of fishing capacity as all boats sat around idle for a significant proportion of time. A better solution would clearly be to have fewer boats harvesting the stock. That way, each boat could be used closer to its full capacity without depleting the fish population. Which fishermen should be asked to give up their livelihood and leave the industry?

The economic-incentive approach addressed this problem by imposing transferable catch quotas on all fish harvested from the fishery. Revenues derived from the annual fee charged for renewing these quotas were used to buy out fishermen who were willing to forgo any future fishing for the relevant species. Essentially, each fisherman stated the lowest price that he or she would accept for leaving the industry; the regulators selected those who could be induced to leave at the lowest price, paid the stipulated amount from the tax revenues, and retired their catch quotas for the affected species. It wasn't long before a sufficient number of licenses had been retired and the fish population was protected. Because the program was voluntary, those who left the industry only did so when they felt they had been adequately compensated. A difficult and potentially dangerous pressure on a valuable natural resource had been avoided by the creative use of an approach that changed the economic incentives.

The fishery example shows how economic incentives can be used to reduce the conflict between economic development and the sustainable use of a renewable resource. Economic incentives can also be used to make economic development the vehicle by which greater environmental protection is achieved. Recall the offset policy. Under this U.S. policy, firms already established in nonattainment areas that chose to voluntarily control their emissions by more than the degree required under the prevailing regulations had those excess-emission reductions certified as "emission reduction credits" (or ERCs). Once the credits were certified, the firms operating permits were tightened to assure that the reductions were permanent. These ERCs could then be sold to new firms seeking to move into the nonattainment area, provided that the acquiring firm bought at least 1.2 ERCs for each 1.0 units of emissions added by the new plant. Air quality improved every time a new firm moved into the area. With this policy, the confrontation between economic growth and environmental protection was diffused. Not only were new firms allowed to move into polluted cities, they became one of the main vehicles for improving the quality of air. Economic development facilitated, rather than blocked, air quality improvement.

It now remains only to show how the entire menu of economic-incentive policies can be woven together in a manner that facilitates international cooperation in the resolution of international environmental problems. Economic analysis suggests five principles that can provide the foundation for this approach.

The Full-Cost Principle. According to *full-cost principle,* all users of environmental resources should pay their full cost. Those using the environment as a waste repository, for example, would be presumed responsible not only for controlling pollution to the full extent required by the law, but also for restoring environmental resource damaged beyond some *de minimus* amount and for compensating those suffering damage.

This principle is based upon the presumption that humanity has a right to a reasonably safe and healthy environment. Because this right has been held in common for the stratosphere and the international sections of the oceans, no administrative body has either the responsibility or the authority to protect that right. As a result, it has been involuntarily surrendered on a first-come, first-served basis without compensation.

Although global warming and ozone depletion impose both an international and intergenerational environmental cost, currently that cost is not being borne, or even recognized, by those who ultimately control the magnitude of the problem. Furthermore, those choosing unilaterally to reduce their emissions expose themselves to the higher costs associated with mitigating strategies. Applying the full-cost principle would send a strong signal to all users of the environment that the atmosphere is a scarce, precious resource and should be treated accordingly. Products produced by manufacturing processes that are environmentally destructive would become relatively more expensive; those produced by environmentally benign production processes would become relatively cheaper. Implementing the full-cost principle would end the implicit subsidy that all polluting activities have received since the beginning of time. When the level of economic activity was small, the corresponding subsidy was also small and therefore probably not worthy of political attention. Because the scale of economic activity has grown, however, the subsidy has become very large indeed; ignoring it leads to significant resource distortion.

What policy implications would flow from the acceptance of the full-cost principle? A first implication is that emissions of harmful substances should bear an emission charge. For the global-warming problem, this could take the form of a tax on all greenhouse gases emitted into the atmosphere. The "carbon tax," which is currently being widely discussed in Europe and the United States, could be one component of this package. However, because carbon dioxide is only one of the greenhouse gases, taxes would necessarily be imposed on other gases, as well. The appropriate level of this tax for each gas would depend upon its per unit contribution to the global-warming problem; gases posing a larger per unit risk would bear higher tax rates.

Substances contributing to ozone depletion would also be taxed according to the full-cost principle. Because the ozone depletion tax and the global-warming tax would be separately assessed, substances such as CFCs that contribute to both global warming and ozone depletion would bear both taxes.

The transition to a more sustainable economic system will depend upon the development of new technologies and upon much greater levels of energy efficiency than are currently being achieved. Those transitions will not occur unless the prevailing economic incentives support and encourage them. Once the greenhouse gas and ozone depletion taxes were in effect, the incentives would be changed; greater energy efficiency and the development of new technologies would become top-priority objectives.

Implications for the legal system would flow from the full-cost principle, as well. For example, international laws should permit full recovery for damage caused by oil spills or other environmental incidents. Not only should the contaminated sites be restored insofar as possible, but those suffering demonstrable losses should be fully compensated.

Making explicit environmental costs that have heretofore been hidden is only one side of the coin; the other is eliminating inappropriate subsidies. Subsidies that are incompatible with the full-cost principle should be eliminated. Implicit subsidies should be targeted as well as explicit ones. For example, when the pricing of environmental resources is subject to government regulation (e.g., water in the U.S. Southwest), prices should not simply be determined by historic average cost, they should reflect the scarcity of the resource.

For one way to accomplish this, recall our discussion of incremental block pricing. Incremental block pricing provides a practical means of introducing the appropriate conservation incentives without jeopardizing the traditional legal constraint that water distribution utilities earn no more than a fair rate of return. With incremental block pricing, the price of additional water consumed rises with the amount consumed per unit of time. Although the first units consumed per month up to some predetermined threshold would be relatively cheap, units consumed beyond the threshold would face a much higher price that truly reflects the scarcity of the resource. By assuring that the marginal units consumed were priced at full cost, adequate incentives to conserve would be introduced.

The transition to the full-cost principle could proceed gradually, beginning in certain sectors and moving to others as greater familiarity with the approach was gained. A complete, immediate transition is not an essential ingredient of a rational approach.

The Cost-Effectiveness Principle.   According to the cost-effectiveness principle all environmental policies should be cost-effective. A policy is cost effective if it achieves the policy objective at the lowest possible cost. Cost-effectiveness is an important characteristic, because it can diminish political backlash by limiting wasteful expenditures.

Appropriate implementation of the full-cost principle would automatically produce cost-effectiveness as a side benefit. Should acceptance of the full-cost principle falter, however, cost-effectiveness could be elevated to a primary policy goal, worthy in its own right. It provides a desirable, if less than perfect, fallback position.

Political acceptance of the full-cost principle is by no means a foregone conclusion. Although taxes on greenhouse and ozone depletion gases can go a long way toward rectifying some of the current distortions in resource pricing, they will do little to reassure those whose vision of the future is defined in terms of specific limits on emissions, not on correcting price distortions. It would be very difficult to establish a set of tax rates that could guarantee a specific emissions target.

If international agreements were to proceed by establishing global limits for greenhouse gases (the approach taken for ozone-depleting gases), allocating the proposed reductions among the nations of the world would be one of the most difficult aspects of this alternative approach. Fairness will no doubt be one critical aspect of the negotiations, and it is likely that some form of cost-sharing will result. How are the costs to be shared?

Recall our discussion of transferable carbon-emission rights. Emissions trading becomes a reasonable approach for implementing the cost-effectiveness principle while providing opportunities for cost-sharing. The process of establishing emissions trading in greenhouse gases would be initiated by setting transferable limits on the amounts each nation could emit on an annual basis. Nations achieving reductions greater than those required by the agreement could receive transferable ERCs that could be sold to other nations. By purchasing these credits, the acquiring nation could increase its quota by the amount covered by the ERCs.

An international market in ERCs would facilitate the movement of credits from those countries with the capacity to create them most cheaply to those countries faced by very high costs of additional control. The capacity to achieve cost-effectiveness regardless of how the initial emission allowances are allocated is a significant attribute of an emissions-trading approach that could be exploited for developing a market approach to cost-sharing. With emissions trading as the strategy of choice, those forging new international agreements would have a very large latitude in attempting to establish emission limitations that are fair and politically feasible without jeopardizing cost-effectiveness. As the Western nations acquired by purchase the necessary production allowances at market prices from those nations selling them, significant financial transfers would take place. The size of these transfers would be dictated by market forces, not by negotiation.

The Property-Rights Principle. Part of the evident loss of efficiency in modern environmental problems involves misspecified property rights, which create perverse incentives. According to the *property-rights principle,* local communities should have a property right over flora and fauna within their border. This property right would entitle the local community to share in any benefits created by preserving the species. Assuring that local property rights over genetic resources are defined and respected would give local communities a much larger stake in some of the global benefits to be derived from the use of those resources and would enhance the prospects for effective enforcement.

Recall our discussion of the problem of stemming the decline in the elephant population. Insofar as permitted by the migratory nature of the herd, the property-rights principle would confer the right to harvest a fixed number of elephants upon the indigenous peoples who lives in the elephant's native habitat. Ownership of harvesting rights and the possibility of continued employment as long as the herd was preserved would assure an income to the local community, giving it a stake in preserving the herd. Preventing poaching would become easier, because poachers would become a threat to the local community, not merely a threat to a distant national government that inspires little allegiance.

A somewhat related application of the property-rights principle could provide an additional means of resolving the diminishing supply of biologically rich tropical rain forests. One of the arguments for preserving biodiversity is that it offers a valuable gene pool for the development of future products such as medicines or food crops. Typically, however, the nations that govern the forestland containing this biologically rich gene pool have not shared in the wealth created by the products derived from it. Currently, nations cutting down their tropical forests have little incentive to protect the gene pool harbored within those forests because they are unlikely to reap any of the rewards that will ultimately result. Exploitation of the gene pool and the economic rewards that result from it typically accrue only to those nations and those companies that can afford the extensive research.

Recall our discussion of the use of royalties to provide an economic return to gene preservation. By establishing the principle that stipulated royalty payments would accrue to the nation from which the original genes were extracted, local incentives would become more compatible with global incentives.

The Sustainability Principle. According to the *sustainability principle,* all resources should be used in a manner that respects the needs of future generations. Adopting the foregoing three principles would go a long way toward restoring efficiency. And restoring efficiency would set in motion the transition toward producing sustainable outcomes. As we have seen, however, restoring efficiency would not be sufficient. Other policies would be needed in order to satisfy the sustainability principle.

Restoring intergenerational fairness in the use of depletable resources might be an appropriate place to start. As the economic models have made clear, current incentives for sharing the wealth from the use of depletable resources are biased toward the present, even in efficient markets. Clearly, this could be rectified by transferring some of the created wealth into the future, but how much wealth?

Salah El Serafy has developed an ingenious, practical way to answer this question.[17] Calculate the present value of the net benefits received from the extraction of a depletable resource over its useful life. This becomes the wealth to be shared. Using standard annuity tables, calculate the constant annual payments that could be made from this fund forever. (In essence, these payments represent the dividends and interest derived from the wealth; the principle would be left intact.) This constant annual payment is what can be consumed from the wealth created from the depletable resources. Receipts in excess of this amount (in the years the resource is being extracted and sold) must be paid into the fund. All succeeding generations receive the same annual payment; the payments continue forever.

The payments could be invested in research rather than in instruments producing a financial return. Such a strategy might envision, for example, setting aside through taxation a certain proportion of all proceeds from depletable resources for funding research on substitutes likely to be used by future generations. In the case of fossil fuels, for example, one might subsidize research into solar energy or the use of hydrogen as a fuel so that, as fossil fuels are depleted, future generations would have the ability to switch to alternative sources easily, without diminishing living standards in the process.

Another adjustment would confront the possibility of species extinction. Compensating future generations for extinct species (the implicit strategy in an efficient allocation) may not be adequate. Not only do we not know the appropriate level of compensation, it is possible that the preferences of future generations would be such that the value of the preserved species would exceed any possible compensation our generation would be willing to offer. Given this uncertainty about the preferences of future generations, one strategy would be to incorporate species preservation into our concept of sustainability in order to allow future generations to make their own valuations. With this approach, strategies that lead to species extinction would simply be infeasible, regardless of the net-benefit calculations. The interests of future generations would be protected by preserving their options rather than by attempting to second-guess their preferences.

Adjusting the national income accounts would be another immediate implication of the sustainability principle. The income accounts must conform with the Hicksian definition of *income*. All of the costs, including the depreciation of natural capital, should be subtracted from the gross receipts in producing a national income figure. Failure to do this, as is the current practice, provides very misleading signals to the public sector. These misleading signals provide powerful incentives for public figures to engage in economic activities that violate the sustainability principle.

---

[17]Salah El Serafy, "Absorptive Capacity, the Demand for Revenue, and the Supply of Petroleum," *The Journal of Energy and Development* 7, No. 1 (autumn 1981): Appendix A.

The Information Principle. Polls generally show that, regardless of their social circumstances, people care about the environment and are willing to commit resources to its preservation. To energize and focus that reservoir of goodwill, however, it is necessary to assure that the citizens are informed. Recognizing the wisdom of this simple observation has paved the way for a new set of strategies designed to improve citizen participation in environmental policy.

Implementing the *information principle* can take a number of forms. In some countries, it has meant increasing the freedom of the press to report on environmental matters. In others, it has meant providing better access to government records that reveal the quantities and types of pollutants being injected into the air and water.

It can also mean labeling "green" products to allow environmentally conscious consumers to use that characteristic as one element of their choice. "Dolphin-safe tuna" provides a classic example of how this approach has been used quite successfully.

One of the appeals of information strategies is their ability to achieve results when more traditional approaches prove inadequate. In many developing countries, for example, human and financial resources are so scarce as to preclude traditional regulatory approaches to pollution control. Fortunately, that does not necessarily mean that pollution goes uncontrolled. Appropriately designed information strategies may result in significant pollution control, even in the absence of traditional monitoring and enforcement (Example 21.4).

FORCED TRANSITION

Let's suppose that current levels of welfare were shown to be unsustainable and that an immediate transition to a new, lower standard of living were necessary to protect future generations. Let's suppose further that a "guided forced transition" would be less painful than a laissez-faire forced transition. How could that more abrupt transition be negotiated?

The most concrete proposals for a forced transition to the steady state come from Herman Daly, an economist with the University of Maryland.[18] Daly is very sympathetic to the goal of a rapid transition to sustainable development and has spent a good deal of his professional life looking into the best way to achieve that objective. We will focus on his proposals in examining how an economy might be forced to this new sustainable path more rapidly than would normally be the case.

Defining the Target

Daly begins by attempting to define the *steady state,* the target of his approach, and how we know when it is achieved. His definition is couched in physical, rather than value, terms. For Daly, the *steady-state economy* is characterized by constant stocks of people and physical wealth maintained at some chosen, desirable level by a low rate of throughput. This throughput—flows of resources and energy—provides direct consumption benefits (e.g., food and shelter) and investment, insofar as necessary to counteract depreciation of the capital stock.

Conceiving of the steady state in physical rather than value terms is significant because it forms an important difference between Daly and others who see the steady state as simply the absence of any development. Daly recognizes that some development would and should occur

---

[18]Herman E. Daly, *Steady-State Economics* (San Francisco: W. H. Freeman, 1977). Expanded 2nd edition published by Island Press, 1991.

Example 21.4

Reputational Strategies for Pollution Control in Indonesia

Inhibited by a regulatory structure that was not able to produce widespread compliance with water pollution control laws because of a lack of resources, in 1993 the government of Indonesia instituted a unique complementary program to increase compliance. Known by its acronym, *PROPER* (Program for Pollution Control, Evaluation, and Rating), this system evaluated 187 factories. Depending upon their pollution output, these factories were assigned to one of five color-coded categories. The categories ranged from black (no effort to control pollution) to gold (polluter exceeds legal limits by at least 50% for air, water, and hazardous waste and makes extensive use of clean technology, pollution prevention, etc.).

The key to the system was not only that the names of the factories and their ratings would be made public, but that the ratings would be conducted periodically, allowing factories to gain public acknowledgment for improving their ratings. The hope was that firms would be sufficiently motivated by possible damage to their reputations by adverse publicity that they would improve their environmental performance.

Though still in its infancy, the early results are encouraging. In the first six months following the announcement of the ratings, the number of firms in the black ("no-effort") category fell by half (from 6 to 3), whereas the number of factories meeting or exceeding legal requirements went from 66 to 76.

Sources: S. Afsah and D. Wheeler, "Indonesia's New Pollution Control Program: Using Public Pressure to Get Compliance," *East Asian Executive Reports* 18, No. 5 (May 1996): 11–13; and Shakeb Afsah, et al., "What Is PROPER?: Reputational Incentives for Pollution Control in Indonesia," World Bank Working Paper (November 1995).

even in the steady state in spite of a constant stock of people and physical wealth. For example, as society learns more efficient ways to use energy, the value derived from the flow of energy may increase, even when the flow itself does not. Because of technological progress, the value of the services received can grow, even if the physical stocks and flows are unchanging. *The steady state and zero economic growth are not necessarily the same thing.*

Institutional Structure

Daly sees three institutional modifications as necessary for the rapid attainment of the steady state:

1. An institution for stabilizing population
2. An institution for stabilizing the stock of physical wealth and throughput
3. An institution to ensure that the stocks and flows are distributed fairly among the population

Allocation among alternative uses is handled by the market. Collective decisions are made on scale and distribution, but allocation remains with the market. Daly argues that the questions of scale, distribution, and allocation involve three separate policy goals and cannot all be served by the single instrument of prices. Market prices achieve the goal of efficient allocation; the other institutions are designed to achieve an optimal (sustainable) scale and an optimal (fair) distribution.

Population Stabilization. According to the Daly proposals, population would be stabilized over the long run using an idea first put forth by Kenneth Boulding.[19] In this scheme, each individual would be given the inalienable right to produce one (and only one!) child. Because this scheme over a generation allows each member of the current population to replace himself or herself, births would necessarily equal deaths, and population stability would be achieved.

This scheme would award each person a certificate entitling the holder to have one child. Couples could pool their certificates to have two. Every time a child was born, a certificate would be surrendered. Failure to produce a certificate would cause the child to be put up for adoption.

Certificates would be fully transferable. Families who placed a particularly high value on children could purchase extra certificates, whereas those who viewed parenting with something less than enthusiasm could sell certificates. As one of its virtues, this system would ensure that the overall objective of population stability would be achieved, but no family would be required to maintain a particular family size. Though every couple would be guaranteed the right to have two children, they could choose to have fewer or more than two.

Stock and Throughput Stabilization. Daly suggests that *throughput* (the flow of energy and resources) should be held at some minimum level using depletion quotas for all depletable resources. These quotas would define the amount of the resource that could be extracted and used. Any extraction and use in excess of this quota would be illegal.

The size of these quotas would be determined by bureaucrats, but according to Daly, these bureaucrats would follow a specific rule. The quotas would be set at a level sufficiently stringent that the price of the resource in question would equal the price of the closest renewable substitute. When no close renewable substitute was available, the bureaucrats would be empowered to decide the most ethical level. Because the quotas would be auctioned off by the government, the government would extract all of the scarcity rent associated with the depletable resources. The quota prices would equal the scarcity rent of the covered resources.

Ensuring Distributional Fairness. Daly also sees a need to override the normal channels for distributing income in the steady-state economy. In a growth economy, tensions between the rich and poor can be ameliorated by the opportunities for social and economic mobility that a growth economy provides. In a steady-state economy, those opportunities are diminished, as the number of new jobs created is smaller.

To alleviate these tensions, Daly proposes establishing a maximum and minimum income level as well as a maximum limit on wealth. The minimum income level would be financed in

---

[19]Kenneth E. Boulding, *The Meaning of the Twentieth Century* (New York: Harper & Row, 1964).

part by progressive taxes, with 100 percent marginal rates above the maximum income and wealth limits. Because these 100 percent tax rates would presumably yield very little revenue (the incentive to earn more having been eliminated), most of the revenue would come from the sale of depletion quotas and from lower tax rates on income levels between the minimum and maximum.

Administration

Critics point out that the Daly system would be expensive to implement. Large bureaucratic staffs would be needed to define the quotas, run the actions, and ensure compliance. In an age where public sentiment seems to be for decreasing rather than increasing bureaucracy, this proposal would buck the trend. A universal quota system for depletable and renewable resources, in addition to being bureaucratically cumbersome, holds the potential to disrupt a smoothly operating institutional structure. Historically, the only time a system such as this has been acceptable is during a war.[20]

Child certificates would also be administratively cumbersome and, in most of the industrialized world, unnecessary in light of rapidly declining fertility trends. In addition, child certificates raise moral questions. For example, this system tends to preserve the existing racial status quo. To minority groups with above-average birth rates and below-average incomes, this looks like a policy to limit their proportion in the population. Even though that is not the intended result, the suspicions raised create unnecessary tensions.

SUMMARY

Sustainable development refers to a process for providing for the needs of the present generation (particularly those in poverty) without compromising the ability of future generations to meet their own needs.

Market imperfections frequently make sustainable development less likely. Intergenerational externalities such as climate modification impose excessive costs on future generations. Free access to biological common-property resources can lead to excessive exploitation and even extinction of the species.

Even efficient markets do not necessarily produce sustainable development. Restoring efficiency is a desirable and helpful, but insufficient, means for producing sustainable welfare levels. Although, in principle, dynamically efficient allocations produce extraction profiles for depletable resources that are compatible with the interests of future generations, in practice this is not necessarily the case. Guaranteeing sustainability frequently requires compensation from the present to future generations, but profit-maximizing behavior produces compensation levels that are too low. Furthermore, adequate compensation levels may be difficult to define, at best, and it is not clear that financial payments can adequately compensate future generations for all of the options they might be asked to forgo.

---

[20]In a personal communication honoring my request that he review this chapter and the one that precedes it, Herman Daly responded, "In my view the real threat to freedom and stimulus to bureaucratic control is *crisis,* and avoidance of crisis with a bit of collective action now seems a good strategy for maximizing freedom over the long run."

New sustainable forms of development are possible, but they will not automatically be adopted. Economic incentive policies can facilitate the transition from unsustainable to sustainable activities. Five principles provide a framework for using economic incentives to manage this transition:

1. All users of environmental resources should pay their full cost to ensure a level playing field between those resources that damage the environment and those that don't (the "Full Cost" Principle).

2. All environmental policies should be implemented in a cost-effective manner to ensure that the maximum environmental quality is received for the expenditure (the "Cost-Effectiveness" Principle).

3. Rights over environmental resources should be designed in such a manner as to promote stewardship (the "Property Rights" Principle).

4. All current uses of resources should be compatible with the needs of future generations, and the present value criterion should be used only to choose among allocations that meet this sustainability test (the "Sustainability" Principle).

5. All citizens should be kept as informed as practical about the environmental consequences of current decisions to allow citizens to participate as fully as possible in the transition to sustainable development (the "Information" Principle).

If it turns out that universally higher standards of living are not possible without exceeding the carrying capacity of the planet, a rapid transition to a new, steady state involving levels of welfare lower than current levels would be needed. To examine how this might occur, we considered the proposals of economist Herman Daly. He sees three institutional modifications as necessary: (1) a plan to control population, (2) a system of annual quotas to govern the rate of consumption of both depletable and renewable resources, and (3) a new mechanism to control the distribution of income and wealth. The institutional modifications suggested by Daly would be implemented at a very high cost.

The search for solutions must recognize that market forces are extremely powerful. Attempts to negotiate agreements that seek to block those forces or to meet them head-on are probably doomed to failure. Nonetheless, it is possible to negotiate agreements that harness those forces and channel them in directions that enhance the possibilities of international cooperation. To take these steps will require thinking and acting in somewhat unconventional ways. Whether the world community is equal to the task remains to be seen.

FURTHER READING

Battie, Sandra S. "Sustainable Development: Challenges to the Agricultural Economics Profession," *American Journal of Agricultural Economics* 71 (December 1989): 1083–1101. Contrasts the viewpoints of "deep ecology" sustainable development advocates with those of traditional economists and suggests some things each can learn from the other.

Costanza, Robert et al. "The Ecological Economics of Sustainability: Making Local and Short-Term Goals Consistent with Global and Long-Term Goals," Working Paper No. 32 (Washington, DC:

World Bank Environment Department, 1990). A catalogue containing abstracts of nearly 200 works in ecological economics presented at a 1990 conference on sustainability in Washington.

Jansson, Ann Mari, et al., eds. *Investing in Natural Capital: The Ecological Economics Approach to Sustainability* (Washington, DC: Island Press, 1994). Proceedings of an international workshop involving ecologists and economists in a joint search for new approaches to sustainable development.

OECD. *The Environmental Effects of Trade* (Paris: Organization for Economic Co-operation and Development, 1994). Contains background documents for OECD discussions on the environmental effects of trade, including sector studies on agriculture, forestry, fisheries, endangered species, and transport.

Pearce, David, Anil Markandya, and Edward B. Barbier. *Blueprint for a Green Economy* (London: Earthscan, 1989). Seeks to answer the question, "If we accept sustainable development as a working idea, what does it mean for the way we manage a modern economy?"

Sterner, Thomas, ed. *Economic Policies for Sustainable Development* (Norwell, MA: Kluwer Academic Publishers, 1994). A collection of 17 essays that describe the state of the art in the use of new economic instruments to achieve sustainable development.

Stewart, Richard B. "Environmental Regulation and International Competitiveness," *Yale Law Journal,* 102 (June 1993): 2039–2106. A comprehensive survey of the trade and environment literature.

Weiss, Edith Brown. "In Fairness to Future Generations," *Environment* 32 (April 1990): 7–11, 30–31. A lawyer proposes a new doctrine to protect the interests of future generations and a set of principles and procedures for implementing that doctrine.

ADDITIONAL REFERENCES

Aniansson, Britt, and Uno Svedin. *Towards an Ecological Sustainable Economy* (Stockholm: Swedish Council for Planning and Coordination of Research, 1990).

Baumol, William J. "On the Possibility of Continuing Expansion of Finite Resources," *Kyklos* 39 (1986): 167–179.

Becker, Robert A. "Intergenerational Equity: The Capital-Environment Trade-Off," *Journal of Environmental Economics and Management* 9 (June 1982): 165–185.

Brown, Lester R., Christopher Flavin, and Sandra Postel. "Picturing a Sustainable Society," in Lester R. Brown et al., eds. *State of the World: 1990* (New York: W. W. Norton, 1990): 173–190.

Daly, Herman E. "The Economic Growth Debate: What Some Economists Have Learned But Many Have Not," *Journal of Environmental Economics and Management* 14 (December 1987): 323–336.

Goldin, Ian, and L. Alan Winters, eds. *The Economics of Sustainable Development* (Cambridge, UK: Cambridge University Press, 1995).

Hawken, P., A. Lovins, et al. *Natural Capitalism: Creating the Next Industrial Revolution* (Boston: Little, Brown and Company, 1999).

Howarth, Richard B., and Richard B. Norgard. "Intergenerational Resource Rights," *Land Economics* 66 (February 1990): 1–11.

McNeeley, Jeffrey A., et al. "Strategies for Conserving Biodiversity," *Environment* 32 (April 1990): 16–20, 36–40.

Parris, T.M. "Comparative International Indicators of Sustainable Development," *Environment* 38, No. 4 (1996): 3.

Pearce, David, et al. "Measuring Sustainable Development: Progress on Indicators," *Environmental and Development Economics* 1, No. 1 (1996): 85–102.

Pezzey, John. "Sustainable Development Concepts: An Economic Analysis," working paper. Washington, DC: World Bank Environment Department, 1992).

Redclift, Michael. *Sustainable Development: Exploring the Contradictions* (New York: Methuen, 1987).

Toman, Michael A. "Economics and 'Sustainability': Balancing Trade-offs and Imperatives," *Land Economics* 70 (1994): 399–413.

Turner, R. Kerry. *Sustainable Environmental Management: Principles and Practice* (Boulder, CO: Westview Press, 1988).

VandenBergh, J. C. J. M., and M. W. Hofkes. "Economic Models of Sustainable Development" in J. C. J. M. VandenBergh, ed. *Handbook of Environmental and Resource Economics.* (Cheltenham, UK: Edward Elgar): 1108–1122.

World Resources Institute. *Natural Endowments: Financing Resource Conservation for Development* (Washington, DC: World Resources Institute, 1989).

WEB SITES OF INTEREST

1. *http://www.ulb.ac.be/ceese/meta/sustvl.html*
   The World Wide Web Virtual Library Sustainable Development site.

2. *http://www.eeeee.net/ee01026.htm*
   A comprehensive listing of Sustainable Development web sites.

3. *http://www.colby.edu/personal/thtieten/sustain.html*
   Sustainable Development/Economics web site.

DISCUSSION QUESTIONS

1. Discuss the mechanism favored by Daly to control population growth. What are its advantages and disadvantages? Would it be appropriate to implement this policy now in the United States? For those who believe that it would be, what are the crucial reasons? For those who believe it is not appropriate, are there any circumstances in any countries where it might be appropriate? Why or why not?

2. "Every molecule of a nonrenewable resource used today precludes its use by future generations. Therefore, the only morally defensible policy for any generation is to use only renewable resources." Discuss.

3. "Future generations can cast neither votes in current elections nor dollars in current market decisions. Therefore, it should not come as a surprise to anyone that the interests of future generations are ignored in a market economy." Discuss.

22

Visions
of the Future
Revisited

*Mankind was destined to live on the edge of perpetual disaster. We are
mankind because we survive. We do it in a half-assed way, but we do it.*

PAUL ADAMSON, A FICTIONAL CHARACTER IN JAMES A. MICHENER'S *CHESAPEAKE* (1978)

We have now come full circle. Having begun our study with two lofty visions of the future, we
proceeded to dissect the details of the various components of these visions—population, the
management of depletable and renewable resources, pollution, and the growth process itself.
During these inquiries a number of useful insights were gained about individual environmental and natural resource problems. Now it is time to step back and coalesce those insights into
a systematic assessment of the two visions.

◆ ADDRESSING THE ISSUES

In Chapter 1 we posed a number of questions to serve as our focus for the overarching issue of
growth in a finite environment. Those questions addressed three major issues: (1) How is the
problem correctly conceptualized? (2) Can our economic and political institutions respond in
a timely and democratic fashion to the challenges presented? (3) Can the needs of the present

generation be met without compromising the ability of future generations to meet their own needs? Can short-term and long-term goals be harmonized? The next three segments of this section summarize and interpret the evidence uncovered.

Conceptualizing the Problem

At the beginning of this book we suggested that if the *Beyond the Limits* team had correctly conceptualized the problem, theirs was the only conclusion that could be drawn. An exponential growth in demand coupled with a finite supply of resources implies that the resources must eventually be exhausted. If those resources are essential, society will collapse when they are exhausted.

We have seen that this is an excessively harsh characterization. The growth in the demand for resources is not insensitive to their scarcity. Though the rise in energy prices was triggered more by politics than by scarcity, it is possible to use higher energy prices as an example of how the economic system reacts.

The growth in demand following the increase in prices fell dramatically, with petroleum experiencing the largest reductions. In the United States, for example, total energy consumption in 1981 (73.8 quadrillion BTUs) was lower than it was in 1973 (74.6 quadrillion BTUs), despite increases in income and population. Petroleum consumption went from 34.8 quadrillion BTUs in 1973 to 32.0 quadrillion BTUs in 1981. Though some of this reduction was caused by sluggishness of the economy, price certainly played a major role.[1]

Price is not the only factor that retards demand growth. Declines in population growth also play a significant role. Because the developed nations appropriate a disproportionate share of the world's resources, the dramatic decline in population growth in those countries has had a disproportionate effect on slowing the demand for resources.

Characterizing the resource base as finite—the second aspect of the model—is also excessively harsh: (1) This characterization ignores the existence of a substantial renewable resource base; (2) it focuses attention on the wrong issue; and (3) it supports ill-conceived attempts to measure the size of the resource base. We will consider each problem in turn.

In a very real sense, a significant proportion of the resource base is not finite. Plentiful supplies of renewable resources (including, significantly, energy) are available. The normal reaction to increasing scarcity of depletable resources is to switch to renewable resources. That is clearly happening. The most dramatic examples can be found in the transition to solar energy in its various forms.

Labeling the resource base as finite is also misleading, because it suggests that our concern should be "running out." In fact, for most resources, we shall never run out. Millions of years of finite resources are left at current consumption rates. The rising cost of extracting and using those resources (including the cost to the environment), not the potential for exhausting them, is the chief threat to future standards of living. The limits on our uses of these resources are not determined by their scarcity in the crust of the earth, but rather by what we would have to sacrifice to extract and process the ores. We may not be willing to pay the price required to extract some of the lower-grade sources of those minerals.

---

[1]Lower prices can also promote consumption, however. After an extended period of lower prices (in real terms), energy consumption had risen to 92.5 quadrillion BTUs by the end of 1999.

Ignorance of this basic point has led to a number of ill-fated attempts to measure the size of this finite resource base. The timing of the societal collapse in the *Beyond the Limits* forecast was quite sensitive to the techniques used to forecast resource exhaustion. Conventional physical indicators, such as the static and the exponential reserve indices, are excessively pessimistic, because they fail to take into account possibilities for expanding current reserves. Historically, no forecast based on these techniques has stood the test of time. There is no reason to expect any similar forecast to do so in the future. They are convenient because they can be readily calculated and easily interpreted, but they are also usually dead wrong.

Current reserves can be expanded in many ways. These include finding new sources of conventional materials as well as discovering new uses for unconventional materials, including what was previously considered waste. We can also stretch the useful life of these reserves by reducing the amount of materials needed to produce the products. Striking examples include the diminishing size of a typical computer system needed to process a given amount of information and the substantially diminished amount of energy needed to heat a superinsulated home.

Although our ability to assess what is happening to cost is far from perfect, two things seem clear. Historically, very little, if any, evidence supports a fear of impending scarcity of minerals. Our ability to develop lower-cost technologies for processing resources has dominated the necessity to extract lower-grade sources. As a result, in real terms, extraction costs have fallen rather than risen over time. However, the most recent evidence suggests that, for a number of minerals, a turning point has been reached in the last few years. For those resources, evidence of scarcity—in the form of rising relative prices and increased exploration activity—has appeared.

Not all errors in resource-base measurement have been committed by those having a tendency to understate the adequacy of the resource base. Errors in the other direction are committed by those who point to the abundance in the earth's crust and atmosphere of almost all substances on which we depend. Although the abundance of those substances may be supported by the evidence, the amounts we actually use will no doubt fall far short of the amounts available.

Paradoxically, some of the most obvious cases where limits are being approached and the carrying-capacity concept has the most validity involve renewable resources rather than depletable resources. Population growth is a key contributor to this phenomenon. Expanding populations force the cultivation of marginal lands and the deforestation of large, biologically rich tracts. The erosion of overworked soils diminishes their fertility and, ultimately, their productivity. Biological resources such as fisheries can be overexploited, even to the point of extinction. The problem with these resources is not their finiteness, but the way in which they have been managed.

Correct conceptualization of the resource scarcity problem suggests that both extremely pessimistic and extremely optimistic views are wrong. Impenetrable proximate physical limits on resource availability are typically not the problem; incentives and information are frequently a much more serious problem. But believing in unlimited amounts of all resources that could support continued economic growth at current rates forever is equally naive. Plenty of resources are available if we are willing to pay the price, but that price is now rising. Transitions to renewable resources, recycled resources, and less costly depletable resources have already begun.

Institutional Responses

One of the keys to understanding how society will cope with increasing resource scarcity and environmental damage lies in understanding how social institutions will react. Are market systems, with their emphasis on decentralized decision making, and democratic political systems, with their commitment to public participation and majority rule, equal to the challenge?

Our examination of the record seems to suggest that, although our economic and political systems are far from infallible and some rather glaring deficiencies have become apparent, there are apparently no fatal flaws.

On the positive side, markets have responded swiftly and automatically to deal with those resources experiencing higher prices. Demand has been reduced and substitution encouraged. Markets for recycling are growing, and consumer habits are changing. No one has had to oversee these responses to make sure they occur. As long as property rights are well-defined, the market system provides incentives for consumers and producers to respond to scarcity in a variety of useful ways. This characteristically rapid and smooth response illustrates none of the overshoot-and-collapse behavior anticipated by the *Beyond the Limits* team.

Compelling as the evidence is for this point of view, it does not support the conclusion that, left to itself, the market would automatically choose a dynamically efficient or a sustainable path for the future. Market imperfections frequently make sustainable development less likely. The most serious limitations of the market become evidence in how it treats common-property resources, such as the fish we eat, the air we breathe, and the water we drink. Left to its own devices, a market will overexploit common-property resources, substantially lowering the net benefits received by future generations. If it is not compensated for by sufficient increases in net benefits elsewhere in the economy, such overexploitation could result in a violation of the sustainability criterion.

Even efficient markets do not necessarily produce sustainable development. Restoring efficiency is a desirable, but insufficient, means for producing sustainable welfare levels. Although, in principle, dynamically efficient allocations produce extraction profiles for depletable resources that are compatible with the interests of future generations, in practice, this is not necessarily the case. Guaranteeing sustainability in the face of declining supplies of depletable resources requires compensation from present to future generations, but profit-maximizing behavior produces compensation levels that are too low. Furthermore, adequate compensation levels may be difficult to define, at best, and it is not clear that financial payments could adequately compensate future generations for the options they might be asked to forgo.

The market has some capacity for self-correction. The decline of common-property fish catches, for example, has led to the rise of private-property fish farming. The artificial scarcity created by imperfectly defined property rights gives rise to incentives for the development of a private-property substitute.

This capacity of the market for self-healing, although comforting, is not always adequate. In some cases, cheaper, more effective solutions (e.g., preventing the deterioration of the original natural resource base) are available. Preventive medicine is frequently superior to corrective surgery. In other cases, such as when our air is polluted, no good private substitutes are available. To provide an adequate response, it is sometimes necessary to complement market decisions with political ones.

The need for government intervention is particularly acute in controlling pollution. Uncontrolled markets not only produce too much pollution, they also tend to underprice commodities that contribute to pollution either when produced or consumed. Firms that unilaterally attempt to control their pollution run the risk of pricing themselves out of the market. Government intervention is needed to ensure that firms that neglect environmental damage in their operating decisions do not thereby gain a competitive edge.

Significant progress has been made in reducing the amount of pollution, particularly conventional air pollution. Recent regulatory innovations, such as the bubble and offset policies, represent major steps toward the development of a flexible but potentially viable framework for controlling air pollutants. By making it less costly to achieve environmental goals, these reforms have limited the potential for a backlash against the policy. They have brought perceived costs more in line with perceived benefits. Emission charges have played a similar role for water pollution control in Europe.

It would be a great mistake, however, to assume that government intervention in resolving environmental problems has been uniformly benign. The acid rain problem was almost certainly initially made worse by a policy structure that focused on local rather than regional pollution problems. Requiring scrubbers for all new coal-fired electrical generating stations was done for purely political reasons and served to raise the cost of compliance unnecessarily.

Perhaps the most flagrant examples of counterproductive government intervention are to be found in the treatment of energy and water resources. By imposing price ceilings on natural gas and oil, the government removed much of the normal resiliency of the economic system. With price controls, the incentives for expanding the supply are reduced and the time profile of consumption is tilted toward the present. As was the case with natural gas, these controls can even cause biases that interfere with the transition to renewable resources. By holding water prices below the marginal cost of supply, water authorities have subsidized excess use. With price controls, resources that in a normal market would have been conserved for future generations are consumed by the current generation. When price controls are placed on normal market transactions, the overshoot syndrome anticipated by the *Beyond the Limits* team can occur. The smooth transition to renewable resources that characterizes the normal market allocation is eliminated by price controls; shortages can arise.

Price controls also play a key role in the world hunger problem. By controlling the price of food, many developing countries have undervalued domestic agriculture. The long-run effect of these controls has been to increase these countries' reliance on food imports at a time when foreign exchange to pay for those imports is becoming increasingly scarce. Whereas developed countries have gone substantially down the road to price decontrol, less developed countries have not yet been able to extricate themselves to a similar degree.

One aspect of the policy process that does not seem to have been handled well is the speed with which improvement has been sought. Public opinion polls have unambiguously shown that the general public supports environmental protection, even when it raises costs and lowers employment. Policymakers have reacted to this resolve by writing very tough legislation designed to force rapid technological development.

Common sense suggests that tough legislation with early deadlines can achieve environmental goals more rapidly than weaker legislation with less tight deadlines. Common sense is frequently wrong. Writing tough legislation with early deadlines can have the opposite effect. Unreasonably tough regulations are virtually impossible to enforce. Recognizing this, polluters have repeatedly sought (and received) delays in compliance. It has frequently been better, from the polluter's point of view, to spend resources in order to challenge the regulations than to spend resources in order to comply with them. This would not have been the case with less stringent regulations, because the firms would have had no legally supportable grounds for delay.

In summary, the record compiled by our economic and political institutions has been mixed. It seems clear that simple prescriptions such as "leave it to the market" or "more government intervention" simply do not bear up under a close scrutiny of the record. The relationship between the economic and political sectors has to be one of selective engagement, complemented in some areas by selective disengagement. Each problem has to be treated on a case-by-case basis. As we have seen in our examination of a variety of environmental and natural resource problems, the efficiency and sustainability criteria allow such distinctions to be drawn, and they provide a powerful basis for policy reform.

Sustainable Development

Historically, increases in inputs and technological progress have been important sources of economic growth in the industrialized nations. In the future, some factors of production, such as labor, will not increase as rapidly as they have in the past. The effect of this decline on growth depends on the interplay among the law of diminishing marginal productivity, substitution possibilities, and technological progress. The law of diminishing marginal productivity suggests slower growth rates, whereas technological progress and the availability of substitution possibilities counteract this drag.

Our examination of empirical evidence suggests that increased environmental control has not currently had a large impact on the economy as a whole, although certain industries have been hit quite hard. Environmental policy has triggered only a small rise in the rate of inflation and a mild reduction in growth. Environmental policy has apparently contributed more jobs than it has cost. The notion that respecting the environment is incompatible with a healthy economy is demonstrably wrong.

The situation is similar for energy. Though rather large increases in energy prices have occurred, the portion of the slowdown in productivity growth during the 1970s attributed to these increases is not large. Some diminution of growth has certainly occurred, but it seems premature to suggest that rising energy prices have already forced a transition to a period of substantially lower productivity growth.

The economy is being transformed, however. It is not business as usual. Two particularly important aspects of this transformation are the decline in population growth and the rise in the importance of information as a driving economic force. Both aspects tend to reduce the degree to which physical limits constrain economic growth and increase the degree to which current welfare levels would be sustainable.

Recognizing that conventional measures of economic growth shed little light on the question, some crude attempts have been made to estimate whether or not growth in the industrialized countries has made the citizens of those countries better off. Results of these studies suggest that, because growth has ultimately generated more leisure, longer life expectancy, and more goods and services, it has been beneficial. But more recent studies suggest that the benefits from growth have been steadily diminishing over time. One study found that further growth in the United States now lowers the economic well-being of the average U.S. citizen; at this stage of affluence, the negative aspects were estimated to outweigh the positive aspects.

Our examination of the evidence suggests that the notion that all of the world's people are automatically benefited by economic growth is naive. Growth has demonstrably benefited the poor in the developed countries, but mainly through transfers from more well-off members of society, not exclusively from the direct effects of growth.

The future outlook for the less industrialized nations is, at best, mixed. Solving many of their future environmental problems will require higher standards of living. However, following the path of development pioneered by the industrialized nations is probably not possible without triggering severe global environmental problems; the solution would become the problem. New forms of development will be necessary.

The less industrialized countries must overcome a number of significant barriers if development is to become a reality. At the local level, rising populations face increasingly limited access to land or productive assets. At the national level, corruption and development policies discriminate against the poor. Globally, their situation is worsened by rising debt burdens, falling prices for exports, and the flight of capital that could be used to create jobs and income.

New sustainable forms of development are possible and desirable, but they will not automatically be adopted in either the high-income or the low-income nations. Are cooperative solutions possible? Can any common ground be established?

The experience in the United States suggests that cooperative solutions may be possible, even among traditional adversaries. Environmental regulators and lobbying groups with a special interest in environment protection in the United States have traditionally looked upon the market system as a powerful and potentially dangerous adversary. That the market unleashed powerful forces was widely recognized and that those forces clearly acted to degrade the environment was widely lamented. Meanwhile, development proponents have traditionally seen environmental concerns as blocking projects that had the potential to raise living standards significantly. Conflict and confrontation became the *modus operandi* for dealing with this clash of objectives.

The climate for dealing effectively with both concerns has improved dramatically within the last few years. Not only have development proponents learned that, in many cases, short-term wealth-enhancement projects that degrade the environment are ultimately counterproductive, but environmental groups have come to realize that poverty itself is a major threat to environmental protection. No longer are economic development and environmental protection seen as an "either-or" proposition. The focus has shifted toward the identification of policies or policy instruments that can promote the alleviation of poverty while protecting the environment.

In the last decade or so, the economic-incentive approach to environmental and natural resource regulation has become a significant component of environmental and natural resource policy. Instead of mandating prescribed actions, such as requiring the installation of a particular piece of pollution control equipment, this approach achieves environmental objectives by changing the economic incentives of those doing the polluting. Incentives can be changed by fees or charges, transferable permits, deposit-refund systems, or even liability law. When the incentives an individual agent faces are changed, that agent can use his or her typically superior information to select the best means of meeting his or her assigned responsibility. When it is in the interest of individuals to change to new forms of development, the transformation can be amazingly rapid.

Public policy and sustainable development must proceed in a mutually supportive relationship. The government must ensure that the market is sending the right signals to all participants so that the sustainable outcome is compatible with other business objectives. Economic-incentive approaches are a means of establishing that kind of compatibility. The experience with the various versions of this approach used in the United States, Europe, and Asia since the mid-1970s suggests that economic-incentive approaches in general are both feasible and effective.

How about global environmental problems? As the scale of economic activity has proceeded steadily upward, the scope of environmental problems triggered by that activity has transcended both geographic and generational boundaries. Whereas the nation-state used to be a sufficient form of political organization for resolving environmental problems, that may no longer be the case. Whereas each generation of humans used to have the luxury of being able to satisfy its own needs without worrying about the needs of those generations to come, that is no longer the case either. Solving problems such as poverty, global warming, ozone depletion, and the loss of biodiversity requires international cooperation.

Economic-incentive approaches could be helpful here as well. Emissions trading facilitates cost-sharing among participants while assuring cost-effective responses to the need for additional control. By separating the question of what control is undertaken from the question of who ultimately pays for it, the government widens the control possibilities significantly. Conferring property rights for biological populations on local communities provides an incentive for those communities to protect the populations. Strategies for reducing debt can diminish the pressure on forests and other natural resources that may be "cashed in" to pay off the debt.

The courts are beginning to use economic incentives as well; judicial remedies for environmental problems are beginning to take their place alongside regulatory remedies. Take, for example, the problem of cleaning up already closed toxic waste sites. Current U.S. law allows the government to sue all potentially responsible parties who contributed to the contaminated site (e.g., waste generators or disposal site operators). These suits accomplish a double purpose: (1) They assure that the financial responsibility for contaminated sites is borne by those who directly caused the problem, and (2) they encourage those who are currently using those sites to exercise great care, lest they be forced to bear a large financial burden in the event of an incident. The traditional remedy of going to the taxpayers would have resulted in less revenue raised, fewer sites restored, and less adequate incentives for users to exercise care.

Europe has tended to depend more on another type of economic incentive, the effluent or emission charge. This approach places a per unit fee on each unit of pollution discharged. Faced with the responsibility for paying for the damage caused by their pollution, firms recognize it as a controllable cost of doing business. This recognition triggers a search for possible ways to reduce the damage, including changing inputs, changing the production process, transforming the residuals to less harmful substances, and recycling by-products. The experience in the Netherlands, a country where the fees are higher than in most other countries, suggests that the effects can be dramatic.

Fees also raise revenue. Successful development, particularly sustainable development, requires a symbiotic partnership between the public and private sectors. To function as an equal partner, the public sector must be adequately funded. If it fails to raise adequate revenue, the public sector becomes a drag on the growth process, but if it raises revenue in ways that distort incentives, that, too, can act as a drag on development. Effluent or emission charges offer the realistic opportunity to raise revenue for the public sector without producing inefficient incentives. Whereas other types of taxation discourage growth by penalizing legitimate development incentives, emission or effluent charges provide incentives for sustainable development. Some work from the United States suggests that the drag on development avoided by substituting effluent or emission charges for more traditional revenue-raising devices such as capital gains, income, and sale taxes could be significant.

Incentives for forward-looking public action are as important as those for private action. The current national income accounting system provides an example of a perverse economic incentive. Though national income accounts were never intended to function as a device for measuring the welfare of a nation, in practice, that is how they are used. National income per capita is a common metric for evaluating how well off a nation's people are. Yet the current construction of those accounts sends the wrong signals.

Rather than recognizing the *Exxon Valdez* spill for what it was—namely, a decline in the value of the endowment of natural resources in the area—it is recorded as an increase in the national income. The spill boosted GDP! All the cleanup expenditures served to increase national income, but no account was taken of the consequent depreciation of the natural environment. Under the current system, the accounts make no distinction between growth that is occurring because a country is damaging its natural resource endowment, with a consequent irreversible decline in its value, and sustainable development, where the value of the endowment remains. Only when suitable corrections are made to these accounts will governments be judged by the appropriate standards.

The power of economic incentives is certainly not inevitably channeled toward the achievement of sustainable development. They can be misapplied, as well as appropriately applied. Tax subsidies to promote cattle ranching on the fragile soil in the Brazilian rain forest stimulated an unsustainable activity, which has done irreparable damage to an ecologically significant area. They must be used with care.

A Concluding Comment

Our society is currently evolving a complementary relationship among the economic system, the court system, and the legislative and executive branches of government that holds promise. We are not yet out of the woods, however. We the public must learn that part of the responsibility is ours. The government cannot solve all problems without our significant participation.

Not all behavior can be regulated. It costs too much to catch every offender. Our law enforcement system works because most people obey the law, whether anyone is watching or not. A high degree of voluntary compliance is essential if the system is to work smoothly.

The best resolution of the toxic substance problem, for example, is undoubtedly for all makers of potentially toxic substances to be genuinely concerned about the safety of their products and to bite the bullet whenever their research raises questions. The ultimate responsibility for developing an acceptable level of risk must rest on the integrity of those who make, use, transport, and dispose of the substances. The government can assist by penalizing and controlling those few who fail to exhibit this integrity, but it can never substitute for integrity on a large scale. We cannot and should not depend purely upon altruism to solve these problems, but we should not underestimate its importance either.

The notion that we are at the end of an era may well be true, but we are also at the beginning of a new one. What the future holds is not the decline of civilization, but is transformation. As the opening quote to this chapter suggests, the road may be strewn with obstacles and our social institutions may deal with those obstacles with less grace and less finesse than we might hope for, but we are unquestionably making progress.

Glossary

Acid Rain—The atmospheric deposition of acidic substances.

Acute Toxicity—The degree of harm caused to living organisms as a result of short-term exposure to a substance.

Aerobic—Water containing sufficient dissolved oxygen concentrations to sustain organisms requiring oxygen.

Age Structure Effect—Changes in the age distribution induced by the rate of population growth.

Alternative Fuels—Unconventional fuels such as ethanol and methanol.

Ambient Permit System—A type of transferable permit system in which permits are defined in terms of the right to affect the concentration at a receptor site by a given amount. This design can achieve a cost-effective allocation of control responsibility when the objective is to achieve a prespecified concentration objective at a specific number of receptor locations.

Ambient Standards—Legal ceilings placed on the concentration level of specific pollutants in the air, soil, or water.

Anaerobic—Water containing insufficient dissolved oxygen concentrations to sustain life.

Anthropocentric—Human-centered.

Aquaculture—The controlled raising and harvesting of fish. (Called "mariculture" when, as is the case with some salmon fisheries, the facilities are in the ocean.) Aquaculture can provide the opportunity to create a private property regime for affected fisheries.

Asset—An entity which has value and forms part of the wealth of the owner.

Average-Cost Pricing—When prices charged for resource use are based on average costs. (Sometimes used by regulatory agencies to assure that regulated firms make zero economic profits, but it is not normally efficient.)

Banking—Firms are allowed to store emissions reduction credits or allowances for subsequent use or sale.

Base-Load Plants—Electric generators that are functioning virtually all the time. (They generally have high fixed costs, but low variable costs.)

Benefit-Cost Analysis—An analysis of the gains and losses of an action which attempts to quantify both the benefits and costs in order to compare them.

Best Available Technology Economically Achievable—A more stringent effluent standard than best practicable control technology which has been defined by EPA as "the very best control and treatment measures that have been or are capable of being achieved."

Best Practicable Control Technology—An effluent standard considering the cost of the pollution control technology in relation to the benefits received from its use.

Biochemical Oxygen Demand—The measure of the oxygen demand placed on a stream by any particular volume of effluent.

Bubble Policy—Specific transferable permit program. Allows existing sources to use emission reduction credits to partially or completely satisfy State Implementation Plan emissions standards.

By-Catch—Untargeted fish which are unintentionally caught as part of the harvest of targeted species.

Carbon Tax—One proposed policy which would control climate modification by placing a per-unit emissions tax on all carbon emitting sources.

Carrying Capacity—The level of population a given habitat can sustain indefinitely.

Cartel—A collusive agreement among producers to restrict production and raise prices. In this case the group tends to act like a monopolist and to share the gains from collusive behavior.

Cash Crop—An agricultural commodity which can be directly sold for money (as opposed, for example, to a crop raised purely for consumption by the family).

Cash for Clunkers—Under this transferable permit program, emission reduction credits can be earned by removing high-polluting vehicles from service and recycling them. Usually owners of these vehicles are offered a cash payment to surrender their vehicles.

Certification Program—The testing of automobiles at the factory for conformity to federal emissions standards.

Choke Price—The maximum price anyone would be willing to pay for a unit of the resource. At higher prices, the demand for that resource would be zero.

Chronic Toxicity—The degree of harm caused to living organisms as a result of continued or prolonged exposure to a substance.

Clawson-Knetsch Method—One method for using travel costs to estimate the recreational value of a resource.

Closed System—No inputs enter the system, and no inputs leave the system.

Coase Theorem—A remarkable proposition, named after Nobel Laureate Ronald Coase, which suggests that in the absence of transactions costs an efficient allocation will result regardless of the property rule chosen by the court.

Cobweb Model—A theory in which long lags between planting decisions and harvest can influence farmer's production decisions in such a way as to intensify or dampen price fluctuations.

Common-Pool Resource—A resource which is characterized by nonexclusivity and divisibility.

Common-Property Regimes—A property rights system in which resources are managed collectively by a group.

Comparative Advantage—A comparative advantage prevails for products which have the lowest opportunity cost of production.

Competitive Equilibrium—The resource allocation at which supply and demand are equal when all agents are price takers.

Composite Asset—An asset made up of many interrelated parts.

Composition of Demand Effect—Shifts in demand brought about by changes in the relative cost of inputs. (For example, rising costs of ores coupled with stable prices for recycled inputs could make the products of firms relying more heavily on recycled inputs relatively less expensive and hence more attractive to consumers.)

Congestion Externalities—Higher costs resulting from an attempt to use resources at a higher-than-optimal capacity.

Congestion Pricing—Charging higher tolls during peak hours to discourage vehicle traffic (and the resulting air pollution) and encourage public transit ridership.

Constant Dollar—Eliminating increases in output measures due purely to inflation.

Consumer Surplus—The value of a good or service to consumers above the price they have to pay for it. Calculated as the area under the demand curve which lies above the price.

Consumption—The amount of goods and services consumed by households.

Contingent Ranking—A valuation technique which asks respondents to rank alternative situations involving different levels of environmental amenity (risk). These rankings can then be used to establish tradeoffs between more of the environmental amenity (risk) and less (more) of other goods which can be expressed in monetary terms.

Contingent Valuation—A survey method used to ascertain willingness to pay for services or environmental amenities.

Conventional Pollutants—Relatively common substances found in most parts of the country, and presumed to be dangerous only in high concentrations.

Cost-Benefit Ratio Criterion—No activity where the present value of net benefits is less than zero should be undertaken.

Criteria Pollutants—Conventional air pollutants with ambient standards set by the Environmental Protection Agency (includes sulfur oxides, particulate matter, carbon monoxide, ozone, nitrogen dioxide, and lead).

Current Reserves—Known resources that can profitably be extracted at current prices.

Dampened Oscillation—In the absence of further supply shocks, the amplitude of price and quantity fluctuations decreases to the point of equilibrium.

Debt-Nature Swap—The purchase and cancellation of developing country debt in exchange for environmentally related action on the part of the debtor nation.

Degradable—Pollutants which degrade, or break into component parts, within water.

Demand Curve—A function that relates the quantity of a commodity or service consumers wish to purchase to the price of that commodity.

Descriptive Economics—The branch of economics that is concerned with describing alternative resource allocations without forming a judgment as to their desirability. Concerned with "what is."

Differentiated Regulation—Imposing more stringent regulations on one class of sources (such as new vehicles) than on others (such as used vehicles).

Discount Rate—The rate used to convert a stream of benefits and/or costs into its present value.

Dissolved Oxygen—Oxygen which naturally occurs in water and is usable by living organisms.

Divisible Consumption—One person's consumption of a good diminishes the amount available for others. (For example, if I use some timber to build my house, you receive no benefits from the timber.)

Durability Obsolescence—A depreciation in the value of a current product when its usefulness declines due to wear and tear.

Dynamic Efficiency—The chief normative economic criterion for choosing among various allocations occurring at different points in time. An allocation satisfies the dynamic efficiency criterion if it maximizes the present value of net benefits that could be received from all possible ways of allocating those resources over time.

Dynamic Efficient Sustained Yield—The sustained yield that produces the highest present value of net benefits.

Economies of Scale—The percentage increase in output exceeds the percentage increase in all inputs. Equivalently, average cost falls as output expands.

Efficient Level of Durability—The level of durability which maximizes the present value of net benefits society receives from the product.

Efficient Pricing—A system of prices which supports an efficient allocation of resources. Generally efficient pricing is achieved when prices are equal to total marginal cost.

Elasticity of Substitution—A measure of the degree to which two factor inputs complement or substitute for one another in production.

Emission Charge—A charge levied on emitters for each unit of a pollutant emitted into the air or water.

Emission Permit System—A type of transferable permit system in which the permits are defined in terms of the right to emit a stipulated amount of emissions. This design can be used to achieve a cost-effective allocation of control responsibility for uniformly mixed pollutants.

Emission Standard—A legal limit placed on the amount of a pollutant an individual source may emit.

Emissions Reduction Credit—Part of a transferable permits system. Any source reducing emissions beyond required levels can receive a credit for excess reductions. These can be banked for future use or sold to other sources.

Enforceability—Property rights should be secure from involuntary seizure or encroachment from others.

Entropy—Amount of energy not available for work.

Eutrophic—A body of water containing an excess of nutrients.

Exclusivity—All benefits and costs accrued as a result of owning and using the resources should accrue to the owner, and only the owner, either directly or indirectly by sale to others.

Expected Present Value of Net Benefits—The sum over possible outcomes of the present value of net benefits for a policy, where each outcome is weighted by its probability of occurrence.

Expected Value—In situations where the value of a resource depends on which of several outcomes might prevail, the expected value of a resource is the sum over all outcomes of the likelihood of each outcome multiplied by the value which would prevail in that outcome.

External Diseconomy—The affected party is damaged by an externality. (For example, my well is polluted by chemicals from a factory next door.)

External Economy—The affected party is benefited by an externality. (For example, my neighbor decides not to develop a wetland that serves as a recharge area for my water supply.)

Externality—The welfare of some agent, either a firm or household, depends on the activities of some other agent.

Fashion Obsolescence—A depreciation in the value of current products when consumers prefer new products for reason of taste.

Feedback Loop—A closed path that connects an action to its effect on the surrounding conditions which, in turn, can influence further action.

Female Availability Effect—A reduction (increase) in the labor force participation of women due to an increase (reduction) in the rate of population growth.

Fixed Cost—Production costs which do not vary with output.

Free Rider Effect—When goods exhibit both the consumptive indivisibility and nonexcludability properties, consumers may enjoy the benefits of goods purchased by others without paying anything themselves. (For example, countries that decide not to take any steps to control global warming can "free ride" on the steps taken by others.)

Functional Obsolescence—A depreciation in the value of a current product caused by the arrival of a new product that can perform the function in a superior manner.

Fund Pollutants—Pollutants for which the environment has some absorptive capacity; if the rate of emission exceeds this capacity, then fund pollutants accumulate.

Gini Coefficient—One measure of the degree of inequality in income or owned assets such as land or financial wealth. Values can range from 0.0 (perfect equality—every household is the same) to 1.0 (perfect inequality—one household owns everything).

Global Environmental Facility—An international organization, loosely connected to the World Bank, which provides loans and grants to developing countries to facilitate projects which contribute to solving such global problems as protecting the oceans, preserving biodiversity, protecting the ozone layer and controlling climate modification. The fund uses the "marginal external cost" rule to allocate funds.

Global Pollutant—A pollutant which travels to the upper atmosphere and causes damage. (Examples include ozone-depleting and greenhouse gases.)

Government Failure—An inefficiency produced by some government action.

Greenhouse Gases—Global pollutants which contribute to climate modification by absorbing the long-wave (infrared) radiation, thereby trapping heat which would otherwise radiate into space. (Includes carbon dioxide, methane, and chlorofluorocarbons, among others.)

Groundwater—Subsurface water that occurs beneath a water table in soils, rocks, or in fully saturated geological formations.

Groundwater Contamination—Pollution that leaches into a water-saturated region.

Health Threshold—A standard to be defined with a margin of safety sufficiently high that no adverse health effects would be suffered by any member of the population as long as the air quality was at least the minimum standard level.

Hedonic Property Studies—A valuation technique that allows the value of an environmental amenity (risk) to be determined from differences in the values of property exposed to different levels of the amenity (risk).

Hedonic Wage Studies—A valuation technique which allows the value of an environmental amenity (risk) to be determined from differences in the values of wages paid to workers exposed to different levels of the amenity (risk).

High-Grading—Discarding low-value fish in favor of high-value fish in order to increase the income derived from a harvest quota.

Horizontal Equity—Treating people with equal incomes equally.

Hypothetical Bias—Ill-considered responses that may arise in surveys based on contrived rather than actual situations or choices.

Impact Analysis—An analysis that attempts to make explicit, to the extent possible, the consequences of proposed actions. May mix quantitative with qualitative information and monetized with nonmonetized information.

Income Elasticity—Measures the percentage change in demand for commodities or services in response to a 1 percent change in income.

Individual Transferable Quotas—A means of protecting a fishery and the income derived from it by limiting the number of fish caught. Individual fisherman are allocated quotas that entitle them to portions of the authorized total allowable catch. These quotas can be transferred to other fisherman or used to legalize their harvest.

Indivisible Consumption—One person's consumption of a good does not diminish the amount available for others. (For example, the benefits I receive from controlling greenhouse gases do not diminish the benefits you receive.)

Information Bias—Arises when contingent valuation survey respondents are forced to value attributes with which they have little or no experience.

Information Worker—A person whose income originates primarily in the manipulation of symbols or information.

Intangible Benefits—Benefits that cannot be easily assigned a monetary value.

Interactive Resources—The size of the resource stock is determined jointly by biological considerations and actions taken by humans.

Joint and Several Liability—A common law doctrine used to assign the cost of cleaning up Superfund sites that states that any subset of parties responsible for the contamination can be assessed the entire cost regardless of the magnitude of their individual contribution.

Joint Implementation—A process in the Climate Change Convention by which nations can work together to reduce the emission of greenhouse gases cost-effectively. Lays the groundwork for a possible tradable carbon permits system.

Latency—The period between exposure to a toxic substance and the detection of harm caused by that substance.

Law of Comparative Advantage—A country or region should specialize in the production of those commodities for which it has a comparative advantage.

Law of Diminishing Marginal Productivity—In the presence of a fixed factor, successively larger additions of variable factors will eventually lead to a decline in the marginal productivity of the variable factors.

Law of Diminishing Returns—The relationship between inputs and outputs when some inputs are increased and others are fixed, eventually leading to the decreased productivity of the variable inputs.

Lead Phaseout Program—A transferable permit program designed to lower the costs of phasing out lead in gasoline as well as to eliminate lead earlier than otherwise would have been possible. It allocated transferable rights to use lead in refining gasoline to refiners. The number of rights declined over time until at the end of the program they expired.

Liability Rules—Rules that award monetary compensation from an injurer to an injured party after damage has occurred. Valuation must be accomplished by the courts.

Low Emission Vehicles—A class of vehicles that can satisfy much more stringent emissions standards than currently imposed on conventional vehicles.

Marginal Cost of Exploration—The marginal cost of finding additional units of the resource.

Marginal Cost Pricing—Basing the prices charged for resource use upon marginal costs. (This pricing scheme is generally consistent with efficiency.)

Marginal External Cost Rule—Used by the Global Environmental Facility to disperse funds. According to this rule the facility will fund additional expenses associated with investments that contribute to the global environmental (produce positive global net benefits), but cannot be justified domestically (since the domestic marginal costs exceed domestic marginal benefits). Countries are expected to pick up that portion of the expenses that can be justified domestically (where the domestic marginal benefits exceed domestic marginal costs).

Marginal Extraction Cost—The cost of mining an additional unit of resource.

Marginal Opportunity Cost—The additional cost of providing the last unit of good as measured by what is given up.

Marginal User Cost—The user cost of the last unit of the resource used.

Marginal Willingness to Pay—The amount of money an individual is willing to pay for the last unit of a good or service.

Market Economy—An economic system in which resource allocation decisions are guided by prices which result from the voluntary production and purchasing decisions by private consumers and producers.

Market Failure—An inefficient allocation produced by a market economy.

Maximum Net Present Value Criterion—Resources should be allocated to those uses which maximize the value of the net benefits received from all possible uses of those resources.

Maximum Sustainable Yield—The maximum harvest that could be sustained forever.

Mean Annual Increment—The cumulative volume of a forest stand at the end of each decade divided by the number of years the stand has been in existence.

Microeconomic Theory of Fertility—A theory that attempts to attribute differences in fertility to the economic environment within which childbearing decisions are made.

Mineralogical Threshold—A sharp discontinuity in the manner in which minerals are extracted; the existence of this threshold implies a sharp discontinuity in the marginal extraction cost.

Minimum Viable Population—The level of population below which regeneration is negative, leading ultimately to extinction.

Model—Formal or informal frameworks for analysis that highlight some areas of the problem in order better to understand complex relationships.

Monopoly—A situation in which the seller side of the market is dominated by a single producer.

Myopia—Near-sightedness; excessive concern for the present.

Natural Equilibrium—Stock levels which persist in the absence of outside influences.

Negative Feedback Loop—A closed path of action and reaction that is self-limiting rather than self-reinforcing.

Negligence—A doctrine in tort law suggesting that the party responsible for pollution contamination owes a duty to the affected party to exercise due care. Failure to fulfill that duty can lead to a requirement for the injurer to pay compensation to the victim.

Net Benefit—The excess of benefits over costs resulting from some allocation.

Netting—A transferable permit program for air pollution control in which firms undergoing modifications or expansion may avoid New Source Review requirements if the resulting increase in emissions falls under a prespecified threshold.

New Scrap—Waste composed of the residual materials generated during production.

New Source Bias—A bias in investment choices related to the decision whether to build a new source versus keeping an old source running longer. The bias is against building a new source because new sources of pollution face more stringent control requirements than existing sources, resulting in higher compliance costs.

New Source Review Process—All large new or expanding sources are subject to preconstruction review and permitting. These firms are typically subjected to more stringent requirements. The specific requirements depend on whether the source is attempting to locate in an attainment or nonattainment area.

New Source Performance Standard—A legally specified amount of emission control required of new market entrants regardless of production location. States can require more, but not less, than this degree of control.

Nonattainment Region—A region in which the pollution concentrations exceed the ambient standards.

Noncompliance Penalty—A charge used to reduce the profitability of noncompliance with pollution control requirements. It is designed to eliminate all the economic advantage gained from noncompliance.

Nonexcludability—No individual or group can be excluded from enjoying the benefits a resource may confer, whether they contribute to its provision or not.

Nonpoint Sources—Diffuse sources such as runoff from agricultural or developed land.

Nonrenewable Resources—Resources that cannot be reproduced during a human time scale, so their supply is finite and limited.

Nonuniformly Mixed Pollutants—For these pollutants, the damage they cause is a function not only of the amount of emissions, but also the location of the emissions sources. (Examples include particulates and lead.)

Nonuse (Passive Use) Values—Resource values that arise from motivations other than personal use.

Normative Economics—The branch of economics that is concerned with evaluating the desirability of alternative resource allocations. It is concerned with "what ought to be."

Occupational Hazards—Risks undertaken during the course of a job.

Offset Policy—One specific transferable permit program. New emitters attempting to enter a nonattainment area must secure sufficient emissions reduction credits from existing sources to cover 120 percent of their emissions.

Old Scrap—Waste recovered from products used by consumers.

Open-Access Resources—Resources for which access is unrestricted.

Open System—A system that imports and exports matter or energy.

Opportunity Cost—The net benefit foregone because the resource providing the service can no longer be used in its next most beneficial use.

Optimal—Best or most favorable option.

Optimization Procedure—A systematic method for finding the optimal means of accomplishing an objective.

Option Value—The value people place on having the option to use a resource in the future.

Output Measure—A measure currently used in national income accounting to indicate how many goods and services have been produced.

Overallocation—More than the optimal level of a resource is dedicated to a given use or time period.

Overshoot and Collapse—Behavior forecasted by the *Beyond the Limits* model which involves exceeding the natural carrying capacity of the environment, with the consequence that society collapses.

Oxygen Sag—A point of low dissolved oxygen concentration generally located around effluent injection points.

Ozone-Depleting Gases—Global pollutants that destroy the stratospheric ozone layer. (Includes chlorofluorocarbons and halons, among others.)

Pareto Optimality—An allocation such that no reallocation of resources could benefit any person without lowering the net benefits for at least one other person. (Named after economist Vilfredo Pareto.)

Peaking Units—Those electricity producing facilities used only during peak periods. (They generally have low fixed costs, but high variable costs.)

Peak-Load Pricing—Charging resource users during the peak period the higher cost of supplying resources during that period. The surcharge during the peak period is designed to cover the cost of expansion since the need to expand is triggered by increased demands during the peak period.

Peak Periods—Times of especially high resource demand. (For example, the demand for electricity during the hottest part of the summer when air conditioning is in heavy use.)

Pecuniary Externalities—External effects that are transmitted through higher prices. (For example, the value of my land increases because surrounding employers expand their operations, thereby creating a scarcity of housing in the immediate area.) Unlike most externalities pecuniary externalities do not generally result in inefficient allocations.

Persistent Pollutants—Inorganic synthetic pollutants with complex molecular structures that are not effectively broken down in water.

Planned Obsolescence—Attempts by producers to increase production by selling products with a shorter life span.

Planning Horizon—The time period over which the benefits and costs are considered in time-related decisions. For a specific investment such as a power plant, for example, the planning horizon might correspond to the useful life of the project. For forestry, it could either correspond to the age of the stand of trees when harvested (the finite planning horizon) or it could extend forever (the infinite planning horizon). In addition to considering the age at which to harvest the stock (the focus of the finite planning horizon model) the infinite horizon model must also take into account a perpetual sequence of forestry decisions (such as restocking, harvesting, preservation, and so on).

Point Sources—Sources of pollution that discharge effluent through a readily identifiable emission point such as an outfall or discharge pipe. (Most industrial and municipal sources are point sources.)

Pollution Absorptive Capacity—The ability of the environment to absorb pollutants without incurring damage.

Pollution Haven Hypothesis—Stricter environmental regulations in one country either encourage domestic production facilities to locate in countries with less stringent regulations or encourage increased imports from those countries.

Porter Hypothesis—Firms facing stringent environmental regulations derive a competitive advantage because they are forced to innovate. Innovation typically increases productivity.

Positive Feedback Loop—A closed path of action and reaction that is self-reinforcing rather than self-limiting.

Positive Net Present Value Criterion—This criterion requires the present value of benefits to be larger than the present value of costs for any project that is to be undertaken.

Potential Reserves—The amount of resource reserves potentially available at different price levels.

Present Value—The current discounted value of a stream of benefits and/or costs over time.

Price Controls—The establishment of maximum or minimum prices by the government.

Primary Effects—The immediate, measurable effects of an action.

Primary Standard—An ambient air pollution standard designed to protect human health.

Prior Appropriation Doctrine—Entitlements for water are allocated to the agent who diverts and first puts water to a beneficial use.

Private Marginal Cost—The cost of producing an additional unit of the resource that is born by the producer.

Producer Surplus—The value of a good or service to producers above the cost to them of producing it. Calculated as the area below the price line that is above marginal cost.

Production Function—A mathematically expressed relationship between inputs and outputs.

Property Rights—A bundle of entitlements defining the owner's rights, privileges, and limitations for use of the resource.

Property Rules—Legal rules that govern the initial allocation of entitlements. Valuation of the entitlements is left to the market.

Proportional Distribution—The net benefits from a policy received by various income groups are proportional to income.

Public Good—A resource characterized by nonexclusivity and indivisibility.

Real Consumption Per Capita—Constant-dollar consumption divided by population.

Real-Resource Costs—As opposed to transfer costs, these are costs born by both private parties and society as a whole because they involve the loss of net benefits, not merely their transfer.

Regional Pollutants—Pollutants that can cause damage some distance from the emission source. (Examples include the precursors for acid rain and tropospheric ozone.)

Regressive Distribution—Net benefits from a policy received by various income groups represent a larger portion of the income of the rich than of the poor.

Renewable Resources—Resources that can be naturally regenerated over time.

Rent-Seeking—The use of resources in lobbying and other activities directed at securing increased profits through protective regulation or legislation.

Replacement Rate—The level of total fertility that is compatible with a stationary population.

Res Nullius Regime—A property rights system in which no one owns or exercises control over resources. Resources covered by this regime can usually be exploited on a first-come, first-served basis.

Resource Endowment—The natural occurrence of resources in the earth's crust and atmosphere.

Retirement Effect—The increase (decrease) of the percentage of the population composed of individuals over 65 years of age induced by a low (high) population growth rate.

Riparian Rights—Allocates the right to use water to the owner of the land adjacent to the water, as long as no adverse effects are imposed on other rights holders.

Risk-Free Cost of Capital—Rate of return earned on an investment when the risk of earning more or less than expected returns is zero.

Risk Neutrality—An agent who has no preference between options that produce the same expected value.

Risk Premium—Additional rate of return required to compensate the owners of the capital when the expected and actual returns may differ. It represents compensation for a willingness to undertake some risk.

Scale Effects—How the size of an operation affects average costs.

Scarcity Rent—Producer's surplus that persists in long-run equilibrium due to fixed supply or increasing costs.

Secondary Effects—Further consequences that follow primary effects.

Secondary Standard—An ambient standard designed to protect those aspects of human welfare other than health.

Severance Tax—A tax levied on minerals as they are extracted.

Socialist Economy—A centrally planned economy where the means of production are controlled by the government.

Social Marginal Cost—The cost of producing an additional unit of the resource that is borne by society at large. Generally includes private marginal costs plus external marginal costs.

Stable Equilibrium—A level of stock that will be restored following temporary shocks.

Starting Point Bias—Arises when a contingent valuation survey respondent is asked to check off his or her answer from a predetermined range of possibilities and the answers depend on the range specified by the survey instrument.

Static Efficiency—The chief normative economic criterion for choosing among various allocations when time is not an important consideration. An allocation satisfies the static efficiency criterion if it maximizes the net benefits from all possible uses of the resource.

Static Efficient Sustained Yield—The sustained catch level in a fishery that produces the largest annual recurring net benefit.

Stationary Population—A population in which age- and sex-specific fertility rates yield a birthrate that is constant and equal to the death rate, so the population growth rate is zero.

Stationary Source—An immobile pollution source. (Industrial sources, for example, as opposed to automobiles.)

Statistically Significant—Observed differences are unlikely to result from pure chance.

Steady-State Economy—Characterized by constant stocks of people and physical wealth maintained at some chosen, desirable level by a low rate of throughput.

Stock Pollutants—Pollutants that accumulate in the environment because the environment has little or no absorptive capacity for them.

Strategic Bias—A respondent provides a biased answer to a contingent valuation survey in order to influence a particular outcome.

Stratosphere—The atmosphere that lies above the troposphere. It extends to about 31 miles above the earth's surface.

Strict Liability—A tort law doctrine requiring that the party responsible for pollution contamination compensate victims for damage caused. Differs from negligence in that the victim does not have to prove negligence by the injurer.

Strong Global Scarcity Hypothesis—According to this hypothesis, scarcity becomes sufficiently deep that the output of food is not able to keep pace with population growth; per capita food production declines.

Suboptimal Allocation—An allocation that could be rearranged so that one or more people could be made better off while no one was made worse off. Also called an inefficient allocation.

Subsidies—Payments from the government that make the cost to the buyer lower than the marginal cost of production. Various types of subsidies exist, such as direct payments and tax breaks.

Substitution—Replacing one resource with another. May occur, for example, when the original resource is no longer cost-effective or is diminishing in quantity or quality.

Sulfur Allowance Auction—Run by the Chicago Board of Trade, this annual auction requires utilities to place a proportion of these allowances up for sale each year. The proceeds are returned to the utilities. (This is called a "zero revenue auction" since the government derives no revenue from it.) It assures

the continual availability of permits and provides good public information on prices.

Sulfur Allowance Program—A transferable permit program targeted at electric utilities that is designed to reduce sulfur emissions from 1980 levels by 10 million tons. Involves an auction and an emissions cap.

Surface Pollutants—Pollutants that can cause damage mainly on the earth's surface or lower atmosphere. (Examples include industrial particulates and lead.)

Surface Water—The fresh water in rivers, lakes, and reservoirs that collects and flows on the earth's surface.

Sustainability Criterion—A criterion for judging the fairness of allocations of resources among generations. Generally requires that resource use by any generation should not exceed a level that would prevent future generations from achieving a level of well-being at least as great.

Sustainable Yield—Harvest levels that can be maintained indefinitely; achieved by setting the annual harvest equal to the annual net growth of the population.

Synergistic—The dose-response relationship is dependent upon several interrelated factors.

System Dynamics—A computer technique developed by Professor Jay Foster and colleagues at MIT, which depicts likely future outcomes of the world economy; this technique specifically incorporates positive and negative feedback loops.

Tangible Benefits—Benefits that can reasonably be assigned a monetary value.

Theory of Demographic Transition—A theory that shows how population growth is related to the stages of industrial development.

Thermal Pollution—Pollution caused by the injection of heat into a watercourse.

Third Parties—Victims who have no contractual relationship to a pollution source. (They are neither consumers of the product produced by the source nor employed by the source.)

Throughput—Flow of resources and energy.

Total Cost—The sum of fixed and variable costs.

Total Fertility Rate—The number of live births an average woman has in her lifetime if, at each year of age, she experiences the average birthrate occurring in the general population of similarly aged women.

Toxicity—The degree of harm caused to living organisms as a result of exposure to the substance.

Tradable Carbon Permits—A proposed transferable permits system designed to control climate modification by setting a limit on carbon emissions and allocating transferable quotas to nations. Quotas would be transferable. All nations would have to stay within their quota (allocated plus acquired.)

Transactions Costs—Costs incurred in attempting to complete transactions. (For example, in buying a home, these might include payments to the broker for arranging the sale, to the bank for one-time special fees, and to the government for the required forms. The value of the time expended in negotiating would also be a transactions cost.)

Transferability—Property rights can be exchanged among owners on a voluntary basis.

Transferable Emission Permit—A pollution control policy requiring each emitter of a pollutant to possess permits for the amount of pollution it releases. The total number of permits (and, hence, the total amount of emissions) is typically limited. Permits are transferable and may be bought or sold.

Transfer Coefficient—A coefficient used in simulating pollutant flows. It relates the degree to which pollution concentrations at a specific receptor site are increased by a one-unit increase in emissions from a specific source.

Transfer Cost—A cost to a private party that is not a cost to society as a whole, because it involves a transfer of net benefits from one component of society to another.

Troposphere—The atmosphere which is closest to the earth. Its depth ranges from about 10 miles over the equator to about 5 miles over the poles.

Underallocation—Less-than-optimal levels of a resource are dedicated to a given use or time period.

Uniform Emission Charge—A charge on effluent that applies the same per-unit rate to all sources regardless of their size or location.

Uniformly Mixed Pollutants—For these pollutants, the damage done to the environment depends on the amount of emissions that enters the atmosphere. The location of emissions is not a matter of policy concern. (Examples include ozone-depleting gases and greenhouse gases.)

Uniform Treatment—A strategy to reduce effluent levels by a specified percentage at each emissions level.

User Cost—Opportunity cost created by scarcity. It represents the value of an opportunity foregone when the resource can no longer be used in its next best use. (For example, for a unit of a depletable resource used now, the user cost is the net benefits that would have been received by saving it and using it during the next time period.)

Usufruct Right—Holders of this right may use a resource (normally subject to restrictions), but do not have full ownership rights.

Variable Cost—Production costs which vary with output.

Vertical Equity—Treating people with different incomes differently. Generally interpreted as treating the poor more favorably.

Weak Global Scarcity Hypothesis—According to this hypothesis, production is able to keep pace with population growth, but the supply curve is sufficiently steeply sloped that food prices increase faster than other prices in general; the relative price of food increases over time, and the problem is affordability rather than physical availability.

Welfare Measure—A measure of development that increases or decreases in relation to how well off society is.

Youth Effect—The increase (decrease) of the percentage of the population composed of individuals under 15 years of age induced by a high (low) population growth rate.

Zero-Discharge—No emissions of the targeted pollutant are allowed.

Zero Emissions Vehicle—Automobiles that directly emit no air pollutants. (Examples include vehicles powered by solar energy and fuel cells. Electric automobiles are also normally included despite the fact that producing the electricity typically results in pollution.)

Zoned Effluent Charge—A charge on effluent that applies different per-unit rates to sources depending on their location. Generally sources closer to, and upstream from, locations with more serious pollution problems face higher rates.

Index

A

Absorptive capacity, 244
Acacia alba, 444
Accumulating pollutants, 341
Acidification, in Adirondack
    Mountains, 290
Acid rain. *See also* Air pollution
    dilution approach to, 290-291
    explanation of, 288
    national study of, 289
    policy in past to control,
        289-290
    strategies to control, 291-296
Acre-foot, 164-165
Adaptation strategies, 301
Adirondack Mountains (New York
    State), 290
Africa. *See also specific countries*
    lead emissions in, 328
    population density and, 108
    population growth in, 108
Age structure effect, 103
Agricultural policies
    environmental costs of, 182-
        184
    feeding the poor and, 190-192
    poverty and, 429-430
    role of, 185
    water pollution and, 353
Agriculture
    allocation of land for, 181-182
    energy costs and, 182
    environmental costs and,
        182-184
    increases in net benefits
        from, 204
    price trends in, 180
    productivity of, 180, 186
    sustainable, 183-185, 190, 444
    technological progress in, 181
    water pollution from, 338
Air pollution. *See also* Acid rain
    coal and, 147
    hazardous, 280-283
    stationary sources of, 263

Air pollution control
    command-and-control approach
        and, 264-273
    emission charges and, 279-280
    emissions fees and, 282-284
    emissions trading program and,
        273-279
    empirical studies of, 272
    legislation and, 263-264
    smog trading and, 276
Air Pollution Control Act of
    1955, 263
Air quality
    command-and-control approach
        and, 273
    vehicle emissions controls and,
        327-328
Air quality standards, 53
Alkaline carbonate sludge, 446
Allied Chemical Corporation,
    392, 446
Allocations. *See also* Market
    allocations; Water allocation
    efficient intertemporal,
        128-131
    market, 131-134
    Pareto optimal, 26
    suboptimal, 27
    sustainable, 94 (*See also*
        Efficient allocation;
        Sustainability; Sustainable
        development)
Alternative fuels/vehicles
    cost effectiveness and, 327
    regulations for use of, 318-319
Aluminum recycling, 367, 370
Amazonia, 207
Ambient air quality standards
    dilution to meet, 265-266
    EPA and, 265-266, 320-321
    explanation of, 264-265
    level of, 268-269
Ambient sampling, 341
Ambient water quality standards,
    347-348

American Cyanamid, 389
American Lung Association, 295
Amoco Cadiz oil spill, 356
Amundsen, E. S., 228
Aquaculture, 228-230
Aquifers
    as common-property resource,
        165, 166
    explanation of, 159
Arizona Public Service Company, 295
Arthur D. Little, 392
Asheim, Geir B., 439
Asia. *See also specific countries*
    carbon monoxide emissions
        in, 328
    lead emissions in, 328
    mobile-pollution control in,
        329-330
    poverty rate in, 427
Associated enforcement
    program, 317
Associated gas, 138
Assurance bonds, 405, 406
Atkinson, S. E., 271-272
Atlantic Richfield Company, 445,
    446
Australia, 29
Austria
    agricultural chemical use in,
        183-184
    approaches to vehicle emissions
        in, 319
Automobiles
    diesel, 312-313
    emission controls and, 312
    increased durability of, 378
Average costs, 165
Averting expenditures, 39, 40

B

Bangladesh, 116-118
Banking programs, 276
Barnett, Harold, 180
Basel Convention on the Control of
    Transboundary Movements of

Hazardous Wastes and Their Disposal, 397
Belize, 216
Bell, Daniel, 419
Benefit-cost analysis
  benefit estimation methods and, 44-45, 48-51
  benefits and drawbacks of, 50-51, 54
  cost estimation methods and, 45-46
  discount rate and, 48, 49
  evaluation of specific actions and, 18-25
  global warming and, 302, 306
  optimal approaches and, 25-27
  pollution control and, 27-29
  of population control, 109
  preservation vs. development and, 29
  treatment of risk and, 46-48
Benefit estimation
  approaches to, 48-51
  issues related to, 44-45
Benefits
  net, 23
  techniques to value, 32-51
  total, 21-22
Benzene, 283
Best available control technology (BACT), 267
Best available technology economically achievable (BAT) requirement, 43, 344, 345, 348, 349
Best practicable control technology currently available (BPT), 343, 348, 351
Beyond the Limits model
  demand for food and, 176
  explanation of, 3, 7
  exponential reserve index and, 125
  flaws in, 9
  treatment of resources in, 11, 139
  vision of future in, 122, 464
Bhopal explosion, 383
Bias, contingent valuation methods and, 36
Bible, 76
Big Thompson Project, 164

Biochemical oxygen demand (BOD), 340
Biodiversity. *See also* Deforestation; Forestry; Forests
  deforestation as threat to, 199, 207
  explanation of, 69-70, 72
  trust funds for preservation of, 216
Biological decision rule, 201
Biomass, 152
Birthrates
  in China, 116
  in United States, 100, 101
  world trends in, 99-100
Bison harvesting, 68, 69
Bjorndal, T., 228
Bolivia, debt-nature swap and, 213
Boston Air-Quality Control Region, 325
Boulding, Kenneth, 458
Brazil
  deforestation in, 205-206
  extractive reserves in, 213
  population density and, 108
  sustainable development in, 446
Bribery, 76-77
Brominated flame retardants (BFRs), 406
Brookshire, David S., 302
Brown, Jerry, 167
Brundtland, Gro Harlem, 434
Bubble policy, 274-275, 404
Bureau of Economic Analysis, 422
Bush, George, 141
Bus transportation, 330

C

Cale, William G., Jr., 213-214
California
  hazardous substance exposure and, 390-391
  organic produce in, 184
  Regional Clean Air Incentives Market, 276
  vehicle emission controls in, 316, 318, 319, 323, 330, 447
  water conservation in, 167
California Air Resources Board (CARB), 319
Canada, acid rain and, 288

Cancer
  saccharin and, 403
  toxic substance exposure and, 384
Capital
  constant total, 92
  economic growth and, 412-414, 441
  energy and, 416
  natural, 92, 422
  risk-free cost of, 74
  social opportunity cost of, 24f, 48
Carbon dioxide emissions, 299, 301
Carbon monoxide emissions
  ambient air quality standards for, 265
  CAC approach and, 273
  decline in, 328
  from mobile sources, 312
  national standards for, 316
Carbon tax, 303
Carrying capacity, 221
Carson, R. T., 357-358
Cartels
  compatibility of members in, 144-146
  explanation of, 73
  oil, 142-146
Carter, Jimmy, 49, 138
Cash for clunkers, 331
Cell fusion, 181
Central Arizona Project, 159
Centrally planned economies, 60, 61
Central Valley Project Improvement Act of 1992, 167-168
Certificate program, vehicle emissions standards, 316-317
Cesium-137, 148
Chekhov, Anton, 363
Chernobyl nuclear accident, 147
Chevron Corporation, 168
Chicago, air quality standards and, 53
Chicago Board of Trade, 295
Childbearing
  external costs and decisions regarding, 110
  as inalienable right, 112
Children, expenditures to raise, 107, 114-117

Chile
population growth in, 110
sustainable agriculture in, 190
China
environmental taxation in, 249
population control in, 116
Chlorofluorocarbons (CFCs), 297
Chronic toxicity, 386
Citizen suits, 346, 356-357
Civil law. *See also* Negligence;
Strict liability
criminal vs., 393-394
explanation of, 393
statutory remedies and, 394, 396
Civil Rights Act of 1964, 389
Clean Air Act
benefits and costs of, 28, 268
compliance with, 277
emissions fees and, 282
EPA standards and, 269
hazardous pollutants and, 280
lead in gasoline and, 317-318
purpose of, 263
regional pollution and, 291
stationary source control
and, 268
vehicle emissions standards
and, 323
warranty provisions in, 317
Clean Air Act Amendments of 1965,
emissions standards in, 316
Clean Air Act Amendments of 1970
emissions standards in, 316,
320, 324
purpose of, 264
vehicle emission control
systems tampering and, 317
Clean Air Act Amendments
of 1977
deadline extensions in, 322
nonattainment areas and, 318
primary ambient standards and,
266, 267
vehicle emission control
tampering and, 317
Clean Air Act Amendments of 1990
alternative fuels and, 318
benefit-cost analysis and, 27-29
sulfur allowance program
and, 293
Clean Water Act
citizen suits and, 357

ocean discharges and, 346
oil discharge and, 345
provisions of, 343
waste treatment plants and, 344
Clean Water Act Amendments
of 1977
BAT standards and, 348, 349
municipal waste treatment
and, 352
provisions of, 344
Clean Water Act of 1987, 344
Climate change, 441
Climate engineering, 301
Closed system, 17
The Closing Circle (Commoner), 20
Coal
air pollution and, 147
availability of, 146
as depletable resource, 126
Coale, Ansley J., 104
*The Coal Question: An Inquiry
Concerning the Progress of the
Nation and the Probable
Exhaustion of our Coal Miles*
(Jevon), 4
Coase, Ronald, 77-78
Cobweb model, 193
Cogeneration, 143
Colombia, 190-191
Columbus, Christopher, 4
Combined approach, 45-46
Command-and-control (CAC) policy
cost-effectiveness of, 270-273
efficiency of, 267-270, 279
emission reduction and,
291-293
explanation of, 264-267
Commoner, Barry, 20
Common law
explanation of, 391
joint and several liability
doctrine and, 400-401
judicial-legislative
complementarity and,
397-399
limitations of judicial remedies
and, 399-400
negligence and, 391-392
statutory remedies and,
394, 396
strict liability and, 393
Common-property regimes, 66-68

Common-property resources
access limits and, 229
free-access and, 227
ocean fisheries as, 225, 237
water and, 165-166
Communal Areas Management
Program for Indigenous
Resources (CAMPFIRE), 238
Comparative advantage law,
87, 188
Composition-of-demand effect, 364
Comprehensive Environmental
Response, Compensation, and
Liability Act (Superfund Act),
33, 396-397, 400
Conable, Barber, 427
Congestion externalities, 111, 112
Congestion pricing, 329, 330
Congestion tolls, 330
Congressional Budget Office
(CBO), 291
Conrad, J. M., 228
Conservation
electrical energy demand and,
150-152
trust funds for, 216
Conservation easements, 213-215
Conservation Reserve Program,
183, 344
Constant-dollar GDP, 421
Constant-dollar NDP, 421
Constant marginal extraction cost,
128, 129
Constant total capital, 92
Consumers' Union, 377
Consumer surplus, 61-62
Consumption, 421
Contemporaneous externalities,
225, 227
Contingent ranking, 39, 41
Contingent valuation
ecotourism and, 42
explanation of, 36
Northern Spotted Owl and, 37
studies of, 37-39
Contraception, income-generating
projects and, 117
Conventional pollutants
command-and-control policy
framework for, 264-273
explanation of, 264
Copper, recycled, 365

Cost effectiveness
    of command-and-control
        approach, 270-273
    effluent water quality standards
        and, 348
    equimarginal principle for, 52
    water pollution control
        and, 358
Cost-effectiveness analysis
    approaches to, 51-52
    example of, 53
    explanation of, 33
Cost-effectiveness principle,
    453-454
Cost estimation, 45-46
Cost of capital, risk-free, 74
Costs
    environmental, 133, 134, 151,
        182-183
    opportunity, 22
    total, 22-23
    variable, 22*f*
Council on Environmental Quality
    benefit estimation and, 48-50
    function of, 54
Criminal law, 393-394
Criteria pollutants, 264. *See also*
    Conventional pollutants
Current reserves, 123
Czechoslovakia, 350

D

Daly, Herman, 456-459
Dante Alighieri, 1
d'Arge, Ralph C., 302
Dasgupta, Partha, 112, 438
Death of a Salesman (Miller), 373*n*
Debt
    deforestation and, 208
    poverty and, 208, 430-431
Debt-nature swaps, 212-213, 215
Decision making, 18-25
Declining-block pricing, 170
Defensive expenditures, 39
Deforestation. *See also* Forest
    harvesting; Forests
    in Brazil, 205-206
    global warming and, 207-208
    incentives for landlords and,
        205-207
    incentives for nations and,
        207-208
    land conversion and, 202-204

poverty and debt and, 208
profit-maximizing decisions
    and, 205
rate of, 199
Degradable wastes, 339
Delaney clause, 402
Delaware Estuary, 349, 350
Demand
    income elasticity of, 144
    price elasticity of, 142-143
    willingness to pay and, 21
Demand curve, 19-21, 70, 71
Demographic transition theory,
    108, 109
Denmark
    agricultural chemical use
        in, 183
    approaches to vehicle emissions
        in, 319
    wind power in, 154
Dennison, Edward, 105
Depletable resources
    allocation of abundant, 86
    classification of, 123
    current reserves of, 125-126
    efficient allocation of, 88-89
    explanation of, 123
    management of, 127-128
    storage of, 127
Deposit-refund systems, 369, 371
Depreciation, 422
Dickens, Charles, 336
Diesel emissions, 41, 312-313
Diminishing marginal productivity
    law, 104
Dioxin contamination, 396
Direct observation methods, 35
Discounting, 24
Discount rates
    choice of, 48
    forest harvesting and, 202, 203
    importance of, 49
    social vs. private, 74
Disposal. *See* Waste disposal
Dissolved oxygen (DO), 340
Diversity
    biological, 69-70, 72
    genetic, 70
Divine Comedy: The Inferno
    (Dante), 1
Dominant policy, 46
Douglas fir, 200, 201
Doyle, Sir Arthur Conant, 15

Du Pont Corporation, 278
Durability obsolescence, 376-378
Dynamic efficiency
    examples of, 84
    explanation of, 27, 85, 127
    sustainable outcomes and, 441
    two-period model and, 85-88
    use of, 84-85
Dynamic efficient allocations
    application of, 91-92
    explanation of, 90-91
    sustainability criterion and, 91
Dynamic-efficient sustainable
    yield, 223

E

Earth Summit. *See* United Nations
    Conference on Environment
    and Development (Earth
    Summit)
Easterlin, Richard, 426
Eastern Europe
    acid rain and, 296
    carbon monoxide emissions
        in, 328
    pollution in, 61
Economic development
    affecting population growth,
        108, 412
    effects of population growth on,
        101-108
    sustainability and, 435-442 (*See
        also* Sustainability;
        Sustainable development)
Economic growth
    alternative measures of, 423-425
    conventional measures and,
        420-423
    energy and, 416-418
    income inequality and, 425, 426
    by increase in inputs, 412
    less industrialized nationals
        and, 426-431
    population trends and, 419
    post-industrial society and,
        419-420
    reduced input flows and,
        412-414
    by technological progress, 412,
        414-415
    zero, 457
Economic rent, 206
Economic replenishment, 125-126

Economics, 18
Economies of scale
    output per worker and,
        105-106
    population growth and, 104
Ecotourism, 42
Efficiency
    court system and, 77-79
    dynamic, 27
    government intervention and,
        79-80
    legislative and executive
        regulation and, 79
    level of diversity and, 70
    monopolies and, 72, 73
    population growth and, 109
    private resolution through
        negotiation and, 75-77
    static, 26-27
    strict liability and, 393
    sustainability and, 209, 438-442
    waste disposal costs and, 367
Efficient allocation
    determination of, 85
    explanation of, 72-73, 128
    fairness of, 90-91
    of fisheries, 225, 232
    of forest resource, 199
    nature of, 92-93
    of pollution, 245-247
    property rights and, 60, 74
    of surface water and
        groundwater, 160-161
Efficient harvests
    biological dimension of,
        221-223
    static-efficient sustained yield,
        223-225
Efficient intertemporal allocations
    explanation of, 127-128
    exploration and technological
        progress and, 131
    N-period model and, 128-130
    transition to renewable
        substitute and, 130-131
    two-period model and, 128
Efficient sustainable yield, 223, 224
Effluent water quality standards.
    See National effluent standards
Ehrlich, Paul, 379
Einstein, Albert, 287
Electricity generation
    conservation and, 150-152

environmental problems with
    transition fuels and, 146-150
peak periods and, 151
solar energy for, 143, 153
Eliot, T. S., 382
Emerson, Ralph Waldo, 59, 410
Emission charges
    acid rain and, 292-293
    explanation of, 253-254
    in France, 279
    function of, 256-258
    in Japan, 279, 280
    permit system vs., 259
    process to determine, 280
    types of, 279
Emission-permit system
    emission charges vs., 259
    explanation of, 255-256
    function of, 256-258
Emission reduction. *See also*
    Mobile-source pollution control
    cost-effective allocations and,
        250-251
    cost-effective policies and, 252
    emission charges and, 253-255
    emission standards and, 252
    transferable emission permits
        and, 255-256
Emission reduction credits (ERCs)
    cost-effectiveness principle and,
        453-454
    explanation of, 274, 280
    netting and, 275-276
    for retirement of old vehicles,
        331
    revenue from sale of, 277
    transaction costs of, 277-278
    use of, 451
Emissions. *See also* Mobile-source
    pollution
    clustered, 313
    dispersed, 313
    relationship between pollution
        damage and, 244
    taxation on, 249
    timing of, 270, 313
    vehicle, 311-313
Emissions fees, 282-284
Emissions standards
    EPA and vehicle, 316-318
    European vehicle, 319
    explanation of, 252
Emissions trading programs

cost-effectiveness principle
    and, 453
effectiveness of, 276-279,
    95-296
explanation of, 273-276
lead phaseout and, 326-327
sulfur allowance program and,
    293-295
Employment, 415-417
Endangered Species Act of
    1973, 20, 37
Energy. *See also specific types
    of energy*
    agriculture and cost of, 182
    allocation of, 138
    economic growth and, 416-418
    overview of, 136-138
    sustainable development and,
        418, 444-445
Energy efficiency, 445
Energy intensity, 445
Energy Policy Act of 1992,
    318-319
Enforceability, 60
Engineering approach, 45
England
    fishing rights in, 166-167
    instream uses of water in,
        166-167
    wind power in, 154
Enke, S., 109, 111n
Entrophy, 17
Entropy law, 17-18
Environment
    as asset, 16-18
    economic approach and, 18
Environmental costs
    agricultural policies and,
        182-185
    extraction of natural resource
        and, 133-134
    internalizing, 151
Environmental Defense Fund
    (EDF), 167, 295
Environmental economics, 3, 10
Environmental policy
    economic growth and, 415-416
    effects of, 415-416
    efficient allocations and, 92-94
    employment and, 415-417
    international cooperation and,
        449-450
Environmental projects, 44-45

Environmental Protection Agency
(EPA)
Allowance Tracking System,
293, 294
ambient air standards and,
265-269
benefit-cost analysis of air
pollution control policy
and, 27-29
cost forecast study and, 50
function of, 264
lead in gasoline and, 317-318,
327, 328
ozone depletion and, 297
pesticide regulation and, 395
point and nonpoint sources
and, 354
pretreatment standards and,
353, 354
toxic substances and, 280, 395,
396, 401, 402, 404
tradable permit system and, 300
vehicle emissions standards and,
316-318, 320-322, 325,
327-329
water pollution control and,
343-345, 347-350, 352, 354
Environmental sustainability,
92, 94
Equimarginal principle, 26, 52
Espenshade, Thomas, 107
Ethics
greenhouse gases and, 302
toxic substances and, 388
Etnier, David A., Jr., 20
Europe. *See also specific countries*
acid rain in, 296
agricultural subsidies in, 185
carbon monoxide emissions
in, 328
car sharing in, 321
lead emissions in, 328
organic farming in, 184
peak-load pricing in, 152
toxic chemical accidents in, 383
vehicle emission controls in,
319-320
water pollution control in,
350-352
wind power use in, 154
Eutrophication, 340, 353
Ex ante estimates, 50, 418
Exclusivity, of property rights, 60

Expected present value of net
benefits, 47
Exploration, 131
Exponential growth, 6
Exponential reserve index, 125
Export taxes, 190
Ex post estimates, 50, 418
External diseconomy, 66
External economy, 66
Externalities
congestion, 111, 112
contemporaneous, 225, 227
explanation of, 64-66
intergenerational, 225, 227
pecuniary, 66
road transport, 314, 315
shrimp farming, 67
types of, 66
Extinction, 221, 455
Extraction costs
constant marginal, 128, 129
environmental costs and,
133-134
Extractive reserves, 213, 215
Exxon Valdex oil spill, 32, 471

F

Family-size decisions
congestion externalities
and, 112
economic approach to,
112-118
Fashion obsolescence, 375-376
Federal Environmental Pesticide
Control Act, 395
Federal Food, Drug, and Cosmetic
Act, 394
Federal Insecticide, Fungicide, and
Rodenticide Act, 395
Federal Power Commission
(FPC), 138
Federal reclamation projects, 164
Feedback loops
explanation of, 3
negative, 7
positive, 6-7
Ferdinand, King of Spain, 4
Fertility
microeconomic theory of, 113
toxic substance exposure and,
384-385, 389
Fertility rates
in China, 116

in Korea, 115
in United States, 100, 102
world trends in, 99-100
Fertilizers, 338
Finland
agricultural chemical use
in, 183-184
approaches to vehicle emissions
in, 319
First law of thermodynamics, 17
Fisheries
appropriability and market
solutions for, 225-227
economic incentive approach
to, 451
efficient harvests and, 221-225
efficient vs. market exploitation
of, 234
high-grading in, 237
poaching and, 238-239
property rights and, 225-226, 230
public policy toward, 227-237
Fishery regulation
aquaculture and, 228-230
individual transferable quotas
and, 233, 235-236-237
local approaches to, 238
raising cost of fishing and,
230-232
taxes and, 233
200-mile limit and, 237
Fish farming, 230
Fishing rights
in England, 166-167
in Sri Lanka, 68
Fish ranching, 230
Food, Agriculture, Conservation,
and Trade Act of 1990, 185
Food additives, 394
Food and Agricultural Organization
(United Nations), 178, 195
Food and Drug Administration
(FDA), 394
Food distribution
India and, 193
malnourishment and, 186
overview of, 186-187
Food/food supplies. *See also*
Agriculture
feast or famine cycles and,
193-195
global scarcity of, 177-180
malnourishment and, 176-177

outlook for, 180-184
for poor, 190-192
stockpiles of, 194-195
Food production
decline in per capita, 180
in least developed countries,
186-188
poverty and population growth
and, 187
undervaluation bias and, 188-190
Food Security Act of 1985, 185
Forest, tropical, 207, 214
Forest and Rangeland Renewable
Resources Planning Act, 211
Forest concessions, 206, 211
Forest harvesting
cost of, 206
costs of, 205
decisions regarding, 208
economics of, 201-203
as threat to biodiversity, 199, 207
Forest Reserve Act of 1891, 210, 211
Forest reserves, 210
Forestry
conservation easements and,
213-215
debt-nature swaps and,
212-213, 215
extractive reserves and, 213, 215
losers from inefficient, 206-207
plantation, 209
sustainable, 209, 211, 212
water pollution from, 338
Forests. *See also* Deforestation
biological dimension of, 200-201
conversion of, 202-204
decreases in net benefits for, 204
legislation related to, 210, 211
overview of, 198-199
perverse incentives for
landowner and, 205-207, 220
perverse incentives for nations
and, 207-208, 220
poverty and debt and, 208
public ownership of, 209-210
public policy and, 210-215
special attributes of, 199
Forest Service (USDA), 210
Forest Stewardship Council
(FSC), 212
Forrester, Jay, 3
Fossil fuel energy, 301, 303
Fox River, 350, 351

France
emission charges in, 279
nuclear energy and, 147
Frederick, Ken, 164
Free-access resources
externalities created by, 225, 227
whale harvesting and, 228
Freeman, A. Myrick, 357
Free riders, 388
Full-cost principle, 451-453
Functional obsolescence, 375
Fund pollutants
efficient allocation and, 245-247
explanation of, 244
water, 339-341

G

Gaia hypothesis, 7
Gasoline, lead in, 317-318, 326-328
Genetic diversity, 70
Geothermal energy, use of, 153
Germany
approaches to vehicle emissions
in, 319, 320
carbon monoxide emissions
in, 328
car sharing in, 321
nitrogenous fertilizer use in, 183
pesticide use in, 183
recycling in, 372
water pollution control in,
350-352
wind power in, 154
Gibbon, Edward, 1-2
Gini coefficient, 429
Global Environmental Facility
(GEF), 304
Global Environmental Monitoring
System (GEMS), 273
Global Environmental Trust
Fund, 304
Global pollutants
explanation of, 245
global warming and, 299-306
ozone depletion and, 297-299
Global warming
agriculture and, 299-301
deforestation and, 207-208
emissions trading and, 305
explanation of, 299
full-cost principle for, 303
Kyoto Protocol and, 304-305
positive feedback loops and, 6-7

strategies to control, 301-304
treatment of risk and, 46
uncertainties related to, 305-306
United Nations Framework
Convention on Climate
Change and, 304
Global warning, 452
Goldman, Marshall I., 61
Grameen Bank, 116, 117
The Grapes of Wrath (Steinbeck), 157
Grazing rights, 67-68
Greenhouse gases
ethics, risk aversion and, 302
explanation of, 299
Green revolution
in India, 193
origins of, 191-192
Gross domestic product (GDP), 420,
421, 431, 444
Groundwater
efficient allocation of, 160-161
explanation of, 159, 337
sources of contamination for,
337-339
supplies of, 159
valuing damage from
contamination of, 40
Guyana, 430

H

Hahn, Robert W., 271, 278
Haigh, John A., 281
Handy, William Christopher, 157
Happiness, income and, 426
Hardin, Garrett, 177, 220
Harrison, David, 281
Hartwick Rule, 91, 92
Hassanein, Saad A., 416
Hatwick, John, 91, 439
Hausman, Jerry, 376
Haveman, Robert, 50, 415
Hazardous and Solid Waste
Amendments of 1984,
395-396
Hazardous pollutants. *See also*
Toxic substances
benzene as, 283
EPA and, 280-281
explanation of, 280
regulatory issues related to,
281-282
Hazardous Substance Response
Trust Fund, 401

Heal, G. M., 438
Health issues, 384-385
Health threshold, 268
Hedonic property value, 39
Helium, 126
Henderson, J. V., 234
Hicks, Sir John, 421
High-grading, in fisheries, 237
*The History of the Decline and Fall
  of the Roman Empire* (Gibbon), 1
Hoffer, Eric, 84
Hofman-La Roche & Co., 383
Honduras, 446
Hong Kong, 329, 330
Hooker Chemical, 382
Hoover, Edgar M., 104
Howe, Chuck, 164
Human development index (HDI),
  424-425
Human-environment relationship,
  16-18
Human life, 39-43
Hungary, 328
Hybrids, 192
Hydrocarbon emissions, 316
Hydrogen, 153
Hydro power, 152
Hypothetical bias, 36-37
Hypothetical resources, 124

I
Iceland, 328
Iglesias, Enrique, 427
Impact analysis
  explanation of, 52
  National Environmental Policy
    Act of 1969 and, 53-54
Income
  ensuring distributional fairness
    in, 458-459
  explanation of, 421, 455
  happiness and, 426
  national, 455
Income elasticity of demand, 144
Income inequality
  demand to reduce, 112
  effects of, 425, 426
  population growth and, 107-108
  results of, 111-112
Increased-block rate pricing, 169
India
  green revolution in, 193
  sustainable agriculture in, 190

Indicated resources, 124
Individual demand curve, 19-21
Individual transferable quotas
  (ITQs), 233-237
Indivisible consumption, 69
Indonesia, 422, 457
Industrial Revolution, 419
Inferred resources, 124
Infertility, 384-385
Inflation, 415
Information bias, 36
Information economy, 419-420
Information principle, 456
INHALE, 295
Inputs, 412-414
Inspection and maintenance (I&M)
  programs, 318, 324-325
Intangible benefits, 44-45
Intemporal scarcity, 88
Interactive resources, 221
Interest groups, 75
Intergenerational externalities,
  225, 227
Intergovernmental Panel on
  Climate Change (IPCC), 299
International agreements, 397
International Fund for Agricultural
  Development, 176-177
International Tropical Timber
  Agreement (ITTA), 215
Interstate market, 139
Intertemporal allocations, 127-131
Intertemporal fairness
  assessment of, 91
  explanation of, 89-90
Intrastate market, 139
Iron ore industry, 132
Irrigation, 184
Isabella, queen of Spain, 4
Itai Itai disease, 341
Italy, 330

J
Japan
  agricultural subsidies in, 185
  aquaculture in, 230
  emission charges in, 279, 280
  nuclear energy and, 147, 149
  ocean dumping and, 341
  recycling in, 365
  toxic substances and,
    399, 400
Jevons, Stanley, 4

Joint and several liability doctrine,
  400-401
Jorgenson, Dale W., 416, 417

K
Kakadu Conservation Zone (KCZ)
  (Australia), 29
Kakadu National Park (KNP)
  (Australia), 29
Kashmanian, Richard M., 354
Katzman, Martin T., 213-214
Kelley, Allen C., 106
Kenya
  sustainable development
    and, 446
  wildlife protection in, 238, 239
Kepone case, 392, 393
Keynes, John Maynard, 4
Kolstad, Charles, 259
Korea
  fertility decline in, 115
  industrialization in, 427
Kyoto Protocol, 304-305

L
Lake Nakuru National Park
  (Kenya), 42
Lakes, 337-338
Land
  allocation of agricultural,
    181-182
  conversion of, 202-204
  food scarcity and, 178, 179
Land ownership, 429
Land use
  sustainable development and,
    447-448
  transferable development rights
    and, 448
  transport costs and, 315
Latency
  explanation of, 384
  toxic substances and, 386
Law. *See* Common law; Criminal
  law; Statutory law
Lead
  ambient air quality standards
    for, 265
  decline in emissions from, 328
  in gasoline, 317-318, 326-328
  recycling of, 366
Lead phaseout program, 326-328
Learned hand formula, 391-392

Least-cost (LC) approach, 350
Less developed countries (LDCs)
  average diet in, 186
  food production in, 187-188
Legal remedies
  limitations to, 399-400
  oil spills and, 355, 356
  toxic substance control and,
    392, 397-405
Legal system, 77-79
Lethal-dose determination, 386
Lewis, D. H., 271-272
Liability
  court system and, 77-79
  strict, 393
Liberia, birthrates in, 100
Life Science Products Company, 392
The Limits to Growth, 3
Lindert, Peter, 107, 419
Liquid natural gas (LNG), 140
Littering, 369, 370
Load management, electricity,
  151-152
Lobsters, 229, 234
Local pollutants
  dilution to control, 290
  explanation of, 244, 288
Logging, 199, 206
Love Canal, 382-383
Lovelock, James, 7
Lovins, Amory, 143
Lowest achievable emission rate
  (LAER), 266, 274

M

MacNeill, Jim, 427
Maine, fisheries in, 229
Malaysia, 440
Malnourishment
  facts regarding, 176-177
  food distribution and, 186
Maloney, Michael T., 273, 278, 279
Malthus, Thomas Robert, 2, 98
Marginal cost
  efficient pricing and, 165
  of exploration, 131
  pollutants and, 245, 246
  of water consumption, 169-171
Marginal-external-cost rule, 304
Marginal opportunity cost curve, 22
Marginal user costs, 88
Marginal willingness to pay, 85
Marietta, Georgia, 370

Marine Protection Research and
  Sanctuaries Act of 1972, 346
Market allocations
  adequacy of, 127
  environmental costs and,
    133-134
  for fisheries, 225
  of pollution, 247-248
  property-right structures and,
    132-133
  questions regarding, 131
  sustainable development and,
    437-438
  toxic substances and, 387-391
Market economies, 60
Marketing boards, 189-190
Maryland Environmental Law
  Society (MELS), 295
Materials balance model, 17n
Maximum sustainable yield, 222
McKibben, Bill, 2
Mean annual increment (MAI), 201
Measured resources, 124
Measure of economic welfare
  (MEW), 424
Mendelsohn, Robert, 300
Meridian National, 445
Meta analysis, 38
Mexico
  acid rain and, 288
  age structure of population
    in, 103, 104
  oil reserves in, 144
Meyer, Stephen, 442-443
Meyers, Norman, 207
Microeconomic theory of fertility, 113
Miller, Arthur, 373n
Minamata disease, 341
Minke whales, 228
Mitchell, R. C., 357-358
Mitigation, 301
Mobile-source pollution
  consequences of, 315
  externalities and, 314, 315
  historical background of, 316
  implicit subsidies and, 313
  overview of, 311-313
Mobile-source pollution control
  air quality change and,
    327-328
  alternative fuels and, 327
  alternative fuels and vehicles
    and, 318-319

associated enforcement program
  and, 317
car sharing and, 321
certification program and,
  316-317
deterioration of new-car
  emission rates and, 323-326
differentiated regulation and,
  322-323
economic and political
  assessment of, 320-322
European approaches to,
  319-320
innovative approaches to,
  329-331
lead phaseout program and,
  326-327
lead regulation and, 317-318
local responsibility and, 318
technology forcing sanctions
  and, 322
uniformity of control and, 323
U.S. policy toward, 316-319
Monopolies, 72-73
Montreal Protocol, 298-299
Muir, John, 210
Multi-Fiber Arrangement, 429-430
Multiple cropping, 444
Multiple regression analysis, 39
Multiple Use-Sustained Yield Act,
  210, 212
Municipal waste, 368
Municipal waste treatment
  subsidies, 344, 352

N

Namibia, 216
National Academy of Engineering,
  323
National Academy of Sciences, 323
National Coal Model, 291
National Commission on Air
  Quality, 323-324
National effluent standards
  allocating control responsibility
    and, 349-350
  enforcement of, 348-349
  European experience with,
    350-352
National Environmental Policy Act
  of 1969, 53-54
National Institute for Occupational
  Safety and Health (NIOSH), 394

National Oceanic and Atmospheric Administration (NOAA), 38
National Priorities List, 404
National Research Council, 106-109
National Science Foundation, 325
Natural capital, 92, 422
Natural equilibrium, 221
Natural gas
    as depletable resource, 126
    regulation of, 138-141
    reserves of, 137
    shortages of, 138
    use of, 136, 138
Natural Gas Act of 1938, 138
Natural Gas Policy Act of 1978, 141
Natural Resource Defense Council, 320, 346
Natural resource economics, 3
    efficient intertemporal allocations and, 127-131
    function of, 10
    market allocations and, 131-134
    resource taxonomy and, 123-127
Natural Resources Defense Council, 164
Nature Conservancy, 72, 168
Naurita, Colorado, 149
Nauru, 93
Negative feedback loops, 7
Negligence, 391-392
Negotiation
    court system and, 77-79
    private resolution through, 75-77
Net benefits
    for agriculture, 204
    derivation of, 23
    expected present value of, 47
Net domestic product (NDP), 421, 424
The Netherlands
    agricultural chemical use in, 183-184
    approaches to vehicle emissions in, 319, 320
    carbon monoxide emissions in, 328
    wind power in, 154
Netting, 275-276
New Guinea, 216

New scrap, 367
New source performance standard (NSPS), 267
New Zealand
    agricultural chemical use in, 184
    agricultural subsidies and, 185
    fisheries in, 451
    individual transferable quotas in, 235
Niagara Mohawk Power Corporation, 295
Nicaragua, 430
Nichols, Albert L., 281
Nitrogen dioxide
    ambient air quality standards for, 265
    from mobile sources, 312
Nitrogenous fertilizer
    environmental damage from, 183
    water pollution from, 353
Nitrogen oxides, 316
Noll, Roger G., 271
Nonattainment regions, 266
Noncompliance penalty, 267
Nonexcludability, 69
Nonuse value, 35, 37, 38
Nordhaus, William D., 306, 423, 424
Normative economics, 18
Northeast Utilities of Connecticut, 295
Northern Spotted Owl, value of, 36, 37
Northern spotted Owl, 205
Norway
    approaches to vehicle emissions in, 319, 320
    congestion tolls in, 330
Nuclear accidents
    effects of, 147
    liability issues and, 148-149
Nuclear energy
    compensation approach to, 149, 150
    safety issues and, 147-149
Nuclear waste
    disposal sites for, 149-150
    storage of, 147-149

O
Obsolescence
    durability, 376-378
    fashion, 375-376
    functional, 375
Occupational hazards
    susceptible populations and, 389
    toxic substances and, 387-389
Occupational Safety and Health Act, 389, 394-395, 402
Occupational Safety and Health Administration (OSHA), 389, 394-395, 404
Ocean fisheries, as common-property resources, 225, 237
Ocean pollution
    from dumping, 339, 341, 346
    from oil spills, 339, 345-346, 355, 356
    sources of, 339
Offset policy, 274, 275
Oil
    compatibility of member interests and, 144-145
    as depletable resource, 126
    income elasticity of demand and, 144
    non-OPEC suppliers and, 144
    OPEC and, 142-146
    price elasticity of demand and, 142-143
    use of, 136, 138
Oil, Chemical and Atomic Workers Union, 389
Oil prices, 154
Oil reserves
    list of largest, 146
    in Saudi Arabia, 145, 146
    in United States and Western Europe, 137
Oil spills
    current approach to, 355
    legal remedies to, 355, 356
    water pollution from, 339, 345-346
Old scrap, 367
Opaluch, James J., 354
Open-access resources, 68, 69
Open system, 17
Opportunity costs
    explanation of, 22

intemporal scarcity and, 88
Optimal global population, analysis of, 99
Optimist model
    conclusions of, 8
    environmental problems and, 10-11
    nature of, 8-10
    origin on, 7
Optimization procedure, 52
Options, predefined, 18-25
Option value, 35
Organic farming, 184
Organization for Economic Cooperation and Development (OECD), 397
Organization of Petroleum Exporting Countries (OPEC)
    explanation of, 142
    income elasticity of demand and, 144
    member interests and, 144-146
    non-OPEC suppliers and, 144
    price elasticity of demand and, 142-143
Output
    explanation of, 102-103
    measurement of, 420
Oyster industry, 226. *See also* Fisheries
Ozone
    ambient air quality standards for, 265, 269, 327-328
    concentrations of, 313n
    explanation of, 297
    from mobile sources, 312
Ozone depletion
    explanation of, 297
    full-cost principle and, 452
    hazards of, 297
    Montreal Protocol and, 298-299
    Rand Corporation study and, 297-298
    tradable permits and, 300

P

Packard, Vance, 373, 373, 375
Palmini, Dennis J., 353
Pareto, Vilfredo, 26
Pareto optimality, 26-27
Parking subsidies, 331

Parry, Martin L., 301
Particulates, 265, 269
Passamaquoddy Bay, 49
Passive-use values, 35, 38
Peak-load pricing, 151-152
Pecuniary externalities, 66
Pelletization, 132
Per capita income, 109
Perfect equality, 429
Perfect inequality, 429
Performance bonds, 406
Persistent pollutants, 341
Perverse incentives
    for landowners, 205-207, 220
    misspecified property rights and, 454
    for nations, 207-208, 220
Pessimist model
    conclusions of, 3-6
    environmental problems and, 10-11
    nature of, 6-7, 10
    origin of, 3
Pesticides
    environmental damage from, 183-184
    registration of, 395
    water pollution from, 338, 353
Pezzey, John, 439
Philippines, 190
Phillips Petroleum Co, v. Wisconsin, 138
Phosphorus control, 354-355
Photovoltics, 153
Pimentel, David, 98-99
Pinelands Development Credits (PDCs), 448
Pinchot, Gifford, 210
Plantation forestry, 209
Poaching, 238-239
Point-of-production strategy, 312
Point sources
    explanation of, 337
    water pollution control for, 343-344
Poland, 328
Politics
    poverty and, 429
    water pricing and, 171
Pollutants
    accumulating, 341

classification of, 244-245
    conventional, 264-273
    fund, 245-247, 339-341
    hazardous, 280-283
    local, 244, 288, 290
    persistent, 341
    regional, 244, 288, 291 (*See also* Acid rain)
    stock, 244, 248, 340
    surface, 245
    toxic organic chemical, 337
    water, 337-341
Pollution. *See also* Air pollution; Emissions, Emission reduction; Mobile-source pollution; Toxic substances; Water pollution; *specific types of pollution*
    assessing damage caused by, 33-34
    efficient allocation of, 245-247
    market allocation of, 247-248
    stationary source, 311-312
Pollution control
    benefit-cost analysis and, 27-28
    bribery and, 76-77
    cost-effectiveness analysis and, 33, 51
    costs of, 415-416
    reputational strategy for, 457
Pollution-control policy
    charges and transferable permits and, 256-258
    cost-efficient emission reduction, 250-256
    efficiency and, 249-250
Pollution havens hypothesis, 442
Population control
    Daly system and, 458
    economic approach to, 109-118
    elements of successful, 112-113
    value of averted birth and, 111
Population density
    environmental effects of, 108
    recycling and, 365
Population growth
    affecting economic development, 101-108, 419
    demand for food and, 178
    effects of economic development on, 108

food production and poverty
and, 187, 188
poverty and, 428
in United States, 100-102
views of, 98
world, 99-100
Porter, Michael, 442
Porter hypothesis, 442, 443
Positive economics, 18
Positive feedback loops
explanation of, 6
global warming and, 6-7
Post-industrial society, 419-420
Potentially responsible parties
(PRPs), 400, 401
Potential reserves, 123
Poverty
agricultural policies and,
190-192
deforestation and, 208
environmental problems and,
410-411
food distribution and, 186
food production and, 187
income inequality and,
425, 426
land ownership and, 429
in less industrialized countries,
426-431
population growth/density and,
108, 428
trade policies and, 429-430
traditional economic growth
model and, 427-428
Preferential-use doctrine, 163
Pregnancy, hazardous workplace
and, 389
Present value
of allocations, 85-86
explanation of, 24
Pretreatment standards, 353, 354
Prevention of significant
deterioration (PSD) program,
266-267, 269
Prevention strategies, 301
Price-Anderson Act, 148
Price controls, 138-141
Price elasticity of demand, oil
market and, 142-143
Primary ambient air quality
standard, 264-265
Prior-appropriation rights, 162, 163

Private discount rates, 74
Producer surplus, 62, 63
Product durability
durability obsolescence and,
376-378
fashion obsolescence and,
375-376
functional obsolescence
and, 375
overview of, 373, 375
Product safety, 389-390
Profit maximization
deforestation and, 205, 208
forest harvesting and, 201-202
Prognostication, dangers of, 4
PROPER (Program for Pollution
Control, Evaluation, and Rating
in Indonesia), 457
Property rights, 59
court system and, 77-79
efficient allocations and, 60, 74
efficient market allocations
and, 60, 61
enforceability of, 60
exclusivity of, 60, 64
explanation of, 60
fisheries and, 225, 226, 230
improperly designed systems
of, 66-69
scarcity rent and, 64
structure of, 60-64
unclaimed land and, 206
Property-rights principle, 454
Property-rights structures, 132-133
Public goods
biological diversity and, 69-72
explanation of, 69
privately provided, 72
Public policy
enforcement of, 346
fisheries and, 227-237
forestry and, 209-215
forests and, 210-215
recycling and, 369-371
sustainable development
and, 471
Public Utility Regulatory Policies
Act of 1978, 143

R
Radioactivity, 147
Radon-222, 148

Ramsey Canyon Preserve, 168
Rand Corporation, 151, 297-298
Rand Institute for Civil Justice, 401
Rawls, John, 89
Real consumption per capita, 421
RECLAIM program (California), 276
Recombinant DNA, 181
Recyclable resources
current reserves of, 125-126
explanation of, 123, 125
Recycling. *See also* Solid waste;
Waste disposal
extraction and disposal costs
and, 364
lead, 366
manufacturing process changes
and, 365-366
population density and, 365
waste disposal and, 366-371, 373
Reforestation, as mitigation
strategy, 301
Refundable deposits, 369, 371
Refuse Act 1899, 342, 343
Regional Clean Air Incentives
Market (California), 276
Regional pollutants. *See also*
Acid rain
Clean Air Act and, 291
explanation of, 244, 288
Regulation
differentiated, 322-323
legislative and executive, 79
Religion, environmental problems
and, 76
Renewable resources
cereal grain as, 177, 178
explanation of, 126-127
finiteness of, 127n
forms of, 152-153
management of, 127
storage of, 127
sustainable development
and, 439
transition to, 130-131, 146-150,
152, 154
Rent
economic, 206
scarcity, 64, 140-142, 160 (*See
also* Scarcity rent)
Rent seeking
explanation of, 75
natural gas policy and, 139-141

Repetto, Robert, 422
Replacement rate, 100
Reproductive health, 384-385
Reputational strategy, 457
Residual, 248
Res nullius regimes, 66, 68
Resource Conservation and
    Recovery Act, 395-396, 398, 402
Resource endowment, 123
Resources
    classification of, 122-127
    open-access, 68, 69
Retirement effect, 103
Ricardo, David, 64
Right-to-know laws, 398
Riparian rights, 161-162
Risk
    acceptable, 402
    treatment of, 46-48
Risk-adverse behavior, 47, 48
Risk aversion, 302
Risk-free cost of capital, 74
Risk-loving behavior, 47
Risk-neutrality, 47
Risk premium, 74
Rivers, 337-338
Road transport
    air pollution from, 314, 315
    car sharing and, 321
    congestion pricing and,
        329, 330
    congestion tolls and, 330
    consequences of, 315
    construction and maintenance
        and, 313
    parking subsidies and, 330
    social costs of, 329
Roman Empire, 1-2
Rosenzweig, Cynthia, 301
Ruckelshaus, William, 322
Russell, Clifford, 358
Ruttan, Vernon, 116
Rwanda, birthrates in, 100

S

Saccharin, 403
Sadik, Nafis, 98, 118
Safe Drinking Water Act
    Amendments of 1986, 345
Safe Drinking Water Act
    of 1974, 345
Salmon fishery, 230-231

Sathirathai, Suthawan, 67
Saudi Arabia, 145-146
Scarcity
    opportunity cost and
        intemporal, 88
    potential for water, 158-159
    views on impending, 379
    in world food market, 177-180
Scarcity rent
    capital and, 439
    explanation of, 64
    monopolists and, 142
    natural gas policy and, 140-141
    water scarcity and, 160
Schaefer, M. D., 221
Schmidt, Robert M., 106
Schultze, William D., 302
Scotland, 166-167
Scrap, 367
Scrubbers, 292, 295-296
Secondary ambient air quality
    standard, 265
Second law of thermodynamics,
    17-18
Self-extinction premise, 1-2
Serafy, Salah El, 455
Seventh Special Session of the
    United Nations General
    Assembly, 194
Sewage, 337, 339
Shakespeare, William, 32
Shrimp farming, 67
Sierra Club, 266, 346
Simon, Julian, 7-9, 98, 99, 176, 379
Singapore
    industrialization in, 427
    mobile-pollution control in,
        329, 330
Smog trading, 276
Social costs
    of road transport, 329
    of vehicle accidents, 313
Social discount rates, 74
Social opportunity cost of capital,
    24*f*, 48
Soil erosion
    agricultural productivity and,
        182-183
    water pollution and,
        338-339, 353
Solar energy
    cost of, 143

for electricity generation,
    143, 153
market penetration of, 150
in United States, 143
uses for, 152
Solid waste. *See also* Recycling;
    Waste disposal
    disposal costs and efficiency,
        366-367
    disposal costs and scrap market
        and, 369
    disposal decisions and, 367-369
    durability obsolescence and,
        376-378
    efficient recycling of, 364-366
    fashion obsolescence and,
        375-376
    functional obsolescence and, 375
    overview of, 363
    pollution damage and, 371-373
    product durability and, 373, 375
    public policies and, 369-371
South America, 328
South Coast Air Quality
    Management District, 327, 417
Southeast Asia, 108. *See also*
    specific countries
Soviet Union
    nuclear safety standards in, 147
    pollution in, 61
Speculative resources, 124
Squatting, 206
Sri Lanka
    fishing rights in, 68
    food stamp programs in, 190
Stable equilibrium, 221
Starting-point bias, 36
State implementation plan (SIP),
    265-266
State-property regimes, 66-67
Static efficiency
    examples of, 84
    explanation of, 26-27, 62, 72-73
    function of, 84
    use of, 84-85
Static-efficient sustainable yield,
    223-225
Static reserve index, 125
Stationary population, 100
Stationary-source pollution, 311-312
Statutory law
    balancing costs and, 402-403

common law as complement to, 397
degree and form of intervention and, 403-404
scale of problem and, 404-405
toxic substances and, 394-397
Steady-state economy, 456-458
Steel industry, 65
Steinbeck, John, 157
Stock pollutants, 244, 248, 340
Storm-water runoff, 338
Strategic bias, 36
Strict liability, 393
Strong sustainability, 94
Stronium-90, 148
Stumpage value, 206
Suboptimal allocations, 27
Subsidies
    agricultural, 185
    implicit, 313
    municipal waste treatment, 344, 352
    parking, 331
Substitution bias, 140
Sulfur allowance program, 293-295
Sulfur oxides, 265
Sulfur-reduction emission permit system, 293
Summers, Lawrence, 117-118
Superfund Act. *See* Comprehensive Environmental Response, Compensation, and Liability Act (Superfund Act)
Supreme Court, U. S.
    benzene standard and, 402
    natural gas regulation and, 138
Surface pollutants, 245
Surface water
    efficient allocation of, 160
    explanation of, 159, 337
    near groundwater, 161
Survey approach, 45
Sustainability
    application of, 91-92
    economic growth and, 435-437
    efficiency and, 209, 438-442
    environmental, 94
    explanation of, 90
    market allocations and, 437-438
    Nauru island and, 93
    population growth and, 101
    strong, 94
    weak, 94

Sustainability principle, 454-455
Sustainable agriculture
    elements of, 183-184
    farmer income and, 190
    governmental encouragement of, 185
Sustainable development
    agriculture and, 444
    cost-effectiveness principle and, 453-454
    economic incentives for, 450-451
    energy and, 418, 444-445
    explanation of, 434-435
    fairness of efficient allocations and, 90-91
    full-cost principle and, 451-453
    implications for environmental policy and, 92-94
    international cooperation and, 449-450
    intertemporal fairness and, 89-90
    outlook for, 468-471
    property-rights principle and, 454
    sustainability principle and, 454-546
    trade and, 442-443
    transition to, 447-448, 456-459
    two-period model and, 85-89
    waste reduction and, 445-446
Sustainable forestry
    certification and, 212
    elements of, 209
    standards for, 211
Sustainable yield
    fisheries and, 222-223
    static-efficient, 223-225
Sweden
    agricultural chemical use in, 183-184
    approaches to vehicle emissions in, 319, 320
    nuclear energy and, 147
Switch point, 130-131
Switzerland
    agricultural subsidies in, 185
    approaches to vehicle emissions in, 319
    car sharing in, 321
    grazing rights in, 67-68
    water pricing in, 170
Synergistic effects, 386
Synthetic natural gas (SNG), 140
Systems dynamics, 3

T
Taiwan, 427
Take-back principle, 372
Talavera, Fray Hernando de, 4
Tangible benefits, 44
Taxes
    environmental, 303-304
    export, 190
    fishing industry and, 233
    on fossil fuels, 303
    input, 183-184
    pollution, 249
    to promote recycling, 371
Tax incentives, 319, 320
Technological progress
    economic growth and, 412
    explanation of, 126, 127
    in iron ore industry, 132
    limits on, 414-415
Tellico Dam, 20
Thailand
    mobile-pollution control in, 329-330
    poverty rate in, 427
    price responsiveness of supply in, 189
    shrimp farming externalities in, 67
A Theory of Justice (Rawls), 89
Thermal pollution, 340
Thermodynamics, first and second law of, 17-18
Third parties, hazardous substance exposure and, 390-391
Thorium-230, 148
Three Mile Island, 149
Times Beach, Missouri, 396
Tissue culture, 181
Tobin, James, 423, 424
Tohoku Electric Power Company, 149
Total benefits, 21-22
Total costs, 22-23
Total fertility rate, 100
Total marginal cost, 128
Total maximum daily load (TMDL) program, 345
Total willingness to pay (TWP)
    explanation of, 21-22
    value and, 35
Toxicity
    chronic, 386
    explanation of, 383

Toxic substances
   accidents releasing, 382-383
   assurance bonds and, 405, 406
   common law and, 391-393,
      397-401
   criminal law and, 393-394
   health effects of, 384-385
   international agreements
      and, 397
   latency period and, 386
   legal remedies for, 397-405
   number of, 385
   occupational hazards related to,
      387-389
   overview of, 383-384
   product safety and, 389-390
   scientific evidence regarding,
      386-387
   statutory law and, 394-397,
      401-405
   third-party issues related to,
      390-391
Toxic Substances Control
   Act, 396, 405
Tradable permits
   global warming and, 305
   for ozone-depleting
      chemicals, 300
Trade
   environment and, 442-443
   poverty and, 429-430
Tragedy of the commons, 68, 443
Transaction costs, 79, 80
Transferability
   of property rights, 60
   water, 162-164, 166
Transferable development rights
   (TDRs), 448
Transferable emission permits
   emission charges vs., 259
   explanation of, 255-256
   function of, 256-258
Transfer costs, 298
Transition fuels, 146-150
Transportation, 311-313. *See also*
   Mobile-source pollution;
   Mobile-source pollution control;
   Road transport
Trash collection, 368-370
Travel-cost methods
   ecotourism and, 42
   explanation of, 38, 39
Tredgold, Thomas, 4

Trees
   growth of, 200-201
   as saleable commodity, 199
Trichloroethylene (TCE), 40
Tropical forests
   biodiversity in, 207
   successes in, 214
Trust funds, 216
Tucson, Arizona, 159, 171
Tugwell, M., 234
Twain, Mark, 347

U

The Ultimate Resource (Simon), 7
Ultraviolet radiation, 297
Undiscovered resources, 124
Uniform treatment (UT) strategy, 350
United Nations Children's Fund
   (UNICEF), 427
United Nations Conference on
   Environment and Development
   (Earth Summit), 434
United Nations Development
   Program (UNDP), 424-425
United Nations Environment
   Program, 273
United Nations Food and
   Agricultural Organization, 178
United Nations Framework
   Convention on Climate Change
   (UNFCCC), 304
United States
   acid rain and, 288
   age structure of population in,
      103, 104
   agricultural productivity in, 180
   agricultural subsidies in, 185
   ambient air quality standards in,
      264-265
   carbon monoxide emissions
      in, 328
   childrearing expenditures in, 107
   economic growth in,
      105-106, 425
   electricity peak-load pricing in,
      151-152
   fertility rates in, 100, 102
   fisheries in, 229
   food stamp programs in, 190
   lead emissions in, 328
   mobile-source emissions control
      in, 316-319, 329
   nitrogenous fertilizer use in, 183

   population growth in, 100-101,
      104, 105
   salmon fishery in, 230-231
   solar energy in, 143
   water allocation in, 161-162
Uranium
   availability of, 146
   disposal of, 147-148
   safety issues and, 147
Uri, Noel D., 416
U.S. Geological Survey, 4
Use value, 35
Usufruct rights, 162, 206

V

Valuation techniques
   discount rate and, 48, 49
   human life and, 39-42
   overview of, 32-33
Values
   methods to estimate, 35-39
   types of, 34-35
Vehicles
   alternative, 318-319, 327
   diesel, 312-313
   retirement of, 331
Vincent, Jeffrey R., 440

W

Warranty provisions, 317
Waste, 25. *See also* Solid waste
Waste disposal
   cost of, 364, 366-367, 369
   decisions regarding, 367-369
   efficiency and, 367
   public policy and, 369-371
   scrap market and, 369
   sustainable development and,
      445-446
Waste flows, 243
The Waste Makers (Packard),
   373, 375
Water
   importance of, 157-158
   instream uses of, 166, 168
   potential for scarcity of,
      158-159
   remedies to problems with,
      166-172
Water allocation
   efficiency in groundwater,
      160-161
   efficiency in surface, 160

prior-appropriation doctrine
and, 162
riparian doctrine and, 161
sources of inefficiency in, 162-166
Water pollutants
accumulating, 341
fund, 339-341
sources of, 337-338
Water pollution
ocean, 339
river and lake, 338-339
sources of contamination and,
337-339
state of, 159
types of, 337
Water pollution control
ambient standards and zero
discharge goal and, 347-348
assessment of, 357-358
characteristics of, 336-337
citizen suits and, 356-357
early legislation for, 342-343
in Europe, 350-352
municipal waste treatment
subsidies and, 344, 352
national effluent standards and,
348-352
nonpoint, 338, 353-355
for nonpoint sources, 337,
338, 344
for ocean dumping, 346
for oil spills, 345-346, 355, 356
for point sources, 337, 343-344
pretreatment standards and,
353, 354
private enforcement of, 346
Safe Drinking Water Act
and, 345

TMDL program and, 345
Water Pollution Control Act
Amendments of 1956,
342-343
Water Pollution Control Act of
1948, 342
Water prices
Central Valley Project
Improvement Act and,
167-168
federal reclamation projects
and, 165-166
increased-block rate, 169
as source of inefficiency, 165
user cost in, 169
Water pricing
declining-block, 170
flat fee, 169
politics and, 171
in Switzerland, 170
Weak sustainability, 94
Weeks Act, 210
Welfare measure, 420
West, Mae, 263
Wetlands Water District,
164-165
Whale harvesting, 228
White, C. M., 132
White, Lynn, Jr., 76
Wilderness Act of 1964, 210, 211
Wildlife protection
ecotourism and, 42
in Zimbabwe, 238
Willingness to pay
actual expenditures and, 37
contingent valuation and, 38
demand and, 21
marginal, 85

wildlife preservation and, 42
Wilson, J. A., 229
Wind power
to drive turbines, 152
for electricity generation, 153
tax credits for development of,
153-154
Women, income-earning potential
of, 116-118
Working Assets Funding Source, 295
Workplace
Occupational Safety and Health
Act and, 394-395
pregnancy and hazardous, 389
World Bank, 181, 190, 249, 427, 430
World Emergency Stockpile, 194
World Health Organization, 273
World Heritage Convention, 214
World Heritage Fund, 214
World Neighbors, 446
World Resources Institute,
190, 422
Worldwide Fund for Nature (WW1),
212, 238
World Wildlife Fund, 216

Y
Yandle, Bruce, 273, 278, 279
Yellowstone River Valley, 166
Yost, Charles, 243
Youth effect, 103, 104

Z
Zero discharge goal, 347-348
Zero economic growth, 457
Zimbabwe, 238
Zinc, R., 109, 111n
Zurich, Switzerland, water pricing
in, 170